MW01620221

LEGAL METHOD and WRITING

EDITORIAL ADVISORS

Rachel E. Barkow
Vice Dean and Charles Seligson Professor of Law
Segal Family Professor of Regulatory Law and Policy
Faculty Director, Center on the Administration of Criminal Law
New York University School of Law

Erwin Chemerinsky
Dean and Jesse H. Choper Distinguished Professor of Law
University of California, Berkeley School of Law

Richard A. Epstein
Laurence A. Tisch Professor of Law
New York University School of Law
Peter and Kirsten Bedford Senior Fellow
The Hoover Institution
Senior Lecturer in Law
The University of Chicago

Ronald J. Gilson
Charles J. Meyers Professor of Law and Business
Stanford University
Marc and Eva Stern Professor of Law and Business
Columbia Law School

James E. Krier
Earl Warren DeLano Professor of Law Emeritus
The University of Michigan Law School

Tracey L. Meares
Walton Hale Hamilton Professor of Law
Director, The Justice Collaboratory
Yale Law School

Richard K. Neumann, Jr.
Alexander Bickel Professor of Law
Maurice A. Deane School of Law at Hofstra University

Robert H. Sitkoff
Austin Wakeman Scott Professor of Law
John L. Gray Professor of Law
Harvard Law School

David Alan Sklansky
Stanley Morrison Professor of Law
Faculty Co-Director, Stanford Criminal Justice Center
Stanford Law School

ASPEN COURSEBOOK SERIES

LEGAL METHOD and WRITING

NINTH EDITION

CHARLES R. CALLEROS
PROFESSOR OF LAW
ARIZONA STATE UNIVERSITY

KIMBERLY Y.W. HOLST
CLINICAL PROFESSOR OF LAW
ARIZONA STATE UNIVERSITY

Copyright © 2022 Charles R. Calleros and Kimberly Y.W. Holst

No part of this publication may be reproduced or transmitted in any form or by any means, electronic or mechanical, including photocopy, recording, or utilized by any information storage or retrieval system, without written permission from the publisher. For information about permissions or to request permissions online, visit us at visit us at www.AspenPublishing.com.

To contact Customer Service, e-mail customer.service@aspenpublishing.com, call 1-800-950-5259, or mail correspondence to:

Aspen Publishing
Attn: Order Department
PO Box 990
Frederick, MD 21705

Printed in the United States of America.

1 2 3 4 5 6 7 8 9 0

ISBN 978-1-5438-4951-6

Library of Congress Cataloging-in-Publication Data

Names: Calleros, Charles R., author. | Holst, Kimberly Y.W., author.
Title: Legal method and writing / Charles R. Calleros, Professor of Law, Arizona State University; Kimberly Y.W. Holst, Clincial Professor of Law, Arizona State University.
Description: Ninth edition. | Frederick, MD: Aspen Publishing, [2022] | Series: Aspen coursebook series | Includes index. | Summary: "A comprehensive text covering both objective and persuasive writing components of the first-year Legal Writing law school course"—Provided by publisher.
Identifiers: LCCN 2021054884 (print) | LCCN 2021054885 (ebook) | ISBN 9781543849516 (hardcover) | ISBN 9781543849523 (epub)
Subjects: LCSH: Legal composition. | Law—United States--Methodology.
Classification: LCC KF250 .C345 2022 (print) | LCC KF250 (ebook) | DDC 808.06/634—dc23/eng/20211109
LC record available at https://lccn.loc.gov/2021054884
LC ebook record available at https://lccn.loc.gov/2021054885

About Aspen Publishing

Aspen Publishing is a leading provider of educational content and digital learning solutions to law schools in the U.S. and around the world. Aspen provides best-in-class solutions for legal education through authoritative textbooks, written by renowned authors, and breakthrough products such as Connected eBooks, Connected Quizzing, and PracticePerfect.

The Aspen Casebook Series (famously known among law faculty and students as the "red and black" casebooks) encompasses hundreds of highly regarded textbooks in more than eighty disciplines, from large enrollment courses, such as Torts and Contracts, to emerging electives such as Sustainability and the Law of Policing. Study aids such as the *Examples & Explanations* and *Glannon Guide* series, both highly popular collections, help law students master complex subject matter.

Major products, programs, and initiatives include:

- **Connected eBooks** are enhanced digital textbooks and study aids that come with a suite of online content and learning tools designed to maximize student success. Designed in collaboration with hundreds of faculty and students, the Connected eBook is a significant leap forward in the legal education learning tools available to students.
- **Connected Quizzing** is an easy-to-use formative assessment tool that tests law students' understanding and provides timely feedback to improve learning outcomes. Delivered through CasebookConnect.com, the learning platform already used by students to access their Aspen casebooks, Connected Quizzing is simple to implement and integrates seamlessly with law school course curricula.
- **PracticePerfect** is a visually engaging, interactive study aid to explain commonly encountered legal doctrines through easy-to-understand animated videos, illustrative examples, and numerous practice questions. Developed by a team of experts, PracticePerfect is the ideal study companion for today's law students.
- The **Aspen Learning Library** enables law schools to provide their students with access to the most popular study aids on the market across all of their courses. Available through an annual subscription, the online library consists of study aids in e-book, audio, and video formats with full text search, note-taking, and highlighting capabilities.
- Aspen's **Digital Bookshelf** is an institutional-level online education bookshelf, consolidating everything students and professors need to ensure success. This program ensures that every student has access to affordable course materials from day one.
- **Leading Edge** is a community centered on thinking differently about legal education and putting those thoughts into actionable strategies. At the core of the program is the Leading Edge Conference, an annual gathering of legal education thought leaders looking to pool ideas and identify promising directions of exploration.

Dedications

To the much loved additions to our families:
Miles, Archie, Bernie, Daisy, Freddy, and Penelope
(one grandson and five rescue dogs, all adorable)
Charles and Debbie Calleros

To my parents, Yong Sun and Lyle Wilson,
for never telling me that things were impossible
Kimberly Holst

In Loving Memory of Mary Lawrence,
A pioneer in our field, and
A lovely human being,
Whose generous spirit
brought us together in celebration,
to her great joy and ours.
Charles Calleros and Kimberly Holst

SUMMARY OF CONTENTS

CONTENTS

TABLE OF CHARTS AND SAMPLE DOCUMENTS

CHARTS

SAMPLE DOCUMENTS

PREFACE

The activities of practicing attorneys speak volumes about the importance of legal writing classes in law school. Although analytic skills and a general knowledge of legal principles form the intellectual foundation of the practice of law, legal analysis is only as effective as the quality with which it is expressed. In your practice, you undoubtedly will devote a substantial proportion of your time and effort to drafting legal documents such as office memoranda, letters, pleadings, motions, briefs, contracts, and wills. Moreover, techniques of expression are closely linked to the underlying substantive analysis; indeed, problems in writing style often betray confusion in the analysis.

Unfortunately, as a first-year law student, you might have difficulty seeing the relationship between your efforts in legal writing classes and your short-term objectives for success in law school. With this book, we hope to reassure you that the work in your first-year legal writing courses will directly contribute to your success with law school exams as well as with legal documents that you draft in a summer clerking position or in postgraduate employment. We hope to demonstrate in Parts I-IV that the skills you develop in analyzing a client's legal problem and drafting an office memorandum are directly transferable to your task of analyzing an essay exam and writing the exam answer.

The remainder of the book examines techniques of advocacy and client representation that should appeal to a broad spectrum of readers: participants in a first-year moot-court program, students in an advanced writing seminar, student law clerks, and practicing attorneys. For example, Parts V through VII examine written advocacy in the context of pleadings, pretrial motions, and appellate briefs. Moreover, they thoroughly examine principles of writing and persuasion that apply generally to any litigation document. Part VIII provides a step-by-step approach to drafting simple contracts, advice letters, and demand letters. Finally, the extensive citations in endnotes, most of which first-year law students can pass over, will provide attorneys with a valuable source of authorities.

Apart from special considerations in advocacy, the book addresses general matters of writing style in Chapters 1 and 8-10. These chapters use problems and examples to outline a general approach to style that focuses on the policies underlying conventions of composition. They encourage you to adopt the following philosophy: We should not memorize and mechanically apply rules of composition any more than we would mechanically apply "black letter" rules of law. Instead, we must understand the goals and purposes of the conventions of legal writing, and we should apply them flexibly to satisfy those goals and purposes. Much the same can be said about persuasive writing style, addressed in Chapter 13.

Of course, this book reflects our own style quirks and biases. We freely split infinitives but always use the serial comma, and we wish a gender-neutral singular pronoun in the third person would win universal acceptance. Unfortunately, the disjunctive phrase "his or her" often needlessly clutters already complex sentences, and plural pronouns such as "they" are not always consistent with content— although we no longer comment on student papers that pair "they" or "their" with a singular noun. When some reference to gender is inevitable, we have alternated between male and female pronouns, for example, by referring to an associate in a law firm with the pronoun "he" and to his assigning attorney with the pronoun "she." We hope this technique permits readers to identify with characters in the text regardless of gender identity. And, for those whose identify as nonbinary, we simply avoid gender references when possible, such as by using plural nouns and pronouns or by avoiding pronouns when possible.

The notes at the end of each chapter cite to source material and acknowledge the brilliant colleagues whose ideas inspired the text. Readers may find some of the additional information in the endnotes to be illuminating or to be helpful in practice as a starting point for research. Otherwise, however, busy students can focus on the text and skip the endnotes without missing any significant points.

January 2022
Charles R. Calleros and
Kimberly Y.W. Holst

ACKNOWLEDGMENTS

Attorneys, judges, and colleagues contributed to the first edition with their comments on early drafts. I especially thank the late Thomas Gordon, who was a staff attorney for the Arizona Court of Appeals, fellow legal writing instructor, and former classmate at the University of California at Davis School of Law. Mr. Gordon's keen analytic insights into the art of legal writing contributed greatly to this book. Other important contributors include the rigorous reviewers who strongly influenced the organization and content of the book, and Janet Wagner, an attorney who skillfully and artfully critiqued my writing style. Several colleagues contributed to selected portions of the book. They include Fred Cole, Amy Gittler, Mark Hielman, Susan E. Klemmer, Christopher Mason, William Monahan, Roger Perry, Frank Placenti, Thomas Quarelli, Jeffrey P. Travers, Paul Ulrich, Sherin Vitro, Judge Noel Fidel, and Professors Jane Aiken, Rebecca Berch (later Chief Justice of the Arizona Supreme Court), Paul Brand, Susan Chesler, Betsy Grey, Mark Hall, David Kader, Amy Langenfeld, Robert Misner, Cathy O'Grady, Mary Richards, Judy Stinson, Bonnie Tucker, James Weinstein, and Larry Winer.

The truly indispensable contributors to the early editions of this book, however, are the students and attorneys who used the early versions of the teaching materials from which this book is derived. I especially acknowledge the Phoenix law firm of Streich, Lang, Weeks & Cardon, now merged with Quarles & Brady, for its dedication to continuing education in legal writing during those years.

I also thank staff and student research assistants for their contributions to the nine editions, in the order of their participation over the years: Donna Blair, Gail Geer, Kay Winn, and Vera Hamer-Sonn provided word-processing assistance; Janice Fuller, Mark Burgoz, Michael Rutledge, Virginia Vasquez, Toby Schmich, Victoria Stevens, Jane Proctor, Lizzette M. Alameda, Brian M. Louisell, Lauren Elliott Stine, Robert Stultz, Jason Zasky, Ashley Stallings, Sarah Weimer, Nora Nuñez, Natalya Ter-Grigoryan, Alyssa Whetstine, Daniel Rubinov, Molly Walker, Carina Arellano, Emily Mahana, and Nicholas Hodder provided student research, cite-checking, and proofreading assistance. Ms. Ter-Grigoryan was especially conscientious and tireless in assisting in preparing the much improved sixth edition after compositor's errors in the fifth edition had introduced typos in the files. For the ninth edition Mr. Hodder applied excellent editing skills to simplify or streamline sentence structure in many places. I am also grateful to the law library staff at Arizona State University. Finally, I am indebted to Arizona

State University College of Law, and especially to Deans Paul Bender, Richard Morgan, Patricia White, Paul Berman, and Douglas Sylvester, who fully supported our efforts to produce the nine editions of this text.

I fondly acknowledge my late mother, Emily, for her early guidance in grammar and for creating the drawings (one for the first three editions, and a new one in its place for the fourth edition, and an updated version appearing in the fifth) illustrating the discussion of restrictive and nonrestrictive pronouns.

Finally, I am pleased to be collaborating with my colleague, Kimberly Holst, who first joined as co-author for the eighth edition, published in 2018. I welcome the contributions that she brings to this and future editions, as she increasingly influences the shape and content of the texts.

Charles Calleros
2022

LEGAL METHOD and WRITING

Part I

Law School—Getting Started

Welcome to law school! For many of you, law school will present at least two new educational challenges. First, the professor in your legal writing course may encourage you to adopt a legal writing style that differs from the writing style you cultivated in undergraduate studies. Second, most of your law school courses will help you develop skills of legal analysis through the "case method," a teaching and study technique that complements your work in your legal writing course. However, this teaching technique differs markedly from the simple lecture format used in many undergraduate courses.

Chapters 1 and 2 facilitate your orientation to law school by introducing you to some fundamental principles of legal writing style and the case method of study. Later, after you have a few weeks of legal education under your belt, you will reexamine these topics in much greater detail in Part IV.

Your first reading of each chapter in this book will provide essential guidance for your legal writing assignments and for general success in law school. You likely will not be able to take full advantage of the book's lessons on first reading, however, because they will frequently address topics with which you do not yet have any concrete experience. As you gain experience throughout the first year of law school, you will find that chapters assigned earlier in the year will make even more sense to you on a second reading. By then, you will have the experience to connect the text to tasks that you have undertaken and to questions that have since come to mind. To get the full benefit of this book, therefore, read each chapter carefully when it is initially assigned, and then periodically review earlier reading assignments after you have gained experience and generated new questions. You will find that the assigned text is even more meaningful and informative on second reading, as it addresses issues that have only recently come into sharp focus in your studies.

After your 1L year, this book can serve as a reference tool in summer clerkships or externships and in your first job after graduation. The chapter endnotes include hundreds of citations to authorities that you will find useful in the practice of law. Perhaps most important, the chapters in Part V provide guides to drafting pleadings and pretrial motions. Trial court filings are often neglected in law school coursework, but they dominate a typical litigation practice.

To get started, turn to the next page, and have a fruitful journey.

Chapter 1

Introduction to Writing Style: Policy, Purpose, and Audience

I. General Approach

Much of this book addresses matters of content or substance in legal writing, which are qualities relating to sound legal analysis and to the accuracy of statements on which courts and clients rely. As a matter of style, however, a substantively good analysis of facts or law will be effective only if expressed clearly and concisely.

The importance of clarity in legal writing should be obvious: your legal memorandum will not enlighten, nor will your brief persuade, unless the reader can understand it. To appreciate the significance of concise writing, you need only consider the time pressures that a supervising attorney or a judge faces; neither has time to glean from 20 pages ideas that you could have clearly expressed in 10.[1]

The dual goals of clarity and concision are often compatible: improving concision by omitting surplus words and by organizing your points more efficiently will frequently enhance clarity as well. After successive revisions, however, further concision may come only at the expense of clarity; in those circumstances, you must give priority to clarity.

II. The Perspective of the Legal Writer

Law students sometimes complain that legal writing's emphasis on clarity and concision compels them to abandon the literary eloquence that they strove to develop in college and to replace it with a dry, uniform style. They may overstate their complaints; effective legal writing reflects the application of principles of good writing generally. Nonetheless, as an inevitable consequence of the substance and purpose of legal documents, legal writing often differs in both substance and style from other kinds of writing.

For example, consider how different writers might treat the subject of a male supervisor's sexual harassment of a female subordinate in the workplace. A poet might create an image of the pain and frustration of the harasser's victim, so vivid an image that readers who had never experienced sexual harassment could appreciate the victim's plight.[2] A writer for a political journal might describe the specific incident as a symptom of more general oppression within a sexist society. A novelist might describe the harassment in particularly dramatic prose, perhaps either as a vehicle for character development or purely to engage or shock the reader.

On the other hand, an associate for the law firm representing the victim of the harassment is understandably preoccupied with the legal significance of the supervisor's actions. In preparing an office memorandum, the associate will analyze whether the harassment constituted "extreme and outrageous conduct," thus satisfying an element of a claim under the tort of intentional infliction of emotional distress. The extent of the victim's injury will interest the associate, at least partly, as an indication of the damages that the victim can recover. Moreover, the associate may discuss events or circumstances that other writers would ignore completely. For example, the associate may confirm the status of the harassing employee as an office supervisor, so that the institutional employer could more easily be held liable for the supervisor's harassment under Title VII of the Civil Rights Act of 1964.[3]

The different perspectives of these writers necessarily influence their writing styles. The poet's meaning may be obscured in the interest of "avoiding dull exposition" and of gaining dramatic effect through rhythm and metaphor.[4] Similarly, the novelist may seek to entertain or stimulate the reader through elegant variation or deliberate ambiguity.[5] But the legal writer can seldom afford to entertain at the expense of communicating clearly. On occasion, legal writers may have legitimate reasons for ambiguity, but deliberate ambiguity should be the exception, not the rule. A supervising attorney is not interested in dwelling on each sentence of an office memorandum to divine its meaning as he might dwell on each line of a poem. Similarly, a judge is not likely to be persuaded by a brief that she does not fully comprehend, even though it entertains her.

This does not mean that lawyers must always write from a legal perspective. If you desire to retain or develop literary eloquence, you may write poetry by night and legal briefs by day.

Nor does it mean that legal writing must be dull, dry, and technical. Clear, concrete, concise legal writing can and should be active, vivid, and engaging. Indeed, you can enhance the persuasive effect of your writing with a telling metaphor, a dramatic phrase, or an engaging description of events that tells a client's story accurately but in a compelling fashion. In short, "law does have a poetic dimension,"[6] and the narrative techniques employed in a novel retain a role in legal advocacy.[7] If you can grab and hold the reader's rapt attention with clear, concise, and engaging writing,[8] your memorandum or brief will drive your points home like a home run with the bases loaded.

Moreover, the legal perspective does not doom legal writers to a uniform writing style. The goals of clear communication and persuasion leave room for individuality. Indeed, you should approach rules of writing style in much the same way that you approach legal rules: apply the rules no further than necessary to serve the underlying policies. Even seemingly inflexible conventions, like rules of punctuation or sentence structure, may simply reflect a desire for clarity or proper emphasis, leaving room for writers' discretion about how best to achieve those objectives.

III. A Policy-Oriented Approach

Many rules of composition are nothing more than conventions that reflect generalities about the best way to achieve clear, concise writing with effective emphasis and flow. Even the traditional rule against splitting infinitives appears to have given way to a more flexible discretionary approach: "Some infinitives seem to improve on being split, just as a stick of round stove wood does."[9] You should familiarize yourself with rules of composition, including the recommendations summarized in Chapter 9, as general guides to achieving the objectives of clarity and concision rather than as ends in themselves.

For example, many writers believe that they may never start a sentence with "However," because their teachers or editors strictly applied a rule against such placement. But it is difficult to justify an inflexible rule to that effect; instead, the placement of transitional words such as "however" should be influenced by considerations of emphasis and flow in the sentence. Those considerations often call for placement of "however" at a natural, mid-sentence breaking point. That placement subordinates "however" as a parenthetic transition guide and permits more substantive parts of the sentence to enjoy the prominence of the position at the beginning of the sentence:

> The statute of frauds does not apply, however, because Vasquez could have performed the contract within one year.

However, if you wish to draw immediate attention to a shift in position or perspective, such as from point to counterpoint, you can appropriately signal that shift at the beginning of the sentence, as in this one.

The debate about the "serial" comma rule further illustrates the benefit of understanding the justifications for rules or conventions of composition. According to the traditional rule, you should use a comma to separate each element of a series of three or more things, as in "meat, vegetables, and dairy products." During the "new English" and "new math" movements of the 1960s, elementary school teachers began teaching a discretionary trend to omit the last comma of the series on the ground that the conjunction "and" or "or" adequately separates the last two elements of the series. The trend never fully displaced the traditional rule. Strunk and White have never wavered in their support for the final comma,[10] and many elementary schools later returned to the traditional teachings. Unfortunately, many students in the meantime had adopted an inflexible practice of always omitting the final comma.

In fact, omitting the final comma may hamper clarity in a series in which some elements have multiple sub-elements. Consider, for example, the possible meanings of this clause: "imprisonment for a maximum of 30 days, a fine of $5,000 and community service for 90 days or probation for a maximum of five years." Depending on the location of a final comma, which would pinpoint the final element of the series, this clause could mean either:

1. [imprisonment for a maximum of 30 days], [a fine of $5,000 and community service for 90 days], or [probation for a maximum of five years];

   OR

2. [imprisonment for a maximum of 30 days], [a fine of $5,000], and [community service for 90 days or probation for a maximum of five years].

Subtle, temporary ambiguities in structure sometimes arise even if the series uses only the coordinating conjunction "and" and not the disjunctive conjunction "or."[11]

Armed with these insights, you can choose either of two approaches to the comma controversy, depending on the emphasis that you place on different policies of composition. If you value consistency as well as clarity, you could reasonably adopt a convention of always using the final comma, because you know that it will sometimes be necessary for clarity and will never cause confusion.[12] Alternatively, if you prefer to restrict punctuation to the necessary minimum, you could exercise stylistic discretion to insert the final comma when it is necessary for clarity and to omit it otherwise.

IV. Purpose and Audience

In every legal document, you should adapt your writing style to achieve the purpose of the document and to suit the needs of your intended audience. By its nature, legal writing is audience focused. In particular, legal writing is designed to meet the expectations of the law trained reader. Part IV thoroughly examines this feature of writing style in the context of office memoranda. Parts V through VII address the needs of intended audiences in the context of briefs to trial and appellate courts, advice letters to clients and demand letters to opposing parties, and contracts on behalf of a client. An overview here will serve to introduce some fundamental principles.

A. Purpose

Many legal documents can be classified as having either of two essential purposes: (1) to communicate a balanced analysis or (2) to persuade. For the most part, essay exam answers, office memoranda, and advice letters to clients fall into the first category. Ordinarily, the purpose of each is to help your reader understand the strengths and the weaknesses of a legal claim or defense. Briefs to a court and demand letters to an opposing party, on the other hand, fall into the second category. The purpose of a brief is to persuade a judge to make a ruling that favors your client. The purpose of a demand letter is to persuade another party to take some practical action, such as pay a debt, drop a claim, or cease some activity that is causing injury to your client. Identifying the purpose of the document should be a conscious and active part of your writing process.

Accordingly, you should adapt the content and style of the writing in each of your documents to suit these distinct purposes. For example, in an office memorandum or an advice letter, you must communicate the strengths as well as the weaknesses of your client's claims or defenses. Thus, if your client seeks to prove that her employer breached an employment contract by discharging her without good cause, you should candidly reveal to her and to your supervisor that the contract language is ambiguous on that point:

> Each of the five grounds for discharge specifically listed in section IX of the employment contract describes some kind of misconduct or unsatisfactory performance by the employee. However, the prefatory phrase "such as" suggests that the list is not exhaustive, but illustrative. If so, the employer may argue that he retained the right to fire an employee for any reason and that he listed only the most obvious reasons in the contract.
>
> To establish that the contract instead requires just cause for dismissal, we should....

In contrast, in your brief to a court, you will attempt to persuade a judge or panel of judges to interpret the contract language in a way that limits grounds for discharge. Accordingly, you should adopt a writing style that reflects confidence in your client's position:

> Section IX of the contract explicitly lists five types of employee misconduct or poor performance as grounds for discharge. Even if the five grounds listed in section IX are illustrative rather than exhaustive, as argued by the defendant, they all illustrate cases in which the employer has good cause for terminating the employment contract. Thus, section IX describes a limited category of grounds for discharge, one that does not justify the arbitrary discharge in this case....

B. Audience

Even when you seek to achieve similar purposes with different documents, you might need to adapt your writing style to the needs of each audience. For example, in both an office memorandum and an advice letter, your purpose is to present a balanced analysis of your client's claims and defenses. The readers of these documents, however, may vary greatly in legal sophistication. The experienced attorney who reads your office memorandum will appreciate your use of fundamental legal terminology and legal authority, as in this excerpt from an analysis of a police officer's defense in a civil rights action:

> If the district court denies Officer Tippett's motion for summary judgment on a question of law, Officer Tippett can file an interlocutory appeal on the issue of qualified immunity. *See Mitchell v. Forsyth*, 472 U.S. 511, 524-30 (1985).

On the other hand, your client, Officer Tippett, presumably has little or no legal training in pretrial and appellate civil procedure. Accordingly, in an advice letter to Officer Tippett on the same issue, you should explain your analysis in plain language:

> Even if the trial court denies your request to dismiss the action against you before trial, you need not face a trial immediately. In many cases, you can immediately appeal the trial court's rejection of your immunity defense. In the meantime, the trial will be delayed while the appellate court determines whether your conduct was indeed sufficiently reasonable that you should be immune from liability for damages.

In some cases, your task is complicated by the presence of multiple purposes and audiences. You will explore these matters further in later chapters, in the context of various documents.

V. Overview of the Process of Legal Writing

Chapter by chapter, this book introduces you to steps in the process of analyzing a legal problem and effectively expressing your analysis in a legal document. The following overview provides a road map to what lies ahead.

A. Developing Skills of Legal Method and Analysis

First and foremost, you must have something to say. You cannot expect to communicate clearly or persuasively unless you comprehend the ideas you wish to express. Parts I through III of this book provide you with tools to identify legal issues, analyze the issues, and develop legal arguments. Specifically, after the next chapter introduces you to the case method of study, Chapters 3 and 4 explore the roles of common law and legislation in our legal system. Chapters 5 and 6 introduce you to important legal concepts and tools of analysis: deference to prior case law and the application of deductive and inductive reasoning to legal problems. Chapters 7 through 10 then capitalize on the foundation built in previous chapters by exploring the content and style of an office memorandum of law. Remaining chapters address other forms of writing, such as briefs to a court, letters to clients or opponents, and contracts.

B. Researching the Law

Once you understand how the law operates, how to identify legal issues, and how to analyze a legal problem, you must find the legal authorities that state the applicable law. Unless your professor or assigning attorney provides you with a file of legal authority, you must research the law in the library or online, a process explored in separate, specialized texts on legal research.

C. Prewriting

As you draft a legal document, you will find that the process of putting your thoughts into writing will sharpen and deepen your understanding of the analysis, enabling you to improve your analysis throughout the drafting process. Nonetheless, you will produce a better final product, and will do so more efficiently, if you carefully plan your writing before you begin to write.

In its earliest and most tentative stages, this "prewriting" process may take the form of refining the issues that you intend to research, filing and indexing your research notes in an organized manner, and developing your analysis of the law as your research proceeds. The most important stage of prewriting, however, is the process of organizing the points that you wish to express after you have completed your research. If you take this step seriously, you can develop an outline to clarify your analysis, allowing you to focus more attention on matters of composition when you begin writing.

To effectively organize your thoughts, you must have a general idea of the format of your document. Thus, Chapter 7 introduces the elements of an office memorandum of law. Parts VI and VII of this text examine the formats of various kinds of briefs submitted to courts.

D. Writing

If you have conscientiously researched and analyzed your problem and have carefully organized your thoughts in outline form, you will be better prepared to focus your attention on the process of writing your document in full. The process of writing an objective analysis is examined thoroughly in Part IV, with further discussion of persuasive writing style appearing in Part V of this text.

An important thread, introduced in this chapter, runs through the discussion of writing style in Chapter 9: good writers do not mechanically apply inflexible rules of composition, nor do they reflexively react without attention to goals or guiding principles. Instead, good writers consciously choose between alternatives, and they flexibly adapt conventions of composition to the needs of their audience and to the purpose of their document. All these considerations are undertaken with the aim of achieving distinctly identified goals, such as clarity, concision, and persuasiveness.

E. Revising Your Writing

The quality of your prewriting and writing processes will influence the time and effort needed for revision. Nonetheless, regardless of the care with which you planned and drafted your document, you can always improve it through proofing and polishing. Strategies for revising your writing, as well as economic limitations on multiple revisions, are discussed in Chapter 9.

F. Revisiting Earlier Stages

This process of researching, analyzing, prewriting, writing, and revising might not proceed in a perfectly linear fashion because later stages of the process will often reveal the need to "circle back" to previous stages. While prewriting or writing, you might encounter gaps in your analysis that require you to supplement your research. During the writing stage, you might find problems with transitions between the sections of your document, leading you to return to your outline to reconsider the organization of your document. Thus, any stage of the thinking and writing process could pave the way for further progress on an earlier or later stage.

VI. Proceeding with Purpose and Enthusiasm

This chapter and Chapters 8 through 10 develop and describe a method of approaching and resolving problems of composition, much as Chapters 3 through 6 describe a method of approaching legal problems.

As you proceed through the book and through your legal writing course, consider this reflection from a student who had just completed a first-year course in legal method and writing in 2013:

> As I reflect on my year in legal methods, I know I have become a better student. I would like to talk about how my writing has improved, but I think this class has taught me much more than that. I learned how to manage my time, how to research, how to work with others, how to solve disputes, how to write persuasively, how to advocate, how to build personal relationships with my classmates, how to hold myself accountable, how to hold my partners accountable, and how to become a better overall law student. This was not a writing class for me. This class taught me how to excel in all my classes, and I feel it is by far the most important class I have taken this semester. I understand that we are learning law in our other classes, and the interpretation of that law. However, this class is the foundation for everything else. Going into practice, I am confident that the education I received in this course has prepared me to excel. I do not think a single individual has received a better education, and the confidence that I have leaving this course is what I value the most.[13]

Of course, reaping such rewards from a course requires dedication, hard work, and willingness to learn from constructive feedback. If you bring that commitment to your study of legal method and writing, you will greatly enhance your legal knowledge and your skills of analysis and expression.

Exercise 1-1

Examine your previous education and experiences relating to writing. Consider whether the special characteristics of legal writing require you to depart from writing styles that you have used successfully in other contexts. Use this self-examination to prepare for constructive criticism from your writing professors.

To begin a dialogue with your writing professor, write an essay in response to one or more of the questions posed at the end of the following problem, and discuss your response with your professor. Do not feel compelled to identify a "correct answer" or to couch your response in any special legal format or style. Instead, simply develop an honest response based on your personal values and opinions and express your response freely in a style that comes to you naturally and comfortably. Ask your writing professor to assess the extent to which your natural writing style is consistent with or deviates from your professor's view of effective legal writing.

Survival of the Fittest and the Common Law

Imagine that you are deciding cases in the nineteenth century as the chief justice of a state's highest appellate court. Your state has no criminal statutes; instead, the criminal law of the state is exclusively common law, a law fashioned by judges and based on custom, common sense, and community values.

Before you is an appeal from a murder conviction in the case of *State v. Blight.* After a full trial, the jury found that Fletcher Blight, the defendant and appellant, had killed Davie Jones by pushing him off a life raft and into the ocean.

The trial record shows that both men boarded the life raft after their vessel had sunk on the high seas. After days of drifting, and with no ship or land on the horizon, it became apparent that the water rations would not sustain both men until a rescue ship arrived. Blight, the stronger of the two, decided to (1) save the remaining water supply for himself; (2) stop administering water to Jones, who was too weak to move; and (3) allow Jones to die. Jones suffered great pain as he slowly died of dehydration. To end Jones's misery and to spare himself the emotional distress of watching Jones suffer, Blight tearfully pushed the helpless Jones into the sea, where Jones quickly died. When Blight was rescued by a passing ship a few days later, he was near death himself. Physicians testified at trial that both men undoubtedly would have died before the rescue ship arrived if Blight had continued sharing the water rations with Jones until the water was exhausted.

1. **Were Blight's actions morally justified?** Speaking as an individual with no connection to the case, do you think Blight's actions were morally justified? Why or why not?
2. **Should the Court expand the legal justifications?** Now, imagine that you are an attorney or a judge in the criminal prosecution of Blight in State *X*, which you can assume has jurisdiction. At the time of the prosecution, criminal law in State *X* is still a matter of "common law," developed by judges, and has not yet been codified into statutes by the State *X* legislature. In State *X*, the courts have defined the common law crime of murder as the "unlawful killing of a human being without justification." At the time of Blight's prosecution, the Supreme Court of State *X* had recognized only one justification for killing another person: self-defense in the face of a potentially deadly attack from the other person. Because Jones had not attacked Blight, Blight's actions were not justified under current law, and he was convicted at trial. On appeal, Blight asks the State *X* Supreme Court to expand the common law justifications to cover the circumstances of his case. In your view, should the law evolve to find justification in Blight's acts?
3. **Precisely what new common law rule or rules would justify Blight's deeds?** As Blight's attorney, draft Blight's proposed rule or rules in the form of proposed trial court instructions to the jury: "You must acquit the defendant of the charge of murder if he was justified in killing Jones. In this case, the defendant was justified in killing Jones if you find that. . . ." This will help to define the expanded justification that the Supreme Court is being asked to approve.

a. As the Chief Justice of the State *X* Supreme Court, would you adopt the proposed rule? What reasons would you give for supporting or opposing an extension of the common law doctrine of justification that would result in Blight's acquittal?

b. Would you support a new common law rule that would improve the law but would not necessarily result in acquittal for Blight? If so, describe the rule and explain your reasons for proposing it.

Checklist for Chapter 1

- ✔ Aim for writing that is clear and concise. When these two goals conflict, give priority to clarity.
- ✔ Do not dogmatically adhere to rules of composition. Instead, appreciate the policies underlying these general rules, and apply them to the extent necessary to achieve those policies. Flexibly depart from overly broad rules to achieve a legitimate writing goal.
- ✔ Adapt your writing style to your purpose and your audience.
- ✔ Adopt an effective process for legal writing:
  - Identify legal issues and develop your analysis, through effective legal research and reasoning, as explored in later chapters.
  - Then plan, write, and revise.
  - Be prepared to circle back to previous stages of this writing process if the need arises.

Endnotes

1. *See, e.g.*, Westinghouse Elec. Corp. v. NLRB, 809 F.2d 419, 424-25 (7th Cir. 1987) (imposing $1,000 penalty on counsel for evading federal rule limiting the number of pages of its opening brief); Morgan v. S. Bend Cmty. Sch. Corp., 797 F.2d 471, 480 (7th Cir. 1986) ("A [page] limitation induces the advocate to write tight prose, which helps his client's cause."); Reliance Ins. Co. v. Sweeney Corp., Md., 792 F.2d 1137, 1139 (D.C. Cir. 1986) ("this court encourages short, tightly argued briefs in all cases, regardless of their complexity").
2. *Cf.* Elisabeth W. Schneider, POEMS AND POETRY 3 (1964) (discussing the difficulty of transferring an "experience whole and alive into the mind, emotions, and sensations of another person").
3. *See* Faragher v. City of Boca Raton, 524 U.S. 775, 802-09 (1998) (subject to some limitations and defenses, an employer is liable for supervisor's sexually harassing conduct under Title VII, 42 U.S.C. § 2000e-2(a)(1) (2012)).
4. Schneider, *supra* note 2, at 25-26.

5. *See* William Strunk, Jr. & E. B. White, The Elements of Style 79 (5th ed. 2009) ("There are occasions when obscurity serves a literary yearning, if not a literary purpose . . . .").
6. Gary Watt, Equity Stirring: The Story of Justice Beyond Law 145 (2009); *see also* Stephen E. Smith, *The Poetry of Persuasion: Early Literary Theory and Its Advice to Legal Writers*, 6 J. ALWD 55, 56 (2009) ("The poem's aim of producing aesthetic pleasure may provide an avenue to persuasion that the legal writer should consider in drafting her own persuasive pieces.").
7. *See, e.g.*, Elizabeth Fajans & Mary R. Falk, *Untold Stories: Restoring Narrative to Pleading Practice*, 15 Legal Writing: J. Legal Writing Inst. 3 (2009) (arguing for pleadings that tell a compelling story rather than merely meet the minimum requirements of modern notice pleading); Bret Rappaport, *Tapping the Human Adaptive Origins of Storytelling by Requiring Legal Writing Students to Read a Novel in Order to Appreciate How Character, Setting, Plot, Theme, and Tone (CSPTT) Are as Important as IRAC*, 25 T.M. Cooley L. Rev. 267 (2008) (storytelling is a powerful, persuasive tool that is part of the lawyer's tradition).
8. *See* Mark K. Osbeck, *What Is "Good Legal Writing" and Why Does It Matter?*, 4 Drexel L. Rev. 417 (2012).
9. Strunk & White, *supra* note 5, at 78; *see also id.* at 58 (arguing against routine adherence to the traditional rule against splitting infinitives). A contemporary dictionary argues that the traditional rule against splitting infinitives was never well founded:

   > Writers who long ago insisted that English could be modeled on Latin created the "rule" that the English infinitive must not be split: *to clearly state* violates this rule; one must say *to state clearly*. But the Latin infinitive is one word (e.g. amare, "to love") and cannot be split, so the rule is not firmly grounded, and treating two English words as one can lead to awkward, stilted sentences.

   The New Oxford American Desk Dictionary 1637 (2d ed. 2005).
10. William Strunk, Jr. & E. B. White, The Elements of Style 1-2 (1st ed. 1959); *id.* at 2 (2d ed. 1972); *id.* at 2 (3d ed. 1979); *id.* at 2 (4th ed. 2000); *id.* at 2 (5th ed. 2009) (50th anniversary edition, reprinting the 4th edition text).
11. *See, e.g.*, Bryan A. Garner, The Elements of Legal Style 16 (2d ed. 2002) (providing illustrations).
12. Strunk & White, *supra* note 5, at 2 ("Always Use the Serial Comma").
13. This quotation is taken from a student blog authored by 1L Richard Sgrignoli, in response to a reflection assignment from his Legal Methods professor, Anna Hemingway, Widener University School of Law.

Chapter 2

Overview of the Case Method of Study

In your first-year contracts course, you probably will study the case of *Hadley and Another v. Baxendale and Others.*[1] By examining the history of this case now, you can become acquainted with the methods by which you will study law in most of your classes.

I. *Hadley v. Baxendale*: A Case Study

The dispute between the Hadleys and Baxendale began as a business transaction during an economic boom amidst England's industrial revolution. Operators of a flour mill in Gloucester entered into a contract with a carrier for the transportation of a broken engine shaft to a manufacturer in Greenwich, on the other side of England.

The operators of the mill, the Hadleys, were anxious to transport the broken shaft to the manufacturer as quickly as possible. The failure of the shaft had halted the milling of corn, and the broken shaft would serve as a model for the manufacture of a new shaft. An employee of the carrier, Pickford and Co., promised that the shaft would be delivered to the manufacturer within two days after the date that the carrier took possession of the shaft. For this, the mill operators paid £2 4s. The carrier could have transported the shaft as promptly as promised had it immediately used available means of land transportation. Presumably to reduce costs, however, it held the shaft for several days in London before loading it onto a canal barge along with a shipment of iron that was bound for the same manufacturer. Consequently, the carrier delivered the shaft to the manufacturer on the seventh day after the carrier received it, resulting in an additional delay of five days during which the mill was stopped.

The mill operators demanded that the carrier compensate for an estimated £300 in lost profits that the mill suffered because of the additional delay. The carrier refused, and the mill operators sued the carrier's managing director, Baxendale, in a trial court in Gloucester, claiming approximately £200 in damages. Although the carrier offered to settle the dispute for £25, the mill operators rejected the offer, and the case went to trial before a jury. The mill operators presented witnesses who testified to £120 in damages, and the jury awarded the mill operators £50 in a compromise verdict that became the judgment of the trial court.

The carrier appealed to the Court of Exchequer. The carrier ultimately persuaded a panel of three judges on this appellate court to reverse the judgment of the trial court and to grant a new trial because the trial judge had given the jury excessive latitude in awarding damages for lost profits.

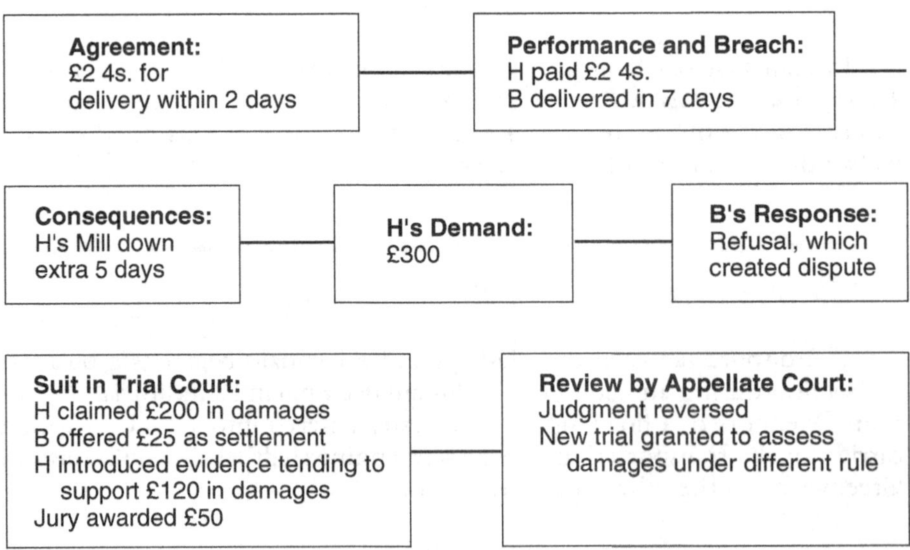

Dispute and Litigation in *Hadley v. Baxendale*

In the appellate court's written opinion, the authoring judge explained that a jury may award only those damages that would flow naturally from the breach of such a contract or that would be reasonably within the contemplation of the parties because of special circumstances communicated at the time of contracting. The appellate judges assumed that the mill would ordinarily have a spare shaft to replace a broken one; consequently, they concluded that lost profits stemming from an idle mill would not be the natural consequence of the breach of the contract for prompt carriage. Whether the possibility of lost profits would nonetheless have been in the contemplation of the parties would depend on whether, at the time of contracting, the mill operators had communicated to the carrier the special circumstances that the broken shaft was the mill's only shaft and that the mill would be idle in its absence.

The appellate court concluded that the mill operators had informed the carrier only that they operated a mill and that the article to be transported was the broken shaft of a mill.[2] On this premise, the appellate court held that the trial judge should not have allowed the jury to consider any lost profits in its calculation of damages.

The case of *Hadley v. Baxendale* illustrates both how a case makes its way through the legal system and how you typically encounter the case only at the final destination in its legal journey. Reacting to a pressing commercial need, the mill operators entered into an agreement with the carrier to exchange money for certain services. Disappointed with the services rendered, the mill operators demanded compensation. Failing to secure the compensation through less formal means, they filed an action in a trial court to obtain a judgment compelling the carrier to pay compensation.

At trial, each party discovered that his claims or defenses were limited by his ability to present credible supporting evidence to the jury, to whom the court had delegated the task of finding facts. Hence, the mill operator's original demand dropped first from £300 to £200, and then to the £120 of losses for which it could produce evidence. Relying on centuries of development of law and custom, the court honored the contractual relationship and permitted the jury to award damages for the carrier's breach of the contract. The jury awarded less in damages than the trial court's instructions and the evidence would have allowed, but more than the carrier thought the law should permit. Accordingly, the carrier took the dispute before a court of higher authority, which ordered a new trial and ruled that the mill operator should not be entitled to recover for lost profits in the new trial. The higher court explained its decision in a written judicial opinion.

II. The Litigation Pyramid

In only a tiny percentage of disputes do the parties complete this process of full trial followed by review of the trial court's judgment in one or more appellate courts. Countless people become entangled in disputes that could give rise to legal claims, yet they seldom take the formal step of filing lawsuits to test their claims. In even fewer cases do they fully litigate their disputes in the trial court. In most lawsuits, the parties manage to settle their disputes before trial by agreeing to a compromise, thus avoiding the expense and risks of full trial. In many others, a full trial of the facts is unnecessary to resolve the dispute, and the trial court grants judgment for one of the parties before trial.

In cases that result in judgment after a full trial, only a small percentage of losing parties seek review of the adverse judgment in an appellate court. When further review in an even higher appellate court is available, still fewer seek that review. Thus, the proportions of disputes that proceed to various levels of dispute resolution form a pyramid:

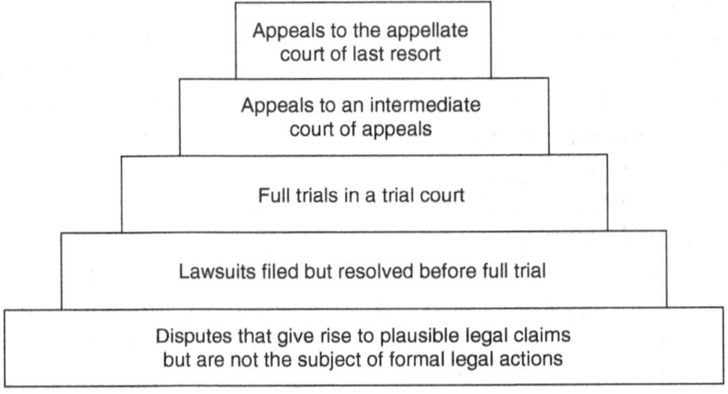

Litigation Pyramid

III. The Casebook Method of Study

Law school courses will direct your attention primarily to appellate court decisions. In nearly all first-year courses in law school, you will encounter the law in casebooks, each of which presents judicial opinions on various topics that relate to a general field of law such as property, contracts, crimes, procedure, or torts.

The cases in a casebook are the disputes that parties bring to courts for resolution. Most of the judicial opinions that analyze the cases are the opinions of appellate courts. These opinions are edited by casebook authors. The edited appellate opinions published in casebooks often summarize the facts of the dispute and the proceedings in lower courts as concisely as possible,[3] sometimes providing no more than a bare outline of the human drama that has preceded the appellate litigation. Most appellate opinions focus instead on using the cases before them as vehicles for developing and articulating general legal rules or principles. In addition to resolving the dispute before the court, these rules provide guidance to courts and litigants in future disputes of a similar nature, as well as to persons who desire to conform their actions to the law.

Judicial opinions may mystify you in your first weeks at law school. They are peppered with legal terminology that will become part of your working vocabulary only after weeks and months of study. Even worse, some of the judicial language, particularly in the older cases, will be antiquated or overly formal and should not influence your own legal writing style; yet you must immerse yourself in the language to understand the opinions.

Moreover, the opinions assume that the reader is familiar with the legal system and the legal method that courts use when working within that system. For example, you might wonder how an early English decision such as *Hadley v. Baxendale* is relevant to your study of law in the United States. Also confusing to some new law students is the relationship between "common law" and "statutory law," both of which may be addressed in the same judicial opinion. Parts II and III of this book answer these and many other questions by introducing you to our legal system and to fundamental principles of legal method.

You undoubtedly will be preparing case briefs or undertaking a process for reading and understanding cases in preparation for the first day of class. You will learn that your professors discuss appellate opinions in a manner that suits their individual pedagogic preferences, which can help you select details for highlighting in your preparation for class discussion. Until you learn more about those preferences, or those of your legal writing professor, you may follow these steps when briefing cases.

Before you begin studying and briefing the case, briefly note the context with a few words at the top of your page. To identify context, consult the syllabus or your casebook's section headings to note the current topic of study, which the assigned case must be illustrating. Then, read the opinion once for a general overview. During your second reading, study the opinion carefully and fill in the elements of your case brief, according to your understanding and interpretation of the opinion:

1. Identification of the Case (state the case name, authoring court, and year of decision)
2. Facts (summarize the facts that led to the legal dispute)
3. Procedural History (summarize the judgments or rulings of the lower courts preceding this court's decision, and state this court's ruling on appeal, such as affirmed, reversed, or remanded for further proceedings)
4. Issue(s) and Holding(s) (state the questions the court addresses, followed by the court's conclusion on each question)
5. Reasoning (explain the court's reasons for its conclusions by summarizing the legal rule or rules adopted by the court and the court's application of those rules to the facts, including any policy considerations that inform its analysis)
6. Evaluation (explain your agreement or disagreement with the court's conclusions and reasoning)

7. Synthesis (explain how this opinion's holding and reasoning compare to those of other assigned opinions that address the same issue and that you have previously briefed)

Actively engage with the case as you are reading and briefing it. Ask yourself how the decision is supported by existing legal authority or policy considerations, take a stand on whether you agree with the decision, and compare the decision with others in the casebook that address the same issue. If you desire further instruction in briefing cases for class, Appendix I provides comprehensive guidance on that topic, as well as three sample cases with which you can practice briefing and synthesizing cases. You will discover that the process for briefing cases is essential to understanding case law and preparing for class discussion, but it does not directly translate to a case summary for a legal document such as an office memorandum or a brief. Later chapters of this book will explore the analysis and presentation of cases in legal documents.

Checklist for Chapter 2

- ✔ Recognize that few cases are litigated through appeal, but
- ✔ Embrace the case method as an important tool for studying law and legal method.
- ✔ Do your best to brief every case assigned for class discussion, with active engagement.
- ✔ Unless and until you learn that a professor prefers to analyze cases in a different manner, follow the guide to briefing cases set forth above in Section III and explained in greater detail in Appendix I.

Endnotes

1. 9 Ex. 341, 156 Eng. Rep. 145 (1854).
2. Interestingly, this represents a departure from the summary of the trial proceedings prepared by the court reporter, who had reported at the beginning of the appellate opinion that the mill operators had informed the carrier that the mill was stopped. Richard Danzig & Geoffrey R. Watson, The Capability Problem in Contract Law 62 (2d ed. 2004) (characterizing the finding of the Court of Exchequer as "remarkable").
3. Indeed, many of the details of *Hadley v. Baxendale* described in this book do not appear in the report of the Court of the Exchequer, much less in a casebook's edited version of that report. The source of this book's more detailed recounting of the case is Danzig & Watson, *supra* note 2, at 48-90.

Part II

Introduction to the Legal System

Chapters 3 and 4 thoroughly examine two important modes of lawmaking in our common law system. Chapter 3 examines common law principles that English and American courts have developed over centuries. Chapter 4 addresses statutes adopted by legislatures, approaches to interpreting statutes, and the relationship between legislation and common law.

Chapter 3

Common Law

I. Overview—Sources of Lawmaking Powers

The United States Constitution allocates powers between the state and national governments and thus establishes the framework for our federal system of government. In turn, each state's constitution establishes the framework for that state's government. A fundamental tenet of these state and federal constitutions is the separation of powers between the legislative, judicial, and executive branches of government. Although lawmaking functions rest primarily with the legislative branch, all three branches exercise some form of lawmaking power.

A. Legislative and Executive Branches

The state and federal legislatures create law by enacting statutes within the authority granted to them by the state and federal constitutions.

Although the primary function of the executive branch is enforcement of laws, the executive branch may lead in policy development by proposing legislation to a legislature. Moreover, a legislature may delegate some of its lawmaking power to the executive branch by statutorily authorizing an executive agency to issue rules and regulations designed to help implement a statutory scheme.

For example, in the exercise of its federal constitutional authority to regulate commerce, the United States Congress has enacted comprehensive labor relations statutes, such as the National Labor Relations Act.[1] It has also created the National Labor Relations Board (NLRB), an agency of the United States, and has authorized the NLRB to issue administrative rules and regulations necessary to help the NLRB enforce the labor relations statutes.[2]

Legislatures cannot amend a constitution in the same way that they enact statutes. For example, Article V of the United States Constitution authorizes Congress to propose constitutional amendments, but such proposals do not become effective until ratified by the legislatures or constitutional conventions of three-fourths of the states. For convenience, this book uses the term "enacted law" to refer to both statutes and constitutions.

B. Judicial Branch

The judicial branch of government develops law in two ways, both in the context of specific disputes. First, state and federal courts contribute to the development of constitutional and statutory law by interpreting the necessarily general terms of such enacted law when applying those terms to the facts of disputes. Second, as offspring of the English judicial system, courts in the United States have adopted, and continue to develop, a substantial body of common law: judge-made law that applies to issues that constitutional or statutory law does not address. State courts are the primary source of common law, because federal courts no longer create and develop "federal general common law."[3] Nonetheless, the federal courts retain the power in a few restricted fields, such as admiralty law, to develop "specialized federal common law."[4]

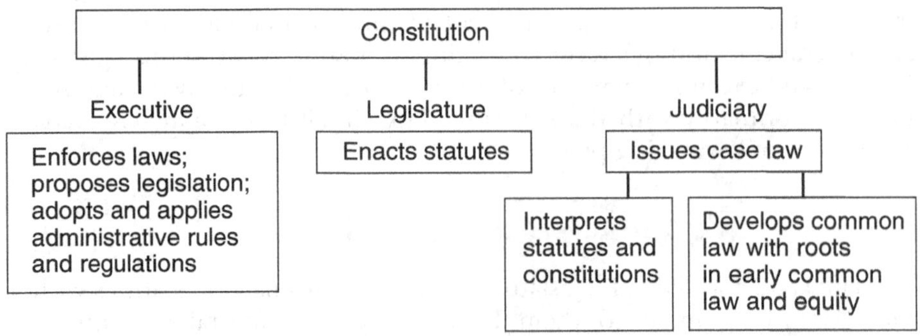

Lawmaking Authority in U.S. Legal System

C. Common Law as a Backdrop for Legislation

An example of the interplay between statutory law and common law is provided in your first-year contracts course. Many principles of contract law—such as consideration, offer and acceptance, performance and breach, and remedies—find their source in a substantial body of common law, developed by judges, first in England and later in the United States.

The common law of contracts forms a backdrop against which state legislatures have enacted statutes, which supersede some of the common law rules. In the resulting hybrid system, the statutes provide the rule of law on issues to which they apply, while common law applies to gaps within and between statutes, and to whole topics that statutes have not addressed.

D. Local and Tribal Governments

These fundamental principles of state and federal lawmaking apply only in limited fashion to two other kinds of governments in the United States: (1) local governments, such as those of cities and counties, and (2) American Indian tribal governments.

Local governments come in a variety of models. Although many of them exercise legislative, executive, and judicial powers, they do not always separate these powers to the same degree as state and federal governments. Moreover, they have opted to enact ordinances through a single legislative body, such as a city council, rather than the bicameral model in Congress and most state legislatures. A state's constitution and statutes may partially define the legal structure that a local government in the state can adopt and the powers that it can exercise. Typically, a municipality further defines its structure with a city or county charter that operates within limits set by state law.

Similarly, American Indian tribal governments take on a number of forms. Although their powers may be limited by federal law, they are otherwise sovereign governments with inherent powers to exercise tribal authority. Not all the tribes have chosen to adopt every fundamental tenet of the state and federal governments. For example, the Navajo Nation of the southwestern United States has no constitution, and it has not always recognized complete separation of legislative, judicial, and executive powers. Nonetheless, its legal system is similar to the state and federal systems in several important respects. Constituents elect the members of the Navajo Tribal Council, which enacts statutory law in the form of codes. The executive power rests primarily in the president, an elected official. Finally, the Navajo trial courts and the Navajo Supreme Court apply federal law and tribal codes, and they develop and apply a common law based on Navajo custom and cultural values or compatible state laws.

This book primarily addresses state and federal common law and statutes. The remainder of this chapter explores common law analysis. Chapter 4 examines statutory analysis before further addressing the relationship between legislation and the common law.

II. Common Law

A. Historical Roots

The common law that courts in the United States develop and apply has its roots in the English common law, which was dispensed in the courts of the English king or queen. This English law came to be known as the "common law" because it applied generally throughout medieval England. For many kinds of claims, the common law partially replaced a less uniform system of customary law dispensed in local courts and in the private courts of feudal lords. The English Court of Chancery supplemented early common law courts by developing and applying a form of "equity" that provided relief when common law remedies were inadequate.

Distinctions between common law and equitable claims, defenses, and remedies continue to have significance for some purposes, such as determining the right to a jury trial in some circumstances.[5] Most United States jurisdictions, however, have eliminated the dual court system and have largely merged law and equity procedure.[6] Accordingly, this book uses the term "common law" to refer generally to laws created and developed by the courts, regardless of whether the principles have their roots in early common law or equity law.

Oliver Wendell Holmes traced the origins of some English and United States common law to early Germanic and Roman law.[7] Other common law principles simply reflect judicial recognition of community needs, habits, or customs, and are "accounted for by their manifest good sense."[8] More generally, common law is "the embodiment of broad and comprehensive unwritten principles... inspired by natural reason and an innate sense of justice."[9]

The term "common" may be misleading when applied to common law in the United States. The courts in each state are free to develop the common law of that state in a manner that reflects local policies; therefore, variations in common law from state to state are inevitable. Nonetheless, to a surprising degree, courts in different states share common views on general principles of law. For example, a federal appellate court has noted that "the principles of contract law do not differ greatly from one jurisdiction to another."[10] Perhaps more important for law students and practitioners, the method employed by courts in deciding disputes and developing common law does not vary substantially among the states.

B. Examples: Common Law Crimes and the Tort of Negligence

Criminal law is now comprehensively addressed by statutes, but it was once primarily within the domain of the common law. The early common law crime of burglary, which was punishable by death, illustrates the judicial development of common law rules to serve the needs of the community. In imposing capital punishment for this crime, the common law courts sought to deter a serious invasion of the home during hours of darkness, when the inhabitants were most vulnerable to attack and the invader most likely to escape recognition. Efforts by the courts to narrowly address that evil are reflected in the general definition of common law burglary, which separates the crime into distinct elements: (1) the breaking and (2) entering (3) of the dwelling house (4) of another (5) in the night (6) with the intent to commit a felony.

In the context of successive cases, the courts defined and applied these elements of common law burglary. However, because of the severity of the punishment, they were reluctant to extend the crime to anything beyond the strict definition of each element. For example, the courts viewed an intruder as less culpable if the occupant of a dwelling failed to properly secure the dwelling. Accordingly, many courts held that a trespasser who gained entry by further opening a partially open door or window had not committed the "breaking" necessary for a burglary.[11]

The history of another common law crime, murder, illustrates the manner in which courts gradually developed common law doctrine "over several centuries of time as a parade of cases, involving different fact situations, came before the judges for decision."[12] The common law decisions generally defined murder as the unlawful killing of another human being with malice aforethought. Early decisions defined "malice aforethought" narrowly by requiring proof of both premeditation and intent to kill. Subsequent cases, however, presented unpremeditated or even unintentional killings that nonetheless warranted classification as murder. In those cases, courts effectively expanded the definition of "malice aforethought" by recognizing other circumstances that would justify conviction for murder: intentional but unpremeditated killing without sufficient provocation; unintentional killing during the commission of another felony; unintentional killing through conduct that reflects a reckless disregard for the lives of others; and killing while engaged in conduct with the intent to do serious bodily harm short of death.[13] Although homicide is now addressed by state legislation, the criminal codes of many states still retain some elements of these developments in the common law of murder.

Turning from criminal law to forms of civil liability, much of tort law is still governed by common law without wholesale replacement by legislation. An important branch of the common law of torts developed to impose civil liability for negligence—careless action that causes injury to another. Over the course of many cases, courts developed a legal standard for measuring the degree of carelessness associated with a negligent act: failure to act as would a "reasonable man of ordinary prudence."[14] This nineteenth-century standard can be modernized and generalized to refer to a reasonable person in the community.

Subsequent cases arose in which liability turned on the alleged negligence of children. Through resolving such cases, courts developed a relaxed standard of care for children, recognizing that they should be able to enjoy childhood activities without the burden of adult responsibilities. Accordingly, the common law developed a special standard of care in such cases based on "a reasonably careful child of the same age, intelligence, maturity, training and experience."[15]

The facts of still other cases, however, justified an exception to the special standard carved out for children. When children caused injury through participation in inherently dangerous activities—suitable for adults rather than children—courts returned to the adult standard of care. Over the course of many cases, the courts continued to develop the common law to classify a variety of activities as "inherently dangerous," such as operating an automobile, motorboat, tractor, snowmobile, motorcycle, snowmobile, or gas-powered mini-bike.[16]

In this manner, the common law typically develops incrementally. As each case presents new facts, courts determine whether the existing common law rule ought to extend to those facts. Through a process called rule synthesis, you can compare the facts and holdings of successive cases addressing the same issue, allowing you to construct a more general legal rule for that topic.

C. Common Law in Constant Change

This process of incremental development of the common law does not always proceed in an unbroken line. Courts sometimes abandon previously adopted lines of authority to chart new courses that better reflect current social, economic, and technological realities:

> The inherent capacity of the common law for growth and change is its most significant feature. It is constantly expanding and developing to keep up with the advancement of civilization and the new conditions and progress of society, and adapting itself to the gradual changes in trade, commerce, arts, inventions, and the needs of the country.... The vitality of the common law can flourish if the courts remain alert to their obligation and have the opportunity to change it when reason and equity so demand. The common law requires that each time a rule of law is applied, it must be carefully scrutinized to make sure that the conditions and needs of the times have not so changed as to make further application of the rule an instrument of injustice.[17]

A change in conditions is not the only possible inspiration for abandoning existing common law; a court will occasionally conclude that a previous decision was flawed from its inception. Hindsight may show that the previous court premised its decision on erroneous factual assumptions about conditions existing at that time. Alternatively, the current court, which itself may have changed in intellectual composition, may find intolerable flaws in the reasoning of the previous decision.[18] This process of evolution, however, is restricted by the doctrine of stare decisis, explored in Chapter 5.

Exercise 3-1

Wrongful Conception, Wrongful Life

In general, the common law of torts imposes civil liability on a physician who breaches a duty of care to a patient. By applying this general common law rule to new medical procedures, courts and juries necessarily refine the content of the rule. In the following problem, assume that the common law of the jurisdiction has not previously addressed the issues that are raised by the facts. You must decide how you would fashion the common law that applies to the issues if you were a judge approving instructions to a jury on the applicable legal rules. Specifically, you must decide to what extent you think the common law should impose liability on a physician for negligently permitting a child to be conceived.

Problem

When Sonia and her husband, Eddie, had their third child, they agreed that they desired no additional children and that Eddie should undergo sterilization. They consulted Dr. Leonard, who performed a vasectomy. Although Dr. Leonard pronounced the operation a success, he in fact performed the vasectomy carelessly and neglected to order routine follow-up tests. Eddie impregnated Sonia within six months after the failed sterilization procedure.

a. In the process of developing the state's common law of torts, should a state court permit Sonia and Eddie to sue Dr. Leonard on a negligence theory of "wrongful conception"? If so, should the damages include only the medical expenses and other costs associated with the childbirth, or should they more broadly include the costs of raising the fourth child?
b. Suppose that the fourth child was born with severe birth defects, but that the failed sterilization procedure did not contribute to the birth defects. Should these facts affect the court's evaluation of the parents' claims based on wrongful conception? Should the court recognize a cause of action on the behalf of the fourth child for "wrongful life," permitting the child herself to collect damages on the theory that she would have been better off had she not been conceived?
c. Should the analysis of any of these questions be affected by the fact that Sonia could have legally aborted her fetus soon after discovering her pregnancy?

Checklist for Chapter 3

- Legislatures enact statutes with authority granted to them by state and federal constitutions.
- Courts create case law in the context of individual disputes by
  - interpreting and applying the provisions of constitutions and statutes and
  - developing and applying a separate body of judge-made common law.
- The common law continually grows as new cases present the courts with opportunities to keep the common law current with social, economic, and technological developments.

Endnotes

1. 49 Stat. 449 (1935).
2. 29 U.S.C. §§ 153, 156 (2012); Am. Hosp. Ass'n v. NLRB, 499 U.S. 606, 609 (1991).
3. Erie R.R. v. Tompkins, 304 U.S. 64, 78 (1938).
4. Henry J. Friendly, *In Praise of Erie — And of the New Federal Common Law*, 39 N.Y.U. L. Rev. 383, 405 (1964).
5. *See, e.g.*, City of Monterey v. Del Monte Dunes at Monterey, 526 U.S. 687, 708-09 (1999) (discussing whether federal statutory claim was "legal" rather than "equitable," for purposes of applying the Seventh Amendment's guarantee of a jury trial to common law actions); Hutchinson v. Spanierman, 190 F.3d 815, 823 (7th Cir. 1999) (applying Indiana law and finding that stale claim was barred by the equitable doctrine of laches even though the legal statute of limitations had not expired); 1 Dan B. Dobbs, DOBBS LAW OF REMEDIES § 2.6(1), at 150-53 (2d ed. 1993) (discussing continuing limitations on equitable remedies, such as injunctive relief, that do not apply to legal remedy of money damages).
6. *See, e.g.*, FED. R. CIV. P. 2 ("There is one form of action — the civil action."); Ross v. Bernhard, 396 U.S. 531, 539-40 (1970) (discussing the procedural joinder of legal and equitable claims and remedies under rules of procedure for federal courts); Dobbs, *supra* note 5, at 149 ("In most states and in the federal system, there are no longer separate equity rules of procedure.").
7. Oliver Wendell Holmes, Jr., THE COMMON LAW 2, 18, 34, 340-44, 360 (Dover Publ. 1991) (1881).
8. *Id.* at 2, 337-39.
9. Stanley Mosk, *The Common Law and the Judicial Decision-Making Process*, 11 HARV. J.L. & PUB. POL'Y 35 (1988) (citing Rodriguez v. Bethlehem Steel Co., 525 P.2d 669, 682- 83 (Cal. 1974)). Indeed, some scholars believe that humans have a biological predisposition to prefer some forms of legal order. *See generally, e.g.*, Richard D. Alexander, THE BIOLOGY OF MORAL SYSTEMS (1987); *cf.* John R. Alford, Carolyn L. Funk, & John R. Hibbing, *Are Political Orientations Genetically Transmitted?*, AM. POL. SCI. REV., May 2005, at 153-67 (study supports conclusion that political attitudes and ideologies are partly shaped by genetics).
10. *E.g.*, *In re* Cochise College Park, Inc., 703 F.2d 1339, 1348 n.4 (9th Cir. 1983).
11. Wayne R. LaFave, CRIMINAL LAW § 21.1(a), at 1070 (5th ed. 2010).

12. *Id.* § 14.1, at 725.
13. *Id.* at 725-26.
14. Robinson v. Lindsay, 598 P. 2d 392, 393 (Wash. 1979).
15. *Id.*
16. *Id.* at 393-94.
17. Mosk, *supra* note 9, at 36.
18. *See generally* Geoffrey R. Stone, *Precedent, the Amendment Process, and Evolution in Constitutional Doctrine*, 11 Harv. J.L. & Pub. Pol'y 67, 71 (1988).

Chapter 4

Legislation

I. Roles of Constitutional and Statutory Law

"The Constitution states the framework for all our law. Legislation is one great tool of legal change and readaptation."[1] As noted by a state supreme court, constitutional and statutory law reflect collective expressions of public policy: "As the expressions of our founders and those we have elected to our legislature, our state's constitution and statutes embody the public conscience of the people of this state."[2]

Of the three branches of government, the legislature is the paramount policymaking body. Consistent with that role, a legislature often enacts statutes to address problems that it concludes are not adequately addressed by the common law.

A. Example: Embezzlement

The early common law crime defined theft as a trespassory taking and carrying away of personal property of another with intent to steal.[3] The requirement of a trespassory taking created a major loophole. One who took possession of property with the owner's permission, but subsequently converted the property to his own use with the intent to permanently deprive the owner of it, did not engage in a trespassory taking and thus did not commit theft.

Legislators in England and the United States were aware that the common law did not impose criminal liability for the latter misappropriation, and they were determined to criminalize such conduct. Consequently, they created the statutory crime of embezzlement, generally defined as the fraudulent conversion of another's property by one who is already in lawful possession of it.[4] Had the legislatures not acted, the courts might have eventually achieved the same result through further development of the common law, but legislative action sometimes provides a quicker and more certain change of course.

B. Example: Consumer-Protection Legislation

A more contemporary example deals with the process of reaching a legally binding agreement through the process of offer and acceptance. Under the common law of contracts, a store's general advertisement typically amounts to an invitation to negotiate rather than an offer by the store to enter into a binding contract. In most cases, a customer makes the first offer after entering the store, by requesting to purchase the advertised goods. Under common law, the store owner is free to reject the customer's offer without incurring any contractual liability.[5]

Unfortunately, this allocation of legal rights and obligations has encouraged some sellers to use bait-and-switch tactics. First, they lure customers into their stores with the "bait" of goods advertised at spectacularly reduced prices; then they "switch" goods by resisting the customer's desire to purchase the advertised goods and by persuading the customer to purchase a more expensive item instead. In response, state legislatures enacted statutes that restrict or prohibit such bait-and-switch tactics.[6] These statutes promote public policy favoring consumer protection by altering rights and obligations as they were previously defined solely by the common law of contracts.

Common Law of Contracts:
If store's ad is not an offer,
Customer makes first offer.
Store can reject that offer and
can "switch" Customer to more
expensive item.

Consumer-Protection Legislation:
Legislature concludes that
common law is deficient and
enacts protective legislation
to address the "bait-and-
switch" problem.

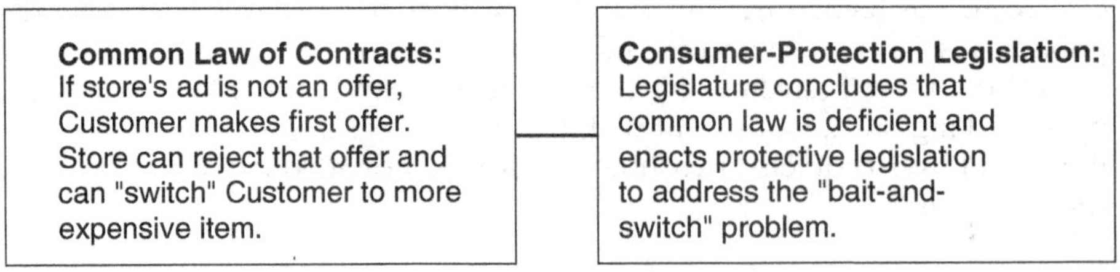

Legislative Reaction to "Bait and Switch"

C. Increasing Significance of Legislation

Prior to the mid-nineteenth century, legislatures in the United States seldom replaced common law wholesale with a comprehensive system of statutes. Instead, they typically enacted statutes to correct specific defects or fill gaps in a well-developed body of common law. Statutes thus assumed a role of secondary importance in the United States, inspiring one scholar to characterize them as "warts on the body of the common law."[7]

State and federal legislation, however, has so proliferated in the intervening decades that "most American jurisdictions now are Code states."[8] Codes are collections of legislative enactments, organized by subject matter. This new prominence of statutory law in the United States warrants an examination of methods of statutory analysis.

II. Judicial Interpretation and Application of Statutes

A federal statute imposes liability on certain employers for discrimination against any individual in the "terms" or "conditions" of employment "because of such individual's ... sex." Would the statute impose liability on an employer who fired your clients, lesbian and gay employees, because of their sexual orientation? Would it impose liability on an employer who made sexual advances toward only female employees, thus adversely affecting their working environment, but who did not withhold tangible job benefits in retaliation for the subordinate rejecting his advances? The answers to these questions depend on the intended meaning of the statutory language "because of ... sex" and "terms" or "conditions" of employment.

A. Vagueness and Ambiguity

Questions such as these arise because statutory language sometimes is vague or ambiguous. A vague term is uncertain in its meaning and indefinite in its scope, making it difficult to identify the meaning or meanings that it encompasses.[9] An ambiguous term has multiple meanings, although each of the meanings may be precise and all the meanings may be easily identified.

As discussed more fully below, some statutes are *ambiguous* because the legislature unintentionally failed to state its desired meaning with precision. On the other hand, some statutes are necessarily *vague* because the legislature—knowing that it could not foresee every possible application of a statute—deliberately used general language, leaving clarification to the courts.

Consequently, opposing parties may reasonably disagree about the application of statutory language to the facts of their dispute. Courts give greater specificity and precision to the vague or ambiguous statutory language by interpreting and applying the statute in the context of specific disputes.

According to one judge, legislatures should not be faulted for keeping judges so busy with cases requiring statutory interpretation,

> because however careful, wise and farseeing the Legislature, the abstract words of a statute often require fitting and tailoring when applied to real-life cases, which may be more bizarre than anyone could possibly have imagined. Fitting and tailoring are what judges do, and what they are supposed to do—they make judgments.[10]

On the other hand, a court does not engage in a wholly creative process when it interprets a vague or ambiguous statute. Judges overstep their authority if they substitute their own policy preferences for those enacted by the legislature. Instead, they traditionally have sought to determine and give effect to the intent of the enacting legislature. A court begins this process by analyzing the statutory language. If helpful, they will also consider context, such as the stated or apparent purpose of the statute and the legislative activities related to enactment of the bill.[11]

This search for the intended meaning of a statute is governed by a separate layer of judicially developed rules of interpretation and construction. "Interpretation" refers to the process of determining legislative intent. "Construction" refers to the process of giving the statutory language a meaning that is consistent with general legislative and public policies, but only in the absence of conclusive evidence of legislative intent.

B. Interpretation Through Intrinsic and Extrinsic Evidence of Legislative Intent

Evidence of legislative intent may be intrinsic to the statute, extrinsic to it, or both. *Intrinsic* evidence of legislative intent is the statutory text itself. This includes the statutory language in question and other provisions of the statute that cast light on the meaning of the term in dispute. Some statutes include a section of defined terms, which may provide partial guidance even when a definition does not conclusively resolve a dispute over the proper interpretation of the language in question. More broadly, companion legislation might reveal the larger legislative context within which a statute operates:

> "[A] statute should be construed in conjunction with other statutes that relate to the same subject or purpose...." Our construction should harmonize related statutes together "as though they constituted one law."[12]

When federal legislation applies to the dispute, courts have frequently consulted legislative history as a source of *extrinsic* evidence of legislative intent. This includes the text of congressional debates, preliminary drafts of the legislation, and hearings or reports of congressional committees assigned to study the proposed legislation. Some legislative history might directly address the meaning of the disputed text, by including a legislator's statement on the floor about the scope of a provision in a bill. Legislative history might also reveal the broad purpose of the legislation, which in turn could help reveal the intended reach of a statutory provision. Unfortunately, the history of state legislation in many states is less comprehensive and less accessible than is federal legislative history.[13]

C. Approaches to Statutory Interpretation

In some states, legislation or case law describes the steps that a court may or must take when interpreting a statute. In federal courts and many states, however, judges and justices have held a variety of views about approaches to statutory interpretation, sometimes defending their competing views in a majority opinion and a concurring or dissenting opinion.

One hybrid textualist approach to interpretation has gained favor to the point of near consensus. Under the "plain meaning" rule of interpretation, if the statutory language in question has a single plain meaning on its face, a court will refrain from considering legislative purpose or legislative history supporting a different meaning, unless the plain meaning would lead to an absurd result.[14] Of course, whether statutory text does indeed have a single plain meaning might be subject to dispute. Accordingly, some judges and scholars have argued that an assertion of plain meaning in statutory text does not preclude a court from considering context to confirm or question the plain meaning.[15] In one case, for example, a state court of appeals gave effect to legislative purpose by determining that the term "shall" in a statute did not impose a mandatory duty.[16] In another case, a federal court of appeals engaged in an exhaustive analysis of legislative history and statutory policy to interpret the statutory term "or" to mean the conjunction "and," rather than the disjunctive "either/or."[17]

When assessing the plain meaning of a statutory clause, courts generally apply accepted conventions of grammar, punctuation, and usage, some of which have solidified into canons of statutory interpretation. For example, a long-standing canon often expressed in Latin—*expressio unius est exclusio alterius*—states that statutory expression of one thing implies exclusion of others. Another canon, however, reminds judges that the word "include" or "includes" normally introduces illustrative examples, and not an exclusive list. Such canons of interpretation often give rise to a presumption about statutory meaning, which might be overcome with other intrinsic evidence.[18]

If statutory text is indisputably ambiguous—if it might readily convey either of the competing meanings advanced by the parties—courts normally will consider extrinsic evidence of legislative intent, such as legislative history and statements of legislative purpose. Even so, legislative history is increasingly viewed as a less legitimate and reliable source of legislative intent than statutory text. "After all, only the words on the page constitute the law adopted by Congress and approved by the President."[19]

Moreover, misuse of legislative history may mislead more than enlighten. The search for legislative intent is an attempt to reconstruct the collective intent of numerous legislators whose views on the wisdom or scope of the statute may vary or conflict. Opposing advocates often can draw on different portions of legislative history to support conflicting views about the proper interpretation of a statute. They simply quote isolated statements of legislators taken out of the context of the complete debate on a bill. A court might then justify its decision by selectively drawing on portions of legislative history that support that result.

These and other pitfalls led the late Justice Scalia to decry the "level of unreality that our unrestrained use of legislative history has attained."[20] In his view, "[t]extualism, in its purest form, begins and ends with what the text says and fairly implies."[21]

Most judges, however, give priority to statutory text without slamming the door on other aids to interpretation. They start with the statutory text but seldom end with it. Judge Learned Hand, for example, explained the importance of legislative purpose as a supplementary guide to meaning:

> Of course it is true that the words used, even in their literal sense, are the primary, and ordinarily the most reliable, source of interpreting the meaning of any writing: be it a statute, a contract, or anything else. But it is one of the surest indexes of a mature and developed jurisprudence not to make a fortress out of the dictionary; but to remember that statutes always have some purpose or object to accomplish, whose sympathetic and imaginative discovery is the surest guide to their meaning.[22]

D. Originalism v. Living Statutes

Should a court give effect to legislative intent and statutory meaning at the time of enactment, or instead to a meaning that reflects advances in knowledge, science, and social views that have taken place between enactment and adjudication? Although this question might be debatable in some state courts, the Supreme Court has provided a general answer for the federal courts:

> This Court normally interprets a statute in accord with the ordinary public meaning of its terms at the time of its enactment.... To do so, we orient ourselves to the time of the statute's adoption....[23]

Even when a court moves beyond statutory text to consult legislative purpose and legislative history, those forms of extrinsic evidence relate to legislative statements and activity when the legislature drafted, considered, and debated the bill.

Still, original meaning need not freeze the law's application to contexts existing at the time of enactment. Consider a state statute enacted in the 1950s that elevates the crime of robbery to a higher degree if the robber used a "deadly firearm" to help accomplish the crime. Ordinary meaning and legislative history at the time of enactment might limit the scope of "deadly firearm" to instruments commonly known as "guns" that fire bullets and can cause death or serious bodily harm, excluding less dangerous instruments such as BB guns, even if they look like a gun that fires bullets. Although unchanged 70 years later, that original meaning could apply to

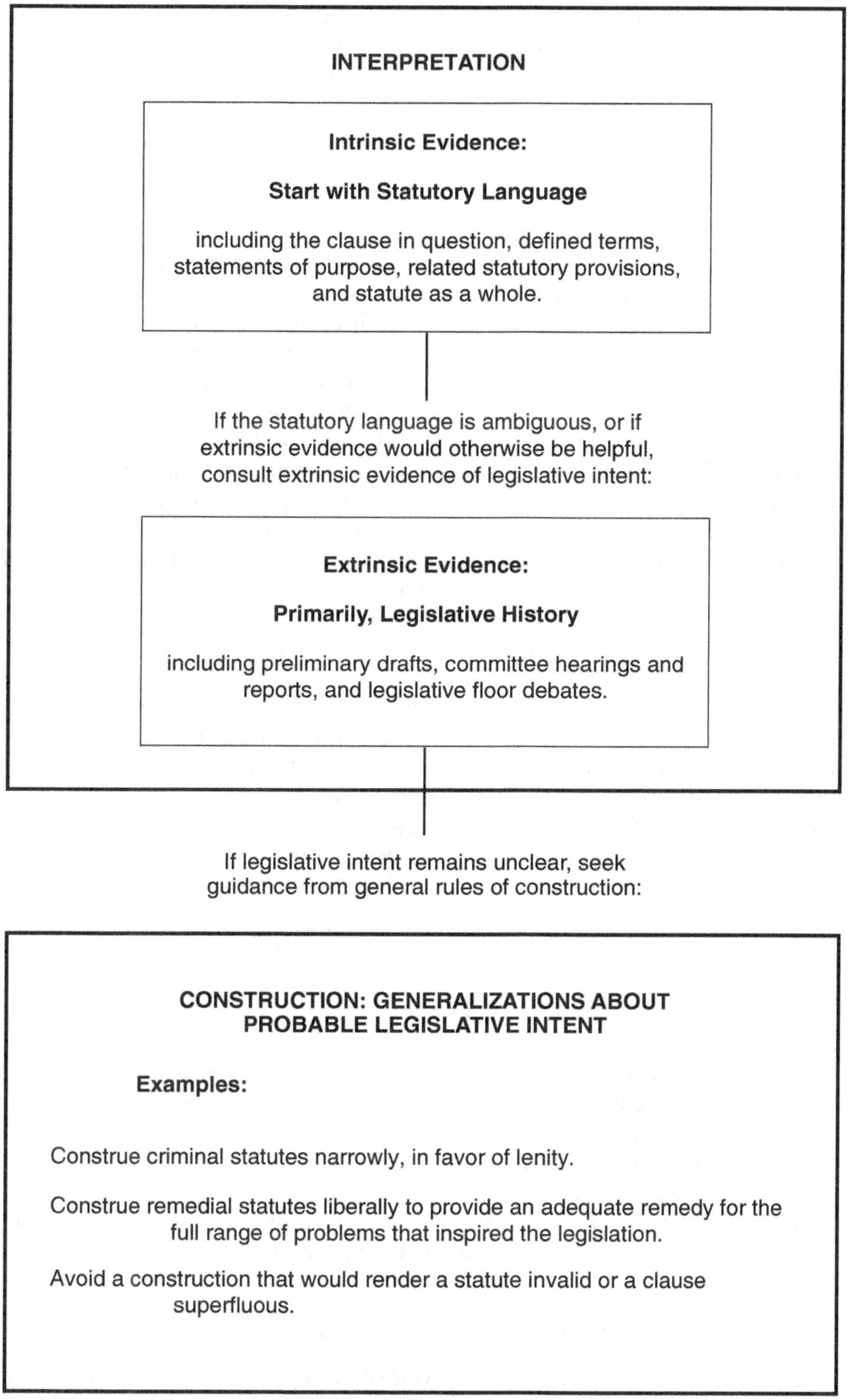

INTERPRETATION

Intrinsic Evidence:

Start with Statutory Language

including the clause in question, defined terms, statements of purpose, related statutory provisions, and statute as a whole.

If the statutory language is ambiguous, or if extrinsic evidence would otherwise be helpful, consult extrinsic evidence of legislative intent:

Extrinsic Evidence:

Primarily, Legislative History

including preliminary drafts, committee hearings and reports, and legislative floor debates.

If legislative intent remains unclear, seek guidance from general rules of construction:

CONSTRUCTION: GENERALIZATIONS ABOUT PROBABLE LEGISLATIVE INTENT

Examples:

Construe criminal statutes narrowly, in favor of lenity.

Construe remedial statutes liberally to provide an adequate remedy for the full range of problems that inspired the legislation.

Avoid a construction that would render a statute invalid or a clause superfluous.

Statutory Interpretation and Construction

new types of firearms not known or considered at the time of enactment. Accordingly, the original meaning of "deadly firearm" could apply decades later to include a plastic gun created by 3D printing that can fire a single projectile to deadly effect.

E. Statutory Construction When Interpretation Fails

If a court cannot obtain clear evidence of legislative intent through intrinsic or extrinsic evidence, it may resort to a judicial rule of construction, such as the general rule that ambiguities in criminal statutes "should be resolved in favor of lenity,"[24] or lenience. This rule advances the policy that an act should result in a criminal charge only if the law clearly prohibited the act. Another long-standing rule of construction arguably saved the Affordable Health Care Act in 2012: "[I]f a statute has two possible meanings, one of which violates the Constitution, courts should adopt the meaning that does not do so."[25] In addition, under a contemporary convention of construction, when applying a provision of a uniform code that reflects a goal of minimizing variations between states, a court should lean toward adopting the statutory meaning chosen by a majority of other states that have interpreted the provision.[26]

A rule of construction may reflect general policies with which the legislature is likely to agree, but it does not necessarily reflect the legislative intent or purpose of the particular statute in question.[27] Moreover, statutory rules of construction are sufficiently varied and nuanced that advocates frequently can find opposing rules of construction that provide at least general support for different statutory meanings.[28] Accordingly, a court will resort to a general rule of construction only if a "statute's language, structure, purpose, and legislative history leave its meaning genuinely in doubt."[29]

III. Case Studies in Statutory Interpretation

In the following subsections, analyses of two kinds of uncertainty in statutory language provide vehicles for examining techniques that the courts use to clarify the scope and effect of statutes. First, an analysis of ambiguous statutory language illustrates general rules of statutory interpretation and construction. Second, an analysis of vague statutory language illustrates the manner in which courts gradually give concrete meaning to abstract statutory language by applying general terms to particular disputes.

A. Illustration: Imprecision Leading to Ambiguity

Ambiguity may result from imprecision in the words or phrases selected by the drafter. The question concerning sexual orientation raised at the beginning of Section II above addresses the proper interpretation of a federal statute, Title VII of the Civil Rights Act of 1964. Section 703(a) of the Act prohibits certain kinds of employment discrimination:

> It shall be an unlawful employment practice for an employer ... to discriminate against any individual with respect to his compensation, terms, conditions, or privileges of employment, because of such individual's race, color, religion, sex, or national origin....[30]

1. The Problem

Does the quoted language prohibit an employer from discriminating against gay and lesbian employees because of their sexual orientation? Perhaps Title VII's reference to "sex" as a protected classification would prohibit such an employment policy. It would clearly do so if Congress used the term "sex" to refer broadly to any sexual characteristic, including an individual's sexual orientation, gender identity, or sexual activities, rather than only to the characteristic of being male or female. The journey of the courts in addressing this issue is remarkable.

2. Intrinsic Evidence

Judicial interpretation of a statute should start with the most direct intrinsic evidence of legislative intent: the statutory language in question.[31] Prior to 2020, most courts found no single, plain meaning of the statutory term "sex." Dictionaries and common usage define "sex" as, among other things, either (1) the division of species between male and female or (2) more general sexual behavior and characteristics.[32]

Other provisions of Title VII might provide intrinsic evidence of the intended meaning of "sex" in section 703(a). In a different subsection of the same legislative act, section 703(h), Congress used the term in the narrow sense of the division of species between male and female.[33] There it used "sex" in a reference to the Equal Pay Act of 1963, which more clearly prohibits only certain kinds of discrimination based on the status of an employee as male or female.[34] If Congress consciously used "sex" in that sense in section 703(h), the obvious virtues of consistency in statutory drafting suggest the likelihood that Congress used the term "sex" in the same way in section 703(a) of the same legislative act.

3. Extrinsic Evidence

If a court found intrinsic evidence to be inconclusive, it could seek guidance from extrinsic evidence, such as legislative history of section 703(a). The original House bill did not include "sex" as a prohibited basis of discrimination. Instead, Howard Smith, a southern Democrat and chair of the House Rules Committee, proposed the addition of "sex" as a protected classification in a last-minute amendment on the House floor. Some believe that he hoped that the amendment would spark sufficient controversy to cause the defeat of the entire bill.[35]

Smith's unsuccessful strategy left the courts with "little legislative history to guide us in interpreting the Act's prohibition against discrimination based on 'sex.' "[36] However, the few statements made on the House floor about the proposed amendment, both by Smith and by more sincere advocates of the amendment, suggest that the speakers were using the term "sex" to refer narrowly to the characteristic of being male or female.[37] That interpretation is consistent with post-enactment evidence of congressional intent. First, the House report on the 1972 Amendments to Title VII demonstrates that this later Congress was primarily concerned with putting women on equal economic footing with men. Second, successive congressional rejections of several bills proposing to amend Title VII by adding "sexual preference" as a protected classification suggest that the narrow judicial interpretation was acceptable to members of those later sessions of Congress.[38]

Relying on this legislative history, for decades courts consistently interpreted the word "sex" in section 703(a) to refer only to male or female status and not also to sexual orientation.[39] Accordingly, they concluded that Title VII does not prohibit an employer from discriminating against employees because of their sexual orientation, provided that the employer applies the same policy to male employees of a specified sexual orientation as it does to female employees of that orientation.[40]

4. Second Thoughts in Some Federal Courts of Appeals

But that restrictive interpretation was not inevitable. The sparse legislative history on the addition of "sex" to Title VII was also consistent with the conclusion that Congress had not taken the time to consider all the possible applications of the statutory term "sex." Even the later congressional rejection of bills to add sexual preference or orientation as a protected classification is a "hazardous basis" on which to draw inferences about the intent of a previous Congress.[41]

More tellingly, even the narrow binary definition of "sex" as one's status as male or female could logically encompass sexual orientation. An employment policy discriminates on the basis of an individual employee's status as male or female if it permits a male employee to date Susan without an adverse employment action but results in discharge or discipline if a female employee dates Susan. Moreover, a sex stereotyping theory embraced by the Supreme Court,[42] if applied expansively, would arguably encompass sexual orientation discrimination, such as when an employer requires male employees to possess traditionally masculine traits, including heterosexual attraction.[43]

Finally, Title VII is remedial in its purpose of redressing the pervasive social and economic problem of employment discrimination. In light of ambiguity in the statutory language, uncertainty about the range of applications of even a narrow definition, and gaps in the intent of the 1964 Congress, the courts could have applied the general rule of liberal construction of remedial statutes.[44]

In a stunning turn of events, these and other arguments in favor of expansive coverage began to bear fruit a half century after enactment of Title VII. In the wake of the Supreme Court's decision invaliding state marriage laws that excluded same-sex couples,[45] a few federal appellate courts broke with early case law and ruled that discrimination based on sexual orientation or transgender status is a form of sex discrimination under Title VII.[46] These courts were free to do so because the Supreme Court had not ruled on this issue. If a panel of a U.S. Court of Appeals had previously ruled against Title VII coverage, that court could overrule its precedent with an en banc decision.[47] Such a decision typically requires participation by all the members of the court, as well as a firm conviction that the previous decision was clearly wrong or is inconsistent with intervening legal developments.[48]

In this movement to reconsider precedent, one judge adopted a controversial premise. Judge Posner viewed Title VII and other legislation as living legal documents whose meaning can evolve with major shifts in knowledge and social attitudes:

> Title VII of the Civil Rights Act of 1964, now more than half a century old, invites an interpretation that will update it to the present, a present that differs markedly from the era in which the Act was enacted. But … this third form of interpretation—call it judicial interpretive updating—presupposes a lengthy interval between enactment and (re)interpretation. A statute when passed has an understood meaning; it takes years, often many years, for a shift in the political and cultural environment to change the understanding of the statute.[49]

Presumably, a legislature could adopt a statute that explicitly invites evolution of its meaning over time through judicial "updating" of its terms. Absent such direction from the legislature, however, Judge Posner's view will likely be rejected by the vast majority of judges as an inappropriate exercise of legislative authority.[50] Nevertheless, as discussed earlier and again in the next subsection, the original meaning of statutory language can apply to new factual contexts over time, including ones not contemplated by legislators or most members of the public at the time of enactment. The Supreme Court's resolution of the dispute about the scope of sex discrimination under Title VII reveals room for debate when defining the line between judicial "updating" of a statute's terms and applying the same meaning to new contexts.

5. The Supreme Court Decides, with a Focus on Text

In June 2020, in *Bostock v. Clayton County*,[51] the United States Supreme Court decided that Title VII's prohibition of discrimination because of an individual's sex necessarily encompasses sexual orientation and transgender discrimination. Justice Gorsuch wrote the majority opinion, applying a textual approach to statutory interpretation. Justices Roberts, Ginsburg, Breyer, Sotomayor, and Kagan joined in his opinion.

The Court granted the employer's argument that, at the time of enactment in 1964, members of Congress and the general public understood the word "sex" in Title VII to refer to status as male or female.[52] Title VII refers to discrimination because of an "individual's" sex, so it matters not whether an adverse employment policy applies broadly to both gay male and lesbian female employees.[53] Instead, from the perspective of an individual employee, the discriminatory policy turns on whether that employee is male or female:

> Imagine an employer who has a policy of firing any employee known to be homosexual. The employer hosts an office holiday party and invites employees to bring their spouses. A model employee arrives and introduces a manager to Susan, the employee's wife. Will that employee be fired? If the policy works as the employer intends, the answer depends entirely on whether the model employee is a man or a woman. To be sure, that employer's ultimate goal might be to discriminate on the basis of sexual orientation. But to achieve that purpose the employer must, along the way, intentionally treat an employee worse based in part on that individual's sex.[54]

Justice Gorsuch found that the relevant statutory terms had a single plain meaning in Title VII, which prevailed over a more restrictive interpretation suggested by legislative history or legislative purpose.[55] The majority opinion asserts that its interpretation and application has been the correct one since the enactment of Title VII, even though the statutory text produced unexpected outcomes that courts recognized only years or decades after enactment.[56]

A dissent by Justice Alito, joined by Justice Thomas, and a separate dissent by Justice Kavanaugh, also employed textual approaches but departed from the majority in their application of textualism. Justice Alito's dissent viewed sexual orientation discrimination to be distinct from sex discrimination rather than implicating one's status as male or female. Justice Alito also concluded that the statutory term "sex" was ambiguous and thus should be interpreted in light of legislative history and its broader historical context.[57] Justice Kavanaugh opined that the majority had employed an overly literal definition of sex, rather than giving effect to the ordinary meaning of sex discrimination as generally understood in 1964.[58]

Notably, all Justices joined an opinion that adopted a textualist approach of one form or another. The three opinions in *Bostock*, however, demonstrate that a consensus to give priority to statutory text can leave much room for dispute and debate.

B. A Second Illustration: Generality Resulting in Vagueness

Even if the legislature chooses its words carefully, most statutory language is necessarily general, because almost all legislation addresses broad categories of activities or disputes rather than specific cases. Legislators simply do not possess the stamina and prescience required to consider every potential dispute within the scope of legislation and to provide a specific resolution for each. Instead, courts put flesh on the bones of legislation by applying the general terms of the statute to the facts of specific disputes. Thus, courts adding precision to statutory language in much the same way that they develop common law—incrementally and in the context of successive disputes.

For example, section 703(a) of Title VII of the Civil Rights Act of 1964 prohibits discrimination only with respect to an individual's "compensation, terms, conditions, or privileges of employment."[59] That statutory phrase is necessarily general, because Congress could not practicably describe in more specific terms all the possible kinds of discriminatory acts that would trigger congressional concern about equal opportunity in the workplace. That generality results in vagueness that promotes disputes over the interpretation and application of the statute in specific cases.

For instance, parties have reasonably disputed whether unwelcome sexual advances made by an employer to an employee affect the employee's "terms, conditions, or privileges of employment" if the employer does not withhold tangible benefits of employment in retaliation for rejection.[60] Courts have given more specific meaning to the statutory phrase by adopting a legal standard for determining the circumstances in which the statute is satisfied: sexual advances by an employer's agent may affect "terms, conditions, or privileges of employment" if they create "a substantially discriminatory work environment, regardless of whether the complaining employees lost any tangible job benefits as a result of the discrimination."[61]

Although the "discriminatory work environment" standard adds a judicial gloss to the statutory language, the judicial standard is itself abstract and suffers from its own problems of vagueness. The United States Supreme Court provided a small measure of guidance by approving liability only if the harassment is "sufficiently severe or pervasive 'to alter the conditions of ... employment and create an abusive working environment.'"[62] Additionally, the Supreme Court later provided more detailed guidance by listing a number of factors that courts should consider in determining whether a working environment has become abusive.[63] Still, the precise parameters of the judicial standard, and thus of the statutory language that it seeks to effectuate, will take form only when courts repeatedly apply the standard to the facts of different disputes.

Unfortunately, you should be prepared to encounter cases at the margin that complicate the bigger picture. Courts in different jurisdictions are free to draw lines differently on the same issue of statutory interpretation, and they often do. You can hope, however, that the cases within a jurisdiction form a coherent pattern, thus illuminating the line between satisfaction or non-satisfaction of the statutory test in that jurisdiction.

Exercise 4-1

1. Judicial Interpretation of Legislation

A statute of State *Y* provides without qualification that "any landlord of a residential unit may prohibit tenants from keeping pets in their units and may evict any tenant who violates such a prohibition and fails to cure the violation within one week of receiving notice of the violation." Does this statute permit a landlord of residential apartments in State *Y* to evict a tenant who refuses to get rid of a single goldfish that the tenant keeps in a two-gallon fishbowl in her apartment? You may assume that State *Y* has no helpful legislative history relating to this statute. Can opposing attorneys reasonably argue for and against application of the statute? Can different judges reasonably reach opposite conclusions on the proper interpretation and application of the statute in this case?[64]

2. Statutory Policy and Classification

The Highway Patrol of State *X* informed legislators of State *X* that motorists were causing accidents by consuming soft drinks while driving. The Highway Patrol was not overly concerned that drivers could keep only one hand on the wheel while consuming soft drinks. Instead, they were concerned that drivers often obstructed their own vision, and thus lost partial control of their automobiles, when they tilted their heads back and tipped their soft drink containers upward to consume the last of their soft drinks. In response, state legislators amended the State *X* Vehicle Code to make it a misdemeanor "to operate a motor vehicle while consuming any beverage from a can or bottle." If the concerns that motivated this bill are recorded in legislative history, should the new law apply to:

a. a driver who tilts her head back to drink water from a paper cup?
b. a driver who keeps his head level while he sips a soft drink through a straw from a bottle?
c. a driver who eats a sandwich in a way that distracts her and obstructs her vision?

In addressing these cases, ask yourself to what extent a court should adhere to the strict terms of the statute, even if such an interpretation in a specific case is not perfectly consistent with the legislative purpose. To what extent should the court interpret the statutory language flexibly to more closely achieve the legislative purpose?

3. Legislative History

The current codification of a Reconstruction-era civil rights act prohibits certain kinds of discrimination:

> *All persons* within the jurisdiction of the United States shall have the same right in every State and Territory to make and enforce contracts ... *as is enjoyed by white citizens*....

42 U.S.C. § 1981(a) (2019) (emphasis added). The original predecessor to this statute contained similar language:

> [C]itizens of the United States ... of every race and color, without regard to any previous condition of slavery or involuntary servitude, ... shall have the same right, in every State and Territory in the United States, to make and enforce contracts ... *as is enjoyed by white citizens*....

Civil Rights Act of 1866 § 1, 14 Stat. 27 (1866) (emphasis added); *see also* Civil Rights Act of 1870 §§ 16, 18, 16 Stat. 144 (1870) (reenacting and adding to 1866 Act). The "immediate impetus" for the original statute was "the necessity for further relief of the constitutionally emancipated former Negro slaves."[65] However, to allay fears among some legislators that the proposed bill would favor nonwhites, proponents of the bill defended it at several stages of the legislative process as one that would protect *all* citizens.[66] More than a century after the initial enactment, the United States Supreme Court applied the modern version of this statute to prohibit private, commercially operated, nonsectarian schools from discriminating on the basis of race against African-Americans in admission to the schools.[67]

a. Should a court apply the statute to protect nonwhites other than African-Americans from race discrimination in contractual relations?
b. Should a court apply the statute to protect white citizens from race discrimination? *See McDonald v. Santa Fe Trail Transp. Co.*, 427 U.S. 273 (1976).
c. If the statute applies to protect racial groups other than African-Americans, how does one distinguish between different races for purposes of finding prohibited discrimination? Would the statute apply to prohibit discrimination against a person because he is Arab-American rather than Anglo-American? *See St. Francis College v. Al-Khazraji*, 481 U.S. 604 (1987) (looking to racial classifications recognized at time of enactment of predecessors to 42 U.S.C. § 1981). Would it apply to discrimination because one is Jewish? *See Shaare Tefila Congregation v. Cobb*, 481 U.S. 615 (1987) (analysis under companion statute, 42 U.S.C. § 1982).

IV. Legislative Enactment and Change

British law professor Gary Watt reminds us to constantly critique the current state of the law:

> We should acknowledge the present state of the law, but we should also acknowledge that it is only a starting point. It is important that we then use

> our imagination as the philosophers do . . . to imagine how we might move away from the worst errors of the present law. . . . We will not find Utopia there. Just humanity.[68]

As a serious student of the law, possibly a future legislator, or simply an engaged citizen, you should not be content to comprehend and interpret statutory law. You should also carefully evaluate the merits of current or proposed legislation.

When you encounter a social problem that you believe is not adequately addressed by current constitutional or common law, consider whether you would support legislation to address the problem. In light of questions of statutory interpretation explored in the previous sections, consider how you would draft legislation to achieve your statutory purpose with minimum ambiguity.

Of course, a legislature that has the power to enact legislation also has the power to repeal or amend it. A constant critique of current legislation helps to fuel the dynamic process of the growth and development of statutory law.

Exercise 4-2

1. Enacting Mandatory Safety Rules

Do you support state legislation requiring a person to wear a protective helmet while driving or riding as a passenger on a motorcycle on a public street or highway? What policy arguments support or oppose such legislation?

2. Enacting Legislation Permitting Physician-Assisted Suicide

In 1997, the United States Supreme Court refused to recognize a constitutional right to physician-assisted suicide, and it left the matter of prohibition, regulation, or permission of physician-assisted suicide to be resolved in other legal arenas, such as state criminal legislation.[69] As a state legislator, what position would you take on this issue? Would you vote for a bill making it a crime for a physician to actively assist in the death of any patient, regardless of the circumstances? Conversely, would you legislatively grant immunity to a physician who hastened the death of a terminally ill patient who requested such assistance? Would you permit physician-assisted suicide, but regulate it by restricting it to certain circumstances? How would you draft your legislation?

3. Immigration Reform

How would you craft a federal bill that seeks to accomplish comprehensive immigration reform? If one of your goals is to gain complete control of our borders, what measures would you propose to achieve that result? What provisions would you include with respect to undocumented aliens who now reside and work in the United States? Would you include a path to citizenship? If so, on what conditions?

Would you include any special provision for undocumented immigrants whose parents brought them to the United States as minors and who are now successfully pursuing a college education or military service in the United States?

4. Overruling Common Law

In August 1997, a North Carolina jury awarded $1 million to an abandoned wife who sued her husband's secretary for committing adultery with her husband and breaking up their marriage.[70] The award was based partly on the common law tort of alienation of affection, defined as wrongful conduct that deprives a married person of the love and companionship of his or her spouse by interfering in a harmonious marriage.[71] Most states have legislatively abolished this and related torts, partly because the torts invite abusive legal tactics and are based on outdated notions about the nature of intimate relationships.[72] Indeed, the North Carolina Court of Appeals had judicially abandoned the common law tort of alienation of affection in 1984, but the North Carolina Supreme Court reversed on the ground that *it* had recognized the tort of alienation of affection in its own case law, which the court of appeals was not free to ignore.[73]

Do you believe such torts should be retained or abandoned? As a member of the state's highest court, would you abolish the tort of alienation of affection in the course of developing the state's common law, or would you view such a major policy change as one best left to the state legislature? As a state legislator, would you support or oppose a bill to abolish the common law tort of alienation of affection?

V. Interplay between Legislation and Common Law

A. Relationship between Legislation and Common Law

1. Legislative Primacy

Although the legislature and the judiciary both exercise lawmaking powers, the legislature is the paramount lawmaking authority. Therefore, legislative enactments supersede inconsistent common law. The following United States Supreme Court statement about the federal system applies as well to the state governments:

> [W]e consistently have emphasized that the federal lawmaking power is vested in the legislative, not the judicial, branch of government; therefore, federal common law is "subject to the paramount authority of Congress."[74]

Accordingly, the legislature may enact statutes that modify, overrule, or codify existing common law.

2. Legislation as Guidance for Common Law

Even if no statute currently applies to a dispute, a court may decline to extend common law principles to the area if it concludes that the matter is better left to legislative action.[75] Moreover, if the court decides to develop and apply the common law, it may find guidance by looking for expressions of public policy in legislation. A provision in the Uniform Commercial Code, for example, authorizes courts to strike out grossly unfair contract terms for "unconscionability."[76] In turn, this statute influenced courts to develop, or further develop, a common law doctrine of unconscionability in contexts to which the Code did not apply.[77]

3. Common Law as Background for Legislation

Although statutory law supersedes common law, the common law at the time of a statute's enactment may provide a helpful context for analyzing legislative intent.[78] If a statute overrules a common law rule or seeks to address a problem left untouched by the common law, a court can better understand the statute's intended scope if it appreciates which deficiencies of the common law elicited a legislative response.[79] Conversely, if a statute codifies existing common law, cases that developed the common law rule will provide guidance in interpreting the statute.

Moreover, a statute often addresses only selected issues within a general subject matter, thereby leaving gaps that common law may fill. In some cases, the statute itself provides for reference to common law, as in the Uniform Commercial Code:

> Unless displaced by the particular provisions of [the Uniform Commercial Code], the principles of law and equity, including the law merchant and the law relative to capacity to contract, principal and agent, estoppel, fraud, misrepresentation, duress, coercion, mistake, ... and other validating or invalidating cause supplement its provisions.[80]

In other cases, statutes only implicitly incorporate common law principles. For example, a federal civil rights statute imposes liability for certain conduct without any express qualifications or limitations. Yet, courts have assumed that Congress intended the statute to implicitly incorporate common law defenses of immunity from liability for money damages:

> It is by now well settled that the tort liability created by [42 U.S.C.] § 1983 cannot be understood in a historical vacuum. In the Civil Rights Act of 1871, Congress created a federal remedy against a person who, acting under color of state law, deprives another of constitutional rights.... One important assumption underlying the Court's decisions in this area is that members of the 42d Congress were familiar with common-law principles, including defenses previously recognized in ordinary tort litigation, and that they likely intended these common-law principles to obtain, absent specific provisions to the contrary.[81]

B. Judicial Power and Limitations Regarding Legislation

Although legislatures can modify or overrule judicially developed common law, the courts retain an important role in the development of statutory law. Courts review statutes for consistency with constitutional requirements, and they will refuse to enforce unconstitutional legislation.[82] Additionally, as discussed in Section III above, courts determine the scope and effect of legislation by interpreting statutes and applying them to specific disputes.

Nonetheless, courts have less flexibility in interpreting statutory law than in developing common law. True, if a court finds good reason to abandon its previous analysis of legislative intent, it may overrule its earlier interpretation of a statute, just as it sometimes overrules its previous statement or application of common law.[83] However, the court may not ignore a statute or modify its terms to reflect contrary judicial views. In contrast, a court may directly reject the substance and reasoning of a common law principle that it had announced and applied in a prior decision: "[W]e have not hesitated to change the common law ... where ... such course was justified."[84]

Interestingly, some American Indian tribal court judges have boldly hinted that they may challenge the conventional hierarchy of laws in tribal governments. Just as a federal or state legislature enacts statutes, a tribal council has adopted the tribal codes. According to assumptions adopted by our state and federal systems, tribal codes should have priority over tribal common law. However, even though tribal codes are formally enacted by tribal councils, many were conceived and drafted by European-Americans and might reflect a poor understanding of tribal culture. In contrast, most tribal courts consciously seek to promote tribal culture and policies when they develop and apply tribal common law.

This phenomenon may justify a departure from U.S. legal method in tribal courts. For example, the Navajo Supreme Court has hinted that it may refuse to give effect to outdated tribal code sections that fail to promote Navajo values or are inconsistent with long-standing Navajo custom. In gestures acknowledging the role of the legislative branch of government, the Navajo Supreme Court has explicitly recommended that the Navajo Tribal Council amend tribal codes that do not promote Navajo culture and policies.[85] This kind of communication between branches of government is not foreign to the state and federal legal systems. However, not content to wait for action from its legislative branch, the Navajo Supreme Court has considered a more assertive legal method. When necessary to preserve important values of tribal culture or sovereignty, the Navajo Supreme Court has hinted at its willingness to elevate Navajo common law or custom above otherwise applicable tribal codes.[86]

One scholarly judge supports similarly skeptical treatment of outdated state statutes.[87] Nonetheless, in the state and federal legal systems in the United States, the conventional hierarchy of laws is firmly entrenched: A constitution defines the reach of statutory authority, and statutes can limit the application of common law.

Checklist for Chapter 4

- Statutory Interpretation and Construction
  - Intrinsic evidence of statutory meaning lies in the statutory text itself, including provisions in the same statute as the term in dispute.
  - Plain Meaning Rule: Most courts give effect to the single plain meaning of unambiguous statutory text, without resorting to extrinsic evidence.
  - Extrinsic Evidence: If the statutory text is ambiguous, courts will seek to clarify legislative intent by consulting extrinsic evidence such as legislative history and statements of legislative purpose.
  - Originalism: Federal courts and most state courts will give effect to the ordinary meaning of a statute when it was enacted. Nonetheless, that original meaning can later apply to new contexts that did not exist and were not contemplated at the time of enactment.
  - Rules of Construction: If the search for legislative intent is inconclusive, courts sometimes rely on rules of construction that reflect general policies, such as favoring a statutory meaning that avoids a constitutional defect or other invalidity of the statute.
- Relationship between Legislation and Common Law
  - Legislation can replace common law with a contrary, superseding rule, and legislative policies might influence continuing development of related common law doctrines,
  - but common law can fill gaps in statutory schemes.

For more problems and exercises related to the legal system, consult Appendix II.

Endnotes

1. Karl N. Llewellyn, THE BRAMBLE BUSH 10 (10th prtg. 1996).
2. Wagenseller v. Scottsdale Mem'l Hosp., 710 P.2d 1025, 1033 (Ariz. 1985).
3. Wayne R. LaFave, CRIMINAL LAW § 19.2, at 971 (5th ed. 2010).
4. *Id.* § 8.6.
5. *See* 1 Arthur L. Corbin, CORBIN ON CONTRACTS § 25 (1963); John D. Calamari & Joseph M. Perillo, CONTRACTS § 2.6(d), at 32 (6th ed. 2009).
6. *See, e.g.*, David Adam Friedman, *Explaining "Bait-and-Switch" Regulation*, 4 WM. & MARY BUS. L. REV. 575 (2013); Note, *State Control of Bait Advertising*, 69 YALE L.J. 830 (1960).

7. Llewellyn, *supra* note 1, at 89; *see also* Roscoe Pound, *Common Law and Legislation*, 21 Harv. L. Rev. 383 (1908).
8. Stanley Mosk, *The Common Law and the Judicial Decision-Making Process*, 11 Harv. J.L. & Pub. Pol'y 35 (1988).
9. *See generally* William Van Orman Quine, Word and Object 85, 129 (1960).
10. Judith S. Kaye, *Things Judges Do: State Statutory Interpretation*, 13 Touro L. Rev. 595, 608 (1997).
11. *See, e.g.*, Jackson Transit Auth. v. Local Div. 1285, Amalgamated Transit Union, 457 U.S. 15, 22-29 (1982); Mohasco Corp. v. Silver, 447 U.S. 807, 815 (1980). Those who advance textualism in its purest form may argue that legislative intent is a fiction and should play no role in interpretation of statutory text. *See* Antonin Scalia & Bryan Garner, Reading Law 16, 349-51, 391-98 (2012). As discussed in the next section, however, courts are more apt to apply a hybrid form of textualism, which still pays at least lip service to a notion of legislative intent.
12. Ariz. Dep't of Economic Sec. v. Lee, 228 Ariz. 150, 152, 264 P.3d 34, 36 (Ct. App. 2011) (citations omitted from quote); *see also* Return Mail, Inc. v. United States Postal Service, 139 S. Ct. 1853, 1863 (2019) (confirming this generalization, but finding that a statute used the term "person" in different ways in different provisions).
13. Kaye, *supra* note 10, at 600.
14. *See, e.g.*, Hall Street Assoc. L.L.C. v. Mattel, Inc., 552 U.S. 576, 589 (2007) ("whatever the consequences of our holding, the statutory text gives us no business to expand the statutory grounds"); Connecticut Nat'l Bank v. Germain, 503 U.S. 249, 253-54 (1992) (giving priority to the plain language of the statute over legislative history and canons of construction); Ziotas v. Reardon Law Firm, P.C., 997 A.2d 453, 457 (Conn. 2010) (refusing to consider extrinsic evidence if the statutory text, considered in relationship to other statutes, is "plain and unambiguous and does not yield absurd or unworkable results"); Note, *Looking It Up: Dictionaries and Statutory Interpretation*, 107 Harv. L. Rev. 1437, 1440-44 (1994) (tracing increasing use of the plain language rule, supported by dictionary definitions, in the United States Supreme Court).
15. *E.g.*, *Return Mail*, *supra* note 12, at 1871-72 (Justice Breyer, dissenting, joined by Justices Ginsburg and Kagen); Maine v. Thiboutot, 448 U.S. 1, 13-14 (1980) (Powell, J., dissenting); Kent Greenawalt, Legislation: Statutory Interpretation: 20 Questions 57 (1999) (concluding that judges may have reason to depart from the "evident meaning" of statutory text in the case of an obvious "slip" in drafting and, "[s]omewhat more controversially," when "a straightforward reading of the text ... is clearly at odds with underlying statutory purpose, is manifestly absurd, or is undoubtedly unjust").
16. Ariz. Dep't of Economic Sec. v. Lee, 264 P.3d 34, 38-39 (Ariz. Ct. App. 2011).
17. Unification Church v. INS, 762 F.2d 1077, 1083-90 (D.C. Cir. 1985); *see also* Tomka v. Seiler Corp., 66 F.3d 1295, 1313-17 (2d Cir. 1995) (plain meaning of statute is not controlling in rare cases in which the literal meaning of statutory language clearly conflicts with legislative intent).
18. For more examples of canons of statutory interpretation, see Scalia & Garner, *supra* note 11. Many of the canons classified in that book as "semantic," "syntactic," or "contextual" arise from conventions of grammar and English usage. *Id.* at xxii–xiv (Table of Contents).
19. Bostock v. Clayton County, 140 S. Ct. 1731, 1739 (2020).
20. Blanchard v. Bergeron, 489 U.S. 87, 98 (1989) (Scalia, J., concurring); *see also* Scalia & Garner, *supra* note 11, at 369-90 (explaining why committee reports and floor speeches are not worthwhile aids in statutory construction). Perhaps due to Justice Scalia's influence, the Supreme Court's reliance on legislative history declined in the 1990s. Lori L. Outzs, *A Principled Use of Congressional Floor Speeches in Statutory Interpretation*, 28 Colum. J.L. & Soc. Probs. 297, 305-06 (1995).
21. Scalia & Garner, *supra* note 11, at 16 (2012).

22. Cabell v. Markham, 148 F.2d 737, 739 (2d Cir. 1945), *aff'd*, 326 U.S. 404 (1945).
23. *Bostock*, 140 S. Ct. at 1739.
24. Bell v. United States, 349 U.S. 81, 83 (1955); *accord*, State v. Tarango, 914 P.2d 1300, 1302 (Ariz. 1996); Johnson v. State, 602 So. 2d 1288, 1290 (Fla. 1992). *But cf.* F. Andrew Hessick & Carissa Bryne Hessick, *Constraining Criminal Laws*, forthcoming in 106 MINN. L. REV. (2022) (arguing that the modern rule of lenity is an inadequate successor to earlier rules of interpretation that favored criminal defendants).
25. Nat'l Fed'n of Indep. Bus. v. Sebelius, 567 U.S. 519, 561 (2012) (construing the Act's insurance mandate to be a tax, which offered an avenue for upholding its constitutionality). "[E]very reasonable construction must be resorted to, in order to save a statute from unconstitutionality." Hooper v. California, 155 U.S. 648, 657 (1895) (quoted in *Sebelius*, 567 U.S. at 536). For more canons of construction, *see* Scalia & Garner, *supra* note 11. Most of the canons categorized in that book as "Principles Applicable Specifically to Governmental Prescriptions" provide good examples of rules of construction. *Id.* at xiv–xvi (Table of Contents).
26. *See, e.g.*, Northrop Corp. v. Litronic Industries, 29 F.3d 1173, 1178 (7th Cir. 1994) ("uniform nationwide application" of the UCC "argues for nudging majority views, even if imperfect").
27. *See, e.g.*, Bell v. United States, 349 U.S. 81, 83-84 (1955).
28. Karl N. Llewellyn, *Remarks on the Theory of Appellate Decision and the Rules or Canons about How Statutes Are to Be Construed*, 3 VAND. L. REV. 395, 401-06 (1950).
29. United States v. Otherson, 637 F.2d 1276, 1285 (9th Cir. 1980). Some commentators are more critical of established canons of statutory construction and would replace them wholesale with other means of resolving legislative ambiguities. *See, e.g.*, Richard A. Posner, *Statutory Interpretation — In the Classroom and in the Courtroom*, 50 U. CHI. L. REV. 800 (1983); *cf.* EEOC v. Arabian Am. Oil Co., 499 U.S. 244, 260-61 (1991) (Marshall, J., dissenting) (arguing that majority of the Court gave undue weight to a rule of construction disfavoring extraterritorial application of congressional legislation).
30. 42 U.S.C. § 2000e-2(a) (2019).
31. Laurence H. Tribe, *Judicial Interpretation of Statutes: Three Axioms*, 11 HARV. J.L. & PUB. POL'Y 51 (1988) ("Axiom one is: *Language first*."); Unification Church v. INS, 762 F.2d 1077, 1083 (D.C. Cir. 1985).
32. *E.g.*, WEBSTER'S SEVENTH NEW COLLEGIATE DICTIONARY 347 (1970), as quoted in Holloway v. Arthur Andersen & Co., 566 F.2d 659, 662 n.4 (9th Cir. 1977).
33. Section 703(h) incorporates a limitation set forth in the Equal Pay Act: "It shall not be ... unlawful ... to differentiate upon the basis of *sex* ... if such differentiation is authorized by the provisions of [the Equal Pay Act]." 42 U.S.C. § 2000e-2(h) (2019) (emphasis added).
34. The Equal Pay Act refers to members of the "opposite sex": "No employer ... shall discriminate ... between employees on the basis of *sex* by paying wages to employees ... at a rate less than the rate at which he pays wages to employees of the *opposite sex* ... for equal work. ..." 29 U.S.C. § 206(d) (2019) (emphasis added). The phrase "opposite sex" is commonly used to refer only to distinctions between males and females. Therefore, the Equal Pay Act is nearly unambiguous in its classifying only on the basis of employees being male or female. That might still leave unanswered questions about defining a transgender or non-binary person as male or female, but it does appear to rely on status as male or female in its test for discriminatory pay for equal work.
35. Charles Whalen & Barbara Whalen, THE LONGEST DEBATE 84, 115-16 (1985).
36. Meritor Sav. Bank, FSB v. Vinson, 477 U.S. 57, 64 (1986).
37. *See* Whalen & Whalen, *supra* note 32, at 116-17.
38. Holloway v. Arthur Andersen & Co., 566 F.2d 659, 662 (9th Cir. 1977).
39. *E.g., id.* at 662-63; Spearman v. Ford Motor Co., 231 F.3d 1080, 1084-85 (7th Cir. 2000).
40. *See, e.g.*, De Santis v. Pac. Tel. & Tel. Co., 608 F.2d 327 (9th Cir. 1979); Bibby v. Philadelphia Coca-Cola Bottling Co., 260 F.3d 257, 261-64 (3d Cir.

2001) (distinguishing between sexual orientation discrimination, which is not prohibited by Title VII, from same- sex gender discrimination, which is).

41. Pension Ben. Guar. Corp. v. LTV Corp., 496 U.S. 633, 650 (1990).
42. Price Waterhouse v. Hopkins, 490 U.S. 228 (1989).
43. Zachary A. Kramer, *The Ultimate Gender Stereotype: Equalizing Gender-Conforming and Gender-Nonconforming Homosexuals Under Title VII*, 2004 U. ILL. L. REV. 465.
44. *See* Bell v. Brown, 557 F.2d 849, 853 (D.C. Cir. 1977). *But see* Antonin Scalia & Bryan Garner, READING LAW 364 (2012) (noting this rule of construction as "an oft-repeated and age-old formulation," but critiquing it as a "false notion.")
45. You will read more about overturning precedent in Chapter 5.
46. Hively v. Ivy Tech Cmty. Coll. of Ind., 853 F.3d 339 (7th Cir. 2017) (en banc) (sexual orientation discrimination is a form of sex discrimination); Zarda v. Altitude Express, Inc., 883 F.3d 100 (2d Cir. 2018) (en banc) (same); EEOC v. R.G. & G.R. Harris Funeral Homes, Inc., 884 F.3d 560 (6th Cir. 2018) (transgender discrimination constitutes sex discrimination).
47. Cristiansen v. Omnicom Grp., Inc., 852 F.3d 195, 201-07 (2d Cir. 2017) (Katzman, C.J., concurring on the basis of circuit precedent but calling for the full court to revisit its precedent on this issue).
48. This passage invites you to revisit our discussion of stare decisis in Chapter 5.
49. *Hively*, 853 F.3d at 353 (Posner, J., concurring).
50. *E.g., id.* at 360 (Sykes, J. dissenting) (referring to a "statutory amendment courtesy of unelected judges"); Bostock v. Clayton County, 140 S. Ct. 1731, 1738 (2020) ("If judges could add to, remodel, update, or detract from old statutory terms inspired only by extratextual sources and our own imaginations, we would risk amending statutes outside the legislative process reserved for the people's representatives.")
51. 140 S. Ct. 1731 (2020).
52. *Id.* at 1739.
53. *Id.* at 1740-43.
54. *Id.* at 1742.
55. *Id.* at 1749.
56. *Id.* at 1753 ("This elephant has never hidden in a mousehole; it has been standing before us all along.")
57. *Id.* at 1754 (Alito, J., dissenting).
58. *Id.* at 1822 (Kavanaugh, J., dissenting).
59. 42 U.S.C. § 2000e-2(a) (2019).
60. Such conduct constitutes sex discrimination if the harasser would not have engaged in the conduct but for the employee's status as a man or a woman; that requirement normally is satisfied in the case of a heterosexual or homosexual harasser, but not necessarily in the case of a bisexual harasser. *See* Barnes v. Costle, 561 F.2d 983, 990 n.55 (D.C. Cir. 1977). That analysis, however, does not answer the question whether the discrimination alters conditions of employment, as required by Title VII.
61. Bundy v. Jackson, 641 F.2d 934, 943-44 (D.C. Cir. 1981).
62. Meritor Sav. Bank, FSB v. Vinson, 477 U.S. 57, 67 (1986) (quoting Henson v. Dundee, 682 F.2d 897, 904 (11th Cir. 1982)).
63. Harris v. Forklift Sys., 510 U.S. 17, 23 (1993). The Supreme Court has also emphasized the value of employing "[c]ommon sense and an appropriate sensitivity to social context" in distinguishing "ordinary socializing in the workplace" from unlawful harassment. Oncale v. Sundowner Offshore Serv., Inc., 523 U.S. 75, 81-82 (1998).
64. This problem is derived from a hypothetical case posed by Shirley Abrahamson, chief justice of the Wisconsin Supreme Court, and related by New York Court of Appeals Judge Judith S. Kaye in *Things Judges Do: State Statutory Interpretation*, 13 TOURO L. REV. 595, 606 (1997).
65. McDonald v. Santa Fe Trail Transp. Co., 427 U.S. 273, 289 (1976).

66. *Id.* at 289-95.
67. Runyon v. McCrary, 427 U.S. 160 (1976).
68. Gary Watt, Equity Stirring: The Story Of Justice Beyond Law 247-48 (2009).
69. Washington v. Glucksberg, 521 U.S. 702 (1997); Vacco v. Quill, 521 U.S. 793 (1997); *see also* Gonzales v. Oregon, 546 U.S. 243 (2006) (rejecting U.S. Attorney General's attempt to change this result through interpretive rulemaking that exceeded rulemaking authority under the federal Controlled Substances Act).
70. *See* Foon Rhee, *Jury Award Turns Attention to "Homewrecker" Law*, Wash. Post, Aug. 10, 1997, at A25.
71. *See, e.g.*, Fitch v. Valentine, 959 So. 2d 1012 (Miss. 2007).
72. *See, e.g.*, Susan L. Thomas, *Proof of Alienation of Affections*, 54 Am. Jur. 3d *Proof of Facts* § 135 (2009); Jill Jones, *Fanning an Old Flame: Alienation of Affections and Criminal Conversation Revisited*, 26 Pepp. L. Rev. 61 (1999).
73. Cannon v. Miller, 322 S.E.2d 780 (N.C. Ct. App. 1984), *vacated*, 327 S.E.2d 888 (N.C. 1985).
74. Northwest Airlines, Inc. v. Transport Workers Union, 451 U.S. 77, 95 (1981) (quoting New Jersey v. New York, 283 U.S. 336, 348 (1931)).
75. *See, e.g.*, City & County of S.F. v. United Ass'n of Journeymen etc. of U.S. & Can., 42 Cal. 3d 810, 815-20, 726 P.2d 538, 541-43 (1986); *see also* Raftopol v. Ramey, 299 Conn. 681, 710-11, 12 A.3d 783, 800 (2011) (stating this proposition but enforcing surrogacy agreement by interpreting ambiguous statute); Heard v. Stamford, 3 P. Wms. 409, 411 (1735) (in explaining why an English court of equity should not intervene, stating that "[i]f the law as it now stands be thought inconvenient, it will be good reason for the legislature to alter it, but till that is done, what is law at present, must take place") (as quoted in Gary Watt, Equity Stirring: The Story of Justice Beyond Law 20 (2009)).
76. U.C.C. § 2-302 (2011).
77. Williams v. Walker-Thomas Furniture Co., 350 F.2d 445, 448-49 & n.5 (D.C. Cir. 1965).
78. 2B Norman J. Singer, Sutherland Statutory Construction § 50.01 (6th ed. 2000); *see* Wayne R. LaFave, Criminal Law § 2.2(d), at 94-96 (5th ed. 2010) (discussing interpretation of criminal statutes in light of common law); City of Okla. City v. Tuttle, 471 U.S. 808, 835-38 (1985) (Stevens, J., dissenting).
79. *See, e.g.*, Heydon's Case, 76 Eng. Rep. 637, 638 (1584), quoted in Singer, *supra* note 78, § 45.05, at 25-26.
80. U.C.C. § 1-103(b) (2001).
81. City of Newport v. Fact Concerts, Inc., 453 U.S. 247, 258 (1981).
82. *See* Marbury v. Madison, 5 U.S. (1 Cranch) 137 (1803) (setting forth seminal dictum regarding judicial authority in the federal system); Dickerson v. United States, 530 U.S. 428 (2000) (striking down congressional attempt to legislatively overrule the celebrated *Miranda* decision, which protected constitutional rights).
83. *See, e.g.*, Monell v. Dep't of Soc. Servs. of N.Y., 436 U.S. 658 (1978) (overruling the Court's previous decision that the term "person" in 42 U.S.C. § 1983 does not include municipalities); Wayne R. LaFave, Criminal Law § 2.2(m), at 107-08 (5th ed. 2010).
84. Kelley v. R.G. Indus., 497 A.2d 1143, 1150-51 (Md. 1985).
85. *E.g.*, *In re* Validation of Marriage of Francisco, 16 Indian L. Rep. 6113, 6115 (Navajo S. Ct. 1989).
86. *See id.* ("This court ... does not rely on [the tribal code], but instead on Navajo custom.").
87. *See* Guido Calabresi, A Common Law for the Age of Statutes 163-66 (1999) (recommending that Anglo-American courts refuse to enforce outdated statutes unless reaffirmed by the legislature).

PART III

Legal Method and Analysis

Chapters 5 and 6 will introduce you to concepts and modes of reasoning that are crucial to your success in the study and practice of law. Chapter 5 explores the doctrine of stare decisis, which ensures that published judicial opinions by appellate courts—case law—have the force of law in our system. Finally, Chapter 6 explores modes of legal reasoning that you will apply throughout law school and indeed throughout your career in law.

Chapter 5

The Role of Precedent: The Court System and Stare Decisis

I. Introduction to Stare Decisis

In the United States, previous court decisions may influence, or even dictate, the result in a dispute currently before a court. The legal effect of the previous decisions is governed by a complex set of conventions commonly referred to as "stare decisis."

"Stare decisis," sometimes called the rule of precedent, means standing by what has been decided. Under the doctrine of stare decisis, a court endeavors to decide each case consistently with its own previous decisions, which are called its "precedent." Moreover, the deciding court ordinarily is strictly bound by the precedent of a higher court that reviews the decisions of the deciding court, if the precedent addressed essentially the same question currently before the deciding court.

Judicial adherence to the doctrine of stare decisis serves several significant goals:

- it promotes efficiency in judicial administration by relieving judges of the burden of revisiting settled legal questions in each case;
- it facilitates private and commercial transactions by ensuring a degree of certainty and predictability in the law that regulates such transactions; and
- it satisfies the common moral belief that persons in like circumstances should be treated alike.[1]

The strength of an authority as precedent depends in part on the relationship between the court that created the precedent and the court that may subsequently apply it. Therefore, our exploration should begin with an introduction to the court system.

II. The Court System

A. Structure of State, Federal, and Tribal Courts

1. State Courts

Most state court systems include courts of limited jurisdiction, which hear disputes on limited matters such as domestic relations, traffic violations, and civil suits with small amounts in controversy. All other disputes are tried in branches of a trial court of general jurisdiction, typically named "Superior Court," "Circuit Court," or "District Court."

In most states, final decisions of this trial court may be reviewed in appellate courts at two different levels. Initially, a disappointed litigant may appeal a trial court judgment to an intermediate court of appeals. The losing party in that appellate court can then seek further review in a court of last resort, known as the "Supreme Court" in nearly all states. A few states have no intermediate appellate court; instead, a single state court of last resort hears appeals directly from judgments of the trial court.[2] Under either model, a disappointed litigant in state court may seek further review on questions of federal law in the United States Supreme Court.[3]

The state court system in California is representative of those systems with two levels of appellate review:

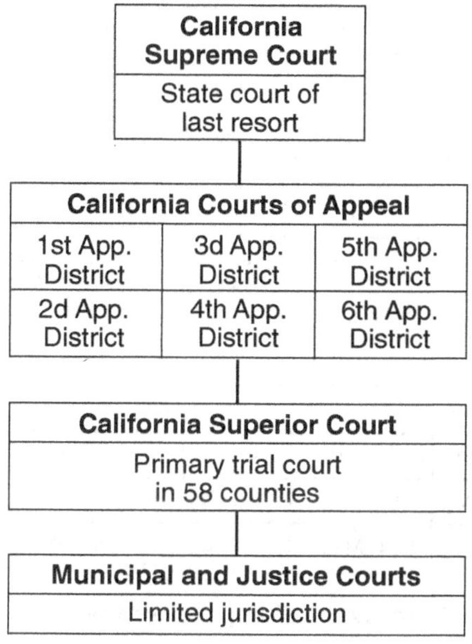

California Court System

In California, two courts of limited jurisdiction, Justice Courts and Municipal Courts, hear restricted classes of cases. The trial court of general jurisdiction is the Superior Court, which serves each of 58 counties throughout the state. The Superior Court hears appeals from the courts of limited jurisdiction, and it entertains original actions in a wide variety of civil and criminal cases. Disappointed litigants in a criminal or civil case may appeal a Superior Court judgment to the California Court of Appeal. This intermediate appellate court is divided into six districts, each of which hears civil and criminal appeals from Superior Courts in counties assigned to that district. A disappointed litigant in the Court of Appeal may appeal to the California Supreme Court in certain kinds of cases and may petition for discretionary review in others.[4]

For example, California's Second Appellate District includes the counties of Los Angeles, San Luis Obispo, Santa Barbara, and Ventura. The California Court of Appeal for the Second Appellate District would hear appeals from the decisions of the California Superior Court in those counties. A litigant disappointed by a decision of the Court of Appeal for the Second Appellate District could appeal to the California Supreme Court or petition it for discretionary review.

2. Federal Courts

The structure of the federal court system is similar to that of the California court system:

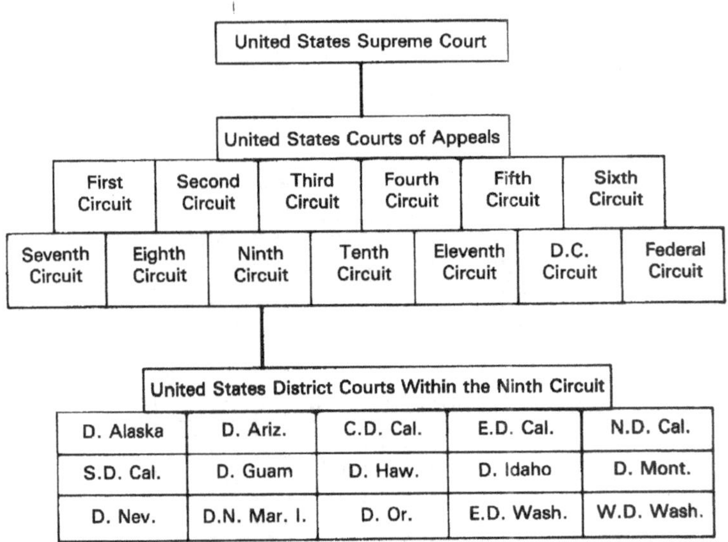

United States Court of Appeals for the Ninth Circuit

The primary federal trial courts are the United States District Courts. With few exceptions, disappointed litigants appeal from a judgment of a district court to the appropriate one of 13 "circuits" of the United States Courts of Appeals. Petitions for further review are taken to the United States Supreme Court. The chart above shows the line of review from judgments of the United States District Courts within the jurisdiction of the United States Court of Appeals for the Ninth Circuit.

The Ninth Circuit encompasses a large portion of the United States. Although Congress has repeatedly considered proposals to split this circuit into two circuits, the Ninth Circuit still includes the states and territories of Alaska, Arizona, California, Guam, Hawaii, Idaho, Montana, Nevada, the Northern Mariana Islands, Oregon, and Washington. Each of those states and territories has at least one district court; California and Washington have more. For example, California is divided into four: the United States District Courts for the Central, Eastern, Northern, and Southern Districts of California.

3. Tribal Courts

Tribal communities in the United States typically employ a two-level court system, with a trial court and a single appellate court, as illustrated by the judicial system of the Navajo Nation:

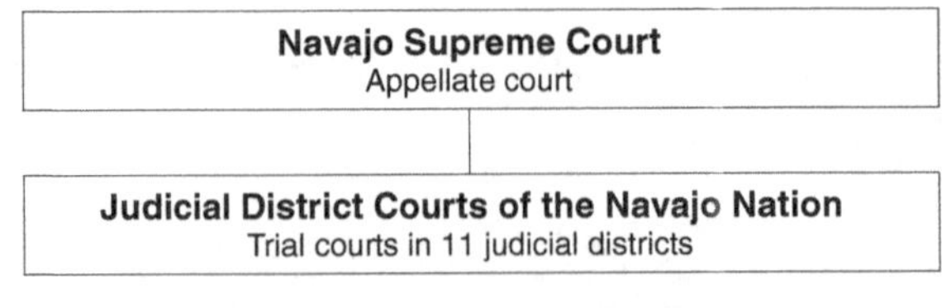

Navajo Nation Court System

The Navajo Judicial Branch alternatively offers the opportunity to resolve disputes in the Navajo Peacemaker Court. Rooted in traditional Navajo culture, the Peacemaking Program seeks to restore harmony in disrupted relationships through engagement, healing, and consensus.[5]

Some tribes are sufficiently small that they join with other tribes to share a single court system. For example, 12 tribes in San Diego County have formed a judicial consortium, the Inter-Tribal Court of Southern California.[6]

B. Court Structure and Stare Decisis

Precedent is not strictly binding on the decision-making of the court that created the precedent: a lthough a court will do so only in unusual circumstances, it can depart from its own prior rulings. For lower courts within the same court system, stare decisis is less flexible: a trial court or intermediate court of appeal must respect the precedent of a higher court that acts as a court of review for the lower court.[7] Such binding precedent, like legislative acts, is *mandatory* authority for the lower courts. The California Court of Appeal, for example, is bound by decisions of the California Supreme Court. As discussed further in Section III below, the lower court must either distinguish the reviewing court's precedent or apply it as *controlling* authority, which is precedent that dictates the outcome of the current case.

Stare decisis generally does not require a court to follow the precedent of coequal autonomous courts, of lower courts within the same court system, or of any courts outside that system. For example, the Florida Supreme Court is not bound by the decisions of the other Florida courts or by those of the California Supreme Court. Similarly, the United States Court of Appeals for the First Circuit is not bound by the decisions of either the United States Court of Appeals for the Second Circuit or any United States District Court. Nonetheless, the deciding court may consider such nonbinding precedent as persuasive authority and follow its reasoning as a matter of choice, provided that the *persuasive* authority does not contradict *binding* precedent.

In some courts, a judicial unit of fewer than all members of the court may create precedent for the entire court. For example, the United States Court of Appeals for the Ninth Circuit has more than two dozen judges, but most appeals in the circuit are heard by panels of three judges each. Each three-judge panel creates precedent that must be followed by all other three-judge panels in the circuit. Within the circuit, a decision of a three-judge panel can be overruled only by an "en banc" panel of 11 members of the court.[8]

III. Scope and Application of Stare Decisis

A. Building a Wall of Case Law, Brick by Brick

Courts add to existing common law or statutory interpretations incrementally, as they decide individual disputes on specific facts. Each resolution of a dispute, when published as a written opinion, adds one more "brick" of precedent to a wall of case law. When courts adhere to precedent under stare decisis, they build on the foundation of judicial "bricks" laid in previous decisions.

Some form of stare decisis is justified in any society that values efficiency, certainty, and equal treatment of similarly situated parties. On the other hand, unquestioning adherence to precedent may inappropriately extend the rule of previous decisions beyond the rationale and policy of the original decision, or it may retain outdated or otherwise unsound precedent. A wall that rises ever higher on a flawed or outdated foundation will eventually fall.

Two limits to stare decisis help to avoid rigidity in the law while maintaining consistency:

(1) A court may *distinguish* a prior decision if it concludes that the prior decision addressed a significantly different dispute from the one now before the court. If so, even if the prior decision was issued by the same court or by a higher court within the jurisdiction, the prior decision does not control the result in the case now before the court. Of course, if the prior decision was issued by a lower court or by a court from another jurisdiction, it would never be *binding* on the current court. Moreover, if such a prior decision is distinguishable from the current case, the prior decision may lose even the persuasive value that it might otherwise have had.

(2) Alternatively, a court's own precedent may be indistinguishable from the dispute currently before the court. If so, the court normally would apply the doctrine of stare decisis to follow its precedent. Nonetheless, the doctrine of stare decisis is not an inexorable mandate. In special circumstances, the court may depart from the normal dictates of stare decisis and overrule its own precedent, replacing it with new case law.

The following sections thoroughly examine each of these limits on stare decisis. Section B addresses whether a prior decision is sufficiently analogous to the current issue that it applies to the issue now before the court, or whether the prior decision instead is distinguishable. Section C assumes that a court's own prior decision is not distinguishable and therefore would normally be controlling in the current dispute. It then discusses the special circumstances in which a court may overrule such precedent.

B. Analogizing and Distinguishing Precedent

1. An Inexact Science with Ample Room for Argument

Few disputes are so similar in their facts and legal issues that resolution of the first dispute provides a clear basis for resolving the second. In those relatively rare cases, the prior decision is "controlling" precedent in the same court or a lower court within the jurisdiction. Such controlling precedent will dictate the result of the subsequent case in a lower court, or at least will control the outcome of an individual issue in that case. Indeed, even the court that created the precedent will normally adhere to it when the issue arises again in that court.[9]

More often, however, differences between two cases in the facts or in the nature of the legal issues are sufficiently substantial that the prior decision should not dictate the resolution of the second. However, even assuming the precedent is not nearly identical to the current dispute and thus is not strictly controlling, it may still be sufficiently analogous to provide a strong basis for deciding the current dispute. Whether the prior decision is analogous or distinguishable is a matter of judgment and analysis, which provides opposing attorneys with plenty of room for argument.[10]

In analyzing the precedential value of arguably distinguishable authority, you should pay attention to the rationale underlying the prior decision. Differences between the cases may reveal that the reasons for the result in the prior decision do not apply to the current case. If so, the distinctions between the two cases justify a different result in the current case, or at least an analysis without deference to the prior decision. Conversely, even though different facts or issues in a prior decision prevent it from clearly resolving the current case, many of the *reasons* for the legal result in the prior decision might apply equally to the current case. If so, the prior case—although not clearly controlling—might supply a rationale that justifies the same legal result in the current case.

Of course, this process of either restricting or extending the application of precedent in relation to a new dispute is far from an exact science. It sometimes implicates the most deeply held values of those who must interpret and apply the precedent:

> Like the antebellum judges who denied relief to fugitive slaves... the Court today claims that its decision, however harsh, is compelled by existing legal doctrine. On the contrary, the question presented by this case is an open one, and our Fourteenth Amendment precedents may be read more broadly or narrowly depending upon how one chooses to read them. Faced with the choice, I would adopt a "sympathetic" reading, one which comports with dictates of fundamental justice and recognizes that compassion need not be exiled from the province of judging.[11]

Although uncertainty about the reasons for a prior decision often complicates the analysis, courts regularly engage in the processes of distinction and analogy to limit, extend, refine, and clarify the rules of prior decisions. Indeed, the scope of a decision typically does not become clear until courts analyze it in subsequent decisions in the context of other disputes. This inquiry is largely one of defining, limiting, and extending the holdings of prior decisions; you will revisit it when you study techniques of briefing cases in Chapter 7.

Moreover, by noting distinctions between some cases and drawing analogies between others, you can synthesize cases that address the same issue on different facts, leading to a fuller picture of the law. From this vantage point, you can incorporate all the relevant cases into a synthesized legal rule that will govern the legal issue in a new case. In some cases, the applicable law will consist of your synthesis of various types of authority that all play a role —— for example, a constitutional provision, one or more statutes, administrative regulations, and case law. Your interpretation of the authority, however, will often be open to debate, allowing the opposing attorney to offer a different synthesis of authority leading to a different synthesized rule. This process of constructing a synthesized rule—and showing your support for it—is discussed and illustrated in later chapters, including Chapters 8 through 10.

2. Gaining Comfort with Legal Uncertainty

The room for debate retained in a flexible doctrine of stare decisis illustrates a more general characteristic of uncertainty or indeterminacy in our legal system. New law students are often eager to write down the "right answer" to every legal question posed by their professors. But, as periodically pointed out in this book, the most interesting legal questions—the ones that are fully litigated and appealed—are ones to which the answer is uncertain prior to the final judicial determination. If the resolution of the legal dispute were perfectly certain, the parties likely would have settled the dispute well short of full litigation. And, if the answer were certain during litigation, why would parties and attorneys wait with great anticipation for the jury's verdict on the evidence? If not for legal uncertainty, why would so many appellate decisions be decided on a split vote of learned judges or justices, who frequently disagree on the merits of the appeal?

British law professor Gary Watt describes the uncertainty in the outcome of legal disputes in a particularly colorful manner:

> There is never only one answer to a legal dispute; indeed it is a rare case that has only one right answer. As Lord Macmillan admitted: "in almost every case except the very plainest, it would be possible to decide the issue either way with reasonable legal justification." Ronald Dworkin fantasizes that there is always one right answer to every case and that a hypothetical Herculean judge could find it. Perhaps Hercules might, but then perhaps Zeus would find another answer on appeal.... [T]he outcome often turns in large part on the purely practical contingency of running out of courts. The nature of the law in such a system is less like a scientific experiment and more like a wheel of fortune: the nature of the legal outcome is determined at the point the wheel stops spinning, and would have [been] determined earlier if the litigants had been at any stage unwilling, or financially unable, to give it an extra push. From the judges' perspective it is a living conversation across a range of reasonable alternative possibilities, and it just happens that the conversation must stop sometime.[12]

The example in the next subsection illustrates Professor Watt's metaphor of a roulette wheel signifying the outcome of a dispute by stopping its spinning and "running out of courts." It reminds us that the main task of law students and attorneys alike is not to know or discover the "right answer" to a novel legal question. Your main task instead is to identify issues—matters that are reasonably in dispute on the facts and the existing law—and to recognize or develop the arguments that can be persuasively advanced on either side of the dispute.

3. Example: Warrantless Searches of Cars, Houses, and Mobile Homes

Supreme Court decisions interpreting and applying the Fourth Amendment to the United States Constitution[13] illustrate the techniques of analogy and distinction as well as the difficulty of predicting legal outcomes. In *Carroll v. United States*,[14] the Supreme Court held that the Fourth Amendment permitted federal officers to search an automobile without first obtaining a warrant. The Court reasoned that, although a suspect may have privacy interests in the contents of an automobile, the ready mobility of the automobile makes obtaining a warrant before searching impracticable.[15] Seven months later, in *Agnello v. United States*,[16] the Supreme Court held that the Fourth Amendment prohibited the warrantless search of a suspect's home when the suspect had been arrested in another location.[17] In disapproving the warrantless search, the *Agnello* Court distinguished *Carroll* on the bases of the immobility of the house and the particularly great privacy interests the owner has in the contents of a house.[18]

Sixty years after *Carroll* and *Agnello*, in *California v. Carney*,[19] the Court considered whether the Fourth Amendment prohibited law enforcement officers from engaging in a warrantless search of a fully mobile motor home. Neither *Carroll* nor *Agnello* clearly controlled, because a motor home arguably combines the mobility of an automobile and the privacy interests associated with a house.[20] Consequently, the result in *Carney* under the doctrine of stare decisis depended on whether the Court found the facts of the case to be more nearly analogous to those of *Carroll* or to those of *Agnello*.

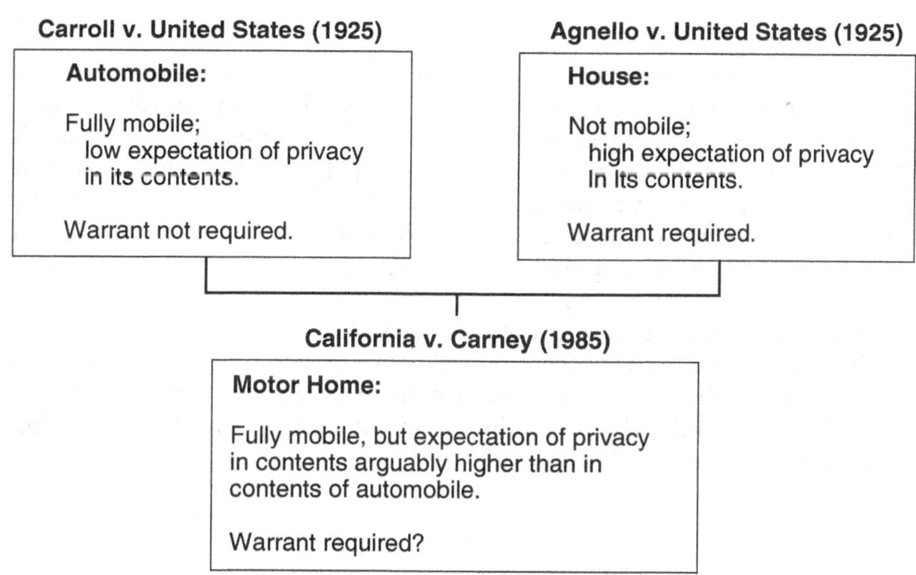

Analogizing and Distinguishing Fourth Amendment Precedent

On a vote of eight to one, the California Supreme Court disapproved the search on two grounds. First, it had analogized *Carney* to cases like *Agnello*, reasoning that the nature of the contents of the motor home, in which the defendant was residing, created similarly high expectations of privacy that one has in the contents of a house. Second, it distinguished *Carroll* on the basis of the comparatively low expectation of privacy that an owner has in the contents of an automobile.[21]

On review, the United States Supreme Court voted six to three to reverse the decision of the California Supreme Court and to approve the warrantless search. It analogized the case to *Carroll*, reasoning that an automobile and a motor home are not only similarly mobile but are similar in the reduced expectations of privacy in their contents. The expectations of privacy in a motor home are low partly because of the pervasive governmental regulation applicable to all licensed motor vehicles.[22]

The majorities in the state and federal Supreme Courts applied the precedent differently because they differed in their analyses, primarily factual, of the expectations of privacy that one has in the contents of a motor home. The United States Supreme Court's decision to approve the warrantless search was not unanimous, and it was not the only "correct" or reasonable decision open to it. Indeed, if you count the combined votes of the justices in both the California and United States Supreme Courts, you will find that a total of eleven state and federal justices voted to require a warrant in the case, while only seven voted to approve the warrantless search. However, because the United States Supreme Court is the highest court in the land, no further appeals are possible. Consequently, the majority of its justices have the last word.

C. Overruling Precedent

1. Standards for Departing from Normal Application of Stare Decisis

A court's own precedent, or that of a higher court within the same jurisdiction, normally is controlling if it is materially indistinguishable from the dispute now before the court. With rare exceptions, a lower court is absolutely bound by the precedent of the appellate courts that review its decisions.[23] However, the doctrine of stare decisis is more flexible in the courts that created the precedent.[24] In exceptional circumstances, a court may depart from a strict application of stare decisis and refuse to follow its own, otherwise controlling precedent. In so doing, it overrules the prior decision and substitutes new precedent in its place.

To return to our metaphor of a wall of precedents, a court may change the direction of its own brickwork, if it has a very good reason to do so. After all, a brick wall will not remain strong if it continues to rise ever higher on a flawed or outdated foundation.

More than a century ago, the United States Supreme Court endorsed this flexibility in stare decisis with surprising liberality:

> The rule of stare decisis, though one tending to consistency and uniformity of decision, is not inflexible. Whether it shall be followed or departed from is a question entirely within the discretion of the court, which is again called upon to consider a question once decided.[25]

In the 2010 decision of *Citizens United*, however, the Court announced a more demanding standard: "Our precedent is to be respected unless the most convincing of reasons demonstrates that adherence to it puts us on a course that is sure error."[26] Even under that standard, the Court overruled its precedent in that case, but the Justices debated at length about whether the Court accorded proper respect to the policies underlying stare decisis.

In a decision in 1992 dealing with the contentious issue of abortion rights, the Supreme Court identified a number of factors that a court should consider when determining whether to overrule its own precedent. A court is justified in doing so if that decision is outdated in light of intervening changes in law and society or if the prior decision has otherwise come to be viewed as hopelessly flawed. More specifically, a court can abandon its prior decision if:

1. "related principles of law have so far developed as to have left the old rule no more than a remnant of abandoned doctrine"; or
2. "facts have so changed or come to be seen so differently, as to have robbed the old rule of significant application or justification"; or
3. "a prior judicial ruling should come to be seen so clearly as error that its enforcement was for that very reason doomed"; or
4. "the rule has proved to be intolerable simply in defying practical workability."[27]

2. Changes in Social and Legal Context

In accordance with the first two justifications, a court may overrule a previous decision that was sensible in its original social, economic, technological, and legal context but nonetheless fails to serve important policies in current conditions. In one case, for example, a court overruled its own precedent when it recognized a legal right on behalf of a deceased fetus under wrongful death and survival statutes.[28] The court justified its departure from precedent partly because of intervening advances in medical knowledge and changes in the laws of other states.[29] Although some precedents retain their force for centuries, "it must be true that most cases will eventually become obsolete because society as a whole does not stand still."[30]

3. Abandonment of Erroneous or Unworkable Precedent

Even absent an intervening change in conditions, a court may overrule a prior decision because it thinks that the prior decision was poorly reasoned at the outset or has proved to be unworkable.[31] In 2013, for example, the California Supreme Court overruled its own decision issued in 1935, on the grounds that the precedent had misconstrued statutory and case law on point, was out of step with prevailing views of the law, and had been difficult to apply.[32]

In a notable departure from a strict application of stare decisis, the United States Supreme Court twice overruled precedent on the same issue in the span of 17 years. In 1985, it overruled a decision it had issued in 1976 on a question of state sovereignty under the Tenth Amendment,[33] even though that precedent had itself overruled another decision that the Supreme Court had issued in 1968.[34] In the last of these three decisions the Court explained:

> We do not lightly overrule recent precedent. We have not hesitated, however, when it has become apparent that a prior decision has departed from a proper understanding of congressional power under the Commerce Clause.[35]

4. Flexible Application of Stare Decisis to Constitutional Issues

In constitutional interpretation, the Supreme Court adopts a more flexible approach to stare decisis than with statutory interpretation, as exemplified by its double reverse on the proper interpretation of the Tenth Amendment in the span of 17 years. Stare decisis can safely apply with full force in cases of federal statutory interpretation, because Congress can correct judicial mistakes in statutory analysis by passing new legislation.[36] In contrast, Article V of the Constitution provides that an amendment to the Constitution is not effective unless approved by two-thirds of each house of Congress and ratified by three-fourths of the states. Thus, Congress cannot easily amend the Constitution to reflect changing social or economic conditions or to overrule judicial interpretations of the Constitution with which Congress disagrees.[37] Consequently, some scholars and judges believe that the Supreme Court should "keep [constitutional] law in accord with the dynamic flow of the social order," with less than the normal restraints of stare decisis.[38]

Nonetheless, countervailing considerations may justify adherence to stare decisis in some cases, even when they address challenges to previous interpretations of the Constitution. First, people may have so substantially relied on an established proposition of law that overruling the prior decision would result in "special hardship" and "inequity."[39] Second, an extraordinarily divisive issue may call for a ruling that is sufficiently durable to erase all doubts about its vulnerability to continuing political pressures. This second consideration is present

> whenever the Court's interpretation of the Constitution calls the contending sides of a national controversy to end their national division by accepting a common mandate rooted in the Constitution.
>
> The Court is not asked to do this very often .... But when the Court does act in this way, its decision requires an equally rare precedential force to counter the inevitable efforts to overturn it and to thwart its implementation.... [O]nly the most convincing justification under accepted standards of precedent could suffice to demonstrate that a later decision overruling the first was anything but a surrender to political pressure and an unjustified repudiation of the principle on which the Court staked its authority in the first instance.[40]

In *Planned Parenthood of Southeastern Pennsylvania v. Casey*,[41] the Supreme Court invoked both these considerations in declining to abandon the central rule of *Roe v. Wade*,[42] which established a woman's limited constitutional right to terminate a pregnancy.

The Court conceded that the reliance factor weighs most heavily in commercial contexts, "where advance planning of great precision is most obviously a necessity."[43] However, even in the noncommercial contexts of reproduction and sexual equality, reliance could not be discounted:

> [F]or two decades of economic and social developments, people have organized intimate relationships and made choices that define their views of themselves and their places in society, in reliance on the availability of abortion in the event that contraception should fail. The ability of women to participate equally in the economic and social life of the Nation has been facilitated by their ability to control their reproductive lives.... The Constitution serves human values, and while the effect of reliance on Roe cannot be exactly measured, neither can the certain cost of overruling Roe for people who have ordered their thinking and living around that case be dismissed.[44]

Indeed, in the context of extraordinary national division over abortion rights, a dramatic change in the course of constitutional law might fan the flames of controversy by suggesting that continued strife could inspire further changes in course:

> The Court's duty in the present case is clear. In 1973, it confronted the already-divisive issue of governmental power to limit personal choice to undergo abortion, for which it provided a new resolution based on the due process guaranteed by the Fourteenth Amendment. Whether or not a new social consensus is developing on that issue, its divisiveness is no less today than in 1973, and pressure to overrule the decision, like pressure to retain

> it, has grown only more intense. A decision to overrule Roe's essential holding under the existing circumstances would address error, if error there was, at the cost of both profound and unnecessary damage to the Court's legitimacy, and to the Nation's commitment to the rule of law.[45]

Moreover, the central rule of *Roe* had not proved unworkable and had not been eroded by changes in facts or in related principles of law. Accordingly, although the Court departed from *Roe* in other respects, it reaffirmed *Roe*'s "essential holding,"[46] staying substantially within the boundaries dictated by stare decisis.

Stare decisis and the longevity of *Roe v. Wade* will face another test as this book goes to press, when the Supreme Court reviews the constitutionality of a state ban on most abortions after 15 weeks of gestation.[47] When the Court issues its decision, probably in June 2022, we will know whether the Court gives the same deference to precedent as it did when deciding *Planned Parenthood* almost 30 years ago.

Exercise 5-1

Analyze the following problems based on decisions of the fictitious Calzona Supreme Court. For further practice in analyzing precedent, perform Problem 1 in Appendix II.

Precedent: *Smith v. Collier*, 47 Calz. 78 (1891)

On February 1, Smith and Collier agreed to marry before the end of the year. They later announced a wedding date of December 1. In November, Smith complained about Collier's habit of playing poker on Saturday nights. In retaliation, Collier broke off the engagement. Smith sued Collier for breach of contract, requesting compensatory and punitive damages. Smith did not allege that Collier committed a tort.

The opinion of the Calzona Supreme Court includes the following excerpt:

> We affirm the trial court's factual findings that Collier breached the marriage contract with the malicious intent to cause Smith injury. Although the courts of this state recognize a general rule against punitive damages for breach of contract, the trial court correctly instructed the jury that it could award punitive damages as well as compensatory damages in this case. Unlike breach of an obligation to deliver coal or repair a carriage, Collier's callous decision to break his commitment to Smith caused such grave injury to her sensibilities and honor, and to the expectations of the community, as to justify vesting the jury with discretion to voice the full measure of its disapproval.

1. Distinguishing *Smith v. Collier*

In the following cases, you represent the defendant. Identify the facts in *Smith v. Collier* that appear to have motivated the court to permit an award of punitive damages. Identify factual differences in your case that might motivate the Calzona Supreme Court to distinguish *Smith v. Collier* and to rule that punitive damages cannot be awarded against your client. Explain why those factual differences justify a different result from the ruling in *Smith v. Collier*. Identify any factual similarities between your case and *Smith v. Collier*. Explain why those similarities do not justify the same result as in *Smith v. Collier*. Which of the following cases is easiest to distinguish from *Smith v. Collier*?

a. *White v. Strunk* (1955)

White agreed to pay Strunk $25,000 for construction of a house on White's property. Strunk agreed to complete construction by August 1, regardless of weather or labor conditions. Unfortunately, abnormally frequent rainfall and faulty workmanship by subcontractors delayed Strunk's work. Despite Strunk's best efforts, he breached the contract by failing to complete construction by August 1, causing White to suffer economic losses.

b. *Roget v. Webster* (1966)

Roget agreed to pay Webster $100,000 in exchange for Webster's promise to construct a retail store on Roget's property. Before either Roget or Webster began performance, Ballentine offered to pay Webster $150,000 to construct an office building on Ballentine's property. Because he could not perform both jobs at once, and because a contract with Ballentine was more profitable, Webster committed a total breach of contract by repudiating his contract with Roget and accepting Ballentine's offer, causing Roget to suffer damages.

c. *White v. Benkowski* (1974)

White's property had no water supply. White agreed to pay Benkowski a monthly fee in exchange for fresh water supplied through pipes from Benkowski's well. After personal animosity developed between White and Benkowski, Benkowski maliciously breached the contract by shutting off the water supply to White's property, causing White to suffer damages.

2. Overruling *Smith v. Collier*

You represent the defendant in *Statler v. Corbin*, a contemporary case that is factually and procedurally indistinguishable from *Smith v. Collier*. Explain why the Calzona Supreme Court should overrule *Smith v. Collier* and disallow punitive damages for breach of a marriage agreement.

3. Distinguishing *Statler v. Corbin* (2018)

In *Statler v. Corbin*, the Calzona Supreme Court overruled *Smith v. Collier* and held that punitive damages are not available to remedy even a malicious breach of a marriage contract. In the following case, *Jones v. Marsh*, you represent the plaintiff. Identify factual or procedural differences between *Statler v. Corbin* and your case, and explain why those differences justify an award of punitive damages in your case.

Jones v. Marsh—In July, Jones and Marsh agreed to marry on November 1. At a family reunion in August, Marsh broke off the engagement in a public statement in which he maliciously and cruelly humiliated Jones. In addition to proving breach of contract, you have alleged and proved that Marsh intentionally inflicted emotional distress on Jones, conduct that is actionable as a tort in Calzona. In opposing Jones's request for punitive damages, Marsh relies on *Statler v. Corbin*.

Exercise 5-2

In his State of the Union address in January 2010, President Obama criticized a Supreme Court decision issued less than a week earlier, prompting one of the Justices attending the address to react momentarily in apparent disagreement. The decision was *Citizens United v. Federal Election Commission*, 558 U.S. 310 (2010), in which a nonprofit corporation challenged the constitutionality of federal legislation that arguably prohibited it from using its general treasury funds to broadcast a movie critical of Hillary Clinton within 30 days of the 2008 Democratic presidential primary election. The Supreme Court held in a 5 to 4 decision that the federal statute could not be enforced because it violated the corporation's free speech rights guaranteed by the First Amendment. Because the *Citizens United* decision required rejection of principles embraced by previous Supreme Court decisions, the lengthy combination of majority, concurring, and dissenting opinions includes a remarkable debate within the Court about the application of stare decisis to the case.

For an advanced exploration of stare decisis, read the excerpts of the *Citizens United* opinions below, and ponder the following questions:

1. **The Debate.** In what way do the dissenting Justices differ in their views about application of stare decisis from the Justices who joined the majority and concurring opinions?
2. **Is the Test Changing?** Is the majority signaling that it is embracing a newly relaxed test for stare decisis, such as one that permits the Supreme Court to accord less deference to a precedent if the precedent has remained controversial within a divided Court since it was decided, or if the party seeking to retain a precedent relies on a supporting rationale other than the one originally adopted in the precedent? Or one that minimizes the significance of legislative reliance on precedent, as contrasted with citizen reliance? Or does the Court's analysis of stare decisis fit comfortably within standards previously announced?
3. **Opinions as Advocacy.** How do you rate each opinion as persuasive writing? Do the majority and concurring opinions persuade you that the Court can overrule precedent in this case without offending or relaxing the doctrine of stare decisis? If so, does the dissenting opinion then cause you to reconsider?
4. **Judging Stare Decisis.** After considering this debate about the application of stare decisis, what is your view of stare decisis generally? Does

it perform an important function of facilitating orderly development of the law, yet leaving ample opportunity to correct serious mistakes? Or does it unwisely encourage retention of outdated or ill-advised judicial decisions? Alternatively, do you view stare decisis as an overly flexible doctrine that is easily manipulated so that it allows the majority of the Court to accept or reject a precedent at its will depending on how it views the merits of the precedent?

CITIZENS UNITED v. FEDERAL ELECTION COMMISSION

Supreme Court of the United States

558 U.S. 310 (2010)

[*Footnotes and parallel citations omitted.*]

Justice Kennedy delivered the opinion of the Court [joined by Justices Roberts, Scalia, and Alito, and by Justice Thomas except with respect to Section IV].

Federal law prohibits corporations and unions from using their general treasury funds to make independent expenditures for speech defined as an "electioneering communication" or for speech expressly advocating the election or defeat of a candidate. 2 U.S.C. § 441b. Limits on electioneering communications were upheld in *McConnell v. Federal Election Comm'n*, 540 U.S. 93, 203-209 (2003). The holding of *McConnell* rested to a large extent on an earlier case, *Austin v. Michigan Chamber of Commerce*, 494 U.S. 652 (1990). *Austin* had held that political speech may be banned based on the speaker's corporate identity.

In this case we are asked to reconsider *Austin* and, in effect, *McConnell*. We . . . hold that *stare decisis* does not compel the continued acceptance of *Austin*. The Government may regulate corporate political speech through disclaimer and disclosure requirements, but it may not suppress that speech altogether. We turn to the case now before us.

. . . .

III

. . . .

C

Our precedent is to be respected unless the most convincing of reasons demonstrates that adherence to it puts us on a course that is sure error. "Beyond workability, the relevant factors in deciding whether to adhere to the principle of *stare decisis* include the antiquity of the precedent, the reliance interests at stake, and of course whether the decision was well reasoned." *Montejo v. Louisiana*, 556 U.S. 778, 792-93 (2009) (overruling *Michigan v. Jackson*, 475 U.S. 625 (1986)). We have also examined whether "experience has pointed up the precedent's shortcomings." *Pearson v. Callahan*, 555 U.S. 223, 233 (2009) (overruling *Saucier v. Katz*, 533 U.S. 194 (2001)).

These considerations counsel in favor of rejecting *Austin*, which itself contravened this Court's earlier precedents in *Buckley* and *Bellotti*. "This Court has not hesitated to overrule decisions offensive to the First Amendment." *WRTL*, 551 U.S., at 500 (opinion of SCALIA, J.). "*[S]tare decisis* is a principle of policy and not a mechanical formula of adherence to the latest decision." *Helvering v. Hallock*, 309 U.S. 106, 119 (1940).

... [I]t must be concluded that *Austin* was not well reasoned. The Government defends *Austin*, relying almost entirely on "the quid pro quo interest, the corruption interest or the shareholder interest," and not *Austin*'s expressed antidistortion rationale.... When neither party defends the reasoning of a precedent, the principle of adhering to that precedent through *stare decisis* is diminished....

Austin is undermined by experience since its announcement. Political speech is so ingrained in our culture that speakers find ways to circumvent campaign finance laws.... Our Nation's speech dynamic is changing, and informative voices should not have to circumvent onerous restrictions to exercise their First Amendment rights. Speakers have become adept at presenting citizens with sound bites, talking points, and scripted messages that dominate the 24-hour news cycle. Corporations, like individuals, do not have monolithic views. On certain topics corporations may possess valuable expertise, leaving them the best equipped to point out errors or fallacies in speech of all sorts, including the speech of candidates and elected officials.

....

No serious reliance interests are at stake. As the Court stated in *Payne v. Tennessee*, 501 U.S. 808, 828 (1991), reliance interests are important considerations in property and contract cases, where parties may have acted in conformance with existing legal rules in order to conduct transactions. Here, though, parties have been prevented from acting—corporations have been banned from making independent expenditures. Legislatures may have enacted bans on corporate expenditures believing that those bans were constitutional. This is not a compelling interest for *stare decisis*. If it were, legislative acts could prevent us from overruling our own precedents, thereby interfering with our duty "to say what the law is." *Marbury v. Madison*, 1 Cranch 137, 177 (1803).

Due consideration leads to this conclusion: *Austin*, 494 50 U.S. 652, should be and now is overruled. We return to the principle established in *Buckley* and *Bellotti* that the Government may not suppress political speech on the basis of the speaker's corporate identity. No sufficient governmental interest justifies limits on the political speech of nonprofit or for-profit corporations.

D

Austin is overruled, so it provides no basis for allowing the Government to limit corporate independent expenditures....

... The *McConnell* Court relied on the antidistortion interest recognized in *Austin* to uphold a greater restriction on speech than the restriction upheld in

Austin, ... and we have found this interest unconvincing and insufficient. This part of *McConnell* is now overruled.

....

Chief Justice Roberts, with whom Justice Alito joins, concurring.

....

II

....

A

Fidelity to precedent—the policy of *stare decisis*—is vital to the proper exercise of the judicial function. "*Stare decisis* is the preferred course because it promotes the evenhanded, predictable, and consistent development of legal principles, fosters reliance on judicial decisions, and contributes to the actual and perceived integrity of the judicial process." *Payne v. Tennessee*, 501 U.S. 808, 827 (1991). For these reasons, we have long recognized that departures from precedent are inappropriate in the absence of a "special justification." *Arizona v. Rumsey*, 467 U.S. 203, 212 (1984).

At the same time, *stare decisis* is neither an "inexorable command," *Lawrence v. Texas*, 539 U.S. 558, 577 (2003), nor "a mechanical formula of adherence to the latest decision," *Helvering v. Hallock*, 309 U.S. 106, 119 (1940), especially in constitutional cases, *see United States v. Scott*, 437 U.S. 82, 101 (1978). If it were, segregation would be legal, minimum wage laws would be unconstitutional, and the Government could wiretap ordinary criminal suspects without first obtaining warrants....

Stare decisis is instead a "principle of policy." *Helvering*, *supra*, at 119....

... [W]e must keep in mind that *stare decisis* is not an end in itself. It is instead "the means by which we ensure that the law will not merely change erratically, but will develop in a principled and intelligible fashion." *Vasquez v. Hillery*, 474 U.S. 254, 265 (1986). Its greatest purpose is to serve a constitutional ideal—the rule of law. It follows that in the unusual circumstance when fidelity to any particular precedent does more to damage this constitutional ideal than to advance it, we must be more willing to depart from that precedent.

Thus, for example, if the precedent under consideration itself departed from the Court's jurisprudence, returning to the "'intrinsically sounder' doctrine established in prior cases" may "better serv[e] the values of *stare decisis* than would following [the] more recently decided case inconsistent with the decisions that came before it." *Adarand Constructors, Inc. v. Peña*, 515 U.S. 200, 231 (1995).... Abrogating the errant precedent, rather than reaffirming or extending it, might better preserve the law's coherence and curtail the precedent's disruptive effects.

Likewise, if adherence to a precedent actually impedes the stable and orderly adjudication of future cases, its *stare decisis* effect is also diminished. This can happen in a number of circumstances, such as when the precedent's validity is so hotly contested that it cannot reliably function as a basis for decision in future cases, when its rationale threatens to upend our settled jurisprudence in related areas of law, and when the precedent's underlying reasoning has become so discredited that the Court cannot keep the precedent alive without jury-rigging new and different justifications to shore up the original mistake. *See, e.g., Pearson v. Callahan*, 555 U.S. 223, 234-35 (2009); *Montejo v. Louisiana*, 556 U.S. 778, 792 (2009) (stare decisis does not control when adherence to the prior decision requires "fundamentally revising its theoretical basis").

B

These considerations weigh against retaining our decision in *Austin*.... *Austin*'s reasoning was—and remains—inconsistent with *Buckley*'s explicit repudiation of any government interest in "equalizing the relative ability of individuals and groups to influence the outcome of elections." 424 U.S., at 48-49. *Austin* was also inconsistent with *Bellotti*'s clear rejection of the idea that "speech that otherwise would be within the protection of the First Amendment loses that protection simply because its source is a corporation." 435 U.S., at 784....

Second, the validity of *Austin*'s rationale ... has proved to be the consistent subject of dispute among Members of this Court.... The simple fact that one of our decisions remains controversial is, of course, insufficient to justify overruling it. But it does undermine the precedent's ability to contribute to the stable and orderly development of the law. In such circumstances, it is entirely appropriate for the Court—which in this case is squarely asked to reconsider *Austin*'s validity for the first time—to address the matter with a greater willingness to consider new approaches capable of restoring our doctrine to sounder footing.

Third, the *Austin* decision is uniquely destabilizing because it threatens to subvert our Court's decisions even outside the particular context of corporate express advocacy. The First Amendment theory underlying *Austin*'s holding is extraordinarily broad. *Austin*'s logic would authorize government prohibition of political speech by a category of speakers in the name of equality—a point that most scholars acknowledge (and many celebrate), but that the dissent denies....

....

These readings of *Austin* do no more than carry that decision's reasoning to its logical endpoint. In doing so, they highlight the threat *Austin* poses to First Amendment rights generally, even outside its specific factual context of corporate express advocacy. Because *Austin* is so difficult to confine to its facts—and because its logic threatens to undermine our First Amendment jurisprudence and the nature of public discourse more broadly—the costs of giving it *stare decisis* effect are unusually high.

Finally and most importantly, the Government's own effort to defend *Austin*—or, more accurately, to defend something that is not quite *Austin*—underscores its weakness as a precedent of the Court....

Instead of endorsing *Austin* on its own terms, the Government urges us to reaffirm *Austin*'s specific holding on the basis of two new and potentially expansive interests—the need to prevent actual or apparent quid pro quo corruption, and the need to protect corporate shareholders. *See* Supp. Brief for Appellee 8-10, 1213. Those interests may or may not support the result in *Austin*, but they were plainly not part of the reasoning on which *Austin* relied.

....

To the extent that the Government's case for reaffirming *Austin* depends on radically reconceptualizing its reasoning, that argument is at odds with itself. *Stare decisis* is a doctrine of preservation, not transformation. It counsels deference to past mistakes, but provides no justification for making new ones. There is therefore no basis for the Court to give precedential sway to reasoning that it has never accepted, simply because that reasoning happens to support a conclusion reached on different grounds that have since been abandoned or discredited.

Doing so would undermine the rule-of-law values that justify *stare decisis* in the first place. It would effectively license the Court to invent and adopt new principles of constitutional law solely for the purpose of rationalizing its past errors, without a proper analysis of whether those principles have merit on their own. This approach would allow the Court's past missteps to spawn future mistakes, undercutting the very rule-of-law values that *stare decisis* is designed to protect.

[T]he Government's new arguments must stand or fall on their own; they are not entitled to receive the special deference we accord to precedent....

Because continued adherence to *Austin* threatens to subvert the "principled and intelligible" development of our First Amendment jurisprudence, *Vasquez*, 474 U.S., at 265, I support the Court's determination to overrule that decision.

* * *

... Congress violates the First Amendment when it decrees that some speakers may not engage in political speech at election time, when it matters most.

Justice Stevens, with whom Justice Ginsburg, Justice Breyer, and Justice Sotomayor join, concurring in part and dissenting in part.

The real issue in this case concerns how, not if, the appellant may finance its electioneering. Citizens United is a wealthy nonprofit corporation that runs a political action committee (PAC) with millions of dollars in assets. Under the Bipartisan Campaign Reform Act of 2002 (BCRA), it could have used those assets to televise and promote *Hillary: The Movie* wherever and whenever it wanted to. It also could have spent unrestricted sums to broadcast *Hillary* at any time other than the 30 days before the last primary election. Neither Citizens United's nor any other corporation's speech has been "banned," *ante*, at 886. All that the parties dispute is whether Citizens United had a right to use the funds in its general treasury to pay for broadcasts during the 30-day period. The notion that the First Amendment dictates an affirmative answer to that question is, in my judgment, profoundly misguided. Even more misguided is the notion that the Court must rewrite the law relating to campaign expenditures by for-profit corporations and unions to decide this case.

....

The majority's approach to corporate electioneering marks a dramatic break from our past. Congress has placed special limitations on campaign spending by corporations ever since the passage of the Tillman Act in 1907, ch. 420, 34 Stat. 864. We have unanimously concluded that this "reflects a permissible assessment of the dangers posed by those entities to the electoral process," *FEC v. National Right to Work Comm.*, 459 U.S. 197, 209 (1982) (NRWC), and have accepted the "legislative judgment that the special characteristics of the corporate structure require particularly careful regulation," *id.*, at 209-210. The Court today rejects a century of history when it treats the distinction between corporate and individual campaign spending as an invidious novelty born of *Austin v. Michigan Chamber of Commerce*, 494 U.S. 652 (1990).

....

II

The final principle of judicial process that the majority violates is the most transparent: *stare decisis*. I am not an absolutist when it comes to *stare decisis*, in the campaign finance area or in any other. No one is. But if this principle is to do any meaningful work in supporting the rule of law, it must at least demand a significant justification, beyond the preferences of five Justices, for overturning settled doctrine. "[A] decision to overrule should rest on some special reason over and above the belief that a prior case was wrongly decided." *Planned Parenthood of Southeastern Pa. v. Casey*, 505 U.S. 833, 864 (1992). No such justification exists in this case, and to the contrary there are powerful prudential reasons to keep faith with our precedents. The Court's central argument for why *stare decisis* ought to be trumped is that it does not like *Austin*. The opinion "was not well reasoned," our colleagues assert, and it conflicts with First Amendment principles. *Ante*, at 47-48. This, of course, is the Court's merits argument, the many defects in which we will soon consider. I am perfectly willing to concede that if one of our precedents were dead wrong in its reasoning or irreconcilable with the rest of our doctrine, there would be a compelling basis for revisiting it. But neither is true of *Austin*, as I explain at length in Parts III and IV, *infra*, at 23-89, and restating a merits argument with additional vigor does not give it extra weight in the *stare decisis* calculus.

....

The majority also contends that the Government's hesitation to rely on *Austin*'s antidistortion rationale "diminishe[s]" "the principle of adhering to that precedent." *Ante*, at 48; .... Why it diminishes the value of *stare decisis* is left unexplained. We have never thought fit to overrule a precedent because a litigant has taken any particular tack. Nor should we. Our decisions can often be defended on multiple grounds, and a litigant may have strategic or case-specific reasons for emphasizing only a subset of them. Members of the public, moreover, often rely on our bottom-line holdings far more than our precise legal arguments; surely this is true for the legislatures that have been regulating corporate electioneering since *Austin*. The task of evaluating the continued viability of precedents falls to this Court, not to the parties.

Although the majority opinion spends several pages making these surprising arguments, it says almost nothing about the standard considerations we have used to determine *stare decisis* value, such as the antiquity of the precedent, the workability of its legal rule, and the reliance interests at stake. It is also conspicuously silent about *McConnell*, even though the *McConnell* Court's decision to uphold BCRA § 203 relied not only on the antidistortion logic of *Austin* but also on the statute's historical pedigree, *see, e.g.*, 540 U. S., at 115-132, 223-224, and the need to preserve the integrity of federal campaigns, *see id.*, at 126-129, 205-208, and n. 88.

We have recognized that "*[s]tare decisis* has special force when legislators or citizens 'have acted in reliance on a previous decision, for in this instance overruling the decision would dislodge settled rights and expectations or require an extensive legislative response.'" *Hubbard v. United States*, 514 U.S. 695, 714 (1995) (quoting *Hilton v. South Carolina Public Railways Comm'n*, 502 U.S. 197, 202 (1991)). *Stare decisis* protects not only personal rights involving property or contract but also the ability of the elected branches to shape their laws in an effective and coherent fashion. Today's decision takes away a power that we have long permitted these branches to exercise. State legislatures have relied on their authority to regulate corporate electioneering, confirmed in *Austin*, for more than a century. The Federal Congress has relied on this authority for a comparable stretch of time, and it specifically relied on *Austin* throughout the years it spent developing and debating BCRA. The total record it compiled was 100,000 pages long. Pulling out the rug beneath Congress after affirming the constitutionality of § 203 six years ago shows great disrespect for a coequal branch.

By removing one of its central components, today's ruling makes a hash out of BCRA's "delicate and interconnected regulatory scheme." *McConnell*, 540 U.S., at 172. . . .

Beyond the reliance interests at stake, the other *stare decisis* factors also cut against the Court. Considerations of antiquity are significant for similar reasons. *McConnell* is only six years old, but *Austin* has been on the books for two decades, and many of the statutes called into question by today's opinion have been on the books for a half century or more. The Court points to no intervening change in circumstances that warrants revisiting *Austin*. Certainly nothing relevant has changed since we decided *WRTL* two Terms ago. And the Court gives no reason to think that *Austin* and *McConnell* are unworkable.

In fact, no one has argued to us that *Austin*'s rule has proved impracticable. . . . In the end, the Court's rejection of *Austin* and *McConnell* comes down to nothing more than its disagreement with their results. Virtually every one of its arguments was made and rejected in those cases, and the majority opinion is essentially an amalgamation of resuscitated dissents. The only relevant thing that has changed since *Austin* and *McConnell* is the composition of this Court. Today's ruling thus strikes at the vitals of *stare decisis*, "the means by which we ensure that the law will not merely change erratically, but will develop in a principled and intelligible fashion" that "permits society to presume that bedrock principles are founded in the law rather than in the proclivities of individuals." *Vasquez v. Hillery*, 474 U.S. 254, 265 (1986).

. . . .

V

....

... At bottom, the Court's opinion is thus a rejection of the common sense of the American people, who have recognized a need to prevent corporations from undermining self-government since the founding, and who have fought against the distinctive corrupting potential of corporate electioneering since the days of Theodore Roosevelt. It is a strange time to repudiate that common sense. While American democracy is imperfect, few outside the majority of this Court would have thought its flaws included a dearth of corporate money in politics.

I would affirm the judgment of the District Court.

Checklist for Chapter 5

- Under the doctrine of stare decisis, a court endeavors to decide each case consistently with its prior decisions.
- Even so, a court may depart from its prior decisions, or precedent, if those decisions are distinguishable from the current dispute.
- Even if a prior decision is not distinguishable, a court may overrule its own precedent in special circumstances.
- Stare decisis is less flexible with respect to the precedent of a higher court in the same jurisdiction. A trial court or intermediate court of appeals must distinguish or apply the precedent of a court that reviews its decisions.
- A court is never bound to apply the precedent of a lower court or any court in another jurisdiction, although it may treat such decisions as persuasive authority.

Endnotes

1. *See* Edgar Bodenheimer, Jurisprudence: The Philosophy and Method of The Law 425-28 (rev. ed. 1974); Frederick Schauer, *Precedent*, 39 Stan. L. Rev. 571, 595-602 (1987); *see also* Payne v. Tennessee, 501 U.S. 808, 827 (1991) (stare decisis "promotes the evenhanded, predictable, and consistent development of legal principles, fosters reliance on judicial decisions, and contributes to the actual and perceived integrity of the judicial process").
2. In 2017, those court systems included those of the District of Columbia and the following states: Delaware, Maine, Montana, New Hampshire, Rhode Island, South Dakota, Vermont, West Virginia, and Wyoming. Catherine A. Kitchell, BNA's Directory of State and Federal Courts, Judges, and Clerks xi-xiv (2019) [hereinafter, BNA's Directory of Courts].
3. 28 U.S.C. § 1257 (2012).
4. BNA's Directory of Courts, *supra* note 2, at 90.

5. For more information about this program, see http://www.courts.navajo-nsn.gov/indexpeacemaking.htm.
6. This consortium is described as part of tribal and state programs in California at http://www.courts.ca.gov/14902.htm. For more information on tribal courts, see http://www.tribal-institute.org/lists/justice.htm.
7. *See* State Oil Co. v. Khan, 522 U.S. 3, 20 (1997) ("The Court of Appeals was correct in applying [Supreme Court precedent] despite its disagreement with [it], for it is this Court's prerogative alone to overrule one of its precedents."). In limited circumstances, however, a trial court may depart from precedent of the intermediate court of appeals in its system. *E.g.*, Miller v. Gammie, 335 F.3d 889, 899-900 (9th Cir. 2003) (en banc) (federal district court could disregard precedent of court of appeals that reviews its decisions, if a decision of a yet higher authority, the U.S. Supreme Court, even though not precisely on point, has undermined the theory or reasoning underlying the court of appeals precedent); Auto Equity Sales, Inc. v. Super. Ct. of Santa Clara County, 369 P.2d 937, 940 (Cal. 1962) (if trial court is faced with conflicting decisions of two coequal panels or divisions of its reviewing court, it cannot follow them both but must choose between the two). Indeed, even United States Supreme Court precedent can lose its binding effect before being overruled. A summary dismissal of an appeal by the United States Supreme Court, although constituting a decision on the merits, will no longer bind lower courts if subsequent Supreme Court decisions undermine its reasoning, even though they do not directly overrule the earlier decision. *E.g.*, Bostic v. Schaefer, 760 F.3d 352, 373 (4th Cir.), *cert. denied*, 135 S. Ct. 308 (2014) (Supreme Court summary dismissal of constitutional marriage claim on behalf of same-sex couple was undermined by later Supreme Court authority, allowing lower courts to consider such claims without being bound by that precedent).
8. *See, e.g.*, United States v. McLennan, 563 F.2d 943, 948 (9th Cir. 1977); 9th Cir. R. 35-3.
9. *See generally* Hutto v. Davis, 454 U.S. 370 (1982).
10. *Compare id.* at 372-75 (majority opinion), *and id.* at 375-81 (Powell, J., concurring), *with id.* at 381-88 (Brennan, J., dissenting).
11. DeShaney v. Winnebago County Dep't of Soc. Serv., 489 U.S. 189, 212-13 (1989) (Blackmun, J., dissenting).
12. Gary Watt, Equity Stirring: The Story of Justice Beyond Law 12-13 (2009) (footnotes with citations are omitted from the quoted text).
13. The Fourth Amendment to the United States Constitution prohibits unreasonable searches and seizures by government officials:

    > The right of the people to be secure in their persons, houses, papers, and effects, against unreasonable searches and seizures, shall not be violated, and no Warrants shall issue, but upon probable cause, supported by Oath or affirmation, and particularly describing the place to be searched, and the persons or things to be seized.

    U.S. Const. amend. IV.
14. 267 U.S. 132 (1925).
15. *Id.* at 153; California v. Carney, 471 U.S. 386, 390 (1985) (quoting and interpreting *Carroll*). Under *Carroll*, even if a warrant is not required, the searching officers must have probable cause to believe that the car contains contraband before they can search it. *Carroll*, 267 U.S. at 153-62. Discussion of the issue of probable cause, however, is not necessary to the analysis in the text above.
16. 269 U.S. 20 (1925), *overruled in part*, United States v. Havens, 446 U.S. 620 (1980).
17. Long before Carroll v. United States, the Supreme Court had assumed that police generally could not search a house without a warrant, unless the search was incidental to a lawful arrest in the house. *Agnello*, 269 U.S. at 32 (interpreting Boyd v. United States, 116 U.S. 616 (1886)). The Court did not directly decide that question, however, until *Agnello*, a few months after *Carroll*. *Agnello*, 269 U.S. at 32.
18. *Agnello*, 269 U.S. at 31-33; *see also* Payton v. New York, 445 U.S. 573, 585-90 (1980).
19. 471 U.S. 386 (1985).
20. *See id.* at 395 (Stevens, J., dissenting).
21. People v. Carney, 668 P.2d 807, 810-14 (Cal. 1983).

22. California v. Carney, 471 U.S. 386, 390-94 (1985); *see also* New York v. Class, 475 U.S. 106 (1986).
23. *See, e.g.*, Hutto v. Davis, 454 U.S. 370, 375 (1982); *see also supra* note 7 (identifying rare exceptions).
24. *See, e.g.*, Jaffree v. Wallace, 705 F.2d 1526, 1532 (11th Cir. 1983), *aff'd*, 472 U.S. 38 (1985).
25. Hertz v. Woodman, 218 U.S. 205, 212 (1910).
26. Citizens United v. Federal Elections Comm'n, 558 U.S. 310, 362 (2010); *see also* Arizona v. Rumsey, 467 U.S. 203, 212 (1984) (departure from precedent requires "special justification").
27. Planned Parenthood of S.E. Pa. v. Casey, 505 U.S. 833, 854-55 (1992); *see also* Montejo v. Louisiana, 556 U.S. 778, 792-93 (2009) ("Beyond workability, the relevant factors in deciding whether to adhere to the principle of *stare decisis* include the antiquity of the precedent, the reliance interests at stake, and of course whether the decision was well reasoned.").
28. Amadio v. Levin, 501 A.2d 1085 (Pa. 1985).
29. *Id.* at 1094-97.
30. Gary Watt, Equity Stirring: The Story of Justice Beyond Law 77 (2009).
31. *See* Geoffrey R. Stone, *Precedent, the Amendment Process, and Evolution in Constitutional Doctrine*, 11 Harv. J.L. & Pub. Pol'y 67, 71 (1988).
32. Riverisland Cold Storage, Inc. v. Fresno-Madera Production Credit Ass'n, 291 P.3d 316 (Cal. 2013).
33. The Tenth Amendment to the United States Constitution reserves power to the states:

    > The powers not delegated to the United States by the Constitution, nor prohibited by it to the States, are reserved to the States respectively, or to the people.

    U.S. Const. amend. X.
34. Garcia v. San Antonio Metro. Transit Auth., 469 U.S. 528 (1985), *overruling* Nat'l League of Cities v. Usery, 426 U.S. 833, 854-55 (1976) (which itself had overruled Maryland v. Wirtz, 392 U.S. 183, 198 (1968), explaining that *Wirtz* had relied on "simply wrong" dicta in United States v. California, 297 U.S. 175, 184-85 (1936)).
35. *Garcia*, 469 U.S. at 557.
36. *See* Pearson v. Callahan, 555 U.S. 223, 233 (2009); Edelman v. Jordan, 415 U.S. 651, 671 & n.14 (1974).
37. In an exceptional reaction to a ruling of the Supreme Court, Congress proposed, and the states ratified, the Eleventh Amendment as a way of overruling Chisholm v. Georgia, 2 U.S. (2 Dall.) 419 (1793).
38. Edgar Bodenheimer, Jurisprudence: The Philosophy and Method of the Law 430 (rev. ed. 1974); *see also* Seminole Tribe of Fla. v. Florida, 517 U.S. 44, 63 (1996) (adopting flexible approach to stare decisis in abandoning Supreme Court precedent interpreting the Eleventh Amendment). *But cf.* Arizona v. Rumsey, 467 U.S. 203, 212 (1984) (even though stare decisis may be relaxed in constitutional cases, departure from precedent still "demands special justification").
39. Planned Parenthood of S.E. Pa. v. Casey, 505 U.S. 833, 854 (1992); *see also* Dickerson v. United States, 530 U.S. 428 (2000) (invoking stare decisis in declining to overrule Miranda v. Arizona, 384 U.S. 436 (1966), which spawned the *Miranda* warnings and which in turn "have become part of our national culture").
40. *Casey*, 505 U.S. at 867.
41. 505 U.S. 833 (1992).
42. 410 U.S. 113 (1973).
43. *Casey*, 505 U.S. at 855-56.
44. *Id.* at 856.
45. *Id.* at 868-69.
46. *Id.* at 846.
47. Dobbs v. Jackson Women's Health, 945 F.3d 265 (2019), *cert. granted*, S. Ct. (2021).

Chapter 6

Deductive Reasoning and IRAC— Introduction to Legal Analysis

I. Overview—Solving Legal Problems

Attorneys perform many tasks for clients that do not directly relate to litigation of legal disputes, including estate and tax planning, business counseling, and legislative lobbying. Even these tasks are influenced by the desire to avoid or control future litigation. Moreover, many people consult an attorney only when litigation has commenced or is imminent. With a little luck and skill, the parties or their attorneys might still avoid formal litigation in court by using alternative dispute resolution (ADR) such as negotiation, mediation, or informal arbitration.[1] Even in that event, these methods of ADR often require the parties to evaluate or present their cases within a general legal framework.

Consequently, legal method relating to litigation of legal disputes is an important component of nearly every attorney's practice. As discussed in Chapter 1, legal writing is audience focused. Because most readers of legal writing are trained in litigation, they expect the writing to conform to this general legal framework.

A lawsuit commences with the filing of pleadings: The plaintiff files a complaint against the defendant, and the defendant responds by filing an answer. If you represent a party in the early stages of such litigation, you must assess the strengths and weaknesses of your client's claims or defenses to prepare for various stages of advocacy, from the pleadings and settlement negotiations to trial and appeal.

In a large or medium-sized law firm, you often will communicate your evaluation to other members of the firm in an office memorandum of law, discussed in detail in Part IV of this book. The principal means of persuading a judge or other adjudicatory body to accept your client's legal claims or defenses is a written brief, discussed in Parts V through VII. To prepare either kind of document, you must apply fundamental skills of legal method and analysis that you develop in the first year of law school, as discussed in Parts II and III of this book.

This chapter examines methods of solving legal problems in the context of litigation of legal disputes. It builds on the groundwork laid in Chapters 3 through 5, and it provides an overview for more detailed discussions of legal method and analysis found throughout the remaining chapters.

II. Overview of Deductive Reasoning and IRAC

A. Deductive Reasoning in the Law—Uses and Limitations

1. The Legal Syllogism

Most essay exams, office memoranda, and briefs require more than purely abstract explanations of the law. They require you to apply legal rules to specific facts to reach a conclusion. In many cases, the analysis follows a pattern of deductive reasoning known as the "syllogism," which derives a conclusion from a major premise and a minor premise.

A common example of syllogistic reasoning addresses the issue of Socrates's mortality:

Major Premise:	All humans are mortal.
Minor Premise:	Socrates is human.
Conclusion:	Therefore, Socrates is mortal.[2]

In a legal argument, the major premise is a legal rule that helps resolve the issue raised by the parties to the dispute. It may represent the terms of a statute, the holding of a single judicial decision that acts as precedent, or a general principle derived from a series of previous decisions. The minor premise of a legal argument generally is a set of facts taken from the dispute that you are analyzing. The conclusion represents your answer to the question of whether the facts stated in the minor premise satisfy the legal standard stated in the major premise.

2. Validity and Correctness of Legal Syllogisms

A deductive argument is *valid* if its conclusion follows necessarily from its premises, but the *correctness* or *truth* of the conclusion of a valid argument depends on the truth of its premises.[3] For example, the Fourth Amendment to the United States Constitution ordinarily requires a police officer to obtain a search warrant from a judicial officer before searching an enclosed structure such as a house. Under the automobile exception, however, an officer may search an automobile without a warrant if she has probable cause to believe that it contains evidence of a crime. Suppose that a police officer searched Jack Greenberg's motor home without a warrant and found illegal drugs. In the state's criminal prosecution of Greenberg for possession of the illegal drugs, the state might advance the following valid deductive argument:

Major Premise:	The automobile exception to the Fourth Amendment's warrant requirement applies to all vehicles with mobility similar to that of an automobile on a street or highway.
Minor Premise:	Even while parked in Greenberg's backyard, Greenberg's motor home was a vehicle with mobility similar to that of an automobile on a street or highway.
Conclusion:	The automobile exception to the Fourth Amendment's warrant requirement applied to Greenberg's motor home while it was parked in Greenberg's backyard.

Although the conclusion of this valid argument follows necessarily from the premises, the conclusion is not true if either of the premises is untrue. The attorney for each party will attempt to persuade the judge to reach a certain conclusion by inviting the judge to accept some formulations of the major and minor premises and to reject others. For example, Greenberg's attorney could raise the Fourth Amendment issue by asking the judge to exclude the evidence obtained in the warrantless search of Greenberg's motor home. In response, the state prosecutor would advance the deductive argument above to demonstrate that the Fourth Amendment did not require the police to obtain a warrant to search Greenberg's motor home. Greenberg's attorney could attack this argument in two ways. He could either argue as a matter of law that the prosecutor's major premise exaggerates the scope of the automobile exception, or he could establish as a matter of fact that the prosecutor's minor premise exaggerates the mobility of the motor home parked in Greenberg's backyard.

A deductive argument is not even valid if its conclusion does not follow necessarily from its premises. For example, if Greenberg's attorney proved that Greenberg's motor home was significantly less mobile than an automobile on the street or highway, the judge would undoubtedly replace the prosecutor's untrue minor premise with the minor premise established by Greenberg's attorney. As reconstructed, the deductive argument would no longer be valid, because the prosecutor's conclusion would not follow from the original major premise and the new minor premise.

3. Limitations of the Legal Syllogism

Deductive reasoning provides at least a rough organizational framework for most legal analyses in office memoranda, answers to essay exams, and briefs. The usefulness of the syllogism in legal reasoning, however, is limited by the flexibility and uncertainty inherent in legal analysis. For example, to establish the major premise of your argument, you might state your interpretation of a previous decision's holding. Until a judge expresses his opinion on the matter, however, you cannot be certain whether he will agree with your interpretation of the previous decision and thus with your statement of the major premise.

Indeed, the dominant understanding of legal method since the twentieth century, known as "legal realism," rejects the notion that the law is external to the judges and other officials who apply and enforce it. Instead, it pragmatically asserts that the law is a prediction about what such officials will do in the face of a dispute. Moreover, their decisions will be based partly on a complex set of motivations, including personal values and judicial approaches that are not explicitly accounted for in the formal abstract rule of law. Thus, judges or juries can take advantage of uncertainty in law or facts by shaping them to support results that they reach on other than purely logical grounds.[4]

In short, legal disputes cannot be analyzed with mathematical certainty:

> The life of the law has not been logic: it has been experience. The felt necessities of the time, the prevalent moral and political theories, intuitions of public policy, avowed or unconscious, even the prejudices which judges share with their fellow-men, have had a good deal more to do

than the syllogism in determining the rules by which men should be governed.[5]

Nonetheless, the syllogism provides a useful starting point for discussing general techniques of presenting a legal analysis.

B. IRAC—The Analytical Paradigm

Most law students use the acronym "IRAC" to help them remember the elements of deductive reasoning. IRAC provides the analytical paradigm, an organizational framework for creating and communicating legal analysis. IRAC stands for Issue, Rule, Application, and Conclusion. Thus,

1. after identifying an **I**ssue, you should
2. state the legal **R**ule that will help resolve the issue,
3. **A**pply the rule to the relevant facts, and
4. Reach a **C**onclusion on the question of whether the facts satisfy the legal rule.

For example, the following excerpt from an essay exam answer discusses the availability of punitive damages in a tort action. Although the exam answer itself should not explicitly refer to IRAC, the margin notes represent the elements that a student should keep in mind when formulating a complete response. In this example, after raising an issue about punitive damages, the student summarized general legal rules regarding the availability of punitive damages, applied them to the facts of the exam, and reached a conclusion.

Punitive Damages—In addition to demanding compensation for his actual losses, Ling may request punitive damages, designed to punish the tortfeasor and to deter others from engaging in similar wrongdoing.	**Issue**
A jury has the discretion to award punitive damages if the tortfeasor acted with the malicious intent to cause harm. In most states, punitive damages are also permitted if the tortfeasor acted with reckless disregard for the risk of harm to others. Unless exceptional circumstances justify the risky conduct, a person acts recklessly if he consciously engages in conduct that he knows or should know poses a great risk of harm to others.	**Rules**

Application to Facts

In this case, Con Motor Co. did not maliciously intend to cause injury when it designed its Backfire sports car. In fact, the discussion at the May meeting shows that the board of directors genuinely hoped that the risky design would not cause accidents. However, Con's chief engineer informed the board of her opinion that placement of the gas tank near the rear exterior of the car would create a risk of deadly explosion in even minor rear-end collisions. Yet, the directors approved that design solely because it would save production costs of $200 per car, a trivial sum when compared to the $40,000 price of the car. In so doing, Con's directors knowingly created a great risk of death or serious injury to consumers without any socially significant justification.

Conclusion

Con Motor Co. thus acted recklessly, permitting a jury in many jurisdictions to assess punitive damages against it. Indeed, in a jurisdiction that requires proof of malicious intent to injure, this would be a good case for a liberalization of the standards to include recklessness as a basis for an award of punitive damages.

This example illustrates a relatively simple essay exam answer, because the conclusion is fairly certain. Many other examples of legal analysis in this book illustrate uncertainty in the conclusions to legal questions, inviting reasonable arguments for both sides of the dispute. Moreover, in an office memorandum of law, without the time constraints of an exam, the rule section of the analysis will examine the law in much greater detail. For example, it might summarize analogous case law, distinguish dissimilar case law, or otherwise synthesize a line of cases, as explored later in this chapter and again in Part IV.

Moreover, you should view your analytical framework, IRAC, as a starting point rather than an inflexible formula. To help you avoid the oversimplification that could result from an excessively mechanical application of IRAC, later chapters of this book explore sophisticated techniques of analysis that build on the general framework of deductive reasoning. For example, Chapter 8, Section III.D tackles problems of organization that arise when an issue or subissue presents different layers or levels of syllogisms.

In the meantime, the remainder of this chapter thoroughly examines each of the elements of IRAC. In the next four sections, you will learn more about identifying **I**ssues, formulating **R**ules, **A**pplying rules to facts, and reaching **C**onclusions.

III. "I"—Identifying Issues for Analysis

A. Defining Issues

A legal issue is a question that a judge, jury, agency hearing officer, arbitrator, or other adjudicator must resolve to determine the outcome of a legal dispute. Whenever an event creates the conditions for a legal dispute, you can identify potential legal issues immediately after the event, even though no party has yet begun to litigate a claim or has even made any demands on another.

Constitutions, statutes, agency regulations, case law, and even the mutual promises set forth in contracts between parties impose duties on some parties and correlative rights on others in the context of the event. Armed with a general knowledge of the law and the facts of the event, you can address the question of whether any party is guilty of a crime or is liable to pay damages to another for breach of a legal duty. If the law and its application to the facts are governed by settled law, the question of liability might be easily answered. If so, a settlement between the parties is more likely than litigation. In a surprising proportion of cases, however, uncertainty in the content of the law, or in its application to novel facts, will block your efforts to supply a definite resolution to a legal dispute. In those cases, you can advance arguments in support of either a potentially wronged victim or a potentially liable party. If the arguments for both parties have potential merit, you have identified a legal issue that warrants full discussion.

1. Issues and Subissues

A general issue may encompass discrete subissues. For example, case law establishes that a defendant generally will be liable to the plaintiff for damages caused by breach of contract if (A) the parties formed an enforceable contract and (B) the defendant failed to perform his contractual promises, thus breaching the contract. At the broadest level, the facts of a dispute might raise the general issue of whether the defendant is liable for breach of contract for failing to perform her contractual obligations by the specified date of March 1. More specifically, the facts may raise separate subissues about (A) contract formation and (B) performance and breach.

You can further subdivide these subissues to recognize multiple legal elements associated with each. For example, case law establishes two primary requirements for contract formation: (1) an agreement reached through a process of offer and acceptance and (2) "consideration" in the form of a mutually induced exchange. These elements are distinct, because parties could *agree* to a transaction that does not satisfy the consideration requirement. Thus, within the subissue of contract formation, the law and the facts could raise a second level of subissues regarding (1) offer and acceptance and (2) consideration. Similarly, within the subissue of performance and breach, the law and the facts could raise a second level of subissues regarding, for example, (1) interpretation of the defendant's contractual promises and (2) possible discharge of the defendant's obligations because unforeseen circumstances made his performance impossible. The law and facts might raise further issues regarding remedies for breach.

Without yet making the issues more specific by referring to critical facts, you can state these issues and subissues in outline form:

Is Defendant (D) liable to Plaintiff (P) for breach of contract by failing to perform by March 1?

I. Did D and P form a valid contract?
   A. Did D accept P's offer?
   B. If so, is the agreement between D and P supported by consideration?

II. Assuming a valid contract between D and P, is D liable to P for failing to deliver by March 1?
   A. Does the contract require D to perform by March 1?
   B. Did unforeseen circumstances excuse D from performing by March 1?

III. Assuming D breached a valid contract with P, is D liable for P's lost profits?

2. Continuing Development of Issues

At the inception of a dispute, your identification of issues might be tentative because your knowledge of the facts is incomplete and the law might be uncertain. As the dispute proceeds through stages of litigation, the issues will become increasingly well defined.

For example, a demand letter or complaint might reveal which potential legal claims the plaintiff will advance after a reasonable investigation of the law and facts. Under modern rules of civil procedure, each party to a civil lawsuit must disclose some kinds of information to the opposing party, and each party can use various "discovery" devices to obtain certain other kinds of information from witnesses and from the opposing party.[6] This court-supervised discovery and disclosure process might reveal that some claims or defenses lack merit, and it might raise new questions about others. Moreover, as explored in Part VI, a litigant may request that the court help define the issues by making rulings before trial. For example, such a pretrial motion might request the court to exclude certain evidence from trial or even to grant judgment without trial on one or more issues. In turn, these pretrial motions might raise separate issues under applicable rules of evidence or procedure concerning the admissibility of evidence or the proper application of standards for summary disposition. Finally, if the dispute goes to trial, the nature of the disposition in the trial court and the factual record developed in the trial court will help determine which issues the losing party might reasonably raise on appeal.

As illustrated by these examples, our adversarial system relies largely on the parties to shape the dispute by raising issues on trial and on appeal. With few exceptions, courts will decline to address questions that are not raised by either party to a dispute.[7] The parties help to define the issues by making strategic decisions about which claims and defenses to assert and about which procedural vehicles are used to assert them.

3. Materiality

Not every potential disagreement about the facts or the law amounts to a legal issue. Even a hotly disputed question of fact or law would not be "in issue" if it were immaterial. A disputed point is immaterial if it could not affect the outcome of the lawsuit in light of other facts and rules of law.

To take an obvious example, suppose evidence shows that the defendant drove his car through an intersection and struck the plaintiff in a pedestrian crosswalk. The defendant's liability for negligence would not be affected by even a heated disagreement over the color of the socks that the defendant wore that day. Assuming that the identity of the driver of the car is conclusively established through some means other than the color of the socks he wore, the issues of law and fact would instead include such material questions as the following:

1. Which party had the green light?
2. What injuries did the plaintiff sustain?
3. Does the law permit the jury to reduce the plaintiff's recovery if his own negligence combined with that of the defendant to cause his injuries?

Of course, many cases raise closer questions of materiality than that in the example above. As discussed in the next section, some questions of materiality may be a matter of degree requiring the exercise of judgment in selecting issues for discussion or argument in a legal document.

Exercise 6-1

Although United States jurisdictions have enacted criminal codes that largely supersede the early criminal common law, imagine a state that still applies the common law definition of burglary: the breaking and entering of a dwelling of another at night with the intent to commit a felony. The law relating to this crime reflected a concern about a serious invasion of the right of habitation during hours of darkness, when the inhabitants were most vulnerable to attack and the invader most likely to escape recognition. The element of a "breaking" does not require damage or destruction; it requires only the opening of a barrier to entry.

Armed only with this general knowledge of the law, identify the issues relating to the common law crime of burglary raised by the following facts:

In June, Leova Rosales left her San Francisco apartment and drove her VW bus down the coast for a three-week vacation near Monterey Bay. Although she occasionally ate at restaurants or stayed with friends, she mostly slept in the back of the bus and prepared simple meals in the bus with groceries that she purchased at local stores.

On the evening of June 20, Leova parked her bus in an overnight recreational-vehicle parking space at Seacliff State Beach. She prepared dinner from an ice chest in the back of the bus. At 11:00 P.M., she fell asleep in the back of her bus, leaving the driver's door closed but unlocked, with her new laptop computer sitting on the driver's seat. A curtain separated the sleeping area of the bus from the driver's cab; other curtains blocked light from the windows in the back of the van, enabling Leova to sleep late in the morning.

At 5:15 A.M., just as the first hints of a sunrise glowed from the hilltops opposite the ocean, Robert Glass approached Leova's van. Through the closed window next to the driver's seat, Robert spied the laptop lying on the seat. Robert opened the closed but unlocked driver's door, leaned into the cab with his feet still planted on the ground, and placed his hand on the laptop, intending to take it and keep it. At that moment, a patrolling police officer drove up to Leova's VW bus and arrested Robert for burglary and attempted larceny. Leova awoke only when the officer knocked on her bus after the arrest.

You may assume that theft of the laptop would constitute felony larceny in the jurisdiction. In the prosecution of Robert Glass on the burglary charge, what elements of the common law crime of burglary would the prosecutor and defense attorney likely dispute? What elements of burglary are not reasonably in dispute? Would further facts help define or resolve the issues? Would case law that refines the law of burglary help define or resolve the issues? If you were assigned the task of preparing an office memorandum on this problem, what facts or law would you desire to investigate further?

B. Scope of Analysis

Any dispute of at least moderate complexity presents a range of potential legal theories and arguments that you might raise in litigation. At the near end of the spectrum are persuasive and conventional legal theories or arguments that a court would almost certainly address in analyzing the dispute. At the far end are dubious legal theories or factual analogies that a court might view as frivolous or immaterial to the outcome of the dispute.

The extent to which you discuss topics toward the far end of the spectrum is a question of "scope of analysis" and depends partly on the nature of your document. The scope of analysis typically is quite broad in a law school essay exam answer, somewhat narrower in an office memorandum addressed to a supervising attorney, and narrower still in a good brief addressed to a judge.

1. Exam Answers

You will often touch on a broad range of issues in an exam answer because most law professors are specifically testing your ability to spot issues. Indeed, on many exams, you will maximize your grade if you identify and briefly discuss all plausible issues, including the less obvious ones. You should not waste precious exam time on irrelevant matters or theories devoid of legal support. However, if time permits, you can stretch a bit to present creative ideas after discussing the more obvious issues.

2. Office Memoranda

In comparison, your supervising attorney likely will expect a slightly narrower scope of analysis in your office memorandum. She will want detailed discussion of significant issues and will generally encourage creative and aggressive analysis, but she might not have time to thoroughly examine more exotic theories or approaches if they are unlikely to affect the outcome of the dispute. Unfortunately, you might be tempted to impress your supervisor with the breadth of your research by describing in detail every legal theory or authority that made its way into your library notes. Your supervisor will not be impressed. She realizes that you will regularly investigate leads that bear no useful fruit, and she expects the final draft of your memorandum to shield her from the burden of retracing your steps down paths that led only to distracting tangents.

On the other hand, the materiality of a fact or theory could be difficult to assess in the early stages of litigation and fact investigation. Accordingly, if you draft an office memorandum in the early stages of a dispute, you should consider discussing the appropriate scope of analysis with your supervising attorney before beginning to write. Absent specific direction from your supervisor, you probably should at least mention any argument of potential significance, even if only in a sentence or two. You can distinguish between a major theory and a less significant one in the depth of your analysis of each. Then, if later developments in the litigation establish the significance of an issue of previously questionable importance, you can analyze that issue in greater depth in a supplemental memorandum.

3. Briefs

As discussed in greater depth in Parts V through VII, when drafting a brief, you often must exercise even stricter control on the scope of analysis. Although creative and novel arguments often win appeals by inspiring changes in the law, some arguments are so clearly marginal that they might detract from the cumulative persuasiveness of the entire brief. If you add a weak argument to one with much greater merit, you reduce the number of pages within the maximum page limit that you can devote to the meritorious argument. Even worse, you might lose credibility on the whole brief.

This general advice about limiting the scope of briefs may apply with less force in criminal cases, in which a party's liberty, or even life, is at stake.

In such cases, defense counsel might be reluctant to waive any argument that could possibly gain relief for her client, and she can realistically hope that some courts will carefully consider all plausible arguments.

IV. "*R*"—Formulating the Legal Rule

Consistent with the general pattern of deductive reasoning, your first step in discussing a legal issue is to identify and analyze applicable legal rules. You will seldom find these rules clearly set forth in a single source of authority. The law that an adjudicator applies to resolve a legal issue may require application of several rules, any one of which may represent a synthesis of several sources of law.

A. Types of Rules: Elements, Factors, and Balancing Tests

Legal rules come in a variety of types. Many statutory or common law rules have multiple required *elements*, each of which must be met to satisfy the rule. For example, a statutory crime might consist of four elements, all of which the prosecution must prove to establish the guilt of the defendant. Alternatively, a rule might dictate certain consequences if one or more elements are present, while requiring proof of fewer than all listed elements. For example, a criminal statute might provide that the crime of robbery is elevated to "aggravated robbery" if, during the course of the robbery, the defendant *either* (1) causes the victim to suffer physical injury, *or* (2) brandishes a firearm, regardless of physical contact.

In contrast, some legal rules set forth a more general standard and then identify *factors* that a court should consider in determining whether the facts satisfy the standard. Such a test will not require satisfaction of all the factors, and the list of factors might not be exclusive. For example, a common law rule provides that an owner may cancel a construction contract if the contractor has committed an uncured "material breach" of the contract. The determination of materiality of a breach is influenced by several factors that serve as general guidelines to a court or jury.[8]

Still other tests could require the *balancing* of two or more opposing factors or values. For example, the reasonableness of a search under the Fourth Amendment often requires balancing (1) the constitutional interest in protecting people from intrusions into their privacy against (2) the legitimate needs of law enforcement in protecting the community.[9] Federal Rule of Evidence 403 more explicitly describes a balancing test, while listing alternative elements that could tip the balance in favor of exclusion of evidence, either singly or in combination with others:

> The court may exclude relevant evidence if its probative value is substantially outweighed by a danger of one or more of the following: unfair

prejudice, confusing the issues, misleading the jury, undue delay, wasting time, or needlessly presenting cumulative evidence.

Parts V through VII present sample arguments that further illustrate the differences between these types of rules. At this point, however, you will gain more by examining the relative strength of different kinds of authorities that help to establish and define the legal rule.

B. Sources of Authority

The relative importance of legal authorities to your analysis of the issue depends on such factors as

1. the primary or secondary nature of the authority;
2. the jurisdiction, in the sense of the political or geographical body, in which primary authority is controlling; and
3. if the primary authority is case law, the strength of the case law as precedent.

1. Primary and Secondary Authority

So far, this book has addressed only primary legal authority: direct statements of law issued by lawmaking bodies. Primary authority includes constitutions, treaties, statutes and local ordinances, administrative rules and regulations, and judicial opinions. Subject to limitations discussed in Sections 2 and 3 below, a primary authority or combination of primary authorities typically supplies the applicable rule in a legal dispute.

Secondary authorities, such as treatises, restatements of the law, and law review articles, do not directly supply the rule of law in a legal dispute. They do not constitute mandatory authority that a court must consider. Instead, they express a commentator's explanation of the law or her opinions about what the law should be. A secondary authority has persuasive value only. It might influence a court or legislature to act in a particular way, and it might be the only available authority to invoke in a case of first impression, but it will not be binding authority on any issue.

An example of a popular treatise is Prosser and Keeton on Torts. This secondary authority generally describes tort law in United States jurisdictions and examines the relevant policies supporting competing approaches in the tort law of different states.

Another frequently cited example of secondary authority is the collection of Restatements of Law issued by the American Law Institute (ALI). The ALI has drafted two Restatements of Contracts, the Restatement (First) of Contracts (1932) and the Restatement (Second) of Contracts (1981). Each of these is divided into numerous sections and subsections, most of which attempt to summarize the common law of contracts as it was generally accepted when the Restatement was drafted. A few sections, however, are meant to influence the law by promoting trends that had not yet been widely accepted. Section 90 of the First Restatement, for example, represented a relatively innovative view of a common law theory of recovery based on reliance, now commonly known as "promissory estoppel." Although no court is required to follow the approach of either Restatement, section 90 influenced many courts. Indeed, more than a few courts adopted the precise language of section 90 of the First or Second Restatement, thus incorporating it into their own case law and giving it the force of primary authority.[10] Further still, some courts have adopted a general policy of following the latest Restatement rules on matters of common law if no statute or case law addresses the point.[11]

Unless a court has adopted such a policy, however, or has already incorporated the content of a secondary authority into its case law, you should limit your reliance on secondary authority. You may use secondary authorities to help you locate and understand primary authority or to help develop an argument not fully addressed or supported by primary authority. However, you should not base your legal analysis or argument on a secondary authority when helpful primary authority is available.

2. Jurisdiction in Which Primary Authority Controls

Some federal constitutional, statutory, and special common laws apply broadly to all domestic jurisdictions. For example, the Thirteenth Amendment to the United States Constitution abolishes the institution of slavery within the United States, whether practiced by a governmental or private entity.

In contrast, the constitutional, statutory, and common laws of a state are mandatory authority only within that state. For example, the Civil Code of California and the case law of the California courts interpreting that code do not have any binding effect on the law of torts, contracts, or property in New York. Similarly, the courts of one state are free to develop the common law of that state independently of the judicial development of common law in other states. True, in an interstate transaction, a New York court might determine that it should apply California law to the dispute; if so, however, it will apply the law of California as the legislature and courts of California have developed it.

In some circumstances the laws of one state could have at least persuasive influence on the development of law in another state. For example, in recognizing a common law tort of wrongful discharge of an employee, the Arizona Supreme Court drew guidance from the emerging common law of California and of other states.[12]

Indeed, case law interpreting a statute of one state could be persuasive in the interpretation and application of a different state's statute, if the statutes in both states have similar or identical language and purposes. For example, the New York and New Hampshire legislatures have adopted identical versions of Uniform Commercial Code section 2-302, which authorizes a court to deny enforcement of a contract provision that is "unconscionable."[13] A New York trial court interpreting section 2-302 of New York's commercial code drew support from, even though it was not bound by, a decision of the New Hampshire Supreme Court interpreting the identical language in New Hampshire's commercial code.[14]

3. Hierarchy of Constitutional, Legislative, and Common Law Authority

Within a relevant jurisdiction, constitutional law can strike down or limit the reach of statutory law, and statutory law can modify or replace common law rules. Admittedly, most first-year courses still focus your attention largely on common law. When researching a legal problem, however, be sure to determine whether any legal issue is governed by one or more constitutional provisions, statutes, or administrative regulations.

On the other hand, courts interpret constitutional and statutory law, so interpretive case law helps to define the constitutional or statutory rule. Consequently, even when your analysis begins with a constitutional or statutory provision, interpretive case law will frequently dominate the legal analysis.

Section C.2 illustrates the hierarchy of authority with an excerpt from a legal memorandum that addresses several kinds of legal authority. The remainder of this Section B, however, focuses on analysis of case law.

4. Strength of Case Law as Precedent

As discussed in Chapter 5, the controlling or persuasive force of case law will depend on its strength as precedent under the doctrine of stare decisis.

Section 2 above further examined one element of this relationship: the relationship of the authority to the forum jurisdiction. The strength of case law as precedent also depends on

1. the relative levels of the court that created the precedent and the one applying it, and
2. the degree to which the precedent is directly controlling, rather than merely analogous, to the current dispute.

a. Level of Court

To summarize some of the lessons of Chapter 5, a trial court or intermediate court of appeals is strictly bound by squarely applicable precedent of a higher court that reviews its decisions. Moreover, although an appellate court can overrule its own precedent, it will do so only in special circumstances. On the other hand, when applying or developing its own state's law, a court need not defer to the decisions of a lower court within the same system or decisions of courts from other systems; at most, those decisions would have persuasive effect. Thus, whenever possible, you should support your analyses or arguments with case law from an appellate court in your jurisdiction that is higher than the court in which your dispute is currently being adjudicated.

The basis for a helpful illustration is provided by the description of the United States Court of Appeals for the Ninth Circuit in Section II.A of Chapter 5. When writing a brief to that court of appeals, you should try to support your argument with United States Supreme Court precedent, which is binding on the court of appeals. If no Supreme Court authority applies, you can strongly support your argument with a previous decision of the Ninth Circuit Court of Appeals itself. If no such authority is available, you can derive some support for your argument from a published decision of the United States District Court for the Northern District of California, a federal trial court. However, decisions of the district court are not binding on the court of appeals. Accordingly, you will assume the burden of persuading the court of appeals that the district court's decision represents the best legal approach—the approach that the court of appeals should adopt as its own. You might more strongly support your argument with a decision from the United States Court of Appeals for the Tenth Circuit, but that decision too would have only persuasive value.

b. Controlling, Analogous, and Distinguishable Authority

To once again summarize a portion of Chapter 5, the strength of case law as binding or persuasive authority also depends on the degree to which it squarely applies to the current dispute. Even precedent of a higher court within the same court system will not control the outcome of the dispute if it is distinguishable. The more significant the distinctions between the precedent and the current dispute, the less likely will the precedent from a higher court control or even influence the outcome of the current dispute. Similarly, the persuasiveness of nonbinding authority from lower courts within the jurisdiction or from courts of other jurisdictions will depend in part on the degree of similarity between the precedent and the current dispute.

When evaluating the legally significant similarities or distinctions between precedent and the current dispute, you should resist the temptation to overemphasize superficial factual similarities appearing in legally distinct contexts. Consider, for example, a current dispute in which the plaintiff's new television set spontaneously generated an electrical fire, causing major damage to the plaintiff's home. The parties might raise the issue of whether the retailer is liable to the plaintiff on a claim of breach of the warranty of merchantability implied in the sales contract under the state's version of the Uniform Commercial Code (UCC).[15] Suppose further that an appellate opinion in the state, issued in 1957, addresses another case in which a television set spontaneously burst into flames, setting fire to the plaintiff's home. The 1957 opinion, however, holds only that the plaintiff, a consumer, failed to file his complaint within the time prescribed by the state's statute of limitations, which barred his action for negligent manufacture of the television set.

At first glance, the prior decision might appear significant because of the factual similarities of the events giving rise to the actions. In fact, however, the prior decision is completely inapplicable. It does not interpret the UCC's warranty of merchantability in a contract for a sale of goods because it addresses a legally distinct cause of action in tort for negligence; indeed, the prior decision was issued before state enactment of the UCC and before the widespread adoption of more contemporary tort doctrines of products liability. Most important, the prior decision discusses only the statute of limitations; it does not directly address the elements of any claim for relief other than timely filing. The precedent would be more helpful if it addressed the scope of a retailer's warranty of merchantability, even if in the context of different goods causing different kinds of accidents and injuries.

5. Summary

Only primary authority within the forum jurisdiction is mandatory and potentially controlling. Primary authority from other jurisdictions and all secondary authority are persuasive only.

If the primary authority is case law within the forum jurisdiction, its strength as precedent will depend partly on the relative levels of the court that created the precedent and the court that will apply it. It will depend also on how closely analogous the precedent is to the current dispute.

Professor Mary Dunnewold illustrates the relative strength of precedent with issue and authority dartboards,[16] which this text has combined into a archery target to the right. A bull's-eye represents a precedent of the highest court within the relevant jurisdiction that decided the same issue on facts nearly identical to the facts in the current case. Just outside the bull's-eye, an appellate court decision within the same jurisdiction with facts that can be analogized to those in the current case might be highly persuasive, thus hitting one of the inner rings of the target. Precedent of a court from another jurisdiction—especially one whose issue and facts are only arguably analogous to those in the current case— might be useful, but it would have less persuasive value, thus hitting one of the outer rings. Of course, a precedent that has no relationship to the facts, issues, reasoning, and policies implicated in the current dispute would miss the target altogether and have no persuasive value.

In practice, it is exceedingly rare to find precedent that scores a bull's-eye. More often, an advocate must explain why a previous case is analogous to the current one, or why a decision on the same issue from another jurisdiction is so persuasive in its reasoning that it should be followed in the current forum. Conversely, the advocate must try to distinguish or undermine the soundness of precedent that is advanced as persuasive authority by opposing counsel.

Exercise 6-2

The Hazardous Materials Transportation Act (HMTA) of State *X* makes it a criminal offense to transport certain hazardous materials, such as toxic chemicals, except with statutorily specified safeguards. For example, the statute requires a transporter of regulated materials to first confine the materials in steel drums and then secure the drums within a cargo bay that is enclosed on the top and on all sides with material of specified strength. Leek Chemical Co. violated the HMTA by transporting highly toxic chemicals in steel drums secured to an open flatbed truck. The truck overturned on an icy highway, causing several of the barrels to roll across lanes of oncoming traffic. An automobile driven by Daniel Stein collided with one of the barrels, bursting the barrel and spreading the toxic chemical onto and into Stein's automobile. Stein was not seriously injured by the initial impact with the barrel; however, he was permanently injured by contact with the toxic chemical.

Stein sues Leek Chemical Co. in tort for damages, alleging both (1) strict liability for causing injury while engaged in an abnormally dangerous activity and (2) negligent transportation of the toxic chemicals. In State *X*, Leek Chemical Co. will be liable on the second claim for negligence if it engaged in a negligent act or omission through breach of a duty of care owed to Stein, causing Stein to suffer injury. Stein hopes to establish the element of negligent act through the doctrine of "negligence per se," which other states recognize but which the Supreme Court of State *X* has never squarely adopted. Under the strongest version of the doctrine of negligence per se, proof of Leek Chemical Co.'s violation of the HMTA, a safety statute, would conclusively establish the element of negligent act, without any further showing of a breach of a duty of care.

To help her evaluate proposed jury instructions at the close of the trial in Stein's lawsuit, the trial judge requests briefing and oral argument on the question of whether State *X* recognizes the doctrine of negligence per se. Stein has the following authority at his disposal:

1. abundant case law from other states recognizing the doctrine of negligence per se in a variety of contexts;
2. an opinion from the highest appellate court of neighboring State *Y* approving application of the doctrine of negligence per se to a violation of a similar hazardous materials transportation statute in State *Y*;
3. an opinion of the State *X* intermediate court of appeals holding that evidence of violation of the State *X* speed limit laws, proximately causing injury, supported a jury verdict of negligence, even in the absence of any other evidence of lack of due care; and
4. an opinion of the Supreme Court of State *X* holding that a transporter of regulated hazardous materials may be criminally liable under the HMTA for intentional violations of that act's criminal provisions, even if the illegal transportation does not result in any accident or injury.

Discuss the relative strength of these authorities to Stein's position. How should Stein's attorney use each authority, if at all?

C. Analysis of Legal Standards

1. Depth of Analysis

In some legal disputes, formulation of the applicable legal rules is a simple task: The applicable laws are easily identified and their general content is clear, at least in the abstract. For example, a dispute over the jury's authority to grant punitive damages in a tort action may be governed by clearly defined rules in the forum state's case law. If so, you could summarize those rules directly and concisely in an office memorandum:

> In this state, a jury may award punitive damages against a person who has committed a tort with either (1) intent to cause injury or (2) reckless disregard for the risk of harm to others. *Ray v. Bradbury*.... Unless exceptional circumstances justify the risky conduct, a person acts recklessly if he consciously engages in conduct that he knows poses a great risk of harm to others. *Id.* at 327.

In such a dispute, once the facts are found, any significant uncertainty about the outcome of the dispute typically derives from a mixed question of fact and law: Do the facts of the case satisfy the legal rule? Although analysis of such a mixed question necessarily involves refinement of the content of the legal rule, it also requires careful evaluation of the facts. Thus, assuming *Ray v. Bradbury* reflects current policy in the jurisdiction, the alleged tortfeasor will not likely dispute the abstract rule governing the availability of punitive damages. Instead, the central issue is a mixed question of fact and law: Do the facts of the case satisfy the legal rule by reflecting recklessness or an intent to injure?

In other disputes, however, the parties may raise substantial issues about the fundamental content of applicable legal rules, such as the issue discussed in Chapter 4 of whether the prohibition of sex discrimination in Title VII of the Civil Rights Act of 1964 encompasses discrimination based on sexual orientation. Compared to the dispute described in the preceding paragraph, resolution of this question required less comprehensive fact analysis and more thorough analysis of the content of the rule at an abstract level. An even more extreme example is provided by the question of whether a court should change the course of the common law by adopting a new theory of tort liability for wrongful discharge of an employee. Although such a question would arise in the context of the facts of a specific dispute, the question of whether to adopt a new common law theory of liability would be analyzed as a nearly pure question of law.

If an issue in a brief, office memorandum, or answer to a law school essay exam raises a question about the fundamental content of a legal rule at a general level, you should analyze the legal rule thoroughly, or "in depth," before engaging in substantial fact analysis. The discussions of common law and statutory law in Chapters 3 and 4 provide a foundation for the development of techniques of legal analysis. Four considerations are especially important:

1. the hierarchical nature of authority,
2. policy analysis,
3. synthesis of incremental authority, and
4. recognizing arguments for both sides.

2. Hierarchy of Authority: Start with Constitutional or Statutory Text

Constitutional, statutory, and common laws form a hierarchy in descending order of priority: Assuming the applicable state or federal constitution authorizes the exercise of state or federal power, a legislature can overrule or modify the common law by enacting statutory law. Accordingly, you should not assume that an issue is governed by common law; instead, you should first consider the possible applicability of constitutional or statutory law.

If a statute applies, you should begin your research and analysis with the relevant language of the statute, even though it may be insufficiently narrow to clearly resolve the issue by itself. Only after you have studied the letter of the statute and its context within an act or a code system can you fully appreciate interpretive case law on the matter. The following passage from an office memorandum illustrates the hierarchy of authority and the focus on statutory language.

Constitution

The Arizona Constitution grants municipalities the right to engage in industrial activities: "The State of Arizona and each municipal corporation within the State of Arizona shall have the right to engage in industrial pursuits." Ariz. Const. art. II, § 34. The Arizona Public Utilities statutemore specifically grants municipal corporations the power to acquire water utility corporations either within or without their corporate limits":

Statute

> A municipal corporation may engage in any business or enterprise which may be engaged in by persons by virtue of a franchise from the municipal corporation, and may construct, purchase, acquire, own and maintain within or without its corporate limits any such business or enterprise....

Ariz. Rev. Stat. Ann. § 9-511(A) (2005). The statutory reference to corporate limits appears without qualification to permit a municipal corporation to acquire utilities that provide service outside the municipality's corporate limits. Arizona case law, however, hints at a narrower interpretation of the statute that recognizes two limitations on the acquisition power.

First, it is unclear whether a city may acquire a water company's property outside the city corporate limits unless the city has shown that it genuinely and reasonably anticipates future growth into that area. *See Sende Vista Water Co. v. City of Phoenix*, 617 P.2d 1158 (Ariz. Ct. App. 1980). In *Sende* . . . .

Case Law

As illustrated in the example above, the principle of analyzing statutory language before turning to interpretive case law also applies to constitutional provisions. As a practical matter, however, some constitutional provisions are so general that their actual language provides quite limited guidance. If so, interpretive case law takes on special significance. For example, the reference to "equal protection" in the Fourteenth Amendment to the United States Constitution is purposefully vague; its generality invites the courts to shape its contours in a way that best satisfies its underlying policies. The mass of case law interpreting the Equal Protection Clause has embellished this simple clause with rich detail. Accordingly, when researching and analyzing an equal protection problem, you would not begin with a grammatical analysis of the words "equal protection." Instead, after identifying the Fourteenth Amendment as the source of the clause, you could appropriately turn immediately to interpretive case law.

3. Policy Analysis

Almost by definition, policy analysis lies at the heart of most lawmaking. A legislature pronounces public policy when it enacts public legislation within the framework of applicable constitutions. Any such enactment represents elected officials' choice among alternative means to address the socioeconomic needs of the jurisdiction. Unless statutory text is devoid of ambiguity, the search for statutory meaning typically does not end with a conclusive grammatical analysis of language or with a reference to definitive legislative history. Instead, statutory interpretation most often takes the form of a multifaceted analysis reconciling the statutory language, legislative history, and general rules of construction with the apparent policies or purposes on which the legislation is based. Constitutions are less specific than most statutes and are not so easily amended; consequently, analysis of policy and general purpose often is even more important in constitutional interpretation.

Similarly, common law rules are largely a reflection of judicial recognition of community needs, habits, or customs. Accordingly, they constitute the judiciary's pronouncement of public policy within the framework of constitutional and statutory law. Any further development of the common law, such as adoption of a new theory of common law liability, necessarily raises policy questions about the effect that the new rule will have on the community and about the relationship of the new rule to legislative policies.

A policy argument may be based on moral, economic, political, institutional, or other social values.[17] When developing or evaluating a legal argument, you should identify the values underlying the legislative purpose or judicial policy of each applicable authority, and you should determine which policy arguments would best advance your client's position.[18]

Exercise 6-3

Policy Analysis—Surrogate Motherhood and Baby Selling

State *X* has a criminal "baby selling" statute, enacted in 1932, making it a felony "to relinquish custody of one's child to another for payment, or to pay or offer to pay another to relinquish custody of the other's child." What conditions spurred the need for this legislation, and what kind of conduct appears to be its primary concern? Does the statutory text plainly and unambiguously prohibit a surrogate mother from charging a fee for carrying the fertilized ovum of another couple to full term and surrendering custody of the child to the couple after birth? If the statutory text is not conclusive, does the act of the surrogate mother pose the same kind of moral and social problem that the statute was designed and intended to address? Should the analysis turn on whether the person charging the fee agrees to artificial insemination of her own ovum, thus making her the biological mother? Rather than applying the 1932 statute, should a court develop a common law rule for enforcement or invalidation of surrogate mother contracts? Or should it defer to the legislature, awaiting its policy analysis and its enactment of new legislation more specifically addressing surrogate mother contracts?

4. Recognizing Arguments for Both Sides

With few exceptions, essay exams and office memorandum assignments call on you to present a balanced discussion of legal issues. Although one party might be identified as your client, your professor or supervising attorney expects you to explore the weaknesses of the client's claims and defenses as well as the strengths.

When writing a brief, you should not take such a balanced approach; instead, you must advocate your client's position and attempt to discredit your opponent's arguments. Nonetheless, to maximize your own advocacy, you must anticipate and evaluate the arguments of your opponent before you write your brief. You might express that more balanced analysis in an office memorandum, or you might simply contemplate it as you outline the arguments for your brief.

Thus, to analyze a legal dispute effectively, you must identify arguments for both sides of the dispute. In synthesizing case law, you should consider alternative formulations of the general principles that emerge from a series of holdings. Similarly, in analyzing statutory language, you should consider intrinsic and extrinsic aids that support alternative interpretations.

For example, the common law of negligence imposes tort liability on a person who proximately causes injury to another by breaching a duty of care owed to the injured person. As a specific application of this tort law, physicians in most circumstances are liable for injuries caused by their failure to exercise reasonable skill and care in their practices. Suppose that the courts of the fictitious State of New Maine have developed an additional common law doctrine of strict liability—which does not require proof of negligence—for injuries resulting from abnormally dangerous activities. The courts, however, have refused to apply this common law doctrine to medical practices, even risky or experimental ones. Against this background of common law, New Maine has enacted a statute that makes any "commercial enterprise strictly liable" for injuries caused by its use "of any toxic material."

Now suppose that a medical patient in New Maine died from a reaction to general anesthesia triggered by the patient's rare disorder of the nervous system. Much of the legal dispute in a malpractice action brought by the deceased patient's estate and surviving family members might center on the applicability of the statute. Assuming anesthesiology is "a commercial enterprise," if the anesthetic is "a toxic material" within the meaning of the statute, the anesthesiologist or her employer would be statutorily liable without regard to the care that she exercised. In contrast, a companion claim based on common law negligence would require an inquiry into the duty of care that the anesthesiologist owed and the degree of care she actually exercised.

In preparing for advocacy, counsel for either side of this dispute would want to evaluate arguments for both sides on the question of the applicability of the statute. For example, counsel for the deceased patient's estate and survivors could argue that the statutory requirement of "toxic materials" is satisfied because the ordinary meaning of "toxic" is "poisonous," and the anesthetic acted like a poison on the nervous system of the patient. Counsel for the estate and the survivors would also want to anticipate a strong counterargument: it is doubtful that the legislature intended to inhibit physicians' use of substances that produce medically beneficial results in almost all cases in which they are administered. Rather, the statutory term "toxic materials" is likely intended to apply only to materials that are generally harmful to all persons, such as potent acids or pesticides. After formulating and evaluating the anesthesiologist's probable counterargument, counsel for the estate and the survivors should try to present their argument in a way that will reduce the impact of the counterargument.

Exercise 6-4

Review your responses to Exercise 6-3 above. Did you explore arguments for both sides on the question of interpretation? Summarize and list the opposing arguments for application of the criminal statute to the case of a "surrogate" mother who in fact is the biological mother. If you did not explore arguments on both sides of each of these issues, do so now.

5. Synthesis of Incremental Law

In few research problems is the legal standard set forth in a single, clearly controlling authority. More often, the legal rules that apply to a dispute are the products of a synthesis of multiple authorities. For example, a Reconstruction-era civil rights statute imposes liability for racial discrimination in private contractual relations,[19] but its application is tempered by constitutional interests in privacy and free association.[20] Thus, the true reach of the statute is defined both by the language of the statute and by values reflected in the First Amendment to the United States Constitution.

Synthesis of authority is particularly important in analysis of case law. Whether judicial opinions interpret statutory or constitutional law or develop common law, the resulting case law is inherently incremental. Courts express their legal analyses in the context of individual controversies, and a holding in a single judicial opinion is often too limited to support an accurate prediction about how the decision will influence subsequent cases. Instead, a series of cases addressing the same topic in a variety of factual contexts will better support a generalization about the case law. The generalization, or synthesis of the cases, provides the reader with a "big picture" view of the law, often as a prelude to more detailed exploration of specific cases.

Many judicial opinions summarize previous relevant cases, leading to the court's formulation of a synthesized rule. A court's synthesis of precedent can save you a good deal of work while providing you with a broader understanding of the law and its historical evolution. In the famous "palimony" case of *Marvin v. Marvin*, for example, the California Supreme Court stated that it could "abstract a clear and simple rule" by comparing and contrasting previous decisions, even though "the past decisions hover over the issue in the somewhat wispy form of the figures of a Chagall painting."[21] Similarly, in *Robinson v. Lindsay*, the Washington Supreme Court traced the history of the reasonable-person standard in negligence law, showed that case law had relaxed this standard of due care for children, but explained that still other case law returned to an adult standard of care when children participated in various inherently dangerous activities, as exemplified in the facts of several such cases.[22]

Even with a judicial synthesis, however, you might find a more recent decision that you must add to the previous synthesis. Indeed, you will often collect several judicial opinions that address the same or similar issue without attempting to explain how the cases relate to each other. If so, you will engage in your own original synthesis of the cases.

The process of generalizing from specific cases is a form of inductive reasoning. The first step in synthesizing cases is to compare the cases' substantive results as conveyed by their holdings. For example, assume that two appellate decisions from different jurisdictions, States *X* and *Y*, both addressed the question of whether a newspaper advertisement amounts to an "offer," defined at common law as an expression of willingness to enter into a contract that empowers the offeree to create a contract by accepting the offer. In Case *A*, an appellate court of State *X* affirmed a trial court judgment that a newspaper advertisement amounted to an offer to sell the advertised goods. In Case *B*, an appellate court of State *Y* affirmed a trial court judgment that a different newspaper advertisement communicated only an invitation to negotiate rather than an offer to sell.[21]

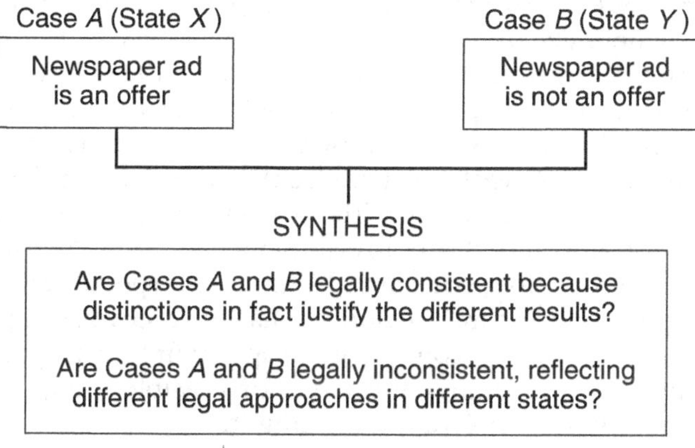

Synthesis of Cases with Differing Results

In the next step of the synthesis, you should determine whether Cases *A* and *B* are materially distinguishable and therefore warrant different results on application of the same legal principles, or whether they are legally inconsistent and simply represent different views of the law adopted by courts in different states. As a general approach, you should first attempt to reconcile the cases by searching for distinctions in facts, procedure, or both that reveal the cases to be legally consistent. For example, unusually specific and detailed language of commitment in the advertisement in Case *A* might clearly communicate a willingness to conclude a contract for sale on a customer's assent. In contrast, more general language in the advertisement in Case *B* might leave important terms of sale unaddressed, suggesting a need for further bargaining before the advertiser is willing to commit to a contract for sale. If so, the courts could be applying the same general legal rule, while adopting different conclusions after applying that rule to different facts.

In these circumstances, you could compose a synthesized legal rule that is consistent with the reasoning of both cases and that appropriately produces different results when applied to the contrasting facts of the cases:

> A newspaper advertisement is an offer only if it expresses definite commitment on complete and specific terms, leaving no important detail for future negotiation.

You could cite to both cases as authority for the proposition above, perhaps with parenthetic explanations briefly summarizing their holdings. This would serve as a suitable introduction to the law. You could then follow with more detailed discussions of each case, and with a comparison of each of those cases to the facts of your case.

If you fail to find material distinctions in facts or procedure between Cases *A* and *B*, you can safely conclude that the appellate decisions are legally inconsistent. In that event, you should analyze the reasons for the different views of the law. Perhaps States *X* and *Y* apply different legal approaches because they emphasize different policies. Such a synthesis helps you to put conflicting case law into perspective and to develop the ability to persuade a court in a future case to adopt one line of conflicting authority over another.

Different results in cases decided by the same court present particularly interesting questions of synthesis, because the court cannot depart from its prior decision under stare decisis without overruling the prior decision. If the cases are not obviously distinguishable but the court does not explicitly overrule the prior decision, you should search with special care for possible distinguishing features before concluding that the court has implicitly overruled the prior decision. Of course, the proper synthesis may lie in middle ground: a decision might limit the range of possible interpretations of a prior holding without completely overruling it.

6. Reorganization of Notes: Synthesis as a Bridge to Outlining

If you prepare an outline before writing an office memorandum or brief, it should be organized not around individual cases but around legal issues or legal rules that the cases address. For example, after examining the narrow holding and reasoning of each of four cases on a topic, you should synthesize the cases and then organize your outline around the synthesized rule you derived from the specific cases.

After you present that synthesized rule in your office memorandum or brief, or your outline of it, you can then use the cases as illustrations of the rule, explaining how each applied the rule to specific facts. Thus, the rule, or the issue that it addresses, becomes the topic of a section of your outline. The cases are just explanations and applications of legal rules. You would not lead with them in an analysis, nor should you organize your outline around individual cases.

Sometimes your synthesis will reveal competing rules in different jurisdictions or exceptions to a general rule within a jurisdiction. If so, your analysis of legal rules will be more complicated. Nonetheless, you will still organize your analysis around the rules, with cases serving as illustrations of the rules.

7. Synthesis as a Step in Deductive Reasoning

After you synthesize a series of cases to construct a general rule from a series of cases, you can use that rule to form the major premise of your deductive analysis, as discussed earlier in this chapter. In an office memorandum or a brief, you could represent this process by stating the rule and then using several paragraphs or pages of in-depth analysis of case law to show how you inductively arrived at your understanding of the rule. The discussion of law in the first sample memorandum toward the end of Chapter 7 illustrates moderately in-depth analysis. For each topic, you can exercise judgment about whether to (1) apply the *synthesized rule* to the facts of your case after completing your explanation of the rule, or (2) apply *each case* to relevant facts as you proceed with your explanation.

Alternatively, if the rule is undisputed and is simply a premise to a contested issue, you could state the rule as a simple proposition, followed by citation to the authority or authorities from which you derived the rule, before applying it to the facts:

> The UCC applies only to transactions that are predominantly for the sale of goods. *See* .... The parties to our case agree that the proposed Contract for Painting Services is predominantly one for services and only incidentally for the supply of paint. Therefore, the issues will be governed by common law rules rather than by the UCC.
>
> Under the common law, an offeree can accept an offer only by agreeing to all its terms without alteration....

Exercise 6-5

Imagine that a parent, Katherine, is developing rules governing the social activities of her teenage daughter, Lina, who is a senior in high school. Katherine has not articulated a comprehensive set of rules in the style of a statute or set of administrative regulations. Instead, Katherine provides guidance by admonishing Lina when she disapproves of Lina's actions and by expressing satisfaction when she approves, just as a court might develop the law incrementally by deciding disputes one case at a time.

In each of the following four "cases," put yourself in Lina's place by examining the facts, Katherine's statements, and Katherine's apparent or stated concerns. Then identify one or more reasonable interpretations of the "holding" of each case and translate it into a rule or set of rules that will govern Lina's future behavior.

Specifically, first determine the "ruling" in each case by determining whether Lina has apparently met or disappointed Katherine's expectations. Then, try to determine the "holding" of each case by identifying the facts that seem to be important to Katherine's ruling. Finally, engage in an ongoing process of "synthesis," by comparing each new holding to previous ones. Through this comparison, and by using inductive reasoning to generalize from specific cases, try to infer a rule or set of rules that will apply to Lina's future actions. This rule should evolve as more cases are added to your ongoing synthesis.

Is the first case ambiguous, inviting several reasonable arguments about the factual basis for Katherine's disapproval? If so, does its holding become clearer as you synthesize it with the second case? How does the third case add a second rule, or a second branch to the rule? How do you reconcile the fourth case with the previous ones?

1. Case #1: The Pizza Hideout

On the first Friday night of the school year, Lina and Lynn, two seniors in high school, went to JJ's Pizza after their school's first football game of the season. They ate and talked until 11 P.M.; indeed, Lina was so engaged in conversation that she didn't answer a call to her cell phone from her mother, Katherine. When Lina walked into her house shortly after 11 P.M., she and Katherine had the following exchange:

Katherine:	"Lina, where have you been? The game ended at 9:30, and you're coming home after 11."
Lina:	"Well, some of us went to JJ's afterwards for pizza."
Katherine:	"So you were at JJ's! And you didn't answer your cell phone!"
Lina:	"Sorry."
Katherine:	"Well, being sorry is not good enough. You're not going out for the rest of the weekend."

2. Case #2: Pizza Reprise

On the second Friday night of the school year, Lina attended the second football game and again went to JJ's afterwards for pizza. Before entering JJ's, Lina called her mother, Katherine, from the parking lot and informed Katherine of her plans. In response, Katherine wished Lina a good time and reminded her to drive carefully. When Lina entered her home shortly after 11 P.M., she had the following exchange with Katherine:

Katherine:	"Did you have a good time?"
Lina:	"We lost the football game, but the pizza was good."
Katherine:	{hugging Lina} "Good. Well, goodnight."

3. Case #3: Closing Out JJ's

On the third Friday night of the school year, Lina attended the football game with Lynn and watched her school's team win for the first time this season. After Lina notified Katherine by cell phone that she planned to go to JJ's for pizza, Lina and Lynn celebrated by eating and talking at JJ's until JJ's closed at midnight. When Lina entered her home shortly after midnight, she and Katherine had the following exchange:

Katherine:	{angrily} "Lina, it's after midnight!"
Lina:	"I told you we were going to JJ's afterwards."
Katherine:	{firmly} "It's good that you called me, but it's after midnight now. I need to draw the line somewhere."
Lina:	"So you mean I can't stay out past midnight? Why? Why do you care? Why do we have to set rules and limits like this? I always do my homework, and I get straight As."

Katherine:	"Yes, I'm really proud of you. But I care what you do at night. I worry about your safety, and I want you to get enough sleep and stay healthy. That's why I have rules. Now goodnight."

4. Case #4: The Obligatory Wedding Reception

On the Saturday night of the fourth week of the school year, Lina accompanied her mother to a relative's wedding and reception. When they entered the house after midnight, they had the following exchange:

Lina:	{wearily} "I can't believe you made me stay at your nephew's wedding all night; I was so bored."
Katherine:	"Hey, John is your cousin, too. And we had a blast on the dance floor, dancing to those old tunes."
Lina:	{complaining} "Yeah, I know. You even talked to everybody after the band stopped playing. And it's after midnight! We have to go to church tomorrow morning."
Katherine:	"Yes, I know, but this was an important family event. Thank you for staying up late with me."

V. "A"—Application of Law to Facts

A. Basic Patterns

At trial, the critical issues often are questions of purely historical fact. For example, the plaintiff in an employment discrimination suit might assume the burden of proving that an employer in fact exclaimed, "Women can't perform this job!" when he rejected the plaintiff's employment application.

As explored in later chapters, appellate courts will defer to some degree to the factual findings of a jury or trial judge; therefore, issues on appeal inevitably contain a more substantial element of law. However, even nearly pure questions of law are developed in the context of specific disputes and with an appreciation for the probable facts of future disputes. Moreover, most disputes present nontrivial questions about whether the facts satisfy the applicable legal standards, such as whether certain acts of preparation leading up to a murder satisfy the premeditation requirement of a first-degree murder statute.

A pattern should emerge from your treatment of facts in an office memorandum or brief. First, you will state all the important facts of the dispute in a separate section at or near the beginning of the document. Second, in the discussion section of a memorandum or the argument section of a brief, after you have explained the legal rule applicable to a specific issue, you will discuss or argue whether the relevant facts satisfy the legal rule. You and your professor will follow a similar pattern in an essay exam. Your professor will first state all the facts in the essay question, and—after you have identified an issue and supplied a rule—you will analyze the subset of facts that are relevant to that issue.

If your assignment does not call for great depth of analysis, you might directly explain why particular facts support or undermine the application of a legal rule (assignments requiring greater depth of analysis will rely on inductive reasoning and will be discussed in Chapter 7). Suppose, for example, that you are writing an office memorandum analyzing the claims of a client seeking punitive damages, as introduced in a previous example in this chapter. After stating the legal rule that a malicious or reckless tortfeasor may be liable for punitive damages, you could identify the facts relevant to this issue and explain how each supports or defeats application of the legal rule:

Facts showing no intent

We have no evidence that Con Motor Co. maliciously intended to cause injury when it designed the Backfire sports car. In fact, our notes of the May meeting of the board of directors show that the board members genuinely hoped that the risky design would not cause accidents.

Facts showing recklessness

However, we do have evidence of recklessness. Con's chief engineer informed the board of directors of her opinion that placement of the gas tank near the rear exterior of the car would create a risk of deadly explosion in even minor rear-end collisions. Yet, the directors approved that design solely because it would save production costs of $200 per car, a trivial sum when compared to the $40,000 price of the car. In so doing, Con's directors knowingly created a great risk of death or terrible injury to consumers without any socially significant justification.

In other cases, however, your application to law and facts might require you to closely compare the facts of published precedent to the facts of the current dispute, to assess whether precedent is controlling, analogous, or distinguishable. For examples, see the discussions of illusory promise and proximate cause in Samples 1 and 5 near the end of the next chapter.

B. Developing Arguments for Both Sides

As with your analysis of more abstract legal rules, your fact analysis in an essay exam answer or office memorandum ought to explore arguments for both sides of the dispute. Similarly, when writing a brief, you should consider your opponent's factual arguments as you develop your own. In the typical dispute, some facts will support application of the legal rule and others will suggest that the legal rule is not satisfied. Still other facts may be used in different ways to support both positions. By balancing and weighing the facts, you can reach at least a qualified conclusion about whether the legal rule is satisfied.

This can be illustrated by extending one of the examples in the previous section on analysis of legal rules. If the parties dispute an anesthesiologist's liability on a claim of common law negligence, an office memorandum might call for analysis of the following facts:

1. The anesthesiologist informed a patient scheduled for foot surgery of the advantages and risks associated with the three most appropriate anesthetics. Based on relative costs, the patient rejected the safest anesthetic in favor of a generally safe and more widely used anesthetic.
2. The anesthesiologist administered general anesthesia without assistance, before the surgical team had arrived and while the circulating nurse was occupied with another patient.
3. While administering general anesthesia, the anesthesiologist concentrated intensely on gauges on her equipment that measured the patient's intake of the anesthetic.
4. The anesthesiologist did not maintain visual contact with the patient or with equipment monitoring the patient's vital signs; as a consequence, she failed to terminate the intake of anesthetic until 10 seconds after the first visible signs of an adverse reaction.
5. The patient suffered from a rare disorder of the nervous system that produced the fatal reaction to the anesthetic.
6. The patient died within a minute of the administration of general anesthesia.

The facts in the first paragraph suggest that the anesthesiologist followed a reasonable procedure in prescribing the anesthetic. Indeed, the facts in item 5 suggest that the patient's unusual disorder—rather than the anesthesiologist's conduct—precipitated the fatal reaction. Moreover, the facts in item 3 support an argument that the anesthesiologist used at least reasonable care in administering the anesthetic, because she concentrated intensely on an obviously important function.

In addition to suggesting that the anesthesiologist was not entirely at fault, however, the facts of item 5 emphasize the need for special care in administering the anesthetic. Moreover, the facts in item 2 support an argument that the anesthesiologist breached a duty of care in administering the anesthetic without assistance, and the facts in item 3 raise a question about the appropriate focus of the anesthesiologist's attention. Finally, the facts in item 4 support an argument that the anesthesiologist acted carelessly in failing to monitor the patient and equipment measuring vital signs.

To complete your deductive reasoning in an office memorandum, you must discuss whether the facts establish a breach of a physician's duty of care, an element of the cause of action. Because the facts in this case support opposing arguments, different legal analysts might reasonably reach different conclusions, depending on the significance each analyst assigns to specific facts. Regardless of the author's conclusion, however, the office memorandum should present the factual arguments for both sides of the dispute. Only by doing so can the author adequately assess the strengths and weaknesses of the client's case and recommend the best way to overcome the weaknesses. Of course, an advocate writing a brief would emphasize the facts supporting her argument and then develop her argument in a way that lessened the impact of anticipated counterarguments.

Exercise 6-6

Review your response to Exercise 6-1 at the end of Section III.A. For each issue that you identified in that exercise, discuss whether the relevant facts satisfy the applicable rule relating to the element of burglary that is in issue. Argue both sides of the facts whenever possible, but argue only the facts that help to resolve each issue.

For more practice in evaluating policy considerations and in applying law to facts, perform Problem 2 in Appendix II.

VI. "C"—Reaching Conclusions

The final element of deductive reasoning is a conclusion derived from the law of your major premise and the facts of your minor premise. When writing a brief, you must state a firm conclusion for each argument that you present. Your conclusions represent the critical points that the court must accept before granting your client relief.

You might hesitate to state conclusions on debatable issues in the more balanced analysis of an office memorandum or essay exam answer. Nonetheless, most supervising attorneys and professors will want you to take a position and to reveal your best judgment about the probable outcome of each issue. If necessary, you may hedge your conclusions with qualifiers such as "probably," but you should remember to complete your deductive reasoning by stating a conclusion for each issue:

> On these facts, a jury likely will find that Con Motor Co. acted recklessly, permitting the jury to award punitive damages.

In some cases, you may find it appropriate to make your conclusion contingent on your ability to establish critical facts or law:

> Assuming we can prove that most hospitals require a team of at least two personnel to administer anesthesia, a jury will almost certainly find that Humana Hospital was negligent in this case.

Exercise 6-7

Gaining Comfort and Experience with Uncertainty in the Law and with Making Arguments for Both Sides. The following exercise is set in a nonlegal context but effectively illustrates some fundamental features of common law analysis.[22]

Pat is the mostly absentee owner of a small grocery store sitting adjacent to a busy downtown sidewalk. Pat made a rare appearance at the store one day to post a new rule on the employees' bulletin board. The posted rule instructed employees to place fresh produce in the window display case if the produce would attract pedestrians who had not previously planned to visit the store. The posting explained that the rule was designed to draw impulse shoppers into the store, because they might then buy several items and possibly become regular customers. According to the posting, if the produce did not meet this standard of attracting impulse shoppers, it should be placed in the appropriate section in the middle of the store.

Kim, the store manager, has applied this written rule in two cases. In the first case, she arranged a crate of clean, shiny, round, red apples in the window display case. In the second case, she placed a crate of unwashed, unpeeled carrots in the produce section in the interior of the store.

On Monday at noon, Kim left to attend to family business for the remainder of the day. She instructed employees to promptly display any goods that arrived in her absence. On Monday afternoon, a crate of clean, shiny, nicely shaped red bell peppers arrived. Where should the employees place the bell peppers? In analyzing this problem, consider the following:

a. In the abstract, one may not be able to identify a single correct answer to this question. In practical terms, the "answer" is the location that will most please Kim when she returns, but that is the "answer" only because Kim is the employees' supervisor and has taken the lead in interpreting the new rule, and not because reasonable minds could reach only one conclusion on the best location for the red bell peppers under Pat's general standard. Moreover, in the meantime, employees must display the bell peppers in Kim's absence and so must predict where she would place them.

b. To better predict where Kim would place the red bell peppers, employees might wish to explore her apparent reasoning in the previous two cases. They might ask two questions: (1) On what basis did Kim conclude that the apples satisfied Pat's general standard of placing produce in the window only if it would attract customers into the store? (2) Does that rationale also explain why Kim concluded that the carrots did not satisfy that standard? If the employees can identify a rationale that explains both the previous cases as a consistent application of Pat's general standard, then perhaps the employees could apply the same rationale to the red bell peppers. In that way, they might be able to better predict whether Kim would conclude that the bell peppers satisfied the standard of attracting customers into the store. Assuming Kim did not explain her reasoning in the previous two cases to her employees, the employees might need to speculate on possible rationales.

c. Are the previous two cases potentially explainable through two or more equally plausible rationales? Do competing rationales sometimes point to different conclusions about where the employees should place the red bell peppers? Does this explain why reasonable judges and attorneys can disagree about the application of a general rule to new facts and about the interpretation of previous judicial decisions? Even with the posted rule (which you might compare to a statute) and with Kim's two applications of the rule (similar to judicial interpretations of a statute) it might be uncertain how Kim would apply the rule to new facts.

Accordingly, maybe your professors are not playing "hide the ball" when they raise legal questions and state that they have no certain answers to the questions. Perhaps your task is not to look for a single correct answer, but to identify issues, analyze the facts and the law, recognize arguments for both sides of the dispute, and either advocate for one party or make a prediction about the outcome. After all, cases are litigated precisely because the outcome is uncertain and the parties cannot predict with certainty how a judge or jury will view the dispute. An appellate court in the jurisdiction may eventually issue a definitive ruling in the dispute, providing its authoritative version of the answer. In the meantime, however, the dispute presents an opportunity for each party to work with law, facts, and policy in an effort to influence the judge, jury, or appellate panel in reaching a conclusion.

Checklist for Chapter 6

- As a general organizational structure for legal analysis, begin with IRAC:
  - For each **I**ssue,
  - state the **R**ule,
  - **A**pply the rule to the facts, and
  - reach a **C**onclusion.
- After you have mastered the basics of IRAC, you can more flexibly adapt your method of presentation to various legal analyses and contexts.
- Recognize the frequent uncertainty in the law or in its application to facts, and look for arguments for both sides of the dispute. If the conclusion is debatable, you have found a substantial issue that requires analysis.
- In stating the rule, be mindful of
  - the frequent need to synthesize several legal sources of authority to formulate a general rule that you can apply to the facts;
  - whether authority is mandatory (primary authority within the jurisdiction) or at most has persuasive value (secondary authority, or primary authority from another jurisdiction); and
  - whether authority is binding on a court, such as case law from a higher court in the judicial system.
- In applying a legal rule to facts, consider whether you can argue that binding precedent is
  - controlling because it is squarely on point,
  - persuasively analogous because it is similar in its issue, facts, and reasoning, or
  - distinguishable from the current case.
- Take a stand by stating a conclusion, even if you must convey some degree of uncertainty.
- You will find much more information, advice, and illustration relating to the construction of legal arguments in Parts V through VII.

Endnotes

1. *See, e.g.*, Stephen B. Goldberg, Frank E.A. Sander, Nancy H. Rogers & Sarah Rudolph Cole, DISPUTE RESOLUTION: NEGOTIATION, MEDIATION AND OTHER PROCESSES (7th ed. 2020); Leonard L. Riskin, Chris Guthrie, Richard C. Reuben, Jennifer K. Robbennolt, Nancy A. Welsh, James E. Westbrook & Art Hinshaw, DISPUTE RESOLUTION AND LAWYERS, A CONTEMPORARY APPROACH (6th ed. 2019).
2. *See* Irving M. Gopi, INTRODUCTION TO LOGIC § 1.4, at 12-15 (12th ed. 2005).
3. *See id.* at 13.
4. *See* J. W. Harris, LEGAL PHILOSOPHIES 98-103 (2d ed. 1997). The Critical Legal Studies movement goes beyond legal realism to broadly attack traditional legal method, scholarship, and education as a system that legitimizes and perpetuates an oppressive socioeconomic order. *See generally* Roberto M. Unger, THE CRITICAL LEGAL STUDIES MOVEMENT (1986); Mark Kelman, A GUIDE TO CRITICAL LEGAL STUDIES (1987); *Critical Legal Studies Symposium*, 36 STAN. L. REV. 1 (1984). Scholars of Critical Race Theory and Feminist Jurisprudence more specifically charge that traditional legal reasoning is grounded in and helps to perpetuate racist and sexist institutions and attitudes. *See generally* Frances Schmid Holland, FEMINIST JURISPRUDENCE (1996); Richard Delgado & Jean Stefancic, CRITICAL RACE THEORY: AN INTRODUCTION (2001). Latino and Latina scholars have developed a new branch of Critical Race Theory, popularly known as "LatCrit" theory. *See, e.g.*, Jean Stefancic, *Latino and Latina Critical Theory: An Annotated Bibliography*, 85 CAL. L. REV. 1509 (1997); Keith Aoki & Kevin R. Johnson, *An Assessment of LatCrit Theory Ten Years After*, 83 IND. L.J. 1151 (2008). Some scholars have argued that courts have retreated from legal realism and are returning to a more traditional and mechanical legal "formalism." *See, e.g.*, John E. Murray, Jr., *Contract Theories and the Rise of Neoformalism*, 71 FORDHAM L. REV. 869 (2002).
5. Oliver Wendell Holmes, Jr., THE COMMON LAW 1 (Dover Publ. 1991) (1881); *see also id.* at 312 ("The distinctions of the law are founded on experience, not on logic. It therefore does not make the dealings of men dependent on a mathematical accuracy."); Neil MacCormick, LEGAL REASONING AND LEGAL THEORY 65-72 (1978) (discussing "the limits of deductive justification").
6. *See* FED. R. CIV. P. 26-37.
7. *See, e.g.*, Yee v. Escondido, 503 U.S. 519, 533 (1992) (Supreme Court "has, with very rare exceptions, refused to consider petitioners' claims that were not raised or addressed below."); United States v. Olano, 507 U.S. 725, 733 (1993) (explaining difference between forfeiture and waiver of an issue); Amcel Corp. v. Int'l Exec. Sales, Inc., 170 F.3d 32 (1st Cir. 1999) (discussing reasons for not addressing claims or legal theories that party neglected to raise in the trial court); Hershinow v. Bonamarte, 735 F.2d 264, 266 (7th Cir. 1984) (declining to address claim presented to appellate court in perfunctory manner). *But cf. Yee*, 503 U.S. at 534-35 (if claim was properly presented below, appellate court will entertain a new *argument* in support of that claim); Giannakos v. M/V Bravo Trader, 762 F.2d 1295, 1297 (5th Cir. 1985) (federal trial and appellate courts must address questions of federal subject matter jurisdiction on their own motions); *In re* Pizza of Haw. Inc., 761 F.2d 1374, 1377-78 (9th Cir. 1985) (appellate court must determine appellate jurisdiction on its own motion); *In re* Pac. Trencher & Equip., Inc., 735 F.2d 362, 364 (9th Cir. 1984) (discretionary appellate consideration of pure question of law not raised in the trial court).
8. *See, e.g.*, Frazier v. Mellowitz, 804 N.E. 2d 796 (Ind. App. 2004) (quoting six factors relating to material breach under the Restatement (First) of Contracts and then applying the five slightly different "circumstances" listed in the Restatement (Second) of Contracts, as well as other factors).

9. *See, e.g.*, Safford Unified Sch. Dist. No. 1 v. Redding, 557 U.S. 364, 371-77 (2009) (content of suspicion regarding possession of prescription strength ibuprofen did not justify strip search of middle school student).
10. *See, e.g.*, Bank of Marion v. Robert "Chick" Fritz, Inc., 311 N.E.2d 138 (Ill. 1974); Vigoda v. Denver Urban Renewal Auth., 646 P.2d 900, 905 (Colo. 1982); *see also* Corbit v. J. I. Case Co., 424 P.2d 290, 300-01 (Wash. 1967) (en banc) (quoting section 90 as a "useful guideline").
11. *See, e.g.*, Smith v. Normart, 75 P.2d 38, 42 (Ariz. 1938) ("We have . . . announced that we would follow the Restatement of the Law where we are not bound by the previous decisions of this court or by legislative enactment . . . ."). *But cf.* Reed v. Real Detective Publ'g Co., 63 Ariz. 294, 303, 162 P.2d 133, 138 (1945) ("We think it would be unwise to follow this rule blindly, particularly when to do so would result in the recognition of a new cause of action in this jurisdiction."); Ramirez v. Health Partners of S. Ariz., 972 P.2d 658, 665 (Ariz. App. 1999) ("Rather, we must consider whether the Restatement position, as applied to a particular claim, is logical, furthers the interests of justice, is consistent with Arizona law and policy, and has been generally acknowledged elsewhere.").
12. Wagenseller v. Scottsdale Mem'l Hosp., 710 P.2d 1025, 1030-31 (Ariz. 1985). This Arizona common law was later superseded by state legislation. Ariz. Rev. Stat. Ann. § 23- 1501(3)(b) (West Supp. 2009).
13. N.H. Rev. Stat. Ann. § 382-A: 2-302 (1961); N.Y. U.C.C. Law § 2-302 (McKinney 1964).
14. Jones v. Star Credit Corp., 298 N.Y.S.2d 264 (N.Y. Sup. Ct. 1969) (citing American Home Improvement, Inc. v. MacIver, 201 A.2d 886 (N.H. 1964), for the proposition that § 2-302 applied to "price unconscionability").
15. The UCC's warranty of merchantability implies a promise on the part of a merchant that goods are fit for their ordinary purposes, among other things. U.C.C. § 2-314 (2002).
16. Mary Dunnewold, *How Many Cases Do I Need?*, 10 Perspectives 10-11 (Fall 2001). Credit for the graphic in the text above goes to my colleague, Amy Langenfeld, who developed a more sophisticated version of the graphic for a classroom presentation.
17. *See* P. S. Atiyah & Robert S. Summers, Form and Substance In Anglo-American Law 5 (1987) (defining "substantive reasons" for legal decisions); *see also* Robert S. Summers, *Two Types of Substantive Reasons: The Core of a Theory of Common-Law Justification*, 63 Cornell L. Rev. 707 (1978).
18. *See generally* J. M. Balkin, *The Crystalline Structure of Legal Thought*, 39 Rutgers L. Rev. 1 (1986).
19. 42 U.S.C. § 1981 (2012).
20. *See generally* Runyon v. McCrary, 427 U.S. 160 (1976) (addressing, but rejecting, First Amendment challenges to application of section 1981 to racial discrimination in a private school).
21. Marvin v. Marvin, 18 Cal. 3d 660, 670 (1976) (en banc).
22. Robinson v. Lindsay, 598 P.2d 392, 393-94 (Wash. 1979) (en banc).
23. *Compare* Lefkowitz v. Great Minneapolis Surplus Store, 86 N.W.2d 689 (Minn. 1957) (offer) *with* Craft v. Elder & Johnston Co., 38 N.E.2d 416 (Ohio Ct. App. 1941) (no offer).
22. This exercise is adapted and expanded from one developed by Professor Elisabeth Keller at Boston College Law School. *See* Jane Gionfriddo, *Using Fruit to Teach Analogy*, The Second Draft: Bulletin of the Legal Writing Institute, Nov. 1997, at 4.

Part IV

Predictive Writing—The Office Memorandum of Law

Chapters 7 through 10 discuss various stages of preparing an office memorandum of law, including research strategy, organizing and drafting the memorandum, and citing to authority. In many first-semester legal writing programs, the office memorandum will be your primary vehicle for studying legal method and writing. Nonetheless, remember that the previous chapters have laid the foundation for this part of the book; you should not hesitate to review them when that would be helpful.

In an actual assignment in a law office, your first task in preparing an office memorandum will be to spend substantial time researching the law that applies to the issues raised in your assignment. You can best learn research techniques with hands-on training and with the assistance of separate texts focusing on legal research. Accordingly, the first chapter in Part IV limits its coverage of research to basic research strategies. Moreover, many first-semester writing courses gradually introduce students to the challenges of preparing law office memoranda, initially assigning first a "closed-universe" problem, which includes the necessary legal materials. In such an assignment, students will not need to research the law.

Chapter 7

The Office Memorandum of Law

I. Overview

Before examining the content of an office memorandum, we should address some preliminary matters, such as audience, purpose, perspective, and the role of the office memorandum among various means of communicating a legal analysis. We should also examine some facets of the "prewriting" phase: research strategy, organization of notes, and assessing the analysis at the outline stage. When you have mastered these preliminary matters, you will be ready to proceed to Section II, to begin writing your office memorandum.

A. Oral Report, Email Memo, or Full Office Memorandum?

Predictive analysis may take different forms, depending on the task presented, the depth of analysis required, and the purposes for which the task was requested. To save time and the client's money, an experienced attorney might draft a brief, an advice letter, or a demand letter directly from research notes, thus skipping the intermediate step of an office memorandum. Frequently, however, an office memorandum or other form of predictive analysis will serve as a helpful intermediate step. If a more senior attorney asks you to assist in a project by performing the research and preliminary analysis, the nature and formality of your report to her will vary depending on her needs.

1. Oral Report

When you have completed a very limited research assignment, a quick oral report to the assigning attorney might be the most efficient means to convey your analysis. For example, while she completes the first draft of a brief to a court, or while she prepares for contract or settlement negotiations, the assigning attorney might uncover an issue of law or fact that previous legal research did not address. She could ask you to perform some quick supplementary research to clarify this matter while she completes her task on a deadline. Or, based on her general knowledge of the law, she could be confident that a potential argument has merit, but she asks you to find the latest cases on point to confirm and support her position.

After several hours of research and analysis, you can organize the essential points in rough notes, prepare a succinct presentation, meet with the assigning attorney at the appointed time, and state your findings in a concise and well-organized oral report. If the assigning attorney submitted a specific question to you, get to the point quickly: state the issue posed and the conclusion you have reached. Then explain your reasoning on the law and facts while supplying copies of the statutes and cases on which you rely. Fully disclose weaknesses in your client's position but recommend a strategy for overcoming those difficulties. Be prepared to describe your research methods and the sources you consulted, to help the assigning attorney determine whether further research might bear fruit.

When delivering an oral report to an assigning attorney, do not be intimidated by your audience's greater experience. If you have researched the issue competently, your knowledge of this specific topic could be superior to that of your assigning attorney. Although you should be courteous and deferential, you should state your findings directly, candidly, and with the confidence of one who has studied the issue carefully.

The assigning attorney likely will respond with some helpful ideas or incisive questions. Be prepared to brainstorm the issues thoroughly and creatively, using your initial analysis as a staging point and not as a constraint on the discussion. The assigning attorney might ask you to follow up with a brief email note summarizing your findings. Alternatively, if your preliminary analysis shows that the issues are unexpectedly complex, she might ask you to conduct further research and compose a full office memorandum of law.

2. Traditional Office Memorandum of Law

In major disputes that are advancing through litigation, a client might have sufficient resources to justify your exhaustively researching a case and preparing a comprehensive written memorandum analyzing the law and facts on several issues. A typical office memorandum will include several sections, titled "Issues," "Brief Answers," "Facts," "Discussion," and "Conclusion." As explained below, these sections serve distinct, albeit overlapping, purposes.

Some assigning attorneys will ask you to deliver the legal memorandum in hard copy. Others will prefer an electronic word processing file of the memorandum, either emailed as an attachment or uploaded onto the firm's electronic case management system. If you deliver the memorandum as an attachment to an email, you can provide an executive summary in the body of the email, providing the assigning attorney with an instantly accessible introduction to your memorandum.

3. Streamlined Email Memo

Somewhere between these two extremes are limited research assignments that merit more than a quick oral report but for which you can present a complete analysis in 1-2 pages of text. A report this short could fit into the body of an email and could easily be read on the screen of a small, handheld device, such as a smartphone.[1] The format for such an "e-memo" should be streamlined but otherwise should remain flexible so that you can adapt it to suit the requirements of each assignment. For illustration, you might include the following elements in an e-memo assigned as a follow-up to a previously submitted office memorandum:

- an overview describing the limited issue or assignment that you undertook in the e-memo, perhaps referring to the source of assumed or agreed facts in the previous memorandum,
- a brief answer or conclusion to the assignment, including succinctly stated reasoning that supports the conclusion,
- a concise but complete analysis of the law and its application to the specific facts of the client's case,
- citations to relevant authority including explanatory parentheticals, and
- a summation with recommendation, but
- omitting a restatement of the facts known to the supervisor.[2]

On the other hand, if assigned to find three or four precedents from a specific state supporting a proposition, you could present the fruits of your research in a list of case citations with a parenthetic explanation for each citation. Select or create any format that efficiently achieves the purpose of the e-memo.

A streamlined e-memo will easily copy into the body of the email, regardless of whether you also attach it as a word processing file. Accordingly, this approach should normally be reserved for assignments that are quite limited in scope. If the assignment presents three or four substantial issues that require application of unsettled or uncertain law to complex facts, the analysis undoubtedly will require more than a few pages of text, making it unsuitable for presentation in the body of an email. If the complexity of a project was not apparent at the time of an e-memo assignment, the email memo itself may point out the need for further research and analysis, and for presentation in a longer, more formal memorandum.

Even when an analysis is sufficiently short and simple to be conveyed in the body of an email, you must write with the same precision and care that you would in a more traditional document. You should cite to the authority on which you rely, using proper citation signals and parenthetic explanations, as examined in Chapter 10. Moreover, the email format is not a license to adopt the breezy style used in your personal emails and text messages. As with other legal documents, tone and audience are important considerations in emails. You should address your assigning attorney with the requisite formality and respect.

Carefully proofread the e-memo. Edit it to correct errors and to revise overly casual language or abbreviations. Above all, check the email heading to confirm that you are sending it to the correct recipient with an accurate subject line.

4. Pedagogic Focus on Traditional Office Memoranda

This chapter provides a comprehensive guide to the traditional office memorandum in full format. In many cases, such a document will best meet the needs of a client or lead attorney, perhaps because the issues in the dispute are too complicated for abbreviated treatment in the body of an email message. Moreover, the more complete format of a traditional office memorandum could be helpful to the assigning attorney when she prepares a document in direct representation of the client, such as a brief to a court. Additionally, an office memorandum creates a record of the analysis based on the facts known when the memorandum was drafted. Finally, the memorandum can serve as a comprehensive guide for research and analysis of similar legal issues that arise in the future.

More important to the first-year law student, the full office memorandum is an indispensable tool for developing skills of analysis and articulation of facts and arguments. Once you have mastered the traditional office memorandum, you can easily adapt your presentation style to provide a more streamlined email or oral report when less depth and formality are appropriate.

After first exploring full, traditional legal memoranda in depth, this chapter ends with illustrations of the way in which a more limited report could be conveyed in the body of an email message. Using email to convey a short advice letter or demand letter is addressed in Chapters 20 and 21.

B. Traditional Office Memorandum: Audience, Purpose, and Perspective

1. Audience and Purpose

An office memorandum of law analyzes the law and the facts of a dispute, predicts an outcome, and recommends measures to assist the client. It is one of the most effective means through which you can directly help a senior attorney represent a client. The assigning attorney may be preparing a more formal document such as a pleading or brief to a court, an advice letter to a client, or a demand letter to an opposing party. When preparing any of these documents, the assigning attorney can use the office memorandum as a source of information, or even as a partial rough draft. In other cases, the assigning attorney might use the information in an office memorandum to develop a tax strategy for a business client or a settlement strategy for negotiations on behalf of a litigation client. The careful statement of facts in an office memorandum also helps you confirm the facts with the client, after providing the client with a copy of the memorandum or with an advice letter based on the memorandum.

2. Perspective

Unless an assigning attorney requests a memorandum that serves as the first draft of a brief, an office memorandum informs and predicts rather than advocates. To effectively represent the client, the assigning attorney must know both the weaknesses and the strengths of the client's claims and defenses. This means identifying not only your client's strongest arguments, but also the strongest arguments of the opposing party. If you present a balanced analysis of the dispute, your assigning attorney can focus his attention on his strongest arguments, can more accurately anticipate the counterarguments of the opposing party, and can develop an effective strategy. Indeed, if you find that the client's case has little chance of success, you might recommend that the client accept any reasonable settlement offer or withdraw his claim.

In that light, if you selectively bear only the good news to your assigning attorney, you will mislead him. Your skewed analysis could cause him embarrassment when further proceedings expose problems in his client's case—problems that he might have avoided or at least anticipated had the law firm confronted them at an earlier stage.

On the other hand, an office memorandum is not entirely neutral. In most cases, it anticipates advocacy on behalf of a client. Therefore, even though you explore arguments on both sides of a dispute in your memorandum, you should not convey a detached indifference to the outcome. Many experienced attorneys complain that student law clerks and recent graduates of law school tend to abandon a client's cause too readily after identifying obstacles to the client's claims or defenses. You must neither conceal such weaknesses nor surrender to despair over them. Instead, after identifying weaknesses in a client's case, you should present the best means of overcoming them. Identify ways to exploit the strengths of the client's case and suggest creative solutions to the problems raised by the weaknesses.

In sum, you should be zealous in your search for a winning argument for your client. However, if you believe that problems in your client's claim or defense are insurmountable, then you should candidly convey that conclusion to your assigning attorney.

C. Mastering the Assignment

The surest way to disappoint an assigning attorney is to misunderstand the assignment. Even a thoroughly researched and beautifully written memorandum will fall flat if it fails to address the matters that the supervisor wanted the associate to analyze.

Unfortunately, many assigning attorneys are too busy to communicate their assignments clearly and thoroughly. Even worse, most will not accept blame for confusion about the assignment. Instead, they expect you to assume responsibility for clarifying vague or confusing points. Consequently, you should not be shy about requesting additional information from the assigning attorney. Indeed, even at the risk of momentarily inconveniencing your assigning attorney, you should aggressively dig out the information that you need to master your assignment so that you can draft a memorandum that precisely meets the attorney's needs. On reading such a memorandum, the delighted assigning attorney will remember little about the minor inconvenience.

Confusion about the topics that your assigning attorney expects you to address may take various forms. In some cases, you will be unable to identify narrow, precise issues because the assignment is unavoidably general or abstract. Assigning attorneys occasionally request office memoranda on general, abstract questions of law, such as the likely scope and effect of a new statute. Although they are not yet working on any disputes relating to the assigned issues, they expect that the general legal analysis developed in such memoranda will help them counsel clients who are concerned about their rights or obligations under the new law. You can tailor such a memorandum to your supervisor's needs by requesting clarification on (1) the kinds of topics that your supervisor deems to be essential and (2) the kinds of disputes in which the firm's clients likely would become embroiled.

In many cases, abstraction in the assignment is unnecessary because the assigning attorney intends to use the legal analysis in the memorandum to help represent a client in an active, concrete dispute. In such a case, if your assigning attorney does not provide you with sufficient information to enable you to thoroughly understand the factual context, you should ask her for further factual details or for a convenient source of such information. By anticipating the application of legal standards to facts, you can frame the issues precisely and narrowly, and you can tailor the research and analysis to your supervisor's real needs. You might even wish to be present, if feasible, when the assigning attorney consults with the client, so that you can learn about the case firsthand.

Vagueness in an assignment often is attributable to the same analytical uncertainty on which the memorandum is intended to shed light. Therefore, after receiving the initial assignment but before writing the memorandum, you might benefit from secondary meetings with the assigning attorney. In some cases, your assigning attorney will not even attempt to identify issues, but will instead supply the factual context and ask you to define and analyze the issues. In other cases, the supervisor will state the issues in general and preliminary form, expecting you to refine and supplement them. Even if the supervisor has no such expectation, you likely will acquire information that allows you to focus the assigned issues more sharply. With a thorough knowledge of the factual context, you can clarify the essential issues as your research deepens your understanding of the legal standards.

As your research proceeds and the contours of the issues stand out more sharply, questions could arise about appropriate limits on the range of topics that you should address or about the depth to which the supervisor would like you to analyze a tangential issue. If so, you should consider whether the supervisor can conveniently give brief guidance on these questions before you begin writing. Although you should not become dependent on such guidance, neither should you assume that supervisors are universally hostile to such contacts. A good way to solicit guidance is to provide your supervisor with a skeleton outline of your preliminary research and request feedback.

D. Research Strategy

Legal research skills are best developed through years of hands-on experience, beginning in your first year of law school. To prepare for that experiential learning, you will undoubtedly study a separate textbook on legal research and receive instruction from faculty and from representatives of firms that offer systems for conducting research online. Because the tools and research systems are constantly changing, this text will limit its coverage to a brief discussion of research strategy.

Before setting your sights on specific primary authority, you should acquire a general grasp of the fundamental principles of law relevant to your assignment. Doing so will help you identify issues and exclude unproductive lines of inquiry. If your prior studies or experience do not provide the relevant foundational knowledge, you should consider beginning your research with a secondary source that provides general background information. As their labels suggest, primary authority within the relevant jurisdiction takes analytical precedence over secondary authority. Nonetheless, you will often find and use the primary authority more effectively if you first consult a secondary source—such as a reputable treatise—to enhance your understanding of the broad outlines of the subject. In other words, primary authority will likely form the basis for your legal analysis, while secondary authority will enhance your general understanding of the area of law.

Once you have begun to explore primary authority, you should look for relevant legislation before digging too deeply into case law. A single

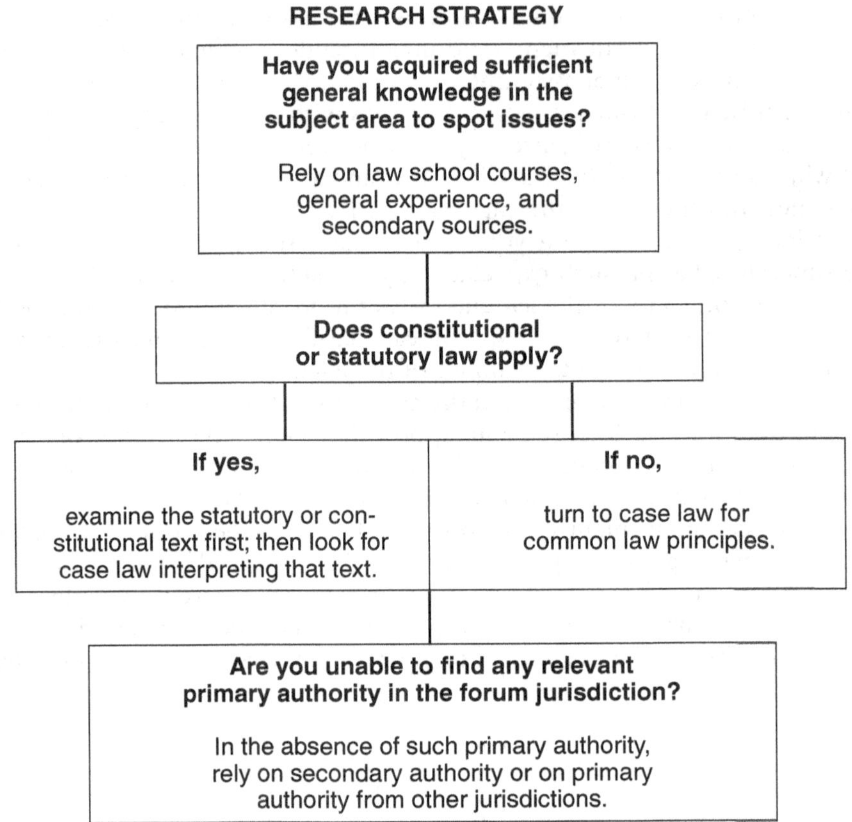

statute can diminish or even destroy the authoritative value of a whole line of case law that developed early common law doctrines or that interpreted previously effective legislation. Thus, you can avoid hours of marginally productive reading by immediately finding the latest applicable legislation.

Even when you know that a body of case law interprets currently effective legislation, you should turn first to the statute itself. The statutory language will provide valuable context for the case law that interprets the statute. If you can find no judicial decisions that interpret the statutory language in question, you should look for helpful legislative history, if any.

Of course, if no statute, constitutional provision, or administrative regulation applies, you may turn to case law for applicable common law. In the absence of any relevant primary authority in the jurisdiction, you can rely on the persuasive authority provided by secondary sources or by primary authority from other jurisdictions to help formulate your analysis.

Once you have identified the issues and the applicable law, consider scheduling a quick conversation with your assigning attorney, bringing along a preliminary outline of your analysis. In most cases, the assigning attorney will confirm that your research and preliminary analysis are addressing the client's needs, giving you the green light to express your analysis fully in a memorandum. Alternatively, your outline might prompt the assigning attorney to clear up a miscommunication about the nature of the assignment, allowing you to redirect your research before you have committed time and energy to the writing process. Or she might ask you to adjust your focus, such as by omitting an issue that another attorney is researching or by adding an issue that the assigning attorney believes might bear fruit. Early collaboration with your intended audience will help ensure that your final product will fully meet her needs.

Even if your early research is on point and appears to be complete, you will likely need to supplement your research after you begin writing. You might discover, for example, that you need additional authority to complete an analysis, or must return to important precedent to clarify some detail of its facts or reasoning. The process of writing your analysis will reveal gaps in your research not previously apparent to you. In sum: Research does not stop once the writing process begins.

E. Reorganizing and Outlining Your Research Notes

An attorney or summer associate researching and analyzing a simple problem might not need to reorganize her modest library notes before expressing her analysis in a short memorandum or brief. On the other hand, long hours of researching a complex, multiple-issue problem could produce a mass of notes dealing with several issues and lines of authority. In those circumstances, the researching attorney might need to summarize and reorganize her notes even before completely analyzing the problem, and certainly before outlining and then writing the memorandum.

When researching a multi-issue project, you will amass many pages of case summaries and other notes addressing several issues, and likely subissues within each issue. To facilitate later outlining of your analysis, you can organize your notes with a web application or other research compilation program.

Alternatively, if you type searchable symbols with your notes in a word processing file, you can later retrieve the notes that relate to a specific issue or point. For example, while researching four legal issues, you can choose a different symbol, such as # or @, for each issue and subissue. Then, every time any authority addresses that topic, precede your notes on that point with the corresponding symbol. Later, when outlining your analysis, you can easily find all your notes relating to that topic by performing a search for the corresponding symbol. Your notes on a single authority might include references to two or more of the issues you are researching, but your symbol search will quickly isolate your notes for that authority relating to the topic you are then outlining.

With such techniques, you can easily find your notes relating to each part of your outline, which could follow this typical pattern:

I. Issue #1
   Authorities for umbrella statement of three elements of a claim or defense
   A. Subissue #1
      Authorities for rules governing element #1
      Important facts relevant to these governing rules
   B. Subissue #2
      Authorities for rules governing element #2
      Important facts relevant to these governing rules
   C. Subissue #3
      Authorities for rules governing element #3
      Important facts relevant to these governing rules
II. Issue #2
   . . . .

A skeleton outline of this nature provides both (1) an excellent guide to the structure of your memorandum, and (2) a useful tool for assessing your organization and analysis. If you detect holes in your analysis requiring additional research or another subsection of discussion, or if your analysis is disorganized, you can more easily address those problems at the outlining stage than after you have drafted your memorandum in full.

To achieve these purposes, the outline should be skeletal, with little meat on its bones, so that you can see the broad structure of your analysis at a glance. Use a shortened form to name an authority in the outline, while indicating where you can find your notes on that authority. And, you should refer only briefly to facts in the record to which the applicable synthesized rule will apply; further detail can await the writing of the memorandum.

If you have organized or coded your research notes with this outlining function in mind, you can easily retrieve authorities relevant to any given issue. And once you are satisfied with your outline of the analysis, you can commence drafting your memorandum in full.

II. Alternative Formats for a Traditional Office Memorandum

A. Choices

A full office memorandum will proceed in deliberate fashion through several stages of information and analysis, with some intentional overlapping of sections. Beyond that traditional structure, however, the format need not be static or inflexible. Like alternative formats for student case briefs or streamlined email memos, several formats for traditional office memoranda are popular.

If your law firm or assigning attorney expresses a strong preference for a certain format, you should respect that preference unless you have a compelling reason to employ an alternative format. In the absence of a stated preference, you should choose a format that suits the needs of the specific assignment. The following are examples of three alternative formats for a traditional office memorandum:

Format A	**Format B**	**Format C**
I. Issue(s)	I. Overview	I. Issue(s)
II. Brief Answer(s)	II. Facts	II. Conclusion
III. Facts	III. Issue(s)	III. Facts
IV. Discussion	IV. Brief Answer(s)	IV. Discussion
V. Conclusion	V. Discussion	
	VI. Conclusion	

B. Format A: Effective for Multi-Issue Memoranda

1. Ordering the Elements to Aid Comprehension

Format A presents the issues first so that the reader of your memorandum can appreciate the legal significance of the facts when he reads them later in the memorandum. Once presented with the questions posed in the Issues section, however, the reader is eager to learn the answers—or probable answers—to which your research and analysis point. Accordingly, prior to the statement of facts, the Brief Answers section provides a succinct preview of your conclusion on each issue:

Issue(s)
Brief Answer(s)
Facts
Discussion
Conclusion

2. Facts in Different Places to Perform Different Tasks

After the statement of all essential facts in the Facts section, the Discussion section of your memorandum analyzes each issue previously stated in the Issues section, usually in a separate IRAC for each issue, set forth in a separate subsection. Within each such IRAC analysis, some of the facts will reappear, but only those that are relevant to *that issue*. In the "A" of IRAC, you will discuss whether those facts satisfy the rules that apply to that issue.

a. Example: Narration of All Essential Facts in Action for Breach of Contract

In a commercial contracts dispute, for example, your Facts section likely would present a chronological narrative of all essential facts, such as those describing (1) the formation of the contract between an owner and a contractor; (2) several complaints by the owner about the contractor's performance of the contract; (3) the unilateral termination of the contract by the dissatisfied owner; and (4) economic injuries suffered by the owner because of the allegedly substandard performance by the contractor, as well as economic injuries suffered by the contractor because of the owner's allegedly unjustified termination of the contract.

b. Example: Analysis of Facts Relevant to Each Issue in the Discussion Section

Suppose that one of the Discussion subsections addresses an issue relating to the owner's right to cancel the contract. Your analysis in that subsection should summarize applicable rules about a contractor's "material breach." Then it should discuss whether the facts ***relevant to that issue*** support a conclusion that the contractor materially breached the contract and thus justified termination by the owner.[3]

In line with the legal rule about material breach, those facts could include the extent and quality of the contractor's performance of obligations spelled out in the contract. Among other factors, they also could include circumstances showing the extent to which the owner's interests could be protected by retaining a right to money damages rather than firing the contractor.[4]

A separate subsection in the Discussion section could address a remedies issue by summarizing rules defining the kinds of injuries that are legally recoverable for breach of contract, and then analyzing the facts relevant to *that issue*. The remedies subsection would include a discussion of whether the legal rule allows recovery for specific economic losses suffered by the victim. For example, if your fact analysis shows that the victim of breach could reasonably have avoided some of his economic losses, those losses would not be included in the category of legally recoverable damages.[5]

3. Conclusions in Different Places to Perform Different Tasks

Each such IRAC analysis in the Discussion section will end with your subsidiary conclusion for *that issue*, as previously previewed in the Brief Answers section. For example, you might conclude in one subsection of the Discussion that the contractor did not materially breach the contract, so that the owner committed a total breach by terminating the contract without justification. You might conclude in another subsection that some of the contractor's injuries are not recoverable as damages because the contractor reasonably could have avoided those losses even after the owner's breach.

To complete the circle, the Conclusion section will gather the conclusions for all the issues, comment on their collective legal significance to the dispute, and reach a recommendation about the actions that might be taken on behalf of the client.

Consequently, the reader is exposed to conclusions in three places: (1) in the Brief Answers, to provide a quick and early bottom line; (2) at the end of the analysis of each issue in the Discussion section, to provide closure to each such analysis; and (3) in a summation and synthesis of all subsidiary conclusions in the Conclusion section, to provide a comprehensive perspective and to establish premises for a recommendation. If you choose to state conclusions—rather than topics or issues—in the section headings in the Discussion section, then each conclusion could appear in four places in the memorandum.

4. Overlapping Sections Are Like Actors Returning to Play Different but Complementary Roles

We might compare a traditional office memorandum to a play with several scenes in two acts. We can readily see that format A contemplates repeat performances of issues, facts, and conclusions, like actors reappearing in slightly different costumes in various scenes or acts of the play.

In a very simple, single-issue dispute, these repeat performances might seem repetitive and inefficient, thus justifying a more streamlined format, such as an e-memo. In a more complex, multi-issue dispute, however, the more deliberate analysis and overlapping sections of format A will provide your assigning attorney with a helpful roadmap to the analysis and with an effective tool for client representation.

If you deliver a full office memorandum as an attachment to an email, you could copy the final Conclusion section into the body of the email. Your email message would then provide a quick "executive summary" of the attached memorandum, easily accessible with any device that can gain access to the Internet.

C. Format B: For Especially Complex Cases

In rare cases, complex multiple transactions and confusing relationships between multiple parties could make statements of the issues incomprehensible to one who has not first read the facts. However, if the reader wades into the facts without first understanding the general nature of the issues, he will be robbed of the opportunity to read the facts with an appreciation for their legal significance.

Format B provides a special format to address this dilemma:

Overview
Facts
Issue(s)
Brief Answer(s)
Discussion
Conclusion

Ideally in a single paragraph, the brief Overview section describes the general nature of the dispute, identifies the nature of the issues in broad terms, and summarizes your assessment of the relative strength of the parties' positions. The Overview section remains concise because it avoids the temptation to prematurely delve into facts, issues, and conclusions in detail.

Nonetheless, its quick glimpse of the full landscape enables the reader to appreciate the legal significance of the events narrated in the Facts section. In turn, both the Overview and Facts sections enable the reader to better comprehend the formal statement of the issues.

If you deliver your memorandum as an email attachment, you could copy and paste the Overview section into the body of the email, providing a useful and readily accessible executive summary.

D. Format C: A Slightly Streamlined Approach for a Full Memorandum

Format C eliminates the Brief Answers section and replaces it with a Conclusion section, so that the Discussion section ends the memorandum by explaining the legal and factual basis for the Conclusion:

Facts
Issue(s)
Conclusion
Discussion

Format C has the disadvantage of ending the memorandum on the final topic of discussion rather than in a Conclusion section that ties all the strands of the analysis together. It also forces the reader to assimilate a full conclusion, including your recommendation, near the beginning of the memorandum without first digesting the analysis in the Discussion section. Nonetheless, some lawyers and law firms prefer format C because it reduces overlap and provides a bottom line and recommendation in the first few pages of the memorandum.

The potential drawbacks of format C are mitigated if the memorandum addresses a single issue. The Discussion section would then present a single analysis, and the reader would not hunger at the end of the memorandum for a consolidated Conclusion section that synthesizes several earlier subsidiary conclusions. Indeed, if the law and relevant facts in a single-issue assignment are simple or limited in scope, the analysis might be suitable for presentation in the body of the email, possibly in an even more streamlined format than format C. If the issue is more complicated and requires more than a few pages of analysis, then a fuller, more traditional memorandum is appropriate. Format C offers a middle ground by providing a slightly more streamlined format than does format A or B, allowing delivery either in the body of an email or attached in a more formal and lengthy legal memorandum, depending on the scope and complexity of the analysis.

E. Flexibility and Adaptation

Unless your law firm or assigning attorney has designated a certain format, you should feel free to adapt a standard format to the needs of a specific assignment. Let's assume, for example, that an assignment raises a single issue and that you are content to state your straightforward answer to the issue only once in the memorandum, as in format C. If you nonetheless determined that the reader would not fully appreciate your recommended action until she has digested the analysis, you could create a new format to suit your purpose. The example below extracts the answer and recommendation from the Conclusion section, states the answer immediately after the Issue section, and returns the recommendation to the end of the memorandum:

Facts
Issue
Answer
Discussion
Recommendation

In any of these formats, an assigning attorney or law firm might ask you to add a short section summarizing your research or to place your research notes in the case file. If another member of the firm later supplements or updates the research, your summary will help avoid wasteful duplication of efforts.

III. Elements of an Office Memorandum

The heading of a memorandum is simple and requires only brief discussion. The heading should identify the recipient of the memorandum; the author of the memorandum; the subject matter stated in a manner that facilitates filing and later retrieval; and the date:

TO:	Susan Elias
FROM:	James Nelson
RE:	Enforceability of Julie Week's Promise to Act as Guarantor for Loan Obligation; File 22 -127
DATE:	July 31, 2022

Some law offices may also include a line above "RE:" for identification of the means of delivering the memorandum, such as "Via: Printed Copy" or "Via: Email Attachment."

The following subsections examine the more substantive elements of format A for an office memorandum: Issue(s), Brief Answer(s), Facts, Discussion, and Conclusion.

A. Issues—Identification and Expression

1. Review

Section III of Chapter 6 discusses the general process of identifying issues for analysis, and Appendix I discusses the process of framing issues for statement in a case brief when preparing for class discussion. These sections lay the foundation for identifying and framing issues in an office memorandum, and you should review them now.

Your professor might refer to the issues as "questions presented" or "issues presented." Whatever the label, the issues are legal and factual questions that a court must answer to resolve the dispute before it.

Identifying issues for analysis in an office memorandum is similar to identifying issues on a law school examination: you must have at least a general knowledge of the applicable law so that you can recognize the legal problems raised by the facts. In many cases, courses that you have taken in law school will enable you to identify the general nature of the issues and to direct your research efforts. Otherwise, a secondary source such as a good treatise can provide the necessary background information.

Be prepared to revise your statement of the issues in the final stages of drafting. When you prepare a case brief for class discussion, you ordinarily cannot state with particularity the issues discussed in the judicial decision until you complete your analysis of the entire opinion. Similarly, when preparing an office memorandum, you ordinarily cannot state with particularity the issues raised by the facts of the dispute until you complete your research and fully analyze the problem. At that time, you must decide which elements of a claim or defense are sufficiently in doubt that they warrant identification and discussion as issues or subissues.

2. Example: Identifying Issues in a Title VII Suit

Title VII of the Civil Rights Act of 1964 imposes liability on employers for engaging in "unlawful employment practices," and it defines "employer" in part as "a person engaged in an industry affecting commerce."[6] Although engagement "in an industry affecting commerce" is always an element of employer liability, in most cases the facts known to all parties leave no doubt that the employer's activities satisfy the statutory rule under any reasonable interpretation. In such a case, the party charged with discrimination could not credibly dispute its status as an "employer" on grounds relating to commerce, and you should not identify that matter as an issue in your memorandum. At most, you might briefly state this conclusion in an introduction to the discussion of a substantial issue.

In the same case, however, unusual facts and uncertainty in the applicable legal standards might raise doubts about whether the employer has committed an "unlawful employment practice." Because the employee plausibly claims that the employer committed an unlawful employment practice, and because the employer plausibly denies it, the parties reasonably dispute that matter, and you should identify it as an issue for discussion.

3. Expressing Issues with Particularity

Once you have identified and analyzed issues for discussion in your memorandum, you should state them with specificity and attention to facts. A complete statement of an issue will succinctly identify the legal element in dispute, as well as the key facts relevant to that analysis.

For example, you should not state the issue—or "question presented"—in such general terms as "whether the employer committed an unlawful employment practice under Title VII of the Civil Rights Act of 1964." Your assigning attorney might present the issue to you in such general terms in the assignment, but only because he or she has not performed the research needed to refine the issue further. After you have researched the law and analyzed the facts, you can more precisely identify the contours of the prospective dispute:

> Did Stalerno create a hostile working environment for the complaining female employees by repeatedly asking them for dates, thus making Stalerno liable for sex discrimination under Title VII by altering the female employees' terms or conditions of employment?

The following formula could help you remember the elements of an issue statement:

> Under (applicable law), does (legal result occur/has legal standard been met, when (relevant facts are present)?

Using this formulation, you could state a compact version of the issue in the Title VII suit:

> Under Title VII of the Civil Rights Act of 1964, did Stalerno create a hostile working environment when he repeatedly made unwelcome sexual advances towards female employees?

If you must omit some details from the issue statement to keep it manageable in length and complexity, you can move some of those details to the brief answer:

> **I. ISSUE**
>
> Under Title VII of the Civil Rights Act of 1964, did Stalerno create a hostile working environment when he repeatedly made unwelcome sexual advances towards female employees?
>
> **II. BRIEF ANSWER**
>
> Probably yes. Stalerno allowed his male employees to work unmolested, but he repeatedly and aggressively asked three female employees for dates, long after the employees expressed their discomfort with the advances. Because Stalerno made his requests in an intrusive and sexually charged manner, he probably created a hostile working environment for the employees. If so, he is liable under Title VII for engaging in sex discrimination that altered the employees' working conditions.

Appendix I discusses a similar technique: drafting a case brief so that the statements of issue and holding share the burden of expressing important details. Alternatively, legal writing expert Bryan Garner recommends that students and attorneys state the premises of an issue in separate sentences within the issue statement.[7] For example, you could state the Title VII issue in the following way:

> I. ISSUE
>
> Title VII imposes liability on an employer that discriminates because of an employee's sex in a way that alters terms or conditions of employment. One way to alter employment conditions is by creating a hostile working environment for employees. In our case, the employer repeatedly directed sexually charged requests for dates to three female employees, even though the employees complained that the advances were unwelcome. The employer discriminated on the basis of sex because he allowed his male employees to work unmolested. Did the employer's discriminatory conduct also amount to a hostile working environment for the female employees sufficient to alter their conditions of employment?

This format for a multi-sentence issue statement might not meet with the approval of every assigning attorney, and it might not be perfectly consistent with some court rules governing the statement of issues in a brief. Still, when supervisors and court rules permit, you might want to experiment with this approach for particularly complex issues.

B. Brief Answer

Each brief answer should be a succinct response to the question presented in each issue. Begin with a direct answer to the corresponding issue, such as "yes," or "no," often coupled with a modifier such as "probably." Then state the applicable law and apply it to the facts of your case, painting with a broad brush.

Unless the assigning attorney requests a detailed statement of your conclusions early in the memo, you should not use the brief answer to explore analytical justifications in great depth. The reader can more easily absorb a complex summary of the analysis after she has read the Discussion section of the memorandum. For example, the medical malpractice dispute discussed in Chapter 6 might raise the following issues and brief answers:

> I. ISSUES
>
> A. Does the phrase "any toxic material" in New Maine's strict liability statute encompass a generally safe anesthetic that produced a fatal reaction in a patient with a rare nerve disorder?
>
> B. Is Humane Hospital liable to Souza's estate for negligent administration of the anesthetic?

1. Did Humane's anesthesiologist breach a duty of care by administering the anesthetic without assistance and by failing to monitor Souza's reactions to the anesthesia?

2. Did Souza's nerve disorder constitute a supervening cause that broke the chain of causation between the anesthesiologist's conduct and Souza's death?

II. **BRIEF ANSWERS**

A. Probably no. A restrictive interpretation is supported by the legislative history and by a general public policy in New Maine encouraging the provision of affordable medical services. The legislature probably did not intend the statutory phrase "toxic material" to include medically prescribed substances that ordinarily produce a beneficial result or otherwise facilitate medical treatment.

B. Probably yes.

1. Probably yes. Under generally accepted hospital procedures, at least two trained medical personnel must monitor the administration of anesthesia, with at least one person monitoring the patient's reactions. In this case, a jury likely will find that the anesthesiologist breached a duty of care to the patient by administering the anesthesia alone.

2. Probably no. The jury likely will also find that the patient's nerve disorder was not a supervening cause and that the anesthesiologist's negligence proximately caused the patient's death.

C. Facts

Some new associates in a law firm regularly omit statements of facts in their legal memoranda. The associates often explain that an assigning attorney obviously knows the facts of an assigned case because she gave the facts to the associate in some oral or written form when she assigned the memorandum.

For several reasons, however, you should include at least a brief statement of facts in a legal memorandum unless your assigning attorney specifically authorizes you to omit it. The assigning attorney might have been familiar with the facts when she assigned the memorandum, but she might need a brief review to refresh her memory when she later reads your memorandum. Alternatively, she could want reassurance that you share her understanding of the facts. Furthermore, the memorandum should be a self-contained document that is helpful to any member of the firm who could be called on to take over the file, including an attorney who knows nothing about the case and does not have time to glean the facts from the file. Your statement of facts can also help you in two ways. First, it can help you focus your research. Second, by revealing the facts on which your analysis is based, it protects you from criticism if newly discovered facts later renders your analysis obsolete.

Your statement of facts should focus on legally relevant facts and necessary background facts as you would in preparing a case brief for class. However, more so in an office memorandum than in a case brief, you can justify mentioning even a marginally significant fact. When briefing a case for class, you must rely on the court's summary of the facts as a complete record on which the court based its decision. Moreover, you can test your analytical abilities by attempting to isolate the material facts and helpful background facts and by omitting the others. In contrast, when preparing an office memorandum at an early stage of a dispute, you know that the facts on which you rely for your analysis are incomplete. Subsequent proceedings may reveal other facts that support new claims, defenses, or arguments. Consequently, previously known facts that appeared to be unimportant when you drafted the memorandum can take on new legal significance. In your statement of facts, therefore, you should recite all material facts in detail, and you should summarize any other information that either provides helpful background material or might take on new significance as the litigation proceeds.

D. Discussion

1. Introducing Your Analysis

In the discussion—or analysis—section of your legal memorandum, you will express your complete legal analysis of each of the previously stated issues. If your memorandum addresses a single issue that you have formally stated at or near the beginning, your discussion of the issue need not begin with any descriptive heading beyond the major section heading "Discussion" or "Analysis." If you address multiple issues, however, you should separately analyze each issue under a descriptive section heading.

Descriptive headings can take a variety of forms. In an office memo, a descriptive heading might be limited to a short phrase that recalls the issue:

> IV DISCUSSION
>
> A. Strict liability for use of toxic materials
>
> . . . .

Some assigning attorneys might prefer that you restate the issue in full or nearly full detail in the corresponding section heading of the discussion:

> IV. DISCUSSION
>
> A. Does the phrase "any toxic material" in New Maine's strict liability statute encompass a generally safe anesthetic that produced a fatal reaction in a patient with a rare nerve disorder?

Other supervisors might prefer that you state your *conclusion* in the section heading because they want your memorandum to develop an argument that they can critique:

> IV. DISCUSSION
>
> A. New Maine's strict liability statute likely does not apply to a generally safe anesthetic that produced a fatal reaction in a patient with a rare nerve disorder.
>
> . . . .

If your legal writing professor teaches the last style above, she might substitute the acronym "CRAC" for IRAC in the Discussion section. Or your professor might invoke CREAC or CRuPAC to remind you that a legal rule that addresses a matter in controversy normally will require *explanation* or *proof*[8] of the rule, such as with case analysis or legislative history, rather than a simple summary in a sentence or two of "black-letter law."

This chapter on office memoranda, however, normally sets forth neutral, issue-oriented subject headings as illustrations. Accordingly, it adheres to the concise acronym IRAC, while Chapter 8 addresses the need to explain the content of a rule as a matter of "depth of analysis."

Indeed, if you adopt a neutral section heading, a topical word or phrase could be sufficient to remind the reader of an issue that is more specifically stated earlier in the memorandum. Moreover, the neutrality of such a heading helps to show that the author examined both sides of the law and the facts:

IV. **DISCUSSION**

A. Strict Liability for Use of Toxic Materials

. . . .

B. Negligence

. . . .

1. Negligent Act

. . . .

2. Proximate Cause

. . . .

Immediately after you identify an issue with a section heading, if helpful, you can illuminate the issue in an introductory sentence or two that refers briefly to facts, arguments, or theories that explain the significance of the issue. For example, the following opening sentence expands on the section heading by explaining the significance of the theory of strict liability:

A. Strict Liability for Use of Toxic Materials

If a statute or the common law imposes strict liability for Souza's death, then Souza's estate can establish liability without proving negligence.

In some instances, the opening paragraph of a section can even draw subsidiary legal conclusions to pinpoint the narrow question in dispute. For example, the following paragraph concludes that a proposed transaction would include a sale of goods. Coupled with other observations, that subsidiary conclusion leads to the primary issue of the section:

> A. Choice of Law—UCC or Common Law
>
> Whether Maldonado accepted Weinstein's offer depends in part on whether the common law of contracts or the Uniform Commercial Code (UCC) applies to the transaction. The UCC applies to "transactions in goods." U.C.C. §2-102 (2011). Weinstein's offer to supply specifically identified, separately priced, movable plumbing parts clearly contemplates a sale of goods as part of the transaction. *See* U.C.C. §2-105(1) (2011). His proposed transaction, however, also involves the service of installing the fixtures, raising a question about the applicability of the UCC to mixed transactions for both services and the sale of goods.
>
> The UCC applies to such a mixed transaction only if....

Of course, if an issue is adequately represented in a section heading and needs no further elaboration, the discussion can proceed immediately to an analysis of the legal standards:

> A. Applicability and Satisfaction of the Statute of Frauds
>
> The Arizona statute of frauds bars enforcement of "an agreement which is not to be performed within one year from the making thereof," unless it, "or some memorandum thereof, is in writing and signed by the party to be charged." Ariz. Rev. Stat. Ann. §44-101(5) (2005) (copy of full text attached)....

2. Analyzing the Law and the Facts

After you have drafted the section heading and the optional elaboration of the issue, you ordinarily should follow the IRAC pattern of deductive reasoning developed in Chapter 6: for each issue or subissue, analyze the law and apply the law to the facts to reach a conclusion. The nature of the analysis in a discussion section will vary with each issue. If the clearly applicable abstract legal rule is simple, you can present the rule and supporting authority directly and concisely, permitting you to direct most of your attention to fact analysis. Other issues might require a choice between competing rules or a clarification of the content of the applicable legal rule. If so, you should discuss the abstract legal rule in depth before applying it to the facts. Of course, determining the content of the rule and applying it to the facts are often related tasks: your discussion of the question of whether specific facts satisfy the legal standard may help to clarify the content of a vague or uncertain rule.

a. Example: Statutory Analysis

Reproduced below is a portion of the discussion section of a sample office memorandum set in the fictitious state of New Maine, whose case law we will assume is published solely in the New Maine Reporter, abbreviated "N. Me." It analyzes the issue of statutory liability for administering anesthesia.

The statutory analysis in the passage focuses on defining the legal rule in a simple factual context, thus requiring relatively little independent fact analysis. In contrast, the memorandum must engage in original statutory analysis because no judicial decision has yet interpreted the statutory language in question. Accordingly, after refining the issue in an introduction, the author of the discussion presents the statutory analysis on three levels, in descending order of priority: the language of the statute, its legislative history (often difficult to find for state legislation, but easily accessible in published materials in this fictitious jurisdiction), and general policy considerations. In this example, the author has applied the law to the relevant facts at each level of the statutory analysis rather than in a single consolidated fact analysis at the end of the discussion. Other means of organizing the discussion, however, are presented in the next chapter.

IV. DISCUSSION

A. Strict Liability for Use of Toxic Material

Introduction

If a statute or the common law imposes strict liability for Souza's death, then Souza's estate can establish liability without proving negligence. New Maine's common law doctrine of strict liability for injuries caused by ultrahazardous activities does not apply to noncriminal medical practices engaged in by licensed physicians. *Stanislaus v. Good Samaritan Hosp.*, 212 N. Me. 113, 115 (1989). New Maine has recently enacted a statute, however, that imposes strict liability for injuries stemming from the use of "any toxic material": "A commercial enterprise is liable for injuries proximately caused by its use of any toxic material, without regard to the degree of care exercised by the enterprise." 12 N. Me. Rev. Stat. Ann. § 242 (Supp. 2021) (effective Jan. 1, 2022). As a profit-making hospital, Humane presumably is a "commercial enterprise" within the meaning of the statute.

Narrow issue

It is less certain, however, that the anesthetic administered to Souza would qualify as a "toxic" material.

Analysis of statutory language

The common meaning of the word "toxic" is "poisonous." *E.g.*, *The Random House Dictionary of the English Language* 1500 (unabridged) (1970). Souza's estate might plausibly argue that the anesthetic was a toxic material because it was poisonous to Souza, even though it would not have been poisonous to most others. The word "toxic," however, applies more naturally to substances that are universally harmful to humans, such as cyanide, DDT, or sulfuric acid. It strains the common meaning of "toxic" to apply it to an anesthetic that might occasionally be harmful to persons with unusual allergies or other extraordinary conditions.

Preliminary fact analysis

Legislative history

Legislative history also supports a restrictive interpretation of the statutory term "any toxic material." The report of the New Maine Senate Committee on Health and Welfare suggests that the legislature was concerned only with the deadliest of substances:

> The purpose of this bill is to reallocate the cost of unavoidable accidents from victims to industry and its consumers, to discourage unnecessary use of deadly chemicals and other hazardous materials, and to encourage the development and use of substitute materials that are generally safe for human contact.

Fact analysis

N. Me. Comm. on Health and Welfare, S. 78-112, 2d Sess., at 2 (2021). The anesthetic in this case is closer to the materials "generally safe for human contact" condoned by the legislature than it is to the "deadly chemicals and other hazardous materials" condemned by it.

Policy analysis

Finally, general state policy appears to support an interpretation that excludes medically prescribed substances from the reach of the statute. The legislature and judiciary of New Maine have recognized a policy of limiting the liability of physicians to encourage the ready availability of affordable medical services. For example, under the New Maine "Good Samaritan" statute, physicians who provide certain emergency medical services are not liable for adverse consequences unless they engage in culpable conduct amounting to at least gross negligence. 12 N. Me. Rev. Stat. Ann. §229 (2010). This protective policy is also reflected in the courts' refusal to extend common law strict liability for ultrahazardous activities to even experimental medical practices. *See Stanislaus*, 212 N. Me. at 115. The legislature presumably was aware of these laws when it enacted the toxic materials statute in 2021.Souza's estate may argue that the legislature intended to retreat from the protective policies of these laws by imposing strict liability on a limited segment of the activities of commercial medical practices. Absent more specific evidence of legislative intent to depart from existing legal policies, however, it is more likely that the legislature retained its protective attitude and assumed that the term "toxic material" would not include routinely prescribed medicines or anesthetics.

Fact analysis

In this case, the prescribed anesthetic, ethane, was not the safest available at the time of Souza's operation. Nonetheless, it is a frequently prescribed substance that produces beneficial results with only minor side effects in all but the most unusual cases.

Conclusion

The strict liability statute almost certainly does not apply to Souza's death.

b. Example: Established Common Law

In contrast to the previous example, the sample discussion below briefly summarizes noncontroversial legal standards—represented in fictitious case law—and places greater emphasis on fact analysis. After illuminating the issue of negligence and summarizing general principles, the discussion separately addresses distinct subissues in different subsections. Within the first of those subsections, devoted to "negligent act," the author has consolidated the relatively simple legal standards in a single paragraph. This allows for a single, uninterrupted line of fact analysis. Nonetheless, the author has divided the fact analysis itself into two paragraphs, presenting opposing factual arguments.

IV. DISCUSSION

A. Strict Liability for Use of Toxic Materials

. . . .

B. Negligence

Introduction

Assuming Humane Hospital is not strictly liable for Souza's death, it may nonetheless be liable to Souza's estate if its agent caused the death through negligence. *See Kityama v. Mercy Hosp.*, 183 N. Me. 752, 759-60 (1974) (hospital liable for negligence of its nurse). An action for negligence requires proof of a negligent act or omission that proximately causes injury. *Baker v. Bruce*, 153 N. Me. 817, 820 (1967).

Narrow issues

In our case, the injury to Souza is obvious. In greater doubt are the elements of negligent act and proximate cause.

1. Negligent Act

Legal rules

A negligent act or omission consists of the breach of a duty of care owed to another. *Id.* at 821. A medical specialist owes a duty to patients to exercise at least the ordinary skill and care that is reasonable and customary nationwide in that medical specialty. *Kityama*, 183 N. Me. at 760. Furthermore, under the "thin-skulled plaintiff" rule, that duty of care encompasses the special care necessary to address increased risks created by a patient's unusual susceptibility to injury. *Id.* In this case, Humane's anesthesiologist, Unger, may have breached duties of care in her unassisted administration of general anesthesia in the face of Souza's known nerve condition.

Fact analysis favoring Humane

Unger exercised care in determining Souza's disorder of the nervous system and in informing her of the risks presented by each of the most suitable anesthetics. Moreover, when administering the anesthetic selected by Souza, Unger took care to provide the prescribed dosage by monitoring the anesthetic intake gauge.

Fact analysis favoring Souza's estate

However, Unger's intense concentration on the anesthetic intake gauge may have been an act of carelessness, rather than enhanced care, because it diverted Unger's attention from Souza and from equipment monitoring Souza's vital signs. Faced with Souza's known nerve disorder, Unger probably had a duty to follow the standard medical practice of summoning a nurse to assist her in administering the anesthesia. Had she done so, the team could have monitored both Souza's vital signs and the intake gauge, and a team member undoubtedly would have detected signs of distress at least 10 seconds before death, arguably enough time to cease anesthesia and take corrective measures.

Conclusion

On these facts, a jury could find that Unger was negligent in her administration of the anesthetic.

2. Proximate Cause

. . . .

c. Rule Synthesis and Illustration

In contrast to the previous sample passage, many legal rules are difficult to define from a single source and must be derived through a comparison, or synthesis, of several judicial decisions. In such cases, you will start your rule section by providing a full statement of the law, composed from a synthesis of multiple authorities. The statement of the synthesized rule may be a single sentence or one or more paragraphs, depending on the complexity of law that governs your legal issue.

Some judicial decisions will give you a head start: they announce a general legal rule after synthesizing previous case law or otherwise developing or interpreting the law. We can refer to such a statement of law as an "inherited rule," one that a court has declared for us. Other judicial decisions might state narrower holdings, each one deciding little more than the case before it, limited to its facts. If so, you will need to construct your own "processed rule," after combining the lessons of several cases in a process of synthesis. Indeed, your final synthesized rule might incorporate both an inherited rule and additional nuances from processed rules that you constructed.

The statement of the rule should encompass the full spectrum of the law applicable to the legal issue. For example, if you are drafting a rule about the unauthorized practice of law, you should set forth a standard that helps to distinguish between actions that constitute the practice of law and those that do not. Your rule statement will be especially reliable if it is derived from examples from each category:

> A nonlawyer engages in the unauthorized practice of law if he advises a client on a question of law, but only if the question is difficult or doubtful. *Gardner v. Conway*, ... (advising on common law marital status and partnership status was practicing law); *Dailey v. Jameson*, ... (advising against signing a contract was not practicing law). A question of law is difficult or doubtful if it requires the expertise of a trained legal mind. *Gardner*, ...

After stating your synthesized rule, you normally will illustrate it with case summaries that illustrate how the courts have applied the rule in previous cases, presumably in the cases from which you derived your rule. These factually rich illustrations will help the reader understand how the courts are incrementally drawing the line between satisfaction and nonsatisfaction of the legal rule.

In turn, the case summaries will support your analogical reasoning when you apply the law to the facts of your case, to predict how a court would resolve your current dispute. You can invoke your case summaries to help analyze which of two or more precedents is more analogous to your case. To facilitate this analysis, you must invest time and energy identifying all the critical facts, reasoning, and holdings that belong in your illustrations of precedents, so that you can profitably compare them to your case. But you should also keep each illustration succinct so that your analysis is tightly focused. Do not muddle a rule illustration with facts and procedural details irrelevant to your analysis.

Your rule illustration should begin with a rule-focused thesis sentence that summarizes the point that your passage illustrates. For example, the thesis sentence might describe a category of facts that satisfied a rule earlier asserted, or that failed to satisfy that rule. You would follow by stating the relevant facts, reasoning, and holding, thus showing in greater detail why those facts satisfied the rule, or did not satisfy it.

In the example of the unauthorized practice of law, let's assume that you have already set forth your complete statement of your synthesized rule, including the test of "difficult or doubtful question of law." If so, each rule illustration might reveal a court's reasoning when it determined that certain advice given did, or did not, relate to "a difficult or doubtful question of law." Your explanation of that reasoning should identify the specific facts that supported and motivated the court's conclusion:

Thesis sentence	For example, applying the legal standards for common law marriage and business partnership requires the expertise of a trained legal mind. *Gardner v. Conway*, 48 N.W.2d 788, 795-96 (Minn. 1951).
Relevant facts	In *Gardner*, an accountant counseled a client about the marital and business partner statuses between the client and his alleged common law wife. *Id.* at 798.
Reasoning	The Minnesota Supreme Court reasoned that the determination of these statuses required legal knowledge greater than that of an ordinary layperson and that the specialized training of an attorney was necessary to safeguard the public. *Id.* at 796-98.
Holding	Consequently, the Court held that the accountant's actions were found to constitute the unauthorized practice of law. *Id.* at 798.
Thesis sentence for second illustration	In contrast, advising against signing a contract does not constitute the practice of law when the advice is based on a general assessment of business risks. *Dailey v. Jameson*....

By explaining the reasoning and factual basis for a judicial decision, the illustration provides the reader with a deeper understanding of the law than could be conveyed by a simple verbal rule statement. The depth of understanding increases when the memorandum presents several illustrations of the rule, especially when cases reach different conclusions. By showing how the facts in one case supported a finding of practice of law, and by explaining why different facts in a second case failed to support such a finding, the memorandum provides a vivid picture of judicial line-drawing between satisfaction and non-satisfaction of the rule.

Alternatively, your passage might illustrate how a case developed a sub-rule or test that provided further definition to the rule. For example, assume that you have set forth the general rule that unauthorized practice of law requires resolution of a difficult or doubtful question of law, but you have not yet added the test that such a question is one requiring application of a trained legal mind to protect the public. If you decide to introduce and explain that test in a rule illustration, your thesis sentence should refer to the test, followed by the facts, reasoning, and holding of the illustrative case:

Thesis sentence	A question of law is difficult or doubtful if it requires the expertise of a trained legal mind. *Gardner v. Conway*, 48 N.W.2d 788, 795 (Minn. 1951).
Relevant facts	In *Gardner*, an accountant counseled a client about the marital and business partner statuses between the client and his alleged common law wife, while assisting the client with his taxes. *Id.* at 798.
Reasoning	The Minnesota Supreme Court recognized that tax preparation could raise questions spanning both the professions of law and accounting, and that the unauthorized practice of law must entail a question that is difficult or doubtful question in its legal facets. Such a question would require "the application of a trained legal mind" to protect the public. *Id.* at 796-98.
Holding	The Court found that the accountant had engaged in the unauthorized practice of law because he had addressed difficult questions of law that required legal training to resolve. *Id.* at 798.

d. Drawing Analogies in the Fact Analysis

When your rule statement includes illustrations similar to your case, you have an opportunity to invoke an analogy, a form of inductive reasoning, to predict the outcome of your case.

Using those facts that you identified as relevant in the rule illustrations, identify facts that are similar to your case, or distinguishable from it. Be explicit in constructing your analogies or distinctions. Use specific facts from your case as well as from the precedent case:

The law clerk's advice in our case addressed whether a tenant should withhold payments from his landlord. That advice addressed a legal question at least as doubtful and difficult as the advice in *Gardner* regarding the client's marital status and partnership status.

After you have asserted a material similarity or difference between the facts of your case and the precedent case, explain your reasoning. Do not assume that the reader will draw the same conclusion from the facts that you have drawn. Explain why the landlord-tenant issue in your case was at least as difficult and doubtful as the legal status issues in the precedent.

As always, examine the weaknesses as well as the strengths of your argument. Consider and articulate how your opponent might argue from the same set of precedent cases. For example, consider how opposing counsel might try to distinguish *Gardner* from the case at hand, by arguing that the landlord-tenant question in fact required no substantial legal analysis.

At the end of a section or subsection that addresses a discrete issue or subissue, state your conclusion about the likely resolution of that issue. State your prediction and a summary of the reasoning that supports it. If a case or line of cases strongly supports your prediction, you could mention that basis for your conclusion. However, do not take up your reader's time by again discussing those cases. Instead, in a very few sentences, succinctly summarize the key legal or factual points that support your prediction.

E. The Conclusion

Even though the questions addressed in an office memorandum may be close, and even though your assigning attorney will not feel bound by your advice, she will expect you to take a position by stating your conclusions. A thorough memorandum will include both (1) a brief resolution of each issue within the part of the discussion section devoted to that issue, and (2) a more general summary of conclusions in a separate section at the end of the memorandum.

In the Conclusion section, you can summarize the individual conclusions that you have reached in the Discussion section of the memorandum. If helpful, you can also summarize the analytical support for the conclusions in a depth that would have been inappropriate in the brief answers stated earlier.

You should not raise new legal arguments in the Conclusion section. However, you can and should use this section to express any strategic recommendations that your analysis inspires. For example, you might recommend that the law firm file a complaint, settle a weak case, investigate certain facts, or concentrate its efforts on a certain legal theory.

Although you may express more information in the Conclusion section than in the brief answers, your conclusion should nonetheless represent a selective summary of your analyses and recommendations. In a simple case, a few sentences will suffice. In a more complex case, your Conclusion section might span a few paragraphs.

For example, the following passage concisely synthesizes the conclusions previewed above in Section B as brief answers, and it adds strategic recommendations:

Summary of analyses

V. CONCLUSION

Considering the legislative and judicial policies favoring limits on physicians' liability, the strict liability statute regulating toxic materials probably will not apply to the administration of anesthetic in this case. The courts will be even less likely to retreat from precedent by applying the common law doctrine of strict liability for ultrahazardous activities. A jury could find, however, that Humane's anesthesiologist was negligent in failing to summon assistance to administer the anesthesia or to monitor the patient closely. We can try to characterize Souza's nerve condition as a supervening cause, but *Rainbow Landscaping* will not be easy to distinguish.

Strategic recommendation

Because the risk of substantial liability is great, I recommend that we advise Humane to settle. Souza's estate might be willing to compromise; its negligence claim is not appropriate for summary disposition and thus is subject to the unpredictability of a jury.

Sample Office Memoranda and E-memos

1. Sample 1: Office Memorandum 1

Imagine that an attorney from the fictitious state of Calzona drafted the following office memorandum using only authority from the Calzona Supreme Court. Study the memorandum and consider the questions that follow it.

Memorandum

To: Susan Elias
From: James Nelson
Re: Enforceability of Julie Week's Promise to Act as Guarantor for Her Cousin's Loan Obligation; File 22-127
Date: July 31, 2022

I. Issue

By stating that he would refrain from demanding payment from Borrower on a loan obligation until he "needs the money," did Lender state a promise that provided consideration for Guarantor's promise to pay the obligation in the event that Borrower failed to pay on demand?

II. Brief Answer

Probably yes. Although the Lender's promise arguably is illusory, it probably satisfies the consideration requirement by committing the Lender to a performance, subject only to economic events not entirely within the Lender's control.

III. Facts

One of our regular business clients, Julie Week (Guarantor), asserted the following facts in an interview.

On December 15, 2021, Guarantor's cousin, Don Caslin (Borrower), purchased two rare antique automobiles from a private owner, Thomas Beatty (Lender), for a total of $200,000. In a self-financing arrangement, Borrower paid $80,000 on delivery and agreed in writing to pay the remainder of the purchase price in 12 monthly installments of $10,000 each, beginning January 1, 2022.

From January to April 2022, Borrower paid Lender a total of $40,000 in monthly installments. In late April, however, Borrower suffered unusual losses in his private business, and he failed to pay the installments due on May 1 and June 1. After Lender threatened to sue for the return of the automobiles, Guarantor and Lender entered into a written agreement (the Guarantee Agreement) designed to give Borrower time to recover from his temporary financial difficulties. Dated June 6, 2022, the Guarantee Agreement refers to the agreement between Lender and Borrower as the "CREDIT/SALE AGREEMENT," and it contains the following statement of mutual obligations:

> 1. LENDER will refrain from asserting his claim against BORROWER and from demanding payment on the CREDIT/ SALE AGREEMENT until LENDER needs the money.
>
> 2. In the event that BORROWER fails to pay all amounts due under the CREDIT/SALE AGREEMENT upon demand by LENDER, GUARANTOR will pay those amounts immediately and will pay further installments as they become due under the CREDIT/SALE AGREEMENT.

On July 1, 2022, Lender demanded payment from Borrower of sums due from May through July, but Borrower explained that he could not yet pay anything. On July 5, 2022, Lender demanded immediate payment of $30,000 from Guarantor; he also stated that he expects either Borrower or Guarantor to pay the remaining five installments as they become due on the first of each month. Borrower states that he will not be able to make further payments for at least the remainder of this year, and Guarantor hopes to avoid responsibility for the debt.

We do not yet have any evidence that Lender engaged in fraud during formation of the Guarantee Agreement or that he lacked a genuine "need" for the money in early July. You have asked me to analyze the question whether the Guarantee Contract is unenforceable on its face for lack of consideration.

IV. Discussion

Lender's promise to refrain from asserting his claim and demanding payment until he "needs the money" arguably is illusory. If so, Guarantor's promise is not supported by consideration and is unenforceable.

An enforceable contract requires consideration in the form of a bargained-for exchange in which a promisor exchanges his own promise for a return promise or performance. *Smith v. Newman*, 161 Calz. 443, 447, 667 P.2d 81, 85 (1984). The exchange can satisfy the consideration requirement even if one party's promise runs solely to the benefit of a third party rather than to the other party to the contract. *Id.* The requirement of an exchange, however, is not satisfied if one party gives only an illusory promise, which does not commit the promisor to any future performance. *Atco Corp. v. Johnson*, 155 Calz. 1211, 627 P.2d 781 (1980).

In *Atco Corp.*, the manager of an automobile repair shop purportedly promised to delay asserting a claim against the owner of an automobile for $900 in repairs. Specifically, he promised to forbear from asserting the claim "until I want the money." In exchange, a friend of the owner promised to act as guarantor of the owner's obligation. *Id.* at 1212, 627 P.2d at 782. The word "want" stated no legal commitment because it permitted the manager at his own discretion to refuse to perform any forbearance at all. Because the manager incurred no obligation, the guarantor's promise was gratuitous and unenforceable. *See id.* at 1213-14, 627 P.2d at 783-84.

On the other hand, even if a promise leaves open the possibility that the promisor will escape obligation, the promise is valid if the promisor does not have complete control over the events on which the promisor's obligation is conditioned. *Bonnie v. DeLaney*, 158 Calz. 212, 645 P.2d 887 (1982). In *Bonnie*, an agreement for the sale of a house provided that the buyer could cancel the agreement if the buyer "cannot qualify for a 30-year mortgage loan for 90% of the sales price" with any of several banks listed in the agreement. *Id.* at 213, 645 P.2d at 888. In enforcing the agreement against the seller, the court distinguished *Atco Corp.* because the word "cannot" referred to the buyer's ability to obtain a loan rather than to his desire. Because his ability to obtain a loan was partly controlled by events and decisions outside his control, the promises in the sale agreement were nonillusory and binding. *Id.* at 214-15, 645 P.2d at 889-90.

Despite the superficial similarity of guarantee agreements in both our case and *Atco. Corp.*, our client's case probably is more nearly analogous to *Bonnie*. Lender's promise to forbear until he "needs" the money appears to condition the length of his forbearance on financial events that are at least partly outside his control: So long as his income and expenses create no need for the money, Lender has a commitment to forbear from demanding payment.

To convince a court to draw an analogy to *Atco Corp.* rather than to *Bonnie*, we could argue that the word "need" refers to a subjective perception of deprivation that is inseparable from one's desires. Lender arguably can control his financial needs through his personal spending decisions, subject only to his own discretion.

Unfortunately for Guarantor, the analogy to *Bonnie* is stronger because financial need is normally viewed as a matter that is controlled at least partly by external factors. Lender's promise probably is not illusory.

V. Conclusion

The promises stated in the Guarantee Agreement appear to satisfy the consideration requirement, because Lender assumed a legal obligation by promising to refrain from asserting his claim and demanding payment until he "needs" the money. Unless we discover other serious defects in the Guarantee Agreement or Lender's performance of it, Guarantor appears to be obligated to pay, and her defenses will not be worth litigating. We should urge Guarantor to settle Lender's claim, and we should try to persuade Borrower to indemnify Guarantor and to assume responsibility for further payments, even if he must sell the cars or other property to generate funds.

Questions on Sample Memorandum 1

a. Did the substantive labels assigned to the parties serve as helpful reminders of the respective roles of the parties, or would you have retained the parties' last names as less distracting references?

b. Does the statement of facts include any facts that you would omit or summarize further? Does it omit any important facts to which the author likely had access?

c. Identify the parts of the "Discussion" section that illuminate the issue, discuss the legal standards, analyze the facts, and state a conclusion.

d. Do you agree with the author's analysis? Does it adequately explore both sides of the dispute? Is it too pessimistic?

2. Sample 2: Essay Exam Answer to Problem in Office Memo 1

The skills that you develop when writing an office memorandum will directly transfer to your law school essay exams, and eventually the bar exam. The example below applies the analytical paradigm of the office memorandum Discussion section to an essay exam answer.

Imagine that the dispute described in the fact statement of Office Memo 1 formed the basis for an essay exam question. A good essay answer might look like the Discussion section of the office memorandum, in a more simplified format. In many courses, for example, the examination answer normally would omit citations and in-depth case analysis.

Identify the elements of IRAC in the following sample:

Q1

. . . .

Lender v. Guarantor

Consideration – Illusory Promise: The lender's promise to refrain from asserting his claim and demanding payment until he "needs the money" arguably is illusory, thus creating doubt about whether the guarantor's promise is enforceable.

An enforceable contract requires a bargained-for exchange in which a promisor exchanges his own promise for a return promise or performance. The requirement of an exchange is not satisfied if one party gives only an illusory promise, which does not commit the promisor to any future performance. Even if a promise leaves open the possibility that the promisor will escape obligation, however, the promise is valid if the promisor does not have complete control over the events on which the promisor's obligation is conditioned.

The lender's promise to forbear until he "needs" the money appears to condition the length of his forbearance on financial events that are at least partly outside his control: So long as his income and expenses created no need for the money, the lender had a commitment to forbear from demanding payment. In an effort to escape obligations, the guarantor could argue that the lender could create financial need at his whim by spending money, or that the word "need" refers to a subjective perception of deprivation that is inseparable from one's desires, which are subject to the promisor's unfettered discretion. More than "want," however, the word "need" normally is viewed as a matter that is subject to the influence of external events. Because the formality of the written agreement suggests that the parties must have intended to create binding obligations, a court probably would interpret the word "need" to impose objective restrictions on the lender's rights and conduct, thereby satisfying the consideration requirement and making the guarantor's promise enforceable.

On balance, I conclude . . . .

3. Sample 3: E-Memo 1

Now imagine that your assigning attorney asked you for a short follow-up memo on a single facet of the office memorandum in Sample 1 above. The following sample assumes that your follow-up analysis is sufficiently short and simple to convey in the body of an email.

From: James Nelson
Sent: Wednesday, August 07, 2022 11:39 A.M.
To: Susan Elias
Subject: Follow-up on File 22 -127: Consideration in Absence of Direct Benefit to Guarantor
Attachments [pdf of *Green v. Day*, or link to a webpage that presents it]

Hello Susan,

Below is my analysis of the consideration issue you assigned to me this morning.

ASSIGNMENT:

You asked me to:

(1) assume the facts as stated in my legal memorandum dated July 31 and

(2) determine whether Guarantor's promise to guarantee payment of Borrower's debt lacks consideration because Lender's "return" promise provided no benefit directly to Guarantor.

CONCLUSION:

Consideration can consist of a promise to provide a service to a third party. Therefore, a commitment by Lender to delay asserting his claim against Borrower could provide consideration for Guarantor's promise. It does not matter that Lender's performance would not directly benefit Guarantor.

ANALYSIS:

Lender's promise to delay collecting a debt from a third party, such as Borrower, can be exchanged for Guarantor's promise to Lender. *See Green v. Day*, 175 Calz. 32, 37, 865 P.2d 1204, 1209 (1993) (finding consideration in similar guarantee context). If Guarantor sought Lender's promise in exchange for her own, it is irrelevant whether she received a direct benefit from Lender's performance of the promise. *Id.* at 38, 865 P.2d at 1210 (citing to Restatement (Second) of Contracts §§71(2), 79 (1981)).

RECOMMENDATION:

On the facts currently known to us, Guarantor's best argument remains her claim that Lender's promise is illusory. As explained in the main memorandum, however, the claim of illusory promise is a relatively weak argument, because the phrase "until Lender needs the money" is not easily interpreted to leave Lender's performance to his unrestricted discretion. Nonetheless, it may introduce enough uncertainty regarding consideration to convince Lender to compromise his claim against Guarantor in a reasonable settlement.

4. Sample 4: Alternative Presentation of E-Memo 1, with Nontraditional Spacing and Paragraphing

From: James Nelson
Sent: Wednesday, August 07, 2022 11:39 A.M.
To: Susan Elias
Subject: Follow-up on File 22 -127: Consideration in Absence of Direct Benefit to Guarantor
Attachments [electronic copy of *Green v. Day*]

Susan,

Please see my analysis below of the consideration issue you assigned to me this morning.

ASSIGNMENT

You asked me to:

(1) assume the facts as stated in my legal memorandum dated July 31, and

(2) determine whether Guarantor's promise to guarantee payment of Borrower's debt lacks consideration because Lender's "return" promise provided no benefit directly to Guarantor.

CONCLUSION

Consideration can consist of a promise to provide a service to a third party. Therefore, t he guarantee promise is supported by consideration even if Guarantor received no direct benefit in return.

ANALYSIS

The absence of a direct benefit from Lender to Guarantor does not undermine a finding of consideration:

* Lender's promise to delay collecting a debt from a third party, such as Borrower, can be exchanged for Guarantor's promise to Lender.

See Green v. Day, 175 Calz. 32, 37, 865 P.2d 1204, 1209 (1993) (finding consideration in similar guarantee context).

* If Guarantor sought Lender's promise in exchange for her own, it is irrelevant whether she received a direct benefit from Lender's performance of the promise.

Id. at 38, 865 P.2d at 1210 (citing to Restatement (Second) of Contracts §§ 71(2), 79 (1981)).

RECOMMENDATION

The additional research does not change the conclusion of the July 31 memo:

* On the facts currently known to us, Guarantor's best argument remains her claim that Lender's promise is illusory.

* As explained in the main memorandum, however, the claim of illusory promise is a relatively weak argument, because the phrase "until Lender needs the money" is not easily interpreted to leave Lender's performance to his unrestricted discretion.

* Nonetheless, it may introduce enough uncertainty regarding consideration to convince Lender to compromise his claim against Guarantor in a reasonable settlement.

5. Sample 5: Office Memorandum 2

The following memorandum, which is set in a fictitious jurisdiction, borrows from examples set forth in previous sections of this chapter addressing individual elements of a traditional office memorandum.

Memorandum

TO:	James Clapton
FROM:	Ginger Jackson
RE:	Souza v. Humane; strict liability and negligence—File No. 22 -63
DATE:	September 9, 2022

I. Questions Presented

A. Under New Maine's strict liability statute, d oes the phrase "any toxic material" encompass a generally safe anesthetic that produced a fatal reaction in a patient with a rare nerve disorder?

B. Is Humane Hospital liable to Souza's estate for negligent administration of the anesthetic?

1. Did Humane's anesthesiologist breach a duty of care by administering the anesthetic without assistance and by failing to monitor Souza's reactions to anesthesia?

2. Did Souza's nerve disorder constitute a supervening cause that broke the chain of causation between the anesthesiologist's conduct and Souza's death?

II. Brief Answers

A. Probably no. A restrictive interpretation is supported by the legislative history and by a general public policy in New Maine encouraging the provision of affordable medical services. The legislature probably did not intend the statutory term "toxic material" to include medically prescribed substances that ordinarily produce a beneficial result or otherwise facilitate medical treatment.

B. Probably yes.

1. Probably yes. Under generally accepted hospital procedures, at least two trained medical personnel must monitor the administration of anesthesia, with at least one person monitoring the patient's reactions. In this case, a jury likely will find that the anesthesiologist breached a duty of care to the patient by administering the anesthesia alone.

2. Probably no. The jury likely will also find that the patient's nerve disorder was not a supervening cause and that the anesthesiologist's negligence proximately caused the patient's death.

III. Facts

On February 17, 2022, our client, Humane Hospital, Inc. (Humane), admitted 22-year-old Teresa Souza to its facility in Greenville, New Maine, for surgery to correct a bone deformity in her foot. Souza's bone deformity was not life threatening, but it severely hampered her mobility. The planned surgery required general anesthesia.

Dr. Roberta Unger, an anesthesiologist for Humane, studied Souza's medical history and discovered that she suffered from a rare nerve disorder that slightly increased the risk that she would suffer an adverse reaction from anesthesia. Unger carefully informed Souza of the advantages and risks associated with each of the three safest and most effective general anesthetics. Souza decided to proceed with the operation and with the administration of general anesthesia. Unger and Souza ultimately agreed that Unger would administer ethane, a widely used and generally safe form of ether. Unger had initially recommended Forane, a potent muscle relaxant that maintains a stable heart rate. Souza, however, rejected Forane because of its greater cost.

At 10:00 A.M. on February 18, Souza was prepared for surgery. While the circulating nurse was occupied with another patient, and before the surgical team arrived, Unger began administering the prescribed anesthetic to Souza. Unger and Souza were alone in the room. Apparently because she was concerned that an overdose might trigger an adverse reaction, Unger concentrated intensely on the anesthetic intake gauge, which monitored the flow of anesthetic. Consequently, she failed to watch either Souza or the equipment monitoring Souza's reactions. Approximately one minute after Unger began administering the anesthetic, the monitoring equipment sounded an alarm, as Souza's heart stopped beating. Efforts to revive her failed. According to computer records, the monitoring equipment reflected growing signs of distress in Souza beginning approximately 10 seconds before her death and before the alarm sounded.

An autopsy showed that the anesthetic combined with Souza's nerve disorder to trigger a reaction that caused cardiac arrest. Mary L. Richards, Ph.D., a professor at the University of New Maine School of Nursing, has told us that hospitals throughout the nation ordinarily require the anesthesiologist to be accompanied by a nurse during the administration of anesthesia. Both the nurse and the anesthesiologist are expected to continuously assess the patient's reaction to anesthesia by reading monitoring equipment and by observing the patient directly. Although she cannot be certain, Richards guesses that the fatal reaction was triggered largely by the final 10 seconds of Unger's administration of anesthesia.

Souza's estate has sued Humane in tort for wrongful death. It advances two theories of tort liability: (1) statutory strict liability for use of toxic materials and (2) negligence in the administration of the anesthetic.

IV. Discussion

A. Strict Liability for Use of Toxic Materials

If a statute or the common law imposes strict liability for Souza's death, then Souza's estate can establish liability without proving negligence. New Maine's common law doctrine of strict liability for injuries caused by ultrahazardous activities does not apply to noncriminal medical practices engaged in by licensed physicians. *Stanislaus v. Good Samaritan Hosp.*, 212 N. Me. 113, 115 (1989). New Maine has enacted a statute, however, that imposes strict liability for injuries stemming from the use of "any toxic material": "A commercial enterprise is liable for injuries proximately caused by its use of any toxic material, without regard to the degree of care exercised by the enterprise." 12 N. Me. Rev. Stat. Ann. § 242 (rev. 2021) (effective Jan. 1, 2022).

The New Maine courts have not yet had an opportunity to interpret the strict liability statute in a published opinion. As a profit-making hospital, Humane presumably is a "commercial enterprise" within the meaning of the statute. It is less certain, however, that the anesthetic administered to Souza would qualify as a "toxic" material.

The common meaning of the word "toxic" is "poisonous." *E.g.*, *The Random House Dictionary of the English Language* 1500 (unabridged) (1970). Souza's estate might plausibly argue that the anesthetic was a toxic material because it was poisonous to Souza, even though it would not have been poisonous to most others. The word "toxic," however, applies more naturally to substances that are universally harmful to humans, such as cyanide, DDT, or sulfuric acid. It strains the common meaning of "toxic" to apply it to an anesthetic that might occasionally be harmful to persons with unusual allergies or other extraordinary conditions.

Legislative history also supports a restrictive interpretation of the statutory term "any toxic material." The report of the New Maine Senate Committee on Health and Welfare suggests that the legislature was concerned only with the deadliest of substances:

> The purpose of this bill is to reallocate the cost of unavoidable accidents from victims to industry and its consumers, to discourage unnecessary use of deadly chemicals and other hazardous materials, and to encourage the development and use of substitute materials that are generally safe for human contact.

N. Me. Comm. on Health and Welfare, S. 78-112, 2d Sess., at 2 (2021). The anesthetic in this case is closer to the materials "generally safe for human contact" condoned by the legislature than it is to the "deadly chemicals and other hazardous materials" condemned by it.

Finally, general state policy appears to support an interpretation that excludes medically prescribed substances from the reach of the statute. The legislature and judiciary of New Maine have recognized a policy of limiting the liability of physicians to encourage the ready availability of affordable medical services. For example, under the New Maine "Good Samaritan" statute, physicians who provide certain emergency medical services are not liable for adverse consequences unless they engage in culpable conduct amounting to at least gross negligence. 12 N. Me. Rev. Stat. §229 (2010). This protective policy is also reflected in the courts' refusal to extend common law strict liability for ultrahazardous activities to even experimental medical practices. *See Stanislaus*, 212 N. Me. at 115. The legislature presumably was aware of these laws when it enacted the toxic materials statute in 2021.

Souza's estate may argue that the legislature intended to retreat from the protective policies of these laws by imposing strict liability on a limited segment of the activities of commercial medical practices. Absent more specific evidence of legislative intent to depart from existing legal policies, however, it is more likely that the legislature retained its protective attitude and assumed that the term "any toxic material" would not include routinely prescribed medicines or anesthetics.

In this case, the prescribed anesthetic, ethane, was not the safest available at the time of Souza's operation. Nonetheless, it is a frequently prescribed substance that produces beneficial results with only minor side effects in all but the most unusual cases. The strict liability statute probably does not apply to Souza's death.

B. Negligence

Assuming Humane is not strictly liable for Souza's death, it may nonetheless be liable to Souza's estate if its agent caused the death through negligence. *See Kityama v. Mercy Hosp.*, 183 N. Me. 752, 759-60 (1974) (hospital liable for negligence of its nurse). An action for negligence requires proof of a negligent act or omission that proximately causes injury. *Baker v. Bruce*, 153 N. Me. 817, 820 (1967).

In our case, the injury to Souza is obvious. In greater doubt are the elements of negligent act and proximate cause.

1. Negligent Act

A negligent act or omission consists of the breach of a duty of care owed to another. *Id.* at 821. A medical specialist owes a duty to patients to exercise at least the ordinary skill and care that is reasonable and customary nationwide in that medical specialty. *Kityama*, 183 N. Me. at 760. Furthermore, under the "thin-skulled plaintiff" rule, that duty of care encompasses the special care necessary to address increased risks created by a patient's unusual susceptibility to injury. *Id.* In this case, Humane's anesthesiologist, Unger, may have breached duties of care in her unassisted administration of general anesthesia in the face of Souza's known nerve condition.

Unger exercised care in determining Souza's disorder of the nervous system and in informing her of the risks presented by each of the most suitable anesthetics. Moreover, when administering the anesthetic selected by Souza, Unger took care to provide the prescribed dosage by monitoring the anesthetic intake gauge.

On the other hand, Unger's intense concentration on the anesthetic intake gauge may have been an act of carelessness, rather than enhanced care, because it diverted Unger's attention from Souza and from the equipment monitoring Souza's vital signs. Faced with Souza's known nervous disorder, Unger probably had a duty to follow the standard medical practice of summoning a nurse to assist her in administering the anesthesia. Had she done so, the team could have monitored both Souza's vital signs and the intake gauge, and a team member undoubtedly would have detected signs of distress at least 10 seconds before death, arguably enough time to cease anesthesia and take corrective measures.

On these facts, a jury could find that Unger was negligent in her administration of the anesthetic.

2. Proximate Cause

Even if its agent was negligent, Humane will not be liable to Souza's estate unless the negligence proximately caused Souza's death. *See, e.g.*, *Baker v. Bruce*, 153 N. Me. 817, 821 (1967). Proximate cause is a flexible doctrine that precludes liability if the relationship between negligence and an injury is so attenuated that it would be unfair to hold the negligent party responsible for the injury. *Id.* at 821-22.

In this case, Humane can argue that the signs of distress appearing for 10 seconds on the monitoring equipment prior to the alarm would not have given even two observant medical workers sufficient time to reverse Souza's fatal reaction. If so, even careful administration of anesthesia would have resulted in death, suggesting that Souza's reaction was truly an unforeseeable accident rather than the proximate result of any negligent act. Unfortunately, the factual premise of this argument may be unsound: According to our own expert, cessation of the anesthesia at the first signs of distress could have prevented the fatal reaction. We may want to investigate this further with other experts.

As a fallback position on proximate cause, Humane could try to characterize Souza's rare nerve condition as a supervening cause. Such an intervening cause may break the chain of causation between the negligence and the injury, particularly if the intervening event was unexpected. *See Safehouse Ins. Co. v. Rainbow Landscaping Co.*, 223 N. Me. 29, 31, 35 (1987) (dictum). Unfortunately, a court may be reluctant to analyze this issue within the framework of supervening cause. Under the more conventional approach, a court would simply apply the "thin-skulled plaintiff" rule to expand Unger's duty of care to encompass responsibility for increased risks of injury created by Souza's known nerve condition. However, if we can persuade the court to depart from the conventional approach and to analyze the increased risk within the less clearly applicable framework of supervening cause, we will gain the opportunity to develop an additional argument to avoid liability.

To develop a supervening-cause argument, we must distinguish *Rainbow Landscaping*, which liberally allocates the risks of some intervening causes to the tortfeasor. In *Rainbow Landscaping*, a landscaping company agreed in writing with a general contractor to install a sprinkler system in the yards surrounding a new house in its final stages of construction. The written contract specifically obligated the landscaper to perform its work "in a manner that does not interfere with the ongoing work of other subcontractors or deface their finished product." *Id.* at 32. On the day that the landscaper began its work, its employees knew that another subcontractor was painting the interior of the house. While welding a sprinkler pipe to a house water line, an employee of the landscaper ignited paint fumes that had accumulated in a room recently painted by the painting subcontractor. The resulting fire entirely destroyed the nearly completed house.

In a suit brought against the landscaper by the owner's insurer, the landscaper argued on its motion for a directed verdict that, even if the landscaper had acted negligently, the paint fumes constituted an intervening cause that precluded a finding of proximate cause. The trial court denied the motion, and the jury returned a verdict for the insurer. The New Maine Supreme Court affirmed. It held that the landscaper was responsible for the consequences of the combustion of paint fumes that it had triggered because its employee should have been aware of the paint fumes and the danger they posed. *Id.* at 35. In dictum, the court stated that it might have reached a different result had the landscaper reasonably failed to foresee that the welding could trigger such a blaze. *See id.*

We can try to distinguish our case from *Rainbow Landscaping* by arguing that the landscaper's agreement to accommodate the work of other subcontractors justified the finding that the landscaper should have known of the hazard. Under this reasoning, the agreement was critical to the allocation of responsibility to the landscaper for the consequences of igniting the paint. That contract has no direct counterpart in our case. Moreover, in light of New Maine's policy of limiting the liability of medical care providers, a court might be willing to apply the doctrine of proximate cause more stringently in a hospital setting than in a construction setting.

On the other hand, although Souza's adverse reaction to the anesthetic was not highly probable, it was certainly foreseeable as a possible consequence of Souza's known nerve condition. Indeed, Unger's intense concentration on the intake gauge shows that she indeed specifically anticipated such a reaction. The absence of a contract such as the one in *Rainbow Landscaping* might be viewed as a technical and immaterial distinction.

Therefore, even if we can persuade a court to analyze Souza's nerve condition within the framework of supervening cause, the court probably will not find the doctrine satisfied on the facts of this case. If Souza's estate can prove that Unger was negligent, it almost certainly can show proximate cause as well.

V. Conclusion

Because legislative and judicial policies favor limits on physicians' liability, the strict liability statute regulating toxic materials probably will not apply to the administration of the anesthetic in this case. The courts will be even less likely to retreat from precedent by applying the common law doctrine imposing strict liability for ultrahazardous activities. A jury could find, however, that Humane's anesthesiologist was negligent in failing to summon assistance for the administration of the anesthesia and to monitor Souza more closely. We can try to characterize Souza's nerve condition as a supervening cause, but *Rainbow Landscaping* will not be easy to distinguish.

Because the risk of substantial liability is great, I recommend that we advise Humane to settle. Souza's estate may be willing to compromise; its negligence claim is not appropriate for summary disposition and thus is subject to the unpredictability of a jury.

Questions on Office Memorandum 2

a. Distinguish between the statutory and common law claims discussed in Office Memorandum 2. How does the legal method differ in the analysis of each claim?

b. Review the statutory analysis in section IV.A of Office Memorandum 2. Its original analysis of language, legislative history, and policy is indispensable precisely because no court had yet interpreted the statute. Imagine instead that the author of the memorandum had found a New Maine case that discusses the applicability of the strict liability statute to a restaurant that sold raw oysters infected with the vibrio vulnificus bacteria. Most oysters naturally absorb these bacteria, and almost all persons who ingest the bacteria after eating raw oysters suffer no ill effects. However, in a tiny percentage of persons, particularly those with liver or kidney problems, the bacteria can lead to septicemia, which often results in death. In the New

Maine case, *Spratt v. Shuck*, a man developed a bacterial infection and died after eating raw oysters served in a restaurant.[9]

Imagine that the New Maine Supreme Court examined the language, legislative history, and policy of the New Maine statute governing strict liability for toxic materials. Imagine further that it found that a raw oyster infected with the vibrio vulnificus bacteria is not a "toxic material" within the meaning of the statute. Would the author of the memorandum discuss the issue of statutory liability in the same manner if a case like *Spratt v. Shuck* were available? Would he rely as heavily on his own analysis of language, legislative history, and policy? How would the analysis differ if it focused on case law such as *Spratt v. Shuck*?

c. Review the subsection discussing the element of proximate cause in a negligence action. Note how the author of the memorandum seeks to manipulate the analytical framework within which to address the legal consequences of Souza's unusual nerve condition. Is this a fair method of argument? Can it be used in other contexts? Most professors of Tort Law readily conclude that a court would analyze Souza's nerve condition within the "thin-skulled plaintiff" rule regarding the scope of duties and not within the framework of proximate cause. In that light, is the argument in the memorandum a welcome exercise in creative argument, or is it a misleading waste of time for the reader?

d. Notice the frequent use of the word "we" in the section on proximate cause. Should the author of a memorandum avoid using such first-person pronouns in a legal analysis? Are first-person pronouns appropriate when referring to the law firm's development of facts or legal theories? Are they better than passive voice or other abstractions?

6. Sample 6: E-Memo 2

From: Ginger Jackson
Sent: Wednesday, November 13, 2021 3:19 P.M.
To: James Clapton
Subject: New Strict Liability Statute for use of Toxic Materials, as Applied to Anesthesia
Attachments [Word file of this e-memo]

James,

Below is my analysis of the strict liability statute's definition of toxic materials as it applies to anesthesia. Please let me know if you have any questions or if you'd like me to conduct additional research.

I. Overview: Background and Issue

Our client, Humane Hospital ("Humane"), is concerned about recent legislation in New Maine. When it becomes effective January 1, 2022, it will impose strict liability for injuries caused by commercial use of toxic materials. Humane is particularly concerned about liability for careful administration of anesthesia to a patient who has an unexpected adverse reaction.

You asked me to address the following issue:

Does the phrase "any toxic material" in New Maine's strict liability statute encompass a generally safe anesthetic that produces a fatal reaction in a patient with a rare and previously undetected intolerance for the anesthetic?

II. Conclusion

Based on the statutory text, legislative history, and state policy, the new legislation almost certainly will apply only to substances that are generally poisonous or otherwise hazardous to health. Humane can safely conclude that its administration of anesthesia will not trigger strict liability under the new statute.

III. Discussion

New Maine recently enacted a statute that imposes strict liability for injuries stemming from the use of "any toxic material": "A commercial enterprise is liable for injuries proximately caused by its use of any toxic material, without regard to the degree of care exercised by the enterprise." 12 N. Me. Rev. Stat. Ann. § 242 (rev. 2021) (effective Jan. 1, 2022).

The common meaning of the word "toxic" is "poisonous." *E.g.*, *The Random House Dictionary of the English Language* 1500 (unabridged) (1970). A generally safe anesthetic conceivably could be viewed as a toxic material under this definition because it could produce a fatal reaction in some patients with a rare intolerance for the anesthetic. The word "toxic," however, applies more naturally to substances that are universally harmful to humans, such as cyanide, DDT, or sulfuric acid. It strains the common meaning of "toxic" to apply it to an anesthetic that might occasionally be harmful to persons with unusual allergies or other extraordinary conditions.

Legislative history also supports a restrictive interpretation of the statutory term "any toxic material." The report of the New Maine Senate Committee on Health and Welfare suggests that the legislature was concerned only with the deadliest of substances:

> The purpose of this bill is to reallocate the cost of unavoidable accidents from victims to industry and its consumers, to discourage unnecessary use of deadly chemicals and other hazardous materials, and to encourage the development and use of substitute materials that are generally safe for human contact.

N. Me. Comm. on Health and Welfare, S. 78-112, 2d Sess., at 2 (2021). The anesthetic in this case is closer to the materials "generally safe for human contact" condoned by the legislature than it is to the "deadly chemicals and other hazardous materials" condemned by it.

Finally, the legislature and judiciary of New Maine have recognized a policy of limiting the liability of physicians to encourage the ready availability of affordable medical services. For example, under the New Maine "Good Samaritan" statute, physicians who provide certain emergency medical services are not liable for adverse consequences unless they engage in culpable conduct amounting to at least gross negligence. 12 N. Me. Rev. Stat. § 229 (2010). This protective policy is also reflected in the courts' refusal to extend common law strict liability for ultrahazardous activities to even experimental medical practices. *See Stanislaus v. Good Samaritan Hosp.*, 212 N. Me. 113, 115 (1989). The legislature presumably was aware of these laws when it enacted the toxic materials statute in 2017. Absent evidence of legislative intent to depart from these legal policies, it is likely that the legislature retained its protective attitude toward the medical profession and assumed that the term "any toxic material" would not include routinely prescribed medicines or anesthetics.

IV. Recommendation

The new statute almost certainly will not impose strict liability for injuries stemming from Humane's administration of generally safe medical procedures such as anesthesia. Thus, negligence will remain the only basis for tort liability stemming from Humane's delivery of medical services. Accordingly, we should advise Humane to avoid negligence by continuing to exercise the utmost care with patients, such as by informing patients of known risks, allowing the patient to choose between alternative treatments when appropriate, and refraining from administering an anesthetic to a patient with a known allergy or intolerance to that anesthetic.

We should monitor our state's case law for any judicial interpretations of the statute, to determine whether we should update our analysis and advice.

Checklist for Chapter 7

- Depending on the nature of the assignment, determine whether you will give an oral presentation, send a short but formal e-memo, or develop a full office memorandum.
- For a full office memorandum, choose a suitable format, such as the following:

  I. Issues
  II. Brief Answers
  III. Facts
  IV. Discussion
  V. Conclusion
- Some sections of the memorandum will partially repeat information from earlier sections, although in different form and depth, to achieve different goals.
- As you draft your office memoranda, remember your audience and purpose.
  - Your goal is to inform an assigning attorney, who typically is preparing to represent a client.
  - The supervisor usually needs a balanced analysis, one that considers the strongest arguments on each side of the legal issue.
  - Nonetheless, the analysis should explore means of overcoming obstacles to the client's claims or defenses, and it should predict the outcome.
- Be certain to cover the elements of IRAC in the discussion section of your memorandum:
  - for each issue or subissue,
  - construct a synthesized rule, and illustrate the rule with complete but succinct case summaries,
  - apply the rule to the facts of your case, comparing your case with the facts and reasoning of precedents when helpful, and
  - reach a conclusion.

Endnotes

1. *See* Kristen Konrad Robbins-Tiscione, *From Snail Mail to E-Mail: The Traditional Legal Memorandum in the Twenty-First Century*, 58 J. LEGAL EDUC. 32 (2008) (reporting on survey of graduates of Georgetown University Law Center regarding the growing use of short and simplified office memos, which can be easily emailed).
2. *See generally* Brad Desnoyer, *E-Memos 2.0: An Empirical Study of How Attorneys Write*, 25 LEG. WRITING 213, 219-21 (2021).
3. *See, e.g.*, Walker & Co. v. Harrison, 347 Mich. 630, 81 N.W.2d 352 (1957) (lessee of commercial neon sign committed first material breach by unilaterally terminating contract when the lessor's failure to maintain the sign amounted to only a minor breach, rather than a material one).
4. *See id.*; RESTATEMENT (SECOND) OF CONTRACTS § 241 (1981) (listing factors relevant to determination of whether breach is material or only minor).
5. *See* RESTATEMENT (SECOND) OF CONTRACTS § 350(1) (1981).
6. 42 U.S.C. §§ 2000e(b) (definition of "employer"), 2000e-2(a) (unlawful employer practices) (2019); *see also* §§ 2000e(g) and (h) (definitions of "commerce" and "industry affecting commerce").
7. *See* Bryan A. Garner, THE WINNING BRIEF: 100 TIPS FOR PERSUASIVE BRIEFING IN TRIAL AND APPELLATE COURTS 92-97 (2d ed. 2004) ("Rule 12: Weave facts into your issues to make them concrete."); Bryan A. Garner, *The Deep Issue: A New Approach to Framing Legal Questions*, 5 SCRIBES J. LEGAL WRITING 1 (1994-95).
8. Richard K. Neumann, Jr., & Kristen Konrad Robbins-Tiscione, LEGAL REASONING AND LEGAL WRITING § 12-2, at 145-47 (7th ed. 2013) (discussing rule proof and explanation and mentioning both "CREAC" and "CRuPAC"); *see* Linda H. Edwards, LEGAL WRITING: PROCESS, ANALYSIS, AND ORGANIZATION 91-96 (5th ed. 2010) (introducing and discussing "rule explanation").
9. The facts for this fictitious case are inspired by those of Simeon v. Doe, 618 So. 2d 848 (La. 1993).

Chapter 8

Organization of Office Memoranda and Briefs

One of the most important features of effective legal analysis and writing is good organization. Techniques of organization are also among the most difficult things to develop and to teach. With a few months of practice, you will steadily improve your skills.

You can develop some basic skills of organization by creating your own outlines of course material, in preparation for law school examinations. By doing so, you will develop skills of classification and organization that you can transfer to office memoranda and briefs. You can find instruction on outlining course material in books on study skills, including one written by a co-author of this book: Charles R. Calleros, LAW SCHOOL AND EXAMS: PREPARING AND WRITING TO WIN (3d ed. 2021).

Although the focus of Part IV is objective analysis in office memoranda, the techniques of organization described in this chapter apply directly to both office memoranda and legal briefs. Accordingly, this chapter uses examples from both predictive and persuasive writing. The following sections explore problems of organization on four different levels, progressing from broader problems of (1) format and (2) relationships among multiple issues, to narrower problems of (3) progression within sections and (4) effective paragraphing.

I. Format

Before drafting any legal document, you must select an appropriate format for the document. The format will determine the essential content of the document and the order in which you present the different parts of that content.

Rules of procedure and local court rules prescribe formats for appellate briefs. With somewhat less detail, they also prescribe or suggest formats for trial pleadings, motions, and briefs. You must follow these rules carefully, because they presumably reflect the court's views about effective content and administrative efficiency. If you depart from the prescribed format, you could irritate the judge or judges who must read the document. Indeed, you might even lead the judge or the clerk's office to reject the document for filing or to impose other sanctions.[1]

The most appropriate format for other documents, such as a contract or an office memorandum, is partly a matter of judgment or style for you or your law firm. For example, Section II of Chapter 7 outlines three different formats for a formal office memorandum; whether one is more appropriate to an assignment than another will depend on the complexity of the memorandum, the preferences of your assigning attorney, and your own personal style. Before beginning to write such a document, you should take a few moments to determine which format will best suit your audience, your personal style, and the purposes of the document.

II. Relationships among Multiple Issues and Subissues

Your statement of the issues and your discussion or argument section of an office memorandum or legal brief should reflect the proper relationships among multiple issues and subissues. Good organization at this broad level requires a thorough understanding of the substantive analysis as well as attention to effective writing techniques. Therefore, if you experience unusual difficulty with this level of organization, you should consider supplementing your research before proceeding further. By reviewing basic principles in a secondary source, you can gain a broad perspective that will help you organize your material.

A. Proper Relationships among Topics

Stated most simply, the section headings of the discussion or argument section of a document should show which topics are distinct and independent, and which are subsets of a more general topic. The statement of the issues should show the same relationships. These relationships are a function of the elements of the legal claims or defenses in question.

For example, suppose that you are preparing an office memorandum to discuss the following theories of employer liability for the discharge of an employee: (1) violation of a promise expressed in the company policy manual to invoke specified hearing procedures before terminating any employee, (2) wrongful discharge for a reason that violates public policy, and (3) intentional infliction of emotional distress.

The following information about the legal content of these claims in one state will help you devise an appropriate organizational structure. The elements of a contract action for breach of promise in a policy manual are (1) a promise in the manual by the employer to restrict the circumstances justifying discharge of the employee; (2) a basis for enforcing the promise, such as incorporation of the manual into the employment contract; and (3) breach of the promise.[2] The elements of the tort of wrongful discharge of an at-will employee in violation of public policy are (1) discharge of the employee (2) for a reason that contravenes a legislative public policy.[3] Finally, the elements of the tort of intentional infliction of emotional distress are (1) extreme and outrageous conduct (2) that is taken with the intent to cause emotional distress or with reckless disregard of the risk of causing such distress, and (3) that causes (4) severe emotional distress.[4]

Although organization of these topics is a matter of judgment rather than an exact science, most legal writers will agree that the following section headings of the discussion section of the memorandum leave room for improvement:

IV. DISCUSSION

A. Wrongful Discharge—Violation of Public Policy or Breach of Promise in Employee Manual

B. Intentional Infliction of Emotional Distress

1. Remedies

First, section A inappropriately encompasses two distinct kinds of claims. True, both claims represent theories of liability in an emerging field known generically as "wrongful discharge." Under this state's law, however, wrongful discharge in violation of public policy is a tort with different elements than those in a claim for breach of a contractual promise to restrict the grounds for terminating the employment contract.

Second, section B inappropriately includes a single subsection on remedies. If remedies were the only topic in section B, a subsection designation would be unnecessary. On the other hand, if section B discusses a theory of liability as well as remedies, both subtopics should be represented in subsection headings if either is. Finally, if the topic of remedies encompasses all of the theories of liability, it should not be buried within a section that addresses only the theory of intentional infliction of emotional distress.

You could address these defects and adopt an improved organizational structure such as the following:

IV. DISCUSSION

A. Breach of Contract
B. Wrongful Discharge in Violation of Public Policy
C. Intentional Infliction of Emotional Distress
D. Remedies

Of course, this sample outline represents only one of many reasonable organizational structures for the memorandum in question. Other organizational structures could reflect different ways of presenting the analysis of remedies. For example, you might recognize that sections A through C present various theories of liability and could be consolidated in a comprehensive section on the same level as the separate topic of remedies. Because the remedies for breach of contract are significantly different from those available for either of the tort claims, the section on remedies could discuss them separately:

IV. DISCUSSION

A. Theories of Liability
  1. Breach of Contract
  2. Wrongful Discharge in Violation of Public Policy
  3. Intentional Infliction of Emotional Distress
B. Remedies
  1. Contract
  2. Tort

Alternatively, you might decide to discuss remedies within each of the sections that introduces a theory of liability, rather than in a separate comprehensive section devoted to remedies. Under this organizational scheme, you could consolidate the two tort theories into a single section if you conclude that the remedies for each would be governed by the same tort principles. Depending on the depth of discussion in the memorandum, you could discuss remedies either in a paragraph at the end of each major section or, as shown below, in separate subsections.

IV. DISCUSSION
- A. Breach of Contract
  - 1. Breach of Promise in an Employee Manual
  - 2. Contract Remedies
- B. Tort
  - 1. Wrongful Discharge in Violation of Public Policy
  - 2. Intentional Infliction of Emotional Distress
  - 3. Tort Remedies

Each of these alternative approaches to organization properly displays relationships among topics in a logical manner. Whether one approach advances the purposes of the document better than another is a matter of judgment for the writer.

B. Order of Topics

1. Logical Organization in an Office Memorandum

In an office memorandum, you should organize your topics in a logical order so that early topics build a foundation for subsequent topics. The clearest example of this is a multiple-issue discussion in which some issues are "threshold issues" in the sense that the resolution of those issues affects the analysis of other issues. Logically, you should discuss the threshold issues before you discuss the issues that are dependent on the outcome of the threshold issues.

For example, suppose that Maya Tortilla Co. alleges that Bakeway Supermarkets (1) formed a contract with Maya; (2) breached its contractual obligations; (3) and is liable to Maya for $20,000 in damages. If Bakeway disputes each of these allegations, the parties have raised three entirely separate issues.

Logically, you should discuss issue #1 first because contract formation is a threshold issue: Bakeway did not assume any contractual obligations and consequent potential liability if it did not form a contract with Maya. Similarly, you should discuss issue #2 before issue #3 for two reasons. First, Bakeway is not liable for damages unless it breached. Second, to determine whether Bakeway breached, you must interpret the contract and define Bakeway's obligation. In turn, the scope of Bakeway's obligation will determine the value of Bakeway's promise to Maya, on which damages will be based.

2. Strategic Organization in a Brief

If you are drafting a brief rather than an office memorandum, you might organize your arguments differently, because strategic considerations could lead you to depart from a purely logical ordering of arguments. Like other people, judges are strongly influenced by first impressions. In many cases, the first argument in a brief influences the judge more strongly than later ones. Also, if pressed for time, a busy trial judge may find herself rushing through the last few pages of a brief before oral argument on a pretrial motion. Accordingly, if one of your arguments is much stronger than the others, you may present it first in your brief, even though another issue is logically prior.

3. Discussing or Arguing the Full Range of Issues

Finally, you should apply all these considerations only to order your topics effectively, not to omit discussing any of the issues. In a close case, you cannot predict with certainty how a court will resolve a threshold issue. Accordingly, even if you tentatively resolve the threshold issue in a way that logically would cut off discussion, you should address all the other substantial issues. In an office memorandum, for example, if you conclude that Bakeway probably did not breach the contract, you should nonetheless discuss the question of the amount of damages for which Bakeway will be liable if—contrary to your prediction—the judge or jury finds that Bakeway breached.

C. Technique

The most efficient way to organize the topics of a memorandum or brief is to outline them in the prewriting stage—after you have researched and analyzed the problem but before you begin to write. Even when you are working under severe time pressure, you should take a few minutes to organize your notes, think deeply and creatively about the analysis, and explore the relationships between topics by comparing different outlines of the discussion or argument. You can much more easily modify your analytical approach and writing strategy at the prewriting stage than you can midway through the first draft.

If you did not prepare an outline before writing the first draft, and if the first draft appears hopelessly disorganized, you can still derive benefits from outlining techniques, albeit with less efficiency than at the prewriting stage. By writing out the section and subsection headings of your first draft in outline form, you can expose and evaluate the organization of your draft and improve the organization by modifying the outline.

Finally, once you have chosen an organizational structure, you should clearly communicate that structure to the reader with descriptive section and subsection headings that at least roughly parallel the structure of the statement of issues. In an answer to a law school examination, such headings normally can take the place of more formal statements of the issues.

III. Progression within Section or Subsection

Once you have divided your topics into separate sections, you are ready to organize the discussion or argument within each section. At the most general level, your analysis should follow the familiar "IRAC" pattern of deductive reasoning: after introducing the issue or argument with a heading and perhaps with a brief introduction in the text, you should discuss or argue the law, apply that law to the facts, and reach a conclusion.

Effective progression within a section also requires attention to one or more of four considerations:

1. hierarchy of authority,
2. progression from general to specific,
3. progression from fundamental to uncertain, and
4. separation or consolidation of logical discussions or arguments.

The first three of these considerations deal mainly with the development of legal standards. The fourth deals with methods of combining legal and factual analysis.

A. Hierarchy of Authority

In statutory analysis, the hierarchy of authority leads to a convention of organization. You should analyze, or at least present, the statutory language in question before analyzing cases that either interpret the statute or that discuss supplemental common law:

> **C. Commercial Impracticability**
>
> The Uniform Commercial Code (UCC) provides that, in limited circumstances, a seller's failure to deliver goods is not a breach of contract "if performance as agreed has been made impracticable by the occurrence of a contingency the non-occurrence of which was a basic assumption on which the contract was made." U.C.C. §2-615(a) (2011). The UCC's use of the term "impracticable" suggests a more liberal standard for discharging obligations than the traditional common law standard of "impossibility of performance." *See Bjorn v. Borg* ....

The normal convention of starting with the statutory language will occasionally apply with less force when you present a well settled principle of constitutional law. Because constitutional provisions are typically even more general than statutory provisions, the enormous body of case law interpreting the text can take on a life of its own, overshadowing the text itself. Thus, you need not quote the language of the Fourth Amendment before explaining the general requirement that police must obtain a warrant before searching a house; reference to case law interpreting the Fourth Amendment in most cases will be sufficient. Nonetheless, you should begin the analysis by at least identifying the Fourth Amendment as the source of the restriction on searches. Moreover, some constitutional issues, like most issues of statutory interpretation, will be sufficiently novel to require attention to text. In such cases you should begin the analysis with the language of the constitutional provision.

B. Progression from General to Specific

Reading a legal analysis or argument should be like viewing a large painting in a museum exhibit. As the viewer enters the room, he sees the general outlines of the subject matter of the painting, and he becomes curious about a few provocative parts. He then moves closer to the painting to separately examine each of these parts. Finally, when he steps back for a final view of the entire painting, he might now appreciate it more fully because of his recent examination of the finer details.

Similarly, overlapping sections in a legal document can

1. provide an overview to the document,
2. separately explore important matters in some detail, and
3. conclude with a summary or with general insights that are easier to appreciate after the discussion of details.

On a broad level, a memorandum or brief performs these functions with (1) the statement of issues or other introduction, (2) the discussion or argument, and (3) the conclusion. On a narrower level, this kind of progression is often appropriate within a section of the discussion or argument.

For an example of progression within a section, let's assume that the plaintiff in a tort action alleges that the defendant intentionally inflicted emotional distress. Assume further that the defendant, your client, contends that the facts in the record fail to satisfy two of the elements of that tort. In such a case, your brief for the defendant might address each of those two elements separately, either in separate paragraphs or in separate subsections of the argument. If so, you can orient the reader by beginning with a paragraph that introduces each of the elements:

II. ARGUMENT

A. Lew's Allegations in Count II Fail to State a Claim for Intentional Infliction of Emotional Distress.

General overview

To establish a right to relief for intentional infliction of emotional distress, Lew must plead and prove that (1) Smith engaged in extreme and outrageous conduct (2) with the intent to cause severe emotional distress or with reckless disregard for the possibility of those consequences, and that (3) his actions caused Lew to suffer (4) severe emotional distress. *See Watts v. Golden Age Nursing Home*, 127 Ariz. 255, 619 P.2d 1032 (1980). Even assuming the truth of Lew's allegations about the manner in which Smith terminated Lew's employment contract, the complaint does not properly allege either the extreme conduct or the severe distress required for liability. Therefore, Lew has failed to state a claim for relief in Count II.

1. Smith's Alleged Conduct Was Not "Extreme and Outrageous."

Only the most deplorable and shocking conduct satisfies the narrow definition of "extreme and outrageous conduct." *Beers v. Bolton*,.... In *Beers*,....

Specific argument

In this case, the complaint alleges only that Smith was a blunt manager who exercised his contractual privilege to fire Lew without advance notice and who stated his reasons for firing him with utmost candor....

2. Lew's Alleged Depression Does Not Amount to Severe Emotional Distress.

Proof of severe emotional distress....

The introduction in the first paragraph above not only provides an overview of the legal standards, it summarizes the overall argument of the section. That argument appears elsewhere as well: the brief (1) states it concisely in the heading for section A; (2) develops it in greater detail in each of the subsections; and (3) should repeat it in general terms at the end of section A, in a separate conclusion section at the end of the document, or both.

At a different level within a section, you might introduce a general principle in a thesis sentence before exploring it in greater detail within the same paragraph:

Thesis sentence

Even if a promise leaves open the possibility that the promisor will escape obligation, however, the promise is valid if the promisor does not have complete control over the events on which the promisor's obligation is conditioned. *Bonnie v. DeLaney*, 158 Calz. 212, 645 P.2d 887 (1982). In *Bonnie*, an agreement for the sale of a house provided that the buyer could cancel the agreement if the buyer "cannot qualify for a 30-year mortgage loan for 90% of the sales price" with any of several banks listed in the agreement. *Id.* at 213, 645 P.2d at 888.

Specific case analysis

In enforcing the agreement against the seller, the court distinguished *Atco Corp.* because the word "cannot" referred to the buyer's ability to obtain a loan rather than to his desire. Because his ability to obtain a loan was partly controlled by events and decisions outside his control, the promises in the sale agreement were nonillusory and binding. *See id.* at 214-15, 645 P.2d 889-90.

In the preceding example, the opening sentence of the paragraph summarizes the general point that the *Bonnie* decision illustrates. That introduction prepares the reader for the detailed analysis of *Bonnie* that follows.

C. Progression from Fundamental to Complex

Some legal discussions or arguments lend themselves to a related method of organization within a section or subsection: progression from fundamental or undisputed points to complex or disputed points. In some cases, the preliminary points provide helpful background information or establish legal premises to the main topic of discussion.

For example, the following passage from a brief provides background information about a legislative policy against punitive damages for breach of contract. That information helps support the ultimate argument that a contractual provision attempting to fix damages for breach is not enforceable:

C. The Liquidated Damages Clause Is Void as a Penalty

Fundamental premises

The contract for the sale of the engine parts is a "transaction in goods" and thus is covered by the Uniform Commercial Code (UCC). U.C.C. §§ 2-102, 2-105 (2011). UCC remedies for breach of contract are designed to compensate the victim of the breach for the loss of the value of the expected performance. *See* U.C.C. § 1-305(a) (2001). They do not permit imposition of a penalty that is designed to discourage breach or to punish the breaching party. *See id.*

Transition to disputed point

Within limited parameters, the UCC permits parties to agree to fix damages for breach in advance by including a provision for "liquidated damages" in their sales contract. However, such damages must be limited to

> an amount which is reasonable in the light of the anticipated or actual harm caused by the breach, the difficulties of proof of loss, and the inconvenience or nonfeasibility of otherwise obtaining an adequate remedy. A term fixing unreasonably large liquidated damages is void as a penalty.

U.C.C. §2-718(1) (2011). In this case, section 5.4 of the contract attempts to fix damages at an amount that is disproportionate to any anticipated or actual harm. Thus, it is an unenforceable penalty clause....

The first paragraph of the preceding passage addresses fundamental matters of statutory policy that are not in issue because the opposing party will not dispute them. It provides a general orientation, however, that will help to place in perspective the argument that the liquidated damages clause constitutes an impermissible penalty under the UCC. True, each major section in a brief should begin with an unqualified statement of the argument. In this example, however, the short and plain section heading arguably meets that strategic requirement, paving the way for immediate establishment of premises that support a fuller statement of the argument.

D. Separation or Consolidation of Analyses

1. Overview—IRAC in Context

In analyzing an issue in a memorandum or a brief, you ordinarily should follow the general structure of the syllogism of deductive reasoning:

major premise—rule of law
minor premise—application of law to facts
conclusion—your prediction or argument regarding the outcome

At the simplest level, you can analyze a topic in a single, undivided IRAC, or in a version of IRAC that begins with an argument or conclusion rather than a neutral, topical reference to the issue. In other words, you would organize your analysis or argument around a syllogism presented in a single, undivided section of your Discussion or Argument:

A. Topic or Argument [stated in a section heading and—if helpful—illuminated in a paragraph below the section heading]

   Legal Rule
   Application to Facts
   Conclusion

If a topic is unusually complex, you might present some elements of a single syllogism in multiple subsections:

A. Topic or Argument [section heading such as "Officer Brown's Assertion of Qualified Immunity from Liability for Using Excessive Force During the Arrest of O'Connor"]
   1. Legal Rule [section heading such as "Law of Qualified Immunity for Police Use of Force"]
      a. General Rules [subsection starting with heading such as "Requirements for Qualified Immunity" and then setting forth precedent establishing that a police officer will be liable in damages for violating the Fourth Amendment only if the unlawfulness of the officer's actions was clearly established by factually similar case law at the time of the incident]

   b. Precedent at Time of Incident [subsection starting with heading such as "State of Clearly Established Law in October 2021," and synthesizing case law prior to October 2021 relating to police use of force on a surrendering suspect]
2. Application to Facts [section heading such as "Analysis of Events of October 2021 under Clearly Established Law"]
   a. Analysis of Facts Relating to Use of Canine Force [subsection analyzing whether officer violated clearly established law by releasing an attack dog on a suspect who was surrendering with hands in the air, but who had not complied with order to drop to the ground]
   b. Analysis of Facts Relating to Use of Taser [subsection analyzing whether officer violated clearly established law by tasing the suspect, prior to handcuffing him, as the suspect lay on the ground with the attack dog's jaws around his ankle]
3. Conclusion [Prediction about whether the officer would be protected by qualified immunity for each use of force]

Conversely, if your main topic of discussion or argument encompasses closely related subtopics that do not warrant separation into formal subsections, you might exercise discretion to discuss more than one topic within an undivided section or subsection. If so, you can present your analysis in either of two ways. First, you can separate the topics into several smaller syllogisms within the section. Each syllogism would include its own legal and factual analyses, set forth in separate paragraphs:

A. Topic or Argument
   Legal Rule 1
      Application to Facts 1
      Conclusion 1
   Legal Rule 2
      Application to Facts 2
      Conclusion 2

Alternatively, you can consolidate the related topics into a single syllogism, a single IRAC with a consolidated statement of multiple rules and analysis of multiple facts:

A. Topic
   Introduction
   Legal Rules 1 & 2
   Application to Facts 1 & 2
   Conclusions

Most writers tend to react to these problems of organization on a subconscious, intuitive level. However, the decision to separate or consolidate is sufficiently important to warrant conscious analysis.

2. Single Syllogism in Undivided Section

At the broadest level, if a topic or argument is sufficiently important and discrete to warrant a separate section or subsection heading, you ordinarily should develop it completely and resolve it within that section or subsection. In the following excerpts from a brief, an advocate divides the arguments about two elements of a tort into subsections. In each of these subsections, the advocate analyzes an element in a single, complete syllogism. For example, in subsection A.1 below, she provides the facts and holding of case law to help define the legal element of "extreme and outrageous conduct." She then applies the law to the facts of her case relevant to that element. Finally, she states a conclusion about the sufficiency of the allegations relating to that element.

II. ARGUMENT	
A. Lew's Allegations in Count II Fail to State a Claim for Intentional Infliction of Emotional Distress	**Major argument**
To establish a right to relief....	
1. Smith's Alleged Conduct Was Not "Extreme and Outrageous"	**First subargument**
Only the most deplorable and shocking conduct satisfies the narrow definition of "extreme and outrageous conduct." *See*.... Conduct that simply reflects normal social and economic adversities is not extreme or outrageous. *See, e.g., Frank v. Boswell*,....	**General rules of law**
In *Frank*, a landlord's eviction notice did not reflect extreme and outrageous conduct, even though it was "rude and intimidating." *Id.* at 289. The court reasoned that....	**In-depth analysis of case law**
In this case, Lew's complaint alleges conduct that is even less extreme than the conduct in *Frank*. It alleges that Smith "fired Lew without severance pay and with full knowledge that Lew's family was facing a desperate financial crisis." Plaintiff's Second Amended Complaint ¶ 7. It further alleges that Smith communicated his decision in a "terse, unfriendly, and unsympathetic conversation, without advance notice." *Id.* at ¶ 8.	**Facts of current dispute**
These allegations state only that Lew was the victim of his own economic distress and that Smith acted to protect the interests of his business. Although some business owners might take it upon themselves to offer personal counseling and financial aid to their employees or ex-employees, Smith has no legal duty to do so.	**Analysis of facts**

Conclusion

Thus, the complaint does not allege circumstances that could establish the requisite "extreme and outrageous conduct."

Second subargument

2. Lew's Alleged "Depression" Does Not Amount to Severe Emotional Distress

Proof of severe emotional distress....

3. Separation of Elements of Single Syllogism into Multiple Subsections

Alternatively, in a particularly complex analysis, you might develop only one element of a complete analysis within a section or subsection. For example, you could develop the legal rules in one section and analyze the facts in a separate section, perhaps even dividing the fact analysis into subsections:

A. Officer Bates Could Not Lawfully Arrest Jones Without Probable Cause to Believe That Jones Had Committed a Felony

Legal rules

Although a police officer may arrest a suspect without a warrant in some circumstances, he may not place a suspect under full custodial arrest without probable cause to believe that the suspect has committed a crime. *See*.... A police officer does not have probable cause unless....

B. Officer Bates Did Not Have Probable Cause

Application to facts

At the suppression hearing, Officer Bates asserted that Jones matched the description of the burglar and that Jones volunteered incriminating statements. Whether taken separately or together, however, these factors did not create probable cause.

1. Jones Did Not Match the Description of the Burglar

First subset of facts

A written transcript of the radio report shows that Officer Bates received the following description of the burglary suspect: white male, six feet tall, 180 lbs., short brown hair, wearing a navy blue windbreaker....

2. Jones's Statements Did Not Create Probable Cause

Second subset of facts

The combined testimony of Jones and Officer Bates creates a clear and consistent picture of their conversation on Washington Street....

Under this approach, section A discusses the law, and section B addresses the fact analysis. It would not be uncommon, however, for the author of such a passage to refer briefly to legal authority within section B when helpful to support the fact analysis.

4. Multiple Syllogisms within a Single, Undivided Section

Conversely, you might occasionally present more than one complete analysis in a discrete section or subsection. If so, you can either (1) fully develop and resolve one syllogism before analyzing the next, or (2) combine the related legal rules of arguably distinct syllogisms and then apply them in combined form to all the relevant facts.

a. Separation of Multiple Syllogisms

Within an undivided section, you can address several closely related topics if none is sufficiently important and discrete to warrant further subdivision into subsections. In many such cases, you can develop these related topics separately within the section or subsection.

For example, you can completely develop and resolve an introductory analysis before moving on to the main topic, as in the following excerpt from a legal memorandum:

A. Option Contract Under UCC	
In some circumstances, a merchant's promise to refrain from revoking an offer to buy or sell goods is enforceable even if gratuitous:	**General statutory rules**
An offer by a merchant to buy or sell goods in a signed writing which by its terms gives assurance that it will be held open is not revocable, for lack of consideration... but any such term of assurance on a form supplied by the offeree must be separately signed by the offeror.	
U.C.C. §2-205 (2011).	
"Merchant" includes "a person who deals in goods of the kind." U.C.C. §2-104 (2011). Stillwell regularly sells computers as part of her wholesale office supply business. Therefore, she is a merchant of the goods that she offered to supply to Azoulay, and section 2-205 thus governs the revocability of her offer.	**Complete syllogism on preliminary matter**
A more difficult question is whether Stillwell "separately signed" the promise not to revoke contained in the form supplied by Azoulay, the offeree. The purpose of the statutory requirement for a separate signing is....	**Transition to main topic of discussion**

The second paragraph of this example quickly resolves the question of merchant status in a complete syllogism, with a statement of the law, an analysis of the facts, and a conclusion. Because that issue is simple and noncontroversial, it does not warrant presentation in a separate subsection with its own heading. On the other hand, it is independent from the analysis of the requirement for a separate signing; therefore, you should develop and resolve it in its own IRAC within a separate paragraph before analyzing other topics raised by the general standards in the first paragraph.

Some legal writers strain this form of separation when using it within a section that features in-depth case analyses of a series of cases. Rather than synthesize these cases and apply the synthesized law in consolidated form to the facts, the writer pauses briefly after each case analysis and applies the holding of that case to the relevant facts. Although this form of argument can work well, it sometimes results in repetition and a rambling, piecemeal effect. You should not use it as a substitute for effective expression of synthesis of authority, as explored in Chapter 10, Section II.B.

b. Consolidation of Multiple Syllogisms

In other cases, you may prefer to combine closely related legal standards and apply them as a group to all the relevant facts. This approach is illustrated by the second and third paragraphs of the following excerpt of a brief:

II. ARGUMENT

A. Bennett Will Prove That Tippett Is Liable Under 42 U.S.C. § 1983 for Violating Bennett's Civil Rights.

General statutory rules

Federal law imposes civil liability on a person who acts under the color of state law to deprive another of a federal right:

> Every person who, under the color of any [state law or custom], subjects, or causes to be subjected, any citizen of the United States or other person within the jurisdiction thereof to the deprivation of any rights, privileges or immunities secured by the Constitution and laws, shall be liable to the party injured....

42 U.S.C. § 1983 (2019).

Consolidated discussion of rules for three subarguments

A private party acts "under the color of state law" if he acts in concert with a state official acting in his official capacity. *See Dennis v. Sparks*, 449 U.S. 24, 27-29 (1980). State action denying a litigant a fair and impartial hearing in civil litigation constitutes a deprivation of due process under the Fourteenth Amendment. *See Catchpole v. Brannon*, 36 Cal. App. 4th 237, 245, 42 Cal.

Rptr. 2d 440, 443 (Ct. App. 1995). Although section 1983 implicitly incorporates the common law doctrine of absolute immunity for judges, that immunity does not protect private parties who conspire with the judge. *See Dennis*, 449 U.S. at 29-32.

Consolidated application of three rules to facts

In this case, Bennett will prove all the elements of his claim under section 1983. First, the evidence will show that Tippett conspired with Judge Bell by bribing Judge Bell to rule against Bennett on his motion for a preliminary injunction; Tippett therefore acted under the color of state law. Second, Tippett's bribe denied Bennett an impartial hearing and therefore deprived Bennett of his federal right to due process. Finally, even though Tippett acted under the color of state law, he had no official state function and therefore does not enjoy the protection of any official immunity.

Conclusion

Thus, the evidence will show that Tippett is liable to Bennett for violating Bennett's due process rights.

c. Discretion to Separate or Consolidate

The decision to separate or consolidate legal analyses often is a matter of judgment on which reasonable writers can disagree. As a general rule, a more superficial treatment of the topics lends itself to consolidation, as in the example above. On the other hand, if you analyze closely related topics in greater depth, you may divide the same discussion of a brief into separate syllogisms that are fully developed and resolved in separate paragraphs within the section:

II. ARGUMENT

A. Bennett Will Prove That Tippett Is Liable Under 42 U.S.C. § 1983 for Violating Bennett's Civil Rights.

General statutory rules

Federal law imposes civil liability on a person who acts under the color of state law to deprive another of a federal right:

> Every person who, under the color of any....

42 U.S.C. § 1983 (2019). In this case, Bennett will prove all the elements of his claim under section 1983.

Full syllogism on first subargument

A private party acts "under the color of state law" if he acts in concert with a state official acting in his official capacity. *See Dennis v. Sparks*, 449 U.S. 24, 27-29 (1980). In *Dennis*, a state judge.... Similarly, the evidence in this case will show that Tippett conspired with Judge Bell by bribing Judge Bell to rule against Bennett on his motion for a preliminary injunction. Therefore, Tippett acted under the color of state law

Full syllogism on second subargument

The Fourteenth Amendment's guarantee of due process in state proceedings is a federal substantive right, the deprivation of which is remediable under section 1983. *See generally Carey v. Piphus*, 435 U.S. 247 (1978). State conduct denying a litigant a fair and impartial hearing in civil litigation constitutes a deprivation of due process under the Fourteenth Amendment. *See Catchpole v. Brannon*, 36 Cal. App. 4th 237, 245, 42 Cal. Rptr. 2d 440, 443 (Ct. App. 1995). In this case, Tippett's bribing the judge directly affected the outcome of the hearing on Bennett's request for a preliminary injunction. Therefore, Tippett caused a deprivation of Bennett's right to due process.

Full syllogism on third subargument

Finally, Tippett is not immune from liability for money damages. Bennett agrees that state judges are absolutely immune from liability for damages for their judicial acts taken within their jurisdiction. *See Stump v. Sparkman*, 435 U.S. 349 (1978). However, such immunity does not extend to a private party who conspires with a state judge, even though by so conspiring the private party acts under the color of state law. *See Dennis*, 449 U.S. at 29-32 (1980). In this case, the record shows that Tippett was not performing an official function and has no official status as an officer of the court. He is a private party who therefore enjoys no official immunity.

General conclusion

Thus, the evidence will show that Tippett is liable to Bennett for violating Bennett's due process rights.

Of course, if the topics are truly independent and warrant extended discussion, you can adopt the conventional approach and present each analysis in a separate subsection and under a separate heading:

II. ARGUMENT	
A. Bennett Will Prove That Tippett Is Liable Under 42 U.S.C. § 1983 for Violating Bennett's Civil Rights.	
Federal law imposes civil liability.... 42 U.S.C. § 1983 (2019). In this case, Bennett will prove all the elements of his claim under section 1983.	**General statutory rules**
1. Tippett Acted Under the Color of State Law.	
A private party acts "under the color of state law" if he acts in concert .... In *Dennis*, ... In this case, the evidence will show that Tippett conspired with Judge Bell .... Therefore, Tippett acted under the color of state law.	**Full syllogism in several paragraphs within first subsection**
2. Tippett Denied Bennett Due Process.	
The Fourteenth Amendment's guarantee of due process in state proceedings is a federal substantive right, ... In *Catchpole*, ... In this case, Bennett will prove that Tippett bribed Judge Bell to rule against Bennett on his motion for a preliminary injunction .... Therefore, Tippett violated Bennett's rights to due process.	**Full syllogism in several paragraphs within second subsection**
3. Tippett Is Not Immune from Suit.	**Third subsection**
Finally, Tippett is....	

5. Summary

These examples primarily illustrate two issues of organization: (1) whether to present topics in separate sections or within a single, undivided section and (2) whether to separate or consolidate analyses within a section. These issues underscore the role of judgment in legal writing and particularly in developing organizational structures. Many problems of this nature have no single, "correct" solution; your resolution will depend on the nature and the depth of the analyses or arguments and on your personal style preferences.

IV. Paragraphs

A. The Role of Paragraphs within a Section

Just as descriptive headings and subheadings communicate the division of a discussion or argument into sections or subsections, good paragraphing helps organize the structure within those sections or subsections. For instance, the paragraphing in the following passage signals the transition from (1) an analysis of the statutory requirements of conduct "under the color of state law" to (2) an analysis of Fourteenth Amendment guarantees:

Statute	A private party acts "under the color of state law" if he acts in concert with a state official acting in his official capacity. *See Dennis v. Sparks*, 449 U.S. 24, 27-29 (1980). *In Dennis*, a state judge .... Similarly, the evidence in this case will show that Tippett conspired with Judge Bell ....
Constitution	The Fourteenth Amendment's guarantee of due process in state proceedings is a federal substantive right ....

The following presentation of the same arguments assumes a greater depth of analysis. Imagine that each of five thesis sentences begins a new paragraph. The five thesis sentences represented by the phrases and clauses in the following example signal the transitions between (1) general legal rules, in-depth case analysis, (3) fact analysis, (4) conclusion, and (5) analysis of potentially adverse authority.

Law	The Fourteenth Amendment's guarantee of due process in state proceedings is a federal substantive right.... *See Catchpole v. Brannon*, ...
Case analysis	In *Catchpole*, ...
Facts of our case	In this case, Bennett will prove ....
Conclusion	Thus, Tippett is liable to Bennett ....
Adverse authority	Tippett has argued..., citing *Parratt v. Taylor*, 451 U.S. 527 (1981). *Parratt* is distinguishable....

B. Paragraph Content and Development

To say that each paragraph should present a single topic or thesis oversimplifies the matter, for the appropriate scope of each paragraph's subject matter may depend on the relationship between the paragraph and the remainder of the discussion. For example, the following analysis of merchant status is superficial, conclusory, and preliminary to the main topic for discussion. Accordingly, you could combine the legal standard, fact analysis, and conclusion of this subsidiary topic in a single paragraph:

> "Merchant" includes "a person who deals in goods of the kind." U.C.C. § 2-104(1) (2011). Stillwell regularly sells computers as part of her wholesale office supply business. Therefore, she is a merchant of the goods that she offered to supply to Azoulay, and section 2-205 thus governs the revocability of her offer.

In contrast, the reader can most easily absorb the more thorough analysis of the main topic if you divide the statement of legal rules and the fact analysis of the main topic into at least two separate paragraphs. At the simplest level, each paragraph could correspond to one of the three elements of deductive reasoning. For example, after it explains the issue, the following sample exam answer analyzes a problem in three paragraphs that (1) summarize the applicable legal rules, (2) apply the rules to the facts, and (3) state a conclusion:

Legal rules

> An enforceable contract requires a bargained-for exchange in which a promisor exchanges his own promise for a return promise or performance. The requirement of an exchange is not satisfied if one party gives only an illusory promise, which does not commit the promisor to any future performance. A promise is illusory if it leaves the promisor free to perform or not according to his unfettered whim or discretion, such as....

Application to facts

> Guarantor should argue that Lender's promise to forbear until he "needs" the money permits Lender to decide at his own whim and unfettered discretion when to demand payment, because he has some control of his own needs. However, that argument would prevail only if the word "need" refers to a subjective perception of deprivation that is inseparable from Lender's purely personal wants or desires. Lender can argue....

Conclusion

> Unfortunately for our client, Lender's promise in the guarantee agreement probably is not illusory, because the word "need" provides some substance to Lender's commitment to forbear. Therefore, Guarantor's promise probably is supported by consideration and is enforceable.

In more complex analyses, the development of legal standards alone will progress through several paragraphs, perhaps beginning with an overview of general standards in one paragraph, followed by two or more paragraphs, each of which explores a significant case or a policy argument. Similarly, the fact analysis might progress through several paragraphs, perhaps displaying different levels of analysis or different categories of facts. For example, the five paragraphs represented by the following phrases and clauses help to signal the transitions between (1) general legal standards, (2) in-depth case analysis, (3) identification of relevant facts, (4) analysis of those facts, and (5) conclusion:

	A. Smith's Alleged Conduct Was Not "Extreme and Outrageous."
General Rules of Law	Only the most deplorable and shocking conduct satisfies the narrow definition of "extreme and outrageous conduct." *See*.... Conduct that simply reflects normal social and economic adversities is not extreme or outrageous. *See, e.g., Frank v. Boswell*,....
Case analysis	In *Frank*, ...
Facts	In this case, Lew's complaint alleges conduct that is even less extreme than the conduct in *Frank*....
Fact analysis	These allegations state only that....
Conclusion	Thus, the complaint does not allege circumstances that could establish the requisite "extreme and outrageous conduct."

In a still more complex example, the explanation of the law could require analysis of several previous cases in separate paragraphs, as well as a synthesis of that precedent.

C. The Role of Sentences within a Paragraph

1. Paragraph Length

A paragraph does not contain some magic number of sentences. The appropriate number of sentences depends in part on the relationship between the paragraph and the topics addressed in surrounding paragraphs.

Of course, if you find that you have set off a single sentence as a separate paragraph, you should always question whether the isolated sentence would better serve as the concluding sentence of the previous paragraph or the thesis sentence of the next one. However, as illustrated by the concluding paragraph of the illustration above, a single sentence may stand by itself as a separate paragraph if it completely addresses a discrete topic or if presentation in a separate paragraph achieves important goals of clarity or emphasis. If you adhere without exception to a rule against single-sentence paragraphs, you might find yourself composing an unnecessary, empty sentence to accompany an informative sentence that could have stood alone.

But legal writing more often suffers from paragraphs that are too long, each one addressing multiple topics in a block of print that covers most of a page. If you find yourself cramming more than four or five sentences into a single paragraph, pause to consider whether you can better present the same ideas in two or three paragraphs. Doing so will reduce the density of the prose on the page and will allow your reader to assimilate the information in smaller chunks.

2. Beginning with a Thesis Sentence

Whenever possible, your first sentence in a multiple-sentence paragraph should communicate your strategy by introducing the topic or thesis of the paragraph, expressing a transition, or both. A thesis sentence asserts the rule that you will illustrate, analyze, or apply in the paragraph. A topic sentence merely describes the information that will follow in the paragraph. As illustrated in many of the preceding examples, thesis statements are especially useful in legal writing, such as when they summarize a synthesized rule, characterize the strength of a factual argument, or compare one case to another.

For example, the first sentence in the following example signals the transition from the analysis of precedent to the identification of the relevant facts of the current dispute, and it provides an overview of the case comparison:

> In this case, Lew's complaint alleges conduct that is even less extreme than the conduct in *Frank*. It alleges that Smith "fired Lew without severance pay and with full knowledge that Lew's family was facing a desperate financial crisis." Pl.'s Second Am. Compl. ¶ 7. It further alleges....

In the preceding sample paragraph, the thesis sentence introduces fact analysis. Similarly, you should use thesis or transition sentences or paragraphs to introduce discussions of legal authority, such as statutes and case law. Section II of Chapter 9 thoroughly discusses and illustrates this critical element of legal writing.

3. Logical Organization within a Paragraph

After you have composed an effective thesis sentence, you should organize other sentences within a paragraph to develop information in a logical, organized fashion. For example, the paragraph below is designed to define the scope of the Uniform Commercial Code and to raise a question about the applicability of the Code to a specific transaction. The awkward placement of the second and third sentences of the paragraph disrupts continuity by stating an intermediate conclusion before establishing its legal premise:

General issue	Whether Maldonado accepted Weinstein's offer depends in part on whether the common law of contracts or the Uniform Commercial Code (UCC) applies to the transaction.
Application to facts	Weinstein's offer to supply specifically identified, separately priced, movable plumbing parts clearly contemplates a sale of goods as part of the transaction. *See* U.C.C. §2-105(1) (2011).
Legal premise	The UCC applies to "transactions in goods." U.C.C. §2-102 (2011).
Specific issue	His proposed transaction, however, also involves the service of installing the fixtures, raising a question about the applicability of the UCC to mixed transactions for both services and the sale of goods.

Reversing the order of the second and third sentences develops points in a more logical order and retains the coherence of transitions:

General issue	Whether Maldonado accepted Weinstein's offer depends in part on whether the common law of contracts or the Uniform Commercial Code (UCC) applies to the transaction.
Legal premise	The UCC applies to "transactions in goods." U.C.C. §2-102 (2011).
Application to facts	Weinstein's offer to supply specifically identified, separately priced, movable plumbing parts clearly contemplates a sale of goods as part of the transaction. *See* U.C.C. §2-105(1) (2011).
Specific issue	His proposed transaction, however, also involves the service of installing the fixtures, raising a question about....

4. Substantive Transition ("Dovetailing") within a Paragraph

Many different organizational approaches can help your reader efficiently paragraph content. Nonetheless, the technique of substantive transition, or dovetailing, is worth highlighting. You can lead a reader from familiar to new information in a paragraph by beginning each sentence with a previously established idea and linking it to a new idea. For example, the phrases in capital letters in the following passage represent new information, and the italicized phrases represent previously introduced information. In each sentence after the first one, previously introduced information is linked to a new idea.

> An enforceable contract requires a bargained-for EXCHANGE in which a promisor exchanges his own promise for a return promise or performance. The requirement of an *exchange* is not satisfied if one party gives only an ILLUSORY PROMISE, which does not commit the promisor to any future performance. A *promise* is *illusory* if it leaves the promisor free to perform or not according to his unfettered whim or discretion, such as....

This technique of consistently linking a familiar idea with a new one is only one of many approaches that you can use in developing a paragraph. You should always retain maximum flexibility to adapt your organizational approach to the characteristics of each passage. The final two chapters of Part IV provide further guidance. They (1) continue to explore paragraphing and paragraph content in the context of presentation of authority and (2) address good organization of words and clauses within a sentence to enhance the clarity or persuasive force of the sentence.

Checklist for Chapter 8

- ✓ When organizing the topics or arguments in an office memorandum or brief,
  - with few exceptions, discuss separate issues in separate sections or subsections;
  - arrange your sections and subsections so that they reflect the proper relationships among topics and subtopics; and
  - present your topics or arguments in a logical order, subject to considerations of strategy.
- ✓ Within a section or subsection,
  - explain the legal rule, advancing from general to specific facets of the rule;
  - apply the rule to the facts; and
  - reach a conclusion.
- ✓ If the topic or argument within a section or subsection is governed by several closely related rules, exercise judgment to either
  - consolidate your statement of all the rules before applying them to all the relevant facts or
  - separately apply some preliminary legal rules to facts before progressing to other rules within the section or subsection.

✓ When composing a paragraph,
- begin with a thesis sentence,
- adopt a logical organization within the paragraph, and
- begin a new paragraph at the earliest reasonable opportunity to avoid overly long paragraphs.

Endnotes

1. *See, e.g.*, N/S Corp. v. Liberty Mut. Ins. Co., 127 F.3d 1145 (9th Cir. 1997) (striking appellant's briefs and dismissing appeal, while citing to similar actions in other cases); Westinghouse Elec. Corp. v. NLRB, 809 F.2d 419, 424-25 (7th Cir. 1987) (imposing $1,000 penalty on counsel for evading federal rule limiting the number of pages of its opening brief).
2. *See* ARIZ. REV. STAT. ANN. § 23-1501(2) (Supp. 2009); Leikvold v. Valley View Cmty. Hosp., 141 Ariz. 544, 688 P.2d 170 (1984) (common law predecessor to § 23-1501(2)).
3. *See* ARIZ. REV. STAT. ANN. § 23-1501(3)(b) (Supp. 2009); Wagenseller v. Scottsdale Mem'l Hosp., 147 Ariz. 370, 376-81, 710 P.2d 1025, 1031-36 (1985) (common law predecessor to § 23-1501(3)(b)).
4. *See, e.g.*, Watts v. Golden Age Nursing Home, 127 Ariz. 255, 619 P.2d 1032 (1980).

Chapter 9

Legal Writing Style in the Office Memorandum

Chapter 1's introduction to writing style identified clarity and concision as the principal characteristics of effective legal writing. This chapter more comprehensively examines those topics, and Chapter 10 addresses effective presentation of legal authority.

This chapter uses selected writing problems as vehicles for developing a method for legal writing. The method it promotes is a flexible approach that provides general guidance for any legal writing assignment. It seeks to show you that effective legal writing style is analogous to the sound practices of legal method and analysis discussed in the preceding chapters. Accordingly, it invites you to treat rules and conventions of writing very much like legal rules: to use them well, you must understand their purposes and policies. As you repeatedly and consciously choose between alternative ways to express your ideas, you will steadily develop good judgment and a personal style. For further practice in recognizing the policies underlying conventions of writing, perform the exercises in Appendix V.

Although this chapter primarily addresses writing style for office memoranda, most of the principles discussed apply equally to briefs, and some of the examples are taken from briefs. Special techniques of persuasive writing are explored in Parts V through VII.

I. Clarity

You cannot write clearly unless you first develop clear ideas. In many cases, muddled legal writing reflects an incomplete understanding of the substantive legal analysis and suggests the need for further research and reflection. Only when you have fully mastered your analysis can you clearly communicate the analysis to your audience.

Moreover, even writing that is clear on its face may be *inaccurate* if you have recorded the wrong citation or statutory text, or have failed to fully comprehend the holding or reasoning of a judicial opinion. Accordingly, the quality of your final written product depends on the care with which you have performed early stages of the research and writing process.

Beyond sound and accurate analysis, an important element of clarity in any legal document is effective organization on all the levels discussed in Chapter 8. Other elements of clarity, discussed below, are simplicity, effective sentence structure, and precise word selection.

A. Simplicity and Plain English

For centuries, people have complained about lawyers' fondness for legal jargon: stuffy, peculiar, archaic legal terminology. They have good reason to complain. For example, some lawyers still end a witness's sworn and notarized written statement with the archaic phrase "Further affiant sayeth not," rather than the perfectly descriptive word "signed."

Although the extent to which you stray from plain and simple terms is partly a matter of personal style, you should tend toward simplicity. If a simple, familiar word will clearly express your idea, your reader may find that a peculiar, complex, or unfamiliar word or phrase in its place is distracting or even unintelligible.

Moreover, simplicity in writing does not limit your expression to simple ideas. Rather, it helps you to express even complex and abstract ideas in such clear, concrete, and simple terms that your reader easily grasps your ideas on first reading.

You can best appreciate the virtues of simplicity by recognizing the ultimate purpose of your document. A legal memorandum should efficiently communicate, and a brief should persuade. A document cannot perform either of these functions if the reader must pause at every sentence to ponder its meaning.

Unfortunately, unnecessary abstraction, complexity, and peculiarity found in some legal writing suggest that the writer's objective is to "sound like a lawyer" or to impress his audience with the breadth of his vocabulary. One judge describes the effect of such writing:

> [T]he use of legalese or "six-bit" college words may help convince your client that you are worth the hourly fee being charged, but it does not help win his case. Indeed, it actually interferes in your communication with the court when the judge is constantly shifting attention from the brief to either a Webster's, Black's Law, or a Latin-to-English dictionary. I know you received a high dollar education. Instead of trying to impress me with some high-brow vocabulary, use your education to figure out how to simplify what you are saying with plain language. After all, the simpler you make it, the easier it is for me to understand.[1]

Occasionally, a peculiar word or phrase earns its place in legal writing as a shorthand term for an unavoidably complex or unfamiliar concept. For example, Chapter 5 uses the term "stare decisis" to refer to a complex set of principles that help to define legal method in the United States. Although this Latin term is unfamiliar to most students entering law school, it is widely accepted among trained lawyers as convenient shorthand for several related ideas whose collective meaning would otherwise require several sentences to convey. Such widely accepted legal phrases qualify as "terms of art."

Similarly, if a statute, regulation, or case law gives special meaning to a legal word or phrase in a relevant context, by all means use that language accordingly. However, surprisingly few forms of peculiar legal language are justified as necessary terms of art. Therefore, you should critically evaluate any unusual language in your writing to ensure that it amounts to an informative term of art rather than distracting legal jargon.[2]

Legal jargon is particularly inappropriate in a document that is addressed to a layperson, who may be unfamiliar with even rudimentary legal terminology. When addressing such an audience, you should exercise special care to avoid unnecessary jargon, and you should explain in plain English the meanings of legal terms of art that other attorneys would easily recognize.

Exercise 9-1

A simple contract should (1) introduce the parties to the contract, (2) recite any background facts that explain the motivations of the parties and thus help to explain their bargain, (3) define the parties' rights and obligations by setting forth their mutual promises, and (4) signify each party's agreement to the terms of the contract.

The following contract is written in antiquated jargon. Parts of it are taken from the contract interpreted in *McMichael v. Price*, 58 P.2d 549 (Okla. 1936). Contract language from formbooks provided further inspiration.

Simplify all or part of the structure and language of the contract so that it expresses the terms of the parties' agreement in plain English. Feel free to use subject headings, section numbers, and paragraphing.

Requirements Contract

This contract for the purchase and sale of sand entered into on this, the ________ ______ day of ____________________, by and between Sooner Sand Co., a general partnership of which Harley T. Price and W. M. McMichael are partners, hereinafter known as the party of the first part, and Bassi Distributing Co., a joint venture of Bassi Trucking Co. and Hardcore Rock & Gravel, Inc., hereinafter known as the party of the second part, Witnesseth:

Whereas, the party of the first part is engaged in the business of selling and shipping sand from Phoenix to various customers in the State of Arizona but has not developed markets outside of Arizona and desires to supply sand wholesale to a distributor with customers outside the state; and

Whereas, the party of the second part has an established business in Phoenix selling and shipping sand to various customers in several states outside Arizona, including California, Nevada, Utah, and Colorado, and desires a stable source of supply of sand for that business;

Now, therefore, in consideration of the mutual covenants herein contained, and other good and valuable consideration the receipt of which is hereby acknowledged, the parties hereby represent, warrant, affirm, promise, covenant, and agree that the said party of the first part will, upon receipt of periodic written orders submitted by the said party of the second part, furnish all of the sand which the said party of the second part requires for shipment to various and sundry points outside of the State of Arizona, for a period of five (5) years from the date hereinabove, said sand to be of a grade and quality at least equal in quality and comparable with the sand of various grades sold by other sand companies in the City of Phoenix, Arizona; furthermore, the said party of the second part agrees to pay as payment and compensation for said sand so furnished a sum per ton which represents sixty percent (60%) of the current market price per ton of concrete at the place of destination of said shipment.

In witness whereof, the said parties have hereunto set their hands and seals the day and year first above written.

____

Sooner Sand Co.—Authorized Agent

____

Bassi Distributing Co.—Authorized Agent

B. Sentence Structure

1. Structuring and Punctuating Long or Complex Sentences

Short, crisp sentences can be powerful:

> Jenkins lived to tell his side of the story. Roberts did not.

On the other hand, a succession of very short sentences can sound stilted or might require empty or repetitive transitional phrases to link the sentences together:

> It was 1:00 A.M. John left the party. He went home. He drove his BMW.

Moreover, long sentences that convey numerous thoughts in multiple clauses are not necessarily problematic; if punctuated and constructed sensibly, they can be clear and readable.

Unfortunately, however, legal writing often suffers from unnecessarily long and complex sentences that are poorly constructed. The readers of such sentences must assimilate too much information before pausing. Consequently, they often lose track of the proper relationships of the ideas expressed.

a. Closure through Punctuation

You can use two devices to avoid or revise unmanageable sentences: closure and visual guides to structure.

Closure usually refers to punctuation that allows a reader to pause to assimilate one or more ideas before moving to the next. For example, the following passages illustrate three levels of closure. The first presents at least three distinct ideas in a single sentence punctuated only by commas:

> Although punitive damages are designed to punish the wrongdoer rather than compensate the victim for actual injury, many courts will award punitive damages only if the plaintiff proves actual injury, and they typically limit punitive damages to an amount that bears a reasonable relationship to the award of compensatory damages.

The sentence above is constructed reasonably well. However, the commas in the sentence invite only brief pauses between ideas, leaving the reader breathless if she is unfamiliar with the subject matter. Periods dividing the passage into three sentences encourage the reader to pause more substantially and to digest each idea before facing the next:

> Punitive damages are designed to punish the wrongdoer rather than compensate the victim for actual injury. Nonetheless, many courts will award punitive damages only if the plaintiff proves actual injury. Moreover, courts typically limit punitive damages to an amount that bears a reasonable relationship to the award of compensatory damages.

If you desire to link the second and third ideas to one another more closely than to the first idea in the paragraph, you can replace the second period with a semicolon. The semicolon provides such a conceptual link with nearly the same level of closure as provided by a period:

> Punitive damages are designed to punish the wrongdoer rather than compensate the victim for actual losses. Nonetheless, many courts will award punitive damages only if the plaintiff proves actual injury; moreover, courts typically limit punitive damages to an amount that bears a reasonable relationship to the award of compensatory damages.

In some passages, visual guides to the structure of a long sentence can effectively substitute for the closure provided by multiple short sentences. The following passages illustrate both techniques. The first sample passage takes advantage of closure by limiting each sentence to a single idea:

> The evidence supports three critical factual conclusions. First, the marijuana, cocaine, and heroin all belonged to Carson and Klein. Second, Rivers was unaware of the presence of those drugs in the house when he entered the living room. Third, when Klein offered to sell the marijuana to Rivers, Rivers declined the offer and attempted to leave the house.

The closure is welcome in this example, because two of the factual conclusions set forth in separate sentences are sufficiently complex to require punctuation within those conclusions.

In the next sample passage, the series of conclusions in the first passage progresses through a single sentence without the disruption of substantial closure. It retains some of the qualities of closure by using numbers as the equivalent of road signs[3] to identify the end of one element of the series and the beginning of the next:

> The evidence supports three critical factual conclusions: (1) the marijuana, cocaine, and heroin all belonged to Carson and Klein; (2) Rivers was unaware of the presence of those drugs in the house when he entered the living room; and (3) when Klein offered to sell the marijuana to Rivers, Rivers declined the offer and attempted to leave the house.

b. Repetition of Prepositions or Other Linking Words or Phrases

If the elements of the series are simpler, you can provide a subtler guide to sentence structure by repeating an introductory word or phrase, such as "that" in the following example:

> Top Notch Co. is not liable on this contract theory unless Jackson can prove that the personnel manual was part of Jackson's employment contract, that the manual contained a promise of job security, and that Top Notch breached such a promise when it discharged Jackson for refusing to shave his beard.

Some writers balk at using "that" in this manner. In many sentence structures, their point is well taken. For example, the word "that" is unnecessary in the following sentence:

> I knew that he would come back.

Although the sentence above does not display any errors of grammar or syntax, a writer could exercise discretion to omit the word "that," thus adopting a more concise style with no appreciable loss of clarity:

> I knew he would come back.

In other cases, the word "that" can help the reader to distinguish quickly between two possible sentence structures. Consider, for example, the following sentences:

> The court held two principles above all others.
> The court held the defendant in custody without bail.[4]
> The court held the defendant had not consented to the search.

In the first two sentences, the word "held" is used in the sense of possessing or retaining something, tangible or intangible. In those two sentences, the word "that" has no place; the writer could not insert it without adding other words. In the third sentence, however, the word "held" is used in a different sense and syntax. Like the word "said" or "concluded" in similar contexts, it introduces a holding or ruling of the court. In this context, a writer could exercise discretion to insert "that" after "held":

> The court held that the defendant had not consented to the search.

Indeed, adding the word "that" in the third sample sentence helps inform the reader that the third sentence has a different structure than the first two. Without the word "that" as a guide to the structure of the third sentence, the reader might momentarily assign the same meaning to "held" that it has in the first two sentences, and might later rely on context to dispel the confusion.

Thus, one should not too quickly adopt an inflexible rule against inserting "that" in such contexts. The decision whether to employ such a guide to structure is a matter of judgment, style, and context.

c. Complex Series

Chapter 1 examined the serial comma rule and its relationship to the goal of clarity in writing. To ensure clarity in complex as well as simple contexts, adherents to the traditional approach consistently insert the final comma in any series of two or more things:

> We braved high winds, driving rain, and flooded streets.

The elements of a series, however, need not be limited to simple nouns, such as "wind, rain, and streets." They may be verb phrases, such as "washed the car, mowed the lawn, and repaired the roof." They may even be independent clauses, each of which could stand alone as a complete sentence with a subject and verb.

Particularly troublesome is a multi-level series in which the primary series is made up of two or more major elements, and at least one of those major elements incorporates its own subsidiary series of two or more subelements. For example, imagine that a sentence includes the following series of two major elements: The defendant (1) had left his car at the garage for maintenance and (2) lacked money for public transportation to another city. Now suppose that the first major element includes three subelements: The defendant (1) had left his car at the garage for (i) repairs, (ii) repainting, and (iii) other maintenance, and (2)...to another city. Unfortunately, many writers fail to distinguish between the major elements and the subelements within a major element:

> The defendant had left his car at a garage for repairs, repainting, other maintenance, and lacked money for public transportation to another city.

The writer has punctuated this sentence as a single series with four elements: "repairs," "repainting," "other maintenance," and "lacked money."

The series is not parallel in structure because the first three elements are objects and the fourth is a verb with an object. If retained as a single sentence, the passage is best structured as a compound sentence with two independent clauses as the major elements and with a series of three subelements within the first major element:

> The defendant had left his car at a garage for repairs, repainting, and other maintenance, and he lacked money for public transportation to another city.

The seemingly minor revisions in the corrected sentence are significant. The addition of the conjunction "and" between the second and third element of the subsidiary series signals the end of that series. Moreover, the addition of the subject "he" in the second major element of the compound sentence transforms that element into an independent clause, parallel with the first major element.

A final point: the clauses in the example above appear as a single sentence to illustrate parallel structure. An alternative revision would split them into two sentences:

> The defendant had left his car at a garage for repairs, repainting, and other maintenance. Unfortunately, he lacked money for public transportation to another city.

d. Toward a Flexible, Policy-Oriented Approach to Punctuation

Many routine conventions of punctuation provide guides to sentence structure and should be applied flexibly to achieve that goal. For example, the insertion of a comma to separate independent clauses joined by a conjunction[5] is not arbitrary; it often avoids temporary confusion in sentence structure, as illustrated by the following unpunctuated sentence:

> Coastal Bank breached its loan commitment to the owner and the contractor threatened to terminate its performance.

Halfway through the sentence, many readers assume that the conjunction "and" joins "owner" to "the contractor." Thus, on encountering "the contractor," those readers conclude for a fraction of a second that the bank owed its loan commitment to the contractor as well as to the owner. By the time they reach the verb "threatened," they realize from context that "the contractor" is the subject of a new independent clause rather than the second in a series of two objects of the prepositional phrase "to the." By that time, however, the ambiguity in sentence structure has caused readers to hesitate for a moment and perhaps even to regress by rereading part of the sentence. This momentary confusion could be even more pronounced in a more complicated compound sentence.

A comma inserted before the conjunction more quickly identifies "the contractor" as the beginning of a new independent clause:

> Coastal Bank breached its loan commitment to the owner, and the contractor threatened to terminate its performance.

This example illustrates two general principles of style. First, some conventions of punctuation or other matters of style enhance the efficiency and ease with which the reader comprehends. The reader of a brief or memorandum likely could glean the meaning of the first sample sentence above from context. However, if multiplied many times in the course of a document, the additional labor and frequent instances of momentary confusion can leave the reader weary and undermine the credibility of the writer.

Second, you should apply rules or conventions of writing style the way that you apply rules of law: apply and extend them as far as necessary to vindicate their underlying purposes or policies, but no further. For example, the following compound sentence is perfectly readable without a comma separating the independent clauses:

> The robber ran and the police gave chase.

Because this sentence is short and simple, the reader can recognize its structure at a glance, arguably making the comma unnecessary as a guide to structure.

You can avoid the comma question and raise others by placing a period after the first independent clause:

> The robber ran. And the police gave chase.

This punctuation gives special emphasis to the action in each clause, but many writers recoil at the idea of beginning a sentence with the simple conjunction "and" or "but." Such usage is not grammatically incorrect; it is simply stylistically questionable in many cases. If the clauses are simple and short, they will normally flow more smoothly if combined in a single sentence with a conjunction in the middle of the sentence.

Moreover, if you want to divide the clauses into two sentences to emphasize each clause or to provide your reader with closure after a long clause, you probably will prefer a stronger transition word than "and" or "but." When writers decide to begin a sentence with a conjunction, most prefer to use a more substantial conjunctive adverb, such as "moreover," "furthermore," "in contrast," "however," or "nonetheless":

> Mr. Blumquist survived the initial explosion. Nonetheless, he died a short time later of smoke inhalation.

Section III of Chapter 1 explains why you should reject an inflexible rule against starting sentences with the transition word "however." Signaling a change of direction at the beginning of a sentence can help you achieve an important objective in legal writing. And it should help you to minimize the need to begin a sentence with "and" or "but." But you should not conclude that the latter construction is universally incorrect. It will simply be a rare passage in legal writing that benefits from such construction. In this entire book, only a handful of sentences begin with "and" or "but." And the three in this paragraph are included primarily to underscore the theme of this subsection: many rules of composition should be viewed as general guides to style rather than absolute prohibitions against unconventional usage.

A few more examples will further underscore this point. Consider, for example, the question of whether to insert a comma after a subordinate phrase or clause to separate it from the main clause that follows it:

> After reviving the victim at the side of the pool[,] the paramedic transported her to the hospital emergency room.

Some writers, including this author, normally insert such a comma, even after a short and simple introductory phrase or clause. Much like the traditional serial comma, the comma after a subordinate phrase or clause never hurts, and it often provides a helpful guide to sentence structure, especially if the introductory phrase or clause is long or complex.

Other writers, however, prefer to avoid unnecessary punctuation. They prefer to insert a comma after an introductory phrase or clause only when necessary for clarity. Such an exercise of discretion is perfectly legitimate, although it requires the writer to determine the degree of complexity or length that would cause a reader to stumble in the absence of a comma.

For example, each of the following five sentences or excerpts begins with a subordinate word, phrase, or clause. The word or phrase beginning the main clause is printed in bold. In which of the examples would you insert a comma before the main clause?

(i) Later **he** mowed the lawn.

(ii) In January 2022 **he** resolved to quit smoking.

(iii) After she examined the patient **Dr. Ong** requested a conference with the chief surgeon.

(iv) In light of Hart's conduct and his oral representations regarding the policy manual **the judge** ruled that....

(v) Although few courts have addressed the question of whether members of a city council enjoy the absolute immunity that protects state legislators **the policy** of protecting the legislative process from....

As stated above, a writer could reasonably choose to insert a comma in each of the five examples. Others might exercise discretion to withhold further punctuation from example (i), and perhaps example (ii), because readers can recognize the simple structures in those examples at a glance. Even those inclined to preserve ink, however, should begin adding a comma at the level of complexity of example (iii) or (iv). The dependent clause at the beginning of example (iii) includes a subject, verb, and object. Moreover, the object, "the patient," might be confused with the subject of the main clause, "Dr. Ong," unless separated by a comma:

> After she examined the patient, Dr. Ong requested a conference....

In examples (iv) and (v), the introductory phrases or clauses are sufficiently long and complex that readers will appreciate a comma, because it invites them to pause to assimilate the information in the introduction before proceeding to the main clause.

A final example will serve to emphasize the role of style and judgment in punctuation and to illustrate the limits of inflexible rules. In the following sentence, a common convention of punctuation justifies each of the commas, at least when viewed in isolation:

> The contract is written, signed, and dated, and, therefore, the statute of frauds does not apply.

In this example, the first two commas appropriately separate three elements of a series. The third comma appropriately separates the two independent clauses joined by the conjunction "and." The last two commas represent a defensible judgment that "therefore" is parenthetic and should be set apart from the rest of the clause with commas.

Nonetheless, most writers would be dissatisfied with the sentence, because the concentration of five commas within six words of text is distracting. In a flawed response, some writers might omit one or more commas without changing the structure of the sentence:

> The contract is written, signed, and dated and, therefore the statute of frauds does not apply.

Although this revision is less cluttered, it incorrectly omits commas that served important functions.

An honest appraisal of the original sentence should reveal structural flaws. None of the five commas is incorrect, but the sentence structure concentrates the commas in a manner that is stylistically displeasing. You can directly respond to this problem by changing the location of "therefore," thus decreasing the need for commas around it by lessening its parenthetic qualities:

> The contract is written, signed, and dated, and the statute of frauds therefore does not apply.

Alternatively, you can replace one of the commas with a period or a semicolon by omitting the conjunction "and" between the two independent clauses:

> The contract is written, signed, and dated. Therefore, the statute of frauds does not apply.

In sum, if you understand the policy justifications for conventions of punctuation, you can more confidently recall them, apply them, and even depart from them when the context justifies an unconventional approach. Conversely, even technically correct writing might display problems of style that invite you to exercise judgment and to consciously choose among alternative sentence structures.

Appendix V describes other common conventions of punctuation and asks you to analyze them.

Exercise 9-2

1. Care with Commas

What further punctuation, if any, would you add to the following sentences? Would you prefer to alter the structure of some of the sentences, or break some of them into two sentences?

a. Two pieces of evidence link Jones to the crime: a witness observed Jones strike the victim with his fist and a glove recovered from the crime scene matches the one found in Jones's car.

b. The court dismissed the action and Romero appealed.

c. The judge dismissed the action because the limitations period had expired.
d. Because the limitations period had expired the court dismissed the action.
e. In some cases even perfectly relevant evidence should be excluded if it would seriously confuse the jury because the prejudicial effect of such evidence frequently outweighs its probative value.
f. The court rejected the defendant's argument that the action should be dismissed because the limitations period had expired reasoning that the plaintiff had established grounds for tolling the limitations period.

2. Closure and Road Signs

Redraft the following sentence to make it easier to read. Break it into multiple sentences or clauses, or use any other device to lead the reader gracefully through the ideas it expresses.

> Plaintiff American Continental Can Co. brought this action against Defendants Conco Sheet Metal Co., Bassi Distributing Co., and Miller Trucking Co., alleging that Conco Sheet Metal Co. had sold it defective sheet metal, that Bassi Distributing Co. had fraudulently misrepresented the description and quality of Conco Sheet Metal Co.'s products, and that Miller Trucking Co. had negligently damaged sheet metal that it agreed to transport from the warehouse of Conco Sheet Metal Co. to the factory of American Continental Can Co., and requesting compensatory and punitive damages.

3. The Ambiguous Series

Identify the major elements of the series in the sentence set forth below. Where does the final element of the series begin? What different interpretations does the sentence invite? How would you use a comma to advance either interpretation over the other?

> In the event of default, the Lessee must vacate the premises, forfeit the security deposit and pay Lessor's actual damages or pay liquidated damages under section 12 of this Lease.

---

2. Concrete Verbs and Active Construction

a. Concrete Verbs

Lawyers often sacrifice vigor and clarity in their legal writing by using vague and abstract verbs such as "involve," "exist," or "occur":

> A modification to the contract occurred on July 1.

Even more frequently, lawyers drain the strength from verbs by building sentences around a form of the phrase "there is":

> There was a modification to the contract on July 1.

The author of the preceding sentence has converted the active verb "modify" into the noun "modification," creating a need for the verb "was," a form of the relatively abstract and passive infinitive "to be." That construction focuses attention on the mere existence or absence of modification.

Unless you have good reason for such abstraction, you can improve this sentence by identifying the actors, abandoning the "be" verb, and focusing on the real action word in the sentence, "modify":

> Nelson and Kubichek modified their contract on July 1.

In some cases, replacing abstract wording such as "there is" with a more concrete, active verb will enable you to add new meaning as well as vigor. For example, the following sentence abstractly comments on the absence of critical evidence:

> There is no evidence in the record that Robert Emery intended to kill the bank teller.

A more concrete verb can emphasize the absence not only of direct evidence of intent but also circumstantial evidence from which a fact finder might infer intent:

> No evidence in the record even suggests that Robert Emery intended to kill the bank teller.

b. Active and Passive Construction

Avoidance of forms of "there is" in legal writing exemplifies a more general preference for active voice in sentence structure. A clause in active voice presents its principal parts in the normal order of actor, verb, and object of the action, such as "curiosity killed the cat."

In contrast, the following sentence features three clauses in passive voice, each of which places the object before the verb and dispenses with the actor altogether:

> The *Allen* doctrine has been criticized, but it continues to be applied because it has been approved in dictum.

The following revision identifies the actors associated with each verb, but it still uses passive voice throughout, as revealed by the inverted order of object, verb, and actor:

> The *Allen* doctrine has been criticized by a few appellate judges, but it continues to be applied by trial judges because it has been approved in dictum by the Supreme Court.

Active voice is more informative than the minimalist passive structure in the first example above, and it more directly and concisely conveys all the information presented in the second example:

> A few appellate judges have criticized the *Allen* doctrine, but trial judges continue to apply it because the Supreme Court has approved it in dictum.

The vigor of active construction can be especially useful in composing strong statements in persuasive writing. For example, the following sentence in passive voice fails to assign responsibility for the repair of the air conditioning:

> The air conditioning was not repaired until 60 days after the tenant gave written notice of the defect.

In contrast, the next sentence uses active voice to identify the landlord as the responsible party and to characterize the landlord's inaction as a culpable omission:

> The landlord neglected to repair the air conditioning until 60 days after the tenant gave written notice of the defect.

Although active voice generally is more direct, concise, or informative than passive voice, you might occasionally prefer passive voice. For example, you may use passive voice to deliberately omit reference to an actor or actors whose identities are unknown or unimportant:

> The bridge was erected in 1923.

Even in this case, some writers so strongly prefer active voice that they refer to the actor or actors generically: "Workers built the bridge in 1923." Most writers, however, would reasonably adopt the passive construction to avoid diverting the reader's attention to unimportant information.

In some cases, you may be aware of the identity of the actor but use passive construction to avoid drawing attention to that identity. For example, a defense attorney might desire to emphasize mitigating factors in a crime while avoiding any reminder to the jury that her client stands accused of the wrongdoing:

> The hostage was not harmed in any way.

Conversely, you may deliberately use passive voice to place unusual emphasis on the actor by placing the actor at the end of the sentence, as in the second of the following sentences:

> The defense wants you to believe that Mr. Cass injected himself with a lethal dose of heroin. To the contrary, the evidence shows that the heroin was injected by the defendant, Ms. Borden.

In some sentences, if you place the actor or actors at the beginning of the sentence, you will unduly delay introducing the verb:

> Ms. Williams, the firm's top expert in tax law, and Mr. Scales, an eloquent oral advocate with 20 years of experience before the state appellate courts, argued the case.

With passive voice, you can introduce the simple verb and its object early in the sentence:

> The case was argued by Ms. Williams, the firm's top expert in tax law, and by Mr. Scales, an eloquent oral advocate with 20 years of experience before the state appellate courts.

In summary, you should prefer vigorous, concrete verbs in active construction unless you have a specific reason to use a vague, abstract, or passive verb.

Exercise 9-3

1. Benefits of Active, Concrete Verbs

Replace the passive, abstract verbs in the following sentences with more active, concrete verbs.

a. There are only two Supreme Court decisions that address this issue.
b. It was argued by government counsel that the tax regulation was applicable to the land exchange.
c. The landlord was ordered by the court to achieve completion of the repairs within 30 days.
d. There was a conspiracy among four distributors to effect an immediate price increase.

2. Occasional Benefits of Passive Construction

By replacing the active verb with a passive verb, restructure the following sentence to minimize the number of words separating the subject, verb, and object and to emphasize the "clearly erroneous" standard.

> Federal Rule of Civil Procedure 52(a)(6), which provides that a federal trial court's findings of fact in a nonjury trial "must not be set aside unless clearly erroneous," limits our review.

3. Effective Placement of Modifiers

For clarity, you should place a modifying word, phrase, or clause close to the part of the sentence that it modifies. On the other hand, to ensure a smooth flow in your writing, you should avoid interrupting important parts of a sentence with a lengthy modifier or other parenthetic information.

The following sample sentences illustrate how these principles relate to one another. If you patiently work through them, you will better appreciate how good writers make conscious choices between alternative sentence structures.

If a subordinate clause is short, you can appropriately emphasize the main clause by placing it after the subordinate clause. The immediately preceding sentence is an example of such construction.

In contrast, the longer and more complicated subordinate clauses in the following sentence inconveniently delay introduction of the main clause:

> Because the consumer fraud statute applies to misrepresentations in either the "advertisement or sale" of merchandise, and because the "sale" of merchandise normally is associated with the passing of title from the seller to the buyer, *see* U.C.C. § 2-106(1) (2011), the statute appears to apply to a seller's misrepresentations made during the delivery of merchandise under a preexisting contract.

You would only increase the reader's frustration by moving the subordinate clauses to the middle of the sentence, between the subject and the verb:

> The consumer fraud statute, because it applies to..., and because the "sale" of merchandise normally is..., appears to apply to a seller's misrepresentations....

You could reveal the information in the sentence more gracefully by starting with the main clause:

> The consumer fraud statute appears to apply to a seller's misrepresentations made during the delivery of merchandise under a preexisting contract, because the statute applies to misrepresentations in either the "advertisement or sale" of merchandise, and because the "sale" of merchandise normally is associated with the passing of title from the seller to the buyer, *see* U.C.C. §2-106(1) (2011).

The revised sentence immediately above is nonetheless too long and complex. You can solve all the problems in this passage simply by breaking it into shorter sentences, as recommended in the discussion of closure in Section I.B.1.a, above:

> The consumer fraud statute applies to misrepresentations in either the "advertisement or sale" of merchandise. The "sale" of merchandise normally is associated with the passing of title from the seller to the buyer. *See* U.C.C. §2-106(1) (2011). Therefore, the statute appears to apply to....

Exercise 9-4

1. Precise Placement of Modifiers

Consider the different positions into which you could insert the word "only" in the following sentence: Officer Jones fired his gun at the suspect three times.

Which of the positions is most consistent with the information in each of the following?

a. Officer Jones fired his gun three times, not five times as reported by a witness.

b. Officer Jones fired his gun three times, but no other officer fired his gun more than once.

2. Modifying Clauses and Sentence Structure

Revise the following sentences. Which of several possible revisions do you prefer, and why?

a. The trial judge, after reviewing the evidence and considering the arguments of the parties, ruled that the contraband was the product of an illegal search.

b. Protesting that he had not finished his testimony, the bailiff escorted the witness from the courtroom.

---

4. Restrictive and Nonrestrictive Clauses

Most writers find it difficult to identify restrictive and nonrestrictive clauses and to choose between the relative pronouns "that" and "which" once they have identified the clause. Most critical for clarity is your remembering to (1) insert a comma before a nonrestrictive clause (and after the clause if it does not end the sentence) and (2) omit such a comma before a restrictive clause. If you wish to go beyond popular usage and satisfy purists in your circle, you will also remember to introduce a restrictive clause with the relative pronoun "that," saving "which" for nonrestrictive clauses. Both considerations are explained in detail below.

a. The Role of the Comma

To illustrate the distinction between restrictive and nonrestrictive clauses, imagine that you and an assigning attorney are standing next to a large conference table in a meeting room of your law firm. The conference table is the only table in the room, and eight chairs are placed around it.

Your supervisor makes a statement that is reproduced below without internal punctuation:

> This table *which we just purchased a year ago* is already showing signs of wear.

Now, imagine the inflection and timing of your supervisor's oral statement. She probably stressed the main clause: "This table is already showing signs of wear." On the other hand, you can imagine a change in tone when she interjected the italicized clause: "which we just purchased a year ago." You can imagine her pausing after "table" and "ago," lending a parenthetic quality to the information between the pauses.

The italicized clause is parenthetic because it is not needed to identify the subject, "this table." Your supervisor was clearly referring to objects in the room, and those objects include only one table. She has directed your attention to that unique object simply by referring to "this table." Her statement about the firm recently purchasing the table helps to reinforce her point about the table's rapid deterioration, but that statement is not needed to identify the table and distinguish it from any others within the range of your perception.

Thus, you could naturally treat the italicized clause as an "aside," an interruption of the main clause. The clause provides interesting additional information, but the rest of the sentence would stand alone coherently without it. The italicized clause is "nondefining" because it is not necessary to define the subject. Stated otherwise, it is "nonrestrictive" because it is not necessary to restrict the universe of tables to the conference table in this meeting room; the phrase "this table" had already accomplished that task.

In an oral statement, you would normally pause before and after such a nonrestrictive clause. In a written statement, you achieve the same effect by setting the clause apart with commas:

> This table, which we just purchased a year ago, is already showing signs of wear.

Imagine now that your conversation turns to the eight chairs surrounding the conference table. You would undoubtedly experience confusion if your supervisor made the following statement without pointing to a particular chair:

> The chair has several small holes in its upholstery.

The subject "the chair" is not sufficiently precise to identify the one chair among eight to which your supervisor is referring. She could avoid the confusion by adding a clause that directs your attention to a single chair. Each of the following revisions contains such a clause:

The chair *next to the potted cactus* has several small holes in its upholstery.

The chair *which sits next to the potted cactus* has several small holes in its upholstery.

The chair *that sits next to the potted cactus* has several small holes in its upholstery.

Regardless of which version your supervisor spoke, she did not pause before the italicized passage; instead, she plowed straight through the sentence at least until she had singled out one of the chairs. The italicized information is not parenthetic; rather than interrupting the main clause, it is a direct continuation of the subject, necessary to identify or to define the chair to which she is referring. In that sense, it is a "defining" or "restrictive" clause because it restricts the universe of eight chairs in the room to the single chair to which your supervisor intends to refer. Just as such a clause would not inspire a pause in an oral statement, it would not require commas in a written statement.

So far, your reaction to these examples is probably a resounding "Who cares?" The following sample sentences, however, illustrate that the distinction between a restrictive and a nonrestrictive clause occasionally will materially affect the content of a sentence in legal writing. The construction of the first sample sentence suggests that all reckless driving constitutes a felony and that a new statute therefore applies to all reckless driving:

> The new statute mandates a jail term for reckless driving, which constitutes a felony violation of the vehicle code.

The meaning of this sentence is conveyed partly by the comma, which suggests to the reader that the sentence would be perfectly sensible if it ended at "reckless driving" and that the clause following the comma simply adds parenthetic information. The clause following the comma is nonrestrictive, or nondefining, because it does not purport to identify a subset of the general category of things denoted by the term "reckless driving."

Even without any changes in wording, the next sample sentence suggests by the absence of a comma that only some forms of reckless driving rise to the level of a felony and that the statute applies only to those forms of reckless driving:

> The new statute mandates a jail term for reckless driving which constitutes a felony violation of the vehicle code.

The absence of a comma invites the reader to rush to the end of the sentence to discover what kind of reckless driving is covered, suggesting that the sentence could not sensibly stop at the term "reckless driving." In this sentence, the clause following "reckless driving" is restrictive, or defining, because it identifies a subset of the things in the general category of reckless driving.

b. The Choice between "That" and "Which"

Both sentences, however, use the relative pronoun "which" to introduce the restrictive or nonrestrictive clauses, leaving the presence or absence of a comma to indicate whether the clause is restrictive or nonrestrictive. To partially relieve the comma of that heavy burden, careful writers—or at least the purists among them—use the relative pronoun "that" in a restrictive clause to emphasize the restrictive nature of the clause and to more clearly distinguish it from a nonrestrictive clause:

> The new statute mandates a jail term for reckless driving that constitutes a felony violation of the vehicle code.

Similarly, in the earlier example of the chair with the holes in its upholstery, a sentence that uses a relative pronoun should use "that" rather than "which":

> The chair that sits next to the potted cactus has several small holes in its upholstery.

Because many writers do not have a natural ear for the purist's use of "that," they tend to use "which" in both restrictive and nonrestrictive clauses. In fact, this practice is so widespread that some might characterize it as the popular approach. Nonetheless, many assigning attorneys will go "which hunting" when reviewing the work of associates.

In most cases, any ambiguity or uncertainty resulting from using "which" in a restrictive clause will be insignificant. For example, the difference in meaning between the following two sentences is insignificant to the writer's analysis:

> The court applied a fairness test, which inquires whether a transaction was consummated through fair dealing and at a fair price.
>
> The court applied a fairness test that inquires whether a transaction was consummated through fair dealing and at a fair price.

Because the sentence singles out one of many possible formulations of a test that incorporates considerations of fairness, the final clause should be restrictive, as in the second example. However, because emphasis of the restrictive nature of the clause is not necessary for analytical clarity, the following popular choice of words would be inoffensive:

> The court applied a fairness test which inquires whether a transaction was consummated through fair dealing and at a fair price.

Moreover, returning to a previous example, a structural revision of the sentence can more clearly convey the intended meaning than use of restrictive or nonrestrictive clauses:

> The new statute mandates a jail term for reckless driving, but only if it constitutes a felony violation of the vehicle code.

Nonetheless, when the choice between relative pronouns will affect clarity, you should follow the example of the United States Supreme Court, which carefully distinguished between restrictive and nonrestrictive clauses in the following excerpt from an opinion:

> Although the Court of Appeals' construction of the Act and of Regulation Z is shared by three of the four other Courts of Appeals *that* have ruled on the question, this view, *which* is essentially a claim that the plain language of the statute and the regulation requires the result reached by the court below, has recently been challenged on several fronts.[6]

c. Procedural Labels

You may also raise questions about restrictive and nonrestrictive clauses when you join procedural labels, such as "plaintiff," to the names of parties to litigation. In that context, you need not worry about a choice between "that" and "which," but you might wonder whether you should insert a comma.

For example, if Robert Jones is one of three plaintiffs in an action, then a phrase that uses his name to define "plaintiff" is restrictive and should omit any comma:

> Plaintiff Robert Jones moves for summary judgment....

In this example, "Robert Jones" restricts the universe of "plaintiffs" to one of the three plaintiffs in the litigation.

In contrast, if Jones is the only plaintiff, you could treat a similar reference as nonrestrictive and include commas:

> Plaintiff, Robert Jones, moves for summary judgment....

In this example, "Robert Jones" arguably supplies parenthetic information about a party who is already identified by the label "Plaintiff."

Alternatively, even if Jones is the only plaintiff, you could reasonably eliminate the commas by characterizing "Plaintiff" as a title that is joined with a name, as in "Dr. Long" or "Secretary-Treasurer Richard King":

> Plaintiff Robert Jones....

This is probably the least distracting stylistic option. However, you cannot adopt this usage of "plaintiff" as a title if you treat "plaintiff" as a common noun by preceding it with an article, such as "the." In that case, you must treat the party's name as a nonrestrictive modifier if he is the only plaintiff:

The plaintiff, Robert Jones, moves for summary judgment against the defendant, Cecelia Ynez.

Exercise 9-5

Relative Pronouns and Wealthy Relatives

Compare the following alternative provisions of a will:

I leave to my daughter my bank account that is in Western Savings.

I leave to my daughter my bank account, which is in Western Savings.

After drafting the will, but before death, the testator closed the bank account at Western Savings and used the funds from that account to open a new one at First Interstate Bank.[7] Which provision would most likely bequeath the First Interstate Bank account to the daughter?

C. Precision

1. Careful Expression of Analysis

Once you clearly understand the idea you want to communicate, you must select the words and phrases that precisely convey your intended meaning. As suggested in Chapter 1, achieving precision in writing may require you to subordinate other potential goals, such as entertaining your reader. For example, many writers believe that they will bore their readers if they repeatedly use a single word or phrase to refer to the same idea throughout a passage. Some writers address this concern by engaging in "elegant variation": using different words or phrases to refer to the same idea. However, any entertainment value of the variation will fail to justify the confusion that typically results in the context of legal writing.

For example, perhaps to elegantly vary their phrasing, many legal writers intermittently use "while" as a synonym for "although," and they use "when" or "where" as a synonym for "if." The following construction is common:

While the court declined to decide the issue of retroactivity in *Fleming*, its dictum in subsequent cases suggests that it has always assumed that the *Fleming* principle applies retroactively.

The primary meaning of "while" in this syntax is duration or simultaneity. But, of course, the writer does not mean that the court offered dictum in subsequent cases *at the same time* that it declined to decide the issue in a previous case. "Although" would more precisely convey the contrast or tension between the court's actions. In the context of the entire sentence, the less precise version does not cause serious confusion or inconvenience. By displaying care with details, however, the more precise wording strengthens the credibility of the writer on more substantive matters.

More substantial risks of confusion arise in the use of synonyms for "because." "Since" is particularly popular:

> Since the employer invited the applicant to read the policy manual at the initial interview, the manual became part of their bargain.

Let's assume that the writer meant to say that the manual became part of the bargain *because* the employer introduced the manual into the negotiations, not simply that the manual became part of the bargain sometime after the initial interview. Although the multiple dictionary definitions of "since" typically include "because," the primary dictionary definition relates to time frame or sequence of events:

> From then till now; in the interval; before this; before now; ago; after that time.—prep. Continuously from the time of; as, since yesterday; subsequent to; after.—conj. In the interval after the time when, as: I have been ill twice since I saw you last. Without interruption, from the time when; as, since we saw you last; because; seeing that; inasmuch as.[8]

Therefore, most readers fail to recognize "since" as a signal for a causal relationship when they first encounter it in a sentence. Although the reader will later discover the intended meaning of "since" from context, that process can produce momentary hesitation or even regression in reading. The ambiguity is most serious when the sentence otherwise refers to a time frame:

> Since Rabin breached the contract on January 1, 2018, the three-year limitations period expired before Smith filed suit on January 10, 2021.

This sentence will appear to some readers to make the marginally useful point that the limitations period expired after the breach of contract as well as before the filing of suit. The word "because" in place of "since" would more clearly convey the intended causal relationship: the breach of contract commenced the running of the limitations period; therefore, the period expired before suit was filed.

You create an even greater risk of confusion if you replace "because" with "as," because causation is not a readily recognized connotation of "as":

> Plaintiff is entitled to the equitable remedy of injunctive relief as his legal remedy is inadequate.

One popular dictionary does not even clearly list "because" as a definition for "as"; the closest it comes is listing "since" as a definition of "as" in its conjunctive form.[9] As explained above, even this reference to "since" is ambiguous.

In each of these three examples, "because" would more precisely and unambiguously convey the writer's intended meaning of causal relationship. Indeed, "because" has no other meaning.[10] Moreover, the word "because" is self-descriptive: the root word "cause" within it suggests its meaning.

2. Beyond Dogma

Popular use of synonyms for "because" illustrates the range of considerations that often influence nuances in writing style. Despite the precision that "because" permits, many writers depart from it in the interest of elegant variation, or they reject it altogether because they think that it has an unsophisticated ring to it. However, few readers demand variation or stimulation from every word in a sentence. As with many other words—such as "the," "with," and "a"—the word "because" precisely and unobtrusively performs its function without diverting the reader's attention from more substantively important parts of the sentence.

The most interesting reason that writers give for substituting "since" or "as" for "because" is an admonition in elementary school never to begin a sentence with "because." Of course, if beginning a sentence with "because" offended some principle of syntax or other consideration of composition, replacing it at the beginning of the sentence with a synonym, and a poor one at that, would not cure the defect. In fact, some elementary school teachers may have invented or repeated such a rule in reaction to students' early tendencies to write incomplete sentences, such as: "Because I missed the bus." Those teachers should have explained the requisite components of a complete sentence rather than place undeserved blame on the word "because."

Another defense of "as" and "since" as expressions of a causal relationship has greater merit. Some writers believe that "as" and "since" are not synonymous with "because" in that context but express slightly different shades of causation. Those writers reasonably use "because" to refer to a direct causal relationship and "since" or "as" to refer to a more attenuated relationship.[11] A style that carefully recognizes such a distinction arguably enhances precision. Unfortunately, few writers use "since" or "as" to connote a causal relationship in such a principled manner. Moreover, to a greater extent than in literary writing, legal writing tends to describe causal relationships that are sufficiently direct to justify use of "because" in place of the softer "since" or "as."

3. Pronouns and Other Gendered Titles

In some documents, gendered pronouns can enhance clarity, such as when the document refers to interactions between two persons, one of whom identifies as male and the other as female. But, conventions in the English language often assign a gender to a person when gender is irrelevant. Sometimes you can finesse this problem by changing the noun from singular to plural. For example, rather than stating that an attorney must file his brief on time, you can refer to attorneys who must file their briefs on time or an attorney who must file briefs on time. In other cases, you can repeat the original noun rather than replacing it with a gendered pronoun, as in: "A police officer is liable for violating constitutional rights only if the officer...."

But the clash between convention and the writer's intention is unavoidable at times. Some documents will require specific pronouns or titles to accurately reflect the roles of parties or actors. Conventional rules of grammar require singular nouns or pronouns to be paired with singular verbs, and plural nouns or pronouns to be paired with plural verbs. For example, when referring to an entity like a court or a company, the appropriate pronoun to use in place of that singular entity would be "it" rather than "they."

But, you should be prepared to depart from convention if you have good reason to do so. While precision and accuracy are important characteristics of legal writing, so too are respect and representation. When possible, honor your client's preferred pronouns. Even pairing "they" with a singular noun will be acceptable for some documents and with some audiences. You can use the non-gendered Mx. in place of Mr. or Ms., and you can safely retire the dated Miss and Mrs. except when the subject has stated a preference for either of those titles.[12]

As language continues to develop, it could offer additional alternatives to the singular "they" or Mx. Society requires time to absorb developments in language, so some supervisors or judges will object to the use of the singular "they" or similar innovations. As with all legal writing, you should know your audience so that you can determine when you should adhere to convention, when you can depart from it without raising an eyebrow, and when you can safely press a colleague to consider a new direction.

II. Concise Writing

When you concisely express clear and persuasive ideas in vivid, active, and precise prose, you can strive to convey the ideas with maximum efficiency and effect. Consider this description by a character in Tom Stoppard's play, *The Real Thing*:

> Henry: ... This thing here, which looks like a wooden club, is actually several pieces of particular wood cunningly put together in a certain way so that the whole thing is sprung, like a dance floor. It's for hitting cricket balls with. If you get it right, the cricket ball will travel two hundred yards in four seconds, and all you've done is give it a knock like knocking the top

> off a bottle of stout, and it makes a noise like a trout taking a fly.... (He clucks his tongue to make the noise.) What we're trying to do is to write cricket bats, so that when we throw up an idea and give it a little knock, it might... travel.[13]

A legal document that effectively conveys its message in 10 pages is more like Henry's cricket bat than one that rambles on for 20 pages to convey the same message.

Still, you must not achieve brevity in your writing by omitting important ideas or sacrificing clarity of expression. You should strive first to express all important ideas in sufficient detail to successfully communicate or persuade. With that accomplished, you can streamline your writing by omitting extraneous ideas and expressing the important ones efficiently. Overworked supervisors and judges will thank you for it, as reflected in one state appellate judge's advice:

> First and foremost, more is not always better....
>
> ....
>
> Conversely, avoid being overly "brief and concise."...
>
> In effect, you are being asked to strike a balance between too much and too little. Including needless matter poses the risk of distracting the court while being conclusory may result in the court holding the argument waived. Exercise your judgment with appropriate regard for the possible consequences when striking the balance.[14]

When you are satisfied that you have expressed all critical points and you have turned to the task of omitting needless matter, you should control the length of your document through content, form, and style. You can control content primarily through the scope and depth of analysis. You can achieve concise form and style through efficient organization, sentence structure, and phrasing.

A. Content: Scope and Depth of Analysis

"Scope of analysis" refers to the range of issues or topics that you address in your legal document. "Depth of analysis" refers to the level of detail with which you address a topic.

1. Scope of Analysis

The range of ideas that you address in your document can dramatically affect the document's length. In analyzing a problem, you need not develop every theory that you have encountered during your research. Instead, you can (1) thoroughly discuss the most important and clearly relevant topics, (2) exclude distracting tangents that are unlikely to affect the outcome of the dispute, and (3) determine whether to discuss topics between the two extremes, perhaps in less detail than would be appropriate for a mainstream theory.

As discussed more fully in Section III.B of Chapter 6, you can apply different scopes of analysis to different kinds of documents. The scope of analysis ordinarily can be broad in your examination answers, because most of your professors will specifically test your ability to identify a wide range of issues. The scope of analysis normally should be narrower in a brief, because briefs generally are most persuasive if they focus on the strongest available arguments.

The scope of analysis in a typical office memorandum is somewhere between the scope of analysis of an examination and that of a brief. An office memorandum should not fail to at least briefly discuss a theory or approach that might ultimately be helpful. On the other hand, to a greater extent than an examination answer, an office memorandum should focus on thorough development of the most helpful theories rather than on identification of every plausible approach. If you are not certain whether a legal theory is worth developing fully, you can always introduce the topic briefly near the end of your office memorandum, while offering to develop a full analysis if requested by the assigning attorney.

2. Depth of Analysis

By properly balancing varying depths of analysis in the discussion or argument section of your memorandum or brief, you can make the document more concise and readable. For convenience, this book will use the terms "light analysis" and "in-depth analysis" to refer to the opposite extremes on the spectrum. You engage in light analysis when you simply state a proposition of law and cite to supporting authority. You engage in in-depth analysis when you analyze legal authority more thoroughly, such as by discussing the facts, holding, and reasoning of case law. You may also control the depth of analysis by choosing between (1) expressing a full deductive argument and (2) expressing an incomplete syllogism, leaving a premise of your deductive argument implicit.

a. Depth of Analysis of Legal Authority

Sample Memorandum 1 near the end of Chapter 7 provides an example of balance between light analysis and in-depth analysis of authority from the fictitious state of Calzona. The second paragraph of the discussion section briefly outlines fundamental principles, which provide helpful background information and which almost certainly will not be disputed by the parties. For this purpose, the author of the memorandum has used light analysis by simply stating propositions of law and citing to supporting authority:

> An enforceable contract requires a bargained-for exchange, rather than a one-sided promise to make a gift. *Smith v. Newman*, 161 Calz. 443, 447, 667 P.2d 81, 85 (1984). In an enforceable exchange, a promisor exchanges his own promise for a return promise or a performance. *Id.* at 86.

However, the memorandum also raises the more difficult issue of whether a particular promise made by a lender was illusory, an issue the parties obviously dispute. An adequate discussion of that issue requires a more thorough analysis of case law to determine which precedent is more nearly analogous to the facts of the current dispute. Such in-depth analysis explores the facts, holding, and reasoning of each significant case. Each of the following rule illustrations begins with a rule-based thesis statement, followed by in-depth case analysis:

Thesis statement

The requirement of an exchange is not satisfied if one party gives only an illusory promise, which does not commit the promisor to any future performance. *Atco Corp. v. Johnson*, 155 Calz. 1211, 627 P.2d 781 (1980).

In-depth analysis of Atco

In *Atco Corp.*, the manager of an automobile repair shop promised to forbear "until I want the money" from asserting a claim against the owner of an automobile for $900 in repairs; in exchange, a friend of the owner promised to act as guarantor of the owner's obligation. *Id.* at 1212, 627 P.2d at 782. The word "want" stated no legal commitment, because it permitted the manager at his own discretion to refuse to perform any forbearance at all. Because the manager incurred no obligation, the guarantor's promise was gratuitous and unenforceable. *See id.* at 1213-14, 627 P.2d at 783-84.

Thesis statement

On the other hand, even if a promise leaves open the possibility that the promisor will escape obligation, the promise is valid if the promisor does not have complete control over the events on which the promisor's obligation is conditioned. *See Bonnie v. DeLaney*, 158 Calz. 212, 645 P.2d 887 (1982).

In-depth analysis of Bonnie

In *Bonnie*, an agreement for the sale of a house provided that the buyer could cancel the agreement if the buyer "cannot qualify for a 30-year mortgage loan for 90% of the sales price" with any of several banks listed in the agreement. *Id.* at 213, 645 P.2d at 888. In enforcing the agreement against the seller, the court distinguished *Atco Corp.* on the ground that the word "cannot" referred to the buyer's ability to obtain a loan rather than to his *desire*. Because his ability to obtain a loan was partly controlled by events and decisions outside his control, the promises in the sale agreement were nonillusory and binding. *See id.* at 214-15, 645 P.2d at 889-90.

The light analysis in the first illustration above quickly establishes noncontroversial points without weighing the reader down with unnecessary detail. The more detailed case analysis in the two immediately preceding sample paragraphs provides the reader with a fuller understanding of a specific legal doctrine—the illusory promise—thus creating a solid legal foundation for the fact analysis that will follow.

Sample Memorandum 2 near the end of Chapter 7 also displays a combination of light and in-depth analyses. Section IV.B.1 of that sample memo presents settled principles of negligence law with light analysis. In contrast, Section IV.B.2 of that sample explores the topic of superseding cause with two paragraphs summarizing the facts, holding and reasoning of a fictitious prior case, *Rainbow Landscaping*, followed by two paragraphs discussing whether *Rainbow Landscaping* is analogous to the current case or is distinguishable from it.

You must strike an effective balance between light and in-depth analyses to achieve the dual goals of clarity and concision. Unless the issue is extremely simple, if you use only light analysis to discuss a point in an office memorandum, you risk defining the applicable legal principles with insufficient clarity to permit thoughtful fact analysis. Moreover, if you use only light analysis to argue a disputed point of law in a brief, you probably will fail to persuade. On the other hand, if you use in-depth analysis excessively, you may cause the reader to grow weary and to lose sight of the general legal theory while wandering endlessly among individual cases.

To help strike this balance, you can use citations with parenthetic explanations as a middle ground between light and in-depth analyses. For example, the following passage uses parenthetic explanations to explain how the cited authorities support the proposition for which they are cited:

> In two other decisions, Arizona courts assumed that the statute of frauds is subject to mitigation to protect a party's reliance on the promise to perform, but they refused to apply the doctrine because the normal requirements of estoppel were not satisfied. *Trollope v. Koerner*, 470 P.2d 91, 98-99 (Ariz. 1970) (insufficient reliance); *Mac Enters. v. Del E. Webb Dev. Co.*, 645 P.2d 1245, 1250 (Ariz. Ct. App. 1982) (no promise).

The brief reference to facts or holdings in the parentheses following the citations provides helpful information for the reader. A full paragraph of in-depth analysis of each case, on the other hand, is unnecessary and would distract from the fuller discussion of the cases that are more nearly on point.

b. Incomplete Syllogisms

So far, this section has discussed depth of analysis of legal principles. You may apply the same considerations to the complete deductive syllogism of major premise, minor premise, and conclusion. Normally, a memorandum or brief presents even a simple legal argument in a full syllogism with a discussion of the applicable legal rule, an application of the rule to the facts, and a conclusion:

> Under the Uniform Commercial Code (UCC), the term "merchant" includes any person who "deals in goods of the kind." U.C.C. §2-104(1) (2011). Wilson deals in used cars because he regularly buys and sells used cars as an adjunct to his car rental business. Therefore, he is a merchant of used cars under the UCC.

Alternatively, particularly if the argument is minor or tangential, you can present it in an incomplete syllogism, leaving the legal rule implicit:

> Wilson is a "merchant" of used cars under the UCC because he regularly buys and sells used cars as an adjunct to his car rental business. *See* U.C.C. §2-104(1) (2011).

A more detailed statement could mention the statutory definition, still without establishing the legal rule in a separate sentence:

> Wilson is a "merchant" of used cars under the UCC because he regularly buys and sells used cars as an adjunct to his car rental business and thus "deals in goods of the kind." *See* U.C.C. §2-104(1) (2011).

B. Form: Efficient Organization, Sentence Structure, and Phrasing

1. Organization and Repetition

By applying the principles of organization discussed in Chapter 8, you can write more concisely as well as more clearly. With good organization, you can eliminate unnecessary repetition and present ideas efficiently by building each subsection on the foundations laid in the previous ones.

You need not adopt an organizational framework that eliminates all repetition. Indeed, Chapter 7 explained how the format for a traditional office memorandum contemplates repetition of certain elements. For example, an early section of Brief Answers previews conclusions appearing later in the Discussion section, followed by a main Conclusion that can both sum up and add strategic advice. That's like an actor appearing as the same character in various scenes of a play, though in different garb each time he appears. This repetition or overlapping is not wasteful in a complicated analysis, particularly if you recognize the distinct purposes of the related elements.

Nonetheless, needless repetition within such a framework may add pages without adding clarity. Good organization on all levels should minimize this problem.

2. Sentence Structure and Phrasing

You can often trace verbosity within a sentence to unnecessary repetition, loose verb structure, and expression of implicit information. In such sentences, the words expressing useful ideas are lost among words that convey marginally useful ideas or simply connect substantive ideas to one another.[15] In editing surplus words from your writing, however, you must not shave your writing so close that you sacrifice clarity.

a. Repetition

As discussed in Subsection 1 above, some repetition is built into the general format of a legal document. Moreover, even at the level of words and phrases, carefully planned repetition may occasionally be justified as a guide to complex sentence structure or as a means of gaining unusual emphasis:

> Jack Bailey has declared his guilt with his own actions. He declared his guilt when he fled the murder scene on the arrival of neighbors; he declared his guilt when he later tried to conceal the murder weapon; and he declared his guilt at trial by offering incredible and inconsistent testimony.

Repetition without purpose, however, merely adds words without contributing to the substance of a sentence. Even worse, it might cause the reader to wonder whether the repetitive words are intended to convey different ideas:

> Section 24 of the lease is null, void, invalid, completely unenforceable, and of no legal force or effect whatsoever.

With a much shorter, cleaner sentence employing only one of the adjectives, you can precisely convey the intended meaning:

> Section 24 of the lease is unenforceable.

On the other hand, even closely related terms are not repetitive if they convey meanings that are materially different. For example, state and federal statutes prohibit various kinds of discrimination based on "race, color, or national origin." Although the classes encompassed by these terms can overlap, they are not identical. Thus, an employer who discriminates against a dark-skinned African-American applicant in favor of a light-skinned African-American applicant arguably discriminates on the basis of color, even though not necessarily on the basis of race or national origin.[16]

b. Verb Structure

You will often add extra words to your sentences when you transform verbs into nouns (nominalization) or use verbs in the passive voice. For example, the author of the following clause added unnecessary bulk to his writing by transforming the verb "objected" into the noun "objection," and substituting "presented" as the verb:

> Defense counsel presented an objection to the testimony.

You add further unnecessary bulk by using the passive voice, adding the words "was" and "by":

> An objection to the testimony was presented by defense counsel.

If you employ the verb "objected" to express the action in active voice, you eliminate surplus words and lead the reader more directly to the main point:

> Defense counsel objected to the testimony.

c. Implicit Information

Legal writers frequently express information that could remain implicit, by referring to procedure when defining a substantive legal principle:

> If a party proves that a contract requires a performance that would violate a criminal statute, the court will strike down the contract as illegal and unenforceable.

Unless you intend to emphasize burdens of proof and court procedures, you can convey all the necessary information in fewer words by focusing exclusively on substance:

> A contract is unenforceable if performance of its obligations would violate a criminal statute.

d. Tension between Clarity and Concision

In your quest to eliminate surplus words, you should remain sensitive to the tension between clarity and concision, taking care to retain words and phrases that communicate important information. For example, the following sentences reflect each kind of verbosity cited at the beginning of this section:

> Robert Jones, who is the plaintiff, brought this action against Mary Smith, the defendant. In this action, Jones filed a complaint that alleges that Smith committed a breach of the contract of employment between Smith and Jones.

You can combine these sentences into a single, much more concise sentence. At the margin, however, further revisions for concision could sacrifice important information, depending on your intended connotation and emphasis.

An initial revision reduces the number of words from 37 to 17, arguably without sacrificing clarity on any level:

> Plaintiff Robert Jones brought this action against Defendant Mary Smith, alleging that Smith breached their employment contract.

Among other things, this revision eliminates the repetition of "this action," recognizes that the filing of a complaint is implicit in other phrases, uses "breached" as a direct verb, and replaces wordy clauses and phrases such as "who is the plaintiff" and "between Smith and Jones" with single but equally precise words.

By treating "Plaintiff" and "Defendant" as implicit, and by replacing "brought this action" with "sued," you can trim another five words from the sentence:

> Robert Jones sued Mary Smith, alleging that Smith breached their employment contract.

This revision, however, may achieve concision at the expense of other considerations of style. To many readers, "sued" carries the negative connotation of harassing litigation; therefore, counsel for Jones might prefer the softer, though less concise, phrase "brought this action." Also, if you wish to refer to the parties subsequently only as "Plaintiff" and "Defendant" or only as "Jones" and "Smith," you should link each party's name to his or her procedural title by initially using the full phrases "Plaintiff Robert Jones," and "Defendant Mary Smith."

On the other hand, if you do not object to the last revision above, you could trim two more words from the sentence and achieve a more direct flow by eliminating the reference to "alleging":

> Robert Jones sued Mary Smith for breaching their employment contract.

Sticklers for precision, however, might argue that you should use the preposition "for" to introduce a description of the requested relief rather than the ground for liability.

To summarize, revisions to achieve concise writing are matters of judgment that require sensitivity to considerations of emphasis, precision, connotation, and other elements of clarity.

Exercise 9-6

Rewrite the following sentence to make it more direct and concise.

The Federal Rules of Civil Procedure, Rule 26(c), provides that the issuance of protective orders to the effect that certain matters ought not to be inquired into in the course of discovery is within the authorization of the court.

III. Review and Revision

To polish your writing, you must critically review and revise early drafts. To do this well, you must approach writing analytically rather than purely intuitively. You must become sufficiently familiar with style problems that you can spot them in your own writing, even though you are comfortable with your own prose. You can best develop these editing skills by studying writing style in books or workshops, by reviewing and critiquing your own work and that of others, and by asking others to review and critique your writing. As with the writing process, it takes time and practice to develop effective editing skills.

Unfortunately, time pressures and limits on the client's resources will sometimes compel you to produce a final draft after only one or two opportunities for revision. The minimally acceptable level of review and revision is easily stated: at the very least, you must proofread your first draft and make necessary changes. Every judge has a horror story about an atrociously written brief, one that obviously was dictated and never proofread. No limitation on time or resources justifies such shoddy work.

The appropriate level of review and revision beyond the minimum is a matter of priorities and economics. A client with ample resources and with a great deal at stake in an important pretrial motion or appeal might expect its legal counsel to spare no expense in writing the best possible brief. You and your colleagues undoubtedly would begin work on the brief as early as possible, subject it to particularly critical review, and polish it through many drafts.

At the other end of the economic scale, in a modest case a firm might find it difficult to justify charging a client for a formal office memorandum prior to settlement negotiations. Instead, an assigning attorney might ask you to deliver your research and conclusions in an oral report or email message. Even when a more formal document is appropriate, you will not serve your client well by piling up billable hours while subjecting a preliminary office memorandum or client letter to repeated scrutiny over half a dozen drafts. Such a document should be clear, complete, and concise, but limits on resources may preclude more than one or two rewrites. Moreover, even if you ordinarily avoid procrastination, you will occasionally be stuck with an emergency "rush job" that leaves you little time for revision.

Consequently, you should strive to produce the best possible written product on the first draft. You can do this by learning to avoid style problems common to your writing and by devoting appropriate attention to the prewriting stage.

To develop the ability to avoid common style problems on the first draft, you must identify and analyze your writing habits. Ironically, this will initially require devoting extra time and attention to your writing over many drafts. With the aid of a colleague or a writing manual, you will gradually become sufficiently conscious of your writing problems and their solutions that you can begin to avoid those problems on the first draft, reducing the need for substantial editing.

For example, one summer associate in a major law firm learned from a writing consultant that he tended to overuse the passive, abstract verb form "there is." For several weeks after this diagnosis, he used his word processing program to highlight this and related phrases in his first drafts, so that he could revise the highlighted passages on second drafts. He eventually became sufficiently attuned to the problem that he avoided it on first drafts.

You can further minimize the need for redrafting, and thus save time in the long run, by carefully formulating and organizing your analysis before beginning to write. You should prepare an outline of your document and consider discussing the outline with your assigning attorney or a peer. Once satisfied with the broad outline of your analysis, you can devote greater attention to the details when you begin writing or dictating.

One final note of caution: word processing provides attorneys with the luxury of blocking and moving passages of text from one computer file to another, such as from a contract for one client to a similar contract for another client. Although this process can reduce the time needed to prepare the initial draft of the second document, it also underscores the need for careful proofreading and revision. The passage in the first document may be helpful as a starting point, but it likely will not be perfectly tailored to the transaction in the second document. Moreover, the imperfection may be sufficiently subtle to require special diligence in evaluating and revising initial drafts of the second document.

Checklist for Chapter 9

- ✔ Apply conventions of composition flexibly, striving to satisfy their underlying purposes and policies, and consciously choosing between alternative words, phrases, or sentence structures.
- ✔ Aim for clarity and concision in your writing, giving priority to clarity when they conflict.
- ✔ To write clearly,
    - use simple, plain English unless a legal term of art will inform more than distract;
    - after comparing alternatives, choose an effective sentence structure and punctuation, with adequate closure and guides to structure;
    - use concrete verbs in the active voice, unless passive construction serves a specific purpose;
    - distinguish between restrictive and nonrestrictive clauses when necessary for clarity; and
    - select the word or phrase that precisely conveys your meaning.
- ✔ To write concisely,
    - maintain reasonable limitations on scope and depth of analysis; and
    - avoid verbosity by adopting efficient organization, sentence structure, and phrasing.
- ✔ To polish your writing,
    - create the best possible product on first draft; and revise and polish your document, with sensitivity to economic constraints.

Endnotes

1. Brian Quinn, *Dispelling Misconception*, 62 TEX. B.J. 890, 891 (1999).
2. *See* Richard C. Wydick & Amy E. Sloan, PLAIN ENGLISH FOR LAWYERS 59, 64-65 (6th ed. 2019).
3. *Cf. id.* at 45-46 (advocating listing of items on separate lines).
4. This sentence would be more precise if it stated that the court ordered the sheriff to hold the defendant without bail, but it suffices to illustrate the point under consideration.
5. *See* William Strunk, Jr. & E. B. White, THE ELEMENTS OF STYLE 5 (5th ed. 2009).
6. Anderson Bros. Ford v. Valencia, 452 U.S. 205, 211-12 (1981) (italics added).
7. The source of this problem is Rebecca W. Berch (former legal writing program director and now a retired Justice of the Arizona Supreme Court), *Words That/Which Cause Problems in Legal Writing*, 25 ARIZ. BAR BRIEFS No. 9 (1987).
8. NEW WEBSTER'S DICTIONARY 902 (encyclopedic ed. 1981).
9. *Id.* at 58.
10. *See id.* at 86.
11. *See generally* William Strunk, Jr. & E. B. White, THE ELEMENTS OF STYLE 23-24 (5th ed. 2009) ("because" presented as concise replacement for the verbose phrase "the reason why is that," and "since" presented as primary replacement for "owing to the fact that"); E. B. White, THE SECOND TREE FROM THE CORNER 17 (1984) ("Parnell was not a playmate of mine, as he was a few years older. . . .").
12. *See* Heidi K. Brown, *Get with the Pronoun*, 17 J. ALWD 61, 71-74 (2020).
13. Tom Stoppard, THE REAL THING 51 (1984).
14. Brian Quinn, *Dispelling Misconception*, 62 TEX. B.J. 890, 891 (1999).
15. One famous textbook recommends that writers maximize the ratio of "working words" to "glue words" in a sentence. *See* Richard C. Wydick & Amy E. Sloan, PLAIN ENGLISH FOR LAWYERS 7-10 (6th ed. 2019).
16. *See generally* Walker v. Secretary of Treasury, I.R.S., 713 F. Supp. 403 (N.D. Ga. 1989).

Chapter 10

Signaling, Presenting, and Quoting Authority

When you assert your analysis or interpretation of the law in a memorandum or a brief, you must support your assertions with citations to legal authority, as illustrated in various examples in previous chapters. One manual on advocacy identifies two functions of citations: "(1) it tells the reader that your rule is supported by legal authority and is not merely a product of your imagination, and (2) it allows the reader to evaluate the persuasiveness of the authority you cited when deciding whether to accept your conclusion."[1]

Comprehensive instruction in basic citation form is best left to a separate citation manual, such as THE BLUEBOOK: A UNIFORM SYSTEM OF CITATION[2] or the ALWD GUIDE TO LEGAL CITATION.[3] This chapter will supplement that instruction with an exploration of three related topics: (1) selecting and using the best citation signal, (2) presenting the law clearly and effectively, and (3) quoting from legal authority effectively but not excessively.

As with Chapter 9's discussion of legal writing style, this chapter occasionally refers to special techniques of advocacy, but it primarily addresses the balanced, nearly neutral analysis that is appropriate for an office memorandum. Techniques of advocacy are explored in greater detail in the second book of this series.

Finally, the citations in the footnotes of this book are in a special format for scholarly publications. Consequently, they differ in some respects from the citation form that you will use in office memoranda and briefs.

I. Citation Signals

Citation signals describe the relationship between the cited authority and either (1) the proposition for which it is cited or (2) other authority. The following subsections present this textbook's interpretations and illuminations of citation signals that were popularized by the Bluebook and are adopted by the ALWD Guide.

In many of the sample citations below, a parenthetic explanation at the end of the citation supplements the signal by more specifically describing the relationship between the cited authority and the stated proposition or other authority. You may prefer to use parenthetic explanations even more liberally than suggested in the examples below. According to the BLUEBOOK, "[p]arenthetical information is recommended when the relevance of a cited authority might not otherwise be clear to the reader."[4]

A. No Signal

Use no signal to introduce a citation if the proposition for which authority is cited (1) quotes from the cited authority, (2) names the authority or otherwise refers to it, or (3) is directly supported by the authority, often because the proposition is a paraphrase or summary of a passage in the authority.[5] Each of these types of propositions is illustrated, in the order set forth above, in the following passage. The second and third citations use "*id.*" to refer to the previously cited authority, *Oncale*, but none of the citations begins with a citation signal:

> Sexual harassment constitutes sex discrimination if "members of one sex are exposed to disadvantageous terms or conditions of employment to which members of the other sex are not exposed." *Oncale v. Sundowner Offshore Servs., Inc.*, 523 U.S. 75, 80 (1998) (quoting *Harris v. Forklift Sys., Inc.*, 510 U.S. 17, 25 (Ginsburg, J., concurring)). In *Oncale*, the Court held that same-sex harassment could meet this standard and thus constitute sex discrimination under Title VII. *Id.* at 80, 82. Such discrimination, however, does not trigger liability under the statute unless it so degrades the working environment that it alters terms or conditions of employment. *Id.* at 78, 81.

B. "*See*"

Introduce a citation with "*see*" if the cited authority supports your proposition, but only indirectly, thus requiring the reader to infer an unstated logical link between the proposition and the authority.[6] For example, if you tailor the holding of the cited authority to the facts of your own case, your proposition will not appear in the cited authority, but it should follow directly from it. In the following example, the cited authority does not mention Gracy's, Inc., Bailey, or Johnson. Therefore, even though the *Oncale* decision clearly supports the proposition about Johnson's claim, it does so only indirectly: It requires the reader to infer that the proposition regarding Johnson's claim follows from the application of general principles stated in *Oncale* or from an analogy to *Oncale*'s application of general principles to the facts of *Oncale*'s claim:

> Gracy's, Inc., will be liable for sex discrimination under Title VII if its general manager, Bailey, selectively harassed Johnson because of his sex and if the harassment was so severe or frequent that it altered Johnson's conditions of employment. *See Oncale v. Sundowner Offshore Servs., Inc.*, 523 U.S. 75, 78-82 (1998).

C. *"Accord"*

According to the BLUEBOOK, if a proposition quotes or names an authority, you should cite to the quoted or named authority without any signal, and you may then use "*accord*" to introduce citations to additional cases that directly support the proposition but are not named or quoted in the proposition:[7]

> "The general rule is that a seller of real estate is under a duty to disclose those material facts which would not be discoverable by the buyer in the exercise of ordinary care and due diligence." *Isaacs v. Bishop*, 249 S.W.3d 100, 114 n.14 (Tex. App. 2008); *accord*, *Robbins v. Capozzi*, 100 S.W.3d 18, 24 (Tex. App. 2002); *Smith v. Nat'l Resort Cmtys., Inc.*, 585 S.W.2d 655, 658 (Tex. 1979).

You can also use "*accord*" to introduce authority from other jurisdictions that adopt the same rule as is stated by the authority to which you have just cited without any introductory signal:[8]

> In Georgia, courts have recognized an affirmative duty to disclose material facts during negotiation of the sale of residential housing. *Condon v. Kunse*, 208 Ga. App. 856, 858, 432 S.E.2d 266, 269 (1993); *accord*, *Hill v. Jones*, 151 Ariz. 81, 725 P.2d 1115 (Ct. App. 1986) (finding seller's duty to disclose termite damage in dwelling as a matter of common law); *Isaacs v. Bishop*, 249 S.W.3d 100, 114 n.14 (Tex. App. 2008) (citing to Texas cases that recognize the duty in both residential and commercial real estate transactions).

D. "See generally"

Use "*see generally*" to signify that the cited authority provides general background information related to the proposition for which the authority is cited:[9]

> In Arizona, an employer may be liable in some circumstances for breach of a promise in a company policy manual. *See Leikvold v. Valley View Cmty. Hosp.*, 141 Ariz. 544, 546, 688 P.2d 170, 172 (1984); *see generally* Michael A. Di Sabatino, Annotation, *Modern Status of Rule that Employer May Discharge At-will Employee for Any Reason*, 12 A.L.R. 4th 544 (1982) (examining erosion of doctrine that employer may terminate without liability an employee hired for an indefinite period).

The annotation cited above does not provide direct support for the proposition about Arizona law, because the annotation predated the *Leikvold* case, which firmly established the Arizona law on point. Instead, the annotation provides general background information about a national trend of expanding employee rights under tort and contract law, background information that can give the reader a fuller understanding of the general topic raised in the proposition.

E. "Cf." and "Compare . . . with"

Use "*cf.*" to introduce an authority that supports the stated proposition by analogy or distinction, followed by parenthetic explanation:[10]

> The "Proposal to Purchase Real Estate" probably is not an offer to buy a lot within the subdivision, because it does not address terms of payment. *Cf. Craft v. Elder & Johnston Co.*, 38 N.E.2d 416 (Ohio Ct. App. 1941) (holding that a newspaper ad for an indefinite quantity of sewing machines was only an invitation to negotiate); *Lefkowitz v. Great Minneapolis Surplus Store*, 86 N.W.2d 689 (Minn. 1957) (holding that a newspaper ad was an offer, but only because it was unusually specific and definite).

Neither of the authorities cited above directly supports your proposition about the real estate proposal, because the authorities address the specialized factual context of newspaper advertisements. Nonetheless, the first citation above supports the stated proposition by showing how analogous facts in the context of a newspaper advertisement supported the same result as the one proposed for a personalized real estate transaction. The second citation indirectly supports the stated proposition by explaining that a different result from the one proposed depended on materially different facts, also in the specialized context of a newspaper advertisement.

To directly compare these two different kinds of support, or to contrast different legal approaches, you can use "*Compare* ... *with*," along with parenthetic explanations.[11] The following example compares two different kinds of support for a proposition:

> A newspaper ad is an offer only if it is sufficiently complete and definite that it leaves no important terms open for further negotiation. *Compare Craft v. Elder & Johnston Co.*, 38 N.E.2d 416 (Ohio Ct. App. 1941) (newspaper ad for an indefinite quantity of sewing machines was only an invitation to negotiate), *with Lefkowitz v. Great Minneapolis Surplus Store*, 86 N.W.2d 689 (Minn. 1957) (newspaper ad was an offer because it was unusually specific and definite).

F. "*See also*"

As an alternative to the signals discussed in Subsections C through E above, you may introduce additional supporting authority with "*see also*." The BLUEBOOK defines "*see also*" so that it arguably lies roughly between no signal, "*accord*," and "*see*," on the one hand, and "*cf.*" or "*see generally*" on the other:

> Cited authority constitutes additional source material that supports the proposition. "See also" is commonly used to cite an authority supporting a proposition when authorities that state or directly support the proposition already have been cited or discussed. The use of a parenthetical explanation of the source's relevance ... following a citation introduced by "see also" is encouraged.[12]

According to the ALWD GUIDE,

> [u]se [see also] to cite authority that supports the proposition in addition to that previously cited in its support. In addition, see also may be used when the cited authority supports a point but is in some respect distinguishable from previously cited authorities.[13]

You likely will use the "*see also*" signal to introduce additional supporting authority that follows authority introduced with a "*see*" signal, or perhaps with no signal. You typically will use "*see also*" to introduce authority that supports your proposition less directly than does the authority preceding it, thus justifying a parenthetic explanation.

For example, suppose the first authority in a citation sentence is introduced with "*see*" because it clearly supports your proposition, but only indirectly, requiring some inference on the reader's part. You might introduce the second authority with "*see also*," rather than with no further signal, if the second authority states or supports your proposition, but not so clearly or obviously that you can dispense with a parenthetic explanation. Of course, in some contexts "*see generally*" or "*cf.*" would be appropriate to signify such an attenuated relationship between the authority and the proposition. Consequently, "*see also*" should be reserved for supporting authority that is not so far removed from the specific topic of your proposition that it provides only general background information, a level of support that is better signified by "*see generally*." Nor should you use "*see also*" to introduce authority that is so contextually different from your proposition that it supports the proposition only by analogy, a relationship better signified by "*cf.*"

For example, the first authority in the following passage, *Rite Realty, Inc. v. Simmons*, is introduced with "*see*" presumably because the court in *Rite Realty* found no offer on facts very similar to those of the "Proposal to Purchase Real Estate," which is the subject of the office memorandum or brief. In contrast, the second authority is introduced with "*see also*" because its more extreme facts moderate the degree of support it provides to the main proposition:

> The "Proposal to Purchase Real Estate" probably is not an offer to buy a lot within the subdivision, because it does not address terms of payment. *See Rite Realty, Inc. v. Simmons*, ... (1968); *see also Frost v. Baker*, ... (finding no offer because document proposed to sell a working farm at a certain price without identifying the farm or its location within the county).

In this example, *Frost v. Baker* requires parenthetic explanation, because the reader should be apprised of how its facts raised more obvious problems in finding an offer than does the "Proposal to Purchase Real Estate" in the case at hand.[14] Nonetheless, *Frost* provides more than general background information. Moreover, neither its reference to a proposal to sell rather than buy nor the more obvious indefiniteness in the terms of its proposal suggest that its support requires the reader to draw an analogy to find support. Accordingly, "*see also*" is a more appropriate introductory signal than "*see generally*" or "*cf.*"

Many writers more naturally and intuitively use "*see also*" in a slightly different context, suggested by the Bluebook's statement that "*see also*" might follow the citation to an authority that has already been ***discussed***. For example, if you have engaged in an in-depth discussion of a case and applied it to the facts to reach a conclusion, you might end your discussion with a "*see also*" citation to provide additional support, particularly if the additional support is somewhat less telling, perhaps because the facts are not as squarely on point or because the authoring court is less authoritative within the jurisdiction:

> Officer Caruso's warrantless search of Kelly's motor home is squarely supported by the Supreme Court's decision in *California v. Carney*, 471 U.S. 386 (1985). In *Carney* .... Similarly, in this case, Kelly had parked his motor home at a parking strip along a state beach.... Thus, Officer Caruso needed only probable cause to search Kelly's motor home. *See id.*; *see also Wisconsin v. Snide* ... (Wis. 1993) (upholding warrantless search of fishing boat with sleeping berths while it was docked lakeside and subject to administrative regulation of government authorities).

G. "*But*" and "*Contra*"

Introduce an authority that opposes your proposition with a new citation sentence beginning with "*but*," combined with another signal, such as "*see*" or "*cf.*," as in "*But see*" or "*But cf.*":[15]

> The "Proposal to Purchase Real Estate" probably is not an offer to buy a lot within the subdivision, because it does not address terms of payment. *Cf. Craft v. Elder & Johnston Co.*, 38 N.E.2d 416 (Ohio Ct. App. 1941) (newspaper ad for indefinite quantity of sewing machines was only an invitation to negotiate). *But cf. Buntz v. Great Calzona Surplus Store*, 251 Calz. 188 (1957) (newspaper ad was an offer at a sale price even though the duration of the sale was left uncertain).

In this example, the fictitious opinion in *Buntz* plays a different role than did the *Lefkowitz* case in Subsection E above. Although *Lefkowitz* reached a different result than stated in your proposition, its reasoning and materially different facts nonetheless supported your proposition by analogy. In contrast, *Buntz* opposes your proposition to some degree because it finds an offer despite an argument that an important term was missing from the ad; therefore, the negative signal "*But*" is appropriate. Because the author viewed the context in *Buntz* as only analogous to that of her case, and because the missing term in *Buntz* was different in character than the missing term in the present case, the author appropriately paired "*But*" with "*cf.*" in introducing *Buntz*. If an authority contradicted your proposition indirectly, requiring some inference but not analogy to a different context, you would introduce it with "*But see*." If an authority directly contradicted your proposition, you would introduce it with "*Contra*."[16]

H. "*E.g.*"

Use "*e.g.*," combined with another signal if necessary, to show that the cited authority is simply an example of numerous cases that might be cited to support the proposition:[17]

> *See, e.g.*, *Dothard v. Rawlinson*, 433 U.S. 321, 323-32 (1977) (height and weight requirement for prison guards).

Alternatively, you may cite to multiple authorities without the "*e.g.*" signal:

> *See Dothard v. Rawlinson*, 433 U.S. 321, 323-32 (1977) (height and weight requirement for prison guards); *Griggs v. Duke Power Co.*, 401 U.S. 424 (1971) (high school diploma or intelligence test); *Blake v. City of L.A. Police Dep't*, 595 F.2d 1367 (9th Cir. 1979) (height and physical abilities test for police officers); ....

As a matter of style, however, you should avoid long string citations of multiple authorities unless you have good reason to cite to more than two or three strong, illustrative authorities. For example, to establish that six circuits of the United States Courts of Appeals have agreed that the same ambiguous statute should be interpreted in a certain manner, you might reasonably cite to a decision in each of six circuits in a long string citation. In most other contexts, however, you can save your reader time and effort by citing to your best one, two, or three authorities and by preceding the citation with the "*e.g.*" signal to signify that numerous other authorities hold similarly.

Exercise 10-1

1. Editing Citations

Using the citation manual designated by your professor, correct the errors in the following citations.

a. Article III, Federal Constitution, sec. 1.

b. U.S. Code, section 1983, title 42.

c. *Crane Co. v. American Standard, Inc.*, C.A.2d, 1973, 490 F.2d 332 at 335 through 336.

d. *Michigan Sugar Co. v. Jebavy Sorenson Orchard Co.*, Mich. Ct. App., 1976, 239 N.W.2d 693, 66 Mich. App. 642. [cited in a brief to a Michigan court].

2. Constructing Citations

Using the citation manual designated by your professor, express the correct citation for the following authorities in a brief to a Connecticut court:

a. In 1980, the Connecticut Supreme Court issued a decision in *Cherwell-Ralli, Inc. v. Rytman Grain Co.* It appeared in volume 180 of the Connecticut Reporter, the official reporter for the Connecticut Supreme Court, beginning at page 714. It also appeared in volume 433 of the unofficial, regional Atlantic Reporter, second series, beginning at page 984.

b. You wish to cite in full to the decision described in paragraph *a* above at page 716 of the official reporter and page 986 of the unofficial reporter. After an additional sentence of text, you wish to cite to the same authority at page 715 of the official reporter and page 985 of the unofficial reporter. No other citation has intervened.

c. You wish to cite to the decision described in paragraph a above at page 717 of the official reporter and page 987 of the unofficial reporter. You last cited to this authority in the previous page of your document, as described in paragraph *b* above; since then, several citations to other authorities have intervened.

3. Selecting Citation Signals

In each excerpt below, select the appropriate citation signal, or mark an "x" to designate that no signal is appropriate.

a. At a minimum, due process requires a hearing before a disinterested, unbiased judge. *Bracy v. Gramley* .... [*Bracy* directly states this proposition, although in slightly different words.]

b. At a minimum, due process requires a hearing "before a judge with no actual bias against the defendant or interest in the outcome of his particular case." *Bracy v. Gramley* .... [*Bracy* is the source of the quote.]

c. Except in special circumstances, police officers must secure a warrant before searching a residence. *Agnello v. United States* ... ; *California v. Carney* ... (permitting warrantless search of a motor home because of its mobility and because of reduced expectation of privacy stemming from administrative regulation of all motor vehicles). Because no special circumstances justified a warrantless search in this case, the discovery of the marijuana was the product of an illegal search. *Agnello v. United States* ... [*Agnello* directly states the opening proposition, though in other words, and it is only the first of many Supreme Court decisions to directly affirm this proposition. *Carney* supports a different result in a limited context that shares some factual elements with those encompassed by the main proposition, but nonetheless is distinguishable from the fixed residence in *Agnello*. *Agnello* indirectly supports the second proposition, because—in the context of a different case, not involving the discovery of the marijuana in the present case—it stated that failure to obtain a warrant in similar circumstances could make a search illegal].

II. Presenting Your Authority Effectively

A. Subordinating Your Citations

1. Citation Clauses and Sentences

Authors of books or law journal articles can gracefully insert case names at the beginning or in the middle of textual sentences, because they customarily drop the remainder of the citations to footnotes. Some attorneys and judges have advocated a similar style for office memoranda and briefs to courts.[18] According to current convention, however, most citations in briefs and in office memoranda remain in the text, raising issues about the best way to combine the citations with the propositions for which they are cited.

Occasionally, a citation to authority is so short that you can unobtrusively insert it into the middle of a sentence as a citation clause:

> Because the employer is potentially liable for punitive damages, 42 U.S.C. §1981a(a)(1) (2012), we should seriously consider the plaintiff's offer to settle for reasonable compensatory damages.

Longer citations at the beginning or middle of a sentence in an office memorandum or brief, however, can divert attention from substantive ideas in the text of the sentence:

> In *Tucson Med. Ctr. v. Zoslow*, 147 Ariz. 612, 614, 712 P.2d 459, 461 (Ct. App. 1985), the court held that, in the absence of an express restriction by contract or statute, a tenant generally has the unrestricted right to assign or sublet.

The passage above draws the reader's attention first to the authority, and only then to the proposition for which the authority is cited. Because the case citation has little independent significance in the example, you could improve this passage by moving the citation to a separate citation sentence, permitting you to reserve the main text for the ideas for which the authority is cited. If you do not wish to emphasize the identity of the authoring court, you can make the strongest substantive statement by presenting the legal proposition as an unqualified statement of truth that at least one court has incidentally discovered:

> In the absence of an express restriction by contract or statute, a tenant generally has the unrestricted right to assign or sublet. *Tucson Med. Ctr. v. Zoslow*, 147 Ariz. 612, 614, 712 P.2d 459, 461 (Ct. App. 1985).

On the other hand, if the decisions of the authoring court are controlling on the court adjudicating the current dispute, you might want to identify the authoring court in the textual sentence, while continuing to subordinate the case name and the rest of the citation:

> The Arizona Court of Appeals has held that, in the absence of an express restriction by contract or statute, a tenant generally has the unrestricted right to assign or sublet. *Tucson Med. Ctr. v. Zoslow*, 147 Ariz. 612, 614, 712 P.2d 459, 461 (Ct. App. 1985).

On rare occasions, you might appropriately retain a full citation to authority in a textual sentence if the citation itself has such great independent significance that it warrants such emphasis:

> In *Brown v. Board of Education*, 347 U.S. 483 (1954), the Supreme Court unanimously held that state-sponsored racial segregation in public schools violates the equal protection guarantee of the Fourteenth Amendment.

In this example, the case name, the identity of the authoring court, and even the date of the decision all trigger recognition in most readers. Alternatively, some writers might refer to the instantly recognizable case name in the textual sentence, saving the remainder of the citation for a separate citation sentence:

> In *Brown v. Board of Education*, the Supreme Court unanimously held that state-sponsored segregation in public schools violates the Equal Protection guarantee of the Fourteenth Amendment. 347 U.S. 483 (1954).

Because it separates the case name from its citation, however, this form is unconventional if it represents the initial citation to this authority in the memorandum or the brief. Therefore, it may not meet with the approval of every editor or assigning attorney.

2. In-Depth Case Analysis

You will have even greater reason to subordinate your citations when you present an in-depth case analysis. The following introduction to the analysis of a fictitious case not only inappropriately begins a textual sentence with a full citation, it also begins exploring the details of the case without first explaining generally why the case warrants in-depth analysis:

> In *Bonnie v. DeLaney*, 158 Calz. 212, 645 P.2d 887 (1982), an agreement for the sale of a house provided that the buyer could cancel the agreement if the buyer "cannot qualify for a 30-year mortgage loan for 90% of the sales price" with any of several banks listed in the agreement. *Id.* at 213, 645 P.2d at 888. In enforcing the agreement against the seller, the court distinguished ....

The reader trudges through such a passage with little interest and at least moderate irritation, because he doesn't discover the point of the case until the end of the passage. A series of such paragraphs presenting a laundry list of cases produces a rambling effect that causes the reader to lose track of the principles that the cases are meant to illustrate.

You can greatly improve the passage quoted above by introducing it with an overview of the point that the in-depth case analysis will illustrate:

> On the other hand, even if a promise leaves open the possibility that the promisor will escape obligation, the promise is valid if the promisor does not have complete control over the events upon which the promisor's obligation is conditioned. *Bonnie v. DeLaney*, 158 Calz. 212, 645 P.2d 887 (1982). In *Bonnie*, an agreement for the sale of a house provided that the buyer could cancel the agreement if the buyer "cannot qualify for a 30-year mortgage loan for 90% of the sales price" with any of several banks listed in the agreement. *Id.* at 213, 645 P.2d at 888. In enforcing the agreement against the seller, the court distinguished ....

The preceding passage uses a topic sentence to summarize the point that the case analysis will illustrate. In more complex analyses, you might precede the case analysis with a paragraph that provides the appropriate overview in two or more sentences.

This method of presenting authority enables you to introduce the case citation in a separate citation sentence and to begin the in-depth case analysis with an unobtrusive, short-form reference to the case name:

> ... events upon which the promisor's obligation is conditioned. *Bonnie v. DeLaney*, 158 Calz. 212, 645 P.2d 887 (1982). In *Bonnie*, an agreement for the sale of a house provided ....

Moreover, if you intend to analyze several cases on the same issue, you can use the topic sentence or overview paragraph to help you to express your synthesis of the case law. Synthesis of authority is a critical component of legal method, warranting further exploration of writing techniques that effectively display synthesis.

B. Synthesis of Case Law

Many legal rules are the products of synthesis of two or more legal authorities. In an office memorandum or a brief, you should present such legal rules with clear guides to your synthesis rather than with isolated and unconnected analyses of the individual authorities.

1. Lack of Synthesis Burdens the Reader

For example, suppose that a section of an office memorandum analyzes the issue of whether a federal civil rights act addresses employment discrimination against a person because he is French-Canadian. The following sample passage presents a "laundry list" of case briefs. It is ineffective because it provides insufficient guidance to the author's synthesis, or perhaps because it betrays the author's failure to synthesize:

I. Racial Classifications Under Section 1981

Section 1981 of title 42 of the United States Code provides in part as follows:

General statutory rules

> All persons within the jurisdiction of the United States shall have the same right in every State and Territory to make and enforce contracts ... as is enjoyed by white citizens ....

In *Runyon v. McCrary*, 427 U.S. 160 (1976), African-American applicants to private, commercially operated, nonsectarian schools sued the schools through their parents. They alleged that the schools refused to admit them because of their race in violation of section 1981. A divided Supreme Court ruled that the school's discriminatory admissions policy violated the statute. It held that the statute applied to private contracts and that application of the statute to the school's admissions policy did not infringe upon the constitutional interests of the students or their parents in association, privacy, and parental control.

In-depth analysis without thesis sentence to express an overview

In *McDonald v. Santa Fe Trail Transp. Co.*, 427 U.S. 273 (1976), white employees sued their employer and their union under section 1981 and Title VII of the Civil Rights Act of 1964. They alleged that their discharge for

In-depth analysis without thesis sentence to express overview or synthesis

misappropriation of property was racially motivated because an African-American employee similarly charged was not dismissed. The Supreme Court acknowledged that the "immediate impetus" for the 1866 predecessor to section 1981 was "the necessity for further relief of the constitutionally emancipated former Negro slaves." *Id.* at 289. Nonetheless, on the strength of legislative history indicating that the bill would protect all races, the Supreme Court held that section 1981 imposes liability for discrimination aimed at any race, including whites. *Id.* at 289-96.

In-depth analysis without thesis sentence to express overview or synthesis

In *St. Francis College v. Al-Khazraji*, 481 U.S. 604 (1987), a college professor of Arab ancestry sued his employer under section 1981 and other civil rights statutes. He alleged that the denial of his application for tenure was racially motivated because similarly situated Caucasians fared better in the tenure process. The trial court dismissed the section 1981 claim for failure to state a claim of race discrimination because Arabs were not a race distinct from Caucasians. *See id.* at 606. The court of appeals reversed and remanded for further proceedings, and the Supreme Court affirmed the decision of the court of appeals.

The Supreme Court held that scientific knowledge and cultural attitudes at the time of enactment of the 1866 and 1870 predecessors to section 1981 shaped the racial classifications addressed by the statute. Legislative history and popular dictionary and encyclopedic sources of the era reflect the view that groups with relatively narrowly defined ancestral roots and ethnic characteristics, such as "Germans," "Greeks," "Jews," and "Gypsies," represent distinct races. The Supreme Court concluded that Arabs would be viewed as a separate race under those standards and that section 1981 therefore addresses discrimination based on Arab ancestry. *See id.* at 610-13.

In our case . . . .

2. The Benefits of Expressing Your Synthesis

The preceding passage does not give adequate notice of the points or issues that each case brief is intended to illustrate, nor does it explain how the authorities relate to one another. The following passage provides a better guide to the author's synthesis. It uses a transition sentence or paragraph to provide a preview of the point illustrated by each case brief and to explain how each authority relates to previously analyzed authorities. The passage below also flows more coherently because it limits its in-depth analysis to the announced topic of the section and refers only tersely to other potential problems in the scope of the statute.

I. Racial Classifications Under Section 1981

Introduction to statutory language

Federal civil rights legislation prohibits certain kinds of racial discrimination in contractual relations:

Statutory language

> All persons within the jurisdiction of the United States shall have the same right in every State and Territory to make and enforce contracts ... as is enjoyed by white citizens ....

42 U.S.C. §1981 (2012).

General guides from case law interpreting the statute

As suggested by the statutory reference to rights "enjoyed by white citizens," the "immediate impetus" for the 1866 predecessor to section 1981 was "the necessity for further relief of the constitutionally emancipated former Negro slaves." *McDonald v. Santa Fe Trail Transp. Co.*, 427 U.S. 273, 289 (1976). Consequently, section 1981 applies most clearly to race discrimination against African-Americans. *See, e.g., Runyon v. McCrary*, 427 U.S. 160 (1976).

Thesis sentence introducing in- depth analysis of *McDonald*

Section 1981's prohibition of discrimination, however, extends beyond discrimination against African-Americans and applies more generally to discrimination based on any racial classification. *See McDonald*, 427 U.S. 273. In *McDonald*, white employees sued their employer and their union under section 1981 and Title VII of the Civil Rights Act of 1964. They alleged that their discharge for misappropriation of property was racially motivated because an African-American employee similarly charged was not dismissed. On the strength of legislative history indicating that the bill would protect all races, the Supreme Court held that section 1981 imposes liability for discrimination against members of any race, including whites. *See id.* at 289-96.

Transition ¶ presenting (1) relationship of *McDonald* to *St. Francis* and (2) overview of *St. Francis*

McDonald did not attempt to identify all the racial classifications protected under section 1981. More recently, the Supreme Court held that the applicable classifications are not those recognized by many contemporary scientific theories, but are the narrower and more numerous classifications generally recognized when Congress enacted the predecessors to section 1981. *See St. Francis College v. Al-Khazraji*, 481 U.S. 604 (1987).

In-depth analysis of *St. Francis*

In *St. Francis*, the Supreme Court reinstated the civil rights claims of a college professor of Arab ancestry who alleged that he was discriminatorily denied tenure because similarly situated Caucasians fared better in the tenure process. The Supreme Court held that scientific knowledge and cultural attitudes at the time of enactment of the 1866 and 1870 predecessors to section 1981 shaped the racial classifications addressed by the statute. Legislative history and popular dictionary and encyclopedic sources of the era reflect the view that groups with relatively narrowly defined ancestral roots and ethnic characteristics, such as "Germans," "Greeks," "Jews," and "Gypsies," represent distinct races. The Supreme Court concluded that Arabs would be viewed as a separate race under those standards and that section 1981 therefore addresses discrimination based on Arab ancestry. *See id.* at 610-13.

In our case . . . .

3. Parallels to Effective Study Techniques

The two passages quoted above illustrate parallels between effective law school study techniques and techniques for preparing documents in a law office. The first passage resembles one of a series of only loosely connected case briefs, such as those you might prepare for class discussion or in your prewriting process for an office memorandum. The case briefs contain useful information, but you can more effectively apply that information to an examination problem if you synthesize the cases and then reorganize them in an outline. Moreover, the outline will help you most if it emphasizes controlling principles and relegates the discussion of cases to the role of illustrating those principles.[19]

In a law office, you will use a similar analytical process in presenting case law in a memorandum or brief. As illustrated in the second passage above, topic sentences or paragraphs introducing each case discussion emphasize principles and often act as transitions that convey case syntheses. The detailed discussion of each case simply illustrates a principle or qualification to a principle that you have already identified in a topic sentence. You should construct such a thesis sentence or paragraph to introduce each in-depth case analysis. Your reader can then make her way through the series of individual case briefs without losing sight of the broader outlines of the analysis.

4. Consolidated Statement of Synthesis

In some analyses, you can state an overview of the complete synthesis in a single introductory sentence or paragraph rather than set it forth incrementally in the thesis sentences of several paragraphs. For example, in a variation of a previous discussion of fictitious case law, the second paragraph of the following passage expresses the author's synthesis of two cases, both of which are immediately cited as support for the synthesis statement, followed by separate paragraphs analyzing each case in depth:

An enforceable contract requires a bargained-for exchange in which a promisor exchanges his own promise for a return promise or performance. *Smith v. Newman*, 161 Calz. 443, 447, 667 P.2d 81, 84 (1984). The requirement of an exchange is not satisfied if one party gives only an illusory promise, which does not commit the promisor to any future performance. *Atco Corp. v. Johnson*, 155 Calz. 1211, 627 P.2d 781 (1980).	**General rules**
Even a conditional promise, however, is valid if the promisor's duty to perform is not dependent solely on the promisor's desire to perform but instead can be triggered by external events over which the promisor does not have complete control.	**Synthesis derived from two cases**
Compare Bonnie v. DeLaney, 158 Calz. 212, 213-15, 645 P.2d 887, 888-90 (1982) (buyer's obligation to purchase a house was not illusory because it was based on his ability to obtain a specified loan), *with Atco Corp.*, 155 Calz. at 1212-14, 627 P.2d at 782-84 (creditor's promise to delay demanding payment was illusory because it allowed him to make a demand as soon as he wanted the money).	**Citation to the two cases, with parenthetic explanations**
In *Bonnie*, an agreement for the sale of a house provided that the buyer could cancel the agreement if the buyer "cannot qualify for a 30-year mortgage loan for 90 percent of the sales price" with any of several banks. . . .	**In-depth analysis of 1st case**
In *Atco*, the manager of an automobile repair shop purportedly promised to delay asserting a claim	**In-depth analysis of 2d case**

> against the owner of an automobile for $900 in repairs. Specifically, he promised to forbear from asserting the claim "until I want the money." In exchange, a friend of the owner promised to act as guarantor.... In contrast to the promise in *Bonnie*, ...

C. Citation within a Citation

If you support your proposition with authority that itself relies on other authority, you may express such reliance with a parenthetic explanation:[20]

> *Meritor Sav. Bank v. Vinson*, 477 U.S. 57, 65 (1986) (quoting 29 C.F.R. §1604.11(a)(3) (1985)). Moreover, the Court referred approvingly to ... *Id.* at 65-66 (describing holding of *Rogers v. EEOC*, 454 F.2d 234, 238 (5th Cir. 1971)).

To reverse the emphasis, you can cite first to the authority that above was viewed as parenthetic:[21]

> 29 C.F.R. §1604.11(a)(3) (1985), *quoted in Meritor Sav. Bank v. Vinson*, 477 U.S. 57, 65 (1986).

If you use this technique, be sure to accurately reflect the manner in which one source refers to the other. Does one cite the other? Quote the other? Overrule the other?

III. Quotations

A. Using Quotations Selectively

If the interpretation or application of a statute or contract is disputed by the parties, the starting point of your analysis is the relevant language of the statute or contract. Accordingly, when presenting such an analysis in a memorandum or brief, you should quote the contractual provisions that must be interpreted or applied.

You should generally quote more sparingly from case law. Judges and assigning attorneys are primarily interested in your original synthesis of case law and your analysis of the facts within the legal framework. They are not impressed by your demonstrated ability to cut and paste lengthy passages written by others. If all or part of a judicial opinion is particularly significant to the analysis in an office memorandum, you need not clutter up your memorandum with lengthy quotations. You can simply attach a copy of the authority in hard copy or as an email attachment.

Occasionally, a passage from case law is so clear, concise, powerful, and narrowly tailored to your dispute that paraphrasing cannot improve it. By quoting such a passage, you will enhance the memorandum or brief. Indeed, this book has presented a few such paragraph-long quotations, often with extraneous words or phrases omitted, but only because they advance the discussion concisely and eloquently, as does this one:

> [W]hen you do decide to quote authority in a brief or an office memorandum, you need not quote at epic length. Indeed, a sure way to induce skimming is the back-to-back employment of two quotes of more than ten lines each.... Select a short helpful quote, and show its application to your case. Give enough to make your point but not so much as to sink your brief from excess weight.[22]

More often, a long passage from case law will seem out of context if quoted, perhaps because it clashes with your writing style or because its relevant portions are unavoidably intermingled with distracting references to points not relevant to your dispute. In such a case, you can help focus the attention of your reader on important ideas, rather than on sudden shifts in style or context, by stating the rule or analysis of a case in your own words.

This general admonition against excessive quotation probably applies most strongly to appellate briefs. Although their workload is heavy, most appellate judges or their law clerks have sufficient time to study the important cases cited in appellate briefs. Moreover, appellate courts have the power to overrule at least some of the precedent likely to be cited in the briefs. Consequently, appellate judges tend to look for original analysis, including policy analysis, rather than extensive quotation from authorities that a judge or a law clerk can easily secure from the library.

In contrast, busy trial judges preparing for hearings on motions may not have time to study carefully all the important cases cited in the briefs.[23] Additionally, they must follow, and cannot overrule, applicable appellate decisions within their jurisdiction. For both these reasons, some trial judges may appreciate passages in briefs that quote arguably controlling holdings from appellate case law. Even so, you should remember the recently quoted advice to "select a short helpful quote" rather than quoting at "epic length."

Of course, when you do quote a source, you should not be so concerned with brevity that you alter the meaning of the quoted source. Neither a judge nor an assigning attorney will appreciate a brief or office memorandum that misleads the reader by concealing important information through material omissions in quotations, or through quotations taken completely out of context.[24]

B. Presenting and Introducing Quotations

1. Presenting Block Quotations

If you quote a substantial portion of any authority, you should set apart the quoted passage in a single-spaced, indented block, without quotation marks other than those that appear within the original quoted text. This blocking technique helps the reader to distinguish the lengthy quotation from the original text. The Bluebook citation manual calls for block quotation only if the quoted passage exceeds 49 words.[25] The ALWD Guide also instructs you to block any quotation that exceeds 49 words, as well as any quotations of poetry or verse, regardless of length.[26] However, the visual benefits of blocking are evident in shorter passages, and you should exercise discretion about whether to block any quotation that takes up all or part of at least three lines of text.

2. Using Substantive Introductions While Subordinating Citations

The principles stated in Section II above about subordinating citations and introducing case analyses with topic sentences apply equally to substantial quotations, especially block quotations. Unless the citation to a block quotation has independent significance, you should relegate it to the end of the quote by placing it at the left-hand margin on a new line below the block. You should also introduce the quoted passage with a thesis statement, a substantive overview that summarizes the point that you intend the passage to convey to the reader.

To start with a bad example, the following passage inappropriately introduces a block quotation of a statutory provision with a citation that has little independent significance. Moreover, the absence of a substantive introduction induced the writer to convey the point of the quote with distracting underlining:

> Title 42 U.S.C. § 2000e-2(a)(1) provides:
>
> It shall be an <u>unlawful</u> employment practice for an employer—
> (1) to fail or refuse to hire or to discharge any individual, or otherwise to <u>discriminate</u> against any individual with respect to his <u>compensation, terms, conditions, or privileges of employment</u>, because of such individual's race, color, religion, <u>sex</u> or national origin.

Using a substantive introduction, you could revise this passage to subordinate the citation, provide the reader with helpful orientation, and minimize the need for underlining as a means of emphasis:

> Federal law prohibits sex discrimination in employment:
>
> > It shall be an unlawful employment practice for an employer—
> > (1) to fail or refuse to hire or to discharge any individual, or otherwise to discriminate against any individual with respect to his compensation, terms, conditions, or privileges of employment, because of such individual's race, color, religion, sex or national origin.
>
> 42 U.S.C. § 2000e-2(a)(1) (2012) (Title VII § 703(a)(1)).

Alternatively, you may want to acknowledge that the title and name of the original legislative act in this example is familiar to most lawyers and therefore has independent significance. You can refer to the act in the introduction, while continuing to subordinate the code citation:

> Title VII of the Civil Rights Act of 1964 makes it unlawful for an employer to engage in sex discrimination:
>
> > It shall be an unlawful employment practice for an employer—
> > (1) to fail or refuse . . . .
>
> 42 U.S.C. § 2000e-2(a)(1) (2012) (Title VII § 703(a)(1)).

Finally, if you want to refer repeatedly to this section of the statute throughout your brief or memorandum, you can emphasize the section number within Title VII, which is more familiar to most lawyers than the code number, by referring to it in the introduction:

> Section 703(a) of Title VII of the Civil Rights Act of 1964 makes it unlawful for an employer to engage in sex discrimination:
>
> > It shall be an unlawful employment practice for an employer—
> > (1) to fail or refuse . . . .
>
> 42 U.S.C. § 2000e-2(a)(1) (2012). Section 703(a) identifies two principal elements of unlawful discrimination . . . .

In rare cases, you may find that an exceptionally long or complex passage should be quoted and cannot be cut to size with judicial editing. Particularly if the quotation addresses multiple themes, you can lead the reader through such material by breaking the quotation into parts and preceding each part with a substantive introduction:

Introduction to U.C.C. §2-207(1)

Under the Uniform Commercial Code, a response to an offer may be an acceptance even though it varies the terms of the offer:

Text of U.C.C. §2-207(1)

> A definite and seasonable expression of acceptance or a written confirmation which is sent within a reasonable time operates as an acceptance even though it states terms additional to or different from those offered or agreed upon ....

Proviso to U.C.C. §2-207(1)

§2-207(1) (2011). However, a proviso to the same statute provides that the offeree may avoid acceptance and state a counteroffer if "acceptance is expressly made conditional on assent to the additional or different terms." *Id.*

Introduction to U.C.C. §2-207(2)

If the original offeree's response is an acceptance, the statute provides that some of the new terms in the acceptance may in some circumstances be added to the contract without the express assent of the original offeror:

Text of U.C.C. §2-207(2)

> (2) The additional terms are to be construed as proposals for addition to the contract. Between merchants such terms become part of the contract unless:
> (a) the offer expressly limits acceptance to the terms of the offer;
> (b) they materially alter it; or
> (c) notification of objection to them has already been given or is given within a reasonable time after notice of them is received.

U.C.C. §2-207(2) (2011).

Exercise 10-2

Rewrite the following passage in an office memorandum to subordinate citations and to introduce the block quotation with a brief substantive overview. You may assume that the case names are not sufficiently independently significant to warrant emphasis in textual sentences.

DISCUSSION

A. Liability for Discrimination Under Section 1981

1. First Amendment Defense

Lilly Prep School has asserted in a letter to our client that it has a First Amendment right to teach and practice racial segregation in its classrooms. We expect it to raise this as a defense in any lawsuit that we file.

In *NAACP v. Alabama*, 357 U.S. 449 (1958), the Supreme Court recognized a First Amendment right "to engage in association for the advancement of beliefs and ideas." *Id.* at 460. In *Runyon v. McCrary*, 427 U.S. 160 (1976), however, the Court stated:

> From this principle it may be assumed that parents have a First Amendment right to send their children to educational institutions that promote the belief that racial segregation is desirable, and that the children have an equal right to attend such institutions. But it does not follow that the *practice* of excluding racial minorities from such institutions is also protected by the same principle.

Id. at 176.

Checklist for Chapter 10

To present authority effectively,

- ✓ subordinate citations, emphasize ideas, and express your syntheses in topic sentences or paragraphs;
- ✓ use quotations selectively, subordinate the citations to the quotations, and introduce quotations with substantive overviews; and
- ✓ use effective citation form and citation signals.

Endnotes

1. Bd. of Student Advisors, Harvard Law School, INTRODUCTION TO ADVOCACY: RESEARCH, WRITING, AND ARGUMENT 5 (Alisha Crovetto & Joshua Skoski eds., 8th ed. 2013).
2. THE BLUEBOOK: A UNIFORM SYSTEM OF CITATION (Columbia L. Rev. Ass'n et al eds., 21st ed. 2020) ("BLUEBOOK").
3. ALWD & Carolyn Williams, ALWD GUIDE TO LEGAL CITATION (7th ed. 2021) ("ALWD GUIDE").
4. BLUEBOOK R. 1.5, at 65.

5. ALWD Guide R. 35.2, at 370; Bluebook R. 1.2(a), at 62.
6. Bluebook R. 1.2(a), at 62; see ALWD Citation Guide R. 35.3, at 370–71 chart 35.1, at 371 (use "*see*" when authority "only implicitly supports the stated proposition").
7. Bluebook R. 1.2(a), at 62.
8. *Id.* The ALWD Guide is in accord with this approach. ALWD Guide R. 35.3, at 371 chart 35.1.
9. *Id.*; Bluebook R. 1.2(d), at 64.
10. ALWD Guide R. 35.3, at 371 chart 35.1; Bluebook R. 1.2(a), at 63.
11. ALWD Guide R. 35.3, at 372 chart 35.1; Bluebook R. 1.2(b), at 63.
12. Bluebook R. 1.2(a), at 63.
13. ALWD Guide R. 35.3, at 371 chart 35.1 (emphasis in original).
14. A parenthetic explanation following the citation to *Rite Realty* might be helpful as well. Still, in the example above, the need for a parenthetic explanation is much stronger in the second citation, reflecting its more attenuated relationship to the stated proposition. If further explanation of *Rite Realty* is appropriate to the document, the author might choose to summarize it in a paragraph or two, explaining in detail its similarities to the case at hand.
15. ALWD Guide R. 35.3, at 371–72 chart 35.1; Bluebook R. 1.2(c), at 63.
16. *See* ALWD Guide R. 35.3, at 372 chart 35.1; Bluebook R. 1.2(c), at 63.
17. Bluebook R. 1.2(a), at 62; ALWD Guide R. 35.3, at 371 chart 35.1.
18. *See, e.g.*, William Glaberson, *Legal Citations on Trial in Innovation v. Tradition*, N.Y. Times, July 8, 2001, at A1 (footnote notation in title of article omitted).
19. *See, e.g.*, Charles R. Calleros, Law School and Exams: Preparing and Writing to Win (3d ed. 2021).
20. ALWD Citation Guide R. 37.4(a), at 388; Bluebook R. 1.6(c), at 67.
21. *See* ALWD Citation Guide R. 37.4(b), at 389; Bluebook R. 1.6, at 67.
22. Noel Fidel, *Some Do's and Don'ts of Motion Writing*, Ariz. Bar J., Aug. 1983, at 9.
23. *Id.* at 10–11.
24. *See, e.g.*, Precision Specialty Metals, Inc. v. United States, 315 F.3d 1346 (Fed. Cir. 2003) (affirming reprimand against lawyer who gave a misleading impression of the law partly by replacing relevant information within a quotation with an ellipsis and by failing to cite and discuss an adverse case appearing in the quoted source).
25. Bluebook R. 5.1(a), at 83.
26. ALWD Guide R. 38.3, at 392.

Part V

Introduction to Advocacy

Written advocacy is a special branch of legal method and writing that combines creative analysis, persuasive writing, and attention to local rules, special formats, and ethical considerations.

Part V provides an overview of advocacy at all stages of litigation. Parts VI and VII thoroughly examine and illustrate written advocacy in the context of four other kinds of pleadings or briefs: (1) complaints, answers, and motions to dismiss, (2) briefs on a motion for summary judgment, (3) briefs on a motion to exclude evidence, and (4) appellate briefs. By studying the general principles in Part V, and then some or all the documents in Parts VI and VII, you will develop a general grasp of the methods and purposes of brief writing, enabling you to prepare a brief for any stage of litigation.

Part VIII examines advocacy in documents that are not directed to a court. It addresses two kinds of correspondence related to litigation: advice letters to clients and demand letters to opposing parties. But it begins with a chapter on drafting contracts, which—if done well—could help the parties avoid disputes and subsequent litigation.

Chapter 11

Advocacy: Overview and Ethics

I. Overview—Procedure and General Format

A. Procedure

In a typical dispute, you will advocate your client's case in various written documents through several stages of litigation. You might engage in written advocacy in the pre-litigation phrase by writing an advice letter to your own client or a demand letter to an opposing party. If correspondence between the parties fails to resolve the dispute in its early stages, the parties can commence formal litigation by filing pleadings, typically a complaint and an answer.

Before trial, you likely will file or respond to motions requesting the judge to take certain actions, such as to rule in advance on the admissibility of evidence or to rule on the merits of some or all the claims and defenses without a trial. During a trial with a jury, you might submit or respond to briefs that request the judge to instruct the jury on the law in a certain way or even to decide the case "as a matter of law" without the jury.

At the outset of a bench trial without a jury, you might submit a trial brief that invites a judge or arbitrator to find certain facts and to apply your interpretation of the law to the facts to reach certain conclusions. Finally, if either party appeals the judgment of the trial court, you will draft one or more briefs to an appellate court, inviting the appellate court to either affirm or reverse the judgment of the court immediately below it.

Throughout these proceedings, the pleadings, motions, and appeals will follow similar briefing schedules:

1. The party seeking relief or seeking reversal of a lower court's judgment files a complaint, petition, or opening brief.
2. The opposing party responds with an answer, response, or answering brief.
3. Finally, the party who filed the petition or opening brief generally has the opportunity to file a reply brief that addresses points raised in the opposing party's answering brief or response. Under federal pleading rules, the drafter of a complaint will file an answer to any counterclaim contained in the defendant's answer;[1] otherwise, the drafter of a complaint or counterclaim will reply to the defendant's answer if the court orders a reply.[2]

B. Basic Formats for Briefs

The format of a complaint or answer, discussed in Chapter 14, differs significantly from that of a brief. Various pretrial, trial, and appellate briefs, however, have much in common. Each will include some statement of the background of the case, followed by an argument and a conclusion.

In some ways, an appellate brief will be more detailed and formal than a pretrial brief. By the time a case reaches an appellate court, the litigants have developed some record of the facts or factual allegations, and they have advanced the dispute through significant procedural steps. Accordingly, an appellate brief's description of the background of a case typically includes a formal statement of facts and a summary of the procedural history. Prior to trial, on the other hand, the facts may be sketchy and the procedural history brief. Consequently, many briefs on pretrial motions combine the procedural history and statement of relevant facts in an "Introduction," "Background," or "Statement of Facts." As explored in Chapter 15, briefs on a motion for summary judgment are exceptional in their unusually formal pretrial presentation of facts.

An appellate brief typically is more formal than a pretrial brief in other ways as well. For example, rules of procedure and local court rules require an appellate brief to include a table of contents, table of authorities, and formal statement of issues. These are customarily omitted from all but the most complex pretrial briefs.

C. Advocacy in an Adversarial System

The differences just described, however, are relatively superficial compared to the universal heart of any brief: the argument. Unlike an office memorandum, your brief will not explore the strengths and weaknesses of both sides of the dispute. Instead, you will use the brief to advocate the legal and factual analysis that best supports the claims or defenses of your client, while anticipating and attacking the claims of the opposing party.

This perspective of a brief is reflected not only in the subtler facets of writing style but also in fundamental elements of format such as section headings. In an office memorandum, you may use any of several types of section headings in the Discussion section, depending on your personal style or the preferences of your legal writing professor or supervising attorney. You could state a conclusion, restate the issue, or use a neutral phrase or sentence that generally describes a topic of discussion and helps your reader recall an issue stated more formally at the beginning of the memorandum. In contrast, in a brief you will uniformly use "point headings" in the argument section to state the conclusions that you want the judge to adopt. In each point heading, you will assert your conclusion in a complete sentence as a prelude to your full deductive argument on that issue.

Chapters 12 and 13 address these and other techniques of written and oral advocacy in greater depth. First, however, Section II introduces you to a few of the many ethical obligations that you assume as an advocate.

II. Good Faith, Reasonableness, and Full Disclosure

A. Assertion of Claims and Defenses

As an attorney, you owe a duty to your client to advocate her case vigorously.[3] In carrying out this duty, you will often argue for creative extension of existing law or for replacement of existing law with new rules.[4] Fundamental principles of professional responsibility, however, impose limits on your advocacy.[5] For example, Federal Rule of Civil Procedure 11 requires attorneys to certify that their written advocacy is supported by a reasonable investigation of the law and facts and is not advanced for an improper purpose:

> (b) REPRESENTATIONS TO THE COURT. By presenting to the court a pleading, written motion, or other paper—whether by signing, filing, submitting, or later advocating it—an attorney or unrepresented party certifies that to the best of the person's knowledge, information, and belief, formed after an inquiry reasonable under the circumstances:
>
> (1) it is not being presented for any improper purpose, such as to harass, cause unnecessary delay, or needlessly increase the cost of litigation;
>
> (2) the claims, defenses, and other legal contentions are warranted by existing law or by a nonfrivolous argument for extending, modifying, or reversing existing law or for establishing new law;

> (3) the factual contentions have evidentiary support or, if specifically so identified, will likely have evidentiary support after a reasonable opportunity for further investigation or discovery; and
>
> (4) the denials of factual contentions are warranted on the evidence or, if specifically so identified, are reasonably based on belief or a lack of information.[6]

Rule 11 authorizes a judge to impose "an appropriate sanction on any attorney, law firm, or party that violated the rule or is responsible for the violation."[7] The sanction may include "nonmonetary directives; an order to pay a penalty into court; or, if imposed on motion and warranted for effective deterrence, an order directing payment to the movant of part or all of the reasonable attorneys' fees and other expenses directly resulting from the violation."[8]

In one notable application of Rule 11, a federal district court found that the heir of Marvel Comics illustrator Stan Lee acted with an improper purpose in advancing a frivolous claim for intellectual property rights. The court imposed a sanction of $1 million, 75% to be paid by the plaintiff and 25% by her attorneys. The Court of Appeals affirmed dismissal of the claim but reversed the order of sanctions, ruling that the record did not justify that extraordinary measure.[9]

Rule 11 contains a "safe harbor" provision that permits a person responsible for a Rule 11 violation to escape sanctions by withdrawing the offending claim or defense within 21 days after receiving service of the motion for sanctions, or within another time set by the court.[10] As explored more fully in the following sections, however, perhaps the best guide to responsible advocacy is not the risk of sanctions but the desire shared by most advocates to maintain their reputations for candor and quality work.

B. Disclosure of Adverse Authority

As an advocate, you have no duty to argue your opponent's case or even to present a balanced analysis such as would be appropriate in an office memorandum. Nonetheless, every advocate is also an officer of the court[11] and owes a general duty of candor and fairness to the court and to other lawyers.[12] Within this framework, the American Bar Association (ABA) Model Rules of Professional Conduct specifically require every advocate to disclose significant authority adverse to the advocate's arguments:

> A lawyer shall not knowingly:
>
> ....
>
> (2) fail to disclose to the tribunal legal authority in the controlling jurisdiction known to the lawyer to be directly adverse to the position of the client and not disclosed by opposing counsel.[13]

As stated by Judge Posner, "When there is apparently dispositive precedent, an appellant may urge its overruling or distinguishing or reserve a challenge to it for a petition for certiorari but may not simply ignore it."[14]

The scope of the duty stated in the Model Rules depends in large part on the interpretation of the phrase "directly adverse." However, the most sensible approach to disclosure is one that maintains your credibility as an advocate. If adverse authority within the forum jurisdiction is sufficiently analogous that the court would consider it in deciding a case, the judge or the judge's law clerk likely will discover the authority sometime before the end of the proceedings, even if it has escaped the notice of the opposing counsel. You can minimize the impact of such adverse authority by acknowledging it early in the proceedings, permitting you to distinguish it, discredit it, or at least frame it in a way that is less damaging to your client than the framing your opponent is likely to present.[15]

The reference to "controlling jurisdiction" in the disclosure rule appears to flatly exclude authority from outside the forum jurisdiction, even if it is squarely on point. In some circumstances, however, your desire to maintain credibility could be a better guide than a specific ethical rule. Suppose, for example, that you are litigating a question of state law not yet addressed by authority within the forum state, but you find adverse case law—arguably closely analogous to your case—from the highest court of another state. In those circumstances, the court will expect you to disclose the nonbinding adverse authority and present your best argument that it is distinguishable or its reasoning flawed.

If an adverse authority does not meet these standards, you need not address it unless the other party relies on it or the court raises a question that encompasses it. In an opening brief, for example, you should not waste time distinguishing marginally analogous adverse case law or criticizing poorly reasoned persuasive authority on which the opposing counsel is unlikely to rely. Instead, you should concentrate on affirmatively presenting your own arguments and supporting authority, and you should attack only the most obvious adverse authority. Then, you can wait to see which authority the opposing counsel advances in the answering brief, and you can attack that adverse authority in your reply brief. Of course, if the court asks you about adverse precedent, you "should make such frank disclosure as the question seems to warrant,"[16] regardless of the scope of ethical duties or strategic considerations that might otherwise apply.

C. Misleading Legal Argument

The ABA Model Rules of Professional Conduct prohibit a lawyer from knowingly making "a false statement of fact or law to a tribunal."[17] However, a legal analysis will not amount to a false statement about the law unless it clearly falls outside the range of plausible interpretations of the legal authorities.

For example, defining the holding of a judicial opinion and determining its effect as precedent is a matter that advocates and judges reasonably debate. As an advocate, you often have room to take an aggressive stance in identifying facts that appear to have been material to a decision and in characterizing the holding and reasoning of the decision.

As with other ethical questions, practical considerations of effective advocacy could provide the best guide to responsible conduct. Published precedent on which you rely is readily accessible to the opposing counsel and to the court. Careless or fraudulent analyses that cross the line separating creative advocacy from misrepresentation almost certainly will be brought to the court's attention. Few things can damage your credibility and effectiveness more than a reputation for stretching legal authority beyond the limits of plausible interpretation.

Every judge has at least one story about a lawyer who ventured past the boundaries of plausible presentation and interpretation of a legal authority. The story always ends with the judge never again trusting the word of that advocate. You will be vastly more effective if you develop a reputation for arguing the law and facts fairly, accurately, and persuasively.[18]

Checklist for Chapter 11

In shifting from predictive analysis to advocacy, you must

- ✓ adopt a suitable format for your document;
- ✓ make the transition from a predictive writing style to a persuasive one, as explored in the following chapters; and
- ✓ take care to satisfy ethical duties in asserting claims and defenses, in disclosing adverse authority, and in representing the content of legal authority.

Endnotes

1. Fed. R. Civ. P. 7(a)(3).
2. Fed. R. Civ. P. 7(a)(7); *see also id.* at Note on 2007 Amendment (referring both to a reply to an answer and to a reply to an answer to a counterclaim).
3. *See, e.g.*, Model Code of Prof'l Responsibility EC 7-4 (2004); *id.* at Canon 7.
4. *See, e.g.*, Hunter v. Earthgrains Co. Bakery, 281 F.3d 144, 156 (4th Cir. 2002) (attorney was "plainly entitled (and probably obligated)" to argue that circuit precedent incorrectly applied Supreme Court precedent and should be overturned).
5. *See, e.g.*, Model Rules of Prof'l Conduct R. (hereafter, "Model Rule") 3.3(a)(1) (2012) (proscribing knowingly false statements of material fact or law).
6. Fed. R. Civ. P. 11(b).
7. Fed. R. Civ. P. 11(c)(1).
8. Fed. R. Civ. P. 11(c)(4).
9. Lee v. POW! Entertainment, Inc., No. 20-55928 (9th Cir. Dec. 6, 2021) (unpublished decision reversing 468 F. Supp. 3d 1220 (C.D. Cal. 2020)).
10. Fed. R. Civ. P. 11(c)(2).
11. *E.g.*, Ex parte Garland, 71 U.S. (4 Wall.) 333, 378 (1867), *cited in* ABA Formal Opinion 146 (1935).
12. Model Rule 3.3 (2012) (candor to court); ABA Formal Opinion 146 (1935).

13. Model Rule 3.3(a)(2) (2012).
14. Gonzalez-Servin v. Ford Motor Co., 662 F.3d 931, 934 (7th Cir. 2011).
15. *See* Charles W. Wolfram, Modern Legal Ethics § 12.8, at 682 (1986).
16. ABA Formal Opinion 280 (1949).
17. Model Rule 3.3(a)(1) (2012).
18. For much more on ethics in legal writing in various contexts, see Melissa H. Weresh, Legal Writing: Ethical and Professional Considerations (2d ed. 2009).

Chapter 12

Developing Your Legal Arguments

Your statements of issues, facts, and procedural history will vary greatly in style and content depending on the stage of the litigation at which you draft a legal document. Consequently, this book separately examines those elements of a pleading or a brief in Parts II and III. Many techniques of advocacy, however, apply broadly to all kinds of briefs and are appropriately introduced in Part I. Specifically, this chapter examines methods of (1) organizing arguments, (2) introducing arguments, and (3) developing the elements of a deductive argument. Chapter 13 examines techniques of persuasive writing and oral argument.

I. Engaging the Reader with an Effective Theme

Before you begin writing, try to develop a theme for your brief—a thread that runs through the fabric of the brief from the Statement of Issues to the Conclusion. If possible, your theme should reflect some facet of the dispute that shows "that your client's position is not only legally correct but also equitably, ethically, and morally 'right.' "[1] Your best arguments are likely to be ones that not only are analytically sound but also help advance your underlying theme throughout your brief.

More specifically, experienced advocates often speak of developing a *theory* of the case, an analytical *framework* for the arguments, a *strategy* for trial or appeal, or a main *point, thrust, direction,* or *idea* that they want to convey to the judge. This process can help you decide which arguments to advance and which facts, case law, and policy arguments to emphasize in your brief so that a persuasive theme emerges.

In its simplest form, a theme may represent an appeal to common sense or justice that translates directly to legal and factual arguments. For example, in litigation of a products liability suit, the injured plaintiff's brief might consistently advance a theme that highlights a dangerous defect in a product. In contrast, the defendant manufacturer's brief might consistently advance a theme that emphasizes the weakness of the causal link between the product's defect and the plaintiff's injuries. Although each brief may necessarily address matters that do not directly advance the theme, each authoring attorney should endeavor to bring the brief's theme to the fore in various parts of the brief, from the issue and fact statements to the argument. In this way, your theme guides the tone, structure, and content of your brief.

For example, imagine that your client is defending against a plaintiff's tort claim. You plan to argue that the plaintiff's choices contributed to his injury and should diminish or eliminate your client's liability. Your theme might be, "dangerous choices lead to devastating consequences." An alternative or parallel theme might be, "You must hold Plaintiff accountable for his risky behavior." To advance either or both themes, you could highlight the different decision points that led to the plaintiff's injuries. Each time, you could emphasize that—when offered a choice between a safe or dangerous option—the plaintiff always chose the dangerous one.

Alternatively, the theme of a brief might encourage the court to embrace a judicial approach or philosophy that would pave the way for acceptance of one or more arguments. For example, various elements of the brief might emphasize that statutory language is unambiguous and should be interpreted according to the plain meaning of its text, rather than in a strained manner that relies heavily on legislative history or statutory purpose. Another brief might advance the theme that expansion of a common law doctrine would enmesh the court in hotly debated issues of social policy that would be best addressed by a democratically elected legislature.

A theme might also consist of a mood or perspective that forms a backdrop to the arguments. One attorney, for example, used the metaphor of a lawless frontier to convey a theme in a motion for summary judgment.[2] The motion challenged an arbitration decision interpreting a collective bargaining agreement, a decision to which a reviewing court would grant substantial deference.[3] Accordingly, the author of the brief bore the burden of showing that the arbitrator's interpretation should not survive even the most deferential judicial review because it did not draw its essence from the terms of the agreement.

Throughout the brief, the author argued those points with sound analysis of the law and facts and with traditional policy arguments. But the author of the brief wanted to create a mood as well, and the case itself invited the author to draw allusions to unrestrained frontier justice in the lawless Wild West: The workplace was a coal mine, and the arbitrator's last name was West. This setting dovetailed perfectly with an excerpt in Supreme Court case law that warned against arbitrators disregarding the collective bargaining agreement to dispense their "own brand of industrial justice."

To introduce this theme, the first sentence of the argument suggested that failure to curb the arbitrator's discretion would render labor relations as chaotic and lawless as in some frontier outpost in the Wild West:

> Despite the deference arbitrators are granted in reaching their decisions, one principle stands clear: the federal labor policy of promoting arbitration of industrial disputes does not create a lawless frontier where arbitrators are free to impose their own brand of "industrial justice."

The phrase "industrial justice" by itself is not pejorative, but the author linked it to an image of arbitrariness and lawlessness associated with untamed frontiers. Subsequently, the author invoked key phrases of his theme in his fact analysis, weaving the theme throughout his brief.

The brief did not belabor this metaphor of a lawless frontier; however, it reminded readers of this image every time it named the arbitrator, West, and every time that it referred to West's "own brand of industrial justice." Finally, the author combined both these reminders with a new play on words at the beginning of the third subsection of the argument:

> Arbitrator West also shot holes through another provision of the [agreement], enforcing his own brand of "industrial justice."

In his response to the opposing party's cross-motion for summary judgment in the same case, this author argued that the arbitrator had refused to choose between two different plausible interpretations of the collective bargaining agreement. Instead, he had compromised inappropriately by choosing an interpretation somewhere between the plausible meanings, arguably an interpretation that no language in the agreement supported. For this brief, the author developed a different theme, one that compared and then contrasted the arbitrator's interpretation with King Solomon's fabled solution:

> Just as King Solomon threatened to do, the arbitrator in this dispute split the baby and imposed an irrational solution when a clear choice was required. Of course, once his threat produced the desired reaction, King Solomon ultimately revealed his wisdom by vacating his irrational decision. Here, the Court should likewise vacate Arbitrator West's irrational decision.

Using colorful metaphors or similes to create a theme is a matter of personal style and can never substitute for sound analysis of the law, facts, and social policies. You should never use a careless or distracting metaphor when a straightforward explanation would be clearer. A telling metaphor, however, may create an effective backdrop for the analysis, encouraging your reader to develop a gut reaction in favor of your client.

II. Organizing Your Arguments

Ordinarily, you should discuss or argue discrete issues in separate sections of your office memorandum or brief. Moreover, your section and subsection headings should show the proper relationships between your topics and subtopics. Beyond these considerations, you also must decide (1) which arguments to advance, (2) the order in which to present your arguments, and (3) the internal organization of each argument.

As you examine these matters in the following sections, reflect on the value of preparing an outline of the argument section of your brief before you begin writing it. The same techniques discussed in Chapter 7, Section I.E for outlining the discussion section of an office memorandum will help you outline the argument section of your brief.

A. Selecting Arguments

1. Include Only Arguments That Earn a Place in Your Brief

You should be more selective in choosing arguments to advance in a brief than in choosing issues to discuss in an essay examination or an office memorandum. For example, a federal appellate judge advises you to "[f]orce yourself to omit fringe issues and far-out theories; they will only dull the thrust of your appeal and obscure the potentially winning point."[4] A professor of trial practice and advocacy emphasizes that this

> means making choices. You throw out arguments that aren't plausible. You pick between the inconsistent legal theories. You cull out the weak points. You toss out whatever gets in the way. You discard what doesn't need to be said, even if it doesn't hurt.
>
> What's left is tight. Lean. Spare. It crackles with power because it's undiluted with stuff that doesn't matter.[5]

2. Consider Your Reader's Burdens

If you can envision two or more equally reasonable theories of your client's case, such as two competing legal frameworks within which to construct your arguments, you normally should choose the one that simplifies the judge's task. If your argument is so complicated that the judge has difficulty following it, the argument will not be persuasive; moreover, the judge will anticipate difficulty explaining a decision based on your arguments. Instead, opt for the approach that is easy to follow, easy to defend as consistent with precedent, and easy to explain in a ruling or opinion. If your brief contains straightforward passages that the judge could easily borrow and adapt for her written opinion, all the better.

3. Presenting Alternative Arguments

If two of your arguments are mutually exclusive, you normally should select the stronger argument and drop the weaker. However, you may choose to present both arguments if they are equally strong and are worth presenting in the alternative.

For example, imagine state law in which a prosecutor can establish the requisite state of mind for homicide in either of two ways: (1) murder, requiring proof of intent to kill, or (2) involuntary manslaughter, requiring proof of reckless disregard for human life. Manslaughter is a lesser included offense of murder. It shares elements with murder (chiefly, causing the death of another), but the required proof of state of mind is less stringent. To argue the sufficiency of the evidence of these crimes in the alternative, you could (1) present the law and facts supporting the charge of murder, including evidence supporting a finding of intent to kill, and (2) argue in the alternative that—even if the evidence is not sufficient to support a finding of intent to kill—the defendant at least acted with recklessness and thus is guilty of manslaughter.

You should use roadmaps, transitions, point headings, and thesis sentences to guide the reader through the alternative arguments. For example, after presenting the argument supporting the crime of murder, your next point heading could assume an adverse outcome on the first argument and present the fallback argument:

> **B. Even if the evidence is not sufficient to support a finding of intent to kill Jan Dobson, the Defendant is guilty of manslaughter because the record shows without contradiction that he fired his gun at least recklessly.**

Whether to argue in the alternative is a matter of judgment based on the relative merits of the arguments, your audience, and other strategic considerations. For example, imagine a defendant in a civil case, Jan Henning, who seeks to avoid liability for breach of a contract allegedly formed through an exchange of emails with Bob Donovan. The parties allegedly agreed to secure a license and funding to grow and distribute marijuana in a state that has legalized such activity. As Henning's attorney, you have studied the facts and the law, and you see three possible avenues for avoiding liability:

> (1) Henning admits that her emailed response to Donovan's offer was quite positive in tone, but part of her response arguably prevented acceptance of the offer because it suggested her desire to consult a friend before she finally committed to the proposed deal. Donovan will argue that a reasonable person would interpret Henning's comment to mean that she had accepted the offer and would consult a friend for advice about performing the agreement.
>
> (2) Although the state permits and regulates the growing and sale of marijuana, an agreement to do so might be unenforceable for violation of public policy, because the federal government still prohibits such actions. Donovan will argue that state contract law will focus on legality under state law, particularly if the federal government is not actively enforcing its law in states that have legalized marijuana.
>
> (3) Depending on whether the contract is interpreted to require Donovan to obtain a business loan for $300,000, Donovan might have materially breached the contract himself prior to Henning's performance coming due, thus releasing Henning from her obligations under state law. Donovan will argue that the contract should not be interpreted to impose that obligation on him.

All three arguments are subject to doubt and debate, but any one of them could succeed in completely defeating Donovan's claim. After assessing the arguments, you might decide to present only the second one in a motion for summary judgment, because it will turn on a purely legal question of public policy—one that is suitable for pretrial disposition. The judge might want to leave the other two issues for a jury to resolve after a full trial of the facts. On the other hand, if the email communications point strongly in favor of Henning's interpretations, a judge might find the first and third arguments to have at least equal merit.

After assessing the arguments in this manner, if you decided to present all of them in the alternative, your points headings can lead the reader through the alternatives:

A. Henning did not accept Donovan's offer because she expressed her intention to consult a friend before reaching agreement.

. . . .

B. Even if Henning and Donovan reached agreement, it is unenforceable under state contract law for violation of public policy, because performance of the agreement would violate the federal Controlled Substances Act.

. . . .

C. Even if the parties formed an enforceable contract, Henning validly terminated the contract and her obligations under it, because Donovan materially breached his contractual obligation to secure a business loan for $300,000.

B. Determining the Order of Your Arguments

Consider beginning your argument with a paragraph that states the theme of your brief or that provides an overview or roadmap to multiple arguments that follow. Such an overview paragraph would appear at the beginning of the Argument section of your brief, even before the subsection heading for the first of several arguments.

Of course, you cannot set forth an effective roadmap without first deciding on an effective ordering of your arguments. If your brief includes a formal statement of the issues, the organization of that statement should mirror the organization of your arguments. To determine the most appropriate order of arguments, you may need to balance neutral analytic considerations against strategic considerations. Moreover, in a responsive brief, you must decide whether to adopt or depart from the organizational structure of the opposing counsel's preceding brief.

1. Leading with Your Strongest Argument

Neutral analytic considerations will lead you to argue threshold issues first and then to argue the issues that are dependent on the outcome of the threshold issues. Strategic considerations, however, may lead you to place your strongest argument first, even if that organization requires you to depart from a purely logical ordering of arguments.

The strategic considerations are based on the varying levels of emphasis associated with different parts of the argument section of the brief. Within a sentence, an idea generally will receive greater emphasis if placed at the beginning than if placed in the middle, but the place of greatest emphasis ordinarily is the end of the sentence.

The same might be true of a short brief submitted to a judge who has plenty of time to study it. The first argument in such a brief would receive the emphasis associated with any initial encounter that makes a first impression. Ideas in the middle of the brief might capture slightly less attention, but they could help lay the foundation for a forceful climax. Presumably, the climactic argument would leave a lasting impression on the judge because it is the last argument that the judge would read.

Unfortunately, briefs are seldom brief, and judges often lack time to read them carefully. Indeed, a trial judge with a full pretrial motions calendar may have time only to skim through your motions brief before oral argument. Far from occupying the place of greatest emphasis, the end of your brief may not be read with the same care that the judge devoted to the beginning of the brief. Consequently, if one of your arguments is much stronger than the others, you can exercise discretion to present it before the others even though another issue is logically prior.

In balancing neutral analytic considerations against conflicting strategic considerations, strategy is secondary to clarity. If strategic ordering creates an organization that is so illogical that it impedes the reader's understanding of the argument, the clarity of logical ordering will be more persuasive.

2. Special Considerations for Responsive Briefs

A special organizational structure is sometimes appropriate for responsive briefs. In the ordinary three-stage briefing procedure, the answering brief will respond directly to the opening brief, and the reply brief will respond to the answering brief. A responsive brief should meet the arguments of the preceding brief "head-on, issue for issue, as they are posited."[6] Nonetheless, the responsive brief can do so on its own terms, within an organizational and analytic framework that places its arguments in the best light.

a. Responding but Still Leading with Your Strongest Argument

When you write a responsive brief, you might choose to adopt the preceding brief's organizational structure and methodically knock down each of your opponent's arguments. On the other hand, if you can more persuasively argue your case with a different organizational structure, you should not hesitate to depart from the structure adopted by your opponent.

For example, suppose that Maya Tortilla Co. has sued Bakeway Supermarkets, alleging that Bakeway (1) formed a contract with Maya; (2) breached its obligations, at least under Maya's interpretation of the contract; (3) and is liable to Maya for $40,000 in damages. Maya has filed a pretrial motion requesting the trial court to grant it summary judgment, which is judgment as a matter of law without a full trial on the facts. Maya has supported its motion with a preliminary showing of facts and with a brief that argues each of the issues in the order presented above. Bakeway can escape summary judgment on any issue by creating a genuine dispute of material fact on that issue, a dispute that must be resolved in a full trial.

As counsel for Bakeway, you could logically begin the argument of your answering brief with Maya's issue 1 because contract formation is a threshold issue: Bakeway did not assume any contractual obligations and consequent potential liability if it did not form a contract with Maya. Moreover, the opening brief begins with issue 1, and you could simplify your task by simply adopting the organizational structure of the opening brief.

However, suppose that you can most easily avoid summary judgment against Bakeway on issue 2. Although you cannot easily refute formation of a contract, you can point to admissible evidence of contract negotiations that supports Bakeway's interpretation of the contract. Moreover, under Bakeway's interpretation of the contract, Bakeway performed rather than breached the contract. Thus, you are confident that you can create a triable issue of fact about the meaning of the contract provision that states Bakeway's obligations. In those circumstances, you could reasonably begin your argument with issue 2, even though that organization departs from a purely logical ordering and from the structure of the opening brief. If you persuade the judge in your first argument that she should deny summary judgment on issue 2, she may then be more strongly disposed to order a trial on other issues as well.

b. Delayed Analysis of Adverse Authority in a Responsive Brief

In responding to an argument in a preceding brief, you can affirmatively develop a legal theory and apply it to the facts, and then separately address authority on which the preceding brief relies. You should address each adverse authority and discredit or distinguish it, or argue that it should be overruled, or concede that it controls one issue and seek to prevail on other issues. You can use the same technique in an opening brief that anticipates a counterargument.

For example, in the following sample passage, the brief writer has affirmatively and confidently argued that Tippett denied Bennett due process under a mainstream legal theory. Only after completing that argument does he seek to persuade the judge to reject an approach based on *Parratt v. Taylor*, on which the opposing party relied in a previous motion:

II. ARGUMENT

A. Bennett Will Prove That Tippett Is Liable Under 42 U.S.C. § 1983 for Violating Bennett's Civil Rights.

1. Tippett Acted Under the Color of State Law.

. . . .

2. Tippett Denied Bennett Due Process.

The Fourteenth Amendment's guarantee of due process in state proceedings is a federal . . . .

In *Catchpole*, ...

In this case, Bennett will prove that Tippett bribed Judge Bell to rule against Bennett on his motion for a preliminary injunction . . . . Therefore, Tippett violated Bennett's rights to due process.

Full syllogism in several paragraphs within second subargument

Tippett argued in the reply brief to his motion to dismiss that Bennett has an adequate remedy under state tort law and that section 1983 therefore affords him no relief, citing *Parratt v. Taylor*, 451 U. S. 527 (1981). *Parratt* is distinguishable . . . .

Separate paragraphs distinguishing adverse authority

In this example, *Parratt v. Taylor* does not clearly address a distinct topic; instead, it helps define the limits of due process in certain contexts. Thus, in a neutral analysis, you may consolidate your discussion of *Parratt* with your discussion of other authorities that establish the legal rule, even though you ultimately distinguish *Parratt* from your case.

In a responsive brief, however, you can invite the judge to analyze your case initially without the distraction of distinguishable adverse authority. By delaying your analysis of the adverse case law in this manner, you can develop the initial argument strongly and positively, without the qualifications inherent in the subsequent discussion of adverse authority.

C. Internal Organization: Deductive Arguments

Once you decide the order of your arguments, you must adopt an effective scheme of internal organization for each argument. You should flexibly adopt any method of internal organization and advocacy that will present your client's argument most effectively. Unless you have good reason to adopt some other approach, however, you should start with the elements and organization of a deductive argument.

"IRAC," which represents the form of deductive reasoning appropriate to an objective analysis in an office memorandum, is thoroughly discussed in Chapter 6. Moreover, Section III and Chapter 8 examine various techniques for organizing points within a deductive argument of a memorandum or a brief. Before writing your brief, you should review those passages.

The deductive reasoning appropriate in the discussion section of an objective office memorandum differs in a key way from the deductive argument appropriate to a brief: an argument in a brief leads with the advocate's desired conclusion rather than with a neutral identification of an issue. Thus, each argument in a brief should include four major elements: **C**onclusion, **R**ule, **A**pplication of the legal rule to the facts, and **C**onclusion. The acronym "CRAC" may help you remember these elements.

Your writing professor may alternatively use a longer acronym, such as "CRuPAC" or "CREAC" to remind you to "prove" or "explain" your asserted rules to a skeptical reader.[7] This chapter, however, will adhere to the simpler acronym CRAC, while addressing the matter of explanation or proof of rules in its discussion of in-depth development of the law.

III. Introducing Legal Arguments

Judges read an enormous volume of material, and they appreciate concise writing that quickly gets to the point. In each of your arguments, you can satisfy this judicial demand with a well-crafted point heading, sometimes supplemented with an introductory paragraph.

A. Point Headings

For each issue in the argument section of your brief, you will discuss the law and apply the law to the facts to reach a conclusion. Before you begin your full argument, however, you will introduce it in an argumentative section heading, or "point heading." In each section or subsection that addresses a discrete issue, your point heading previews the conclusion.

Depending on the style adopted by the author, a section heading in an office memorandum may neutrally identify the issue addressed in that section. The section heading of an argument in a brief, however, always advocates a position by asserting a point and inviting the judge to reach a specific conclusion. It thus sets the tone for the full argument.

If a section or subsection of your argument develops a full deductive argument, its point heading should be tailored to the facts of your case, much like the statement of an issue and holding in a student case brief. Indeed, you may view your point headings as statements of the holdings in your case that you want the court to adopt:

> **II. ARGUMENT**
>
> A. **O'Gorman is not liable for medical costs associated with Wallace's heart failure, because O'Gorman's conduct did not proximately cause that injury.**
>
> ....
>
> B. **O'Gorman is not liable for punitive damages because he did not act with the requisite malicious intent or recklessness.**

Because these point headings refer to the parties and incorporate important facts, they convey a clear, concrete point, even when read in isolation. The bold letters and the indentation help the point headings stand out on the page, providing conspicuous road signs for the reader.[8]

In some cases, you might develop only one element of a deductive argument, such as an abstract legal principle, within a section or subsection. In such cases, of course, each point heading should be limited to stating a conclusion on the point developed in the section or subsection:

> **II. ARGUMENT**
>
> A. **O'Gorman is not liable for punitive damages because he lacked the requisite scienter.**
>
> 1. **The jury may be permitted to award punitive damages only when the evidence is sufficient to permit a jury finding of malicious intent or recklessness.**
>
> ....
>
> 2. **The evidence at trial will show that O'Gorman acted in a careful manner and certainly not with recklessness or malicious intent.**

The advantages of point headings are obvious in multiple-issue briefs, in which you must divide the argument into sections and subsections. Within the argument section of the brief, the point headings pop up periodically as road signs that signal an entrance to a new street or highway of your argument. Additionally, at least in an appellate brief, you will set forth your point headings together in the table of contents near the beginning of the brief, providing a quick summary of all your points and presenting a useful road map for the judge's journey through your brief.

Even in a single-issue brief, however, you should begin your argument with a point heading. It will simply stand alone in the argument section without any number or letter denoting division of the argument into sections:

> **III. ARGUMENT**
>
> **The alleged agreement is unenforceable because it was not signed by the party against whom enforcement is sought.**
>
> The UCC statute of frauds requires . . . .

B. Paragraphs

Immediately after the point heading, but before discussing the legal authority, you might use an introductory sentence or paragraph to illuminate the issue and to expand on the point heading, or to place it within a larger context:

> **A. The alleged agreement is unenforceable under the UCC Statute of Frauds because it is not evidenced in a signed writing, as required for goods priced at more than $500.**
>
> Sun Printing Co. denies that it ever agreed to the contract alleged by Scott Paper Supply. This lawsuit presents precisely the kind of groundless contract claim that statutes of frauds are designed to bar by requiring a signed written contract as a requisite to enforcement.
>
> The Uniform Commercial Code statute of frauds generally bars . . . .

Such an introductory paragraph can be particularly helpful in a responsive brief. Rather than abstractly addressing the issues, an answering or reply brief should respond directly to each of the preceding brief 's arguments.

Nonetheless, the response normally should begin by stating its counter-argument affirmatively rather than by restating the opponent's argument. The introductory paragraph following a point heading can set up your full response by adding more detail to the point heading, thus explaining generally why the opposing argument lacks merit. You may save citation to authority for the more detailed discussion of law that follows:

> **A. Scott Paper Supply's timely confirmation of the agreement satisfied the UCC statute of frauds, because Sun Printing Co. failed to object to it.**
>
> The confirmation signed by Scott Paper Supply satisfied the statutory requirements of a signed writing. The UCC deems Sun Printing Co. to have implicitly adopted that confirmation, as though it had signed it, when Sun Printing Co. failed to object to the confirmation.
>
> The UCC provides that . . . .

In rare cases, you may begin with a summary of your opponent's argument if that serves as an effective means of revealing the weaknesses in that argument and placing your own argument in a favorable light. When using this technique, you must immediately and convincingly refute your opponent's argument in the same breath with which you present his argument.

This technique works best, of course, if the opponent's argument sounds extreme even when presented on its own terms. If so, you can "set up" your opponent's argument for an easy response. Specifically, you should try to restate your opponent's argument fairly and accurately but in a way that fully reveals its weaknesses.

For example, suppose that your opponent's opening brief on appeal argues that the trial judge erred in denying injunctive relief, but it acknowledges the trial judge's broad discretion in such matters only in a vague passage buried in the middle of a lengthy section. In your answering brief, you will take greater pains to emphasize the discretionary nature of such relief. You might begin that emphasis not only in your point heading but also in an opening paragraph that summarizes your opponent's argument in a way that immediately reveals its weakness or the challenges it faces:

> **A. The trial court properly exercised its discretion to deny the extraordinary remedy of injunctive relief.**
>
> Redrock Co. bears the heavy burden of showing that Judge Norris abused her discretion by denying Redrock's demand for an injunction against further construction on the Big River Project. In fact, the record establishes a balance of equities that tip sharply against injunctive relief. Judge Norris's careful decision reflects a routine and proper exercise of discretion.
>
> Injunctive relief is . . . .

IV. Developing the Deductive Argument

A. Arguing the Law

This book has provided you with the legal method and the techniques of organization and writing with which you can construct an argument about the content of applicable law on a specific issue or subissue. An outline of these principles will illustrate the range of considerations that may influence your strategic decisions when arguing the law within the argument portion of your brief.

1. Hierarchy of Authority

First, you must be sensitive to the hierarchy of authority. For example, suppose that (1) your client is not liable under state common law standards for actions that he took as an employer, but (2) a federal statute will impose liability if it applies to your client's business. If applicable, the statutory law will supersede the common law. Therefore, you must analyze the statute and determine whether you can argue either that it is unconstitutional or that it does not apply to your case. This statutory analysis might include arguments concerning the statutory language, the legislative history, the policy underlying the statute, or the limitations imposed by constitutional provisions.

For illustration, consider the first issue addressed in the final sample office memorandum in Chapter 7. It raises a question about the interpretation of a recently enacted, fictitious statute that created a form of liability beyond that recognized under the state's common law. Moreover, the statute is sufficiently new that no published judicial decision has yet interpreted the statutory term that is currently in dispute. One can imagine how the office memorandum's balanced analysis could be transformed into an argument on behalf of the defendant hospital:

A. Recently enacted New Maine legislation does not apply to a hospital's administration of general anesthesia.

A recently enacted statute of New Maine imposes strict liability on commercial enterprises for injuries caused by the use of "any toxic material." 12 N. Me. Rev. Stat. Ann. § 242 (Supp. 2013) (effective Jan. 1, 2014). Although the New Maine courts have not yet had an opportunity to interpret section 242 in a published opinion, the text and purpose of the statute establish that the anesthetic administered to Souza is not a "toxic material." This interpretation of the statute advances sound legal policies that support widespread availability of affordable medical care administered with due care.

The common meaning of the word "toxic" is "poisonous." *E.g.*, The Random House Dictionary of the English Language 1500 (unabridged) (1970). "Toxic" thus applies most naturally to substances that are universally harmful to humans, such as cyanide, DDT, or sulfuric acid. It strains the common meaning of "toxic" to apply it to an anesthetic that medical professionals use daily in surgeries that preserve the lives or improve the health of countless patients. A generally safe anesthetic is not transformed into a toxic substance simply because it may provoke an unusual reaction in a patient with a rare disorder; otherwise, wholesome cow's milk would be classified as poisonous or toxic simply because a small percentage of people may have a serious allergy to it.

Legislative history also supports a restrictive interpretation of the statutory term "any toxic material." The report of the New Maine Senate Committee . . . .

Finally, general state policy supports an interpretation that excludes medically prescribed substances from the reach of the statute. To encourage the availability of affordable medical services throughout the state, the legislature and judiciary of New Maine have recognized a policy of limiting the liability of physicians. For example, under the New Maine "Good Samaritan" statute. . . .

In this case, the prescribed anesthetic, ethane, is a frequently prescribed substance that produces beneficial results with only minor side effects in all but the most unusual cases. Souza's tragic reaction to ethane during her surgery is a product of her rare disorder, rather than any "toxic" characteristics of the ethane. . . .

2. Strength of Case Law as Precedent

Second, in analyzing case law, regardless of whether it interprets a statute or applies common law, you must appreciate the relative strength of different kinds of authorities. Case law from a higher court within the forum jurisdiction is potentially controlling on the facts of your case, and you must argue for a broader or narrower interpretation of its holding, depending on whether it supports or undermines your position. Case law from other jurisdictions may have persuasive value, but only in the absence of controlling law within the jurisdiction.

For example, in the following passage of an argument set in a fictitious jurisdiction and governed by common law, the counsel for Beatty, a lender, encourages the court to synthesize mandatory precedent in a favorable manner and to brush aside adverse persuasive authority from another jurisdiction:

Principles derived from a synthesis of the Calzona cases establish that Beatty's promise is not illusory. The consideration requirement therefore is satisfied, and Weeks's promise is enforceable.	**Introduction to argument**
Even if a promise leaves open the possibility that the promisor will escape obligation, the promise is not illusory if the promisor does not have complete control over the events on which the promisor's obligation is conditioned. *Bonnie v. DeLaney*, 158 Calz. 212, 645 P.2d 887 (1982). In *Bonnie*, an agreement for the sale of a house provided that the buyer could cancel the agreement if the buyer "cannot qualify for a 30-year mortgage loan for 90% of the sales price" with any of several banks listed in the agreement. *Id.* at 213, 645 P.2d at 888. In enforcing the agreement against the seller, the court emphasized that the word "cannot" referred to the buyer's ability to obtain a loan rather than to his desire. Because his ability to obtain a loan was partly controlled by events and decisions outside his control, the promises in the sale agreement were nonillusory and binding. *See id.* at 214-15, 645 P.2d at 889-90.	**In-depth analysis of favorable case law**

The *Bonnie* court distinguished its earlier decision, *Atco Corp. v. Johnson*, 155 Calz. 1211, 627 P.2d 781 (1980). In *Atco Corp.*, the manager of an automobile repair shop promised to forbear "until I want the money" from asserting a claim against the owner of an automobile for $900 in repairs. In exchange, a friend of the owner promised to act as guarantor of the owner's obligation. *Id.* at 1212, 627 P.2d at 782. The word "want" stated no legal commitment because it permitted the manager at his own discretion to refuse to perform any forbearance at all. Because the manager did not incur even a conditional obligation, the guarantor's promise was gratuitous and unenforceable. *Id.* at 1213-14, 627 P.2d at 783-84.

In-depth analysis of adverse case law

Together, these cases show that any limitation on the promisor's freedom will validate his promise. A promise is illusory only if it leaves the promisor complete control over his actions.

Synthesis that emphasizes favorable case law

Under these controlling principles, the parties in this case each assumed valid obligations ....

Application to facts

Thus, *Atco* is distinguishable from our case, and *Bonnie* is controlling.

Weeks attempts to salvage his flawed analogy to *Atco* by interpreting it in light of authority from New Maine. The New Maine cases, however, are not binding on this court and are inconsistent with the reasoning of the controlling authority in *Bonnie* ....

Argument against application of nonbinding authority

In this example, counsel for Beatty placed her affirmative arguments in positions of priority before distinguishing or discrediting authority supporting counterarguments. She summarized her argument in the first paragraph.

In the second and third paragraphs, she synthesized local case law by reconciling two decisions with apparently contrasting holdings, starting with the supporting precedent. In the fourth paragraph, she derived a legal rule by generalizing from the two cases, thus concluding her synthesis while emphasizing the supporting case law. In the fifth paragraph, as illustrated more fully in Section B below, counsel for Beatty applied this rule to the facts of her case, taking care to analogize the favorable precedent and to distinguish the adverse precedent. In the final paragraph, she protected this analysis by explaining why case law from another jurisdiction should not be used to interpret the local case law in a different manner.

The persuasive influence of authority from a lower court or from a court in another jurisdiction may be stronger in the absence of any applicable authority from the forum state. If persuasive authority undermines your client's position, you can try to distinguish it from the facts of your case or to discredit its reasoning as unworthy of adoption in the forum jurisdiction. Conversely, if persuasive authority supports your position, you should argue that its reasoning is sound and is consistent with the policy of the forum jurisdiction. Your opponent will do the opposite, allowing the court to consider the best arguments for both sides before ruling.

For example, in the following passage, in which fictitious case law has interpreted a fictitious federal statute in imaginary courts, an advocate attempts to persuade a court in the state of New Maine to adopt the reasoning of Calzona case law and to reject precedent from the jurisdictions of Floridia and the U.S. Court of Appeals for the Fifteenth Circuit:

In-depth analysis of favorable case law

The federal Food Quality Act (FQA) preempts more stringent state legislation seeking to ensure the quality and purity of food produced or sold in interstate commerce. *State v. Biggs*, 123 Calz. 56, 567 P.2d 765 (2009). In *Biggs*, state officials sought to enjoin the marketing and sale of fruits and vegetables advertised as "organic." The officials invoked a Calzona statute that set criteria for food labeled or advertised to be organic. *Id.* at 57, 567 P.2d at 766. The Calzona Supreme Court held that the FQA's provisions regarding organic produce were intended to be exclusive and to eliminate unreasonable restrictions on commerce. *Id.* at 58-60, 567 P.2d at 767-69. It therefore held that the FQA barred the state from prohibiting such regulation. *Id.* at 61, 567 P.2d at 770.

In reaching its decision, the California Supreme Court exhaustively analyzed the legislative history of the FQA. It noted that ....

Critical analysis of adverse case law

One other state court and one federal court had previously rejected the preemption argument adopted in *Biggs*, but each of them overlooked the critical legislative history that *Biggs* so carefully analyzed. *Arzani v. Matlock*, 332 So. 2d 234 (Fldia. 2008); *Michigan v. Smedley*, 439 F.3d 166 (15th Cir. 2006).

For example, in *Arzani*, the court summarily held that ....

The advocate hopes that the preceding passage will persuade the court to adopt the reasoning of *Biggs*. In the fact analysis, the advocate can argue further that *Biggs* is analogous to the facts of her case and that the rule of law it represents thus applies to those facts.

3. Depth of Analysis

In presenting your legal arguments and authority, you must exercise firm control over depth of analysis, as introduced in Chapter 6, and discussed more thoroughly in Section II.A.2 of Chapter 9. Those passages examine three different levels or depths of analysis:

1. light analysis to present fundamental and undisputed propositions with direct statements of law and citation to authority,
2. direct statements of law and citation to authority with parenthetic explanations for a slightly deeper level of analysis, and
3. in-depth analysis of statutes or case law to explore policy and reasoning or to explain a rule by showing how precedent has applied the rule to facts in previous cases.

For example, the following introduction to an argument uses technique 2 above to quickly establish an undisputed point about federal law before addressing state law claims in greater depth:

> Because Comcon has always employed fewer than fifteen employees [Hart SofF ¶ 1], Rembar has no claim against Hart under federal employment discrimination law. *See* 42 U.S.C. § 2000e(b) (2006) (defining employers covered by Title VII of the Civil Rights Act of 1964).

A good brief typically will employ the full range of depths of analysis. If a dispute reaches a court without a negotiated settlement, the issues are presumably substantial and reasonably contested by both parties. Consequently, neither party will be able to prevail on crucial issues with conclusory statements of the law and application to the facts. Instead, the brief likely will advance in-depth arguments of the law, the facts, or both for all but general background points.

Nonetheless, general legal background may set the context for your more specific legal analyses. Rather than jump too quickly to the details of a complex argument, you should first provide your reader with necessary foundational points, which often can be summarized quickly and succinctly.

In the following argument, for example, the author sets forth basic standards in "light analysis" in a synthesis paragraph, before explaining an element of the legal rule by engaging in in-depth analysis of case law:

> Hart is not liable for intentional infliction of emotional distress unless his conduct was so "extreme and outrageous" that it fell "within that quite narrow range" of conduct "at the very extreme edge of the spectrum." *Watts v. Golden Age Nursing Home*, 127 Ariz. 255, 258, 619 P.2d 1032, 1035 (1980). Moreover, "it is extremely rare to find conduct in the employment context that will rise to the level

of outrageousness necessary to provide a basis for recovery for the tort of intentional infliction of emotional distress." *Mintz v. Bell Atl. Sys. Leasing Int'l, Inc.*, 183 Ariz. 550, 554, 905 P.2d 559, 563 (Ct. App. 1995) (quoting *Cox v. Keystone Carbon Co.*, 861 F.2d 390, 395 (3d Cir. 1988)).

In *Mintz*, an employee was hospitalized after suffering a nervous breakdown as the alleged result of gender discrimination in the workplace. The employer terminated her disability benefits, ordered her to return to work, and then—while the employee was again hospitalized after returning to work for one day—notified her of a reassignment of her duties by a letter delivered to the hospital. *Id.* at 552, 905 P.2d at 561. The Arizona Court of Appeals affirmed a finding that, as a matter of law, this alleged conduct was not extreme and outrageous, even assuming the employer had failed to promote the employee because of gender discrimination and assuming the employer knew that the employee was unusually susceptible to emotional distress. *Id.* at 553-54, 905 P.2d at 562-63.

In light of cases such as *Mintz*, a federal district court has characterized Arizona's standard for extreme and outrageous conduct as one requiring "extraordinary" conduct. *Tempesta v. Motorola, Inc.*, 92 F. Supp. 2d 973, 987 (D. Ariz. 1999). Applying *Mintz*, the *Tempesta* court granted summary judgment for the defendant employer on the employee's claim of intentional infliction of emotional distress, even after assuming the truth of the employee's allegations that he had suffered harassment and wrongful termination because of his sex. *Id.* at 986-87.

It is even clearer in this case that Hart did not engage in extreme and outrageous conduct ....

4. Elements or Factors in Legal Rules

Legal rules come in a variety of types. Some statutory or common law rules require proof of several mandatory elements. Failure to prove any one of the elements prevents satisfaction of the legal rule.

Other legal rules identify factors that a court should consider in determining whether the facts satisfy a general standard. The list of factors may not be exclusive, and the standard may be met without proof of every factor. Some legal rules, including many constitutional tests, contemplate the balancing of two or more competing factors or values.

The nature of a legal rule will influence your presentation and analysis of the rule. For example, the following argument introduces three mandatory elements of a tort and then presents separate arguments on each element.

Each argument in a subsection then presents more detailed legal requirements for the element discussed in that subsection:

C. The undisputed facts show that Hart is not liable for intentional infliction of emotional distress.

The Arizona Supreme Court has adopted the Restatement test for intentional infliction of emotional distress, requiring proof of three elements: (1) extreme and outrageous conduct, (2) engaged in with intent to cause distress or with reckless disregard of the near certainty that distress will result, (3) causing severe emotional distress. *Watts v. Golden Age Nursing Home*, 127 Ariz. 255, 258, 619 P.2d 1032, 1035 (1980) (citing to the Restatement (Second) of Torts § 46 (1965)). Rembar cannot genuinely dispute that the facts fail to satisfy these elements.

1. Hart did not engage in extreme and outrageous conduct.

Conduct is not "extreme and outrageous" unless it is falls "within that quite narrow range" of conduct "at the very extreme edge of the spectrum." *Watts*, 127 Ariz. at 258, 619 P.2d at 1035. Moreover, "it is extremely rare to find conduct in the employment context that will rise to the level of outrageousness necessary to provide a basis for recovery for the tort of intentional infliction of emotional distress." *Mintz v. Bell Atl. Sys. Leasing Int'l, Inc.*, 183 Ariz. 550, 554, 905 P.2d 559, 563 (Ct. App. 1995) (quoting *Cox v. Keystone Carbon Co.*, 861 F.2d 390, 395 (3d Cir. 1988)).

In *Mintz*, an employee was hospitalized after suffering a nervous breakdown as the alleged result of gender discrimination in the workplace. . . .

In light of cases such as *Mintz*, a federal district court has characterized Arizona's standard for extreme and outrageous conduct as one requiring "extraordinary" conduct. *Tempesta v. Motorola, Inc.*, 92 F. Supp. 2d 973, 987 (D. Ariz. 1999). Applying *Mintz*, the *Tempesta* court granted . . . .

In this case, the record on summary judgment will show that . . . .

2. Hart did not act with intent or reckless disregard.

. . . .

3. Rembar did not suffer severe emotional distress.

. . . .

The following argument, in contrast, addresses material breach of contract, which permits the non-breaching party to cancel the contract. The concept of material breach is a standard for which several factors serve as guidelines. The argument rejects an assertion that every factor in the guidelines must be satisfied, and it argues that the preponderance of factors in favor of material breach outweigh a single factor supporting a finding of minor breach:

2. Tarasenko did not materially breach the contract.

In this jurisdiction, materiality of breach is not governed by a "single touchstone." Instead, the Michigan Supreme Court has drawn guidance from the six "influential" factors of section 275 of the Restatement (First) of Contracts:

> In determining the materiality of a failure fully to perform a promise the following circumstances are influential:
>
> (a) The extent to which the injured party will obtain the substantial benefit which he could have reasonably anticipated;
>
> (b) The extent to which the injured party may be adequately compensated in damages for lack of complete performance;
>
> (c) The extent to which the party failing to perform has already partly performed or made preparations for performance;
>
> (d) The greater or less hardship on the party failing to perform in terminating the contract;
>
> (e) The willful, negligent or innocent behavior of the party failing to perform;
>
> (f) The greater or less uncertainty that the party failing to perform will perform the remainder of the contract.

Walker & Co. v. Harrison, 347 Mich. 630, 635, 81 N.W.2d 352, 355 (1957) (quoting the Restatement (First) of Contracts § 275 (1932)).

In 1981, the second Restatement updated the relevant factors, providing a slightly modified guide to material breach, based on five "circumstances" that "are significant." Restatement (Second) of Contracts § 241 (1982). For example, the second Restatement refers to "standards of good faith and fair dealing" in place of the first Restatement's reference to "willful, negligent or innocent behavior." *Id.* at § 241(e). But the precise formulation of the Restatement's guidance is not significant. The Restatements characterize their factors only as "circumstances" that are "influential" or "significant." Moreover, the Court in *Walker* analyzed the facts of its case in a common sense fashion, without specifically relating facts of the case to every factor in the Restatement section that it had quoted. *Walker & Co.*, 347 Mich. at 636, 81 N.W.2d at 356 (adopting trial court's factual analysis and conclusion of no material breach).

Accordingly, Tarasenko misapplies the law in this state when she argues that her breach could not be material because her failure to fully perform was not the product of bad intentions or lack of care. Contrary to the premise of Tarasenko's argument, bad faith or other culpability is not a required element of material breach; instead, it is only one of "many factors" that are relevant. *Id.* at 635, 81 N.W.2d at 355 ("Many factors are involved."). This single factor in Tarasenko's favor is easily outweighed by the other relevant circumstances, which together strongly support a finding of material breach.

First, Jenkins received almost none of the benefit that he had expected ....

Second, ...

5. Presenting and Framing Your Authority

Finally, you must lead your reader through each of your arguments and support your assertions of law with supporting authority. Three techniques are explored in Chapter 10, Sections II and III. You should

1. express your syntheses of authorities or other thesis statements in topic sentences or paragraphs;
2. unless the citations are independently significant, focus attention on your ideas and relegate citations to subordinate citation sentences; and
3. introduce quotations with substantive overviews that invite the judge to adopt your interpretation of the quoted material.

When you present case law, recognize that the scope of nearly every precedent's holding is subject to interpretation and thus to reasonable dispute. Consequently, within reasonable bounds, you can frame the holding of a precedent relatively narrowly or broadly, as dictated by the outcome that favors your client.

For example, one advocate might argue that (1) the holding of a precedent should extend no further than the compelling facts in that case, and (2) the applicable law should apply differently to the facts of the current case, (3) leading to a different result. The opposing advocate can respond that the reasoning of the precedent suggests that the authoring court would apply the legal rule in the precedent broadly, to a wide array of factual contexts. Such a broad interpretation would encompass the current case, supporting a decision reaching the same result.

A case discussed in Chapter 5, provides a good illustration. Imagine a dispute about whether the Fourth Amendment requires a warrant to search a fully mobile motor home, in which the defendant was residing permanently, while the motor home was parked in public parking lot. Supreme Court precedent #1 held that police need only probable cause, and not a warrant, to search a car, because of the car's mobility and reduced expectations of privacy. Supreme Court precedent #2 held that police generally must secure a warrant to enter and search an apartment, because of the exceptional expectations of privacy in one's home. In a motion to suppress evidence found in the motor home, the defense counsel would argue that the reasoning of precedent #2 extends broadly to any permanent home, including a motor home. Like the resident of a more conventional house or apartment, one who dwells in a motor home would have great expectations of privacy in the space in which he keeps his personal effects and performs all the private routines of daily life, from sleeping and dressing to using the bathroom. Counsel for the State would argue instead for a narrow interpretation of the reach of precedent #2, limiting it to fixed homes, and excluding motor homes. Any vehicle that can be driven on public streets is thereby subject to numerous administrative regulations, which reduce expectations of privacy. State's counsel would also attempt to frame the holding and reasoning of precedent #1 broadly, arguing that its holding should apply to any vehicle that can move rapidly to a place of hiding or across state lines.

Opposing advocates normally can offer opposing interpretations of case law whether the precedent develops a common law rule or interprets a statutory or constitutional provision. Further, if the issue turns on the interpretation of a newly enacted statute, one that has not yet been judicially interpreted and applied, advocates typically enjoy particularly rich opportunities to advance opposing interpretations of the statutory mandate. A statute typically states a rule in relatively general language so that it can apply to a broad array of future cases fitting within a defined category. If the facts of a case lie close to the statutory line, this feature of legislation frequently leaves ample room for debate about whether specific facts fall inside or outside the statutory boundary.

As explored in Chapter 1, Section II, your interpretation and framing of the breadth of an authority will be persuasive only if reasonable. If you stretch statutory language or the holding of a case beyond any plausible interpretation, you will lose credibility and might violate ethical rules.

B. Analyzing the Facts

As discussed in greater detail in Chapter 18 in the context of appellate briefs, the opening statement of facts in a brief is most effective if it does not prematurely argue the law or the application of the law to the facts. In contrast, when you analyze the relevant facts in the argument section of a brief, you should explicitly reach a conclusion by relating the facts to the previously discussed legal rules. You may accomplish this by (1) directly applying the law to the facts or (2) using a form of inductive reasoning to analogize or distinguish precedent by comparing the facts and reasoning of the precedent to your own case.

To illustrate the first technique, suppose that you have established in your discussion of the law that a state police officer can be liable for punitive damages for recklessly depriving a citizen of her right to be free from arrest without probable cause. In the fact analysis of your argument, you could directly apply that rule of law to the facts by showing how the defendant police officer acted recklessly. In the following sample passage, the notations within brackets refer to pages of the trial court reporter's transcript on which critical testimony of witnesses is found.

> Substantial evidence in the record supports the jury's finding that Officer Mullins acted with at least reckless disregard for Wong's clearly established Fourth Amendment rights. Mullins's actions show that even he did not believe that Wong fit the dispatcher's description of the robbery suspect. According to his own testimony, when he initially spotted Wong moments after receiving the robbery report, he passed by her and continued looking for the suspect. [RT at 324.] Only after failing to find a suspect who fit the dispatcher's description did he relocate Wong and summarily arrest her. [RT at 326.]
>
> The jury could infer from these facts that Officer Mullins felt compelled to arrest somebody for the robbery and that he recklessly gambled that Wong might have been involved simply because of her general proximity to the robbery. This is precisely the kind of reckless disregard for constitutional rights that an award of punitive damages is designed to deter.

Alternatively, your discussion of the law could include in-depth case analysis and synthesis of arguably controlling, analogous, or distinguishable authority. If so, you may want to use the second technique of inductive reasoning to compare those cases directly to your dispute in your fact analysis:

Analogizing favorable case law on the facts

Bonnie is closely analogous to the current case and thus supports the conclusion that Beatty's promise was not illusory. In both *Bonnie* and our case, the promised performance was conditioned on events not entirely within the control of the promisor. In *Bonnie*, the buyer could escape his obligations only if market conditions rendered him *unable* to obtain a satisfactory mortgage loan. Similarly, in our case, Beatty could terminate his obligation to refrain from collecting on the debt only if economic conditions affected his income and expenses so as to create a need for the money.

Distinguishing adverse case law on the facts

Conversely, *Atco Corp.* is distinguishable from our case. The promisor in that case retained the freedom to escape all contractual obligations if, at his own discretion, he *wanted* to. In contrast, the Guarantee Agreement in this case did not permit Beatty to demand his money whenever he *wanted* it. Instead, ...

C. Conclusions

Immediately after your fact analysis in each argument of your brief, you should briefly repeat the conclusion that you previewed in the point heading for that section or subsection:

> Scott Paper Supply timely objected to Sun Printing Co.'s written confirmation of the alleged agreement. Therefore, the confirmation does not satisfy the requirements of the statute of frauds.

Additionally, every brief should end with a formal conclusion section. Many attorneys squander this opportunity to summarize their analyses. The following boilerplate is typical:

> **III. CONCLUSION**
>
> For the foregoing reasons, Appellant respectfully requests this Court to reverse the judgment of the superior court.

Although this style is conventional, a more substantive conclusion ordinarily is more satisfying, particularly if the brief presents more than one argument.

A substantive conclusion need not take up much space. If your arguments are simple, your conclusion need only briefly and generally repeat the request for relief and the supporting grounds, as in this closing to a brief in support of a motion to exclude evidence before trial:

> **III. CONCLUSION**
>
> Under Rule 403, Powell is entitled to pretrial exclusion of all evidence of his membership in the Black Panther Party. The danger of confusion and the prejudicial effect of the evidence substantially outweigh its probative value, and the prejudice can be avoided only through exclusion of the evidence before trial.

In a more complex case, the conclusion might briefly summarize multiple arguments:

> **III. CONCLUSION**
>
> Yazzi's statement to the police officer is inadmissible on three grounds. First, it is not relevant to any issue in this suit. Second, even if it were relevant, it would be excludable because its prejudicial value substantially outweighs its probative value. Finally, it is inadmissible hearsay not falling within the exception for statements for purposes of medical treatment. This evidence should be excluded before trial to avoid exposing it to the jury and causing irremediable prejudice.

Checklist for Chapter 12

✓ To effectively advocate your client's case in a written document,
- organize your legal arguments in logical order, subject to considerations of strategy if clarity can be retained;
- introduce each of your arguments with an effective point heading and, if helpful, an introductory paragraph; and
- present your analysis of the law, apply the law to the facts, and state the conclusion that you want the court to reach.

The next chapter examines persuasive writing style, as well as oral argument.

Endnotes

1. Hon. Jacques L. Wiener, Jr., *Ruminations from the Bench: Brief Writing and Oral Argument in the Fifth Circuit*, 70 Tul. L. Rev. 187, 190 (1995).
2. The examples in this subsection were supplied in 2000 by Christopher Mason, an attorney with the Phoenix office of the law firm of Bryan Cave LLP.
3. *See* United Paperworkers Int'l Union v. Misco, Inc., 484 U.S. 29, 36-38 (1987).
4. Wiener, *supra* note 1, at 194 (1995).
5. James W. McElhaney, *The Art of Persuasive Legal Writing: Briefs Come Alive When Every Word Sings to the Reader*, A.B.A. J., Jan. 1996, at 76.
6. Wiener, *supra* note 1, at 197.
7. Richard K. Neumann, Jr., & Kristen Konrad Robbins-Tiscione, Legal Reasoning and Legal Writing § 12-2, at 145-47 (7th ed. 2013) (discussing rule proof and explanation and mentioning both "CREAC" and "CRuPAC"); see Linda H. Edwards, Legal Writing: Process, Analysis, and Organization 91-96 (5th ed. 2010) (introducing and discussing "rule explanation").
8. For more tips on designing documents for legibility, *see* Ruth Anne Robbins, *Painting with Print: Incorporating Concepts of Typographic and Layout Design into the Text of Legal Writing Documents*, 2 J. ALWD 108 (Fall 2004).

Chapter 13

Expressing Your Advocacy: Persuasive Writing Style and Oral Argument

Persuasive brief writing begins with your developing a theme and selecting arguments, as discussed in Chapter 12. Additionally, depending on the nature of the brief and the procedural posture of the case, the brief frequently should include a fact statement that tells your client's story in a compelling fashion. This chapter addresses persuasive style in presenting facts and legal arguments.

I. Persuasive Writing Style

Supervising attorneys often complain that law students or recent graduates from law school do not use sufficiently strong language to write persuasively. Admittedly, advocacy calls for a writing style that departs from the more neutral style appropriate for an office memorandum. Unfortunately, however, many supervising attorneys equate persuasive writing style with hyperbole, and they advise writers to pepper every sentence of a brief with exaggerated modifiers. Such a style may grab a judge's attention, but it does not often persuade. Judges recognize overstatement and tend to take everything in such a brief with an extra pinch of salt. Even worse, a writing style that is too obvious in its advocacy tends to divert the judge's attention from the substance of the argument and to the style itself.

The most persuasive writing style is one that the judge hardly notices. It uses an engaging writing style that keeps the judge's attention riveted on the substance of the arguments, and it presents those arguments so reasonably and clearly as to give her the impression that the brief merely confirms her own independent conclusions. The most important element of such writing is good substantive analysis; a few extra hours of research and reflection may lead to an argument that is easily written in a persuasive manner. Beyond that, persuasive legal writing is distinguished by (1) strong, but not exaggerated, language and (2) effective emphasis through sentence structure, specificity, and vivid, concrete language.

A. Persuasive Language

1. The Adversarial Approach

To clearly communicate your legal analysis to a supervising attorney in an office memorandum, you must candidly reveal uncertainties in the law and weaknesses in your client's case. In contrast, a brief in the same litigation should not explore the weaknesses of a client's case. Rather, it should attempt to frame the facts and arguments in a manner that highlights the strengths of a client's case and de-emphasizes the weaknesses. For example, to satisfy ethical duties or maintain credibility, you must disclose adverse case law. Nonetheless, you can lead with your strongest arguments and most favorable authority, and then present reasonable arguments for overruling or distinguishing the adverse case law. The adversary system ensures that opposing counsel will challenge your arguments.

In an office memorandum, you might candidly admit the weakness of the support for a client's argument, as with the following fictitious analysis of a client's preemption argument:

> Only one state court has held that the federal Food Quality Act preempts more stringent state regulation. *State v. Biggs*, 123 Calz. 56, 567 P.2d 765 (2009). Two other courts have interpreted the Act to permit more stringent state controls that are consistent with its policy. *Arzani v. Matlock*, 332 So. 2d 234 (Fla. 2008); *Michigan v. Smedley*, 439 F.3d 166 (15th Cir. 2006). To support our argument that federal law preempts the New Maine regulation of organic food labeling, we should emphasize the thorough reasoning of *Biggs* and try to discredit or distinguish *Arzani* and *Smedley*.
>
> In *Biggs*, ...

In contrast, in a brief to the court in the same case, you must state your client's argument more positively, while acknowledging and attempting to distinguish or discredit the contrary authority:

> The federal Food Quality Act preempts more stringent state regulations. *State v. Biggs*, 123 Calz. 56, 567 P.2d 765 (2009). In *Biggs*, state officials sought to prohibit . . . .
>
> Two courts had previously rejected the preemption argument adopted in *Biggs*, but each of them overlooked the critical legislative history so carefully analyzed in *Biggs*. *See Arzani v. Matlock*, . . . ; *Michigan v. Smedley*, ... For example, in *Arzani* . . . .

The proposition for which *Biggs* is cited in the second example illustrates the power of the simple, unqualified statement:

> The federal Food Quality Act preempts more stringent state regulation.

You should avoid unnecessary qualifiers that weaken arguments, such as the following introduction to the argument of your client, Mason:

> Mason contends that the federal Food Quality Act preempts more stringent state regulation.

Because the argument section of your brief obviously comprises a series of legal contentions, specific introductions to that effect are superfluous. You may set up a response to your opponent's propositions by referring to them as "arguments" or "contentions," but such a characterization of your own conclusions or statements of law tends to weaken them. Instead, assert your argument directly:

> The federal Food Quality Act preempts more stringent state regulation.

2. Clichés That Weaken or Offend

Ironically, modifiers that are designed to reinforce a proposition sometimes sap the strength from an otherwise powerful statement. For example, comments such as "it is abundantly clear that" and "obviously" have little effect on the judge except to make him wonder whether the words were added to shore up a shaky proposition that in fact is subject to great debate. Along with other forms of exaggeration, clichés and empty modifiers such as these tend to make the advocacy in the writing too obvious and distracting. A judge will accept your conclusions more readily if you offer persuasive arguments than if you invoke stock phrases that describe your arguments as persuasive.

The line between strong advocacy and overstatement is most delicate when referring directly to a matter within the court's discretionary power. For example, the word "should" in the following argument reflects lack of confidence in the argument:

> This court should exclude evidence of Jenkins's subjective intentions regarding the lease.

On the other hand, a stronger verb suggests a presumptuous challenge to the power of the court:

> This court must exclude evidence of Jenkins's subjective intentions regarding the lease.

On reading such an argument, the judge might be subconsciously inclined to demonstrate that she does indeed have the discretionary power to admit the evidence, the exercise of which would not likely be overturned on appeal. Restating the proposition in passive voice tends to soften and depersonalize the challenge:

> Evidence of Jenkins's subjective intentions regarding the lease must be excluded.

Nonetheless, the challenge to the judge's power remains implicit in this construction. Perhaps the best statement is one that focuses directly on the character of the evidence rather than on the power of the judge:

> Evidence of Jenkins's subjective intentions regarding the lease is inadmissible.

This proposition is strong and unqualified, yet it avoids expressing or directly implying a personal challenge to the judge.

3. Personal Attacks

Avoid personal attacks on opposing counsel. Although you may become exasperated with apparently unreasonable or offensive conduct by your opponent, judges do not appreciate being caught in a crossfire of personal insults. Unless misconduct by a party or his attorney is properly the subject of a motion, judges are far more interested in your response to the opposing counsel's arguments than in your personal opinion of your opponent's intelligence, research skills, or personality. Thus, you may safely characterize the opposing counsel's argument as internally inconsistent, but you should not comment that he is unable to write a coherent brief. Similarly, if your statement of the procedural history unemotionally records events that reflect the opposing counsel's bad faith, the judge will undoubtedly draw negative conclusions about his advocacy without any further comment from you.

A court's published reaction to a derogatory characterization of opposing counsel's argument is illuminating:

> There are good reasons not to call an opponent's argument "ridiculous".... The reasons include civility; the near-certainty that overstatement will only push the reader away (especially when, as here, the hyperbole begins on page one of the brief); and that, even where the record supports an extreme modifier, "the better practice is usually to lay out the facts and let the court reach its own conclusions." *Big Dipper Entm't, L.L.C. v. City of Warren*, 641 F.3d 715, 719 (6th Cir. 2011).[1]

B. Persuasive Facts

When allowed by the court, you should present facts in a narrative form rather than as a list or as bullet points. The facts should tell your client's story in a way that supports the asserted arguments. Although you must present facts truthfully and in the proper context, you can frame them persuasively without being overtly manipulative. Word choice, sentence structure, and organization are key considerations for creating a story that supports your client's arguments.

It is common to default to a chronological organization of the facts. Although this is a logical choice, it might not serve your client as well as a topical or spatial organization. For example, if your client is accused of murder, it is not helpful to start the narrative with, "The victim was killed on July 1." Instead, you could begin the story by describing your client's location and activities at the time of the crime, or later when she heard about the victim's death. In either of these alternative structures, the reader begins the story with your client's perspective of the events rather than by thinking about the victim's death.

Consider this alternative synopsis of *The Wizard of Oz*:

> Transported to a surreal landscape, a young girl kills the first person she meets and then teams up with three strangers to kill again.[2]

This is not a false or incorrect synopsis of this familiar tale. The framing omits the circumstances in which Dorothy meets her friends and characterizes them as "strangers" who "team" up. The synopsis also uses the word "kill" twice in a short sentence, which grabs the reader's attention. Additionally, it minimizes the circumstances that lead to Dorothy's presence in Oz by placing them in the subordinate clause, and it emphasizes the killing of the two witches by placing them in the independent clause. Finally, all names are omitted and the fact that the two people who were killed were *wicked* witches is not mentioned.

Persuasive fact framing is an essential component of persuasive advocacy.

C. Sentence Structure

To preserve your credibility and ethical standards, you often must candidly acknowledge law that is adverse to your client's case and that you can neither discredit nor distinguish. You can minimize the resulting damage by using techniques of persuasive writing style to de-emphasize the adverse law and to focus attention on more helpful points.

One such technique consists of placing helpful information in the main clause and relegating adverse information to a dependent subordinate clause, a clause that cannot stand by itself as a complete sentence. For example, as counsel for the plaintiff in a contract action, you can de-emphasize the general rule against damages for emotional distress by disposing of it in an opening subordinate clause:

> Although damages for emotional distress are not often awarded for breach of contract, Jones is entitled to such an award because of the exceptional nature of his case: The central purpose of his contract with Runyon Pet Cemetery was to alleviate his grief over the loss of his dog. *See generally* . . . .

You maintain credibility with this passage by facing, rather than evading, the general rule. Moreover, by placing the general rule in a subordinate clause, you invite the reader to give it only brief pause, as you might invite a guest at a restaurant to dine lightly on appetizers in anticipation of the main course.

Location of information within a sentence also affects emphasis. Generally, the end of a sentence conveys the greatest emphasis, the beginning of a sentence conveys secondary emphasis, and a parenthetic phrase or clause at a natural breaking point in the middle of the sentence conveys the least emphasis. For example, if you represent the defendant in the example above, you can emphasize the general rule by placing it at the end of the sentence:

> In demanding an award of damages for emotional distress, Jones runs afoul of the general rule that such damages are not awarded for breach of contract.

Generally, you will emphasize the general rule least by placing it in a parenthetic clause at a natural breaking point in the middle of the sentence:

> Jones is entitled to an award of damages for emotional distress in this exceptional case, even though such awards are rare in contract actions, because the central purpose of his contract with Runyon Pet Cemetery was to alleviate his grief over the loss of his dog.

This passage may be the best of the three for the plaintiff because it places favorable information in the positions of greatest emphasis.

If willing to sacrifice other style objectives, the defendant can create unusual emphasis in the middle of the sentence with an abrupt, dramatic, or unnatural interruption of the sentence:

> Jones unreasonably demands—while admitting that such damages generally are not awarded in contract actions—an award of damages for emotional distress.

D. Introducing Block Quotations

You can use a substantive introduction to a block quotation as effective preliminary advocacy. Your introduction will emphasize the point of the quotation by presenting it in summary form.

Moreover, quotations from contracts, statutes, or case law often are reasonably subject to varying interpretations, and a substantive introduction can encourage the reader to interpret the quoted passage in a favorable manner. For example, the following passage from an employment contract lists several grounds for discharging an employee, but it doesn't expressly state whether the list is exclusive:

> XI. Ajax Co. reserves the right to discharge any employee who
> 1. fails to perform satisfactorily,
> 2. commits gross insubordination, or
> 3. commits a criminal act on the work site.

Assuming an employee hired under this contract is employed for an indefinite term, the traditional common law at-will rule would permit the employer to discharge the employee for any reason if the contractual list of grounds for discharge is not intended to be exclusive. On the other hand, if the contract provision quoted above is interpreted to include an implicit promise by the employer to refrain from discharging an employee except for the listed reasons, then the contract would override the otherwise applicable common law rule.

When quoting this passage in the argument section of the brief for either the employer or a discharged employee, you will achieve the least impact with a stock introduction such as:

> Section XI of the Employment Contract provides, in relevant part, as follows:

Instead, as counsel for the discharged employee, you should use an argumentative introductory sentence to characterize the provision as a restriction on the employer's freedom to terminate the employment:

> The Employment Contract expressly identifies only three grounds for discharge, all relating to poor performance or serious misconduct:
>
> XI. Ajax Co. reserves the right to discharge any employee who
> 1. fails to perform satisfactorily,
> 2. commits gross insubordination, or
> 3. commits a criminal act on the work site.
>
> Employment Contract § XI.
>
> The parties intended this list to be the exclusive, because . . . .

Conversely, as counsel for the employer, you can use an argumentative introduction to characterize the provision as an affirmation of the employer's common law freedom to terminate:

> No provision of the contract expressly limits Ajax Co.'s common law right to discharge any employee at Ajax's will. Indeed, the only provision addressing termination selects three particularly strong grounds for illustration and emphasis:
>
> XI. Ajax Co. reserves the right to discharge any employee who
> 1. fails to perform satisfactorily,
> 2. commits gross insubordination, or
> 3. commits a criminal act on the work site.
>
> Employment Contract § XI.
>
> Nothing in the contract suggests that these listed grounds are exclusive. Instead, ...

You can always begin arguing for a favorable interpretation after neutrally presenting the quoted passage. However, the reader is more likely to adopt your proposed interpretation if a substantive introduction prepares him for the interpretation before he reads the quoted passage.

Exercise 13-1

Foreclosure Falsities

In October 2010, in the wake of class action lawsuits and official investigations, some United States lending institutions suspended their home foreclosures nationwide to review their foreclosure procedures. Litigation challenging a home foreclosure in Maine revealed that GMAC, servicing a home loan for the Federal National Mortgage Association, had routinely engaged in a practice that the media soon dubbed "robo-signing": a "limited signing officer" would prepare hundreds of foreclosures each day, signing affidavits attesting that the requisites for foreclosure had been met even though the officer had not reviewed the relevant documents to confirm the assertions in the affidavits.

After discovering this practice in a deposition, a volunteer attorney for the homebuyer, Thomas Cox, persuaded the trial court in Maine to set aside its earlier partial summary judgment in favor of GMAC and to order GMAC to pay expenses associated with the deposition. Mr. Cox's brief included the following application of law to facts in his argument that the signing official (named in this exercise only as "S.O.") submitted his affidavit in bad faith, a legal prerequisite for an order of sanctions against GMAC:

> When [S.O.] says in an affidavit that he has personal knowledge of the facts stated in his affidavits, he doesn't. When he says that he has custody and control of the loan documents, he doesn't. When he says that he is attaching "a true and accurate" copy of a note or a mortgage, he has no idea if that is so, because he does not look at the exhibits. When he makes any other statement of fact, he has no idea if it is true. When the notary says that [S.O.] appeared before him or her, he didn't, and when the notary says that [S.O.] was sworn, he wasn't. The practice of GMAC Mortgage, LLC in submitting foreclosure affidavits such as this, knowing that they will be relied upon by a judge to enter an order taking away a family's home, must be seen as a quintessential definition of a summary judgment affidavit "presented in bad faith."[3]

1. Impact of the Facts

If you were the judge in this case, how would the preceding fact analysis affect your view of the case? If the case presented close legal issues or ones that permitted exercise of your discretion as the trial judge, would you be inclined to rule in favor of the homebuyer if any reasonable interpretation or application of the law permitted that result?

2. Analyzing the Presentation

Analyze the author's writing style. Explain how the style of presentation helps to maximize the persuasive effect of these compelling facts. Be specific in your description.

3. Persuasive Presentation in Other Styles

Can you rewrite the fact analysis in an alternative style of presentation, while still matching or exceeding the persuasive effect of the original? Describe the techniques of persuasive writing that you employ in your version.

II. Oral Argument to the Court

In many appeals and pretrial or trial motions, you will argue your client's case orally to the court after submitting your written brief. In most cases, your written brief will influence a judge more strongly than your oral argument. Indeed, before oral argument, most judges read both parties' briefs and come to a tentative decision on the merits.

Nonetheless, oral argument is not yet a meaningless formality in our courts. It provides you with a final opportunity to emphasize critical points, respond to judges' questions, change the mind of a judge who had tentatively decided to rule in favor of the opposing party, or strongly influence a judge who has not formed a tentative opinion.

A. General Format

Oral argument format varies based on the level of court, type of case, judicial preferences, and other local factors. The typical appellate oral argument follows a pattern similar to that for filing written briefs: The advocate seeking relief or reversal of a judgment in a lower court argues first, the opposing advocate responds, and the first advocate has an opportunity for rebuttal. In some courts, the advocate arguing first must tell the court before she begins her argument whether she wishes to divide her time between opening argument and rebuttal.

Rebuttal is a powerful weapon. It provides the advocate who opens the oral argument to have both the first and last word on the issues. Therefore, if you give the opening oral argument, you should always preserve the opportunity for rebuttal. Similarly, if you are responding to the opening argument, and if the court permits you to give a brief surrebuttal to the opponent's rebuttal, you should reserve time for a possible response to the rebuttal.

B. Formality and Demeanor

Appropriate courtroom attire is mandatory for any oral argument. For both men and women, this generally consists of a conservative, dark-colored suit. Beyond that, the level of formality of the proceedings will vary among courts.

For pretrial and trial motions, some state trial court judges hold oral arguments in their chambers rather than in the courtroom. After friendly, informal introductions, all are seated. As the judge listens from behind his desk, the attorneys deliver their arguments while seated in office chairs. In some cases and courts, the judge will dispense with formal presentations and simply ask questions designed to clarify the parties' positions. Similarly, oral argument while seated at tables is common in arbitration proceedings and some agency hearings.

Other trial judges and virtually all appellate panels of judges, however, conduct oral arguments with greater formality. In those courts, you deliver your oral argument from a lectern in the courtroom, or—in some arguments in trial court—while standing at the counsel table. These courts typically will designate time limits for oral argument and may have developed other conventions about the structure of oral argument.

If you are uncertain about the customs in a court or the expectations of a judge, you can observe another attorney's oral argument before the judge, speak with a colleague who has practiced before the judge, or seek advice from the staff of the clerk's office or from the judge's personal law clerk. To consult with them, you can contact them by telephone or simply arrive early on the day of the argument.

Your demeanor in oral argument should be as formal as your attire. You should be confident and relaxed, but respectful of the judge, always addressing him or her as "Your Honor." If you disagree with a judge during the argument, you need not be disagreeable. For example, if the judge asks you whether your formulation of a legal rule will have certain adverse policy ramifications, you should answer the question confidently but without arrogantly suggesting that the question is silly.

Thus, you should *not* respond to a judge's question or assertion with a challenge to the judge's analytic skills, such as the following:

> No, Your Honor, you are incorrect on that point.

Instead, you should answer the question without casting doubt on the questioner:

> No, Your Honor, the Court can avoid those potential problems of line-drawing by stating its holding in this appeal narrowly. Appellant suggests the following formulation: . . . .

In some cases, you can even validate the question as you answer it:

> Yes, Your Honor. That question has occupied the attention of many courts and scholars. To explain Appellant's interpretation, I must review the rationale for the exclusionary rule.

C. Content of the Argument

1. Introducing Yourself and Your Argument

In a formal courtroom argument, you should begin your presentation by introducing yourself and your representative capacity:

> May it please the court, I am Terry Malloy. I represent Bakeway Stores, the appellant on this appeal and the defendant in the trial court.

The opening phrase, "May it please the court," oddly suggests that you hope that your name literally pleases the court. However, it also signals respect to the court and a willingness to allow the judges to set the agenda for the dialogue through their questions and comments. Moreover, if a judge expects this traditional salutation, your departing from it could place the judge in an unreceptive mood. Accordingly, you should introduce yourself with this traditional phrase unless you are confident that the judge or judges hearing your argument are comfortable with a more natural greeting, such as "Good morning, Your Honor. I am. . . ."

After the personal introduction, you can capture a judge's attention with a brief characterization of the motion or appeal, advancing your theory of the case. If the facts are compelling, you can describe the general nature of the case in a sentence or two that conveys the theme of your argument, as explored in Chapter 12. For example, suppose that a state is prosecuting an 18-year-old student for felony possession of illegal drugs on the premises of his high school. The attorney for the defendant student has filed a motion in the trial court to exclude evidence obtained in an allegedly illegal detention and search. He might introduce his oral argument at the suppression hearing with the following characterization of the case:

> Your Honor, this motion concerns the reasonableness of a search by armed police officers who—acting solely on information about previous drug sales by a former student—rushed into a high school hallway with a barking police dog, ordered all fifteen high school students in the hallway to fall to their knees with hands behind their heads, and searched them, one-by-one. As the Supreme Court held in *Redding* . . . .

Of course, the prosecutor might respond with a very different characterization of the case:

> Your Honor, the seizure of the crack cocaine in this case was the product of a thorough investigation in an ongoing effort by police and school administrators to protect all students from trafficking in illegal drugs at Richland High School.

2. Body of the Argument

a. *General Strategy*

Many courts impose a time limit on each oral argument. Although some courts of last resort may allow up to 60 minutes for each side in a complex case, 15 to 30 minutes is more typical, and arguments on simple pretrial motions may be limited to an even shorter time. In most motions or appeals, you will not have time to address all the issues in the depth in which you explored them in your brief. Consequently, you should carefully study the arguments presented in both parties' briefs to determine the most effective strategy for oral argument.

Your strategy will differ depending on the circumstances of each case. In one appeal, for example, you might rely on multiple arguments that are both complex and interdependent. You might fear that, even with a well-organized brief to guide them, the judges may not fully appreciate how the arguments fit together to form the larger picture. Accordingly, you could decide to present an oral outline of all the arguments and their relationships, leaving the detail of each to your brief.

More often, you can identify an argument in your brief that you wish to emphasize. Perhaps it addresses a critically important threshold issue or is your strongest theory. In other cases, you might select an argument for oral presentation because it is the weakest link in your argumentative chain and needs extra support.

Whatever strategy you choose, you should communicate your intentions immediately after the introduction to your argument. For example, at a hearing to suppress evidence obtained in an allegedly illegal search, the prosecutor might try to justify the search on several grounds. Although she will introduce evidence at the hearing supporting each of the grounds and will advocate each ground in her brief, she might use her oral argument to focus on the determinative issue of consent to search. If so, she should reveal her plans to the court:

> This hearing presents three major issues, all of which the briefs examine in detail. I will be happy to answer questions on any of the issues. However, I would like to focus my presentation on the issue of consent to search. If the facts show that the defendant consented to the detention and the search, this court need not address difficult legal issues such as those related to expectations of privacy on a high school campus.

b. Using the Facts

Many judges will advise oral advocates before argument that the judges are familiar with the facts of the case and that the advocates should proceed with their legal analyses. Even absent such an instruction, you ordinarily should not begin your argument with a lengthy recitation of the facts beyond a general characterization of the nature of the case. You might depart from this advice if the facts are particularly compelling and your legal arguments are not. In most cases, however, you will make better use of your limited time by arguing the law and applying the law to the facts without a separate introductory recitation of facts.

Whenever you rely on facts in an oral argument, be certain of the source of the facts. Be prepared to cite to the portion of the record that establishes the facts.

c. Responding to Questions

Questions from the bench constitute the most uncertain variable in oral argument. They ensure that oral advocacy in most cases is not a series of speeches but a dialogue, primarily between each advocate and the judges, and secondarily between the advocates as they respond to one another. Oral argument also permits judges on a panel to establish a coy dialogue between the judges, as they attempt to persuade each other with comments and questions ostensibly directed to the advocates.

You should genuinely welcome the opportunity to respond to questions. A judge's questions may reveal areas in which she has doubts, permitting you to directly influence her thinking on those points.

Occasionally, a judge will press you for a concession on your weakest of several alternative arguments. Your waiving the argument might be the most effective way to turn the judge's attention to your stronger arguments. However, you should not too quickly waive a major argument that you had earlier determined was sufficiently meritorious to warrant discussion in your brief. If you are arguing before a panel of judges, the other panel members may not share the doubts of the questioning judge; yet, if you expressly waive the controversial point during oral argument, none of the judges will take up that argument. Thus, even though it appears that you must waive the argument to preserve your credibility, you should first try to shift to a more productive topic of discussion after making a minor concession:

> Your Honor, as explored in detail in the Appellee's Brief, Todd maintains that he has standing to establish unreasonable use of force based on the totality of the circumstances, including evidence showing how the entire police operation affected all the students. However, Todd's principal argument on appeal is that the police violated the Fourth Amendment by detaining and searching Todd without even reasonable suspicion that any illegal activity was taking place.

Except when trying to avoid a waiver of an argument, you should not give the appearance of evading questions from the bench. Instead, you should confront and answer the questions directly. To answer judges' questions effectively, you must come to the argument thoroughly prepared. In particular, you should be ready to

- discuss the facts, holding, and reasoning of any case that you seek to distinguish or on which you rely;
- cite to the record to identify the source of facts on which you rely; and
- discuss the policy implications of alternative holdings among which the court must choose.

An excellent method of preparing for the oral argument is to hold practice sessions with colleagues acting as judges. Your colleagues can provide constructive criticism and can help you anticipate the questions likely to be asked by the judges in the actual oral argument.

Even with excellent preparation, you may not always anticipate every question that a judge will ask you. If you cannot formulate a satisfactory answer to a truly unexpected and excessively challenging question, you probably will do better to acknowledge the difficulty of the question and to offer to address it in your rebuttal or in a supplementary brief than to simply bluff or brush the question aside.

Because you cannot always predict the number of questions from the bench, you must build maximum flexibility into your argument. You should be prepared to do either of the following or anything in between:

- present your arguments without interruption until your time elapses or you otherwise finish your argument; or
- present a brief introduction, respond without break to a series of questions that takes up all your allotted time, and request that the court permit you to end with a prepared conclusion no longer than a few sentences.

3. The Conclusion

You should end your argument on a compelling note, perhaps with a summary of your strongest points. A carefully planned conclusion will be particularly helpful if persistent questioning from the bench prevents you from covering all the points that you had planned to address in your oral argument. Faced with the impending expiration of your allotted time, you can fall back on the conclusion as a quick means of stating your points, if only in summary fashion.

D. Nervousness and Verbal Stumbling

All but the most experienced oral advocates feel some anxiety at the prospect of facing an inquisitive panel of judges in a public setting. If you feel such anxiety, you may be concerned that your nervousness will interfere with your speech patterns, causing your voice to shake or causing you to stumble over your words or to pause to collect your thoughts. You need not worry excessively about such problems for two reasons.

First, so long as the judge can understand you, the substance of your arguments and of your responses to questions will be more important than your charisma and stage presence. Some debate competitions may exalt form over substance: You may earn points if you can glibly respond to a judge's questions without pause, or lose points if you occasionally stumble over a difficult word. In actual oral arguments, however, a judge will be more concerned with establishing a genuine dialogue with you. She will not be uncomfortable with a few moments of silence from you; indeed, most judges will expect you to pause to think deeply before answering a difficult question. Moreover, if you speak sufficiently slowly and clearly to make yourself understood, most judges will forgive you for the occasional verbal stumbling that nervousness may produce.

Second, you can minimize distracting imperfections in your delivery caused by nervousness. Perhaps the best way to bring such nervousness under control is to approach your oral argument with the confidence that comes from thorough preparation. If you have carefully prepared your analysis, mastered the facts and the record, anticipated questions, and rehearsed your argument before colleagues playing the role of inquisitive judges, you can confidently assume that you will bring an expertise to the courtroom that the judge will appreciate.

Just prior to the argument, consider spending a few minutes taking slow, deep breaths, while you clear your mind of doubts and distracting thoughts. Try to focus your thoughts on viewing the oral argument positively, as an opportunity for a constructive dialogue with the judge.

To deal with remaining nervousness at the beginning of your argument, you should prepare a carefully worded introduction that you can commit to memory, so that you will not find yourself groping for words at the outset. Then, after you have warmed up your speaking voice, you can speak more flexibly from a rough outline of your main argument before closing with a carefully planned conclusion. Remember, your oral argument is more akin to a formal conversation with the court than a formal speech. Active engagement in the conversation coupled with solid preparation are key to a successful oral argument.

Checklist for Chapter 13

- Effective written advocacy requires
  - sound analysis,
  - sensible organization, and
  - effective writing style.
- In addition to the matters examined in Chapter 12, you must adopt a persuasive writing style.
- Carefully prepare an oral argument that
  - strategically supplements your brief,
  - follows the rules and customs of the court, and
  - makes essential points within time limits.
- Present your oral argument in an engaging, conversational manner, using only an outline for notes, while welcoming questions from the bench.

The following chapters examine further techniques of persuasive writing in the context of various legal documents.

Endnotes

1. Bennett v. State Farm Mut. Auto. Ins. Co., 731 F.3d 584, 584-85 (6th Cir. 2013).
2. This synopsis has been credited to *Philadelphia Inquirer* writer Lee Winfrey, but is likely the work of writer Rick Polito circa 1998. See http://jimromenesko.com/2012/10/26/wizard-of-oz-synopsis-is-going-to-followwriter-to-the-grave/.
3. The facts for this exercise are taken from court documents in Fed. Nat'l Mortg. Ass'n v. Bradbury, No. BR-OE-09-65 (9th Dist. Ct., ME), and from David Streitfeld, *From This House, a National Foreclosure Freeze*, N.Y. Times, Oct. 15, 2010, at A1. The quoted paragraph from Mr. Cox's brief omits a footnote that appeared in the brief after the third sentence of the paragraph. The author thanks Richard Neumann for bringing this example of persuasive writing to the attention of the legal writing community.

Part VI

Pretrial Advocacy— Pleadings and Motions

You might file different kinds of pleadings and briefs to a court from the inception of a lawsuit to its final disposition in a court of last resort. This part of the book explores a few kinds of pretrial pleadings and briefs with the aim of preparing you to initiate or respond to any form of written advocacy. Part III will examine appellate brief-writing.

The following three chapters introduce you to three kinds of pretrial written advocacy: pleadings (and surviving a motion to dismiss a pleading), motions for summary judgment, and pretrial motions to exclude evidence. When combined with the discussion of appellate briefs in Part III, Part II should provide you with the skills and confidence you need to perform any task of written advocacy.

Chapter 14

Pleadings and Motions to Dismiss

I. The Complaint

"A civil action is commenced by filing a complaint with the court."[1] Because a complaint is such a fundamental and significant document, law schools are increasingly offering students opportunities to draft complaints in legal writing or clinical courses. Still, when faced with the task of preparing a complaint, you might be tempted to turn to canned language in formbooks.

Forms can provide general guidance in some cases. In fact, many jurisdictions have officially authorized pleading forms for certain kinds of suits. Nonetheless, you will more quickly and thoroughly master pleading skills if you understand the components of a complaint well enough to draft one "from scratch." Your primary tools in such a task are the results of your investigation of facts and your knowledge of the applicable law. Beyond that, rules of procedure, local court rules, and case law provide the necessary guidance.

A. Overview: Format and Content

Local court rules on pleading often specify a standard caption that identifies the case and the nature of the document. For example, the Rules of Practice for the United States District Court for the District of Arizona specify the line spacing and precise location in the caption on the first page of a document for, among other things, the following information: (1) the name, address, email address, state bar attorney number, and telephone number of the representing attorney, and whether the attorney represents the plaintiff, defendant, or other party; (2) the title of the court; (3) the names of the parties in a "title of the action"; (4) the docket number (or a space for it if the clerk has not yet assigned one); and (5) a designation of the nature of the document.[2]

More substantively, Federal Rule of Civil Procedure 8(a) requires a complaint to contain three elements:

> (1) a short and plain statement of the grounds for the court's jurisdiction . . . ;
> (2) a short and plain statement of the claim showing that the pleader is entitled to relief; and
> (3) a demand for the relief sought, which may include relief in the alternative or different types of relief.

Each of these elements warrants further examination.

B. Jurisdictional Statement

The jurisdictional statement is particularly important in a complaint filed in federal court, because the subject matter jurisdiction of federal courts is limited to that authorized by Article III of the United States Constitution and by federal statutes.[3] Therefore, in the initial paragraphs of a complaint in federal court, you should allege facts establishing subject matter jurisdiction based on a federal question,[4] diversity of citizenship,[5] or a special statutory grant of jurisdiction.[6] Although the jurisdictional statement is sufficient if it alleges facts that support the court's exercise of jurisdiction,[7] federal pleaders customarily cite to the specific statutes that grant jurisdiction:

> 1. This claim arises under Title VII of the Civil Rights Act of 1964; therefore, this court has subject matter jurisdiction under 42 U.S.C. § 2000e-5(f)(3) and 28 U.S.C. § 1331.[8]

Pleading subject matter jurisdiction is less important in state court than in federal court, because most state trial courts are courts of general jurisdiction. When state pleaders address subject matter jurisdiction at all, it is often with simple introductory allegations that the amount in controversy exceeds the amount reserved for state courts of limited jurisdiction. This is often coupled with a citation to the state constitutional or statutory provision that authorizes the court's exercise of general trial jurisdiction.

Nonetheless, many state rules of civil procedure have adopted all the elements of the governing federal rule of civil procedure, thus requiring some statement of "jurisdiction" in state court complaints. Because a special allegation of subject matter jurisdiction is less clearly necessary in a state court complaint, state pleaders often begin their complaints with allegations of *personal* jurisdiction over the defendants. Such statements typically introduce the parties and allege in conclusory fashion that the defendant has engaged in conduct in the state out of which the claim arises or has otherwise established the requisite contacts with the state.

Some Federal complaints also include allegations establishing that the court has personal jurisdiction over the defendant, even though the appendix of forms to the federal rules, published until 2015, included no such allegations in their samples.[9] Assuming that lack of personal jurisdiction is treated as an affirmative defense for pleading purposes, a complaint will not be insufficient for failure to affirmatively plead personal jurisdiction over the defendant.

C. Claim for Relief

Federal Rule of Civil Procedure 8(a)(2) omits any reference to "facts" in its requirement of a statement of the claim for relief. Nonetheless, "Rule 8(a)(2) envisages the statement of circumstances, occurrences, and events in support of the claim presented."[10] Most people would use the word "fact" to describe allegations of that nature. Moreover, as discussed below, the Supreme Court's interpretation of Rule 8 since 2007 sometimes requires detailed allegations of fact.

Thus, in the main body of the complaint, you will allege facts that establish entitlement to relief. This may require preliminary legal research and a reasonable investigation of the facts, to help satisfy your ethical obligations under Rule 11.[11] Your knowledge of the law will enable you to determine which kinds of facts are legally significant, and your knowledge of the case will help you to identify facts that you can allege reasonably and in good faith.

To draft your claim for relief effectively, you must determine

1. the extent, if any, to which you should supplement fact allegations with references to the law;
2. the specific content of the fact allegations; and
3. the appropriate level of specificity of the allegations.

1. Allegations of Fact and Citations to Law

Your complaint normally should allege facts and ultimate conclusions of fact establishing a claim for relief; you need not cite to supporting legal authority.[12] Thus, you need allege only the minor premise and conclusion of the syllogism of deductive reasoning, leaving the major premise implicit:

~~[**Major premise:** Rule of Law]~~
Minor premise: Allegations of Fact
Conclusion: Allegation of Liability or Other Ultimate Conclusion

Indeed, focusing excessively on legal rules could lead a pleader to state legal conclusions rather than the facts supporting the conclusions. According to the Supreme court, none of the following would meet the requirements for a complaint in federal court: (1) "labels and conclusions," (2) "a formulaic recitation of the elements of a cause of action,"[13] or (3) "conclusory statements without reference to its factual context."[14]

Accordingly, in practice, citation to specific legal authority is much less common in the claim for relief than in the jurisdictional statement. The only references to legal authority commonly found in claims for relief are descriptive headings that introduce counts with general legal theories of relief, such as "Negligence," "Wrongful Discharge," "Employment Discrimination," or "Breach of Contract."

Nonetheless, a pleader will sometimes cite to authority in the claim for relief for a strategic purpose. For example, in cases in which the plaintiff seeks a settlement at the outset of litigation, his attorney might briefly cite to authority in the complaint to demonstrate to the defendant that the claim is substantial and that further litigation is unlikely to reduce the risk of liability. In most cases, however, the attorney could achieve the same result with a demand letter that explains the merits of the claim. Such a letter could either precede or accompany the complaint.

In other cases, an attorney might cite to legal authority in the body of the complaint because the claim is admittedly novel and thus would not be readily recognized as meritorious on the basis of the factual allegations alone. The author of the complaint might hope that the citations will help the judge understand the advocate's legal theory and keep an open mind pending further proceedings.

When the allegations are unusually complex or the underlying legal theories novel or complex, some attorneys recommend a middle ground: limit your allegations to factual matters but explain the nature of the claims and allegations in a short "Introduction" or "Overview" that precedes the specific factual allegations. In one or two paragraphs, you can help the reader see the whole forest before entering dense groves of trees by (1) briefly identifying any novel legal theories on which your claims depend, or (2) summarizing how numerous complicated transactions or other facts relate to one another, or both.

2. Substance of Allegations

Normally, a claim for relief should state the journalist's "five Ws": who, what, where, when, and why.[15]

Who—In some complaints, you will introduce the parties in the jurisdictional allegations. Otherwise, your statement of the claim for relief should identify them and their relationship to one another. It should also identify any other significant actors.

What, *Where*, *When*—The statement of the claim should describe the events that give rise to the claim. You should take care to allege all facts needed to support each element of the claim and the request for relief.

Why—You should allege any state of mind that is material to the claim or to the availability of special relief. For example, a request for punitive damages in a common law tort claim must be supported by an allegation of malice, willful misconduct, or at least recklessness, depending on the jurisdiction.

You need not allege all matters that may ultimately be in dispute; you need allege only the legal elements of your client's claim for relief, with sufficient factual detail to make the claim plausible. The defendant must plead affirmative defenses in the answer,[16] and the complaint need not anticipate them. The federal rules list 18 affirmative defenses;[17] statutes and case law may help you define the burdens of pleading on other matters. In case of doubt, you should plead a matter as part of the claim for relief.

For example, suppose that the jurisdiction in which the complaint is filed recognizes a cause of action for intentional infliction of emotional distress on proof of four elements: (1) The defendant engaged in extreme and outrageous conduct (2) with the intent to cause severe emotional distress or with reckless disregard for the possibility of those consequences, and (3) the conduct caused the plaintiff to suffer (4) severe emotional distress.[18] After introductory allegations establishing personal jurisdiction and identifying Jansen as the plaintiff and Bostich as one of the defendants, the count for this claim should allege facts supporting each of the four elements of the prima facie case:

COUNT I

Infliction of Emotional Distress

Relationship of parties

3. Beginning March 1, 2021, Jansen worked on an assembly line at the Zydeco Radio factory under the direct supervision of Bostich. As Jansen's supervisor, Bostich had the authority to impose production quotas on Jansen and to impose discipline, including termination, for failure to meet quotas.

Conduct	4. From April 5 to June 10, 2021, Bostich engaged in the extreme and outrageous conduct of imposing impossible production quotas on Jansen and threatening to fire Jansen if he failed to meet the quotas.[19]
State of mind	5. During this time, Bostich frequently demeaned Jansen verbally, showing that he harbored ill will toward Jansen and intended to cause him harm. Specifically, Bostich maliciously conveyed the quotas, threats, and other verbal abuse for the purpose of causing Jansen to suffer severe emotional distress. Alternatively, Bostich recklessly disregarded the likelihood that Jansen would suffer such distress.[20]
Causation and severe distress	6. On June 10, 2021, as a direct result of Bostich's conduct, Jansen suffered a complete nervous breakdown requiring bed rest for three weeks and extensive medical care.
Injuries supporting a request for an award of damages	7. Jansen continues to suffer insomnia, headaches, inability to concentrate at work, general nervousness, and other emotional distress as a result of Bostich's conduct. In an effort to address these symptoms, Jansen has frequently consulted a general physician and a psychological counselor, incurring substantial medical expenses.

In contrast, even if the allegations raise some question of whether the statute of limitations has expired, the complaint need not affirmatively allege that the statute of limitations has not expired or has been tolled. Instead, expiration of the statute of limitations is an affirmative defense that the defendant has the burden of pleading.[21]

3. Specificity of Fact Allegations: General Notice Pleading and Plausibility

The early, rigid common law forms of action largely disappeared in this country in the nineteenth century with widespread enactment of versions of the Field Code, named for David Dudley Field. These rules required complaints to set forth a "statement of the facts constituting the cause of action, in ordinary and concise language."[22]

In the twentieth century, the federal system and most states replaced their versions of the Field Code with rules permitting pleadings that give the court and the opposing party more general notice of most claims and defenses.[23] On its face, Federal Rule of Civil Procedure 8(a)(2) requires the main portion of a complaint to include only a "short and plain statement of the claim showing that the pleader is entitled to relief." The federal rules occasionally require greater detail for certain matters. Rule 9(b), for example, provides that allegations of "fraud or mistake" must state the circumstances "with particularity."[24] Otherwise, however, notice pleading permitted very short complaints and allowed plaintiffs to ascertain factual and evidentiary details in the discovery and disclosure process.[25]

But the federal rules governing pleading and motions to dismiss are subject to interpretation. In the twenty-first century, Supreme Court case law nudged the pendulum to swing back toward detailed fact pleading, encouraging longer, more detailed complaints. In 2007 and 2009, the United States Supreme Court held that a federal complaint is subject to dismissal unless it states "a claim to relief that is plausible on its face."[26] This new "plausibility" standard does not require allegations that establish the "probability" of liability,[27] nor does it transfer the more rigid particularity requirement of Rule 9(b) to Rule 8(a)(2).[28] On a motion to dismiss under Rule 12(b)(6), however, the plausibility requirement does direct a federal judge to use "experience and common sense" to determine whether the factual allegations permit a plausible inference of wrongdoing, rather than the "mere possibility" of wrongdoing.[29] For example, if the allegations of fact, assumed to be true, more readily permit an inference of innocent behavior than of wrongdoing, they do not state a plausible claim.[30]

To avoid dismissal for lack of plausibility, a federal court of appeals opines that "the plaintiff must give enough details about the subject-matter of the case to present a story that holds together."[36] Consistent with this advice, some scholars reject the spare style of notice pleading in favor of narratives that present a more complete and detailed portrayal of context, actors, events, and consequences.[31] In addition to increasing the plausibility of the claim, greater detail allows the pleader to introduce elements of persuasion in the complaint, thus advancing a level of advocacy that might otherwise be left to post-complaint motions. For example, details about plaintiffs' status and actions can help the reader identify or sympathize with the plaintiff. Similarly, by alleging the defendant's breach of a legal duty in detail, the pleader can paint a vivid picture of an injustice that the reader consciously or subconsciously desires to redress.

As discussed in Chapter 11, Federal Rule of Civil Procedure 11 requires an attorney to conduct a reasonable investigation into the facts and to plead facts that "have evidentiary support or, if specifically so identified, will likely have evidentiary support after a reasonable opportunity for further investigation or discovery."[38] Accordingly, you cannot provide a more detailed narrative in your complaint through conjecture or wishful thinking. On the other hand, neither can you conduct discovery until you have filed a complaint that survives the trial judge's assessment for plausibility. Consequently, the plausibility standard inevitably will increase the average time, effort, and expense devoted to initial investigation of facts. On the other hand, a detailed complaint could permit the parties to more quickly assess the value of a claim, possibly leading to earlier settlement, which could offset some of the increased costs of gathering facts for a detailed complaint.[40]

States that have adopted notice pleading standards are not bound to adopt the federal plausibility requirement as an interpretation of their state rules of civil procedure, even if modeled on the federal rules.[32] Nonetheless, many drafters of complaints in state court will choose to provide greater detail than the required minimum, to paint a more compelling picture at the outset of litigation.

Aside from requiring more thorough investigation of facts, a more detailed complaint will require greater time and effort in drafting, to tell a clear and compelling story. A lengthy, detailed complaint will not escape dismissal if the allegations are rambling, confusing, and disorganized.[33] Even a detailed narrative can be concisely written, wasting no words and moving briskly. The complaint should lead the reader through all essential elements of the story, but without verbosity, confusion, or unnecessary repetition.

D. Request for Relief

Your complaint should end with a simple statement of the relief sought by your client. The main request for relief typically is for an injunction, an award of money damages, or both. Consult local rules to determine whether you must request a specific dollar amount for some kinds of damages and an unspecified amount for others.

Additionally, you should request an award of reasonable costs and attorneys' fees if your client has a legal basis for such an award. Finally, you can retain flexibility by closing the request for relief with a catch-all request for "other appropriate relief":

> Jansen therefore requests judgment granting the following relief:
>
> 1. an award of compensatory damages in an amount to be set at trial;
> 2. an award of punitive damages in an amount to be set at trial;
> 3. an award of reasonable costs and attorneys' fees; and
> 4. such other relief as the court deems appropriate.

E. Style and Organization

1. Writing Style

Some of lawyers' stuffiest jargon can be found in antiquated pleadings:

> Comes now the plaintiff before this honorable court and, through his attorneys, Jenkins, Brown, and Little, alleges, pleads, and avers as follows:
>
> ....
>
> 3. That the defendant did employ said plaintiff as a designer of clothes . . . ;
>
> 4. That on July 6, 1927, said defendant did . . . ;
>
> Wherefore, the plaintiff prays that this honorable court grant judgment . . . .

The federal rules reject jargon in favor of plain English: "Each allegation must be simple, concise, and direct. No technical form is required."[34] When stated in plain English, the allegations in the preceding example are unquestionably simpler and more concise:

> Plaintiff alleges:
>
> . . . .
>
> 3. The defendant employed the plaintiff as a designer of clothes. . . .
>
> 4. On July 6, 1927, the defendant. . . .
>
> Plaintiff requests the following relief: . . . .

2. Organization

To facilitate analysis of the claims by the court and the parties, set forth the allegations of your complaint in consecutively numbered paragraphs. Separation of different claims for relief into separate counts may be permissible or required, depending on the circumstances.

If you are alleging separate claims for relief based on different transactions or occurrences, federal rules require you to state the claims in separate counts "[i]f doing so would promote clarity."[35] Otherwise, presentation of allegations in separate counts appears to be discretionary.

Even if your client's claims arise out of a single transaction, separate counts should be helpful if you rely on distinct legal theories that are based on different fact allegations. For example, a consumer injured by a faulty electrical appliance may have a cause of action against the retailer on two legal theories: products liability in tort and breach of a contractual warranty. If you divide the allegations into separate counts, you can identify which fact allegations are material to each theory of relief. If some facts are common to both theories, one count can incorporate some of the allegations of the other:

> **COUNT I**
>
> **Tort—Products Liability**
>
> 4. On January 1, 2019, Green purchased a microwave oven from Retailer.
>
> 5. The microwave oven had an unreasonably dangerous defect. . . .
>
> . . . .
>
> **COUNT II**
>
> **Contract—Breach of Warranty**
>
> 8. Green realleges the allegations in paragraphs 4-7.
>
> 9. Babcock Appliance Center warranted the microwave oven to be free of defects. . . .

You must also exercise discretion to determine whether to follow each count with a separate request for relief or to consolidate them in a single request after presenting all counts. As with separation of theories into counts, separation of requests for relief to accompany different counts normally will be helpful if the available remedies vary with each count. For example, if punitive damages are available only on the products liability count and if attorneys' fees are available only on the count for breach of warranty, separate requests for relief after each count could facilitate subsequent analysis of the claims. On the other hand, if the requests for relief on different counts are identical, you can avoids pointless repetition by stating a single request for relief at the end of the complaint.

II. The Answer

To avoid judgment against him by default, the defendant must respond to a complaint by filing an answer or other appropriate response.[36] The defendant may move to dismiss the complaint on its face before filing an answer.[37] The answer must admit or deny each allegation of the complaint.[38] In addition, the answer may set forth any affirmative defenses,[39] assert counterclaims against the plaintiff,[40] or both. If the answer asserts a counterclaim, the original plaintiff must file an answer to the counterclaim to avoid default judgment on the counterclaim.[41]

A. Admissions and Denials

Nearly every complaint will contain some allegations of fact that the defendant admits to be true. Therefore, the typical answer will not generally deny all allegations of the complaint; instead, it will address each paragraph of the complaint and identify areas of dispute.[42] For example, an answer to the complaint partially set forth earlier in this chapter might admit and deny allegations in the following manner:

ADMISSIONS AND DENIALS

1. Defendant Bostich admits the allegations in paragraphs 1-3 of Plaintiff Jansen's complaint.

2. Bostich denies the allegations in paragraph 4 of the complaint that he set impossible goals for Jansen and that he intimidated Jansen in his work. Bostich admits that he warned Jansen of the possibility of termination for failing to meet goals.

3. Bostich denies the allegations in paragraph 5 of the complaint.

4. Bostich has no information on which to form a belief in the truth of the allegations in paragraph 6 of the complaint, and he therefore denies them.

If the complaint is more than a few paragraphs long, it could help to match up the paragraphs of the complaint and answer, rather than admitting several paragraphs of allegations in the first paragraph of the answer:

> 1. Defendant Bostich admits the allegations in paragraph 1 of Plaintiff Jansen's complaint.
>
> 2. Defendant Bostich admits the allegations in paragraph 2 of the complaint.
>
> 3. Defendant Bostich admits the allegations in paragraph 3 of the complaint.
>
> 4. Bostich denies the allegations in paragraph 4 of the complaint that....

One attorney even recommends that each paragraph of the answer restate or summarize the corresponding allegation of the complaint before admitting or denying it. The judge might be disposed to refer repeatedly to such a self-contained answer, rather than refer to the complaint, which would not include the defendant's denials.[43]

Conversely, you can consolidate your admissions and denials to the maximum degree if you prefer the most concise possible answer:[44]

> 1. Defendant Bostich admits the allegations in paragraphs 1-3 of Plaintiff Jansen's complaint.
>
> 2. Bostich admits that he warned Jansen of the possibility of termination for failing to meet goals.
>
> 3. Bostich denies all other allegations.

B. Affirmative Defenses

In a separate section of your answer, you should allege facts and conclusions supporting any affirmative defenses that your client, the defendant, can reasonably assert.[45] Even if the allegations of the complaint are true and are legally sufficient to state a claim for relief, a meritorious affirmative defense to the prima facie case will justify judgment for the defendant.

For example, in the litigation between Jansen and Bostich, suppose that (1) the statute of limitations for tort actions in the jurisdiction is one year, (2) Jansen filed his complaint on June 9, 2022, and (3) Bostich last communicated a supervisory ultimatum to Jansen on June 6, 2021. Bostich might be prepared to argue that the statute of limitations has expired on the ground that Jansen's cause of action accrued at the latest on June 6, 2021, the date of Bostich's last act, rather than on June 10, 2021, the date of Jansen's nervous breakdown. If so, Bostich could assert expiration of the statute of limitations as an affirmative defense:

AFFIRMATIVE DEFENSE

5. Bostich last exercised any supervisory control over Jansen on June 6, 2021. Therefore, Jansen's cause of action accrued more than one year before the filing of his complaint, and the statute of limitations bars his action.

C. Counterclaims

The defendant named in a complaint might wish to assert an independent claim for relief against the plaintiff. If so, the roles of the parties are reversed for purposes of the counterclaim, and the principles of pleading discussed in Section I above apply to the counterclaim.

For example, in the litigation between Jansen and Bostich, additional facts might support a claim against Jansen for battery:

COUNTERCLAIM

Battery

6. On the evening of July 16, 2021, Jansen struck Bostich over the head with a baseball bat as Bostich left the Zydeco Radio factory.

7. Jansen acted maliciously and for the specific purpose of causing serious injury to Bostich.

8. As a result of Jansen's malicious attack, Bostich lost consciousness, required treatment in a hospital emergency room, and suffered debilitating pain for 24 hours.

Therefore, Bostich requests the following relief: ....

III. Motion to Dismiss

A. Standards and Procedure

As discussed above, Federal Rule of Civil Procedure 8(a)(2) requires that a complaint in federal court include "a short and plain statement of the claim showing that the pleader is entitled to relief." Under Rule 12(b)(6), a defendant may move to dismiss all or part of a complaint "for failure to state a claim upon which relief can be granted."

On a motion to dismiss, the defendant is essentially adopting the following strategy:

> If this case proceeds, I will deny some of the factual allegations of the complaint, and I am confident that the plaintiff will not be able to prove those allegations at trial. But we do not need to proceed to trial or even to

> discovery. Even if the allegations in the complaint were true, they would not amount to a claim under applicable law. In this motion and the response to it, the plaintiff and I will present our arguments about the content of the applicable law. Then, after applying the law to the facts of the complaint, the court should rule that the plaintiff's alleged facts, even if true, would not satisfy the legal requirements of any claim for relief.

In a state that has adopted general notice pleading without a plausibility requirement, a court will take the following steps in assessing a motion to dismiss:

- analyze the law without deferring to allegations of the complaint that amount to legal propositions;
- assume the truth of all factual allegations in the complaint, drawing inferences in favor of the nonmoving party;
- limit its analysis to the allegations in the complaint, without considering other allegations or evidence; and
- dismiss only if it appears the plaintiff can prove no set of facts entitling the plaintiff to recover.[46]

In federal court, or in a state court that adopts the equivalent of the federal plausibility requirement, a motion to dismiss the complaint benefits from that additional burden on the complaining party, as described earlier in this chapter. The court will still assume the truth of the allegations in the complaint. However, the court must use its experience and judgment to determine whether the complaint's factual conclusions are ***plausible*** and not merely ***possible***. To deem a claim plausible, the court might require more specific intermediary factual allegations to support a factual conclusion that appears far-fetched to the court, such as the factual conclusion that a high official ordered or condoned the actions of a lower-level official.

B. Format

1. The Motion

As with any motion, you should state your request for dismissal on a free-standing page, as illustrated in Exercise 14-2 below, with a caption title such as "Motion to Dismiss Complaint." You should state your request for dismissal in a simple, plain sentence that cites to Rule 12(b)(6) or its equivalent in the jurisdiction. This request can simply state the legal conclusion that the allegations in the complaint (or in one or more counts of the complaint) do not state a claim for which relief can be granted. If you can explain that conclusion more specifically without adding undue length to your request, you can tailor that standard to the issue in your case:

> Defendant, Hi-Tech Filter Co., moves this Court to dismiss the complaint for failure to state a claim. *See* [Fed. or state] R. Civ. P. 12(b)(6). The complaint fails to allege actions that amount to breach of contract under the plain meaning of the language of the contract.

The plaintiff can respond to the motion with a similar cover page, which might be entitled "Opposition to Motion to Dismiss." The opposition will not advance any motion but will simply request that the court deny the motion to dismiss, while adding a succinct summary of its ground for denial:

> Plaintiff, Crystal Pools, Inc., requests that this Court deny Defendant's Motion to Dismiss. The complaint states a valid claim for breach of contract: It alleges with requisite detail that Defendant delivered goods that materially deviated from the contract specifications in section V of the contract.

2. The Supporting Brief

Appended to your motion will be a legal brief supporting your request. Typically entitled "Memorandum of Law," it will typically include three sections:

I. Facts [or "Introduction," or "Background," or "Statement of the Case"]
II. Argument
III. Conclusion

Section I of your brief can concisely summarize the nature of the dispute, the critical allegations of the complaint, and any relevant procedural developments in the case.

Section II should follow the style, ethical considerations, and organizational structures explored in Part V of this book. In the final section of your brief, concisely conclude by restating your request and the grounds for it, much like your summary in the motion itself.

Exercise 14-1 with Sample Complaints

Compare and critically evaluate the following three versions of a complaint in the same wrongful discharge action. Which level of detail do you prefer? Which level would satisfy a plausibility requirement? What other differences in style do the complaints reflect? Which styles do you prefer? Note that the line spacing of the sample complaints in this book do not conform with the line-spacing requirements of most local rules.

For further practice with pleadings, complete Assignments 1 through 3 in Appendix VI.

ARIZONA SUPERIOR COURT

MARICOPA COUNTY, ARIZONA

GEORGE BRYANT, Plaintiff, v. MARIE JARDON, d.b.a. Chez Marie, Defendant.	No.____________ COMPLAINT

Plaintiff alleges:

COUNT 1

I

Plaintiff George Bryant is a resident of Phoenix, Arizona. Defendant Marie Jardon owns and operates Chez Marie, a restaurant located in Phoenix, Arizona.

II

Bryant worked for Jardon as a waiter at Chez Marie from August 16, 2020 to September 28, 2021.

III

At the time of his discharge on September 28, 2021, Bryant had an employment contract with Chez Marie that imposed substantive and procedural restrictions upon Jardon's right to terminate Bryant's employment.

IV

Acting through her agent, Mario Prieto, Jardon discharged Bryant on September 28, 2021, in breach of her employment contract with Bryant.

V

As a result of Jardon's breach of contract, Bryant has suffered lost wages and other incidental and consequential losses.

COUNT 2

VI

Bryant realleges and incorporates paragraphs I-V above.

VII

Acting through her agent, Jardon maliciously and unlawfully discharged Bryant for reasons that violate public policy, causing Bryant lost wages and other injuries.

Bryant therefore requests judgment granting the following relief:

1. an order reinstating Bryant to his position as waiter at Chez Marie;
2. an award of compensatory and punitive damages;
3. an award of costs and attorneys' fees; and
4. other appropriate relief.

Dated________________

by________________________,
Thomas Sanchez
Simpson, Sanchez & Summers
303 North Central Avenue
Phoenix, Arizona 85002
(602) 229-1111
Bar No. 28371
Attorney for the plaintiff

ARIZONA SUPERIOR COURT
MARICOPA COUNTY, ARIZONA

George BRYANT, Plaintiff, v. Marie JARDON, d.b.a. Chez Marie, Defendant.	No.____________ COMPLAINT

Plaintiff alleges:

I

BREACH OF PROMISE

1. Plaintiff George Bryant is a resident of Phoenix, Arizona. Defendant Marie Jardon owns and operates Chez Marie, a restaurant located in Phoenix, Arizona.

2. Bryant worked for Jardon as a waiter at Chez Marie from August 16, 2020 to September 28, 2021. Mario Prieto acted as the maître d' and supervisor of waiters at Chez Marie during Bryant's employment at Chez Marie. In all the events alleged below, Prieto acted on behalf of Jardon.

3. At the time of his discharge on September 28, 2021, Bryant had an employment contract with Chez Marie that included the terms of an "Employee Handbook."

4. The Employee Handbook contains promises of job security, including promises that (i) Jardon will not discharge any waiter except for inadequate performance and (ii) any waiter recommended for discharge has the right to meet with Jardon and Prieto to persuade them that the waiter should not be discharged. The Handbook also provides that Jardon will make the final determination in the event of disagreement between Prieto and Jardon on a discharge matter.

5. At all times during his employment at Chez Marie, Bryant performed his job in a manner that met the highest standards at Chez Marie. Despite the adequacy of Bryant's performance, Prieto discharged Bryant on September 28, 2021. Although Bryant immediately requested a meeting with Prieto and Jardon to discuss the discharge, both Prieto and Jardon refused to convene such a meeting.

6. As a result of Jardon's breach of promises in the Handbook, Bryant has suffered lost wages and other incidental and consequential losses.

7. Jardon's breach of promises in the Handbook constitutes a breach of her employment contract with Bryant. Moreover, Bryant foreseeably relied on promises in the Handbook, and Jardon's breach has created an injustice that can be avoided only by enforcing the promises.

II

RONGFUL DISCHARGE

8. Bryant realleges and incorporates paragraphs 1-7 above.

9. In discharging Bryant, Prieto was motivated by malice, by an invidiously discriminatory animus, and by concerns unrelated to the successful operation of Chez Marie. Jardon's termination of Bryant's employment therefore violated public policy.

III

REQUEST FOR RELIEF

10. Bryant requests:

i. an order reinstating Bryant to his position as waiter at Chez Marie;
ii. an award of compensatory damages in an amount to be set at trial;
iii. an award of punitive damages in an amount to be set at trial;
iv. an award of costs and attorneys' fees; and
v. such other relief as the court deems appropriate.

Dated__________________

by_______________,
Thomas Sanchez
. . . .

IN THE SUPERIOR COURT OF THE STATE OF ARIZONA
IN AND FOR THE COUNTY OF MARICOPA

GEORGE BRYANT, Plaintiff, v. MARIE JARDON, d.b.a. Chez Marie, and MARIO PRIETO, Defendants.	No.________ COMPLAINT (JURY TRIAL REQUESTED)

Plaintiff George Bryant, by and through his attorneys, Simpson, Sanchez and Summers, alleges the following:

1. This is an action for injunctive relief and for compensatory damages exceeding $50,000. This court has original jurisdiction pursuant to the Arizona Constitution, Article 6, § 14(3).

2. Plaintiff is a resident of Phoenix, Arizona. Defendant Marie Jardon owns and operates Chez Marie, a restaurant located in Phoenix, Arizona. Defendant Mario Prieto acted as the maître d' and supervisor of waiters at Chez Marie during Bryant's employment at Chez Marie. All material events alleged below took place in Maricopa County.

I

FIRST CLAIM FOR RELIEF
(Breach of Contract)

3. Plaintiff worked for Defendants as a waiter at Chez Marie from August 16, 2016 to September 28, 2021. In all the events alleged below, Defendant Prieto acted on his own behalf as well as on behalf of Defendant Jardon.

4. On January 1, 2020, Defendants modified Plaintiff's employment contract to include promises of job security contained in the terms of an "Employee Handbook" and in oral assurances.

5. Among other things, the Employee Handbook contains the following promises of job security: (i) Defendants will not discharge any waiter except for inadequate performance and (ii) any waiter recommended for discharge has the right to meet with Defendants to persuade them that the waiter should not be discharged.

The Handbook also provides that Defendant Jardon will make the final determination in the event of disagreement between Defendants on a discharge matter. (Copy of text of excerpts of Handbook is attached and incorporated by this reference.)

6. At all times during his employment at Chez Marie, Plaintiff performed his job in a manner that met the highest standards at Chez Marie. Despite the adequacy of Plaintiff's performance, Defendants discharged Plaintiff on September 28, 2021. Although Plaintiff immediately requested a meeting with Defendants to discuss the discharge, Defendants refused to convene such a meeting.

7. As a result of Defendant's breach of contract, Plaintiff has suffered lost wages and other incidental and consequential losses.

THEREFORE, Plaintiff demands judgment granting the following relief:

i. an order reinstating Plaintiff to his former position at Chez Marie;
ii. an award of compensatory damages for all consequential and incidental losses;
iii. an award of costs and attorneys' fees; and
iv. such other relief as the court deems appropriate.

II

SECOND CLAIM FOR RELIEF
(Promissory Estoppel)

8. Plaintiff realleges paragraphs 1-7 above and incorporates them by this reference.

9. On January 1, 2020, Defendants gave Plaintiff promises of job security by making oral assurances and by distributing the Employee Handbook. Plaintiff relied to his detriment on those promises by performing extraordinary services and by forbearing from taking other job opportunities. That reliance was reasonably foreseeable by Defendants.

10. Defendants' termination of Bryant's employment on September 28, 2021 constituted a breach of their promises of job security and has created an injustice that can be avoided only by enforcing the promises.

THEREFORE, Plaintiff demands judgment granting the following relief:

i. an order reinstating Plaintiff to his former position at Chez Marie;
ii. an award of compensatory damages for all consequential and incidental losses;
iii. an award of costs and attorneys' fees; and
iv. such other relief as the court deems appropriate.

III

THIRD CLAIM FOR RELIEF
(Wrongful Discharge)

11. Plaintiff realleges paragraphs 1-10 above and incorporates them by this reference.

12. Defendants maliciously discharged Plaintiff because of his sexual orientation and because Plaintiff's exemplary performance made Defendant Prieto jealous. Those reasons for discharge reflect bad faith and violate the public policy of state laws.

THEREFORE, Plaintiff demands judgment granting the following relief:

i. an order reinstating Plaintiff to his position as waiter at Chez Marie;
ii. an award of compensatory damages in an amount to be set at trial;
iii. an award of punitive damages in an amount to be set at trial;
iv. an award of costs and attorneys' fees; and
v. such other relief as the court deems appropriate.

Dated________________

by______________,
Thomas Sanchez
....

Exercise 14-2 and Templates for Motions to Dismiss

Motion to Dismiss—Use the instructions below to draft a brief supporting or opposing a motion to dismiss a complaint.

Study Count I of the sample complaint in Appendix VI, Assignment 1, which alleges breach of a promise to marry. For purposes of this exercise, disregard Count II of the complaint, and assume that Count I, in paragraphs I through XIII, constitutes the entire complaint. Research the law in your state, or in a state designated by your professor, to determine whether state law provides a claim for relief for such a breach, whether the designated state's law instead abandons or restricts such a claim, or whether the state's law has not yet addressed this question. As attorney for the defendant, James Clyde, determine whether you have good legal grounds to file a motion to dismiss the complaint for failure to state a claim, or at least to dismiss some of the complaint's requests for certain kinds of relief.

If you conclude that you can file a motion to dismiss in good faith, consider whether filing the motion represents a good expenditure of your client's resources. You might ask whether the motion has a good chance of succeeding, assuming the truth of the allegations in the complaint.

If you conclude that filing a motion to dismiss represents sound strategy, prepare a motion using the following template, and with any further formatting required by your professor:

CALZONA SUPERIOR COURT

WARMS SPRINGS COUNTY

Georgia Anne TUCKER, Plaintiff, v. James CLYDE, Defendant.	No. CIV-9X-79 MOTION TO DISMISS (Oral argument requested)

Defendant, James Clyde, moves this Court to .... [In plain language, state the disposition you request. If you can do so in a simple clause or sentence, add a brief preview or summary of the general legal ground on which you base your request.]

[Signature of student representing Clyde]
[Name of student signing motion]
[Fictitious address of law firm]
Attorney for Defendant, James Clyde
[Date]

You should accompany the motion with a supporting brief. Unless your professor provides different instructions, you may use the following template for your brief:

MEMORANDUM OF LAW

IN SUPPORT OF MOTION TO DISMISS

I. Facts [or "Introduction," or "Background," or "Statement of the Case"]

II. ARGUMENT

III. Conclusion

Signature block and date (as in the motion)

If the law in your designated state permits good faith argument on both sides of this issue, and if you are assigned to oppose the motion, begin with a cover page that identifies the court, the parties, and the signing attorney in the same manner as in the motion. However, replace "Motion to Dismiss" with "Opposition to Defendant Clyde's Motion to Dismiss," and identify "Plaintiff, Georgia Anne Tucker" as the represented party. Below that, without stating a motion of your own, you can simply state the plaintiff's intent to oppose the motion, perhaps with a very brief reference to the nature of your argument. You can then begin your brief with the same heading as the Memorandum of Law above, except with the phrase "IN OPPOSITION TO" in place of "IN SUPPORT OF."

Checklist for Chapter 14

- When drafting pleadings, follow the format prescribed by applicable rules. For example, federal rules require the drafter of a complaint to allege
  - jurisdiction,
  - a claim for relief, and
  - a demand for judgment.
- In an answer, you
  - must admit or deny the allegations of the complaint, and
  - may also assert affirmative defenses or a counterclaim.
- Generally, pleadings should allege ultimate factual conclusions and supporting facts but not legal rules.
- Under federal rules and some state rules, a court might require relatively detailed factual allegations for some claims, to satisfy a test of plausibility.
- The defendant may challenge the sufficiency of a complaint under the applicable pleading standards by moving to dismiss the complaint for failure to state a claim for relief.

Endnotes

1. Fed. R. Civ. P. 3.
2. D. Ariz. LRCiv. 7.1(a).
3. *See, e.g.*, Mayor v. Cooper, 73 U.S. (6 Wall.) 247, 252 (1868).
4. *See* 28 U.S.C. § 1331 (2012).
5. *Id.* § 1332.

6. *See, e.g.*, 42 U.S.C. § 2000e-5(f)(3) (2012) (granting jurisdiction of actions brought under Title VII of the Civil Rights Act of 1964).
7. Aguirre v. Auto. Teamsters, 633 F.2d 168, 174 (9th Cir. 1980).
8. *See also* Fed. R. Civ. P. app. at Form 7 (2012) (form allegations for federal question jurisdiction, published until 2015, included both requisite fact allegations and citation to federal statute granting jurisdiction), *abrogated* Fed. R. Civ. P. 84 (2015).
9. *See id.*
10. Advisory Committee on Rules for Civil Procedure, *Report of Proposed Amendments to the Rules of Civil Procedure for the United States District Courts* 18-19 (1955), reprinted in Richard H. Field, Benjamin Kaplan & Kevin M. Clermont, Civil Procedure: Materials for a Basic Course 1151 (10th ed. 2010).
11. *See* Chapter 11, Section II.B (discussing ethical duties in filing documents with the court).
12. *E.g.*, Skinner v. Switzer, 562 U.S. 521, 530 (2011) ("a complaint need not pin plaintiff's claim for relief to a precise legal theory" or "provide an exposition of his legal argument"); Doss v. South Cent. Bell Tel. Co., 834 F.2d 421, 424-25 (5th Cir. 1987) (improper to dismiss complaint that pleaded improper legal theory if the allegations state a claim on any other legal theory).
13. Ashcroft v. Iqbal, 556 U.S. 662, 678 (2009).
14. *Id.* at 686.
15. Delmar Karlen, Procedure Before Trial In A Nutshell 41-42 (1972).
16. Fed. R. Civ. P. 8(c)(1). Rule 8(c)(1) formerly listed 19 affirmative defenses, Fed. R. Civ. P. 8(c)(1) (2007), but the reference to "discharge in bankruptcy" was eliminated in 2010 to avoid confusion with a statute that addressed the effect of discharge, 11 U.S.C. § 524(a) (2012).
17. *Id.*
18. *See, e.g.*, Watts v. Golden Age Nursing Home, 619 P.2d 1032, 1035 (Ariz. 1980) (citing Restatement (Second) Of Torts § 46).
19. Whether the allegations of paragraphs 3 and 4 establish "extreme and outrageous conduct" will depend on the law of that jurisdiction and could be litigated on a motion to dismiss for failure to state a claim. *See, e.g.*, Fed. R. Civ. P. 12(b)(6).
20. This allegation of scienter should suffice not only to satisfy the second element of the tort but to support a request for punitive damages as well.
21. Fed. R. Civ. P. 8(c).
22. *See* Richard L. Marcus, *The Puzzling Persistence of Pleading Practice*, 76 Tex. L. Rev. 1749, 1753 & n.28 (1998) (discussing and quoting the Field Code).
23. *See id.* at 753-54.
24. Fed. R. Civ. P. 9(b); *see also* Ziemba v. Cascade Int'l, Inc., 256 F.3d 1194, 1202 (11th Cir. 2001) (explaining purposes of Rule 9(b) but noting that it is not intended to abrogate the concept of notice pleading).
25. *See* Fed. R. Civ. P. 26-37.
26. Ashcroft v. Iqbal, 556 U.S. 662, 678 (2009) (quoting Bell Atl. Corp. v. Twombly, 550 U.S. 544, 570 (2007)). *Iqbal and Twombly* effectively overrule Conley v. Gibson, 355 U.S. 41 (1957).
27. *Iqbal*, 556 U.S. at 678 (quoting *Twombly*, 550 U.S. at 556).
28. *Id.* at 686-87.
29. *Id.* at 678 (quoting or citing *Twombly*, 550 U.S. at 556, 557-58).
30. *Id.* at 678-80. The court will not assume the truth of allegations that amount to legal conclusions. *Id.* at 679-80.
36. Swanson v. Citibank, N.A., 614 F.3d 400, 404 (7th Cir. 2010).
31. *E.g.*, Anne E. Ralph, *Not the Same Old Story: Using Narrative Theory to Understand and Overcome the Plausibility Pleading Standard*, 26 Yale J.L. & Human. 1 (2014); Elizabeth Fajans & Mary R. Falk, *Untold Stories: Restoring Narrative to Pleading Practice*, 15 Legal Writing 3 (2009).

38. Fed. R. Civ. P. 11(b)(3).
40. The authors thank Georgetown Law Professor Jonah Perlin for these and other insights provided in his presentation at the 8th Biennial Applied Legal Storytelling Conference: *Not So Short, Not So Plain: The New Story of Civil Complaints* (July 15, 2021).
32. *E.g.*, Walsh v. U.S. Bank, N.A., 851 N.W.2d 598 (2014) (rejecting plausibility requirement for the State of Minnesota rules of procedure); McCurry v. Chevy Chase Bank, FSB, 169 Wash. 2d 96, 233 P.3d 861 (2010) (same for State of Washington rules of procedure).
33. *See, e.g.*, Vibe Micro, Inc. v. Shabanets, 878 F.3d 1291 (11th Cir. 2018) (affirming dismissal of federal claims in a rambling, repetitive "shot gun" complaint filled with irrelevant matter and failing to distinguish between the acts of various defendants).
34. Fed. R. Civ. P. 8(d)(1). The Federal Rules of Civil Procedure were stylistically revised in 2007 to state the rules more concisely and in plain English. Therefore, much of the case law will refer to rules in their prior form, in slightly different language and organization of subsections.
35. Fed. R. Civ. P. 10(b).
36. *See* Fed. R. Civ. P. 12(a).
37. *See* Fed. R. Civ. P. 12(b).
38. Fed. R. Civ. P. 8(b)(1)(B).
39. *See* Fed. R. Civ. P. 8(b)(1)(A), (c)(1).
40. *See* Fed. R. Civ. P. 7(a), 8(a), (c)(2).
41. *See* Fed. R. Civ. P. 7(a).
42. *See generally* Fed. R. Civ. P. 8(b) (form of denials).
43. Benjamin R. Norris, *Writing Pleadings*, Ariz. Att'y, Dec. 2000, at 37.
44. *See* Fed. R. Civ. P. 8(b)(3).
45. *See* Fed. R. Civ. P. 8(b)(1)(A), (c).
46. Rooney v. Ohio State Highway Patrol, 87 N.E.3d 777, 780-81 ¶¶ 13-14, (Ohio Ct. App. 2017); Greenwood v. Taft, Stettinius & Hollister, 663 N.E.2d 1030, 1031 (Ohio Ct. App. 1995).

Chapter 15

Motion for Summary Judgment

I. Procedural Context

A pretrial motion for summary judgment is a popular means of determining whether the court should dispose of all or part of a dispute before the parties proceed to trial. In most cases, you will have little difficulty alleging facts that state a claim for relief; therefore, your complaints will seldom be susceptible to attack for failure to state a claim. On the other hand, even if you allege a claim or defense in good faith, you may fail to gather substantial admissible evidence supporting the claim or defense. In such cases, the opposing party's motion for summary judgment exposes the absence of a triable issue of fact. It compels you to choose between making at least a preliminary showing of the evidence supporting your allegations or suffering adverse judgment before trial. In other cases, both parties concede the absence of any dispute of fact, stipulate to the facts, and use the motion for summary judgment to argue unsettled questions about the law and its application to the stipulated facts.

Summary judgment litigation often takes place only after each party has thoroughly investigated the case through the discovery and disclosure process.[1] Indeed, the trial judge may delay resolution of a motion for summary judgment if further discovery is needed to permit the nonmoving party to support its opposition. Nonetheless, if you successfully move for summary judgment, you will avoid the greater burdens of a full trial.

On the other hand, if the trial court denies your motion for summary judgment, your unsuccessful motion may hamper your ability to settle the case before trial. If the opposing counsel initially expected to settle the case, he may have only minimally prepared the case prior to summary judgment litigation. Your motion for summary judgment, however, will have forced your opponent to organize his facts and legal arguments. If the motion fails, he likely will be much more demanding in settlement negotiations for three reasons. First, the denial of the motion will strengthen his belief in the potential merits of his client's claims or defenses. Second, he will be more nearly prepared for trial after researching the law and gathering the facts to oppose your motion for summary judgment. Finally, his client will have invested significant resources in opposing the motion, expenditures that his client will likely incorporate into the client's new settlement position.[2] Consequently, you should not move for summary judgment unless you have a reasonable chance of success.

Summary judgment litigation provides you with a stimulating vehicle for developing brief-writing skills. You must remain constantly sensitive not only to the merits of the underlying claims or defenses but also to the standards for summary judgment. Moreover, the local rules of many courts prescribe a special format for summary judgment briefs, providing you a valuable opportunity to examine the role of procedural rules in written advocacy.

II. Standards for Summary Judgment

The federal rules authorize a court to grant summary judgment if the parties do not genuinely dispute any material facts and if the moving party is entitled to judgment as a matter of law.[3]

To illustrate the materiality requirement, let's imagine that the record on summary judgment establishes without dispute that a seller repudiated a binding sales contract with the buyer, compelling the buyer to purchase the goods from another supplier at a higher price. If the buyer moved for summary judgment on her contract claim against the seller, the repudiating seller could not successfully respond to the motion by establishing even a genuine dispute of fact about whether he had changed his mind and retracted his repudiation after the buyer had purchased the substitute goods. Under the governing Uniform Commercial Code, once the buyer had relied on the seller's repudiation by making a substitute purchase, the repudiation was final,[4] and the seller's attempted retraction would have no bearing on his liability. Thus, any dispute of fact about whether the seller in fact had attempted a late retraction would be immaterial to the buyer's contract claim and could not preclude summary judgment for the buyer on that claim.

The court does not resolve genuine factual disputes on summary judgment. Nonetheless, to evaluate the genuineness of a purported factual dispute, the court may undertake a limited evaluation of the strength of the facts presented by the nonmoving party. A factual issue is not genuine if the nonmoving party's factual support is so trivial that "the record taken as a whole could not lead a rational trier of fact to find for the non-moving party."[5] In short, the nonmoving party "must do more than simply show . . . some metaphysical doubt as to the material facts."[6]

When moving for summary judgment, you may request summary judgment on one or more claims or defenses, or even on part of a claim or defense.[7] Alternatively, you may request a ruling that identifies some uncontested material facts without granting any final judgment.[8]

As the moving party, you have the initial burden of showing that the pretrial record supports judgment in your favor. If you move for summary judgment on the strength of a claim or defense on which you would have the burden of proof at trial, you must support your motion for summary judgment with admissible evidence tending to prove all the elements of the claim or defense.[9] You could make such a showing with deposition testimony, answers to interrogatories, admissions, or other information and documents obtained during discovery or disclosure, or with affidavits prepared specifically for the motion.[10]

As an alternative basis for summary judgment, you may demonstrate that the opposing party lacks factual support for an element of her claim or defense. If so, you need not affirmatively produce evidence tending to negate that element. Instead, you may satisfy your initial burden simply by reviewing the existing record and demonstrating that it contains no admissible evidence supporting the critical element.[11]

Once you have satisfactorily supported your motion, the opposing party can avoid summary judgment by establishing a genuine issue of material fact for trial. She may not rely on the allegations or denials in her own pleading but must point to the moving party's admissions or to facts in affidavits, deposition testimony, or other documentary evidence or fruits of discovery, unless she can show that the requisite information is not available to her.[12]

If the materials establish grounds for summary judgment, the federal rules state that the court "shall grant summary judgment,"[13] but some courts and commentators believe that the court nonetheless retains discretion to deny summary judgment and refer the matter to trial.[14]

III. Format for Summary Judgment Briefs—Overview

Rules of procedure, local court rules, and custom suggest that materials supporting a motion for summary judgment should include the following:

1. a motion requesting action by the court;
2. a statement of material facts;
3. affidavits, or other materials not already in the record, that support the fact statement and the motion; and
4. a supporting brief, sometimes referred to in court rules as a "memorandum of law" or, in less modern terms, a "memorandum of points and authorities."

The requirements for the response are similar except that the nonmoving party need not file a formal motion opposing the motion for summary judgment. Under typical local court rules, the nonmoving party's first page would resemble the motion but would identify itself as an "Opposition" or "Response" to the motion, and could briefly introduce the supporting brief and other materials. The moving party's reply, if any, might consist of a brief that replies to the nonmoving parties' legal arguments and a fact statement that responds to additional facts asserted by the nonmoving party.

Some local rules describe parts of the required format in surprising detail. For example, local rules for some United States District Courts specify the information required on designated lines of the caption of the title page of each document filed in support of the motion.[15] The most interesting of the local rules addressing summary judgment, however, are those specifying formats for the statements of facts.

IV. Statements of Facts

Before the advent of local rules governing motions for summary judgment, briefs and supporting materials often failed to pinpoint areas of factual dispute. Often, counsel for the moving party summarized the materials supporting the motion in a general narrative fact statement, and counsel for the nonmoving party summarized supporting materials in a general counter-statement of the facts. Worse yet, in some cases, one or both advocates omitted any consolidated statement of the facts and simply referred to the record in fact analyses dispersed throughout the argument section of the brief.

To help trial judges identify the potential areas of factual dispute, many courts have enacted local rules specifying a methodical point/counterpoint format for the statements of facts in motions for summary judgment. For example, a local rule for the United States District Court for the District of Nebraska requires the moving party to state the facts in numbered paragraphs, similar to allegations in a complaint, while citing to the original source of each fact:

> The statement of facts should consist of short numbered paragraphs, each containing pinpoint references to affidavits, pleadings, discovery responses, deposition testimony (by page and line), or other materials that support the material facts stated in the paragraph.[16]

Unlike allegations in a complaint, this fact statement must include citations to supporting materials: "As to each fact, the statement shall refer to the specific portion of the record where the fact may be found."[17] If you represent the moving party, you could reasonably entitle this section "[Moving Party's] Statement of Material Facts." Alternatively, to reflect the moving party's hopes, you could add "Undisputed" before "Material Facts," although in all but unusual cases, such a title sounds a tad presumptuous before the nonmoving party has an opportunity to respond and identify areas of factual dispute.

Interpreting another court's local rules, one judge has stated that (1) a statement of material facts supporting a motion for summary judgment should "contain only factual allegations . . . limited to facts pertinent to the outcome of the issues identified in the summary judgment motion," and (2) "the numbered paragraphs should be short," containing "only one or two individual allegations, thereby allowing easy response."[18]

The Arizona rules instruct the nonmoving party to respond to the moving party's statement of material facts by identifying areas of factual dispute in much the same way that an answer sets forth denials of allegations in a complaint:

> Any party opposing a motion for summary judgment shall file a statement in the form prescribed by this Rule, specifying those paragraphs in the moving party's statement of facts which are disputed, and also setting forth those facts which establish a genuine issue of material fact or otherwise preclude summary judgment in favor of the moving party.[19]

If you represent the nonmoving party, you might reasonably entitle this section "Response to [Moving Party's] Statement of Material Facts," or "[Nonmoving Party's] Statement of Material Facts," or even "[Nonmoving Party's] Statement of Undisputed and Disputed Material Facts" because you obviously hope that the court will rule that your documents establish a dispute with respect to at least some of the material facts.

Fact statements following this format provide the court with a clear guide to the parties' positions on summary judgment, because the nonmoving party must methodically respond to each factual assertion of the moving party, point by point, organized by numbered paragraphs.

This point/counterpoint format is not popular with all attorneys and in all fields of litigation, so your assigning attorney may prefer a less regimented format when permitted by local rules. Because the point/counterpoint format for fact statements is required by the local rules of many courts, however, and because it provides a systematic guide for the novice litigant, this chapter will adopt it for its instruction and examples.

For illustration, the following represents excerpts from the plaintiff's statement of facts on his motion for summary judgment in a suit alleging race discrimination in violation of federal law:

> 1. Defendant, Irma Barnes, owns and operates "Irma's Diner," a restaurant and bar located in Mesa, Arizona. Barnes employs more than 15 employees in this business. (Ex. D, Barnes Dep. at 3-4.)
>
> 2. Plaintiff, Michael Powell, is African American. He worked as the night manager of the bar at Irma's Diner from January 1, 2018 to June 17, 2018. (Exh. B, Personnel Record for Michael Powell.). . . .
>
> 3. Powell's duties included . . . .
>
> 4. On June 17, 2018, Barnes confronted Powell about Powell's selection of a rhythm and blues band as musical entertainment for the bar. After using several racial slurs in the ensuing discussion, she fired Powell solely because of his race. (Ex. A, Powell Aff. ¶ 8.)

Barnes's response to the motion for summary judgment should specifically identify which portions of Powell's statement of facts she disputes. To highlight areas of dispute with maximum clarity, you can respond to each of the moving party's paragraphs with a corresponding, identically numbered paragraph:

> 1. Barnes does not dispute paragraph 1 of Powell's Statement of Facts.
>
> 2. Barnes does not dispute paragraph 2 of Powell's Statement of Facts.
>
> 3. Barnes does not dispute paragraph 3 of Powell's Statement of Facts.
>
> 4. Barnes does not dispute the assertions in paragraph 4 that Barnes fired Powell on June 17, 2018, after confronting Powell about his selection of musical entertainment. Barnes disputes that she used racial slurs or that race played any factor in her termination of Powell's employment. . . .

In addition, Barnes should identify the specific facts that reflect a genuine factual dispute on the material issue of Barnes's racial animus. Unless these facts appear in Powell's fact statement, Barnes normally would state them as "Additional Facts" in a separate section that follows her identification of areas of dispute:

STATEMENT OF UNDISPUTED AND DISPUTED FACTS

1. Barnes does not dispute . . . .

. . . .

4. Barnes does not dispute the assertions . . . musical entertainment. Barnes disputes . . . Powell's employment.

. . . .

ADDITIONAL FACTS

1. Barnes never used racial slurs in Powell's presence, and she fired Powell solely because he displayed insubordination in the face of direct instructions by Powell to replace the band Barnes had hired. (Plaintiff's Ex. D, Barnes Dep. at 24-25.)

Court rules should then permit the moving party to respond to the nonmoving party's statement of additional facts.[20]

Most court rules requiring separate fact statements for summary judgment can be interpreted to permit you to attach the statement of facts under the same title sheet that states the motion and covers the supporting brief, or that presents the opposition and supporting brief, so long as you set forth the statement of facts separately from the brief itself. Nonetheless, most attorneys prefer to file the formal statement of facts under a caption as a separate document.

V. Supporting Evidentiary Materials

You must support each assertion in your statement of facts with admitted alleged facts from the opposing party's pleading or with facts reflected in affidavits, materials generated through discovery and disclosure, or other evidence. Federal Rule of Civil Procedure 56 specifically provides that the affidavits must "be made on personal knowledge" and "set out facts that would be admissible in evidence."[21] Therefore, even though your opponent may overlook this matter,[22] your summary judgment materials should preliminarily establish the admissibility of (1) documents included in the summary judgment materials[23] or (2) the expected trial testimony represented in the materials, such as in affidavits or deposition testimony.[24]

For example, the following excerpt from an affidavit asserts the admissibility of other documents under the "business records" exception to the "hearsay rule" of evidence:[25]

> 5. The Payroll Action forms in Exhibits B and C are true copies of records that I prepared and kept in the course of my regularly conducted business activity, which includes maintaining such employment records as a uniform practice. Those forms include information within my own knowledge and information that my supervisor transmitted to me on matters within his knowledge.

Some attorneys separately file supporting affidavits and other evidence. If those materials are not voluminous, however, you can more conveniently and appropriately attach them to the formal statement of facts.

VI. The Motion

As with every document that you separately file with the trial court, you should begin your motion with a caption identifying the case and the nature of the document. In the motion itself, you should simply and clearly state your request for action and should briefly introduce the grounds supporting the request.

Unfortunately, many lawyers have developed a tradition of loading motions with abstract boilerplate that says almost nothing about the motion or the dispute:

> Defendant, Sun Printing Co., by and through its undersigned attorneys, Jenkins, Powell, and Smith, P.C., hereby moves, pursuant to the Arizona Rules of Civil Procedure, Rule 56, for an order granting summary judgment against Plaintiff, Scott Paper Supply, on the grounds that there exists no genuine issue of material fact and that Defendant is entitled to summary judgment as a matter of law. This motion is supported by the attached memorandum of law, the Statement of Material Facts separately filed with this Court, and the documents and exhibits filed with this Court.

A judge learns almost nothing from such boilerplate. She does not need a superfluous reference to the legal representation; your identity as legal counsel is revealed in your signature at the end of the motion, and as well at the top of the cover page under the format prescribed by some local rules. In addition, the judge is well aware of the basic abstract standards for summary judgment;[26] repeating those standards in the motion adds nothing to her knowledge about your case.

The judge will read your motion with greater interest if you clearly and concisely state what relief your client wants and why he is entitled to it. You should convey new information to the court by tailoring the abstract standards to the facts:

> Pursuant to Arizona Rule of Civil Procedure 56, the defendant, Sun Printing Co. ("Sun"), moves for summary judgment against the plaintiff, Scott Paper Supply ("Scott"). Sun is entitled to judgment under the UCC Statute of Frauds because Scott cannot genuinely dispute that the agreement alleged by Scott was for paper priced at more than $500 and was never reduced to writing.
>
> This motion is supported by the attached memorandum of law, by the separately filed Statement of Undisputed Facts and accompanying exhibits, and by the record in this case.

By conveying the theme of the full argument, such a motion whets the judge's appetite for the supporting memorandum of law. An even crisper motion could present a more concise summary of the argument:

> Defendant, Sun Printing Co., moves for summary judgment against Plaintiff, Scott Paper Supply. *See* Ariz. R. Civ. P. 56. Sun Printing Co. is entitled to judgment because the oral agreement alleged by Scott Paper Supply is unenforceable under the UCC Statute of Frauds as a matter of law. This motion is supported by . . . .

As terse as this passage may sound, it contains more useful information than the longer string of boilerplate in the first example.

When opposing a motion, you need not state a formal countermotion in the title page of your opposition materials. You may follow the caption immediately with your responsive brief. At the most, you might include a cover page with a brief statement of opposition parallel to the motion:

> Plaintiff, Scott Paper Supply ("Scott"), opposes Defendant's motion for summary judgment. Defendant, Sun Printing Co. ("Sun"), is not entitled to judgment as a matter of law, because Scott's supporting materials show that Sun adopted Scott's written and signed confirmation of the agreement, thus satisfying the UCC Statute of Frauds under Ariz. Rev. Stat. Ann. § 47-2201(B) (2017). This opposition is supported by the attached memorandum of law, by the . . . .

VII. The Brief

Your brief, or Memorandum of Law, is your tool of persuasion. With it, you argue for a favorable interpretation of the law and analysis of the facts. A motion brief typically includes three sections:

1. an introduction,
2. an argument, and
3. a conclusion.

In a complex case, you should consider adding a formal statement of the issues at the beginning of your brief. Such a statement of issues would not be typical in a brief supporting or opposing a motion, but it could be helpful in unusual circumstances.

A. The Introduction

The first section of your supporting brief should summarize the facts, with the brief opposing summary judgment sometimes emphasizing material disputes of facts. In either party's brief, you might reasonably title this section "Introduction" or "Summary of Facts." In this introductory section, you can summarize the facts in a more concise and less formal manner than is possible in the separate, formal statement.

For each statement of a fact in this introduction, you should cite to a source—either to (1) the underlying evidentiary sources already in the record or added to the record in your summary judgment materials, or (2) paragraphs in your separately filed statement of facts, which in turn will cite to underlying evidentiary sources. Some courts prefer, or even require, the brief to cite only to paragraphs in the separately filed statement of facts.[27]

When court rules or other judicial pronouncements do not specify a preference or requirement, you can exercise discretion to cite either to the original source or to your separately filed fact statement. If, for example, each of the fact statements in the Introduction is supported by a single underlying evidentiary source, such as an affidavit or deposition testimony, citation to that original source could be concise, informative, and helpful to the reader. On the other hand, if each of many fact statements is supported by several underlying sources, or if the citations to some underlying sources are quite lengthy, direct reference to those sources could impede the flow of the Introduction, and your reader will probably prefer more concise citations to the numbered paragraphs in your separately filed statement of facts.

In addition, you may use an introductory section to present a summary of your argument or a combination of facts, procedural history, and a summary of your argument. For example, you might begin your Introduction with a paragraph-long overview of your arguments or the issues in the case, to provide a context for a summary of the facts in chronological order. Other passages of this book advise against premature legal argument in a statement of facts in other kinds of briefs, such as an appellate brief. However, this admonition applies with less force in the introduction to your summary judgment brief, because you will separately file a formal statement of facts for summary judgment.

Accordingly, the Introduction may be a suitable place to advance any theme that you have developed for your brief. Alternatively, you can express your theme or brief overview of your arguments in the first paragraph of your Argument section.

B. The Argument

Chapter 12 discusses techniques of constructing legal arguments. Indeed, some of the examples in Chapter 12 are taken from sample summary judgment briefs. This section addresses techniques of persuasion peculiar to summary judgment briefs.

Argument on purely legal questions can be crucial in some summary judgment litigation. If the court determines that material facts are not in dispute, or if the parties have stipulated to the absence of factual dispute, the court will decide whether a moving party is entitled to judgment as a matter of law.

Typically, however, the parties will also argue about the presence or absence of a genuine dispute of fact. In such a case, once you have established the law on an issue or subissue, you should thoroughly analyze the facts. As discussed in greater detail in the immediately preceding section, when you argue the facts, remember to cite to your formal, separately filed statement of facts or to the original evidentiary sources that are already in the record or are included in your supporting materials. The samples in this chapter suggest several ways to cite to either kind of source; unless local rules specify a format, any reasonable citation form is acceptable.

Also, remember to incorporate the standards for summary judgment into your argument. For example, if you are moving for summary judgment, you should not argue that the preponderance of the evidence shows that Sun Printing Co. objected to the contents of the confirmation within ten days after receipt. Such an argument gives the impression that you are inappropriately asking the judge to resolve a factual issue without a trial. Instead, your brief should refer to the "undisputed evidence" and the inferences that can be drawn from it, thus properly asserting the absence of a factual dispute.

Conversely, if you are opposing summary judgment, your brief should remind the judge periodically that nothing more than a genuine and material question of fact is needed to defeat summary judgment. In making this point, you should not simply reiterate the abstract standard; rather, you should identify issues of fact that make summary judgment inappropriate:

Scott Paper Supply's letter confirming the purchase agreement is dated September 1 (Exh. 2), and Scott's Distribution Manager personally mailed it that day (Exh. 3, Connor Aff. ¶ 3). Scott Paper Supply never received any objection to the terms of the confirmation. (*Id.* ¶ 4.) Moreover, Sun Printing Co. concedes that it has no record of making any such objection. (Exh. 4, Sun's Ans. to Scott's First Set of Inter., No. 23.)

Opposition facts

In direct opposition to Sun Printing Co.'s assertions, this evidence shows that Sun Printing Co. received the confirmation and failed to object to it. At the very least, this evidence raises a genuine dispute of fact that must be resolved at trial.

Dispute of fact

C. The Conclusion

You should end each section of the argument of your brief with a conclusion about the topic of that section, similar to the conclusion stated in the point heading that introduces the argument. Together, the point heading and the conclusion provide maximum emphasis in their positions as the first and last statements the judge reads within a section. Finally, as illustrated in Chapter 2, the entire brief should end with a section entitled "Conclusion" that encompasses all the arguments of the brief.

Sample Motion for Summary Judgment

Study the following sample and think about the law and facts that you would need to respond successfully to it. For further practice with summary judgment, perform Assignments 4 and 5 in the Appendix. Along with Assignment 3 in the Appendix, Assignment 5 presents evidence with which the plaintiff in the sample below can oppose the motion for summary judgment, partly by contesting the moving party's factual assertions. Feel free to move the dates of events forward by an appropriate number of years if necessary to make the timing of your response realistic.

ARIZONA SUPERIOR COURT
MARICOPA COUNTY

CHARLOTTE REMBAR, Plaintiff, v. ALEXANDER HART d.b.a. COMCON, Defendant.	No. C732431 Defendant Hart's Motion for Summary Judgment (Judge Wisdom)

Defendant Alexander Hart d.b.a. Comcon moves for summary judgment on all claims in this action. Under Arizona Rule of Civil Procedure 56, Hart is entitled to judgment as a matter of law because the undisputed facts show that Hart did not promise Rembar job security and did not discharge Rembar for an unlawful reason or in a wrongful manner.

This motion is supported by the attached Memorandum of Law, the separately filed Statement of Material Facts, and the entire record before the Court.

August 5, 2018

____

Lisa Hall
Kendricks, Hall, & Oats, P.C.
3310 Alma School Rd., Suite 200
Mesa, Arizona 85283
(480) 839-0365
Bar No. 0076089

MEMORANDUM OF LAW IN SUPPORT OF MOTION FOR SUMMARY JUDGMENT

I. INTRODUCTION

As documented and set forth more fully in Defendant Hart's Statement of Material Facts ("Hart SofF"), Alexander Hart employed Charlotte Rembar as a computer systems consultant for Hart's sole proprietorship, Comcon. (Hart SofF ¶ 2.) Although Hart distributed an employment manual to Rembar, their employment contract permitted either party to terminate the contract at will. (Hart SofF ¶¶ 2-5.)

On November 1, 2017, Hart discharged Rembar because of her "negative attitude." (Hart SofF ¶¶ 7-8.) During her employment, Rembar often flirted with Hart, and Hart sometimes returned the flirtations; however, Hart and Rembar did not have a romantic relationship, and Hart never made any unwelcome advances toward Rembar. (Hart SofF ¶ 6.)

Rembar has asserted four claims for relief in her complaint: (1) breach of an alleged promise of job security, (2) sex discrimination in violation of the Arizona Civil Rights Act ("the ACRA"), (3) wrongful discharge in violation of public policy, and (4) intentional infliction of emotional distress. Because the record shows that Hart employed Rembar at will and that Hart discharged Rembar for a legitimate business reason and in a proper manner, Hart is entitled to judgment as a matter of law on all these claims.

II. ARGUMENT

A. Hart did not breach his employment contract with Rembar by discharging Rembar for her negative attitude.

"The employment relationship is severable at the pleasure of either the employee or the employer unless both the employee and the employer have signed a written contract to the contrary. . . ." Ariz. Rev. Stat. Ann. § 23-1501(2) (2016). In some circumstances, an employee manual can become part of the employment contract, and promises of job security in the manual can restrict the employer's freedom to terminate the contract. *See id.* Nonetheless, even assuming for purposes of summary judgment that Hart and Rembar's employment contract included the terms of the Comcon Policy Manual, Hart did not breach those terms for two reasons. First, neither the Policy Manual nor any other term of the contract imposed any restriction on Hart's freedom to terminate Rembar's employment. Second, even if the contract permitted Hart to fire Rembar only for unsatisfactory performance, her negative attitude created such grounds for discharge.

1. The Employment Contract Remained Terminable at Will.

Even assuming the Comcon Policy Manual was incorporated into the employment contract, the manual did not change the at-will nature of the contract because it did not contain requisite "provisions of job security." *Leikvold v. Valley View Cmty. Hosp.*, 141 Ariz. 544, 547, 688 P.2d 170, 173 (1984) (quoting *Pine River State Bank v. Mettille*, 333 N.W.2d 622, 628 (Minn. 1983)). Because the terms of the contract "are clear and unambiguous, the construction of the contract is a question of law for the court" and thus is appropriate for summary judgment. *Id.* at 548, 688 P.2d at 174.

Comcon hired Rembar for an indefinite term of employment, rather than for a fixed term. (Hart SofF ¶ 2.) The terms of Comcon's Policy Manual unambiguously left Hart free to terminate his contract with Rembar at his will. No provision of the Policy Manual purports to restrict the grounds for discharge of an employee. (Hart SofF ¶ 3.) Instead, the only provisions relating to termination affirmatively reserve Hart's right to discharge employees. (Hart SofF ¶¶ 4-5.) Because Rembar had worked at Comcon for more than 60 days, she was classified as a nonprobationary employee at the time of her discharge. (Hart SofF ¶¶ 2, 4-5.) Under the heading "Nonprobationary Employment," the Policy Manual especially emphasizes a particular ground for discharge: "Comcon reserves the right to terminate the employment of any employee who is not performing satisfactorily." (Hart SofF ¶ 5.) However, it does not state or even suggest that unsatisfactory performance is the exclusive ground for discharge. Absent such a stated restriction, Hart remains free under the general rule to terminate the contract for any reason or for no reason at all.

Hart's employment contract with Rembar was terminable at will.

2. Hart Validly Fired Rembar for Unsatisfactory Performance.

Even if the Policy Manual had identified unsatisfactory performance as the sole ground for discharging nonprobationary employees, Hart would not have breached such a provision.

Hart discharged Rembar because of her "negative attitude." (Hart SofF ¶¶ 7-8.) Because Rembar's position required her to work closely with clients, a pleasant personality and a positive attitude were indispensable qualities for satisfactory job performance. (Hart SofF ¶ 7.) Therefore, even assuming that the employment contract provided for limited job security, Hart did not breach the contract because the undisputed facts show that he discharged Rembar for unsatisfactory performance.

B. Hart did not engage in unlawful sex discrimination.

Because Comcon has always employed fewer than fifteen employees (Hart SofF ¶ 1), Rembar has no claim against Hart under federal employment discrimination law. *See* 42 U.S.C. § 2000e(b) (2012) (defining employers covered by Title VII of the Civil Rights Act of 1964). Comcon is a covered employer under the Arizona Civil Rights Act ("ACRA"), Ariz. Rev. Stat. Ann. § 41-1461(2) (2017); however, he did not violate its provisions.

The ACRA makes it an "unlawful employment practice for an employer:

> 1. To . . . discharge any individual or otherwise to discriminate against any individual with respect to his compensation, terms, conditions or privileges of employment because of such individual's . . . sex . . . .

Ariz. Rev. Stat. Ann. § 41-1463.B (2017). Rembar alleges that Hart discriminated against her by subjecting her to unwelcome sexual advances and discharging her in retaliation for her refusal to submit to the alleged advances. The record, however, contradicts these allegations.

Rembar's own frequent flirtations with Hart showed that she welcomed Hart's harmless flirtations and attentions. Hart never made advances that were not welcomed by Rembar, and he never conditioned benefits of employment on Rembar's acquiescing to his flirtations. (Hart

SofF ¶ 6.) Most important, Rembar's discharge had nothing to do with any flirtations between Hart and Rembar; Hart discharged Rembar solely because of her unsatisfactory job performance. (Hart SofF ¶¶ 7-8.)

As a matter of law, Hart did not engage in sexually discriminatory conduct in violation of the ACRA.

C. Hart is not liable in tort for wrongfully discharging Rembar, because the Arizona Civil Rights Act provides the exclusive remedy for such alleged misconduct.

Before its statutory modification, the common law tort of wrongful discharge imposed liability for a violation of an important public policy reflected in the state's constitution, its statutes, or, in limited circumstances, its judicial decisions. *See Wagenseller v. Scottsdale Mem'l Hosp.*, 147 Ariz. 370, 378-79, 710 P.2d 1025, 1033-34 (1985). Rembar's complaint demands tort damages for common law wrongful discharge in violation of the public policies reflected in the ACRA, a tort claim previously recognized in this state. *See Broomfield v. Lundell*, 159 Ariz. 349, 767 P.2d 697 (Ct. App. 1988). Her claim fails as a matter of law, however, both on the facts in this record and through statutory preemption.

First, as stated in arguments A and B above, Hart did not engage in sexual harassment or any other sexually discriminatory employment practice that would violate the policies of the ACRA. Second, even if Rembar can genuinely dispute those facts, her wrongful discharge claim is now governed by the Arizona Employment Protection Act ("AEPA"), Ariz. Rev. Stat. Ann. § 23-1501 (2016).

The AEPA provides that an employer may be liable for discharging an employee "in violation of a statute of this state." Ariz. Rev. Stat. Ann. § 23-1501(3)(b) (2016). If the violated statute provides its own civil remedies, however, those remedies are exclusive; indeed, the AEPA lists the ACRA as its first example of a source of such exclusive remedies:

> [T]he remedies provided to an employee for a violation of the statute are the exclusive remedies for the violation of the statute or the public policy set forth in or arising out of the statute, including the following:
>
> (i) The civil rights act prescribed in title 41, chapter 9.

Id.; *see also* Ariz. Rev. Stat. Ann. § 41-1481 (2017) (setting forth enforcement procedures and remedies for violations of the ACRA). Because Rembar bases her wrongful discharge claim on alleged violations of the ACRA, her remedy is limited to the relief available in the ACRA. *See Cronin v. Sheldon*, 195 Ariz. 531, 991 P.2d 231 (1999) (finding that the AEPA constitutionally preempted the tort remedy recognized in *Broomfield*).

Accordingly, regardless of whether Rembar can establish a factual dispute about the reasons for her discharge, Hart is entitled to summary judgment on Rembar's tort claim of wrongful discharge.

D. Hart did not engage in extreme and outrageous conduct and therefore is not liable for infliction of emotional distress.

The AEPA would not preempt a claim of intentional infliction of emotional distress for an unlawfully discriminatory discharge. *Cronin*, 195 Ariz. at 541, 991 P.2d at 241 (dictum). However, Hart is not liable for intentional infliction of emotional distress unless his conduct was so "extreme and outrageous" that it fell "within that quite narrow range" of conduct "at the very extreme edge of the spectrum." *Watts v. Golden Age Nursing Home*, 127 Ariz. 255, 258, 619 P.2d 1032, 1035 (1980). As discussed above, Hart discharged Rembar for legitimate business reasons. (Hart SofF ¶¶ 7-8.) Moreover, Hart communicated his decision in a normal professional manner. (Hart SofF ¶ 8.) Because of its economic consequences, termination of employment is often an extremely distressing event for the discharged employee. However, discharge for business reasons is an economic fact of life and hardly amounts to a basis for tort liability.

Moreover, even if Rembar could establish a dispute of fact regarding the reason for her discharge, the dispute would not be material. "[I]t is extremely rare to find conduct in the employment context that will rise to the level of outrageousness necessary to provide a basis for recovery for the tort of intentional infliction of emotional distress." *Mintz v. Bell Atl. Sys. Leasing Int'l, Inc.*, 183 Ariz. 550, 554, 905 P.2d 559, 563 (Ct. App. 1995) (quoting *Cox v. Keystone Carbon Co.*, 861 F.2d 390, 395 (3d Cir. 1988)).

In *Mintz*, an employee was hospitalized after suffering a nervous breakdown as the alleged result of gender discrimination in the workplace. The employer terminated her disability benefits, ordered her to return to work, and then—while the employee was again hospitalized after returning to work for one day—notified her of a reassignment of her duties by a letter delivered to the hospital. *Id.* at 552, 905 P.2d at 561. The Arizona Court of Appeals affirmed a finding that, as a matter of law, this alleged conduct was not extreme and outrageous, even assuming the employer had failed to promote the employee because of gender discrimination and assuming the employer knew that the employee was unusually susceptible to emotional distress. *Id.* at 553-54, 905 P.2d at 562-63.

Based on cases such as *Mintz*, a federal district court has characterized Arizona's standard for extreme and outrageous conduct as one requiring "extraordinary" conduct. *Tempesta v. Motorola, Inc.*, 92 F. Supp. 2d 973, 987 (D. Ariz. 1999). Applying *Mintz*, the *Tempesta* court granted summary judgment for the defendant employer on the employee's claim of intentional infliction of emotional distress, even after assuming the truth of the employee's allegations that he had suffered harassment and wrongful termination because of his sex. *Id.*at 986-87.

It is even clearer in this case that Hart did not engage in extreme and outrageous conduct. Even if Rembar's allegations of mild sexual advances and retaliatory discharge were supported by the record, that conduct would not satisfy the demanding test of egregiousness applied in Arizona courts. As a matter of law, Hart is not liable for intentional infliction of emotional distress.

III. CONCLUSION

Rembar cannot genuinely dispute Hart's showing on the facts that Hart promised Rembar no job security, Hart discharged Rembar for poor performance, and Hart did not engage in sexual harassment. Therefore, Hart is entitled to summary judgment on all claims.

August 5, 2018

____
Lisa Hall for
Kendricks, Hall, & Oats, P.C.
3310 Alma School Rd., Suite 200
Mesa, Arizona 85283

COPY OF THE FOREGOING MAILED
August 5, 2018 to:
Roberts and Cray
101 E. Washington St., Suite 600
Phoenix, Arizona 85001

ARIZONA SUPERIOR COURT
MARICOPA COUNTY

CHARLOTTE REMBAR, Plaintiff, v. ALEXANDER HART d.b.a. COMCON, Defendant.	No. C732431 Defendant Hart's Statement of Material Facts and Exhibits Supporting Motion for Summary Judgment (Judge Wisdom)

For purposes of summary judgment only, Defendant Alexander Hart d. b.a. Comcon presents the following material facts:

1. Alexander Hart is the sole owner and manager of Comcon, a firm that provides expert consulting on computer systems to businesses in the Phoenix metropolitan area. From January to November 2017, Comcon employed eight employees other than Hart himself; Comcon has never employed a greater number of employees before or since. (Hart Aff.¶ 1 (Ex. D).)

2. Effective January 1, 2017, Hart hired Charlotte Rembar for the position of Comcon consultant at a salary of $5,000/month. (Dec. 30, 2016 Payroll Action (Ex. B).) The only written record of Rembar's contract with Comcon is the Payroll Action form that states her date of hire and her salary. (Hart Aff.¶ 2 (Ex. D).) The term of Rembar's employment was left indefinite. (*Id.*)

3. At or before the time of Rembar's hiring, Alexander Hart gave Rembar a Policy Manual that summarizes many of the personnel procedures at Comcon. (Policy Manual (Ex. A).) The Policy Manual includes one example of a ground for discharging a nonprobationary employee, but it does not explicitly limit Comcon's right to discharge an employee for any other reason. (*Id.* at § IV.)

4. Under the heading *Probationary Employment*, section IV.A of the policy manual provides that "Each employee will work on probationary status during his or her first 60 days of employment. During this probationary period, Comcon reserves the right to terminate the employee for any reason or for no reason at all." (*Id.* at § IV.A.)

5. Under the heading *Nonprobationary Employment*, section IV.B of the policy manual provides that "Comcon reserves the right to terminate the employment of any employee who is not performing satisfactorily." (*Id.* at § IV.B.)

6. From the beginning of her employment at Comcon, Rembar sought to attract Hart's attentions with casual flirtations, such as references to his appearance and suggestive smiles. Hart returned the flirtations in a similar manner, but no sexual relationship developed between them. Any flirtations directed by Hart toward Rembar were welcomed, and even invited, by her. Hart never demanded sexual favors from Rembar, and he never conditioned any benefits of employment on Rembar's submitting to a sexual demand or otherwise reacting to a flirtation. (Hart Aff.¶ 3 (Ex. D).)

7. In the fall of 2017, Hart became dissatisfied with Rembar's performance. Specifically, she displayed a negative attitude in her work. Because Comcon consultants must work closely with their clients, a consultant with a negative attitude severely hampers Comcon's business relationships. (Hart Aff.¶ 4 (Ex. D).)

8. Effective November 2, 2017, Hart terminated Rembar's employment because of her negative attitude. (Nov. 1, 2017 Payroll Action (Exh. C).) Hart communicated the discharge to Rembar in a normal, professional manner. (Hart Aff.¶ 4 (Ex. D).)

August 5, 2018

Lisa Hall
Kendricks, Hall, & Oats, P.C.
3310 Alma School Rd., Suite 200
Mesa, Arizona 85283
(480) 839-0365
Bar No. 0076089

Exhibit A

POLICY MANUAL
for Employees of Comcon

I. Introduction

The success of Comcon lies in its ability to recruit and retain the best employees available nationally. To promote a stable and productive workforce, Comcon provides attractive terms and conditions of employment, including those set forth in the following policies.

II. Salary

A. Initial Salary . . . .

B. Change in Salary . . . .

III. Holidays, Vacations, Sick Leave

A. Holidays . . . .

B. Personal Leave . . . .

IV. Termination

A. Probationary Employment

Each employee will work on probationary status during his or her first 60 days of employment. During this probationary period, Comcon reserves the right to terminate the employee for any reason or for no reason at all.

B. Nonprobationary Employment

Comcon reserves the right to terminate the employment of any employee who is not performing satisfactorily.

. . . .

Exhibit B

PAYROLL ACTION

Nature of Action

___X___ New Hire _____ Change in Pay _______ Termination

Previous Pay *N.A.*

New Pay $5,000/mo.

Effective Date *Jan. 1, 2017*

Reason for Change or Termination

Comments

Consultant

Date *Dec. 30, 2016*

Processed By *Leslie West*

Exhibit C

PAYROLL ACTION

Nature of Action

_____New Hire ___________Change in Pay __X__ Termination

Previous Pay *$5,000/mo.*

New Pay *N.A.*

Effective Date *Nov. 2, 2017*

Reason for Change or Termination

Negative Attitude

Comments

Date *Nov. 1, 2017*

Processed By *Leslie West*

Exhibit D

AFFIDAVIT OF ALEXANDER HART IN SUPPORT OF MOTION FOR SUMMARY JUDGMENT

Maricopa County, Arizona

Alexander Hart, under oath, swears to the following information from personal knowledge:

1. I am the sole owner and manager of Comcon, a firm that provides consulting services to businesses on the development and use of computer systems. From January to November 2017, I employed eight employees, the largest workforce that I have employed since I formed Comcon in 2008. Specifically, during that period I employed a secretary, an accountant, and six consultants.

2. Effective January 1, 2017, I hired Charlotte Rembar for the position of consultant. The Payroll Action form identified in this motion as Exhibit B is the only written record of Rembar's hiring and her terms of employment. Rembar and I understood at the time of hiring that her term of employment was indefinite. On or before the time of her hiring, I gave her a Comcon Policy Manual, which reaffirms that Rembar had no definite term of employment or guarantee of continued employment.

3. From the beginning of her employment at Comcon, Rembar sought to attract my attentions with casual flirtations such as suggestive smiles and compliments on my grooming and appearance. She made it clear that she welcomed reciprocation, and I often returned her flirtations with similar smiles and comments. Our personal relationship never advanced beyond these casual flirtations. Specifically, we never had a sexual relationship, and I never made any unwelcome sexual advances toward Rembar, nor did I ever condition any benefits of employment on Rembar's submitting to any sexual demands or otherwise reacting in any way to my flirtations.

4. Sometime in the fall of 2017, I began to notice that Rembar displayed a negative attitude about me, about herself, and about her work. I find it extremely important to maintain a workforce with positive attitudes and pleasant personalities, because the consultants work closely with clients, and our business thus depends on maintaining good personal relationships with clients. To ensure that we maintained those relationships, I discharged Rembar effective November 2, 2017, to rid our workforce of her negativism. I communicated the discharge to Rembar in a normal, professional manner in an office meeting on November 1, 2017.

5. The Payroll Action forms in Exhibits B and C are true copies of records that were prepared and kept under my direction by my personal secretary, Leslie West, in the course of her regularly conducted business activity, which includes maintaining such employment records as a uniform practice. Those forms include information within Ms. West's own knowledge and information that I transmitted to her on matters within my knowledge. The Policy Manual in Exhibit A is a true copy of a manual that I drafted and printed in June 2009 and have since distributed to all employees.

I swear under oath that the foregoing is true:

______________________	______________
Alexander Hart	Date

Checklist for Chapter 15

To prepare a motion for summary judgment,

- ✓ draft a motion that requests summary judgment and briefly introduces the judge to the grounds for your motion;
- ✓ prepare evidentiary materials that will support your statement of facts, if they are not already in the record;
- ✓ draft a separate statement of facts that cites to the supporting materials; and
- ✓ draft a supporting brief that
  - summarizes the facts and procedural history,
  - argues the law and facts relating to the issues, with attention to the standards for summary judgment, and
  - states your conclusions.
- ✓ When opposing a motion for summary judgment, you should prepare a brief and a separate statement of facts with supporting materials.
- ✓ To oppose a motion or to reply to an opposition brief,
  - you need not file a separate motion;
  - instead, you should submit a brief that responds to the arguments presented in the preceding brief.

Endnotes

1. The federal procedures for discovery and disclosure are set forth in Federal Rules of Civil Procedure 26-37.
2. *See, e.g.*, Raymond L. Ocampo, Jr., *Moving Violations*, Cal. Law., Aug. 1984, at 47,
3. *See* Fed. R. Civ. P. 56(a). The citations and quotations in this chapter are based on amendments to Rule 56 effective December 1, 2010. Some of the new language and organization of subsections in Rule 56 depart from references to the rule in much of the case law, but judicial interpretations of prior statements of the rule should be compatible with the substance of the new rule. *See* Joseph Kimble, *Lessons in Drafting from the New Federal Rules of Civil Procedure*, 12 Scribes J. Legal Writing 25 (2008-2009) (discussing project of redrafting federal rules for style only). Beyond the scope of this discussion are state standards for summary disposition that deviate from the federal rules. Many states follow the federal standards closely. *See, e.g.*, Orme Sch. v. Reeves, 802 P.2d 1000 (Ariz. 1990) (en banc) (interpreting Ariz. R. Civ. P. 56); *cf.* Aguilar v. Atl. Richfield Co., 24 P.3d 493, 512-14 (Cal.2001) (amended California summary judgment rules are similar, though not identical to, federal standards).

4. *See* U.C.C. § 2-611(1) (2011).
5. Matsushita Elec. Indus. Co. v. Zenith Radio Corp., 475 U.S. 574, 587 (1986).
6. *Id.* at 586.
7. Fed. R. Civ. P. 56(a).
8. *See* Fed. R. Civ. P. 56(g) (permitting court to find the absence of material fact on an issue not resolved on summary judgment).
9. *See* Celotex Corp. v. Catrett, 477 U.S. 317, 331 (1986) (Brennan, J., dissenting); Fed. R. Civ. P. 56(c)(1)(b), (c)(2) (allowing showing or objection that supporting evidence would not be admissible at trial).
10. *See generally* Fed. R. Civ. P. 56(c)(1)(A), (c)(4).
11. *See* Celotex Corp. v. Catrett, 477 U.S. 317, 322-24 (1986) (majority opinion); *id.* at 329-31 (Brennan, J., dissenting); Fed. R. Civ. P. 56(c)(1)(b), (c)(2).
12. *See* Fed. R. Civ. P. 56(c)-(e); *see also* Southern Rambler Sales, Inc. v. Am. Motors Corp., 375 F.2d 932, 937 (5th Cir. 1967) ("Rule 56 [is] saying in effect, 'Meet these affidavit facts or judicially die.' ").
13. Fed. R. Civ. P. 56(a).
14. *See* Orme Sch. v. Reeves, 802 P.2d 1000, 1008 n.11 (Ariz. 1990) (en banc) (referring to the discretion to deny summary judgment as the "traditional rule"). Indeed, for a few years, the language of Rule 56 was amended to state that summary judgment "should be rendered" when the requirements were satisfied, Fed. R. Civ. P. 56(c)(2) (2007), until the traditional term "shall" was restored in 2010.
15. *See, e.g.*, D. Ariz. LRCiv. 7.1(a).
16. D. Neb. Civ. R. 56.1(a)(2); *see also* Malec v. Sanford, 191 F.R.D. 581, 583 (N.D. Ill. 2000) (quoting and interpreting Local Rule 56.1(a) for the United States District Court for the Northern District of Illinois, setting forth a similar format for the moving party's statement of material facts).
17. Ariz. R. Civ. P. 56(c)(3).
18. *Malec*, 191 F.R.D. at 583.
19. Ariz. R. Civ. P. 56(c)(3). *See also Malec*, 191 F.R.D. at 583-84 (quoting and interpreting N.D. Ill. R. 56.1(b), setting forth a similar format for the opposing party's statement of undisputed and disputed facts). The Arizona rules also permit the nonmoving party to join with the moving party in stipulating to facts not in dispute. Ariz. R. Civ. P. 56(c)(3).
20. *See Malec*, 191 F.R.D. at 584 (citing to N.D. Ill. R. 56.1(a)(3) (final unnumbered paragraph)).
21. Fed. R. Civ. P. 56(c)(4); *see* Vandeventer v. Wabash Nat'l Corp., 867 F. Supp. 790, 798 (N.D. Ind. 1994) (rejecting and expressing displeasure with affidavit that was prepared by attorney and that did not reflect personal knowledge of party who signed affidavit).
22. *See, e.g.*, Catrett v. Johns-Manville Sales Corp., 826 F.2d 33, 37 (D.C. Cir. 1987) (regardless of whether letter qualified as a business records exception to the hearsay rule, trial court properly considered it on summary judgment because other party failed to object to its use).
23. *See* Andrews v. R.W. Hays Co., 998 P.2d 774 (2000) (court disregarded hearsay statements in affidavit because neither the affidavit nor other materials established exception to hearsay rule); *cf.* Olympic Ins. Co. v. H.D. Harrison, Inc., 418 F.2d 669, 670 (5th Cir. 1969) (document produced in ordinary course of business was sufficiently reliable to form basis for summary judgment).
24. *See Malec*, 191 F.R.D. at 585. ("[A]lthough the evidence supporting a factual contention need not be admissible itself, it must represent admissible evidence. For example, a deposition transcript is not usually admissible at trial but (obviously) may be used in support of summary judgment; . . . .").
25. *See* Fed. R. Evid. 803(6).
26. *See* Noel Fidel, *Some Do's and Don'ts of Motion Writing*, Ariz. B.J., Aug. 1983, at 8, 9 (advising legal writers to omit "canned" recitations of basic summary judgment standards).
27. *See, e.g.*, *Malec*, 191 F.R.D. at 586.

Chapter 16

Motion to Exclude Evidence Before Trial

Black's Law Dictionary defines "in limine" as: "preliminary; presented to only the judge, before or during trial."[1] The typical motion in limine is a motion to exclude evidence before trial, or at least to require opposing counsel to raise the question of admissibility outside the presence of the jury if the trial is underway. Conversely, but much more rarely, an advocate may use it to move for admission of evidence before trial if she anticipates an objection to the evidence.[2]

Thus, in contrast to the typical motion for summary judgment, a motion to exclude evidence seeks to define the scope of the trial litigation rather than to dispose of the case before trial. It generally is simpler than a motion for summary judgment. If you can strip the mystery away from the popular Latin phrase, you should have little trouble supporting or opposing the motion.

I. Pretrial Exclusion of Evidence

The Federal Rules of Civil Procedure provide that "the admissibility of evidence" is appropriate for consideration and disposition in a pretrial conference.[3] Additionally, those rules and the Federal Rules of Evidence implicitly authorize a trial court to rule on pretrial motions to exclude evidence other than in pretrial conference, or they at least leave undisturbed the court's inherent power to do so.[4]

During trial, attorneys can and do object to evidence offered for admission.[5] However, pretrial rulings on complex, potentially prejudicial, or especially significant evidentiary matters tend to improve the efficiency and quality of the trial proceedings.[6]

For example, suppose a visitor to your client's factory sues your client for injuries sustained at the factory. At trial, the plaintiff 's counsel asks a defense witness in front of the jury to confirm that your client offered to pay the plaintiff 's medical expenses. You can immediately object that the question seeks a response that may lead the jury to find liability on an improper ground.[7] In most jurisdictions, the judge will sustain your objection and will order the witness not to provide the solicited testimony.[8] However, the damage to your client's case may be irreparable if the question alone improperly influences the jury's deliberations, despite the court's admonishments to the jury to ignore it. You could have protected your client more effectively had you earlier persuaded the judge to exclude the evidence before trial and to order the parties and their attorneys to refrain from referring to the evidence in any way at trial.

Additionally, pretrial litigation of complex evidentiary matters permits more thorough written and oral argument by the parties and more considered deliberation by the court, all without disrupting an ongoing trial. Moreover, pretrial disposition of objections to particularly significant evidence gives the parties an opportunity to modify their trial strategies or to reassess their settlement positions.[9]

II. Format

Unless local court rules specifically address motions in limine,[10] you should follow procedural rules governing motions generally.[11] Beyond that, the common format is a product of custom and common sense. As with any legal document, you can best support or oppose a motion to exclude evidence if you understand the purposes of your document and draft it accordingly.

III. The Motion

In a motion to exclude evidence, you should simply and clearly state the requested action and briefly summarize the grounds for the motion.

In describing the relief requested, you probably should go beyond generally asking for exclusion of certain evidence. To ensure effective protection, you should describe the objectionable evidence as inclusively as possible and should request an order specifically prohibiting the opposing party from referring to the evidence:

> The defendant, Axxon Corp., moves for a pretrial order excluding all evidence that Axxon Corp. offered to provide medical care and to pay the medical expenses of the plaintiff, Herb Taylor. The evidence is inadmissible under Federal Rule of Evidence 409.
>
> Specifically, Axxon Corp. requests an order directing Taylor and his counsel (1) to refrain from referring to such an offer in any way in the presence of the jury during voir dire and all subsequent proceedings, and (2) to take all necessary steps to ensure that their witnesses avoid such references.

To oppose a motion to exclude evidence, you need not file a separate motion; you can simply file a brief that opposes the original motion. At the most, you might want to draft a cover page with a caption and a paragraph that parallels the motion in summarizing the ruling you seek and the supporting grounds:

> Plaintiff Herb Taylor opposes Defendant Axxon Corp.'s motion to exclude evidence of Axxon Corp.'s offer to provide and pay for medical care. The evidence is admissible to show the extent of Taylor's injuries. The court should not exclude the evidence for this limited purpose.

IV. The Brief

A brief supporting or opposing a motion to exclude evidence, or any other motion, is often referred to as a "Memorandum of Law." When preparing a brief supporting a motion to exclude evidence, you ordinarily should follow the familiar pattern of Introduction, Argument, and Conclusion. The party opposing your motion should file a responsive brief that directly answers the arguments in your supporting brief. Similarly, if local rules permit a reply brief, the moving party can rebut the counterarguments presented in the opposing brief.[12]

On a motion for summary judgment, you will address at least some of the claims or defenses of the litigation on their merits. In contrast, on a motion to exclude evidence, you will typically focus more narrowly on the admissibility of certain evidence. Consequently, in your supporting or opposing briefs, you should address the merits of claims or defenses only to the extent necessary to address some element of admissibility, such as relevance. This narrow focus affects the scope of the introduction and argument sections of the briefs.

A. The Introduction

In the introductory section of a brief supporting a motion to exclude evidence, you need not include a full statement of facts and procedural history. In light of the motion's focus on an evidentiary issue, your introduction need summarize only those portions of the facts and procedural history necessary to an understanding of that specific issue. You should accompany your motion with any necessary factual support for your assertions, such as affidavits or documents generated during discovery or prepared specifically for the motion. Additionally, you should cite to such attachments or to other parts of the record. Absent a local rule specifying a specific format, any reasonable citation form is acceptable; two examples are presented below. Finally, your introduction should explain why you expect the nonmoving party to attempt to introduce the evidence at trial and why the court should resolve the matter before trial, unless you choose to address those matters in the Argument section.

For example, the brief supporting the motion might begin with the following introductory points:

MEMORANDUM IN SUPPORT OF MOTION TO EXCLUDE EVIDENCE

I. Introduction

Nature of the case

Herb Taylor, a sales representative for Corbin Heavy Equipment Co., brought this tort action against Axxon Corp. He alleges negligence in the maintenance of the Axxon manufacturing plant in Albuquerque, New Mexico.

Facts

Specifically, Taylor alleges that, while touring the Axxon plant in January 2019 with Axxon General Manager Jerry Olshon, Taylor lost his footing, fell backwards, and struck his head against a forklift. (Compl. ¶¶ 3, 4.) According to Olshon's deposition testimony, as a humanitarian gesture, Olshon immediately offered on behalf of Axxon to provide transportation to the nearest hospital and to pay for Taylor's medical expenses. [Olshon Dep. 18.] Taylor later developed difficulties with his eyesight, which he alleges are the result of his accident at the Axxon plant. (Compl. ¶ 6.)

The critical issue in this case is whether Axxon negligently maintained its plant, causing Taylor to fall. Taylor's counsel has examined Olshon extensively during deposition about Olshon's offer to pay medical expenses, leading Axxon to believe that Taylor's counsel will attempt to introduce that evidence at trial.

Belief that evidence will be introduced

Evidence of Olshon's offer to pay medical expenses is inadmissible to establish Axxon's liability, and Axxon will not introduce it for other purposes. The evidence must be excluded before trial, because reference to it even in a question to a witness would indelibly and improperly influence the jury.

Need for pretrial exclusion

When opposing a motion, you should state any facts and procedural history that are material to your argument and that are not fairly stated in the opening brief:

I. Introduction

Plaintiff Taylor is prepared to prove that Defendant Axxon Corp.'s negligence proximately caused Taylor to lose nearly all sight in his right eye. Axxon apparently seeks to show that Taylor's injuries at the Axxon factory were slight and that Taylor's partial blindness must be unrelated. *See* Answer ¶ 6. Thus, the extent of Taylor's injuries at the factory is in issue.

Issues for trial

Taylor plans to introduce Axxon Corp.'s offer to provide and pay for medical care as evidence that Axxon's agent at the scene of the accident determined Taylor's injuries to be serious. The evidence is admissible for this purpose and should not be excluded.

Relevance of evidence on particular issue

B. The Argument

The argument section of a motion to exclude evidence follows the same general pattern discussed in Chapter 12. Each section or subsection within the argument should state a contention in a point heading, analyze the law and the facts, and restate or summarize the contention in a conclusion.

1. Legal Rules

In the statement of legal standards in the opening brief supporting a motion to exclude evidence, you typically will focus on rules of evidence that restrict admissibility. If you prefer a thorough analysis, you may choose to develop the legal standards in some detail:

> Even relevant evidence is inadmissible "if its probative value is substantially outweighed by the danger" that it will cause "unfair prejudice, confusion of the issues, or misleading the jury." Fed. R. Evid. 403. Evidence presents such a danger if it has "an undue tendency to suggest a decision on an improper basis, commonly, though not necessarily, an emotional one." *Id.*, Advisory Committee Note.
>
> In this case, evidence of Powell's membership in the Black Panther Party a half-century ago has little, if any, probative value. . . .

On the other hand, the general standards for some of the more commonly invoked evidentiary rules are familiar to judges and attorneys. Therefore, you could exercise stylistic discretion to present those standards summarily, or even implicitly, and to move more quickly to the fact analysis:

> Evidence of Powell's former membership in the Black Panther Party should be excluded because its probative value is substantially outweighed by its potential for confusion and unfair prejudice. *See* Fed. R. Evid. 403. The F.B.I. file report shows that Powell was a member of the Black Panther Party more than 50 years ago for the brief period of eight months. During that time, Powell participated in political rallies and peaceful protests against police brutality, and he met with other members in political strategy meetings. . . .

2. Application of Rules to Facts

As in any legal argument, the fact analysis should lead to a conclusion by relating the facts to the legal standard:

Little relevance

> Purely political activities such as these have little or no probative value on the merits of Powell's position that he did nothing to provoke Officer Beatty's assault. As the record shows, when Powell was a member of the Black Panther Party for less than a year in 1970, he did not espouse violence or engage in any violent activities.

> The primary effect of evidence of Powell's membership would be to inflame the passions of the jury. Despite the nonviolent role that Powell played as a member of the organization, many view the Black Panther Party as a radical organization that actively sought confrontation with established institutions such as police agencies. Some jurors undoubtedly would react emotionally to the controversial image of the Black Panthers.
>
> Moreover, some jurors undoubtedly will confuse the original Black Panther Party, a serious political movement, with an unrelated, less constructive, and more controversial "New Black Panthers Party." . . .

Unfair prejudice

The argument section of an opposing brief or a reply brief will contain similar elements, except that each will be narrowly tailored to respond directly to contentions advanced in the brief that preceded it.

C. The Conclusion

Chapter 12's discussion of conclusions includes examples from sample motions in limine. In summary, you should

1. end each argument in a brief with a conclusion on that argument, and
2. end the entire brief with a general summary of all the arguments and with your request for relief.

This sample Conclusion sums up the theme of a brief that presented a single argument:

> **III. Conclusion**
>
> Officer Beatty is on trial in this civil suit. By offering evidence of Powell's membership in the Black Panther Party, Officer Beatty is inappropriately trying to turn the tables and put Powell on trial for his nonviolent political activities more than five decades ago. The evidence should be excluded because its minimal probative value, if any, is substantially outweighed by the danger of confusion and unfair prejudice.

Sample Motion in Limine

The following sample is taken from the files of an actual case, although it is reproduced here with lesser line spacing than in the original.

Deborah E. Driggs
State Bar No. 6081
David L. Keily
State Bar No. 12345
SACKS, TIERNEY, KASEN & KERRICK, P.A.
. . . .
Attorneys for Defendants Rayner

SUPERIOR COURT OF ARIZONA
MARICOPA COUNTY

AGUA FRIA SAND & ROCK, INC., an Arizona corporation, Plaintiff, v. Estate of DALE FAY RAYNER, Deceased; JACK RAYNER, JR., Personal Representative of the Estate of DALE FAY RAYNER, Deceased; Estate of JACK RAYNER, JR., Personal Representative of the Estate of JACK RAYNER, SR., Deceased; JACK RAYNER, JR., Defendants.	No. C-531100 MOTION IN LIMINE TO EXCLUDE TESTIMONY AS TO TRANSACTIONS WITH OR STATEMENTS BY JACK M. RAYNER, SR., AND DALE FAY RAYNER (Oral Argument Requested) (Hon. Gloria G. Ybarra)

Defendants Rayner move for an order excluding testimony by the plaintiff or its agents, or questions or statements by its counsel, about transactions with or statements by Jack M. Rayner, Sr., and Dale Fay Rayner. This motion is made pursuant to Arizona's Deadman's statute, Ariz. Rev. Stat. Ann. § 12-2251 (Supp. 1985), and is supported by the attached Memorandum of Points and Authorities.

DATED December 29, 1986.

By ______________________________
Deborah E. Driggs
David L. Keily, for
SACKS, TIERNEY, KASEN & KERRICK, P.A.
Attorneys for Defendants

MEMORANDUM OF POINTS AND AUTHORITIES

I. FACTUAL BACKGROUND

Plaintiff Agua Fria Sand & Rock, Inc. (Agua Fria) brought this suit against defendants for fraud, breach of a duty of due care, and breach of a lease. Agua Fria was the assignee of a leasehold interest in certain real property owned by defendants. On this property, Agua Fria operated a sand and gravel mine. In February 1980, Agua Fria's plant and equipment were destroyed by a flood. After the flood, Agua Fria moved its operations to a new site on the property.

Agua Fria alleges that the defendants wrongfully evicted them from the new site. Although Agua Fria occupied the land as a tenant at will, it alleges that the defendants promised to execute and deliver a written lease for a term of 20 years.

The defendants deny that they had promised to execute and deliver a written lease for a term of 20 years to Agua Fria. They allege that Agua Fria was evicted because it had failed to make rental payments and to satisfy other lease obligations.

Jack M. Rayner, Sr., died on October 14, 1982. Dale Fay Rayner died on April 17, 1984. Jack M. Rayner, Jr., is the Personal Representative of the Estates of Jack M. Rayner, Sr., and Dale Fay Rayner. Agua Fria has sued Jack M. Rayner, Jr., in his capacity as Personal Representative of the estates of Jack M. Rayner, Sr., and Dale Fay Rayner.

Questions, argument, or testimony before the jury regarding alleged oral promises made by either testator will improperly influence the jury, even if objection at trial or related proceedings is sustained. Therefore, this Court should exclude all such references before trial.

II. ARGUMENT

The Arizona Deadman's Statute bars admission of testimony of transactions with, or statements by, Jack M. Rayner, Sr., and Dale Fay Rayner.

To reduce the danger of fraudulent testimony, the Arizona Deadman's statute restricts the admission of testimony about transactions with, or about statements made by, the testator in certain suits:

> In an action by or against personal representatives, administrators, guardians or conservators in which judgment may be given for or against them as such, neither party shall be allowed to testify against the other as to any transaction with or statement by the testator, intestate or ward unless called to testify thereto by the opposite

> party, or required to testify thereto by the court. The provisions of this section shall extend to and include all actions by or against the heirs, devisees, legatees or legal representatives of a decedent arising out of any transaction with the decedent.

Ariz. Rev. Stat. Ann. § 12-2251 (Supp. 1985).

The statute clearly applies to this case. First, Agua Fria has filed suit against Jack M. Rayner, Jr., in his capacity as personal representative of the estates of Jack M. Rayner, Sr., and Dale Fay Rayner. Judgment may be granted for or against Jack M. Rayner, Jr., in his capacity as personal representative. Finally, Agua Fria plans to introduce evidence of an alleged oral agreement by the deceased, Jack M. Rayner, Sr., and Dale Fay Rayner, to execute a written lease with a term of 20 years.

The statute authorizes admission of testimony of transactions with or statements by the deceased if "required . . . by the court." Therefore, such admission ultimately lies within the discretion of the trial court. *Mahan v. First Nat'l Bank*, 139 Ariz. 138, 140, 677 P.2d 301, 303 (Ct. App. 1984).

The trial court's determination to admit testimony of transactions with or statements by the decedent will be upheld only if (1) independent evidence corroborates the transaction with the decedent, and (2) an injustice will result if the testimony is rejected. *Id.*

Agua Fria has no independent evidence to support its claims that the deceased promised to execute and deliver a written lease of the premises for a term of 20 years. Instead, Agua Fria rests on the bald assertion that the deceased made such promises. This type of uncorroborated testimony is exactly what the statute was intended to proscribe.

Second, no injustice will result from exclusion of testimony of transactions with or statements by Jack M. Rayner, Sr., and Dale Fay Rayner. The exclusion will apply equally to both parties. Moreover, exclusion of the testimony comports strongly with public policy to render incompetent as witnesses persons who will gain from distortion of transactions with the decedent when death has rendered the decedent incapable of refuting these inaccuracies. *See Carrillo v. Taylor*, 81 Ariz. 14, 299 P.2d 188 (1956). The exclusion will simply preclude Plaintiff Agua Fria from making use of self-serving, uncorroborated declarations about what the deceased supposedly said. Agua Fria should not be able to manufacture lease obligations out of the alleged representations of those who are no longer able to refute them.

III. CONCLUSION

The objectionable testimony in this case is uncorroborated, and its exclusion will not result in an injustice. Therefore, this testimony should be excluded under the applicable Deadman's statute. To prevent evasion of the statute, this Court's order should apply broadly to comments or questions of counsel in front of the jury, as well as to testimony.

December 29, 1986.
SACKS, TIERNEY, KASEN & KERRICK, P.A.

____

Deborah E. Driggs
David L. Keily
3300 N16orth Central Avenue
Phoenix, Arizona 85012-1576
Attorneys for Defendants

Checklist for Chapter 16

To prepare a motion to exclude evidence before trial,

- ✓ draft a motion that simply and clearly requests the court to exclude specified evidence and to prohibit the parties from referring to the evidence at trial;
- ✓ draft a supporting brief that
  - introduces the facts and procedural history relevant to the motion,
  - argues the law and facts relating to the evidentiary issues, and
  - states your conclusions; and
- ✓ attach any documentary evidence or affidavits necessary to support your motion, or refer to evidence already in the record.

To oppose a motion to exclude evidence, or to reply to an opposition brief,

- ✓ you need not file a separate motion.
- ✓ Instead, you should submit a brief that responds to the arguments presented in the preceding brief.

For further practice with motions to exclude evidence, complete Assignment 6 in the Appendix.

Endnotes

1. Black's Law Dictionary 858 (9th ed. 2009).
2. *See* Hon. Robert E. Bacharach, *Motions in Limine in Oklahoma State and Federal Courts*, 24 Okla. City U. L. Rev. 112, 114 (1999).
3. Fed. R. Civ. P. 16(c)(2)(C).
4. *See generally* Fed. R. Evid. 103(c) ("In jury cases, proceedings shall be conducted, to the extent practicable, so as to prevent inadmissible evidence from being suggested to the jury by any means, such as making statements or offers of proof or asking questions in the hearing of the jury."); Charles W. Gamble, *The Motion in Limine: A Pretrial Procedure That Has Come of Age*, 33 Ala. L. Rev. 1, 2 & n.6 (1981).
5. *See* Fed. R. Evid. 103(a) (unnumbered paragraph following subsections (1) & (2)) (referring to rulings "admitting or excluding evidence, either at or before trial").
6. *See* Fed. R. Civ. P. 16(a) (stating objectives of pretrial conference).
7. *See* Fed. R. Evid. 409, Advisory Comm. Note. Exclusion of such evidence also promotes a generally humanitarian policy of encouraging such assistance, regardless of liability. *Id.*
8. *See* Fed. R. Evid. 409.
9. *See* Gamble, *supra* note 4, at 8-10.
10. *See, e.g.*, Ariz. R. Civ. P. 7.2(b), (c) (specifying timing for motions in limine and disallowing reply briefs).
11. *See, e.g.*, D. Ariz. LRCiv. 7.2(a)-(e) (specifying requirements for motions and for opening, answering, and reply briefs in this federal trial court); Ariz. R. Civ. P. 7.1(a) (setting forth general requirements for motions in this state's trial practice).
12. *Compare* D. Ariz. LRCiv. 7.2(b)-(d) (for all motions in this federal trial court, referring to the moving party's brief, the responsive memorandum, and the reply memorandum) *with* Ariz. R. Civ. P. 7.2(c) (disallowing reply briefs for motions in limine in this state's trial courts).

Part VII

Appellate Briefs

Writing appellate briefs differs from most pretrial brief writing in three respects. First, if you have fully tried your case before appeal, you will analyze the issues on appeal on a more complete factual record than was available during the litigation of pretrial motions. Second, in developing your arguments on appeal, you must consider standards of appellate review, which require varying levels of deference to trial court rulings and findings. Third, rules of procedure and local rules typically prescribe a more formal and detailed format for appellate briefs than for most pretrial or trial briefs.

Chapter 17

Standards of Appellate Review

I. The Record on Appeal

Aside from physical exhibits and some kinds of documentary evidence admitted into court, the proceedings in the trial court are recorded in two records: the trial court clerk's record and the court reporter's transcript.[1] The trial history of a case can usually be most easily traced in the trial court clerk's record, which contains litigation documents filed with the trial court, from the initial pleadings to the notice of appeal. It also includes the written judgment of the court, along with orders reflecting the court's rulings on procedural and other preliminary matters. A docket sheet attached to the clerk's record contains a brief entry for each document in the record. This provides a convenient index to the record and a summary of the history of the litigation.

The reporter's transcript is a record of all the statements made "on the record" in court during the litigation process. It includes oral arguments of the parties on motions, testimony of witnesses, rulings from the bench, and instructions to the jury.

Shortly after a disappointed litigant has filed notice of appeal from the judgment of the trial court, the parties on appeal designate the portions of the clerk's record and reporter's transcript that are necessary for the appeal.[2] In some circumstances, other original documents and physical exhibits admitted into evidence may also be forwarded to the appellate court.[3]

Before writing an appellate brief, you must master the record on appeal because the evidence and arguments presented to the trial court help to define the scope of the appellate court's inquiry. Indeed, when referring to testimony, arguments, rulings, or other portions of the trial history, you should carefully cite to the pages of the clerk's record or reporter's transcript that reflect that information. Although rules of procedure or local rules may specify a different citation form, common abbreviations for citation to, for example, page 134 of the clerk's record are "CR at 134," for "clerk's record." Page 383 of the reporter's transcript is commonly cited as "RT at 383" or "Trial Tr. at 383." If either record is bound in multiple volumes, you must also cite to the volume number in some reasonable fashion. For example, you might cite to page 115 of the third volume of the reporter's transcript as "III RT at 115" or "RT, vol. 3, at 115." In any of these citations, you can omit the "at," or replace it with an abbreviation for "page," depending on your style or applicable rules; for example, "CR 134," "RT p. 115;" or "RT, vol. 3, pg. 115." If separate records are not designated by volume numbers, include the date or other clarifying information. Finally, if the opening brief is accompanied by an appendix containing relevant parts of the record, appellate rules of procedure or local court rules may require citation to the appendix rather than to the underlying record.[4] One might cite to such an appendix in any of several reasonable ways, such as "Appendix p. 42," "Appendix at 42," or "App. 42."

II. Standards of Review in the Federal Courts

A. Overview

An appellate court cannot necessarily reverse a trial court's judgment simply because the appellate judges would have decided the case differently on the same record. The appellate court will sometimes limit the degree to which it subjects a trial court determination to appellate scrutiny. To accomplish this calibration, the appellate court will apply different standards of review to different kinds of trial court findings or rulings.

For example, on a motion for summary judgment or a motion to dismiss an action for failure to state a claim, a trial court does not resolve any factual disputes; instead, it decides as a matter of law whether alleged or undisputed facts satisfy the applicable legal standards. When reviewing a trial court's granting of such a motion, the appellate court will also be deciding matters of law, rather than fact. It will place itself in the position of the trial court and decide "*de novo*," without deference to the trial court's analysis, whether the moving party satisfied its burden on the motion.[5]

In contrast, a jury's verdict or a trial judge's findings of fact rendered after trial represent the fact finder's resolution of factual disputes. When reviewing such findings, an appellate court will restrict its review, deferring substantially to the fact finder's resolution of conflicting evidence. Not surprisingly, appellate courts rarely overturn findings of fact.

Thus, to effectively argue your case on appeal, you must consider the standard of review, or the degree to which the appellate court will defer to a finding or ruling made in the trial court. Indeed, the outcome of some appeals will depend directly on the standard of review that the appellate court chooses to apply.[6]

Appellate standards of review in the federal court system will serve as a starting point for your understanding standards that apply in a state court. Under the two most important standards—and subject to a "constitutional facts" exception discussed at the end of this chapter—an appellate court restricts its review of questions of fact but not of questions of law.

B. Restricted Appellate Review of Findings of Fact

1. Review of Jury Findings

The Seventh Amendment to the United States Constitution guarantees the right to a jury trial "in suits at common law," and it provides that "no fact tried by a jury shall be otherwise re-examined in any court of the United States, than according to the rules of the common law." Accordingly, a federal appellate court generally will uphold the factual findings of a jury in a civil case unless those findings are not supported by "any substantial evidence."[7] Federal statutes prescribe the same standard of review for the findings of some administrative agencies.[8]

Even though a different set of constitutional considerations applies, an appellate court will also restrict its review of a jury's findings of fact resulting in a criminal conviction. Specifically, rather than reweigh all the evidence, an appellate court may constitutionally uphold a criminal conviction if "the record evidence could reasonably support a finding of guilt beyond a reasonable doubt."[9]

The Seventh Amendment does not apply to state courts. Therefore, some states may permit broader appellate review of jury findings, particularly review of a jury's calculation of damages in a civil suit. New York, for example, has legislatively authorized its state appellate courts to overturn a jury's calculation of damages as excessive or inadequate if the jury award materially deviates from reasonable compensation. More typically, however, a state or federal trial court will set aside a jury's calculation of compensatory damages only if the damages are so excessive as to shock the conscience of the court, and an appellate court typically will overturn the trial court's determination on whether to set aside a jury award only if the trial court abused its discretion.[10]

2. Review of a Judge's Findings of Fact

In civil suits in which the parties have no constitutional or statutory right to a jury, or in suits in which the parties have waived their right to a jury, the trial judge will both find the facts and rule on the law. Under Federal Rule of Civil Procedure 52(a)(6), a federal court of appeals will not overturn the factual findings of a federal trial judge unless the findings are "clearly erroneous." Although Rule 52(a) applies only to civil proceedings and does not directly apply to a trial judge's factual findings on preliminary rulings in a criminal trial, some courts have adopted Rule 52(a)'s "clearly erroneous" standard by analogy for the criminal context.[11]

Under Rule 52(a)(1), a trial judge trying a case without a jury will divide his findings into findings of fact and conclusions of law. For example, he may state as a conclusion of law that a federal antidiscrimination statute requires proof of intent to discriminate, and he may state as a finding of fact that the evidence shows no discriminatory intent. On appeal, the appellate court could review without restriction the trial judge's interpretation of the statute to require proof of intent to discriminate; accordingly, it would reverse the trial court's conclusion on that question if it interpreted the statute differently. In contrast, the appellate court would not overturn the trial judge's factual finding of absence of discriminatory intent unless the record showed that finding to be clearly erroneous,[12] even if the appellate judges might have found discriminatory intent had they been the initial fact finders.

One court has defined the clearly-erroneous standard of appellate review in a colorful manner that seems to require great deference to the trial court's findings of fact: "To be clearly erroneous, a decision must . . . strike us as wrong with the force of a five-week-old, unrefrigerated dead fish."[13] Under a more conventional measure of clear error, however, the reviewing court simply asks "whether 'on the entire evidence,' it is 'left with the definite and firm conviction that a mistake has been committed.'"[14] At least in theory, the clearly-erroneous standard permits slightly broader appellate review than does the substantial-evidence standard, which is typically applied to findings of juries and some administrative agencies:[15]

> Under the substantial-evidence standard, a reviewing court must uphold the findings of a jury or administrative agency if the record contains sufficient evidence to permit a reasonable person to make those findings. In contrast, the clearly-erroneous standard permits the reviewing court to review the entire record, and to overturn a finding of fact if it is convinced that the finding is clearly wrong, even though a reasonable person could have made the finding.[16]

An appellate court's deference to factual findings made in the trial court is supported by practical and policy considerations that recognize distinctions in the roles of trial and appellate courts. The fact finder in the trial court, either the judge or the jury, is generally in a better position than the appellate court to evaluate the evidence. This advantage is strongest when factual findings are based partly on the fact finder's evaluation of the credibility of witnesses. The mannerisms of the witness on the stand may be much more revealing than the cold print of the reporter's transcript. Accordingly, Rule 52(a)(6) specifically directs appellate courts to give "due regard to the trial court's opportunity to judge the witnesses' credibility."

Conversely, the trial court's advantage is weakest when factual findings are based largely on other evidence that is available in identical form to both the trial and appellate courts. Nonetheless, Rule 52(a)(6)'s restricted standard of review applies to "[f]indings of fact, whether based on oral or other evidence," suggesting that restrictions on appellate review must be at least partly based on policies other than a practical advantage enjoyed by the trial court.

In fact, restrictions on appellate review of findings of fact are independently justified by the importance of an appellate court's role in developing general principles of law relative to its role of correcting error in the judgment in a specific case. Admittedly, appellate courts should perform a limited "corrective" function by subjecting each trial judgment to some review for error and thus reducing the risk of injustice.[17] At least as important, however, is the appellate court's "institutional" function of "developing and declaring legal principles that will have application beyond the case that serves as the vehicle for expression of the principles."[18] This institutional function is strongest in the highest appellate court in a jurisdiction.[19] It emphasizes the development of a cohesive body of legal standards rather than the review of evidence supporting findings of fact.

C. Conclusions of Law: Mixed Conclusions of Fact and Law in a Nonjury Trial

In contrast to the restricted appellate review of findings of fact, appellate review of a trial judge's conclusions of law is unrestricted. The appellate court may freely correct the trial court's formulation of legal standards.[20]

Often, however, classifying a finding as more nearly one of law than of fact in a nonjury trial is a difficult task.[21] Without doubt, Rule 52(a)(6)'s clearly-erroneous standard applies to appellate review of a trial judge's findings of historical fact, such as findings about events and actions.[22] It also applies to review of "factual inferences" drawn by a trial court from "undisputed basic facts."[23]

However, some trial court determinations fall between the two extremes of formulation of abstract legal standards and findings of historical fact or factual inference. For example, a trial judge's determination of whether the historical facts satisfy an abstract legal standard is a mixed finding of fact and law, which may contain elements of both factual inference and refinement of the legal standard. Thus, whether a trial court finding is one of fact, subject to restricted appellate review, or one of law, subject to full review, could be subject to dispute and thus be raised as one of the threshold issues on appeal.

1. Review of Discretionary Rulings

A narrow class of mixed findings is protected by an especially restricted standard of review. Specifically, an appellate court will severely restrict its review of certain "discretionary" rulings of a trial judge, such as discovery and evidentiary rulings, the granting or denial of injunctive or declaratory relief, or the determination whether to grant a new trial. Assuming that the trial judge formulated the correct legal rule before applying it to the facts, the appellate court generally will not overturn such a mixed finding of the trial judge unless she abused her discretion.[24]

2. Mixed Findings as Predominantly Fact or Law

Most mixed findings, however, do not fall within this narrow class of discretionary rulings. Instead, for purposes of appellate standards of review, appellate courts must classify the findings under Rule 52(a) as findings of fact or conclusions of law. The proper means of accomplishing this classification is a matter of continuing debate. However, the practical and policy considerations underlying restrictions on appellate review provide some guidance in the debate.

In many cases, the standard of review will turn on the level of court that is in the best position to make the determination. For example, if a mixed question of fact and law requires the application of a simple, noncontroversial legal rule to complex historical facts, its resolution will require the trial judge primarily to refine her understanding of the facts rather than to interpret the legal rule. The trial judge normally is in the best position to make such a determination, and review of the factual record is more in keeping with the trial court's customary role than with the appellate court's institutional function of clarifying the law.[25] Therefore, an appellate court should view the finding as more nearly a finding of factual inference than a conclusion of law, and it should restrict its review accordingly.

Consider, for example, a trial judge's ruling in one case that an employer's series of early retirement offers to employees did not amount to a "plan" subject to regulation under the federal Employee Retirement Income Security Act. The meaning of the statutory term "plan" adopted by the trial judge was a matter of law subject to unrestricted review; however, the mixed question of whether the early retirement offers satisfied the legal test for constituting a "plan" primarily required analysis of the factual characteristics of the offers. The appellate court thus treated this mixed question as "principally a question of fact," and it applied the restrictive "clearly erroneous" standard to its review of the trial judge's finding on that issue.[26]

Conversely, if a mixed question of fact and law requires the application of complex, uncertain, or highly controversial legal standards to simple historical facts, the trial judge's resolution of the question will primarily reflect refinement of her understanding of the content of the legal rules. De novo review of such a mixed finding produces the "normal law-clarifying benefits [of] an appellate decision on a question of law."[27] Accordingly, an appellate court should view such a finding as more nearly a conclusion of law, subject to unrestricted review, than one of factual inference.

Consider, for example, the question in one United States Supreme Court case of whether the government presented "clear, unequivocal and convincing" proof that a naturalized citizen had fraudulently procured his certificate of naturalization during World War II by falsely renouncing his allegiance to Nazi Germany and falsely swearing allegiance to the United States. Because of the technical nature of the special standard of proof, along with the uncertain and politically sensitive nature of the legal concept of "allegiance," this mixed question was primarily one of law. Therefore, the appellate courts could review the trial court's determination without restriction.[28]

3. Constitutional Facts Doctrine

Similarly, courts will freely review the mixed question of whether a jury award of punitive damages violates constitutional guarantees of due process[29] or whether certain speech falls within a category protected by the First Amendment.[30] Judicial determinations on these mixed questions necessarily reflect choices about the scope of important constitutional rights.

Indeed, to safeguard constitutional guarantees of freedom of speech, courts have adopted a limited "constitutional facts" exception to the normally restricted review of findings of historical fact discussed above in Section II.B. In such cases, courts may examine the underlying record and freely review even some purely factual findings of a jury or trial court judge, if the facts are critical to the First Amendment analysis.[31] Even when freely reviewing findings of constitutional fact, however, the appellate court will defer to the fact finder's determinations of witness credibility.[32]

Appellate Standards of Review

The following chart summarizes widely adopted standards of appellate review for various kinds of trial rulings or findings. You should view the chart as only a starting point in your analysis of appellate review, because the precise standard of review in any category can vary between state and federal courts and between states.

TRIAL COURT DETERMINATION	APPELLATE STANDARD OF REVIEW
Finding of fact by civil jury and some administrative agencies	Affirmed if supported by substantial evidence
Finding of guilt by jury in criminal prosecution	Affirmed if rational basis or reasonable support in the evidence for a finding that prosecution met its burden of proof
Trial judge's exercise of discretion	Affirmed unless trial judge abused discretion
Trial judge's finding of fact	Affirmed unless clearly erroneous
Trial judge's ruling on the law or instructions on law to jury	Reviewed without restriction and rejected if appellate court disagrees on the merits
Trial judge's mixed finding of law and fact	Treated as finding of fact or conclusion of law, often depending on whether legal or factual questions predominate

Standards for Appellate Review

Checklist for Chapter 17

- An appellate court will freely review a lower court's statement or formulation of a legal rule, without deference to the lower court's interpretation of the law.
- In contrast, an appellate court will substantially restrict its review of findings of fact in the trial court, with the precise standard of deference varying with the context.
- On appellate review, a trial judge's application of law to facts will be treated in some courts either as a ruling of law or a finding of fact, depending on whether the trial court's analysis on that point is predominantly one of
  - clarifying the legal rule in a factual context or
  - drawing legally relevant factual inferences.
- Finally, an appellate court will restrict its review of a trial judge's exercise of discretion on certain kinds of issues.

Endnotes

1. *E.g.*, FED. R. APP. P. 10(a).
2. *See, e.g.*, FED. R. APP. P. 10(b).
3. *See, e.g.*, FED. R. APP. P. 11(b)(2).
4. *E.g.*, FED. R. APP. P. 28(e).
5. *See* Experimental Eng'g, Inc. v. United Techs. Corp., 614 F.2d 1244, 1246 (9th Cir. 1980) (reviewing dismissal of action for failure to state a claim); Heiniger v. City of Phoenix, 625 F.2d 842, 843-44 (9th Cir. 1980) (discussing standards of review for summary judgment).
6. *See, e.g.*, Chaline v. KCOH, Inc., 693 F.2d 477, 480 n.3 (5th Cir. 1982); Walsh v. Centeio, 692 F.2d 1239, 1241 (9th Cir. 1982).
7. *See, e.g.*, Aetna Life Ins. Co. v. Kepler, 116 F.2d 1, 4 & n.1 (8th Cir. 1941). Interestingly, a finding of negligence is not a pure finding of fact, because it requires the jury to define and apply a standard of care, resulting in a mixed conclusion of law and fact. For purposes of appellate review, however, such jury verdicts are treated as findings of fact. Appellate courts distinguish more finely between a trial judge's findings of fact and conclusions of law.
8. *See, e.g.*, 29 U.S.C. § 160(f) (2012) (appellate review of factual findings of the National Labor Relations Board); 5 U.S.C. § 706(2)(E) (2012) (judicial review of the factual findings of some administrative agency findings, as set forth in the Administrative Procedure Act); *In re* Gartside, 203 F.3d 1305 (Fed. Cir. 2000) (under the Administrative Procedure Act, "substantial evidence" standard of review applies to review of findings of fact of Patent and Trademark Office Board of Appeals).
9. Jackson v. Virginia, 443 U.S. 307, 318 (1979).
10. *See* Gasperini v. Ctr. for Humanities, Inc., 518 U.S. 415, 422 (1996) (comparing earlier judicial standards in New York courts to N.Y. CIV. PRAC. L. & R. § 5501(c) (McKinney 1995)). In *Gasperini*, the Court held that the Seventh Amendment is satisfied in a federal diversity action applying New York substantive law if the federal district court reviews the jury's award under the New York statutory standard and if the federal appellate court reviews the district court's determination only for abuse of discretion. *Id.* at 419, 432-39.
11. *See, e.g.*, Ornelas v. United States, 517 U.S. 690, 699 (1996) (in reviewing determinations of reasonable suspicion and probable cause in suppression hearing, appellate court reviews district court's findings of historical fact for clear error). Of course, the defendant has a right to a jury determination of the ultimate facts regarding criminal liability. *See* U.S. CONST. AMEND. VI.
12. *See* Pullman-Standard v. Swint, 456 U.S. 273, 287-88 (1982).
13. Parts & Elec. Motors, Inc. v. Sterling Elec., Inc., 866 F.2d 228, 233 (7th Cir. 1988).
14. Easley v. Cromartie, 532 U.S. 234, 235 (2001) (quoting United States v. United States Gypsum Co., 333 U.S. 364, 395 (1948))
15. *See, e.g.*, Dickinson v. Zurko, 527 U.S. 150, 162-64 (1999) (recognizing that the "clearly erroneous" standard allows for more searching review, but characterizing the difference as subtle, and observing that the choice between the two standards will not often determine the outcome); Loehr v. Offshore Logistics, Inc., 691 F.2d 758, 760-61 (5th Cir. 1982).
16. Charles R. Calleros, *Title VII and Rule 52(a): Standards of Appellate Review in Disparate Treatment Cases—Limiting the Reach of* Pullman-Standard v. Swint, 58 TUL. L. REV. 411 n.40 (1983) (citations omitted); *see also Zurko*, 527 U.S. at 162 (distinguishing between the "definite and firm conviction" required for clear error and the "reasonable mind" standard for the substantial-evidence test).
17. Calleros, *supra* note 16, at 421-22.
18. *Id.* at 420-21.

19. Indeed, under its "two-court rule," the United States Supreme Court will give special deference to a finding of fact made by a trial judge and upheld on appeal in the intermediate court of appeals. *See, e.g.*, Rogers v. Lodge, 458 U.S. 613, 622-27 (1982).
20. *See* Pullman-Standard v. Swint, 456 U.S. 273, 287 (1982).
21. *See id.* at 288.
22. *See, e.g.*, Washington v. Watkins, 655 F.2d 1346, 1352 (5th Cir. 1981).
23. Commissioner v. Duberstein, 363 U.S. 278, 291 (1960) (citing United States v. United States Gypsum Co., 333 U.S. 364, 394 (1948)).
24. *See, e.g.*, Gen. Elec. Co. v. Joiner, 522 U.S. 136 (1997) (district court's evidentiary rulings—including those on admission or exclusion of scientific evidence—are reviewed only for abuse of discretion); Browning-Ferris Indus. of Vt. v. Kelco Disposal, Inc., 492 U.S. 257, 279 (1989) (district court's decision whether to grant new trial or remittitur after jury award is reviewed for abuse of discretion), *cited with approval in* Gasperini v. Ctr. for Humanities, Inc., 518 U.S. 415, 435 (1996) (review of district court's decision whether to set aside jury award of damages in a diversity suit); Wilton v. Seven Falls Co., 515 U.S. 277, 289-90 (1995) (abuse of discretion standard for reviewing district court's decision whether to entertain a declaratory judgment action); Los Angeles Mem'l Coliseum Comm'n v. Nat'l Football League, 634 F.2d 1197, 1200 (9th Cir. 1980) (abuse of discretion standard for reviewing district court's decision whether to grant injunctive relief).
25. *See* Pierce v. Underwood, 487 U.S. 552, 559-60 (1988).
26. Belanger v. Wyman-Gordon Co., 71 F.3d 451, 453-56 (1st Cir. 1995).
27. *Pierce*, 487 U.S. at 561.
28. Baumgartner v. United States, 322 U.S. 665 (1944).
29. Cooper Indus. v. Leatherman Tool Group, Inc., 532 U.S. 424 (2001).
30. *See, e.g.*, Bose Corp. v. Consumers Union, 466 U.S. 485, 504-06 (1984).
31. *Id.* at 499-514 (freely reviewing district court's finding of actual malice in defamation case and referring to other cases and contexts, including independent review of the record in jury cases); *see also id.* at 515 (White, J., dissenting) (interpreting majority's analysis as applying to a pure question of fact); *id.* at 515 (Rehnquist, J., dissenting) (same); *id.* at 518 n.2 (Rehnquist, J., dissenting) (arguing that full independent review of constitutional facts found by state jury is less controversial than freely reviewing the careful, written findings of a district court judge); Adam Hoffman, *Corralling Constitutional Fact: De Novo Fact Review in the Federal Appellate Courts*, 50 DUKE L.J. 1427 (2001).
32. *Bose*, 466 U.S. at 499-500; Harte-Hanks Commc'ns, Inc. v. Connaughton, 491 U.S. 657, 688 (1989).

Chapter 18

The Brief—Effective Appellate Advocacy

I. Overview of Appellate Briefs: Formats and Filing

Rules of procedure and local court rules typically prescribe more formal and detailed formats for appellate briefs than for motions memoranda and other briefs. As the following examples illustrate, you must follow the latest version of applicable rules in the appropriate jurisdiction to ensure that the clerk's office of the court will accept your brief for filing.

A. Components of the Opening Brief

When you represent the "appellant" (bringing an appeal as a matter of right) or the "petitioner" (if you must petition the court to accept the case for discretionary review), you will file the opening brief, seeking reversal of the judgment below. At a minimum, typical rules will require this brief to include the following substantive components:

1. a statement of the issues raised on appeal;
2. a statement of the procedural history of the case (frequently entitled "Statement of the Case" or "Proceedings Below");
3. a statement of the facts relevant to issues raised on appeal;
4. an argument (often preceded by a summary of the argument, either as mandated by applicable rules or as a matter of the brief writer's discretion); and
5. a conclusion.

In addition, rules of procedure or court rules typically require other substantive and formal components such as a table of contents, an alphabetically arranged table of authorities, and statements of jurisdiction and of standards of review. For example, United States Supreme Court Rule 24. requires nine components in opening briefs to that court, along with a table of contents and a table of authorities in all but very short briefs:

> **Rule 24. Briefs on the Merits: In General**
>
> 1. A brief on the merits for a petitioner or an appellant . . . shall contain in the order here indicated:
>
> (a) The questions presented for review. . . .
>
> (b) A list of all parties to the proceeding in the court whose judgment is under review. . . .
>
> (c) If the brief exceeds 1,500 words, a table of contents and a table of cited authorities.
>
> (d) Citations of the official and unofficial reports of the opinions and orders entered in the case by courts and administrative agencies.
>
> (e) A concise statement of the basis for jurisdiction in this Court, including the statutory provisions and time factors on which jurisdiction rests.
>
> (f) The constitutional provisions, treaties, statutes, ordinances, and regulations involved in the case, set out verbatim with appropriate citation. . . .
>
> (g) A concise statement of the case, setting out the facts material to the consideration of the questions presented,. . . .
>
> (h) A summary of the argument, suitably paragraphed. . . .
>
> (i) The argument, exhibiting clearly the points of fact and of law presented and citing the authorities and statutes relied on.
>
> (j) A conclusion specifying with particularity the relief the party seeks.

For briefs filed with a United States Court of Appeals, Federal Rule of Appellate Procedure 28(a) specifies eight components for the appellant's opening brief, with two others required in certain circumstances. As amended in 2013, Rule 28(a)(6) now combines two previously separate components into a single "statement of the case," which includes both the procedural history and the statement of facts. Rule 28(a) now requires the following format for the opening brief:

Rule 28. Briefs

(a) **Appellant's Brief**. The appellant's brief must contain, under appropriate headings and in the order indicated:

(1) a corporate disclosure statement if required by Rule 26.1;

(2) a table of contents, with page references;

(3) a table of authorities—cases (alphabetically arranged), statutes, and other authorities—with references to the pages of the brief where they are cited;

(4) a jurisdictional statement, including:

(A) the basis for the district court's or agency's subject matter jurisdiction, with citations to applicable statutory provisions and stating relevant facts establishing jurisdiction;

(B) the basis for the court of appeals' jurisdiction, with citations to applicable statutory provisions and stating relevant facts establishing jurisdiction;

(C) the filing dates establishing the timeliness of the appeal or petition for review; and

(D) an assertion that the appeal is from a final order or judgment that disposes of all parties' claims, or information establishing the court of appeals' jurisdiction on some other basis;

(5) a statement of the issues presented for review;

(6) a concise statement of the case setting out the facts relevant to the issues submitted for review, describing the relevant procedural history, and identifying the rulings presented for review, with appropriate references to the record (see Rule 28(e));

(7) a summary of the argument, which must contain a succinct, clear, and accurate statement of the arguments made in the body of the brief, and which must not merely repeat the argument headings;

(8) the argument, which must contain:

(A) appellant's contentions and the reasons for them, with citations to the authorities and parts of the record on which the appellant relies; and

(B) for each issue, a concise statement of the applicable standard of review (which may appear in the discussion of the issue or under a separate heading placed before the discussion of the issues);

(9) a short conclusion stating the precise relief sought; and

(10) the certificate of compliance, if required under Rule 32(g)(1) [*e.g.*, if the brief satisfies length requirements through word or line count under Rule 32(a)(7)(B), rather than through page limitations].

B. Components of Answering and Reply Briefs

If you represent the "appellee" or "respondent," the party seeking a ruling affirming the judgment of the court below, you must file an answering brief. In the United States Courts of Appeals, for example, Federal Rule of Appellate Procedure 28(b) provides that the appellee's answering brief should include all the components listed for the appellant's opening brief except for subsection (a)(9); however, the appellee may adopt the statements of jurisdiction, issues, case, facts, and standard of review presented in the appellant's brief if the appellee is satisfied with them.

According to subsection Rule 28(c), the appellant may respond to the appellee's answering brief with a reply brief, but the reply brief can dispense with most of the statements set forth in the appellant's opening brief. In addition to an argument responding to the answering brief, the reply brief need contain only a table of contents and a table of authorities.

C. Formatting and Other Formal Requirements

Rules of procedure or local court rules typically specify additional formal requirements regarding such things as typeface, line spacing, margins, overall length, and the color of the cover sheets for the opening, answering, and reply briefs.

The specified form for the information on the cover of an appellate brief varies in different jurisdictions. In some jurisdictions, the cover sheet includes the caption of the case in the same basic format as it appeared in trial pleadings and briefs, as illustrated by the sample briefs at the end of this chapter and Chapters 14 through 16. In other jurisdictions, including the United States Courts of Appeals, rules of procedure require the cover to include certain identifying information, which attorneys usually present on several widely spaced lines that are centered on the cover page.[1]

D. Filing the Brief in Hard Copy and Electronically

Court rules traditionally contemplated that appellate advocates will provide multiple copies of briefs in "hard copy," printed or typewritten on paper. More recently, however, most federal courts and many state courts have adopted rules that permit or require parties to file briefs electronically, and some court rules permit electronic briefs to include hyperlinks that connect citations in the brief to cited authorities or to parts of the record.[2]

United States Supreme Court rules require briefs submitted to that court to be filed both electronically and in hard copy.[3]

II. Statement of Issues

The art of stating issues in an office memorandum is discussed in detail in Section III of Chapter 6 and Section III.A of Chapter 7. You should review those principles now as a starting point for drafting the statement of issues in your appellate brief. When drafting an issue statement in a brief, however, you should additionally strive to phrase the issue in a way that suggests a favorable response or otherwise serves to advocate your client's case.

A. Issue Statements as Preliminary Advocacy

Your statement of the issue can invite the court to apply an analytical framework or standard of review that best suits your client's arguments. Of course, you should develop that strategy primarily in the argument section of the brief. However, you can make the judge more receptive to your approach by initially exposing her to the theme of your brief in your statement of the issues.

For example, suppose that you represent an appellant who appeals from a trial judge's decision to deny a preliminary injunction. You know that the appellate court will overturn that decision only if the trial judge abused her discretion, provided that the trial judge applied the proper legal standards to the facts.[4] However, you believe that her ruling leaves some room for questions about the content of the legal rules governing injunctions that she applied to the facts. Accordingly, you might use the statement of the issue to invite the appellate court to find error in the trial judge's formulation of the legal rules, which formulation would be subject to unrestricted review, as discussed in Chapter 17:

> In denying Surge Corp.'s request for a preliminary injunction, did the trial judge apply an incorrect legal rule by requiring a showing of likelihood of success on the merits, rather than using a "sliding-scale" test that would justify a preliminary injunction upon a showing of especially great irreparable harm and at least substantial questions on the merits?

The opposing counsel could argue that the trial judge applied a sliding-scale test and that the judge's balancing of the facts does not reflect an abuse of discretion under the most flexible of legal rules. Nonetheless, he might frame the issue so that it emphasizes the restricted standard of review of the ultimate ruling and refers only abstractly to potential questions about choices among legal rules:

> Did the trial judge properly exercise her discretion to deny preliminary injunctive relief on the ground that Surge Corp. failed to make the requisite showing on the merits under applicable legal rules?

Of course, the nature of the opportunity to promote a favorable approach in the statement of the issue will vary with the circumstances of each appeal. For example, an appeal in a contract dispute might raise a purely legal question about whether the peculiar facts of an exceptional case justify a special exception to the general common law requirement of consideration for contract formation. If so, the parties might use their statements of the issue, as well as their arguments, to appeal either to the appellate judges' senses of fairness and justice or to their appreciation of the benefits of certainty in the law.

In those circumstances, if you represent the party who would benefit from an exception to the general rule, you might use the statement of the issue to promote the value of fairness by vividly and concretely emphasizing the peculiar facts of the case:

> Does McGowin's moral obligation to perform his promise to pay Webb for past services give rise to a legal obligation in light of the serious physical injuries suffered by Webb and the immeasurable benefit he gave to McGowin in heroically saving McGowin's life?

This statement of the issue appeals to the appellate court's corrective function: reaching a just result on the unique facts of the case before it, even if that requires a departure from general principles.[5]

In contrast, if you represent the party who would benefit from application of the general rule, you would advance a different theme. Specifically, you might use the statement of the issue to promote the consideration rule in its abstract form or to emphasize the general policies supporting the rule:

> Did the trial court correctly reject a vague and uncertain "moral obligation" exception to the fundamental principle that a promise made in recognition of past services lacks consideration and therefore is unenforceable?

This issue appeals to the appellate court's institutional function: the wisdom of applying the rule in nearly every context, the importance of maintaining the vitality of a longstanding rule, and the need for certainty and predictability in the law.[6]

B. Credibility of the Advocate

In phrasing the statement of the issue to advocate an approach or a conclusion, you should not be so anxious to invite a favorable response that you state a false issue. For example, assume that you represent a criminal defendant who appeals from a state conviction for illegal possession of cocaine. The applicable criminal statute defines "possession" as contemporaneous intent and ability to exercise physical control over the substance. If the trial judge correctly instructed the jury on the applicable legal rules and definitions, you might still argue that substantial evidence did not support the jury finding of ability to exercise control over the cocaine. If so, the following statement of the issue would not effectively advance your client's cause:

> Is proof of ability to control an illegal substance a requisite element of a conviction for illegal possession of that substance?

Under currently accepted legal definitions in the state, an appellate judge would readily agree that the question presented by this statement of the issue must be answered affirmatively. However, she would object that the question does not fairly characterize any genuine issue on appeal. Because the trial judge correctly instructed the jury on the applicable legal standards, your implicit attack on the completeness of the instructions would be futile. Instead, your issue statement must fairly address your client's true contention on appeal:

> Is the jury's finding of Wade's ability to control the cocaine unsupported by the evidence in light of undisputed testimony that the officers found Wade standing outside the locked automobile containing the cocaine, without a key to the automobile?

Thus, you must recognize limits on your efforts to invite a favorable response to a statement of the issue. Specifically, you must maintain credibility and must fairly link the statement of the issue to your genuine argument on appeal.

III. Statement of Procedural History

Rules of procedure or local court rules will specify whether you must state the procedural history in a separate section or combine it with the historical facts. If the rules require you to state the procedural history in a separate section, they typically designate the section as the "Statement of the Case." If the rules instead require you to combine the facts and procedural history, they typically designate the combined section as either the "Statement of the Case" or the "Statement of Facts." With either format, the essential elements of a statement of procedural history are brief descriptions of "the nature of the case, the course of proceedings, and the disposition below."[7]

In the opening paragraph of the statement of procedural history, you should introduce the parties and generally describe the claims and defenses that they presented in the trial court. Next, you should chronologically recite the portions of the trial history and the rulings of the court that are relevant to the issues on appeal, including the trial court's final judgment and the appellant's filing notice of appeal. In a brief to a second-level court of appeal, you should also summarize the ruling of the intermediate appellate court. As described in Section I above, court rules in some jurisdictions might require you to discuss additional matters.

Once you have identified parties as the appellant and the appellee in your brief, you would do well in any jurisdiction to follow federal appellate rules for referring to parties:

> References to Parties. In briefs and at oral argument, counsel should minimize use of the terms "appellant" and "appellee." To make briefs clear, counsel should use the parties' actual names or the designations used in the lower court or agency proceeding, or such descriptive terms as "the employee," "the injured person," "the taxpayer," "the ship," "the stevedore."[8]

IV. Statement of Facts

A. Telling a Compelling Story

The opening statement of facts in a brief can play a surprisingly important role in your advocacy. A persuasive statement of facts near the beginning of your brief may incline a judge to rule in favor of your client even before the judge has considered the legal analysis. If so, the judge may take advantage of the flexibility or uncertainty in the legal principles to reach the result that the facts show to be just, provided that she can do so without departing from clearly controlling precedent or otherwise upsetting the orderly development of a coherent body of law. A persuasive opening statement of facts will help make the judge receptive to the legal and factual analyses in the argument section of your brief.

As you can imagine, the appellant's statement of facts and the appellee's statement of facts should evoke very different reactions in the reader. Each brings the client's story to the fore while stating the facts accurately, fairly, and completely.

Good examples of fact statements appear in Exercise 18.1. The excerpts in Exercise 18.1 are taken from a case in which a shopper sued a department store and others for wrongfully detaining him after accusing him of shoplifting. The fact statement in each brief tells the story from a very different perspective than that advanced in the opposing brief. The brief for the shopper emphasizes facts that show how events unfolded from the shopper's perspective, detailing how he entered the store twice and made three separate purchases during those visits. The brief for the department store emphasizes facts that show how events unfolded within the perception of store employees, who were confused by the shopper's multiple purchases, some placed in the same shopping bag.

Each brief states the facts fairly, accurately, and completely, with citations to the record. Yet, each also succeeds in presenting the client's perspective in an engaging manner that holds the reader's attention. A simple trip to the store for farm tools unfolds as a drama, complete with the shopper's flirtation with a store employee, tough talk between the shopper and security guards, and a shoving match between the shopper and a police officer resulting in the shopper stumbling headfirst through a wall of the store's security room.

Not every case will present such dramatic events; consequently, it will not always be easy to present your facts in a way that "commands the reader's attention" and "compels the reader to keep reading."[9] Nonetheless, if you develop a good theme as discussed in Chapter 12, if you employ the techniques of persuasive writing style explored in Chapter 13, and if you emphasize facts that tell the story from your client's perspective, any case can lend itself to telling a compelling story.[10]

B. Constraints That Build Trust

To present the facts persuasively, you might be tempted to slant the record misleadingly in favor of your client's case or to introduce legal arguments and conclusions in the statement of facts. Neither technique will succeed. They will only undermine your credibility with the court. Conversely, if you combine persuasive themes and writing style with accuracy and completeness, judges likely will turn to your statement of facts as a trustworthy reference.

1. Advocacy with Credibility

If you riddle your statement of facts with exaggerations or misleading omissions, you will simply diminish your credibility. Instead, your statement of facts should display your client in a favorable light while reflecting a concern for completeness and accuracy. If the judge is convinced that your statement is accurate and complete, he may repeatedly turn to it for a fair summary of the record, resulting in maximum exposure of the subtle advocacy of your statement.

a. Organization of Facts

Rather than omit unfavorable facts, you should place them in a context that minimizes their impact and that helps you emphasize favorable facts. In addition to the techniques of persuasive writing discussed in Chapter 13, you can use the organization of the entire fact statement to emphasize the favorable facts. Chronological order of facts may be the clearest and most logical; it is certainly the order most often recommended by judges. However, you can increase the impact of favorable events by describing them in the places of greatest emphasis: the beginning and end of the fact statement. If you can do so without unduly sacrificing clarity and continuity, you can justify departing from chronological order or at least supplementing a chronological statement with a second reference to a critical and favorable fact at the beginning or end.

For example, if a defendant in a murder case has pled not guilty and is seeking to suppress evidence of an illegal search, the defendant's chronology normally should not begin with the death of the victim, but perhaps with the illegal search. The prosecution in that case, on the other hand, might begin with the defendant's relationship with the victim prior to the victim's death.

b. Variation in Emphasis

You can also emphasize favorable facts by using specific, concrete descriptions and strong verbs in active voice. Conversely, you can lessen the impact of unfavorable facts by describing them in general, abstract terms.

For example, suppose that Samuel Hughes, convicted of first-degree murder, had sought at trial to mitigate the offense by showing that he was intoxicated at the time of the crime and therefore could not have premeditated the killing. On appeal, he hopes to persuade the court to interpret the statutory requirement of premeditation in a restrictive manner so that it will apply only to deliberation with a relatively clear mind.

As appellate counsel for Hughes, you could emphasize the intoxication, while referring to the murder with a light touch, even though you must concede that Hughes struck the fatal blow, as established by several eyewitnesses:

> When he fatally injured the decedent, Samuel Hughes was staggering from the effects of a full pint of whiskey.

This statement refers to both the killing and the victim in abstract terms and in a subordinate clause. Moreover, it humanizes the defendant in the main clause by referring to him by name and describing his intoxication vividly.

Conversely, as the prosecutor on appeal, you could deemphasize Hughes's intoxication by referring to it generally, and you could emphasize his aggressive conduct by describing it in gruesome detail:

> While under the influence of self-induced intoxication, the defendant murdered Grace Smith by bludgeoning her from behind with a baseball bat.

This statement relegates the defendant to anonymity by referring to him with a procedural label. In contrast, it names the victim, thus inviting the reader to recognize her as a person, rather than a statistic. Moreover, the description of the attack as one from behind tends to portray the victim as particularly sympathetic and defenseless. The statement not only refers to the defendant's impaired state of mind abstractly and in a subordinate phrase, it invites the reader to reject intoxication as a mitigating factor by characterizing it as self-induced. Finally, powerful verbs—"murdered" and "bludgeoning"—convey the horror of the assault.

Neither of these statements directly addresses the legal issue of statutory interpretation. Both are designed, however, to remind the judge of the concrete factual context in which the statute will apply in this case. Each statement portrays the event in a light that could make the judge more or less receptive to a restrictive interpretation of the statute.

2. Premature Legal Argument

If your fact statement crosses the line between presenting facts in a favorable light and prematurely introducing legal argument, you could undermine its effectiveness as a vehicle for making the judge receptive to your main argument. A judge knows that the legal argument of a brief will be one-sided, and he generally reserves judgment on legal conclusions until he has read both briefs. But he may be more willing to develop an immediate impression of the case from an apparently complete and accurate statement of facts.

For example, if the prosecutor's statement of facts specifically characterizes an act as premeditated, thus assuming a favorable interpretation of that statutory element, the judge may react defensively; he may warn himself that he should resist such a mixed conclusion of law and fact until he has thoroughly studied the arguments in both briefs. On the other hand, if the prosecutor's statement of facts vividly describes the convicted defendant as seething from a humiliating insult and then selecting a baseball bat as a weapon for retaliation after rejecting a cue stick as insufficiently weighty, the judge is invited to draw his own conclusion that the statutory element of premeditation does not require a restrictive interpretation to account for intoxication. Even if tentative or subconscious, that conclusion could predispose the judge at an early stage to accept the prosecutor's explicit legal arguments and conclusions in the argument section of the prosecutor's brief.

Conversely, when the judge reaches the argument section of the brief, he may resist arguments supporting conclusions that you had bluntly attempted to force on him in the statement of facts. He will be more comfortable with arguments that confirm conclusions he had reached on his own after reading apparently nonargumentative facts.

3. Permissible Sources for the Facts

Your statement of facts on appeal is subject to two further limitations. First, except for matters within common knowledge or otherwise subject to judicial notice,[11] the appellate court and the litigants are constrained by the trial court record as the exclusive source of the facts of the dispute. In a fully tried case, those facts are reflected in testimony recorded in the reporter's transcript, in documentary evidence admitted at trial, and in any physical evidence admitted at trial and retained by the trial court clerk. If the trial court disposed of the case on the pleadings or on summary judgment, the facts are reflected in the allegations of the pleadings or in the preliminary presentation of evidence on the motion for summary judgment. Rules of procedure and local court rules will set forth the responsibilities of the parties, primarily the appellant, in forwarding all or part of the trial court record to the appellate court and in filing relevant portions in an appendix to the appellate briefs.[12]

Second, if findings of fact are made by a jury or by the trial court, those findings take on greater significance than the underlying record of testimony and other evidence because of the restricted appellate review of such findings, as discussed in Chapter 17. If the appellant wishes to challenge the findings of fact, the appellant should refer to the underlying record of evidence to support the challenge; however, the findings will stand unless they are clearly erroneous or unsupported by substantial evidence. If the appellant instead chooses to limit the attack to a challenge of the trial judge's formulation of legal standards or the judge's application of those standards to facts, the appellant must rely on the lower court's findings of fact. Such an argument may include supplementary references to illuminating evidence, but only if consistent with the findings. The appellee should focus on either the findings or the underlying evidence supporting the findings, depending on which response most appropriately meets the appellant's challenge. These strategic considerations are illustrated in Section V.D.1, below.

As discussed in Chapter 17, Section I, when you refer to facts or procedural history in any section of your appellate brief, you must cite to the source. Applicable rules may require you to cite directly to the underlying record on appeal or to an appendix that contains excerpts of the record.[13]

V. The Argument

Earlier chapters and exercises have provided you with the basic information and skills you need to formulate, organize, and express your arguments in any brief. In summary, for each issue you should

1. state the conclusion you want the court to adopt in an argumentative point heading,
2. argue for a favorable interpretation of legal authority,
3. apply the legal rules to the facts, and
4. state the conclusion that you want the appellate court to reach.

This section will supplement the earlier chapters by examining some characteristics that are peculiar to appellate arguments.

A. Summary of Argument

Some rules of procedure and local court rules will require, or at least permit, appellate advocates to include a summary of the argument immediately before the main argument.[14] If applicable rules do not require a summary, you should include one in a separate section if your brief is sufficiently complex that an overview of your arguments will substantially enhance your reader's comprehension. If a summary in a separate section is neither required nor appropriate, you nonetheless should consider beginning your argument with an overview paragraph that outlines your arguments and conveys the theme of your brief.

If you do include a summary of argument in a separate section of your brief, you should place it under a section heading entitled "Summary of Argument." United States Supreme Court Rule 24.1(h) calls for a "clear and concise condensation of the argument made in the body of the brief," and it contemplates a multi-paragraph summary, because it states that the summary should be "suitably paragraphed."

The summary, however, should not stretch into several pages. A summary should do no more than briefly explain your major points in a few paragraphs, citing only to the most significant authorities. Along with the collection of point headings in your Table of Contents, the Summary of Argument can provide your reader with a general road map of her journey through your brief. If the summary delves into your argument in even moderate detail, however, it will make the main argument seem repetitive, to the irritation of your reader.

B. Standard of Review

Standards of appellate review are examined in detail in Chapter 17, and their significance to appellate strategy and argument is evident throughout the current chapter. Not surprisingly, the standard of review for each issue on appeal is a matter of great interest to the court as well as to the advocates. Consequently, even if applicable court rules do not require it, you should state the standard or standards of review, either in a separate section of the brief or at the outset of your argument for each issue on appeal. Your statement might be as simple as a single sentence, such as the following reference to unrestricted review: "This Court will engage in *de novo* review of the district court's summary judgment for the defendant. *See Heininger*. . . ."

Occasionally, the standard of review will be a matter of dispute between the parties; if so, you should devote a section of your argument to this topic, just as you develop other arguments in your brief. In an appeal by your client from a nonjury trial in federal court, for example, the parties might dispute whether the trial judge correctly classified a finding as one of law or fact. You might have reason to argue that a finding classified as a "finding of fact" should be treated instead as a mixed finding of law and fact in which questions about the boundaries of the legal rule predominate. If the appellate court agrees with your description of the finding, it might review the finding without restriction, as a question of law rather than as a finding of fact.

C. Arguing the Law—The Role of Policy Analysis

1. When the Question Is One of First Impression

On questions of first impression in a jurisdiction, courts of all levels will consider policy arguments in an effort to develop the law in a way that best suits the social needs and existing legal framework of the jurisdiction. If the parties advance competing legal approaches from other jurisdictions, or novel approaches based on scholarly commentary, a court typically will seek to determine which proposed rule will best promote the values and policies that are reflected in existing case law or enacted law.

For example, prior to the Supreme Court's recognition of a constitutional right to marriage equality in *Obergefell v. Hodges*, lower courts wrestled with difficult questions relating to the scope of existing precedent and the appropriate standard of constitutional scrutiny of state statutes that barred same-sex marriage. The outcome in these cases, however, was often influenced by broad policy considerations regarding the appropriate role of the judiciary. When lower courts rejected challenges to legislative bans, they frequently invoked a policy of deferring to elected members of the legislature and to democratic deliberation on questions of great social import; in contrast, courts that struck down same-sex marriage bans frequently emphasized equality principles and the duty of the courts to uphold constitutional rights.[15]

2. The Enhanced Role of Policy Analysis on Appeal

Appellate briefs differ in style from pretrial and trial briefs, partly because they examine the underlying policies of legal standards more frequently or to a greater extent. Depending on the procedural posture and other circumstances of an appeal, this difference in approach may be reflected in such factors as the restrictions on appellate review of factual findings, the appellate court's institutional function of developing a cohesive body of law, and the varying degrees to which stare decisis controls decisions at various levels of the court system.

Unless the appellant assumes the difficult burden of challenging factual findings made in the trial court, the appellate briefs likely will explore questions about the content of legal rules, either in the abstract or in the process of determining whether the accepted facts satisfy the rules. Because the appellate court can overrule its own precedents, it will consider policy arguments that favor or oppose extending, limiting, modifying, or overruling those precedents.

The institutional function of the appellate courts further encourages policy analysis in appellate brief writing. For two reasons, this effect is greatest in the highest court of a jurisdiction. First, unlike an intermediate court of appeals, the highest court is not bound by the precedent of any court within that jurisdiction. Second, the highest courts in many jurisdictions will accept review of some kinds of lower court decisions only after a discretionary determination that appellate resolution would help develop a cohesive body of law or otherwise would significantly affect the outcome of many cases other than the one that serves as the vehicle for addressing the questions.

Thus, more often than in trial briefs, appellate advocates will allocate substantial portions of their arguments to the policies underlying legal rules and to the social and jurisprudential consequences of retaining or abandoning those rules. Moreover, these characteristics typically will be even more pronounced in a court of last resort than in an intermediate court of appeals.

For example, the following two passages are excerpts of arguments about the proper application of precedent of the state supreme court, the highest court in the state. The first argument could be addressed to the trial court or even to the intermediate court of appeals. Because neither court can overrule the state supreme court precedent, the argument focuses on the applicability of the precedent to the facts of the dispute:

B. The trial judge erred in instructing the jury that Bramwell could be liable for the tort of wrongful discharge if he discharged Kirkeide in "bad faith" rather than in violation of public policy.

Introduction to argument

The trial court's instruction on the tort of wrongful discharge fails to distinguish between conduct that violates a public policy and conduct that might strike the employee as unfair or unwarranted in the context of a specific employment relationship. This instruction permitted the jury to award damages against Bramwell for conduct that is not a tort in this state.

General legal rule

The New Maine Supreme Court has recently recognized a cause of action in tort for wrongful discharge. However, it carefully limited its holding to discharges that violate public policy:

> Thus, an employer is liable in tort for wrongful discharge if it discharges an employee for a reason that violates an important public policy of the state. Pronouncements of public policy will most often be found in our state's constitution and its legislation.

Blass v. Arcon Co., 337 N. Me. 771, 776 (1996).

In *Blass*, the employer discharged a truck driver in retaliation for the driver's refusal to transport toxic wastes in unsafe containers. The employer was liable in tort for wrongful discharge because its conduct violated the policies of state environmental and occupational safety statutes. *See id.* at 777.

In-depth case analysis

In contrast to *Blass*, Bramwell's discharge of Kirkeide in this case did not violate any public policy. At most, Bramwell acted hastily and exercised poor business judgment, but not in a way that implicates public policy. Yet, the trial court's instruction permitted the jury to impose liability. . . .

Application to facts

In the preceding illustration, the *Blass* decision did not need to address whether a discharge can be tortious for reasons other than a violation of public policy; therefore, it does not preclude future extensions of the new tort of wrongful discharge. Nonetheless, the brief writer has reasonably assumed that a trial court or intermediate court of appeals would not readily extend a newly recognized tort beyond the terms of the Supreme Court's holding. Thus, the brief writer concentrates on explaining the holding of the *Blass* decision and distinguishing it.

In contrast, the following passage is addressed to the New Maine Supreme Court, the mythical author of the *Blass* decision. Because that court can overrule, limit, or extend its own precedent, the argument spends more time on policy analysis. Specifically, it argues that, as a matter of policy, the court should not broaden the tort of wrongful discharge beyond the holding of the *Blass* decision.

B. The trial judge erred in instructing the jury that Bramwell could be liable . . . .

The trial court's instruction on the tort of wrongful discharge fails to distinguish between conduct that violates a public policy and conduct that . . . .

Introduction to argument

Although this Court has recently recognized a cause of action in tort for wrongful discharge, it carefully limited its holding to discharges that violate public policy:

General legal rule

Thus, an employer is liable . . . .

Blass v. Arcon Co., 337 N. Me. 771, 776 (1996).

In *Blass*, the employer discharged a truck driver in retaliation for the driver's refusal to transport toxic wastes in unsafe containers . . . .

In-depth case analysis

Policy analysis

This court should reject Kirkeide's invitation to extend the tort of wrongful discharge beyond the holding of *Blass.* This state has long promoted the policy of freedom of contract, permitting contracting parties to shape their own rights and obligations. *See, e.g., Snell v. Abundes,* 128 N. Me. 217, 221 (1970). Even if limited to violations of public policy, the tort of wrongful discharge effectively limits the parties' freedom to create a contract that is terminable at the will of either party. Any further restriction on the freedom to contract would require courts to review nearly every contested business decision that affects the tenure of an employee. To preserve freedom of contract and to conserve judicial resources, this Court should narrowly tailor the tort of wrongful discharge to impose liability only for discharges that offend the values of society as a whole, and not for employment decisions that merely reflect a failed relationship between two private parties.

Application to facts

In our case, the trial court's instruction, approved by the court of appeals, extended the tort of wrongful discharge beyond the holding of*Blass.* By permitting an award of damages for a "bad faith" discharge, ...

In a final example, the author of an amicus brief, Professor Ralph Brill, helped to persuade the Illinois Supreme Court to broaden the exceptions to the traditional common law rule that a landowner owed no duty of care to protect a trespasser from serious harm. The opening paragraphs of the Argument section of the amicus brief equated the traditional rule with outdated doctrines of property law that courts had already abandoned:

Primogeniture has long ago been abolished. The doctrines of Worthier Title and the Rule in Shelly's Case have faded into history. No longer does a landowner own upward to the heavens and downward to the center of the earth; aircraft may fly overhead without trespassing, and utilities may gain easements for their wires and pipes. The rule of caveat emptor has been tempered or abolished; in fact, sellers now impliedly warrant the habitability of the property they sell. And landlords no longer are free to avoid responsibility for protecting their tenants from harm.

These and other ancient doctrines derived from our English heritage have been altered or replaced out of recognition of their purely

> feudal origins, and their inconsistency with modern life, mores, practices and problems.
>
> However, one major vestige of these bygone times has remained, at least in theory, the limitation on the landowner's duty to trespassers on the land. . . .

3. The Persuasive Value of Warning about Negative Consequences

Of course, an advocate should always explain to a judicial panel why the holding desired by the advocate is consistent with precedent, logical analysis, and sound policy. But advocates should not overlook the persuasive power of combining this positive argument with a negative story about the undesirable consequences of the holding sought by the opposing party.

Judges normally are relatively cautious creatures. When creating precedent, they are sensitive to the risk of taking the law on a path that will be difficult to traverse in future cases, or one that may lead to an undesirable destination. Accordingly, an advocate frequently can dissuade a judge from adopting a proposed holding by describing the difficulties of applying the resulting rule to other factual contexts, or by explaining how the holding could lead to an absurd result if logically extended. In this fashion, the advocate can make the judge more receptive to the holding sought by the advocate's client. Indeed, a negative argument against an adverse holding may pack an even more persuasive punch than the advocate's positive description of the virtues of the holding desired by the advocate.

For example, in a sample passage in the preceding subsection, the writer warns that expansion of the tort of wrongful discharge would launch the judiciary on a path of inappropriately assessing whether every challenged discharge is consistent with sound business practices. Such a path not only would erode the established policy of freedom of contract, it also would divert judicial resources from matters more appropriately assigned to the judiciary.

In a different case, an advocate for the plaintiff might warn of the future repercussions of a holding that fails to recognize a claim on the plaintiff 's facts. The advocate might explain that the plaintiff 's case is not an isolated one and that a negative holding will lead to numerous injustices:

> Defendant correctly points out that this court has not yet based a finding of substantive unconscionability solely on price disparity. Nonetheless, such a finding represents a natural extension of existing precedent and is necessary to vindicate important policies favoring consumer protection. Failing to find unconscionability in grossly inflated and unfair pricing would leave countless consumers at the mercy of unscrupulous vendors, many of them highly trained and experienced in high-pressure sales tactics.

D. Arguing the Law and the Facts

1. Strategic Choices

The appellant will seek to overturn unfavorable findings or conclusions of the trial court. As explained in Section V.B above, the appellant will benefit from unrestricted appellate review of conclusions of law. Moreover, the appellate court is not bound by the trial court's characterization of a finding as one of fact or law. Accordingly, if you represent the appellant, you should try to characterize unfavorable mixed findings of fact and law in a nonjury trial as conclusions of law, which are reviewable on appeal without restriction. In a jury trial, on the other hand, a jury's mixed finding of fact and law normally will be treated as a finding of fact for purposes of restricted appellate review.

If an unfavorable finding is undeniably one of fact, you must make some strategic choices among alternative approaches on appeal. As counsel for the appellant, you must decide whether to challenge the unfavorable finding of fact under a restricted standard of review, argue that the trial court applied the wrong legal rule to the facts, or both.

For example, suppose the plaintiff in a federal civil rights suit won an award for compensatory and punitive damages against your client, a police officer, for false arrest in violation of the Fourth Amendment. At trial, the judge gave the following instructions to the jury over your objection:

> If you find that Officer Mullins arrested Ms. Wong without probable cause, you must find that Officer Mullins violated Ms. Wong's clearly established constitutional rights, and you must award Ms. Wong compensatory damages in the amount of her actual injuries. Furthermore, if you find that Officer Mullins was grossly and inexcusably careless regarding Ms. Wong's constitutional rights, you may exercise discretion to award Ms. Wong punitive damages in an amount that will punish Officer Mullins and discourage him and others from similar violations.

Applying these instructions to the facts, the jury found Officer Mullins liable and awarded Ms. Wong $25,000 in compensatory damages and $100,000 in punitive damages. The trial court also awarded Ms. Wong her reasonable attorneys' fees.

Your client, Officer Mullins, has appealed. As one of your arguments on appeal, you wish to challenge the award of punitive damages, which is necessarily premised on a jury finding that Officer Mullins was "grossly and inexcusably careless." You can attack the award in either or both of two ways.

First, to take advantage of unrestricted appellate review of matters of law, you can try to persuade the appellate court that the trial judge incorrectly instructed the jury on the law:

A. Officer Mullins is entitled to a new trial because the trial judge erroneously instructed the jury that it could award punitive damages for conduct less culpable than reckless disregard for constitutional rights.

The United States Supreme Court has established a recklessness standard for punitive damages in federal civil rights actions:

General legal rule

> We hold that a jury may be permitted to assess punitive damages in an action under § 1983 when the defendant's conduct is shown to be motivated by evil motive or intent, or when it involves reckless or callous indifference to the federally protected rights of others.

Smith v. Wade, 461 U.S. 30, 56 (1983).

A standard based on reckless misconduct or callous indifference requires a greater showing of culpability than simple negligence. *See Johnson v. Lundell* . . . . In *Johnson* . . . .

Related legal rules

The extraordinary nature of punitive damages justifies close scrutiny of the trial judge's instructions to ensure that they recognize even fine distinctions in culpability. Otherwise. . . .

Policy analysis

In this case, the trial court instructed the jury that it could award punitive damages if it found that Officer Mullins was "grossly and inexcusably careless." (III R.T. 52.) This instruction did not adequately convey the requisite standard: reckless or callous disregard of constitutional rights.

Application to facts: the instruction

Even when coupled with the adjective "grossly," the word "careless" connotes only a breach of duty rising to the level of negligence. . . .

Further analysis of instruction

The trial court improperly instructed the jury on the standard for punitive damages. Officer Mullins is entitled to a new trial so that the jury may apply the proper legal standard to the facts.

Conclusion

Alternatively, if you are prepared to labor against a restricted standard of review, you can try to persuade the appellate court to overturn the jury's implicit finding that Officer Mullins was "grossly and inexcusably careless." Under this approach, you must review the underlying evidence, such as the testimony at trial, and explain why the jury's finding is not supported by substantial evidence:

B. Alternatively, this court should vacate the award of punitive damages because substantial evidence does not support the jury's finding that Officer Mullins acted with the requisite culpability to justify punitive damages.

Introduction to argument

Even if the trial court's instructions adequately conveyed the culpability required for an award of punitive damages, the jury did not properly find such culpability on the part of Officer Mullins. At most, the evidence supports the conclusion that Officer Mullins made a reasonable mistake in judgment in chaotic circumstances. Therefore, the trial judge erred in denying Mullins's Motion for Judgment Notwithstanding the Verdict on the issue of punitive damages, and this Court should overturn the jury's award of punitive damages.

Rules governing review of jury's findings

This Court may overturn a finding of the jury if the finding is unsupported by substantial evidence in the record so that no reasonable juror could have made the finding on the evidence. *See* . . . . This substantial evidence standard permits appellate courts to review jury findings to guard against verdicts based on bias, passion, or incompetence. *See* . . . . To satisfy the purposes of such review, this court should scrutinize the record for . . . .

Examination of facts: the testimony

Officer Mullins's uncontradicted testimony establishes the reasonableness of his actions. He testified that the report over his squad car radio identified the robbery suspect only as a young man of slight build with dark, shoulder length hair. (II RT at 335-36.) One block from the robbery site, Officer Mullins spotted Ms. Wong walking at a very brisk pace away from the robbery site. *Id.* at 336. He initially passed her by because he was looking for a male suspect. *Id.* at 337. However, when he found no other suspects in the vicinity, he realized that Ms. Wong fit the description of the robbery suspect except for her gender. *Id.* at 339. He remembered that Ms. Wong was wearing jeans and a sweatshirt, and he realized that an agitated witness might have been mistaken about her gender. *Id.* at 339-40. Consequently, he turned his squad car around, found Ms. Wong again, and stopped her for questioning. *Id.* at 340.

Other testimony supports Officer Mullins's version of the events. Ms. Wong herself testified that she had been walking at an unusually brisk pace. (I RT at 327.) She also admitted that she had trouble answering Officer Mullins's questions. *Id.* at 331. Although in her testimony Ms. Wong offered innocent explanations for her hurried pace and her inability to communicate effectively with Officer Mullins, *id.* at 360, nothing in the record shows that these explanations were apparent to Officer Mullins at the time of the arrest. . . .

Analysis of testimony: permissible inferences

In sum, the evidence leads inescapably to one conclusion: In his eagerness to fulfill his duties as a police officer, Officer Mullins mistakenly arrested the wrong person, but he did not recklessly disregard anyone's constitutional rights in doing so. Quite the contrary, he took steps at several stages to safeguard Ms. Wong's rights.

Conclusion

The record simply does not contain substantial evidence supporting the jury's finding of sufficient culpability to justify an award of punitive damages. Apparently, the jurors misunderstood or ignored the trial court's instructions and based their verdict on irrelevant factors.

For these reasons, this Court should overturn the jury's award of punitive damages. The evidence does not support this extraordinary award.

Counsel for the appellee can respond to either of these arguments directly. In response to the first sample argument, for example, she can argue either that (1) the law permits an award of punitive damages for culpability less than recklessness, perhaps because "callous indifference" denotes a lower standard that equates to gross and inexcusable carelessness, or (2) the trial judge's instructions adequately conveyed the requisite standard of recklessness. In response to the second sample argument, she can (1) emphasize the restricted standard of appellate review, (2) describe evidence in the record that supports a jury finding of recklessness or callous indifference, and (3) explain why that evidence should be viewed as "substantial."

2. Varieties of Fact Analysis

As illustrated in the preceding subsection, the appropriate nature and depth of fact analysis on appeal will depend in part on two factors: (a) the nature of the appellant's challenge to the trial court's judgment, and (b) the procedural posture of the case when the trial court disposed of it.

a. Nature of Appellant's Challenge

For an example of the first factor, suppose that you represent the appellant and that you choose to challenge the trial judge's instructions on the law, as in the first sample passage in Subsection 1 above. Your arguments on such a challenge will often focus on the law and include only modest fact analysis. Specifically, after your arguments on the law, your application of the law to the facts could include no more than a comparison of the correct legal rule to the actual instruction and a statement about the need for a new trial with proper instructions to the jury:

> In this case, the trial court instructed the jury that it could award punitive damages if it found that Officer Mullins was "grossly and inexcusably careless." (III R.T. 52.) This instruction did not adequately convey . . . .
>
> . . . Officer Mullins is entitled to a new trial so that the jury may apply the proper legal standard to the facts.

In contrast, detailed fact analysis will be mandatory if the appellant challenges the findings of fact of the trial judge or jury, as did the appellant in the sample briefs at the end of this chapter. As illustrated in the second sample passage in Subsection 1 above, the parties then must review the record and argue whether the evidence supports the finding of fact under the applicable standard of review:

> Officer Mullins's uncontradicted testimony establishes the reasonableness of his actions. He testified that the report over his squad car radio . . . .
>
> Other testimony supports Officer Mullins's version of the events. Ms. Wong herself testified that she had been walking at an unusually brisk pace. (I RT at 327.) She also admitted . . . .
>
> In sum, the evidence leads inescapably to one conclusion: . . . .

> The record simply does not contain substantial evidence supporting the jury's finding of sufficient culpability to justify an award of punitive damages. . . .

b. Procedural Posture

Your fact analysis may also vary with the second factor: the procedural posture of the case at the time of trial disposition. Specifically, dispositions at different pretrial and trial stages will lead to appellate analyses of different kinds of facts.

For example, suppose that the trial court dismissed the action for failure of the complaint to state a claim for relief. On appeal, you can argue the law, but you will have no findings of fact or even underlying evidence in the record to which to apply the law. Instead, you must argue whether the factual allegations of the complaint state a claim for relief under the correct interpretation of the law.

On appeal from summary judgment, on the other hand, you ordinarily will have a record of preliminary showings of fact with documents, affidavits, and other discovery materials. Therefore, you can argue whether the evidentiary materials submitted by both parties created a genuine issue of fact for trial under the applicable law.

Finally, the record will include formally introduced evidence if either party has appealed from the trial judge's denial of a motion for a directed verdict or for a judgment notwithstanding the verdict after presentation of the evidence in a jury trial. Moreover, on appeal from judgment after a full trial, the record will include both the evidence and the findings of the judge or jury. As explored above, the record in either case may provide a fertile source for fact analysis, depending on the appellant's strategic choices and the nature of her challenge to the ruling or judgment in the trial court.

VI. The Conclusion

The discussion in Section III.C of Chapter 12 about the conclusion section of a brief applies with full force to appellate briefs. At the least, your conclusion must briefly restate the action that your client requests the appellate court to take. In a complex case, your conclusion may also include a brief summary and synthesis of the arguments presented in your brief.

Exercise 18-1

In addition to responding to the appellant's arguments on appeal, an appellee may file its own "cross-appeal" to affirmatively challenge aspects of a lower court's decision. The following excerpts are from the Opening Brief and Answering Brief on a cross-appeal filed by the appellee of the main appeal. The excerpts are limited to portions of the Statement of the Case and the entire Statement of Facts from each of those briefs.

1. Statements of the Case

Study the procedural history traced in the statements of the case in the opening brief and the answering brief. Identify the trial court rulings challenged by each party. Is it clear why both parties were dissatisfied, resulting in cross-appeals?

2. Statements of Fact

Study the statements of fact in the opening and answering briefs. Notice how each brief tells a story in narrative fashion, presenting the perspective of the client. Does each fact statement successfully present an apparently complete and neutral summary of the facts while placing the advocate's client in the best possible light?

Consider the points of conflict between the two fact statements. In what instances is the apparent conflict simply a reflection of each advocate using techniques of writing style to emphasize some facts and deemphasize others? In what instances is the conflict rooted in genuine disagreement about the factual conclusions that find support in the record? What is the legal significance on appeal of conflicting evidence in the record on a material point, given the procedural posture of this case?

APPELLEE'S [Sears Roebuck and Co.] OPENING BRIEF ON CROSS-APPEAL

STATEMENT OF THE CASE

Plaintiff-appellant Max Koepnick ("Koepnick") commenced this action by filing a complaint on December 5, 1983 (C.T. at 1). The defendants named in the complaint were defendant-appellee Sears, Roebuck & Company ("Sears") and the City of Mesa ("Mesa"). The complaint set forth claims in six counts, which were all alleged to have arisen out of an incident that occurred at the Sears store at Fiesta Mall in Mesa, Arizona on December 6, 1982. Sears was named as defendant in only four of the counts. These were Count One for false arrest, Count Four for trespass to chattel, Count Five for invasion of privacy and Count Six for malicious prosecution. Mesa was named as defendant in Count Two for false arrest and Count Three for assault and battery. Mesa was also named as a co-defendant with Sears in Counts Five and Six.

. . . .

The jury returned verdicts against Sears for $25,000.00 in compensatory damages and $500,000.00 in punitive damages on Count One for false arrest and $100.00 in compensatory damages and $25,000.00 punitive damages on Count Four for trespass to chattel (9R.T. at 101-03). The jury also returned verdicts against Mesa for $50,000.00 on Count Three for assault and battery and $100.00 on Count Four for trespass to chattel (9R.T. at 101-03). Judgment was entered on the verdicts on February 25, 1986 (C.T. at 97; Appendix A).

. . . .

A hearing on the post-trial motions was held on April 17, 1986. Upon consideration of the motions, the court granted Sears' and Mesa's motions for judgment N.O.V.[16] on Count Four for trespass to chattel and granted Sears' motion for new trial on Count One for false arrest. The court granted judgment N.O.V. for defendants on the trespass to chattel claim as Koepnick failed to present evidence that the alleged trespass caused any damage or injury, which is an essential element of an actionable claim. The court granted a new trial on the false arrest claim as the court determined that reasonable cause to detain Koepnick existed as a matter of law and that, therefore, it had erred in instructing the jury on the issue of reasonable cause (Minute entry dated May 14, 1986; Appendix B).

. . . .

Koepnick filed a notice of appeal on July 24, 1986, with respect to the trial court's order granting Sears' motion for judgment notwithstanding the verdict on Count Four for trespass to chattel and for a new trial on Count One for false arrest (C.T. at 124). Sears filed a notice of cross-appeal with respect to the portions of the judgment dated February 24, 1986, granting judgment in favor of Koepnick and the portions of the order dated July 18, 1986, denying Sears' motion for judgment notwithstanding the verdict on Count One for false arrest and conditionally denying defendant Sears' motion for new trial on Count Four for trespass to chattel (C.T. at 128). No appeal was taken by either Koepnick or Mesa with respect to the adjudications of the claims asserted by Koepnick against Mesa. Accordingly, Mesa is not a party to this appeal.

. . . .

STATEMENT OF FACTS

On December 6, 1982, Koepnick drove to the Sears store located at Fiesta Mall to get some screwdrivers (4R.T. at 145-47). He arrived at approximately 5 p.m. (4R.T. at 145). Once in the store, he was assisted by Mara Thomas, a sales clerk in the hardware department (4R.T. at 147; 8R.T. at 36). After Koepnick selected the tools he wanted, Thomas carried them to the cash register (4R.T. at 148). Koepnick was waited on at the cash register by Bruce Rosenhan, another sales clerk, who rang up the tools for Koepnick (4R.T. at 150-51; 7R.T. at 88). These tools consisted of a set of screwdrivers, a wrench set, a nut-driver set, an open-end wrench set and a set of pliers (7R.T. at 88-89; Ex. 11). Koepnick asked Rosenhan for an itemized receipt (4R.T. at 151; 7R.T. at 88). Rosenhan bagged Koepnick's purchases, stapling the bag closed with the receipts on the outside (4R.T. at 151; 7R.T. at 89). Koepnick left the cash register area (4R.T. at 171; 7R.T. at 89).

After waiting on Koepnick, Rosenhan went out to work on the sales floor (7R.T. at 90). Rosenhan saw Koepnick again in the hardware department approximately 15 minutes after he had waited on him (7R.T. at 90-91). Koepnick came over to where he and Thomas were in the back of the department (7R.T. at 90). Rosenhan saw Koepnick speak to Thomas and pull a large wrench out of the shopping bag Rosenhan had earlier stapled closed (7R.T. at 91). At that time, Koepnick's bag was open and there were no receipts in view on it (7R.T. at 91). Rosenhan realized that the wrench Koepnick pulled out of the bag was not one of the wrenches from the sets that he sold to Koepnick (7R.T. at 91). When Rosenhan finished with the customer he was helping, he asked Thomas if Koepnick put the wrench back in his bag and whether she had sold it to him (7R.T. at 92). Thomas told him that Koepnick put it back in his bag and that she had not sold that wrench to him or had anything to do with it (7R.T. at 92). Rosenhan asked all the other employees present in the department whether they had sold that particular wrench to Koepnick and learned that none of them had either (7R.T. at 92).

Rosenhan went to the front register and used the phone to call security (7R.T. at 92). He spoke with Steve Lessard, one of the security agents on duty at that time in the store (4R.T. at 77). It was approximately 5:35 to 5:40 when Lessard received the call from Rosenhan (4R.T. at 83). He informed Lessard that he believed that there was a customer in the store who was a shoplifter (4R.T. at 77). Lessard told him to meet in the sewing machine department, which is located next to hardware (4R.T. at 77-78). When Rosenhan and Lessard met, Rosenhan explained what had occurred with the purchase of the tools and the subsequent incident of the large wrench being observed in the bag (7R.T. at 93; 4R.T. at 78-79). Lessard radioed to Dave Pollock, another security agent on duty at Sears, and requested that he come and assist him (4R.T. at 79).

When Pollock arrived, Lessard explained what he had learned from Rosenhan and asked him to watch Koepnick while he spoke with the other employees (4R.T. at 79-80). Lessard went around the hardware department and spoke with each of the employees present there (4R.T. at 80). Among the employees he spoke with was Mara Thomas, who informed Lessard of her contacts with Koepnick and confirmed the fact that she did not sell or help Koepnick with the large wrench he had in his bag (4R.T. at 80-81; 8R.T. at 41).

After Lessard had spoken with all of the employees in the hardware department and confirmed that none of them sold the wrench in question, he observed Koepnick in the socket aisle (4R.T. at 82). Koepnick picked out some sockets and then put the bag he was carrying down at the cash register (4R.T. at 82). Koepnick went back to the socket aisle and picked up another socket (4R.T. at 82). While Koepnick was away from the cash register area, Lessard instructed Pollock to go by the shopping bag and confirm that the large wrench in question was still in it (4R.T. at 82). When Pollock went over to the bag, he observed that the bag was pulled open and the wrench was inside (7R.T. at 41). No receipts were seen in or on the bag by Pollock (7R.T. at 41, 84). Pollock reported back to Lessard and told him what he saw (7R.T. at 41).

Lessard and Pollock observed as Koepnick returned to the cash register and purchased some sockets (7R.T. at 42; 4R.T. at 82-83). As Koepnick began to leave the store, Lessard went to the clerk at the cash register and asked what items had been purchased, verifying that Koepnick had not paid for the crescent wrench in question at that time (7R.T. at 83-84). Lessard and Pollock followed Koepnick out of the store (4R.T. at 84). At no time did either observe Koepnick take any receipts off the shopping bag he was carrying (4R.T. at 84). As they followed Koepnick out of the store, they discussed the information they had and decided to stop Koepnick with respect to the large wrench in question (4R.T. at 84).

Koepnick estimated that it was approximately 6:15 P.M. when he exited the east door of the store (5R.T. at 72). Lessard approached Koepnick as he walked into the parking lot area approximately 20 to 25 feet from the door of the store (4R.T. at 87). Koepnick refused to stop when Lessard first spoke to him (5R.T. at 178; 4R.T. at 87-88). Koepnick testified that Lessard then came around in front of him, pulled the wrench in question out of the bag and told him that he did not have a receipt for it (4R.T. at 178). Koepnick was also told he was under arrest for shoplifting (4R.T. at 178). Both Koepnick and Lessard testified that Koepnick was shown identification by Lessard, although Koepnick testified that he did not see it clearly (4R.T. at 179-80; 4R.T. at 87-88). Koepnick did not show a receipt for the wrench when Lessard stopped him (4R.T. at 91; 5R.T. at 63).

Koepnick initially refused to return to the store with Lessard and Pollock (4R.T. at 179). Koepnick was informed that he had to return to the store with them (4R.T. at 180). After some further discussion, Koepnick was escorted up to the security office in the Sears store (4R.T. at 179-81; 5R.T. at 70-72). He was not handcuffed or physically injured in any way by the Sears employees (5R.T. at 70, 72). Once in the security office, Koepnick was instructed to sit down to wait for the police to arrive (4R.T. at 183).

In the security office, Lessard examined the shopping bag Koepnick had been carrying and found receipts for the purchase of the sockets (4R.T. at 94; 5R.T. at 72-73). No other receipts were found in or on the bag (4R.T. at 95). Although Koepnick had the receipts for his other purchases in his front shirt pocket, he never attempted to show them to the Sears employees (5R.T. at 63, 66). While waiting for the police to arrive, Koepnick asked if he could get a drink of water or go down to his truck, but those requests were refused (4R.T. at 183).

While Pollock watched Koepnick, Lessard continued his investigation and began to prepare his report of the incident (4R.T. at 97-98). Lessard telephoned the hardware department and spoke to Kim Miller, the hardware department manager. Lessard called the hardware department as he needed the stock number for the wrench in question (8R.T. at 72). He also wanted to have the audit tape on the cash register checked as there were no receipts in the shopping bag for the tool sets that Rosenhan had told him he had rung up for Koepnick (8R.T. at 72).

Officer Michael Campbell of the Mesa Police Department arrived at 6:30 P.M., approximately 15 minutes after Koepnick had been brought to the security office (6R.T. at 67; 4R.T. at 186). Campbell and Lessard stepped across the hall to permit Lessard to inform the officer as to what he had observed (4R.T. at 186; 4R.T. at 101-102). As Lessard was talking with Officer Campbell, Koepnick attempted to walk out of the security office (4R.T. at 187; 4R.T. at 58). Officer Campbell came out into the hallway and met Koepnick at the door to the security office (4R.T. at 187; 4R.T. at 59). Koepnick and Officer Campbell became involved in an altercation, resulting in Koepnick striking his head against the back wall of the security office (4R.T. at 187-88; 4R.T. at 60-64). After that occurred, Officer Campbell was able to handcuff Koepnick (6R.T. at 96-98).

Officer Campbell had made the decision to arrest Koepnick when the altercation started (6R.T. at 93). While he was being handcuffed by Officer Campbell, Koepnick took the receipts that had been in his shirt pocket and stuffed them inside his shirt (4R.T. at 189; 6R.T. at 96-97). Once Koepnick was handcuffed, Officer Campbell removed the receipts he had observed Koepnick stuffing inside his shirt (4R.T. at 66; 6R.T. at 100). The receipts that were found on Koepnick were examined and matched to the various tools Koepnick had in his shopping bag (4R.T. at 191; 4R.T. at 68).

During the altercation, Officer Campbell had instructed Pollock to use his radio to call for assistance (6R.T. at 98). Sergeant Reynolds and Officer Gates came to the Sears security office in response to the request (6R.T. at 108).

Lessard learned after the altercation that another sales clerk, Jeff Ward, had also been working in the hardware department that day (4R.T. at 103-104). Ward, however, had left the sales floor before Rosenhan observed Koepnick with the wrench in the shopping bag and called Lessard down to investigate the situation (8R.T. at 9-10). When Ward later returned to the hardware department, Miller informed him of the call from Lessard and that security had some questions about whether a customer paid for a certain wrench (8R.T. at 110). Ward told Miller that he had rung up such a wrench for a customer (8R.T. at 11). Miller took Ward up to the security office (8R.T. at 11). They arrived about the time the altercation occurred between Koepnick and Officer Campbell (4R.T. at 103; 8R.T. at 12).

Once Lessard became aware of Ward's contact with Koepnick, he interviewed Ward (4R.T. at 104). Ward stated that he had first observed Koepnick as Koepnick walked up to the cash register and pulled the receipt off a shopping bag that was lying on the counter (4R.T. at 104; 8R.T. at 6). Ward asked him if that was his package and Koepnick said it was (4R.T. at 104; 8R.T. at 6). Koepnick had a large combination wrench and a smaller set of wrenches with him to purchase (4R.T. at 104; 8R.T. at 6). Ward rang these items up, and Koepnick paid for them (4R.T. at 104). Ward then bagged these wrenches in a smaller brown bag, which Koepnick placed inside the larger shopping bag he already had (4R.T. at 104; 8R.T. at 104; 8R.T. at 8). Koepnick then placed the receipts Ward had prepared for the wrenches in his shirt pocket and left (8R.T. at 8). Ward did not see Koepnick again on the sales floor that night (8R.T. at 9). After Ward finished ringing up the other customers at the cash register, he left the sales floor (8R.T. at 9, 24). Ward told Lessard he had been on a break (4R.T. at 72). Ward could not recall at trial exactly where he went when he left the sales floor (8R.T. at 9).

After questioning Ward, Lessard discussed with the police officers the possibility that Koepnick had taken the wrench he purchased from Ward out to his truck and brought the shopping bag back in and put another wrench in it (4R.T. at 69-70). Lessard was familiar with this method of shoplifting through his work as a security agent (4R.T. at 105). The information Lessard had that caused him to believe that this was a possibility was (1) Ward's statement that he had bagged the large wrench in a separate brown bag that was not present in the large shopping bag Koepnick had when he was stopped, (2) Rosenhan's statement that there was a period of 15 minutes from the time he last saw Koepnick after his first purchase until he saw him again in the hardware department with the wrench, and (3) Koepnick's actions in not exhibiting the receipts for his purchases when he was detained (4R.T. at 105-06, 111).

The police officers made the decision to search Koepnick's truck (6R.T. at 101-02; 6R.T. at 128). Officer Campbell testified that he asked Koepnick for permission to search the truck and Koepnick consented (6R.T. at 130). Koepnick testified that he consented to the search only on the condition that he be allowed to go with them (4R.T. at 194). Lessard accompanied Officer Gates down to Koepnick's truck (4R.T. at 107). Officer Gates opened the vehicle and Lessard assisted him in looking in the truck (4R.T. at 107). No Sears merchandise was found (4R.T. at 107). The search of the truck lasted about two minutes (4R.T. at 72-73). Nothing was taken or damaged in the search (4R.T. at 110-11, 197).

Once Officer Gates and Lessard returned to the security office, the police officers discussed what action they would take (4R.T. at 197-98). Sergeant Reynolds made the decision to cite Koepnick for disorderly conduct for his actions in striking Officer Campbell (6R.T. at 130). After Koepnick received the citation, he was released by the Mesa Police Department (4R.T. at 198).

....

Respectfully submitted this 13th day of April, 1987.

GUST, ROSENFELD, DIVELBESS & HENDERSON

By ______________________________

Fred Cole
Roger W. Perry
Attorneys for Defendant-Appellee/Cross-Appellant

APPELLANT'S [Max Koepnick] CROSS-APPEAL ANSWERING BRIEF

....

STATEMENT OF THE CASE

On December 5, 1983, Plaintiff/cross-appellee Max Koepnick sued Defendant/cross-appellant Sears, Roebuck & Co. ("Sears") and the City of Mesa ("Mesa") for false arrest, assault, trespass to chattel (by further detaining him while searching his truck), invasion of his right of privacy and malicious prosecution. These claims all arose out of Koepnick's arrest for alleged shoplifting on December 6, 1982 (Appendix A, C.T. at 1). The counts in Koepnick's complaint alleging invasion of privacy against both defendants and alleging malicious prosecution, false arrest and punitive damages against Mesa were all disposed of by directed verdicts (Appendix B, C.T. at 97). Those issues are not involved in this appeal.

The remaining portions of Koepnick's complaint were tried to a jury on January 13-22, 1986. The jury awarded Koepnick $25,000 in compensatory damages and $500,000 in punitive damages against Sears for false arrest. It awarded him $100 in compensatory damages against both Sears and Mesa and $25,000 in punitive damages against Sears for trespass to Koepnick's personal property. . . .

....

On July 24, 1986, Koepnick filed a notice of appeal only from the portions of the trial court's order granting Sears' motion for new trial on his false arrest claim and for judgment N.O.V. on his claim of trespass to chattel (C.T. at 124). The portion of the litigation involving Mesa has been settled. Mesa is therefore not a party to this appeal and has not filed a cross-appeal. Sears filed a notice of cross-appeal with respect to other portions of the judgment on August 5, 1986 (C.T. at 128). The parties have stipulated that the cost bonds for their respective appeals are waived. This Court has jurisdiction concerning this appeal pursuant to A.R.S. §12-2101(F)(1).

STATEMENT OF FACTS

I. Koepnick and His Purchases.

Max Koepnick was a manager, foreman, and mechanic for a large Queen Creek farming operation whose assets exceed $2,500,000 (4R.T. at 145, 6R.T. at 21). His lawsuit resulted from his detention and arrest for shoplifting while he was purchasing tools for the farm at the Sears store in Fiesta Mall, Mesa, Arizona, on December 6, 1982 (4R.T. at 145-47). Koepnick paid cash for those tools and had the receipts for all of them in his possession when he was arrested, including the receipt for a 1 5/16 open-end crescent wrench. That wrench was the precipitating cause of his arrest.

Koepnick drove to Sears in the farm pickup truck he used for business purposes (4R.T. at 145-46). He entered the store at approximately 5:00 P.M. (4R.T. at 145, 5T 68). Business in the Sears store happened to be slow at that particular time (3R.T. at 13). Koepnick proceeded to the hardware department. He first purchased a five-wrench set, a nut-driver, an open-end wrench set, a plier set, and a set of screwdrivers (Ex. 11). Bruce Rosenhan, Sears hardware department manager, rang up those purchases on a cash register and stapled portions of the Sears seven-part handwritten receipt used at customers' requests for cash purchases to the outside of the bag (4R.T. at 149, 173). Sears' policy was to staple the register receipt and the original of the seven-part receipt to the outside of the bag (3R.T. at 22, 4R.T. at 45). The customer's purchases were also recorded automatically on the cash register tape (3R.T. at 18-19). The other six copies of the handwritten receipt may have been placed in a trash can on one of the shelves below the cash register (3R.T. at 21).

Koepnick then left his purchases at the cash register counter to look for a wrench (4R.T. at 151). During this time he flirted with a salesperson, Mara Thomas, who showed him various tools. Ms. Thomas then escorted him to the register where he purchased a 1 5/16 open-end crescent wrench. Sales clerk Jeff Ward made this sale. At that time, Ward prepared another handwritten seven-part form, since this sale was also for cash (8R.T. at 8-9, Ex. 12). As had occurred with Koepnick's first purchases, the crescent wrench was bagged and stapled together with the receipt. This bag was placed inside the first, with the wrench handle sticking out (4R.T. at 173). At trial, Koepnick denied the wrench was ever put into a separate brown bag (4R.T. at 173, 174). He also testified all the receipts were stapled onto the original bag (4R.T. at 17). Jeff Ward then left the hardware department to take a break (3R.T. at 12, 8R.T. at 9).

Koepnick picked up the bag from the register counter and started to leave. However, he then remembered he needed some spark plug sockets (4R.T. at 174). He therefore went back to the register, set the bag down and proceeded to look for the sockets (4R.T. at 175).

During this time, manager Rosenhan contacted Sears security guards Steve Lessard and Dave Pollock, who began observing Koepnick. Lessard spoke with all four hardware department employees then on the floor about whether there was a receipt for the open-end crescent wrench (3R.T. at 9). None could remember ringing it up. However, Lessard failed to ask those employees if anyone else was then on a break (*id.*). He simply assumed those four employees were the only ones on duty (3R.T. at 10-11). Moreover, no one checked either the register tape or the receipts tray behind the counter (3R.T. at 34). Doing so would have confirmed that Koepnick had in fact paid for the crescent wrench, since the cash register tape could have been checked against the wrench's stock number (3R.T. at 19-20). Lessard also admitted at trial that he also could have searched for the six discarded copies of Koepnick's three sets of receipts that were probably in the trash container below the cash register (3R.T. at 21-22).

Meanwhile, Lessard had Pollack walk past the bag on the counter to confirm visually that the wrench in the bag was a Sears product (3R.T. at 28). Pollack could see a price tag sticker on the end of the wrench. However, although the stapled receipts on the bag were also in plain view, they were not checked against the merchandise (4R.T. at 175). Lessard himself admitted that Pollack had an "easy view" of the receipts (3R.T. at 29-30).

Lessard himself also saw the bag on the counter. However, he did not notice the handwritten receipts and cash register tape stapled to the top of the bag (3R.T. at 27). He also testified at trial he could not dispute testimony that the register receipts and handwritten receipts were stapled to the top of the bag (*id.*). He "didn't recall" whether anyone bothered to look for those receipts on the bag before Koepnick was stopped, although he conceded that it would have been a "fairly reasonable thing to do" (3R.T. at 30).

While this "investigation" was occurring, Koepnick located and purchased the sockets, returned to the register counter, picked up his bag from the counter, tore off all the receipts, placed them in his shirt pocket and left the store. Lessard and Pollack followed him (4R.T. at 177). Lessard estimated that he had between 20 and 25 minutes to make his investigation before he stopped Koepnick outside the store (3R.T. at 14). He even had time to discuss with Pollack that they had "done a thorough investigation" (3R.T. at 34).

II. Koepnick's Detention, Arrest, Assault, and Eventual Release.

Koepnick placed the time and location of his stop and arrest by Lessard and Pollack at 6:15 P.M., in a dark, dimly lighted area of the Sears parking lot (5R.T. at 72). Koepnick's version of the facts was that in that dimly lighted area two punks accosted him, yelled "Hey," and positioned themselves on each side of him (4R.T. at 178). They then jerked the wrench out of the bag stating, "You don't have a receipt, do you?" (4R.T. at 180-81).

Koepnick thought he was being hustled. He asked who his captors were. Their response was, "We're security guards." (4R.T. at 179). Koepnick asked them to "prove it." In response, one of the guards flashed his badge (*id.*). However, Koepnick could not see it clearly (4R.T. at 179-80). Koepnick was then told that he was going with the guards and that he was under arrest for shoplifting (4R.T. at 180).

Koepnick was escorted to an upstairs security room, denied a drink of water, and seated, with no inquiry as to whether he had a receipt for the wrench (4R.T. at 180). The Mesa police were called. When Koepnick attempted to enter the hallway to obtain a drink of water, he and Officer Campbell (who was wearing a bullet-proof vest) got into a pushing match. As a result, Koepnick fell or was thrown head first through the wall of the security room, causing him to incur neck and other injuries (4R.T. at 60-64).

Koepnick was then handcuffed. While he was recovering from the blow to his head, the Mesa police and the Sears security staff verified every item he had purchased against every receipt on the table of the security room (4R.T. at 68). Lessard had also verified with Jeff Ward that Koepnick had in fact purchased the crescent wrench. The bag which supposedly contained the wrench had already been accounted for in the security office. However, despite all of Koepnick's purchases being fully accounted for, the Mesa police continued to detain him at Sears' insistence while Lessard conducted a non-consensual, unescorted search of his truck, looking for an alleged "brown bag" (4R.T. at 71). Koepnick had approximately $1,200-1,400 in cash and all of his business records in the truck (4R.T. at 197). The search, which required approximately 15 to 20 minutes, proved fruitless

(4R.T. at 197-98). During this time, Koepnick remained under detention. Had Lessard not decided to search Koepnick's truck, Koepnick would simply have been cited immediately for disorderly conduct and then released (6R.T. at 115). Instead, after the search, Koepnick was then freed of his handcuffs and cited for disorderly conduct (4R.T. at 198). He was finally permitted to leave the Sears security room at about 7:00 P.M. (4R.T. at 199).

DATED this day 11th of May, 1987.

Respectfully submitted,
THOMAS J. QUARELLI, ESQ.
WILLIAM J. MONAHAN, P.C.

By ______________
William J. Monahan
and
PAUL G. ULRICH, P.C.

By ______________
Paul G. Ulrich
Attorneys for Appellant
Cross-Appellee

Sample Appellate Briefs

The following opening and answering briefs illustrate all the critical features of an appellate brief. The appeal was successful: The Georgia Supreme Court reversed the convictions. *Debelbot v. State*, 839 S.E.2d 513 (Ga. 2020).

The briefs are edited to omit sections and passages unnecessary for the purpose of displaying samples of their components. This editing extends to omitting the Appellant's reply brief, partly because legal writing programs at law schools typically do not assign one, for pragmatic reasons.

Supreme Court of Georgia

Albert DEBELBOT, Appellant,

v.

THE STATE, Appellee.

No. S19A1474.

August 30, 2019.

On Direct Appeal from the Superior Court of Muscogee County in SU09CR1843

Brief for Appellant Albert Debelbot

Carrie Sperling, WI Bar. No. 1094464, Wisconsin Innocence Project, Univ. Wisconsin Law School, 975 Bascom Mall, Madison, Wisconsin 53706, (608) 262-3646, csperling@wisc.edu, for appellant Albert Debelbot.

Thomas Moffett Flournoy III, GA. Bar No. 265998, Office of the Public Defender, 420 10th Street, Columbus, Georgia 31901, (706) 653-4301, mflournoy@columbususga.org, for appellant Albert Debelbot.

TABLE OF CONTENTS

TABLE OF AUTHORITIES[17]

INTRODUCTION

This Court remanded to address whether Albert Debelbot received ineffective assistance when his trial counsel: (1) failed to object after prosecutors told jurors that, to convict Albert Debelbot of his daughter's murder, jurors could be less than 51% certain; or (2) failed to investigate and present expert testimony that would have shown the Debelbots' daughter died of natural causes. The motion-for-new-trial court analyzed neither. Indeed, the motion-for-new-trial court ignored the first issue entirely.

Instead, the lower court's order focused only on expert testimony presented at the post-trial hearings. Here, too, the motion-for-new-trial court did not engage in any discernible ineffective-assistance analysis. The order doesn't cite *Strickland v. Washington*, the landmark decision that established the test to analyze ineffectiveness. Nor does the order cite a single ineffective-assistance case. In fact, the words "deficiency" and "prejudice," which are the pillars of ineffective-assistance analysis, appear nowhere in the order denying relief.

In lieu of an ineffective-assistance analysis, the court wielded the wrong tools to arrive at a collection of erroneous conclusions. Most significantly, the lower court seemed to fundamentally misunderstand its role. The court explicitly adopted language reserved for thirteenth-juror analysis, which is not relevant on appeal. In this role, the lower court asked whom did it believe: the State's experts or the defense experts. . . .

If the motion-for-new-trial court had applied the correct legal framework, the court would have granted relief.

First, counsel did provide ineffective assistance by failing to object to the prosecutor's incorrect statement of its burden of proof. Counsel was clearly deficient. As this Court noted, "we cannot conceive of any good reason that a competent criminal defense attorney could have to fail to object to such an egregious misstatement of the law." Therefore, the real question is whether this deficiency prejudiced Debelbot. Here, too, this Court offered considerable guidance. This case, this Court noted, was "a close question." Further, this Court observed, "a case like this one, where there was no direct evidence to prove that Albert, Ashley, both of them, or neither of them killed McKenzy, could turn on reasonable doubt, and the verdict could be affected by an argument that 50-50 proof is good enough."

Second, counsel provided ineffective assistance by failing to investigate and present expert testimony that would have shown the Debelbots' daughter died of natural causes. In sum, the Debelbots' trial should have been a battle of the experts. The State's case hinged entirely upon one expert. No other evidence implicated Albert Debelbot. Trial counsel could have presented experts, who would have both attacked the State's theory and presented an alternate cause of death.

Counsel's twin failures, independently or cumulatively, denied Debelbot any meaningful representation at trial.

For these reasons, this Court should reverse with an instruction to grant a new trial.

STATEMENT OF THE CASE

Just sixty hours after witnessing the birth of their first child, the Debelbots suffered her loss, and they were arrested on June 2, 2008, thirty-two hours after her death. (T22. 308-09, 311, 395.) Ashley and Albert were indicted for murder, felony murder, and cruelty to a child. (R. 11.) They both pleaded not guilty and were tried together in October 2009. (T21-22.) They were found guilty on all counts and sentenced to prison for the remainder of their natural lives. (R1. 12-13.)

Albert filed a timely motion for new trial on November 6, 2009. (R1. 147-150.) Upon entry of new counsel in February 2014, Albert's motion for new trial was set for hearing. (R2. 152-54.) Over the course of the following three years, in consolidated proceedings, Albert and Ashley presented evidence to support their motions for new trial. They submitted their motions for decision on August 10, 2017. (T38. 2096-98). The superior court denied relief on all claims. (R15, 2567-69.) Albert Debelbot timely filed his appeal, presenting four claims of ineffective assistance of counsel, and this Court heard arguments on August 7, 2018.

On March 13, 2019, this Court vacated the superior court's denial of Albert's motion for new trial and remanded the case with instructions. *Debelbot v. State*, 305 Ga. 534 (2018). On May 6, 2019, the superior court issued its Order on Remand, again rejecting the motion for new trial without addressing Albert Debelbot's Sixth Amendment right to counsel claims. (R15. 2645-59.) Albert timely filed his notice of appeal on May 31, 2019. The case was docketed with this Court on July 10, 2019, with the initial brief due on July 30, 2019. This Court granted his timely requests for extension of time to file Appellant's opening brief on August 30, 2019. A copy of that order is attached.

STATEMENT OF JURISDICTION

This Court has jurisdiction over this appeal because Albert Debelbot was convicted of the offense of murder. Ga. Const. Art. VI, § 6; Ga. Sup. Ct. R. 19 n.l.

STATEMENT OF FACTS

When Albert and Ashley Debelbots' daughter, McKenzy, died just three days after her birth, the GBI medical examiner's default diagnosis was intentionally inflicted, non-accidental trauma, a homicide. (T21. 150-51.) Dr. Lora Darrisaw arrived at this conclusion based on injuries within Baby McKenzy's head: skull fractures on both sides and bleeding within the brain and between the skull and scalp. (Ex41. (147).) Although Dr. Darrisaw found some evidence that would have been inconsistent with acute, inflicted trauma - the right side of McKenzy's brain was "soft and mushy," the left side was "unremarkable," and there was no external evidence injury (T21. 156-57; T28. 572; Ex. 41. (147))–s he didn't question her diagnosis or investigate alternative causes. She came to her opinion based on the absence of a historical account of any other cause. (T30.719.)

Although police found no evidence of foul play, and neither Albert nor Ashley spoke an incriminating word, they both became the default perpetrators because they were alone with McKenzy the evening she died.

At trial, Dr. Darrisaw's testimony was the sole evidence a crime occurred and was the only evidence that implicated the Debelbots. Dr. Darrisaw assumed that Baby McKenzy's injuries were inflicted "less than four, probably no more than one or two hours" before her death. (T21. 210-11.) Dr. Darrisaw ruled out the possibility that birth trauma caused McKenzy's injuries because the symptoms would have been visible immediately to everyone, and the hospital never would have released McKenzy. (T21. 154-55.)

Albert's counsel never tried to investigate an alternative explanation for McKenzy's death because he trusted Dr. Darrisaw's work. (T21. 154-55.)

At trial the State used the lack of any challenge to its medical expert as a tactical weapon. (T21.118; T22. 288, 313-17, 328, 400-01, 403-05, 409; T29.536, 545,-46, 549, 551.) The prosecutor told the jury that the Debelbots were both responsible because "[t]hey have both, in the face of the medical evidence, just sat here and told you, well, I don't know what happened." (T29.545.) The prosecutor told the jury that because: "They won't tell us what happened. They're both responsible." (T29. 545.)

The State asked the jury to assume McKenzy's injuries didn't occur at the hospital because the Debelbots hadn't sued the hospital:

> And, by the way, . . . , if [defense counsel] actually thought that the . . . injuries could have been caused by the birthing process, they'd be suing the hospital. And you know it. They'd be suing the hospital, the doctors. They'd be suing the nurses. They'd be suing the insurance. That's what they do. They haven't done that. Why? Because they don't have any evidence that the hospital did this or that these injuries were caused by the *birthing process*.

(T29. 533-34.)

The State continued to capitalize on the Debelbots' failure to present an expert:

> And in seventeen months what has the defense brought you? What have they brought you into the court to refute our evidence? Nothing. Except the two people charged with killing their baby telling you, yeah, we don't know what happened; we don't know.

(T29. 536.)

The State argued that the jury didn't need to know which one of the Debelbots inflicted the fatal injury:

> [Defense counsel] says we have to show or we have to tell you which one killed the child; we can't tell you which one killed the child. Here's what I don't want you to do. You should not get in there and say, you know, I'm not really sure which one did it so I'm just going to let both of them go.

(T29. 536, 545.)

The prosecutor wrapped up by patently misrepresenting the meaning of beyond a reasonable doubt:

> You don't have to be ninety percent sure. You don't have to be eighty percent sure. You don't have to be fifty-one percent sure. [Beyond a reasonable doubt] does not mean to a mathematical certainty.

(T29. 546). Even though this misrepresentation seemed calculated to mislead, defense counsel sat silent instead of holding the State to its burden of proof.

When the jury convicted both of the Debelbots, there was no way to discern whether it understood its duty - to acquit unless convinced to an utmost certainty that the State proved each element of the offense against each defendant. See In re Winship, 397 U.S. 358, 364 (1970).

After securing new counsel in 2014, Albert amended his motion for new trial. (R2. 152) Ashley followed suit in early 2015. (T3. 397.) The Debelbots presented evidence in the motion-for-new-trial hearing that should have been presented at trial. The Debelbots' four medical experts, with seven distinct but relevant medical specialties, rendered their opinion that McKenzy suffered a vascular insult in utero that compromised her brain and skull, leading to her untimely death. *Debelbot*, 305 Ga. at 540.

Dr. John Plunkett, a board-certified forensic pathologist with expertise in infant head trauma, had been retained by Ashley's trial counsel prior to trial. Due to a scheduling conflict, he did not testify at the Debelbots' trial. (T26.132-33.). . .

Dr. Plunkett presented at least three significant contributions to the overall diagnosis of McKenzy's brain injury. . . .

The State lodged no objections to any of the exhibits upon which Dr. Plunkett relied, and they were admitted. (T26. 172.)

Dr. Julie Mack, board-certified radiologist with a certificate of added qualifications in pediatric radiology, testified that the CT scans from Martin Army Hospital showed McKenzy's brain had suffered significant loss in volume and her skull hadn't formed properly. (T28. 490-91, 507.). . .

The State conducted voir dire regarding Dr. Mack's credentials, and the motion-for-new-trial court accepted Dr. Mack, stating, "I believe without question that Dr. Mack is qualified as a general radiologist and I believe that she has the education and training as a pediatric radiologist." (T28. 456-457.). . .

Dr. Mack found evidence of this brain loss in the autopsy photos. She compared the CT image to an autopsy photo of McKenzy's brain. (Ex41. (43).) The two images, she testified, show a smaller temporal and occipital lobe on the right side of her brain. (T28. 517-18.) These images were admitted into evidence as DX21 without objection. (Ex41. (16-43); T28. 524-25.)

Dr. Mack linked this evidence to the timing of the injury. She explained, "[T]here's no question the loss of brain occurred intrauterine. You can't lose this amount of volume of brain after birth in three days. Can't happen. Absolutely can't happen." (T28. 492-93.). . .

The State did not object to Dr. Mack's use of 3D reconstructions as demonstrative, and they were admitted as demonstrative exhibits. (T28. 558; Ex41. (181-83).)

Dr. Peter Dehnel, a board-certified pediatrician who specializes in the care and treatment of newborns, testified to matters related to pediatrics. (T27.269.)

Dr. Dehnel testified that he has been a practicing pediatrician in Minnesota for over 33 years and has treated several thousand infants in the course of his career. (T27. 277-78.) . . .

Dr. Dehnel also focused on the medical examiner's finding of a "soft and mushy" right-brain. (T27. 306.) He testified that if blunt force caused injury to McKenzy's skull and brain, the affected area would first swell and the tissue would be "tense, firm brain tissue; not soft and mushy as it's described" in the autopsy report. (T27. 306.) He concluded that McKenzy's brain must have been developing abnormally before her birth. (T27. 307-08.) . . .

Dr. Daniel Sahlein - triple-board-certified in neurology, radiology, and diagnostic neuroradiology with a special certificate in interventional neuroradiology - testified as the final defense witness. (T35. 1544-1546.) Of all the doctors who testified in the motion-for-new-trial hearing, Dr. Sahlein had the most relevant experience and training regarding infant vascular obstructions. . . .

Dr. Sahlein testified that McKenzy's brain and skull injuries began before her birth. (T37. 1700.) He based his opinion on her medical records and CT scans. There, he found evidence of blood clots in McKenzy's brain. (T37.1716.) The clots that formed in the dural sinus were at least 3 to 7 days old. (T37. 1715-17.) Clots and bleeding in other areas of the brain were of different ages, which means the bleeding happened over a period of time. (T37.1717.) Dr. Sahlein's diagnosis was untreated dural sinus thrombosis, a condition he has seen many times. (T37. 1695-1697.) . . .

Dr. Sahlein testified that injuries like McKenzy's, because of their location and the immaturity of her brain, would likely go unnoticed by both the hospital staff and her parents. . . . Given that McKenzy's exam in this case was documented by a medical student and second-year resident, Dr. Sahlein wasn't surprised that her brain injury was missed. (T37. 1729, 1853-54.) . . .

In the motion-for-new-trial hearing, Dr. Darrisaw disagreed with the defense experts' cause of death diagnosis, but she conceded facts that lent support to the Debelbots' conclusion about the timing and causation of McKenzy's death.

Under cross-examination, Dr. Darrisaw agreed that the type of injuries she found in McKenzy's autopsy could have been caused by an accident, birth-related injuries, or "any type of prenatal injuries." (T30. 720-21.) Dr. Darrisaw explained that she came to her original conclusion of a non-accidental cause of death based on "a lack of evidence of an alternative explanation" for McKenzy's injuries. (T30. 719.) In other words, no one informed her that something accidentally happened to McKenzy. (T30. 720.)

Dr. Darrisaw also admitted a crucial point, that the right side of McKenzy's brain was smaller than the left. (T28. 606-08.) She testified that although she didn't note the different sizes of the brain hemispheres in her autopsy report, she did note the consistency of the right side, which was "a lot softer and mushier." (T28. 606.) . . .

Although Dr. Darrisaw testified with near certainty at trial that McKenzy's injuries occurred within a few hours of her death (T21. 209-11), she was much less certain in the motion-for-new-trial hearing. At trial, Dr. Darrisaw told the jury, "This baby after this injury is completely flaccid, unable to do anything and eventually dies very rapidly thereafter." (T21. 210.) But in the motion for new trial hearing, her testimony was nuanced. She said she "narrowed [the time of injury] down to the possibility or probability of [between eight and twelve hours]." (T30. 712.)

Dr. Susan Palasis did not testify at trial. The State's neuroradiologist testified in the motion-for-new-trial hearing. Although a well credentialed pediatric neuroradiologist, Dr. Palasis admitted that she had no expertise in the feeding patterns of newborns. (T31. 1015.)

Dr. Palasis offered evidence that contradicted the medical examiner. Dr. Palasis insisted that the brain shifted right because the left side of the brain, but not the right side, became swollen from the trauma. (T31. 999.) This finding directly contradicted Dr. Darrisaw's autopsy finding that there were no signs of significant brain swelling. (Compare T28. 610-11, with T31. 1024-27.) . . .

Dr. Palasis also contradicted the medical examiner on the timing of the injuries. When asked how long it would take for the right side of the brain to become "soft and mushy," Dr. Palasis testified, "I'm definitely not talking minutes, not even hours. I'm talking most likely within twenty-four hours or less." (T31. 998-99.) She continued, "I would expect the injury could have occurred within a 24-hour period." (T31. 1011.) But, she testified, the process could take 24 hours or more. (T33. 1344-45.) This testimony obliterated the State's contention at trial that McKenzy's brain injuries could only have occurred while she was in the Debelbots' care.

When asked about the age of the bleeding within McKenzy's brain, Dr. Palasis contradicted even further the testimony given at trial. She testified that some of the bleeding was acute to subacute, which she defined as up to 7 to 10 days. (T33. 1332-34.)

These admissions on the timing of the injury - from almost certainly within a few hours to quite possibly up to 7 days—destroyed the State's direct link between the injuries and the identity of the perpetrator. Given that the Debelbots had visitors the afternoon they brought McKenzy home and Albert left the home during the evening, this change in timeline meant that the State could no longer, with certainty, put Albert in the same room with McKenzy when the injuries occurred.

Despite the extensive, well documented evidence from defense experts—evidence that directly contradicted Dr. Darrisaw's conclusion at trial—the motion-for-new-trial court denied the Debelbots' request for a new trial. In November 2017, the court asked the State to draft an order denying relief. (T15. 2564.) The resulting order based the denial on 13th juror grounds under *Lundy v. State* and on *Harper v. State*. (T15. 2567-69.) The order never mentioned Albert's ineffective assistance of counsel claims, which require an entirely different analysis than claims based on general grounds.

The Debelbots appealed the terse order on January 10, 2017. After extensive briefing and oral argument, this Court remanded the case, asking the motion-for-new-trial court to provide more precise findings. (T15. 2594-2617.) The court's resulting Order on Remand ignored Albert's ineffective assistance of counsel claims. The Order cites only 13th juror grounds as the basis for denying Albert relief from conviction. (T15. 2654, 2658.) The Order cites only *Harper v. State*, 249 Ga. 519 (292 S.E.2d 389) (1982), in assessing the admissibility of defense expert testimony and evidence. (T15. 2652.) Absent from the Order was any discussion of the uncontested material facts the defense experts presented in the motion-for-new-trial hearing. The court ultimately concluded that the "verdict was not contrary to the evidence" nor "decidedly and strongly against the weight of the evidence." (T15. 2658.)

ENUMERATION OF ERRORS

In violation of the Sixth and Fourteenth Amendments to the United States Constitution, Albert Debelbot was denied effective assistance of counsel when his trial counsel failed to:

1. object to the State's closing argument that re-characterized proof beyond a reasonable doubt as less than a preponderance of the evidence, and

2. investigate or present medical evidence to challenge the medical examiner's testimony on the cause and timing of McKenzy's injuries.

STANDARD OF REVIEW

Albert's claims of ineffective assistance of counsel are entitled to de novo review. Reviewing courts give no deference to lower courts when they use the wrong legal test. *Strickland v. Washington* requires a two-pronged analysis of deficiency and prejudice. 466 U.S. 668, 687 (1984). The motion-for-new-trial court didn't apply *Strickland*'s two-prong review nor assess the cumulative effects of counsel's alleged deficiencies. The court based its holding on general grounds under O.C.G.A. § 5-5-20 and § 5-5-21. (*See* R15. 2658) (addressing only whether "the verdict was not contrary to the evidence" and "was not decidedly and strongly against the weight of the evidence").) Therefore, de novo review is appropriate.

The motion-for-new-trial court also applied the wrong legal standard to its evidentiary rulings. When the lower court misapplies the legal standard, de novo review is appropriate. *See Williams v. State*, 328 Ga. App. 876, 880 (763 S.E.2d 261) (2014) (stating that "while the abuse-of-discretion standard presupposes a 'range of possible conclusions' that can be reached by a trial court with regard to a particular evidentiary issue, it does not permit a 'clear error of judgment' or the application of 'the wrong legal standard"'). Because the motion-for-new-trial court side-stepped the Georgia Evidence Code and wrongly applied *Harper v. State* to the evidentiary issues presented, the court's rulings on the admissibility of defense-expert testimony and evidence are subject to de novo review.

Finally, when a trial court excludes evidence exculpatory to the defense, this Court must review whether the lower court arbitrarily applied the state's evidentiary rules, thus infringing on a "criminal defendant's right to have a meaningful opportunity to present a complete defense." *Holmes v. South Carolina*, 547 U.S. 319, 324, 331 (2006) (overturning the state trial court's application of an evidentiary rule to exclude third-party guilt evidence because the rule was arbitrarily applied). To resolve Albert's claims of ineffective assistance of counsel, this Court must assess whether the motion-for-new-trial arbitrarily applied Georgia's Evidence Code.

ARGUMENT

In his motion for new trial, Albert Debelbot challenged his conviction based on ineffective assistance of counsel. This Court found at least two claims "deeply troubl[ing]" - counsel's failure to object when the State argued the jury could convict on less than a preponderance of the evidence and failure to investigate and present an alternative medical explanation for McKenzy's death. *Debelbot*, 305 Ga. at 535.

This Court remanded the case with specific direction to clarify what expert evidence, presented in the motion-for-new-trial hearing, was admissible and credible. *Id.* at 542-44. These findings were necessary in order to assess counsel's alleged deficiencies and any resulting prejudice under the *Strickland* test. *Id.* at 542.

On remand, the motion-for-new-trial court made admissibility and credibility findings. Only three findings pertain to the admissibility of defense expert testimony.

- The court found all defense experts were, indeed, qualified as experts in their respective fields but found their theory novel and not credible (R15.2645);
- The court relied on *Harper v. State* to exclude the defenses' images of McKenzy's CT scans because they were displayed on OsiriX viewing software (R15.2653); and
- The court relied on *Harper v. State* to exclude the defense experts' theory that an in-utero stroke caused demineralization of McKenzy's skull (R15.2653-54).

In addition to addressing the admissibility of defense expert evidence, the motion-for-new-trial court made several credibility findings. The court found: (1) defense experts lacked sufficient experience and qualifications to be credible (R15. 2655-56), (2) the jury wouldn't have given much weight to defense experts' opinions (R15. 2656-57), and, (3) in its role as 13th juror, the motion-for-new-trial court believed the State's experts over the defense experts (R15. 2654-55).

Albert's claims of ineffective assistance of counsel are unaffected by the motion-for-new-trial court's admissibility and credibility findings because the court applied the wrong legal principles to exclude defense-expert evidence and inappropriately weighed the credibility of defense experts against the State's experts to determine which were more believable. Strickland calls for a different analysis.

Under an appropriate application of clearly established federal law, Albert was denied his Sixth Amendment right to effective assistance of counsel.

I. Albert was denied effective assistance of counsel when trial counsel failed to object to the State's recharacterizing proof beyond a reasonable doubt as less than a preponderance of the evidence.

In closing, the prosecutor told jurors:

> Reasonable doubt. . . does not mean to a mathematical certainty. Which means we don't have to prove that ninety percent. You don't have to be ninety percent sure. You don't have to be eighty percent sure. ***You don't have to be fifty-one percent sure***. It does not mean to a mathematical certainty.

(T29. 546) (emphasis supplied).

The prosecutor's statement was "obviously wrong." *Debelbot*, 305 Ga. at 543. "Proof beyond a reasonable doubt is the highest standard of proof recognized in our system of jurisprudence." *Id.* at 544 (Bethel, J., concurring). Indeed, the United States Supreme Court has described the reasonable-doubt standard as akin to "near certitude." Jackson v. Virginia, 443 U.S. 307, 315 (1979).

Despite the prosecutor's gross misstatement of the law, defense counsel failed to object.

To prevail on a claim of ineffective assistance, Albert must show that counsel was deficient and that the deficiencies prejudiced him. *Strickland*, 466 U.S. at 687. The motion-for-new-trial court has never addressed counsel's failure to object to the prosecutor's closing. (*See* R.15 at 2567-69; 2645-58). Therefore, this Court conducts its own independent review of the record.

This Court has expressed "serious concern regarding the State's closing argument." *Debelbot*, 305 Ga. at 543. This Court found that the prosecutor's statement was "obviously wrong." *Id.* The statement "invited the jury to apply a significantly lower standard," one that is "repugnant to our system of criminal justice." *Id.* at 544 (Bethel, J., concurring). This Court could not "conceive of any good reason that a competent criminal defense attorney could have to fail to object to such an egregious misstatement of the law." *Id.* And because trial counsel's performance fell below an objective standard of reasonableness, this Court left the question of prejudice for a later cumulative error analysis. *Id.* Absent counsel's failure to object, there is a reasonable probability the result of the proceeding would have been different. *See Strickland v. Washington*, 466 U.S. at 693 (noting the standard does not require that "a defendant. . . show that counsel's deficient conduct more likely than not altered the outcome in the case").

This Court has already observed that the State barely produced sufficient evidence to support a conviction. *Debelbot*, 305 Ga. at 538 ("Although a close question, we conclude that this evidence was sufficient to allow the jury to find both Albert and Ashley guilty of malice murder"). The Court observed, "[a] case like this one, where there was no direct evidence to prove that Albert, Ashley, both of them, or neither of them killed McKenzy, could turn on reasonable doubt." *Id.* at 543. Given the weakness of the State's case, counsel's failure to object prejudiced the outcome. *See Tezeno v. State*, 343 Ga. App. 623, 630 (2017) (noting that even where the court finds sufficient evidence to support conviction, the defendant may still prevail on a Sixth Amendment right effective representation claim).

Even under a plain error analysis, which requires the appellant to make an affirmative showing that the error probably did affect the outcome below, the prosecutor's argument could have provided sufficient grounds to reverse Albert's conviction. *See Nations v. State*, 303 Ga. 221, 223-24 (2018) (noting that plain error requires the opponent of the evidence to show the evidence affected the outcome of his trial); *Gates v. State*, 298 Ga. 324, 327 (2016) (stating that plain error "requires the appellant to make an affirmative showing that the error probably did affect the outcome below").

This Court found plain error when a prosecutor argued in closing that a jury's "honest belief" in the defendant's guilt would suffice as proof beyond a reasonable doubt. *Ward v. State*, 271 Ga. 62, 63 (1999). The Court reasoned that the argument was "more akin to the preponderance standard used in civil trials than the reasonable doubt standard required in criminal prosecutions," and it overturned the defendant's felony murder conviction despite the presence of sufficient evidence to convict. *Id.* at 63; *see also Wetzel v. State*, 298 Ga. 20, 27 (2015) (overturning conviction where lack of guidance from the jury instructions "in conjunction with the blatantly incorrect explanation of the law offered by the State, left the jury without proper guidance on the relevant law").

Given that the prosecutor's remark in *Ward* met the plain error threshold, the prosecutor's misrepresentation in this case certainly meets a lower materiality showing. In this case, the burden of proof was not an isolated incident or a "mere slip of the tongue." *See Ward*, 271 Ga. at 63. The misrepresentation was part of a constant refrain - that the Debelbots' failure to provide an explanation for McKenzy's injuries was evidence of their guilt. (T21. 118; T22.288, 313-17, 328, 400-01, 403-05, 409; T29. 536.) The egregious misstatement on burden of proof was not a stray remark delivered in the heat of argument. It was a calculated crescendo.

Defense counsel, no better than a bump on the log, failed to object to the prosecutor's argument, a misstatement that any first-year law student would have caught. In a case like this, the verdict depended on jurors' understanding of the burden of proof. The State had a weak case, and the State "invited the jury to apply a significantly lower standard, which is repugnant to our system of criminal justice." *Debelbot*, 305 Ga. at 544 (Bethel, J. concurring).

Worse yet, the motion-for-new-trial court never engaged with this error. In 2017 and on remand, the motion-for-new-trial court offered no analysis. Under de novo review, the record in this case demonstrates that absent counsel's failure to correct the prosecutor's misstatement, there is a reasonable probability of a different result.

II. Where the medical examiner's opinion was the only evidence a his counsel failed to investigate or present an alternative cause of death.

Because the State relied solely on the testimony of the medical examiner to prove that Baby McKenzy was murdered by her parents, counsel's complete failure to embark on a medical investigation was objectively unreasonable. Had counsel investigated the medical evidence and presented an alternative explanation for McKenzy's death, there is a reasonable likelihood the outcome would have been different.

A. Trial counsel's decision to trust the medical examiner's opinion rather than investigate alternatives cannot be considered objectively reasonable under the circumstances.

Defense counsel's function is to "make the adversarial testing process work in the particular case." Strickland, 466 U.S. at 690. When the State's case rests on expert medical evidence, trial counsel cannot make strategic judgments about how to defend the case without investigating the strength and nature of the medical evidence. Ottlev v. State, 325 Ga. App. 15, 22 (2013); Goldstein v. State, 283 Ga. App. 1, 6 (2006). Even when counsel forgoes a medical defense to pursue another strategy, counsel's decision must be informed by a reasonable investigation that makes a medical defense unnecessary. *Wiggins v. Smith*, 539 U.S. 510, 522-23 (2003).

In Albert's case, counsel conducted no independent review of the medical evidence because he trusted the medical examiner. (T30. 793.) However, counsel's duty to investigate goes beyond his own side of the case. Counsel must investigate the other side's evidence too. *See Rompilla v. Beard*, 545 U.S. 374, 385-90 (2005). Furthermore, an unwillingness to second-guess a member of the prosecution team when her opinion is central to the case is objectively unreasonable. *See Thomas v. Clements*, 789 F.3d at 769 (finding deficient performance where counsel's failure to reach out "to an expert to review or challenge [the medical examiner's] findings acquiesced to the state's strongest evidence of intent despite its perceivable flaws"); *Elmore v. Ozmint*, 661 F.3d 783, 859 (4th Cir. 2011) (noting that the obligation to test the state's case "cannot be shirked because of the lawyer's unquestioning confidence in the prosecution").

The obvious defense was to challenge the medical examiner, who was not an expert in pediatrics, obstetrics, neurology, or neuroradiology. (T30. 772.) Had trial counsel consulted and presented experts to provide an alternative, non-criminal explanation for McKenzy's cause of death, the testimony would have been plausible, admissible, and could have raised a reasonable doubt about Albert's guilt. There is no strategic reason to have forgone such a challenge to the core of the State's case.

B. Had counsel presented medical experts at trial, their testimony would have been admissible and would have provided a reasonable probability of a reasonable doubt.

In the motion-for-new-trial hearing, the Debelbots presented the kind of defense that could have been presented at trial. Defense experts provided extensive testimony and dozens of exhibits to support their opinion that McKenzy's brain suffered a vascular insult while she was still in the womb. These experts concluded that had Baby McKenzy remained in the hospital the day of her discharge, she would have died at the same time.

The motion-for-new-trial court admitted each of these experts as experts in their respective fields and admitted dozens of exhibits that supported their opinions. (R15. 2645.) The decision to admit the evidence proffered by the defense was correct. The motion-for-new-trial court erred, however, in reversing some of its evidentiary rulings, ultimately applying Harper to exclude CT images "made in OsiriX" and defense experts' "novel theory [of] an in-utero vascular malformation causing demineralization of McKenzy's skull." (T15. 2653.)

1. The motion-for-new-trial court applied the wrong legal framework to erroneously exclude defense expert evidence.

The Georgia Code retains extremely permissive rules on expert admissibility in criminal trials. Section 24-7-707 governs expert testimony, stating that "the opinions of experts on any question of science, skill, trade or like questions shall always be admissible; and such opinion may be given on the facts as provided by other witnesses." Section 24-7-703 further provides that experts may rely on inadmissible facts and data to form their opinions, if they are "of the type reasonably relied upon by experts in the particular field." The threshold for expert admissibility in Georgia's criminal trials is widely considered to be lower than the threshold applied in civil proceedings. Ronald L. Carlson & Michael Scott Carlson, Carlson on Evidence 446-47 (6th ed. 2018).

To the extent that *Harper* applies in criminal trials, its role is limited. The *Harper* court adopted a "gatekeeping" mechanism as a way to exclude "junk science" disguised as expert testimony. Kenneth L. Shigley & John D. Hadden, *Georgia Law of Torts - Trial Preparation and Practice* § 26:5 (2019). *Harper v. State* has been used to exclude the use of truth serum but not accident reconstruction or gang evidence. *Lopez v. State*, 829 S.E.2d 862 (Ga. App. 2019); *Taylor v. State*, 337 Ga. App. 486, 492 (2016). *Harper* doesn't apply to medical experts' cause of death opinions, even where experts disagree. *See Smith v. State*, 302 Ga. 207, 211 (2017) (raising concerns that limitations on expert opinion that injuries resulted from abuse would also block defendants' expert testimony that injuries were consistent with an accident).

Harper doesn't require that experts hold a medical license to give testimony regarding a medical issue, as long as witnesses possess "certain training and experience to testify on issues within the scope of their expertise." *Hyde v. State*, 189 Ga. App. 727, 728 (1988); *Avret v. McCormick*, 246 Ga. 401 (1980).

The motion-for-new-trial court abused its gatekeeping function by side-stepping the Georgia Code and excluding expert evidence under *Harper*. Had the court applied the appropriate legal framework in its Order on Remand, it would have ended up where it started—deeming all the proffered expert evidence admissible. As the court appropriately ruled during the motion-for-new-trial hearing, the attacks on defense expert qualifications and the concerns about manipulation of the CT images go to the weight, not the admissibility of the evidence. (T36. 1645, 1652.) *See Morrison v. Koornick*, 201 Ga. App. 367, 370 (1991) (allowing a vascular surgeon who was not a radiologist nor an orthopedist but had a "fair amount of experience" in reading CT scans and "understanding the differences of expressed retroperitoneal bleeding" to testify about the CT scans because his lack of qualifications goes to weight rather than admissibility).

. . . .

4. Defense experts did not raise a theory of skull "demineralization"; therefore, there is no such theory to exclude under *Harper*.

The motion-for-new-trial court excluded what it characterized as the defense's "novel theory" that an "in-utero vascular malformation [caused] demineralization of McKenzy's skull." (T15. 2653.) It did so even though the State did not raise a specific, contemporaneous objection to such a theory. In fact, defense experts never proffered a theory of skull demineralization. A simple search of the transcripts reveals that no defense expert used the word demineralization. No defense expert testified that an "in-utero vascular malformation [caused] demineralization of McKenzy's skull." (R15. 2653.) The only witness who used the term demineralization was the State's expert, Dr. Palasis. (T31. 1058, 1060; T33. 1361-64, 1366.)

Defense experts described McKenzy's skull as "poorly formed" (T36.1669), "abnormally formed" (T27. 386, T28. 482, 537), "malformed" (T27.374), "underformed" (T27. 374, 394), and "non-mineralized" (T36. 1671-72, 1674, 1766-67). Specifically, Dr. Sahlein cited medical literature on a condition known as lacunar skull—a congenital defect linked to conditions where intracranial pressure interferes with the fetal skull development. (T37.1668-69.) He pointed out dark divots in the skull. (T37. 1668-91; T36. (93).) Dr. Sahlein described how the brain, which consists of ridges and valleys, under conditions of high pressure, press against the skull and leave defects in the developing skull. (T36. 1669.) Dr. Sahlein said this type of congenital defect is one he has seen in his practice. (T36. 1673.)

"Demineralization" is not the same theory. Demineralization suggests that the skull was once mineralized and de-mineralized over time - a condition that Dr. Palasis did not see in McKenzy's skeletal X-rays. (T31. 1056.) Defense experts, on the other hand, observed a skull that never properly formed in utero.

The motion-for-new-trial court wrongly applied *Harper* without establishing whether defense witnesses testified to a demineralization theory, and it excluded the "demineralization theory" absent a specific *Harper* objection. Worse, the motion-for-new-trial court cited only the State's expert testimony to identify and reject this "novel" theory. (R15. 2654 n.44.) Because defense experts offered no theory of demineralization, and the court cited no defense testimony to support its finding, this Court owes no deference to this finding. . . .

III. Where the State's case rested entirely on the medical examiner and the jury was told to convict on less than a preponderance of the evidence, counsel's failure to investigate or present an alternative cause of death undermines confidence in the trial's outcome.

Claims of ineffective assistance of counsel require a cumulative assessment of counsel's errors to determine whether the "decision reached would reasonably likely have been different absent the errors." *Strickland*, 466 U.S. at 696. This does not require a showing that counsel's actions "more likely than not altered the outcome." *Harrington v. Richter*, 562 U.S. 86, 111-12 (2011).

In assessing prejudice from deficient performance, the court must consider all of trial counsel's unprofessional errors against the totality of the evidence. Williams v. Taylor, 529 U.S. 362, 397-98 (2000); *Elmore*, 661 F.3d at 868 (noting that the totality-of-the-evidence standard requires the court to consider all of the motion-for-new-trial evidence favoring acquittal and reweigh it against the evidence the state presented at trial).

In reviewing the cumulative effects of Albert's counsel's errors, this Court does not assess the evidence as the motion-for-new-trial court did—with a simple "I believe the State's experts, not the defense experts." That's akin to a 13th Juror analysis. Instead, this Court reviews the record de novo to assess "how a jury might have reacted to the additional evidence" presented by the defense. *Debelbot*, 305 Ga. at 543 (citing *Humphrey v. Morrow*, 289 Ga. at 870); see also Woodard v. State, 296 Ga. 803, 810 n.5 (2015).

The analysis is qualitatively different. And when the state's medical case at trial is weak, counsel's failure to challenge it is more likely to have prejudiced the defendant. *Debelbot*, 305 Ga. at 543 (citing *Strickland*, 466 U.S at 696).

Defense experts presented a coherent non-criminal explanation for McKenzy's death. Many of defense experts' findings were uncontested, and many went unrebutted. Any of these findings could have caused a juror to doubt the State's cause of death explanation. Together, these findings create a compelling case that McKenzy's parents were not responsible for her death.

Head circumference. The medical records demonstrated that McKenzy's head circumference increased from 33.5 centimeters on the day of her birth to 35 centimeters before discharge, an increase of 1000% the expected growth within a 36-hour period. (T27. 324.) Defense experts concluded that this massive growth meant McKenzy was bleeding between her skull and scalp before her discharge from Martin Army Hospital. (T27. 326; T37. 1739-41.) This objective finding demonstrates that the Debelbots did not cause the swelling underneath McKenzy's scalp. It began well before they left the hospital.

Neither Dr. Darrisaw nor Dr. Palasis had an explanation for this unusual finding. (T31. 1019.)

A juror could have found from this objective measurement alone that McKenzy's injury predated her release from the hospital. The motion-for-new-trial court, however, never addressed it.

Soft and mushy brain. The autopsy report and Dr. Darrisaw's testimony establish that the right side of McKenzy's brain was "soft and mushy." (T28.606.) Defense experts testified that this finding supports a conclusion that the injury to McKenzy's brain could not have occurred within hours of her death. They testified that it takes much longer than a few hours for the brain to become soft and mushy. (T26. 198, 209, 245; T27. 306.)

Dr. Darrisaw offered no explanation for this unusual finding. She testified that although she took many samples of McKenzy's brain to further analysis, she did not take a sample of the soft and mushy part of the brain. (T30. 664-65.) Dr. Darrisaw seemed to agree that the mushy brain finding suggested a longer time period between injury and McKenzy's death than what her trial testimony conveyed. (T30. 611-12.)

Dr. Palasis testified that the brain could not have become soft and mushy within minutes or hours, but possibly more or less than 24 hours. (T31.998; T33. 1344-45.)

This "soft and mushy" brain finding calls into question the State's entire theory of the case. If the jury knew that the injury probably occurred more than a few hours before McKenzy's death, possibly 24 hours or more, how could it, beyond a reasonable doubt, place the Debelbots with McKenzy at the time of the injury?

The motion-for-new-trial court never addressed this finding.

Presence of older bleeding. Both defense experts and Dr. Palasis agreed that the CT scans showed blood clots within McKenzy's brain of different ages, and some were present for more than 24 hours and up to 7 days or more. (T33.1333-34; T37. 1716-17.) This finding supports the conclusion that an untreated dural sinus thrombosis occurred in utero and started an evolving process that led to more clotting and a soft and mushy brain. (T37. 1717.) Had the jury seen and heard this evidence, it would have reason to doubt that McKenzy's injuries were inflicted just hours before her death.

The motion-for-new-trial court never addressed this finding.

Lacunar skull. CT scans showed dark divots in McKenzy's skull. Dr. Sahlein testified that this finding supported the conclusion that the skull formed abnormally in utero due to increases in intracranial pressure that resulted from the ongoing process of blood clotting in the brain. (T36. 1668-70; T37." 1689-92.)

Had a juror seen the divot on the CT scans, it would have reason to believe that McKenzy suffered a vascular insult in the womb that compromised the integrity of her skull.

The motion-for-new-trial court did not address this unrebutted finding. Instead, it addressed a theory the defense experts never advanced - that McKenzy's skull became demineralized before her birth.

Loss of brain mass is hard to detect in newborns. Dr. Sahlein, a board-certified neurologist, testified that infants who suffered massive strokes with extensive loss of brain mass often exhibit only very subtle asymmetries and their injuries are very difficult to detect even when experienced neurologists perform exams. (T37. 1792-94, 1796-97.) Dr. Dehnel, a board-certified pediatrician who has treated thousands of newborns, agreed. Dr. Sahlein presented published research papers that support the conclusion that newborn infant brain injury is extremely difficult to detect because newborns retain their primitive functions such as sucking and eating even with extensive brain loss.

A juror who heard this testimony would have reason to doubt Dr. Darrisaw's testimony at trial - that an infant with this kind of brain injury would become "very rapidly pretty much flaccid, unconscious, unable to move, obviously unable to. . . feed." (T21. 153.)

The motion-for-new-trial court never addressed the research Dr. Sahlein cited.

Had Albert's counsel mounted an informed challenge to the medical examiner's testimony at trial, there's a reasonable probability that the jury would have a reasonable doubt.

At trial, the medical evidence was always and obviously vital to the State's case, but the jury heard a one-sided presentation. The unchallenged testimony of the medical examiner allowed the State to confidently argue during its closing argument:

> The medical examiner explained to you that the injury happened that night. . . . [t]his is all unrefuted evidence. (T22. 538.)
>
> Another reason we know it happened that night, the baby had actually some liquid in its stomach. . . . In other words, this injury happened within four hours of the baby dying. She was at the hospital for two of those hours. So the two hours before that [when] she was at home with the Debelbots. . . . Another reason. . . this injury occurred that night. . . is the fresh blood. . . . [T]he medical examiner explained that that is fresh blood and that it shows that this injury had just happened. This is a fresh blood injury. (T22. 539-40.)
>
> We know this injury was caused before eight hours. We know from the liquid in the stomach it was caused before four hours. We know from the fresh blood that it was caused recently.

(T22. 541.)

Narrowing the timeline with such certainty was the State's only evidence that connected Albert to the injuries. The extremely narrow time frame allowed the prosecutor to effectively argue that the State didn't have to prove which one of the Debelbots inflicted the injuries because they "were the only two people in the room." (T22. 545.)

But in the motion-for-new-trial hearing, the State's expert radiologist, Dr. Palasis contradicted the State's clean timeline. Dr. Palasis refused to narrow the time of injury to within four hours, and "not too close to the time the child came. . . to the emergency room because you need to allow for the brain to react to the injury." (T31. 999.) Instead, she concluded that the injuries occurred not within minutes, and not even within hours, and she "would not be surprised that [the injuries] could have occurred the previous day prior to going to the emergency room." (T31. 1011.)

Even Dr. Darrisaw admitted uncertainty about how long it would take McKenzy's brain to become "soft and mushy," and with that uncertainty, the State could no longer have used the four-hour window as rock-solid proof that Albert and Ashley intentionally inflicted fatal trauma. Had Albert's counsel presented a radiologist to view McKenzy's CT scans, the timeframe would have expanded even further, such that the State could not prove that the injuries occurred after McKenzy left the hospital.

Given the complete absence of evidence, outside Dr. Darrisaw's findings, to support the State's claims that Albert murdered his newborn daughter, the jury would have welcomed defense experts' explanation for how McKenzy died. The uncontested evidence at trial was that McKenzy's parents were excited for her arrival. Albert said she was "a gift from God." (T22. 301.) The Debelbots had moved stateside to raise McKenzy. (T21. 298-99.) They prepared for her arrival, equipping her nursery. (T21. 305.) Albert shared McKenzy's birth with friends and family through texts and calls. (T21. 303.)

Evidence of a non-traumatic cause of death would have bolstered the Debelbots' steadfast and straightforward claims that they didn't know what happened and they didn't do anything to hurt McKenzy. Their inability to explain and their refusal to guess what caused the injuries would have been seen, not as a sign of guilt, but as strong evidence of their innocence.

Had counsel investigated and meaningfully challenged the medical evidence in any way, there's a reasonable likelihood the jury would have reached a different verdict. *See Tezeno*, 343 Ga. App. at 636 (finding defense counsel ineffective for failing to prepare for cross-examination and failing to expose the limitations in the research offered by the State's expert); *Elmore*, 661 F.3d at 868 (finding defense counsel ineffective for failing to challenge the state's forensic evidence, especially the medical examiner's time of death conclusion).

Without evidence to challenge the core of the State's case, the prosecutor's argument—that the jury could convict the Debelbots even if they weren't 51% sure—almost certainly closed the door to Albert's only opportunity for acquittal. Counsel's failure to challenge the medical examiner and to offer medical evidence that aligned with his client's story, when considered with the prosecutor's egregious misstatement of the burden, undermines confidence in the jury's verdict.

CONCLUSION

Albert's experts presented a medical explanation that his jury never heard. Applying their experience and training to mostly undisputed facts, these experts undermined the State's fragile case. Neither the Georgia Evidence Code nor the constitution permit a gatekeeping function that would have deprived Albert the opportunity to present this evidence at trial.

Therefore, Albert Debelbot asks this Court to vacate his conviction and grant him a new trial in which he can meaningfully test the State's evidence against him.

Supreme Court of Georgia.

Albert DEBELBOT, Appellant,

v.

THE STATE OF GEORGIA, Appellee.

No. S19A1474.

October 24, 2019.

Brief of Appellee By the Attorney General

Christopher M. Carr 112505, Attorney General, Beth Burton 027500, Deputy Attorney General, Paula K. Smith 662160, Senior Assistant, Attorney General, Ashleigh D. Headrick 676295, Assistant Attorney General, Office of the Attorney General, 40 Capitol Square, Sw, Atlanta, Georgia 30334, (404) 651-6927, aheadrick@law.ga.gov, for appellee.

TABLE OF CONTENTS

[The Table of Authorities is omitted from this sample brief. Please see the Appellant's Opening Brief for an example.]

STATEMENT OF THE CASE

This is the second appearance of Appellant's case in this Court. In the prior appearance, the Court affirmed his malice murder conviction (and that of his wife/co-defendant) for the death of their newborn daughter, arising from a joint jury trial in Muscogee County Superior Court in October 2009. *See Debelbot v. State*, 305 Ga. 534 (2019). The Court determined that the evidence was constitutionally sufficient to authorize the conviction, but vacated the trial court's order denying the motion for new trial and remanded the case for further proceedings on the claims of ineffective assistance of trial counsel. *Id.* This appeal is from the trial court's ruling on remand. (R. 2645).[18]

In *Debelbot I*, the Court explained that a remand was warranted because the "sweeping nature" of the trial court's conclusions about the admissibility of the medical testimony presented by the defendants at the motion for new trial hearings precluded "meaningful review" at that time. 305 Ga. at 540. Whether their trial attorneys acted reasonably depended on whether the expert evidence was "admissible and credible." *Id.* at 542-43. The Court also noted that, due to the trial court's "limited findings" as to this testimony, it was not clear "what evidence, if any, was properly ruled to be inadmissible" under *Harper v. State*, 249 Ga. 519 (1982), which in turn meant that the Court could not conduct "a meaningful prejudice" analysis under the Sixth Amendment test. *Debelbot*, 305 Ga. at 543. The Court vacated the trial court's order denying the motion for new trial and remanded the case "for further findings, where the court should specify which material medical evidence is properly subject to such a Harper analysis and perform that analysis." *Debelbot*, 305 Ga. at 543.

In accordance with this Court's instructions, the trial court entered a new order denying Appellant's motion for new trial as amended on May 6, 2019. (R. 2645-2658). Appellant timely filed a notice of appeal on May 31, 2019. (R. 1-4). This appeal follows.

STATEMENT OF FACTS

The Court set forth the following facts in the first appeal as to the crime:

Viewing the evidence in the light most favorable to the jury verdict, the trial evidence shows that Ashley gave birth to McKenzy on XX/XX/2008, at Martin Army Community Hospital in Columbus, and they were discharged from the hospital on May 31. There were no signs that the baby was unhealthy or in distress. The Debelbots took McKenzy home and provided the sole care for the infant for the next 13 hours, during which time—according to the Debelbots—they fed and played with McKenzy, changed her diaper, and gave her a bath. In the early morning hours of June 1, the Debelbots took McKenzy to the hospital after noticing a bump on her head. McKenzy died a few hours later.

When police arrived, Albert appeared to be very distraught and cried several times, while Ashley did not appear to be nearly as upset as Albert and was never seen crying. During police interviews, however, Ashley got upset in explaining McKenzy's injuries and claimed not to know what happened to McKenzy. The police conducted a search of the Debelbots' apartment, but there is no indication that anything of evidentiary value was recovered.

A GBI medical examiner, Dr. Lora Darrisaw, performed an autopsy on McKenzy on June 2, 2008. Dr. Darrisaw testified that McKenzy had a fracture on the left side of her head, extensive fractures on the right side of her head, and bleeding in the brain. Dr. Darrisaw noted that McKenzy's birth occurred without any apparent complications and that the infant had food in her stomach at the time of the autopsy. Dr. Darrisaw also examined 19 microscopic slides of McKenzy's brain, found that no inflammatory cells had formed in response to the trauma, and concluded that the injuries preceded McKenzy's death by no more than 12 hours, possibly as little as one or two hours. Dr. Darrisaw opined that McKenzy's birth was not the cause of the trauma, because the extent of the injuries would not have allowed the infant to eat or do anything else and would have caused a very rapid death. Instead, Dr. Darrisaw concluded that McKenzy's death was a homicide and the cause of death was blunt force trauma, either by a series of blows to the head or by a "crushing type of injury."

Based on Dr. Darrisaw's conclusion, the police arrested the Debelbots, who both denied harming their child. *Debelbot*, 305 Ga. at 534-36.

Further facts will be added as necessary to address Appellant's two enumerations of error.

ARGUMENT AND AUTHORITY

I. Trial counsel was effective.

In his two enumerations of error, Appellant asserts that he received ineffective assistance of counsel. In his first enumeration, he asserts that trial counsel was ineffective for failing to object to the State's closing argument as re-characterizing the State's burden of proof. In his second enumeration, he asserts that trial counsel was ineffective when he did not present medical evidence to challenge the medical examiner's testimony that the victim's injuries were caused by intentionally-inflicted trauma. Appellant then argues that he was prejudiced by the alleged errors. Appellee submits that Appellant has failed to demonstrate deficient performance and prejudice under *Strickland v. Washington*, 466 U.S. 668 (1984), to prevail on these claims. . . .

This Court's scrutiny of an attorney's performance must be "highly deferential." *Strickland*, 466 U.S. at 689. . . .

Counsel is "strongly presumed" to have rendered effective assistance and made "all significant decisions in the exercise of reasonable professional judgment." *Strickland*, 466 U.S. at 689. Even where defendant's trial counsel has passed away prior to the hearing on his motion for new trial, the defendant still bears the "heavy burden" of proof to overcome the "strong presumption" and that counsel's conduct falls within the range of reasonable professional conduct and affirmatively show that the purported deficiencies in counsel's performance were indicative of ineffectiveness and not examples of a conscious, deliberate trial strategy. *Rhoden v. State*, 303 Ga. 482, 483-84 (2) (2018); *Morgan v. State*, 275 Ga. 222, 227 (2002).

As to the prejudice prong:

> The defendant must show that there is a reasonable probability that, but for counsel's unprofessional errors, the result of the proceeding would have been different. A reasonable probability is a probability sufficient to undermine confidence in the outcome.

Strickland, 466 U.S. at 694. *See also Fisher v. State*, 299 Ga. 478, 483(2) (2016). When determining prejudice, this Court weighs the prejudice from all deficiencies in deciding whether to reverse. *Debelbot*, 305 Ga. at 544.

A. Appellant has not shown prejudice from trial counsel's failure to object to the State's closing argument

Appellant asserts that he was prejudiced when the prosecutor argued that the jury did not have to be 51% sure to find him guilty. (Appellant's Brief at 23). In *Debelbot I* the Court held that trial counsel performed deficiently when he failed to object to the prosecutor's closing argument, but withheld judgment on prejudice pending the order on remand denying Appellant's motion for new trial. *Debelbot*, 305 Ga. at 543-544. Appellee submits that, because trial counsel emphasized the State's heavy burden of proof, Appellant has failed to demonstrate prejudice.

During trial counsel's closing argument, he argued the following to the jury:

> Another different burden is the law. If this was a civil case - I know some of you have been on a civil jury - there's a different burden. You don't have to prove who ran the light beyond a reasonable doubt. If you're getting divorced you don't have to prove who deserves a toaster beyond a reasonable doubt.
>
> But in a criminal case because of the penalties associated and the seriousness associated with cases like this they must prove the case beyond a reasonable doubt. And the Court will define for you what that means. It means that if you hesitate, if you say, well, wait a minute, no, you just haven't pushed my mind beyond hesitation, then that is doubt based upon reason. And you would be required to acquit Albert.
>
> Now, that's a very heavy burden of proof. It's the heaviest one we have in the law. There are several levels but that's the heaviest one we have because of the seriousness of the penalty of this. And the government has that burden.

(T29. 489-90).

During the State's closing argument, the prosecutor made the following argument to the jury:

> Reasonable doubt. The Judge will charge you on reasonable doubt. Just keep in mind, and he will charge you, reasonable doubt does not mean beyond all doubt. It does not mean to a mathematical certainty. Which means we don't have to prove that ninety percent. You don't have to be ninety percent sure. You don't have to be eighty percent sure. You don't have to be fifty-one percent sure. It does not mean to a mathematical certainty.
>
> And it does not mean beyond a shadow of a doubt. That's just something the TV made up. It's actually beyond a reasonable doubt. And that would be a doubt to which you can attach a reason. And I submit to you there is no reasonable doubt in this case.

(T29. 546).

The trial court charged the jury on the burden of proof in the case in chief as follows:

> The defendants are presumed to be innocent until proven guilty. Each defendant enters upon the trial of the case with a presumption of innocence in his or her favor. This presumption remains with the defendant until it is overcome by the State with evidence that is sufficient to convince you beyond a reasonable doubt that the defendant is guilty of the offense charged.
>
> No person shall be convicted of any crime unless and until each element of the crime as charged is proven beyond a reasonable doubt.
>
> The burden of proof rests upon the State to prove every material allegation of the indictment and every essential element of the crime charged beyond a reasonable doubt.
>
> There is no burden of proof upon the defendant whatsoever, and the burden never shifts to the defendant to produce evidence or to prove innocence.
>
> However, the State is not required to prove the guilt of the accused beyond all doubt or to a mathematical certainty. A reasonable doubt means just what it says. A reasonable doubt is a doubt of a fair-minded, impartial juror honestly seeking the truth. A reasonable doubt is a doubt based upon common sense and reason. It does not mean a vague or arbitrary doubt but is a doubt for which a reason can be given, arising from a consideration of the evidence, a lack of evidence, or a conflict in the evidence.

(T29. 555-56).

Appellee submits that Appellant has not shown prejudice under *Strickland*. Though this Court noted in the prior appeal that the trial court's instruction could potentially have been seen by the jury as reinforcing the prosecutor's misstatement of the law, *Debelbot*, 305 Ga. at 544, Appellee submits that the same could be said about trial counsel's. Trial counsel's argument went further than the trial court's charge in intimating to the jury exactly what "beyond a reasonable doubt" meant, how heavy that burden was on the State, and that if the State had failed to prevent them from hesitating as to Appellant's guilt, that they should acquit him. Appellee submits that trial counsel's argument was incongruous with the prosecutor's argument about reasonable doubt, and that the trial court's instruction could also be read as buttressing trial counsel's argument to the jury regarding the State's heavy burden. For these reasons, Appellee submits that Appellant has not shown prejudice from trial counsel's failure to object.

B. Trial counsel was not ineffective for failing to investigate and offer medical evidence

Appellant next asserts that trial counsel was ineffective when he did not consult or retain an expert to aid in his defense at trial. In subpart A, Appellant asserts that trial counsel's decision not to present the medical examiner's testimony was unreasonable. Appellee submits that Appellant has failed to overcome the "strong presumption" that trial counsel's decision in this regard was reasonable.

In subpart B, Appellant argues in 5 subsections that the trial court erred in its analysis when it excluded much of Appellant's experts' testimony. Appellant takes issue in five subparts with the trial court's analysis of the admissibility of his experts' testimony: that the trial court should have applied O.C.G.A. § § 24-7-703 and 707 to the evidence rather than *Harper*, that trial court erroneously excluded the CT scan evidence because the State acquiesced to their admission at the hearings on his motion for new trial, that O.C.G.A. § 24-9-901 applied to the authentication of the CT images, that the trial court erroneously excluded under *Harper* a theory not offered by the defense, and finally, that the exclusion of the expert testimony at trial would violate Appellant's right to present a defense. Appellee submits that the trial court properly analyzed the evidence under *Harper*.

The Trial Court's Rulings

In its order on remand, the trial court maintained that Appellant's experts were qualified as experts. However, the trial court found that the collective theory of the defense experts, "while novel, is supported by no new evidence, and is not credible in this case." (R. 2645). The trial court additionally found that their "novel theory concerning an in-utero vascular malformation causing demineralization of [the victim's] skull does not meet the standard promulgated by [this Court's] decision in *Harper*." (R. 2653). In so finding, the trial court credited Dr. Palsis' testimony on the subject where she testified that recent medical literature did not support their theory, finding finally that the theory could not be said to have reached a scientific stage of verifiable certainty under *Harper*. (R. 2653-54).

The trial court further found, "after hearing all of the evidence, being the finder of fact, in its[] capacity as 13th juror, this Court believes the state's witnesses and disbelieves Dr. Julie Mack, Dr. John Jerome Plunkett, Dr. Peter John Dehnel, and Dr. Daniel Sahlein," as to the following facts:

1. That the victim did not have a deformed skull or that she was missing any portion of her skull, but that a portion of the victim's skull had been pushed down into the skull (R. 2654);
2. That the victim was not missing any portions of her brain, but that blood clots were covering portions of her brain (R. 2654-55);
3. That Dr. Sahlein's OsiriX scans were not FDA-approved or accurate, and credited instead Dr. Palasis and her demonstration of how images from the OsiriX platform can be manipulated (R. 2655); and
4. That there were external signs of trauma on the victim's head.

(Id.) . . .

1. The trial court did not err when it did not apply O.C.G.A. § 24-7-703 and 707, or O.C.G.A. § 24-9-901, to the admissibility of the scientific evidence at Appellant's 2009 trial.

In section (II) (B) of his brief, Appellant argues that the trial court should have applied O.C.G.A. § 24-7-703 and 707, as well as O.C.G.A. § 24-9-901, to the admission of Appellant's offered scientific evidence. (Appellant's Brief at 29-37). Appellee submits that the trial court applied the proper legal standard when ruling on the admissibility of this evidence.

While the hearings on the motion for new trial took place after the effective date of the new Evidence Code, Appellant's trial did not. He was tried before the new Code went into effect. The determination being made in this appeal is whether trial counsel was ineffective in his representation in Appellant's October 2009 trial, which determination relies on whether the evidence would have been admissible at that time. Because this is a question of whether the evidence was admissible at the time Appellant was tried, Appellee submits that applying the new Code to the admissibility of the evidence, and using that as a measure of the reasonableness of trial counsel's conduct and prejudice from any alleged deficiency, is improper.

First, as to Appellant's Rule 703 argument, this Court has held that *Harper*, former O.C.G.A. § 24-9-67.1, which was carried forward as Rule 703 in the new Code, applies in criminal cases:

> In light of the long-standing history of *Harper* and its progeny, which existed when the legislature enacted the *Daubert* test in OCGA § 24-9-67.1 as a part of Georgia's Tort Reform Act, we do not conclude that the legislature intended to abandon the *Harper* evidentiary test in criminal cases. Indeed, the almost verbatim re-enactment of old OCGA § 24-9-67 as new OCGA § 24-9-67 would seem to affirm Georgia's traditional reliance upon *Harper* in criminal matters, and we expressly hold that new OCGA § 24-9-67, and [neither *Daubert* nor] OCGA § 24-9-67.1 controls the admission of evidence in criminal proceedings.

Vaughn v. State, 282 Ga. 99, 101 (3) (2007) (quoting *Carlson v. State*, 280 Ga. App. 595, 598 (1) (2006)). Therefore, Appellee submits that neither Rule 703 nor its predecessor under the old Code applies here.

Regarding Appellant's Rule 707 argument, Appellant appears to be asserting that the trial court "side-stepped" Rule 707 by applying *Harper*. (Appellant's Brief at 30). However, Rule 707 is based on former O.C.G.A. § 24-9-67, which this Court held was carried forward into the new Code as Rule 707. *Winters v. State*, 305 Ga. 226, n. 2 (2019). Because Appellant was tried in 2009, former O.C.G.A. § 24-9-67 applies. Under this old Code section, "the opinions of experts on any question of science. . . or like questions shall always be admissible. . . ." Indeed, this Court's decision in *Harper v. State*, 249 Ga. at 519, was decided under former O.C.G.A. § 24-9-67, *Walsh v. State*, 303 Ga. 276, 277-78, (quoting *Spencer v. State*, 302 Ga. 133, 135 (2017). In short, *Harper* dictates the manner in which trial courts evaluate the admissibility of scientific evidence under former O.C.G.A. § 24-9-67, now codified as Rule 707. Therefore, Appellee submits that Appellant's argument that the trial court erred by applying *Harper*, rather than Rule 707, does not follow.

Appellant further argues that *Harper* does not apply to bar an expert's opinion on cause of death even where experts disagree, citing to this Court's decision in *Smith v. State*, 302 Ga. 207, 211 (2017). Appellee submits that Appellant has stretched *Smith* beyond its holding. Indeed, *Smith* does not implicate (or cite) *Harper* at all; rather, it relates to the admissibility of expert opinions on an ultimate issue, which in *Smith* was the infant victim's cause of death. That an expert's opinion goes to the ultimate issue is separate and distinct from whether that expert opinion on an ultimate issue is barred by *Harper*. Appellee submits that the trial court properly applied *Harper* to exclude the OsiriX evidence.

Based on the foregoing, Appellee submits that this argument lacks merit.

2. The trial court did not err when it found the CT scan evidence inadmissible when the State did not object to their admissions at the hearing

Appellant next asserts that the trial court was precluded from excluding the 2D and 3D OsiriX evidence because the State did not object to their admission during the proceedings on his motion for new trial. (Appellant's Brief at 32-33). Appellee submits that this is a non sequitur. That the trial court admitted this evidence at the motion for new trial hearing for the purpose of ruling on Appellant's motion does not preclude its determination that the same would not have been admissible at trial under *Harper*, which is the relevant inquiry here. Appellee submits that this argument lacks merit.

. . . .

4. That the trial court excluded a theory the defense allegedly did not offer does not contribute to the ineffective assistance argument

In subpart 4, Appellant contends the trial court erred when it held that *Harper* excluded the defenses theory that "in-utero vascular malformation" that created "demineralization" of the victim's skull because the theory was "novel" and unsupported by medical literature, because the defense never offered a theory of demineralization, but that the victim's skull never properly formed or mineralized at all. He asserts that because "defense experts offered no theory of demineralization, and the court cited no defense testimony to support its finding, this Court owes no deference to this finding." (Appellant's Brief 38). Appellee submits that Appellant's argument offers nothing of consequence for this Court to consider in the context of determining the ineffective assistance of counsel claim. If the defense did not offer a theory of demineralization, then Appellee submits that it is not possible for there to be any error or harm from the trial court in excluding it. . . .

II. Appellant has not demonstrated deficient performance on his second claim, such that he has not shown cumulative prejudice.

Finally, Appellant asserts that he suffered prejudice based on trial counsel's failure to object to the State's closing argument cumulatively with his not presenting medical evidence. Because Appellant has not shown deficient performance on the second claim, Appellee submits that Appellant has not shown cumulative prejudice, as each alleged error must be independently established before an analysis of combined prejudice can be undertaken. *Waits v. State*, 282 Ga. 1, 5-6 (2007).

This Court has held that

> it is well established that the decision as to which defense witnesses to call is a matter of trial strategy and tactics. And tactical errors in that regard will not constitute ineffective assistance of counsel unless those errors are unreasonable ones no competent attorney would have made under similar circumstances. In particular, how to deal with the presentation of an expert witness by the opposing side, including whether to present counter expert testimony, to rely upon cross-examination, to forego cross-examination and/or to forego development of certain expert opinion, is a matter of trial strategy which,

> if reasonable, cannot be the basis for a successful ineffective assistance of counsel claim.

Perdue v. State, 298 Ga. 841, 845 (3) (2016).

Though trial counsel was deceased and not available to testify as to his investigation and strategic decisions, trial counsel's opening statement and closing argument help shed light on his trial strategy: to emphasize a failure of the State to prove its case beyond a reasonable doubt, to cast blame on Appellant's co-defendant, and to intimate to the jury that Appellant was not a person that would inflict this injury on his own child. (T22. 119, 121-123, 491, 494-502).

In his brief, Appellant relies on the testimony of Sandy Callahan, who represented Ashley, to show that trial counsel's performance was deficient. (Appellant' Brief at 28). Appellee submits that Callahan's impressions and opinions of trial counsel's performance are irrelevant to the question of whether trial counsel's performance was deficient, for, as *Strickland* dictates, the inquiry is into trial counsel's perspective at the time, not Callahan's. *See Strickland*, 466 U.S. at 689. Additionally,

> while other counsel, had they represented appellant, may have exercised different judgment, the fact that trial counsel chose to try the case in the manner in which it was tried, and made certain difficult decisions regarding the defense tactics to be employed with which appellant and his present counsel now disagree, does not require a finding that the representation below was so inadequate as to amount to a denial of effective assistance of counsel.

Smith v. State, 283 Ga. 237, 240 (2) (b) (2008).

Based on the foregoing, Appellee submits that Appellant has failed to present this Court with sufficient evidence to overcome the strong presumption that trial counsel's decisions were reasonable. *See Mosby v. State*, 300 Ga. 450, 455-56(2) (2017).

Turning to prejudice, Appellant asserts that he has suffered cumulative prejudice, based on trial counsel's failure to object to the State's closing argument and his failure to offer medical evidence. Appellee submits that Appellant has failed to demonstrate such prejudice.

As for the medical evidence, Appellee submits that based on the inadmissibility of the defense's imaging, as well as issues with the credibility of Dr. Mack, that no reasonable juror would have found Appellant's experts credible. First, Dr. Sahlein and Dr. Mack's testimony was based almost exclusively on OsiriX imaging, which Appellee submits the trial court properly ruled inadmissible under *Harper* based on its unreliability. As for Drs. Plunkett and Dehnel, Dr. Plunket testified that, while he considered other evidence, "the most critical factor was interpretation of the CT scan done" at the hospital in the formation of his opinion for how the victim died, and that he worked with Dr. Mack and correlated the autopsy findings with the CT scan findings. (MNT. 179, 217). To formulate his opinion, Dr. Dehnel had access to x-rays, CT scans, laboratory data, autopsy pictures and photographs; the medical examiner's report; however, he also testified that he also relied on the affidavits of Drs. Plunkett and Mack. (MNT. 280-81, 407).

As the State demonstrated during the motions hearings, and as the trial court found in its order, Dr. Mack used unreliable methods in reaching her conclusions, and even collaborated with someone she knew had been discredited as being disingenuous and testifying in a biased manner. Appellee submits that, at trial, the State would have elicited this testimony, and would have further elicited testimony that Drs. Plunkett and Dehnel collaborated with Dr. Mack in reaching their own opinions. In short, Appellee submits that Dr. Mack's lack of credibility would have infected Dr. Plunkett and Dr. Dehnel's testimony and impugned their credibility before the jury. Based on the foregoing, Appellee submits that no reasonable juror would have accepted the testimony of these doctors, such that Appellant has not demonstrated prejudice.

CONCLUSION

For the reasons set out above, this Court should affirm the Appellant's conviction and sentence.

Checklist for Chapter 18

When preparing an appellate brief, you should:

- Follow procedural and local court rules governing format.
- State the issues in a manner that invites a favorable conclusion but that maintains credibility and accuracy.
- To ensure that your opening statement of facts increases the judge's receptivity to your main argument, you should
  - tell a compelling story from your client's perspective;
  - state the facts completely and accurately, drawn from permissible sources;
  - emphasize favorable facts and deemphasize unfavorable ones through sentence structure, varying levels of specificity and concreteness, and general organization; and
  - avoid premature legal argument.
- Argue the case with attention to the law, the facts, and policy considerations.

Endnotes

1. *See* FED. R. APP. P. 32(a)(2).
2. *See, e.g.*, FED. R. APP. P. 25(a)(2)(D) (authorizing federal courts of appeals to adopt local rules permitting electronic filing of briefs and other documents); 9th Cir. R. 255 (requiring electronic filing of briefs by attorneys, with listed exceptions); 2d CIR. R. 251(i) (permitting hyperlinks).
3. U.S. S. Ct. R. 29.7 (excepting briefs filed by *pro se* litigants).
4. *See, e.g.*, Los Angeles Mem'l Coliseum Comm'n v. Nat'l Football League, 634 F.2d 1197, 1200 (9th Cir. 1980).
5. *See generally* Webb v. McGowin, 168 So. 196, 199 (Ala. Ct. App. 1936) (Samford, J., concurring) (departing from "strict letter of the rule" in the interests of justice).
6. *See generally* Mills v. Wyman, 3 Pick. 207 (Mass. 1825) (rejecting "moral obligation" exception in the interests of maintaining universal application of the consideration doctrine).
7. FED. R. APP. P. 28(a)(6).
8. FED. R. APP. P. 28(d).
9. Mark K. Osbeck, *What Is "Good Legal Writing" and Why Does It Matter?*, 4 DREXEL L. REV. 417 (2012).
10. For much more on telling your client's story, in both legal and factual argument, see Ruth Anne Robbins, Steve Johansen & Ken Chestek, YOUR CLIENT'S STORY (2013).
11. *See, e.g.*, FED. R. EVID. 201 and advisory committee note on subsection (f) (judicial notice of adjudicative facts in trial and on appeal); United States v. Pink, 315 U.S. 203, 216 (1942) (appellate judicial notice of record in other case); Ellie Margolis, *Beyond Brandeis: Exploring the Uses of Non-Legal Materials in Appellate Briefs*, 34 U.S.F.L.

REV. 197 (2000) (arguing for effective use of nonlegal materials to establish "legislative facts" on appeal, as well as at trial).

12. *E.g.*, FED. R. APP. P. 10 (the record on appeal), 11 (forwarding the record), 30 (appendix to the briefs), 32(b) (form of appendix).
13. *E.g.*, FED. R. APP. P. 28(e), 30(c)(2); *see also* Han v. Stanford Univ., 210 F.3d 1038 (9th Cir. 2000) (appeal dismissed for failure to correct opening and reply briefs' omission of citations to the record). For a guide to preparing an appellate appendix containing excerpts of the record on appeal, see Roger J. Miner, *Essay: Common Disorders of the Appendix and Their Treatment*, 3 J. APP. PRAC. & PROCESS 39 (2001).
14. *E.g.*, FED. R. APP. P. 28(a)(7).
15. *See* Charles R. Calleros, *Advocacy for Marriage Equality: The Power of a Broad Historical Narrative During a Transitional Period in Civil Rights, 2015* MICH. ST. L. REV. 1249, 1282-86, 1289-90, 1309-13.
16. Authors' note: "N.O.V." is an abbreviation for the Latin term *non obstante veredicto*, which means "notwithstanding the verdict," the phrase used earlier in the Statement of the Case. A judgment notwithstanding the verdict refers to a ruling by the judge that the jury's verdict on an issue is not supported by the evidence presented at trial and should be replaced by the court's contrary judgment on that issue.
17. Some authorities are omitted for shorter presentation in this book.
18. Omitted in the brief at this point is a footnote in which the authors of the brief explained that citations to the clerk's record are denoted by "R," to the jury trial transcript by "T," and to the hearings on the motion for a new trial by "MNT."

Part VIII

Writing to Parties: Contracts and Correspondence

As a practicing attorney, you will communicate not only with judges and other attorneys but also with your clients and other parties. For example, you might draft a written contract that the parties adopt as the final and complete expression of their negotiated agreement. If your client later complains that the other party has breached the contract, you might draft an "advice letter" to your client, advising her of her legal rights and recommending certain action. Depending on your client's assessment of her options, you might then send a "demand letter" to the opposing party, demanding that he take certain action to satisfy your client's claims.

Part VIII examines contracts and letters as examples of drafting directed to parties. It does not proceed on the premise that your immediate audience will invariably be the parties themselves. On the contrary, if you know that the other party is represented by counsel, you will ordinarily address your contract proposal or your demand letter to counsel. Similarly, if you or your law firm is the outside counsel for a corporation, you might address your advice letter to the corporation's in-house counsel. Nonetheless, more so than with office memoranda and briefs, contracts and letters are directed ultimately to the parties themselves.

Contracts and letters can be useful at various stages of litigation. For example, a contract might lead to a dispute, or it might express the parties' agreement to settle a dispute that has already proceeded through pretrial, trial, or even appellate litigation. Similarly, although you will often draft advice and demand letters at the earliest stages of litigation, you may use them at any stage of the litigation that raises new questions or that creates a new opportunity to state your demands.

Chapter 19

Contracts

I. Basic Approaches

With some limitations, parties can privately shape their legal rights and obligations by exchanging enforceable promises in a contract. Each party's promises impose contractual duties on that party and create contractual rights in the other.

The authors of one contracts casebook believe that the contractual promise is the greatest human invention, even greater than the wheel, the lever, and the pulley:

> [F]or it is the promise that breaks the ultimate physical restraint. It permits us to live a bit of the future today. When two or more employ the tool of promise in concert, they create a unique social engine—the *bargain*.[1]

Although this claim may provoke some debate about the relative merits of the promise and the pulley, none will dispute that enforceable contracts are indispensable to modern commerce.

Moreover, you need not reinvent the wheel with every contract. Some law firms produce high-quality form contracts for common transactions and maintain them in computer files. Whether you find a form contract in your office, online, or in a library, you can use it effectively by following a methodical process like that recommended by Wayne Schiess:

1. Study the entire form contract to secure general understanding of its scope and content.
2. Compose an outline of the component parts of the form contract.
3. Revise the list or outline to conform it to the needs of your client's transaction, such as by:
   - eliminating unnecessary provisions,
   - reorganizing other provisions as needed, and
   - noting the need for additional provisions.
4. As necessary, revise the language of the form contract to:
   - tailor it to the needs of your client's transaction,
   - avoid ambiguities and state the terms in plain English, and
   - add language or provisions needed for your client's transaction but missing from the form.
5. Proofread the entire document for mistakes, and edit the layout and language as needed to ensure readability and flow.[2]

You can best tailor those forms to new transactions if you understand the purposes of each section of a contract and have the drafting skills to express an agreement in plain, simple, clear English. Moreover, for contracts that do not lend themselves to a computerized form system, you should feel comfortable drafting "from scratch" without reliance on a form. You can draft with confidence if you understand the fundamental components of a contract.

II. Fundamental Components

A. General Format

A written contract should always contain the following provisions:

1. an introduction identifying the parties to the transaction,
2. a section describing the rights and obligations of the parties, and
3. signature lines showing the parties' agreement to the terms of the contract.

Among other things, a contract may also include:

1. a statement of "recitals," which describes the background of the transaction and the parties' reasons for entering into the contract,
2. a glossary of defined terms, and
3. a section of miscellaneous provisions addressing such topics as termination or modification of the contract, the relationship of the contract to other transactions, or the parties' choice of law or forum in the event of a dispute.

B. Introduction to the Contract

In the first lines after the title of a contract, you should identify the parties as simply and clearly as possible. If more than two parties join in the transaction, or if at least one of the parties is a complex entity, you should set the parties' names apart from each other on the page.

For example, you can start with a descriptive section heading and use paragraphing to separate the parties' names:

> **I. PARTIES**
>
> The parties to this contract for the purchase and sale of sand are:
>
> 1. SOONER SAND CO., a general partnership consisting of Harley T. Price and W. M. McMichael, general partners, and
>
> 2. BASSI DISTRIBUTING CO., a joint venture of Bassi Trucking Co. and Hardcore Rock & Gravel, Inc.

If you use this format for the introduction, you can refer to the parties throughout the contract by the formal names of their business entities: SOONER SAND CO. and BASSI DISTRIBUTING CO. Alternatively, you can assign descriptive labels to the parties, such as Seller and Buyer, and use that shorthand reference throughout the contract:

> 1. Sooner Sand Co. ("Seller"), a general . . . .
>
> 2. Bassi Distributing Co. ("Buyer"), a joint . . . .

Two experts on transactional documents, Susan Chesler and Karen Sneddon, recommend using the parties' names rather than descriptive labels, because it personalizes the parties and the contract. Doing so helps the parties "identify with the rights and obligations" and "instills ownership" of the agreement.[3]

Many drafters also like to assign a label to the contract itself and to include the date of the agreement in the introductory sentence:

This contract for the purchase and sale of sand (the "Agreement") is entered into on May 1, 2006, by the following parties:

C. Recitals

Although not essential to an enforceable contract, a statement of the factual background of the transaction, popularly known as a statement of "recitals," can help a neutral party interpret the contract if the parties dispute its meaning.[4] Recitals can even help establish consideration for the contract by showing the parties' reciprocal inducements or by providing a basis for implying obligations. For example, in the celebrated contracts case *Wood v. Lucy, Lady Duff-Gordon*,[5] Justice Cardozo of the New York Court of Appeals relied partly on the recitals of a written contract to imply an obligation by an exclusive agent to use reasonable efforts, thus satisfying the consideration requirement.

Chesler and Sneddon also argue that Recitals can help avoid disputes by enhancing the parties' connection to the contract and encouraging performance. The parties can do so by including "comprehensive and personalized descriptions of the parties . . . and their relationship to each other."[6] This can help explain the importance of each party's performance to the other, encouraging collaboration and full performance.

Recitals in an outdated contract are easy enough to spot. Each recital of a background fact appears in a clause beginning with the word "whereas" and is strung together with other recitals in a single, unmanageably long run-on sentence. To provide better guidance to your reader, you should (1) introduce the recitals with a section heading, such as "Recitals" or "Background" and (2) state your recitals in conventional sentences within numbered paragraphs:

II. RECITALS

1. Seller is engaged in the business of selling and shipping sand from Phoenix to various customers in the State of Arizona but has not developed markets outside of Arizona. Seller desires to supply sand wholesale to a distributor with customers outside the state.

2. Buyer has an established business . . . .

When used in a traditional manner, recitals state only the background of the transaction and the motivations of the parties. The contract will state the binding obligations in a different section of the written contract, as discussed below.

D. Statement of Reciprocal Promises

The heart of any contract is the parties' statement of their reciprocal promises. Those promises define the parties' mutual rights and obligations, which form the consideration for the agreement.

1. Introductory Clause; Recital of Consideration

Perhaps in an excess of caution, many drafters still begin their statements of reciprocal promises with outdated recitals of consideration such as the following:

> NOW, THEREFORE, in consideration of the mutual covenants herein contained, and other good and valuable consideration the receipt of which is hereby acknowledged, the parties hereby agree . . . .

Aside from displaying an antiquated writing style, in most cases the reference to "the receipt" of "other . . . consideration" is simply false and is an exceedingly poor way to establish consideration. Expressing a promise in a signed writing raises a presumption of consideration in some states,[7] but a recital of consideration has no additional legal effect under the majority rule.[8]

Especially antiquated is the reference to "good and valuable" consideration. Centuries ago, conventional consideration with economic value—such as money, goods, or services—was known as "valuable consideration." A familial or other personal relationship with the other party was viewed as "good consideration" for a promise to that party. The latter form of consideration, however, has long been abandoned by the common law.[9]

Under modern theory, the consideration in a typical contract consists of the parties' mutual promises, exchanged for one another with reciprocal inducement.[10] Rather than pompously recite the existence of consideration, you should state the mutual promises under a descriptive section heading and a simple introductory clause that refers to the promises as "mutual" or "reciprocal," or otherwise as part of a "bargained-for exchange":

> **III. MUTUAL RIGHTS AND OBLIGATIONS**
>
> Seller and Buyer agree to the following exchange of reciprocal promises:
>
> 1. *Supply.* For a period of five years from the date of formation of this contract, Seller will supply Buyer with all the sand that Buyer requires. . . .
>
> 2. *Delivery.* . . .
>
> 3. *Quality.* . . .
>
> 4. *Price.* For each ton of sand delivered, Buyer will pay Seller a sum equal to . . . .

Some drafters are tempted to begin each statement of an obligation with a phrase such as "Seller promises to supply" or "Seller agrees to supply." The reference to "promises" or "agrees," however, is unnecessary. If you begin your section with an appropriate heading, such as "Mutual Rights and Obligations" or "Mutual Promises," and if you follow immediately with an umbrella statement such as "Seller and Buyer agree to the following bargained-for exchange:" you need not repeatedly invoke the word "agree" in each statement of a promise. Moreover, to state a promise, you need not use the word "promise."

If preceded by the appropriate section heading and umbrella statement, words such as "will" and "must" in the statements of obligation will appropriately convey a party's intent to commit to a future performance:

> **IV. MUTUAL RIGHTS AND OBLIGATIONS**
>
> The parties agree to the following exchange of mutual promises:
>
> 1. Bank will approve a construction loan application submitted by Contractor, if the application satisfies the following requirements: . . . .

In such a construction, the term "will approve" is an obligation, and not just a prediction or statement of intention, because it follows an umbrella term introducing it as one of several mutual "promises." Thus, it is the equivalent of: "1. Bank promises that it will approve . . . ." On the other hand, the permissive term "may" would denote the granting of a discretionary power or authority under the contract:

> 12. If Tenant commits a major default as defined in Section 11, Landlord may demand acceleration of the remaining rent pursuant to Section 13 or may demand liquidated damages pursuant to Section 14, at its option.

Other authors and drafters are wary of the term "will approve" to denote a mandatory obligation. They advocate use of "shall," "must," "may," and "will" to serve different roles in expressing, respectively: mandatory duties, predicates to asserting contractual rights, authorizations of discretionary action, and statements about future events. If you find that such terms help you differentiate between different kinds of contract provisions, you will find support in sample contracts and in drafting books that explore drafting challenges in greater depth than is possible in this chapter.[11] If you employ terms consistently, and if you accurately and precisely express your meaning, you likely can achieve your drafting goals with any of several approaches. If you are concerned that a party or court will attach an unintended meaning to one of these terms, you can always include a definition or umbrella statement that clarifies the function you are assigning to a term.

2. Precision in Drafting

a. Simplicity; Terms of Art

The terms of the exchange are a matter of negotiation between the parties. If you represent your client in the negotiations, you can participate in shaping the substance of the bargain. As part of that process, you might draft proposed contract provisions to serve as offers or counteroffers to the other party. In other cases, your client might ask you to prepare a formal written document expressing a bargain that the parties have previously negotiated. In either case, one of your primary tasks as drafter of the final document is to express the parties' negotiated rights and obligations as precisely as possible to reduce the risk of misunderstanding and costly disputes during performance of the contract.

To draft precisely, you should take advantage of helpful terms of art but avoid unnecessary jargon. For example, the provisions below refer to the buyer's "requirements," a legal term of art that has special meaning and legal consequences under the Uniform Commercial Code.[12] Similarly, the parties could belong to a trade that widely recognizes helpful industrial terms of art, which might earn a place in your contract as well. Otherwise, however, the contract language should be in plain, simple English:

> 1. *Supply.* For a period of five years from the date of formation of this contract, Seller will supply Buyer with all the sand that Buyer requires for Buyer's business of selling and shipping sand to customers outside the State of Arizona.
>
> 2. *Delivery.* Buyer may order sand as Buyer's requirements arise by sending a written purchase order to Seller . . . .

Some legal terms are not necessarily terms of art but may be generally helpful and inoffensive. In the following passage, for example, the seller makes a special kind of promise by "warranting" the quality of the goods:

> 3. *Quality.* Seller warrants that the quality of the sand that is delivered to Buyer will be at least equal to that of sand of corresponding grades sold by other sand companies in the City of Phoenix, Arizona.

The word "warrants" in this passage is not a necessary term of art under the Uniform Commercial Code. The seller would undertake the same legal obligation by simply promising that

> Seller will deliver to Buyer sand of a quality that is at least equal . . . .[13]

Nonetheless, drafters typically and reasonably use the term "warrants" or "warranty" to draw attention to the special nature of a promise that goods or services will meet certain standards.

Similarly, many drafters use special phrases to draw attention to "conditions," which qualify or limit contractual duties. In a standard insurance contract, for example, the insured will assume an absolute obligation to pay premiums to the insurer, but the insurer will pay money to the insured only if the insured suffers a loss covered by the insurance contract. You could introduce the insurer's conditional promise with the simple word "if":

> If Insured suffers a covered loss as defined in section VI above, Insurer will reimburse Insured for . . . .

Many insurers, however, like to emphasize the conditional nature of their promises with special phrases, such as "on the condition that" or "in the event that":

> In the event that Insured suffers a covered loss as defined in section VI above, Insurer . . . .

b. Deliberate Imprecision

Occasionally, precision is neither feasible nor desirable. In some cases, for example, the parties may have failed to reach precise agreement on some difficult issue, even though they are ready to go forward with their general transaction. If so, you might be forced to express their imperfect agreement on the difficult issue in terms that are sufficiently imprecise to encompass the range of interpretations that describes their divergent positions.

For example, imagine that the buyer of factory equipment demands during negotiations that the seller agree to repair or replace defective parts within 10 days after receiving notice of the defect. Imagine further that the seller counteroffers to repair or replace defective parts within 45 days after receiving notice of the defect. If the parties cannot agree to a time limit measured by a specific number of days, they might instead agree to the vague language "within a reasonable time in light of all the circumstances," realizing that they might not share the same interpretation of that language in particular applications.

Language such as this might save the deal if negotiations are stalled on a contentious issue. Moreover, if performance of the contract proceeds smoothly, the parties will never test their divergent interpretations of the language. On the other hand, if adverse circumstances place a strain on performance, the lack of perfect agreement on the precise meaning of the provision could erupt into a serious dispute. Thus, during the negotiation of such a deal, you must help your client weigh the benefits of reaching general agreement against the risks of subsequent disputes over the meaning of vague language.

c. Plain English: Perfection and Pitfalls

A student once told me that his law school training in plain English paid great dividends during a summer clerkship with a law firm. On behalf of its client, the firm had conveyed proposed terms for an international licensing agreement, but the other party had declined to accept or otherwise respond in any meaningful way for many months. The student, who had prior professional experience in the subject matter of the contract, redrafted it in plainer English and simpler sentence structure, while cutting its length in half. When his firm conveyed the redrafted version as an offer, the other party accepted almost immediately. The first version was so formal, dense, and complicated that it intimidated the other party. The revised version was much easier to read and understand, putting the readers at ease and allowing them to be persuaded that the proposed enterprise would be mutually beneficial.

When you replace stuffy jargon with simpler, plain English, however, beware of potential pitfalls. What appears to be needless jargon will sometimes amount to a term of art that carries a precise meaning in an industry. Moreover, a seemingly antiquated legal term can carry special force if courts have interpreted and applied it in numerous contexts over many years, thus reducing the risk of a genuine dispute over its meaning in the current context. Accordingly, when updating a form contract to replace antiquated language with modern prose, you should take steps to ensure that the new language is sufficiently clear and precise that it reliably protects your client's interests and conveys the agreement of the parties.[14] In some cases, you can assure that a party or court will give your intended meaning to a plain-language provision by including plain English definitions to key words or phrases.

When starting with a form contract, you should strive to improve its style while also *tailoring* it to the current transaction and *reducing* the risk of dispute or unintended judicial interpretation. If you can meet these goals, you will realize the full potential of plain English in drafting.

3. Merger Clauses and Parol Evidence

As an example of a typical miscellaneous provision, a "merger clause" states that the written contract is the exclusive statement of the parties' agreement. If the other party subsequently asserts that the total agreement includes rights and obligations not expressed in the written contract, you can refer to the merger clause and seek to exclude evidence of the alleged unwritten obligations under the "parol evidence rule." With some exceptions, the common law parol evidence rule views the final and complete written agreement as the exclusive statement of the terms of the parties' agreement, thus excluding prior written notes or testimony about prior oral statements if offered to alter or add to the written terms.

A typical merger clause refers only generally to the subject matter of the agreement:

> XXV. *Prior Agreements Superseded.* This written contract constitutes the parties' complete and exclusive statement of their agreement on the subject matter covered by this contract, and it supersedes all previous agreements, promises, or representations regarding that subject matter.

Unfortunately, such a clause does not eliminate the risk of litigation of a common question under the parol evidence rule: Does an alleged additional agreement address topics within the subject matter of the main written contract so that the main contract supersedes it, or does the additional agreement address unrelated topics so that it can stand separately as an independent, enforceable contract?[15]

For example, suppose that on July 1 the parties signed a written contract for the lease of restaurant space with a fully equipped kitchen, but without any terms mentioning dining tables and chairs. The lessee later asserted that the lessor also orally agreed on June 28 to sell dining tables and chairs to the lessee at the spectacularly low price of $450. The lessor denies the oral agreement. He also points to the merger clause and argues that, assuming he did tentatively agree on June 28 to sell the dining furniture, such an agreement was simply part of continuing negotiations that the parties abandoned and superseded in their July 1 agreement.

However, to successfully invoke the merger clause to exclude evidence of the oral agreement, the lessor must demonstrate that the alleged agreement to sell dining furniture falls within the subject matter of the July 1 contract; otherwise, the alleged June 28 agreement can stand outside the field occupied exclusively by the July 1 contract. Unfortunately, the merger clause cannot help the lessor much because it fails to define the subject matter of the contract.

If you intend a written contract to broadly supersede prior agreements or promises on related transactions, you must describe the subject matter of your contract expansively so that the merger clause can have the intended effect. If you anticipate specific problems stemming from failed negotiations on collateral matters, you can address those matters explicitly:

> XXV. *Prior Agreements Superseded.* This written contract constitutes the parties' complete and exclusive statement of their agreement on all matters relating to the lease of the Scottsdale premises, the operation of a restaurant on those premises, and the furnishings and equipment needed for the operation. This contract supersedes all previous or contemporaneous agreements, promises, or representations regarding that subject matter.

This merger clause expresses the parties' intent to abandon any prior agreement for the sale of restaurant furnishings or equipment and to replace it with the terms of the lease agreement. To dispel any doubt about this scope of exclusion, the merger clause could specifically identify previous agreements by name and date, stating that the current contract supersedes them. Alternatively, a separate provision entitled "Rescission and Replacement of Previous Agreements" could state the parties' intentions to rescind specified prior agreements and replace them with the current agreement.

4. Allocating the Risk of Unexpected Impediments to Performance

In an era of climate change and recurring pandemics, performance of contracts can be disrupted by major weather events, government-mandated closures of businesses, and other events beyond the control of either party. If the parties do not allocate the risk of such events in their contract, common law or statutory law will provide a default rule to govern the dispute.[16] However, they can greatly reduce uncertainty and litigation costs by addressing this topic in their contract. Such a provision is traditionally known as a *force majeure* clause, addressing the possible intervention of a superior force.

If the parties can identify possible impediments to performance—such as storms that might delay shipping, governmental restrictions on crossing borders, labor disputes, or disruptions due to pandemics—they should explicitly allocate the risks of such events. For example, they could provide that a supplier may delay delivery due to designated impediments, and then cancel its obligations if the impediment persists for a designated time. At the other extreme, the contract might provide that a supplier must perform by the due date even if a listed impediment unexpectedly occurs, unless performance would violate governmental mandates. If a supplier agreed to such a provision, it likely would procure insurance against liability for nonperformance and incorporate the cost of insurance into its contract fee.

Some impediments to performance are truly unforeseeable and thus cannot be specifically addressed by the parties. Nonetheless, they can end their *force majeure* provision with a clause that allocates the risk of an unforeseen impediment to performance. For example, after specifically addressing the risk of certain listed events, they might provide that a supplier or vendor must perform on time unless any other unexpected impediment, beyond either party's control, increases the cost of performance by at least 25%.

E. Signature Line

You may end your contract with any reasonable means of presenting the parties' signatures as evidence of their agreement to the terms of the contract. You do not need to invoke formalistic jargon such as: "In witness whereof, the said parties have hereunto set their hands and seals the day and year first above written."

Instead, you may simply precede the signature lines with the single word "Signed." At most, you might introduce the signatures with a clause such as, "The undersigned parties agree to these terms."

If you have not already dated the contract at the beginning, you can include a space for the date next to each party's signature. The latest date on a signature line will correspond to one party's acceptance of the other party's offer and normally will identify the date of contract formation.

Exercise 19-1

1. Sample Requirements Contract

Study the following contract. Does it require any greater complexity to perform its function?

REQUIREMENTS CONTRACT

I. PARTIES

The parties to this contract for the purchase and sale of sand are:

1. Sooner Sand Co. ("Seller"), a general partnership consisting of the general partners Harley T. Price and W. M. McMichael, and

2. Bassi Distributing Co. ("Buyer"), a joint venture of Bassi Trucking Co. and Hardcore Rock & Gravel, Inc.

II. RECITALS

1. Seller is engaged in the business of selling and shipping sand from Phoenix to various customers in the State of Arizona but has not developed markets outside of Arizona. Seller desires to supply sand wholesale to a distributor with customers outside the state.

2. Buyer has an established business in Phoenix selling and shipping sand to various customers in several states outside Arizona, including California, Nevada, Utah, and Colorado. Buyer desires a stable source of supply of sand for that business.

III. MUTUAL RIGHTS AND OBLIGATIONS

Seller and Buyer agree to the following bargained-for exchange:

1. *Supply.* For a period of 5 years from the date of formation of this contract, Seller will supply Buyer with all the sand that Buyer requires for Buyer's business of selling and shipping sand to customers outside the State of Arizona.

2. *Delivery.* Buyer will order sand as Buyer's requirements arise by sending a written purchase order to Seller. On receipt of such a purchase order, Seller will deliver the ordered sand within 10 days to Buyer's facility at 1531 Range Road in Glendale, Arizona.

3. *Quality.* Seller warrants that the quality of the sand that is delivered to Buyer will be at least equal to that of sand of corresponding grades sold by other sand companies in the City of Phoenix, Arizona.

4. *Price.* For each ton of sand delivered, Buyer will pay Seller a sum equal to 60% of the market price per ton of concrete in the City of Phoenix at the time of Seller's delivery to Buyer.

5. *Term of Payment.* Seller may give an invoice to Buyer for sand on or after Seller delivers the sand to Buyer. Buyer will pay the full amount of such an invoice within 30 days of its receipt of the invoice.

2. Sample Format for More Complex Agreement

a. Compare the following outline of a sample contract with the sample contract in Problem 1 above. The sample below displays an alternative introductory section, and it contemplates more complex provisions that must be subdivided into more numerous subsections.

b. In section 4.2 of the contract, draft a merger clause that identifies your document as the complete and exclusive statement of the parties' agreement. In particular, be certain to supersede prior failed negotiations in which Seller proposed to lease trucks to Buyer for the transportation of the sand to other states.

CONTRACT FOR PURCHASE AND SALE OF REQUIREMENTS FOR SAND

This contract for the purchase and sale of sand (the Agreement) is entered into on [Date]____________ by the following parties:

1. Seller: Sooner Sand Co., a general partnership consisting of Harley T. Price and W. M. McMichael, general partners, and

2. Buyer: Bassi Distributing Co., a joint venture of Bassi Trucking Co. and Hardcore Rock & Gravel, Inc.RECITALS

1. Sooner Sand Co. is engaged. . . .

2. Bassi Distributing Co. has an established. . . .MUTUAL RIGHTS AND OBLIGATIONS

Sooner Sand Co. and Bassi Distributing Co. agree to the following bargained-for exchange:

Article I – Definitions

1. 1 *Grades of sand*—. . . .

1. 2 *Market price*—. . . .

Article II – Supply of Sand

2. 1 *Quantity*—. . . .

2. 2 *Quality*—. . . .

2. 3 *Delivery*—. . . .

Article III – Payment

3. 1 *Price*—. . . .

3. 2 *Terms of Payment*—. . . .

Article IV – Miscellaneous Provisions

4. 1 *No Oral Modification*—. . . .

4. 2 *Prior Negotiations Superseded*—. . . .

4. 3 *Mandatory Arbitration of Disputes*—. . . .

Signed and dated:. . . .

________________________ ________________________

Checklist for Chapter 19

To draft a simple contract, you should

- ✓ identify the parties in an introductory provision,
- ✓ recite the background facts, if helpful,
- ✓ state the reciprocal promises of the parties in plain English except when the legal context calls for special terms of art, and
- ✓ provide signature lines as a means for the parties to express their assent to the terms of the contract.

Endnotes

1. Daniel W. Fessler & Pierre R. Loiseaux, CONTRACTS, MORALITY, ECONOMICS AND THE MARKETPLACE (CASES AND MATERIALS) 1 (1982).
2. Adapted from Wayne Schiess, PREPARING LEGAL DOCUMENTS NONLAWYERS CAN READ AND UNDERSTAND (ABA 2008).
3. Susan M. Chesler & Karen J. Sneddon, *Happily Ever After: Fostering the Role of the Transactional Lawyer as Storyteller*, 20 TRANSACTIONS: TENN. J. BUS. L. 491, 495-96 (2021).
4. *See, e.g.*, Susan M. Chesler & Karen J. Sneddon, *The Power of a Good Story: How Narrative Techniques Can Make Transactional Documents More Persuasive*, 22 NEVADA L.J. § IV.A. (forthcoming 2022) (hereafter, "*Power of a Good Story*").
5. 118 N.E. 214 (N.Y. 1917).
6. Chesler and Sneddon, *Power of a Good Story, supra* note 4.
7. *See, e.g.*, CAL. CIV. C. § 1614 (West 1982).
8. *See* John D. Calamari & Joseph M. Perillo, CALAMARI AND PERILLO ON CONTRACTS § 4.6, at 158 n.3 & accompanying text (6th ed. 2009).
9. *See* EUGEN BUCHER, ENGLAND AND THE CONTINENT: DISTINGUISHING THE PECULIARITIES OF THE ENGLISH COMMON LAW OF CONTRACT 54 (Tony Weir, trans., 2009).
10. *See* RESTATEMENT (SECOND) OF CONTRACTS § 71 (1981).
11. *See, e.g.*, Tina L. Stark, DRAFTING CONTRACTS: HOW AND WHY LAWYERS DO WHAT THEY DO (2d ed. 2013).
12. U.C.C. § 2-306(1) (2011).
13. *See* U.C.C. § 2-313(1)(a), (2) (2011).
14. *See* Lori D. Johnson, *The Ethics of Non-Traditional Contract Drafting*, 84 U. CIN. L. REV. 595 (2016) (as a matter of professional responsibility, drafters should conduct appropriate research and inform the client of the risks of replacing antiquated language).
15. *See, e.g.*, Gianni v. R. Russell & Co., Inc., 126 A. 791 (Pa. 1924).
16. U.C.C. § 2-615 (2011) (impracticability in sales of goods); RESTATEMENT (SECOND) OF CONTRACTS §§ 261-71 (1981) (impracticability and frustration of purpose).

Chapter 20

Advice Letters

As counselor and advocate, you will draft many kinds of letters to your client or to others on your client's behalf. Two of the most important are advice letters and demand letters. These letters are closely related to two kinds of documents examined in previous chapters of this book: office memoranda and briefs. Like an office memorandum, an advice letter communicates a balanced legal analysis of a dispute or proposed action, predicts an outcome, and recommends a course of action. In contrast, a demand letter is like a brief in that it advocates a position and usually requests the addressee to take specific action. This chapter examines advice letters; Chapter 21 examines demand letters.[1]

I. Advice Letters Distinguished from Opinion Letters

Many attorneys and commentators use the term "opinion letter" to refer to any letter addressed to a client that offers a legal analysis, opinion, or recommendation. Within this general class of letters, however, are two important subcategories, each of which warrants a narrowly descriptive label. The term "opinion letter" best describes highly specialized letters that provide clients with formal opinions on certain kinds of legal questions. The term "advice letter" accurately describes the far more common kind of letter in which you will more generally analyze a legal problem and advise your client about the relative merits of alternative courses of action.

More specifically, an opinion letter is a formal document that expresses your definite conclusion, or that of your law firm, about whether a specified act is legally valid. For example, you might issue to a corporate client your formal opinion that the corporation has validly issued certain stock under applicable laws and under the articles and bylaws of the corporation. An opinion letter may also be used by your client to demonstrate to other parties that an action is legally valid. For example, an entrepreneur may seek advice about the probability of securing a patent on an invention and then show that opinion letter to potential investors to raise capital. Because the client will rely significantly on such an opinion, the standards for an opinion letter are high, and its format is fairly rigid.

In contrast, in an advice letter, you will communicate your analysis of a legal problem to a client in much the same way that you would use an office memorandum to communicate the analysis to a supervising attorney. Even if you cannot definitively resolve the legal issues in the analysis, you can evaluate the relative merits of the parties' claims and defenses, estimate the probability of success on the merits, and recommend a course of action or describe alternative courses of action. You can thus provide your client with valuable advice short of giving a definite opinion of the legality of certain actions.

In many law firms, only designated attorneys are authorized to issue formal opinion letters on behalf of the firm. Moreover, those attorneys tend to follow carefully developed forms when drafting their opinion letters, leaving little room for flexibility in format or creativity in analysis. Further examination of opinion letters is beyond the scope of this book. Instead, this chapter will explore the more common advice letter.

II. Purpose, Audience, and Writing Style

The writing style that you adopt for a document is partly a function of your intended audience and the purpose of your document. When you draft an office memorandum, you can easily identify your audience and purpose: you will communicate a balanced legal analysis to an experienced attorney. When you draft an advice letter, however, your audience and purpose may be less clear.

For example, the legal experience and general sophistication of your audience may vary greatly from one letter to the next. One client may be new to his business, have no legal training, and have learned English only after recently arriving from a foreign country. Another client may be a sophisticated, experienced businesswoman with at least a rudimentary knowledge of the laws that affect her business. Still another client may be a corporation with an in-house counsel to whom you will direct your advice letter. You should adapt your writing style to suit the experience and legal training of your audience. In a letter to the legally inexperienced client described above, you should take special care to use plain, simple English and to avoid legal jargon. In letters to more experienced and legally knowledgeable clients, you can safely use legal terminology and assume familiarity with legal method. In each case, however, your goal is the same: to communicate clearly, not to impress the reader with the breadth of your legal vocabulary.

In some cases, your client may wish to share your advice letter with customers, partners, or other attorneys. If so, you should draft the letter with the needs of the secondary audience in mind. For example, if your law firm's client is a corporate manager, she may intend to discuss your advice letter with the corporation's separate, in-house counsel. If so, you may want to provide a full explanation of your underlying legal analysis or even attach a copy of the formal office memorandum on which the advice letter is based.

III. Format

You should adopt any format that suits your audience and the purpose of your advice letter. As a starting point, you can follow the basic elements of a reasonable format for an office memorandum:

Issues
Brief Answers
Facts
Discussion
Conclusion

With this format, your advice letter would

1. restate the questions that your client posed to you,
2. briefly summarize your conclusions,
3. state the facts on which your analysis is based,
4. summarize your analysis of the law and the facts, and
5. state your conclusions and your strategic recommendations.

If your advice letter is simple and brief, you need not use formal section headings to display the transitions between elements of your format. Instead, you can simply use sensible paragraphing to lead the reader from one element to the next. Indeed, some clients prefer to receive short advice letters in the body of an email message, easily accessible to a client who is on the move.

On the other hand, if your letter is long and complex, you should use section headings, just as you would in an office memorandum or a brief. You need not use precisely the same format headings as you would for an office memorandum. One attorney used the following primary headings in an advice letter to introduce the issues, brief answers, facts, discussion, and conclusion:

Issues Addressed
Executive Summary of Conclusions
Background
Analysis (divided into subsections)
Recommendations

IV. Introduction and Statement of Issues

Immediately after the address and before the salutation of your advice letter, you should concisely state the general subject matter of the letter:

> Clay Franks
> Vice-President, Construction
> GRT Developers
> 1212 Central Ave., Suite 2201
> Boomtown, Calzona 81717
>
> RE: TRI Corp.'s possible breach of contract on the Westcourt project.
>
> Dear Mr. Franks,

In the first paragraph after the salutation, take a moment to build rapport with the client. Then, refer to your client's inquiry on this subject matter and state the issues that your letter addresses.

In some cases, your client will pose a general question that asks for strategic advice rather than legal conclusions: "Should we fire TRI and sue it for breach of contract?" If so, you might want to inform your client of the legal issues on which your strategic advice will depend:

> Dear Mr. Franks,
>
> It was a pleasure meeting with you the other day. You exercised good judgment to seek advice about the appropriate response to TRI's actions on this project. Specifically, you asked us at our meeting to advise you whether you should fire TRI from the Westcourt project

and sue it for breach of contract. In formulating our advice on this matter, we have analyzed the following questions:

(1) Did TRI breach the construction contract by using Cohoes pipe rather than the Reading pipe called for in the architect's plans?

(2) If so, was TRI's breach "material," thus permitting you to cancel the construction contract and fire TRI from the project?

(3) If TRI has breached the contract, to what remedies is GRT entitled?

If you decide to introduce the primary parts of your letter with formal section headings, you could begin with "Issues":

Dear Mr. Franks,

It was a pleasure meeting with you the other day. You exercised good judgment to seek advice about the appropriate response to TRI's actions on this project. Specifically, you asked us to advise you whether you should fire TRI from the Westcourt project and sue it for breach of contract.

I. Issues

In formulating our advice on this matter, we have analyzed the following questions:

A. Did TRI breach the construction contract by using Cohoes pipe rather than the Reading pipe called for in the architect's plans?

B. If so, was TRI's breach "material," thus . . . .

C. If TRI has breached . . . .

V. Brief Answers

Some attorneys will discourage you from summarizing your conclusions in brief answers near the beginning of your advice letter. They fear that your client will fail to appreciate or will even misinterpret your conclusions if he has not read your full analysis first. Like an assigning attorney reading an office memorandum, however, a client reading an advice letter is eager to reach the bottom line. You should not withhold it from him out of some misplaced concern that he is not ready to face it. On the contrary, the client may be so apprehensive about the conclusion, that he will not carefully read the letter, skimming until he reaches the conclusion. Moreover, mindful that he has paid for the entire letter, the client is nearly certain to read beyond the brief answers and to appreciate your full analysis. Thus, unless the letter is very short, or unless exceptional circumstances compel you to lay unusual groundwork before revealing an unfavorable conclusion,[2] you should satisfy your client's curiosity early in the letter.

If you use a simple format without section headings, you may briefly summarize your conclusions in a sentence or two immediately following your statement of the issues in the opening paragraph:

> Dear Ms. Price:
>
> Thank you for your telephone call the other day. In that call, you asked us whether you would be liable for damages if you discharged your head chef in retaliation for his testifying against you in a hearing of the state Food and Beverage Commission. As discussed more fully below, we conclude that such a discharge would not constitute a breach of your employment contract, but it would render you liable under the state tort law of "wrongful discharge."

In a more complex letter, you could state your brief answers under some appropriate heading, such as "Brief Answers" or "Summary of Conclusions":

> Dear Mr. Franks,
>
> It was a pleasure meeting. . . . Specifically, you asked us to advise you whether you should fire TRI from the Westcourt project and sue it for breach of contract.
>
> I. Issues
>
> In formulating our advice on this matter, we have analyzed the following questions:
>
> A. Did TRI breach the construction contract by using Cohoes pipe rather than the Reading pipe called for in the architect's plans?
>
> B. If so, was TRI's breach "material," thus permitting you to cancel the construction contract and fire TRI from the project?
>
> C. If TRI has breached the contract, to what remedies is GRT entitled?
>
> II. Summary of Conclusions
>
> A. TRI breached the construction contract, because the architect's plans clearly call for Reading pipe and do not permit substitutes.
>
> B. TRI's breach almost certainly is not material, because Cohoes pipe is nearly identical to Reading pipe in all important specifications. Therefore, you cannot cancel the contract.
>
> C. GRT is entitled to the difference between the value of the Reading pipe and that of the Cohoes pipe, a difference that appears to be insubstantial.

In addition to providing these answers to the specific legal issues that you have formulated, you might add a sentence to your overview paragraph that summarizes your response to the client's general strategic question:

> Dear Mr. Franks:
>
> It was a pleasure meeting . . . . Specifically, you asked us to advise you whether you should fire TRI from the Westcourt project and sue it for breach of contract. In this letter, we summarize our legal analysis and advise you not to fire TRI or withhold its payments.

VI. Facts

In every advice letter, you should state the facts on which your analysis is based. By making a record of the factual premises of your analysis, you can protect yourself against criticism or liability if subsequently discovered facts render your legal analysis obsolete. Additionally, you should explicitly ask clients to correct or update the facts if they see any errors or haves received new information. Indeed, if a client has supplied you with the facts, you may want to disclaim responsibility for any fact investigation:

> III. Facts
>
> The advice in this letter is premised on the following facts, which you have supplied and which we have not yet independently investigated. If the following facts prove to be incomplete or incorrect, you should not rely on the advice in this letter without first consulting us. Please advise me of any corrections or changes to the facts stated in this letter.

VII. Legal Analysis

In the body of your letter, you should reach a conclusion on each issue by applying the relevant law to the facts. In a letter to a corporate client's inhouse counsel or to a sophisticated client who has some legal knowledge, you can develop your legal analysis and cite to authority in much the same way that you would in an office memorandum. Other clients, however, will have little use for your in-depth analysis of authority or for legal citation. They would rather read a simplified summary of your legal analysis, and they are willing to assume that your underlying research and analysis has been thorough.

Thus, even if you have more fully expressed your analysis in another document, you may want to simplify the discussion in your advice letter. For example, as an initial reaction to a client's inquiry, you might draft a full office memorandum addressed to a supervising attorney. The memorandum will then serve as a basis for formulating advice to the client. In the advice letter, however, you need not analyze the legal authority with the same depth and formality that you found useful in the memorandum. Instead, you can more simply and briefly convey your analysis of each issue by (1) abstractly summarizing the law with little or no citation to authority, (2) identifying the relevant facts, and (3) stating your conclusion:

> Under state tort law, you are liable for damages if you discharge an employee for a reason that violates public policy. Legislation of this state establishes public policies of maintaining health standards in restaurants and encouraging witnesses to testify fully and truthfully at state administrative hearings. Therefore, if you discharge Chef Boyardi in retaliation for his testifying about violations of hygiene standards in your restaurant, you will be liable for violation of public policy.

In some cases, you can even leave the legal rule implicit by simply stating a conclusion, after identifying the facts on which it is based:

> Your contract with Chef Boyardi does not commit the parties to a definite term of employment, and it does not restrict your right to terminate the contract. Therefore, under state contract law, you can discharge Chef Boyardi at any time and for any reason without breaching the contract.

If your client has some legal training or expects to share your letter with another attorney, you may want to analyze authority to an extent that approaches the depth of analysis in your office memorandum. Alternatively, you can summarize your analysis in the letter and simply attach the office memorandum on which the advice in your letter is based. In this way, the client can rely primarily on the more accessible information in the letter, but he also has access to your more thorough and formal memorandum if the need for it arises.

Some clients may even prefer to receive short and simple advice letters in the body of an email message, to which they can easily gain access with a laptop computer or handheld device while on the move. If a longer and more formal legal document would be helpful as well, you can attach it to the email message. In some cases, however, you might have communicated the analysis to your supervising attorney in a brief email memo, rather than a formal office memorandum. If so, your advice letter to the client, even if sent in the body of an email, might be a bit longer, if necessary to explain legal points that are readily understood by a fellow attorney but foreign to a client without legal training.

VIII. Conclusion; Strategic Recommendations

In a final paragraph or section of your advice letter, you should summarize your subsidiary conclusions and offer your ultimate advice. If your client's legal rights and obligations are unclear, do not hesitate to convey the uncertainty with words and phrases such as "probably," or "although the question is close, TRI probably committed a material because" or "although our client has some chance of success on her claim, we likely cannot prove. . . ." Even so, you should reach a conclusion, even if only a qualified one:

> Although the question is a close one, the noncompetition agreement probably is unreasonable in scope and therefore unenforceable as a violation of public policy. In particular, the geographic scope of the restrictions likely exceeds the area in which Exco has business interests now or in the foreseeable future. I recommend. . . .

Your ultimate advice likely will be strategic, such as a recommendation to change a term in a proposed contract, file a lawsuit, communicate a settlement offer, or refrain from discharging an employee. If the ultimate decision for the client is essentially a business decision, such as whether to purchase property for development, you should outline the legal consequences of the purchase but leave the business decision to the client. On the other hand, if the ultimate decision is more clearly tied to the legal merits of a claim or defense, such as whether to settle a legal dispute, you can more strongly recommend a specific course of action.

Be sure to fully articulate the merits of any recommendations so that the client understands the likely consequences, including nonlegal considerations, of alternative courses of action. For example, even though you determine that a client has a strong claim for breach of contract, you might recognize that your client and the breaching party have a long-standing business relationship that is worth preserving. If pursuing the claim would damage or destroy that relationship, an alternative course of action might compare favorably to a lawsuit.

Ultimately, the client must make the final decision. When advising a client to settle, for example, you should recommend a range of settlement offers within which your client can exercise some judgment to choose a position or to reject settlement altogether.

Exercise 20-1 and Sample Advice Letters

1. Sample Advice Letter without Section Headings

The following advice letter is addressed to a restaurant owner with no legal training. The author has used only paragraphing to signal the transition from one element of the letter to the next, and he has not cited to authority.

a. Identify the purpose or purposes of each paragraph in the letter.

b. At its current length and format, would the letter be suitable for delivery in the body of an email message if the client has easy access to the Internet?

c. Research the problem and rewrite the letter so that it conveys additional information to a client with legal training. Specifically, cite to authority and briefly analyze the authority. If appropriate, divide the expanded letter into sections with section headings.

August 1, 2022
Leona Price
Hep Crepe Restaurant
123 Washington St.
Spinach Village, New Maine 10307

RE: Liability for terminating Chef Boyardi's employment

Dear Ms. Price,

Thank you for reaching out to our firm regarding your potential legal claim. You have asked us whether you would be liable for damages if you discharged your head chef in response to his testifying against you in a hearing of the state Food and Beverage Commission. As discussed more fully below, we conclude that such a discharge would not constitute a breach of your employment contract, but it would render you liable under the state tort law of "wrongful discharge."

Our analysis is premised on the following facts, as you have supplied them. Because a change in the facts may impact our analysis and conclusion, please contact us to correct any errors or to update us with any changes to the facts. The state Food and Beverage Commission has recently held hearings on violations of state health and hygiene regulations at various restaurants within the Village. The Commission requested your head chef, Anthony Boyardi, to testify at the hearings. Under examination by Commissioners, Chef Boyardi testified that employees have failed to control rat and insect infestations at Hep Crepe, resulting in continuing violations of state regulations. Because you view Chef Boyardi's act of testifying as disloyal conduct, you wish to fire him.

Your contract with Chef Boyardi does not commit the parties to a definite term of employment, and it does not restrict your right to terminate the contract. Therefore, under state contract law, you can discharge Chef Boyardi at any time and for any reason without breaching the contract.

Under state tort law, however, you will be liable for damages if you discharge an employee for a reason that violates public policy, regardless of whether the discharge would constitute a breach of contract. Legislation of this state establishes public policies in favor of maintaining health standards in restaurants and encouraging witnesses to testify fully and truthfully at state administrative hearings. Therefore, if you discharge Chef Boyardi in retaliation for testifying at the administrative hearings, you will be liable for violation of public policy. Your liability will include damages designed to compensate Chef Boyardi for his losses and may extend to additional damages designed to punish you for your intentional misconduct.

In conclusion, if you discharge Chef Boyardi in retaliation for his testimony, he will have a valid claim against you for damages. We advise you not to discharge him unless you are prepared to justify the discharge on other grounds. We recommend that you address the infestations in your restaurant, repair your relationship with Chef Boyardi, and capitalize on the continued popularity of your restaurant.

If you have any questions on this matter, please call me at (898) 123-4567.

Sincerely,

____

Robert Linzer
for Avila and Celaya, P.C.
222 N. 3d St.
Spinach Village, New Maine 10307

2. Sample Advice Letter with Section Headings

a. Compare the following letter with the one above. Describe each way in which the letters differ in style and format.

b. Assume in the letter below that your client, Clay Franks, is an Anglo-American with racist tendencies and that the opposing party's representative, Cal Dunlap, is African-American. Do those facts affect your analysis of the problem? Does the letter below adequately address the problems potentially caused by your client's racism without unduly offending him? Should you be worried about offending him?

c. The letter below is addressed to a client who has at least a basic knowledge of the law relating to performance and breach of construction contracts. Rewrite the letter so that it is appropriate for a client who has no legal training or knowledge. Specifically, summarize your analysis without citing to specific authority. If appropriate, eliminate the section headings and guide your reader through the simpler letter with good paragraphing and transition sentences.

Marcia Todd
Todd, Brown & King
1212 Central Ave., Suite 401
Boomtown, Calzona 81717
July 5, 2022

Clay Franks
Vice-President, Construction
GRT Developers
1212 Central Ave., Suite 2201
Boomtown, Calzona 81717

RE: TRI Corp.'s possible breach of contract on the Westcourt project

Dear Mr. Franks,

It was a pleasure meeting with you the other day. You exercised good judgment to seek advice about the appropriate response to TRI's actions on this project. Specifically, you asked us to advise you whether you should fire TRI from the Westcourt project and sue it for breach of contract. In this letter, we summarize our legal analysis and advise you not to fire TRI or withhold its payments.

I. ISSUES

In formulating our advice on this matter, we have analyzed the following questions:

A. Did TRI breach the construction contract by using Cohoes pipe rather than the Reading pipe called for in the architect's plans?

B. If so, was TRI's breach "material," thus permitting you to cancel the construction contract and fire TRI from the project?

C. If TRI has breached the contract, to what remedies is GRT entitled?

II. SUMMARY OF CONCLUSIONS

A. TRI breached the construction contract, because the architect's plans clearly call for Reading pipe and do not permit substitutes.

B. TRI's breach almost certainly is not material, because Cohoes pipe is nearly identical to Reading pipe in all important specifications. Therefore, you cannot cancel the contract.

C. GRT is entitled to the difference between the value of the Reading pipe and that of the Cohoes pipe, a difference that appears to be insubstantial.

III. FACTS

The advice in this letter is premised on the following facts, which you have supplied. We have not yet independently investigated the facts. If the following facts prove to be incomplete or incorrect, you should not rely on the advice in this letter without first consulting us.

GRT Developers is constructing a shopping center at the southwest corner of 27th Ave. and Marconi Way in Boomtown. As Vice-President of the Construction Division, you have hired TRI to install the plumbing system. GRT's contract with TRI incorporates the architect's plans, which you first transmitted to TRI in a letter soliciting its bid on the project. Those plans clearly call for the plumbing subcontractor to use Reading brand pipe for all plumbing: "All pipes in the plumbing system must be Reading pipe, in the sizes and grades specified in these plans, and no other brand pipe."

From the beginning, you have had difficulty working with TRI's foreman, Cal Dunlap. When TRI had completed about half of the plumbing on the project, you discovered that TRI had installed Cohoes brand pipe rather than Reading pipe. In a heated conversation with Dunlap, you demanded that TRI remove the Cohoes pipe, install Reading pipe, and compensate GRT for the resulting delay in construction. Dunlap agreed to install Reading pipe in the remainder of the plumbing, but he refused to replace the previously installed pipe. You now want to know whether you can fire TRI if Dunlap does not meet your demands.

Your own engineers have concluded that Cohoes pipe is equal to Reading pipe in durability and other relevant specifications. You do not know why the architect required Reading pipe, but you know that his brother-in-law is a sales manager for Reading Manufacturing Co.

IV. ANALYSIS

If TRI has breached the construction contract, GRT may sue it for all foreseeable damages caused by the breach, provided that GRT can prove the damages with reasonable certainty. *See Johnson v. Coombs Constr. Co.*, 345 Calz. 2d 331, 334 (1979). However, you may not fire TRI from the project unless TRI's breach is so substantial that a court would characterize it as "material," rather than "minor." *Lehman Brothers, Inc. v. Steenhook Enters.*, 401 Calz. 2d 112, 115 (1985). If a breach is only minor, you may not terminate the contract; instead, you must permit TRI to complete its performance, while reserving GRT's claim for damages resulting from its minor breach. *See id.* If you terminate the construction contract for only a minor breach, GRT will itself be guilty of the first material breach and will be liable to TRI for damages. *See id.*

A. *Breach of Contract*

The construction contract plainly requires TRI to use Reading pipe and no other. TRI has admitted that it used Cohoes pipe in approximately half of the plumbing. Therefore, TRI has breached the contract, and it is liable to GRT for foreseeable damages that GRT can prove with reasonable certainty.

B. *Materiality of Breach*

TRI's breach is material if it is so substantial that it either (1) robs GRT of the primary benefit that it expected from the contract, or (2) demonstrates that TRI is not competent to perform the work and therefore should not be allowed to continue. *See id.* at 116. Stated conversely, the breach is minor if TRI is competent to complete the contract and GRT can be fully compensated for its losses by an award of money damages that is small in proportion to the value of the entire contract. *See id.*

In this case, TRI's breach probably is not material under either branch of the test of materiality. First, GRT's primary benefit from the plumbing contract presumably is high-quality durable plumbing. Cohoes pipe is equal to Reading pipe in durability and other relevant specifications. The architect apparently required Reading pipe for personal reasons and not because it is superior to Cohoes pipe. Therefore, unless GRT has some special need for Reading pipe, it will receive its primary benefit from the contract even though half of the plumbing consists of Cohoes pipe.

Second, although TRI's use of Cohoes pipe shows that Dunlap departed from the architect's plans, we have no evidence that he has failed to follow more important specifications of the plans or that his crews have performed poorly in the actual installation. Dunlap probably knows that Cohoes pipe is equal to Reading pipe, and he may have decided not to take that architect's requirement seriously. Therefore, the events do not suggest that TRI is incompetent to perform Dunlap's promise to complete the installation of plumbing with Reading pipe.

In summary, a court likely would infer that your unhappiness with TRI stems more from your personal dislike for Dunlap than from problems caused by TRI's use of Cohoes pipe. Therefore, a court almost certainly will find that TRI's breach is not material.

C. *Remedies*

Assuming TRI's breach was only minor, you have no right to fire TRI from the project. Instead, you must permit TRI to complete its performance, and you may demand that it compensate GRT for any damages that result from its minor breach. If you are reasonably certain about the breach and the extent of damages, you may collect the damages yourself by withholding an appropriate amount of payments that GRT otherwise would owe to TRI. *See Johnson*, 345 Calz. 2d at 335. On the other hand, if you wrongfully withhold a substantial portion of TRI's payments above any amount that it owes GRT for breach, GRT may itself be liable for breach. *See id.*

Unfortunately, without further evidence that the choice between Reading pipe and Cohoes pipe will affect the value of your project in any way, you will have difficulty proving any damages. Therefore, we advise you not to withhold any payments owed to TRI.

V. CONCLUSION

Although TRI has breached its contract with GRT, the breach almost certainly is not material, and it probably did not cause any recoverable damages. In these circumstances, if you fire TRI from the project, GRT will be liable to TRI for breach of contract. Indeed, even withholding TRI's payments to cover damages caused by its breach is risky, because we have difficulty identifying any such damages.

We recommend that you work in a cooperative fashion with Dunlap to ensure the best possible performance of TRI's remaining duties under the contract. In the meantime, you might want GRT's engineers to calculate the damages, if any, the installation of Cohoes pipe has caused. If you find any damages, we will be happy to advise you about the best possible means of demanding compensation from TRI.

Please do not hesitate to call me if you have any questions about this matter. My direct line is (111) 232-3232.

Sincerely,

____

Marcia Todd
for Todd, Brown & King

Checklist for Chapter 20

In an advice letter, you should

- ✓ use plain English whenever possible,
- ✓ adapt your format and depth of legal analysis to your audience and your purpose,
- ✓ restate the questions that your client has posed to you and identify the legal issues that they encompass,
- ✓ briefly answer the issues,
- ✓ state the facts on which your analysis and advice are premised,
- ✓ discuss the law and apply the law to the facts to reach a conclusion for each issue, and
- ✓ summarize your subsidiary conclusions and state your advice.

Endnotes

1. Many of the ideas in Chapters 20 and 21 are taken with permission from lecture materials prepared by Frank M. Placenti and Mark Hileman, shortly before submission of the first edition of this book in 1989, when they worked for the Phoenix law firm Streich, Lang, Weeks & Cardon, P.A., which later merged with the law firm of Quarles & Brady.
2. *See* Henry Weihofen, LEGAL WRITING STYLE 178, 199 (2d ed. 1980).

Chapter 21

Demand Letters

I. Purposes of a Demand Letter

With a demand letter, you may seek to achieve one or more of three goals. First, you may seek to persuade another party to take or cease some action. For example, you might send a demand letter to your client's commercial tenant in an office building, demanding that he stop entering into unauthorized subleases and that he pay past due rent.

Second, you may seek to revoke a waiver of rights to permit your client to assert those rights in the future. For example, even though your client's lease agreement clearly requires payment of rent on the first of each month, your client might have implicitly waived her right to demand timely payment by frequently accepting late rent payments over the previous year without complaint. If so, you can help your client reassert her rights by sending a demand letter that (1) revokes any implied consent, (2) demands prompt payment of rent strictly according to the contract for the remainder of the lease, and (3) warns of your client's resolve to pursue legal remedies for future breaches of the lease.

Third, you may seek to obtain information or concessions from the opposing party to help your client assert rights in the future. In such a letter, you do not really expect the opposing party to accede to your client's demand; rather, you hope to provoke a reaction that you can use to your client's advantage. For example, suppose that your client orally agreed to purchase goods from a supplier for a total price of $10,000, but the supplier has balked at performing. You know that your client will have trouble enforcing the oral agreement, because the Uniform Commercial Code generally requires such agreements to be evidenced in a writing signed by the party against whom enforcement is sought.[1] You might nonetheless send a letter to the supplier setting forth the terms of the oral agreement and demanding performance pursuant to those terms. In so doing, you may hold out little hope that the supplier will immediately perform as promised; instead, you hope that the supplier will either (1) respond by repeating its decision not to perform but admitting that it had entered into the oral agreement or (2) fail to respond within ten days of receiving the letter, thus implicitly adopting your letter's description of the agreement.[2] Either reaction to the demand letter will satisfy the Uniform Commercial Code's requirement that the oral agreement be evidenced by a signed writing, thus enabling your client to assert a contract claim.[3]

II. Audience, Tone, and Writing Style

The audience for your demand letter is the opposing party, his attorney, or both. Your purpose is to persuade the other party to take or cease some action or to otherwise modify his relationship to your client. In addition to establishing the legal and factual soundness of your client's claim, you will seek to convince the other party that acquiescence to your demand is a more positive outcome than the alternatives, such as litigation.

Of course, you should adopt a tone that will most likely achieve your goals. Your task is complicated, however, by the multiplicity of audiences and goals. For example, although your primary audience is the opposing party, his attorney, or both, your own client is an important secondary audience. Even if you think that a conciliatory tone will achieve the best results with the opposing party, your client may make it clear that she has hired you to take the strongest possible stance and to intimidate the opposing party. On the other hand, the community is a possible tertiary audience, because the opposing party may seek to gain public support by airing the dispute in the news media. If a particularly strident passage in your demand letter is published, adverse public reaction may hinder your client's ability or willingness to assert her claims. Thus, you should adopt a tone that is firm but not nasty.

Indeed, because a demand letter frequently is the first step in a process of negotiation, one author believes that the letter should "prime" the recipient in a positive manner, to encourage compromise and settlement.[4] Under that view, you might adopt a more collaborative approach if the value of your client's claim is uncertain so that you seek a cooperative process of mutual compromise. On the other hand, if your client's claim is quite certain on the merits and in amount, you might be less interested in compromise and more determined in your assertion of your client's demand for payment or other action that is clearly due.

Aside from tone, your style should be straightforward, businesslike, and professional. As is true in a brief, the most persuasive style in a demand letter is one that the reader does not notice, one that focuses the reader's attention on your demands, your justifications, and the consequences of his failure to satisfy the demands. Thus, you should write in plain English and avoid legal jargon or florid, distracting prose.

III. Format

You may adopt any reasonable format that will achieve the goals of your demand letter. At a minimum, your demand letter should include

1. an introductory sentence or overview paragraph,
2. a statement of the legal and factual support for your demands, and
3. a specific statement of the demands and the consequences of the opposing party's failure to satisfy the demands.

You need not divide a simple demand letter into sections; good paragraphing will suffice. If you divide a long or complex demand letter into sections, you should use whatever section headings suit the purposes of your letter.

IV. Overview

Immediately below the address and before the salutation of your demand letter, you should identify the general subject matter of the letter:

> Arnold G. Hooper
> Hooper Construction Co.
> General Contractor
> 4094 Industrial Way
> Fairbanks, New Maine 10713
>
> RE: Damages for Delay in Completion of the Office Bldg. on Center St.
>
> Dear Mr. Hooper,

In the first paragraph of your demand letter, you should provide any introductory information necessary to orient your reader. If this is your initial correspondence to the addressee, your opening paragraph should identify your representative capacity. Beyond that, the opening paragraph can provide such information as a general description of the relationships of the parties and an overview of your client's demands.

For example, the following opening sentence states the author's representative capacity and captures the reader's attention with a demand and the threat of a lawsuit:

> Dear Mr. Hooper:
>
> Our client, Dawn Development, Inc., has directed us to prepare legal proceedings against you if you delay further in paying the liquidated damages owed under the Center St. construction contract.

In contrast, the following opening paragraph in a settlement proposal develops the background and purpose of the letter more deliberately, and it introduces the demand for payment in a more conciliatory fashion:

> RE: *Araiza v. Udave*
>
> Mr. Phillips:
>
> I met last Wednesday night with my clients, the plaintiffs in the suit against Max and Josephine Udave. All the plaintiffs are keen to press their claims. Nonetheless, they have agreed to make the following settlement offer: They will withdraw their suit if Max and Josephine Udave pay them a total of $10,000, conditioned on actual payment by noon on June 30, 2022. In light of my following evaluation of the case, I think you will find this offer to be quite reasonable.

V. Factual and Legal Basis for the Demands

A. Stating Your Legal Premises

Your explanation of the factual and legal justification for your client's demands may take many forms. In a routine collection letter, you can simply state the amount that is past due under an identified loan agreement, installment contract, or liquidated damages clause. In such a demand letter, the opposing party ordinarily will not dispute the general enforceability of such contracts, and you need not discuss the legal principles that make contractual obligations enforceable:

> As you have conceded in correspondence with our client, your firm completed construction on the Center St. office building 22 days beyond the deadline in the Construction Contract dated September 8, 2017 (attached). This delay has caused Dawn Development to suffer damages, which you and Dawn Development reasonably estimated at the time of contracting would be $1,000 for each day of delay in completion. Accordingly, pursuant to the liquidated damages clause in section 15 of the contract, you are liable to Dawn Development for liquidated damages of $22,000. Our client has informally requested payment of these damages on several occasions, but has not received a satisfactory response from you.

In other cases, the fact or amount of the opposing party's liability may be more doubtful, prompting you to explain more thoroughly the legal basis for your client's demands. Such an explanation—at least if directed to the opposing party's attorney—can look very much like the legal analysis and application to facts in a brief. For example, the following passage justifies a demand for consequential damages stemming from a breach of contract:

> In addition, the plaintiffs will be entitled to foreseeable consequential damages stemming from the breach. *See Southern Ariz. Sch. for Boys, Inc. v. Chery*, 119 Ariz. 277, 280, 580 P.2d 738, 741 (1978). Those will include the plaintiffs' expenditures on specialized accessories that were suitable only for the wedding and that some plaintiffs were unable to use. *See A.R.A. Mfg. Co. v. Pierce*, 86 Ariz. 136, 142, 341 P.2d 928, 932 (1959) (victim of breach entitled to award of damages for wasted promotional expenditures). Those members of the wedding party who could not fully participate in the wedding, the sole event for which the specialized gowns were ordered, can also recover damages for that lost opportunity. *See, e.g., Mieske v. Bartell Drug Co.*, 593 P.2d 1308 (Wash. 1979) (in UCC case, upholding award of $7,500 for emotional value associated with contracting parties' loss of home movies of significant events). Indeed, the opportunity to participate in the wedding formed the basis for the contracts for the gowns.

In all cases, be sure to determine whether any statute or regulation requires your letter to provide the other party with notice of specified legal rights, to use specific language in the demand, or otherwise to include certain information.

B. Audience

The appropriate level of formality of your legal analysis will depend on the sophistication of your audience. If you address your demand letter to the opposing party's attorney, or if you are certain that the opposing party will consult an attorney, you can reasonably cite to legal authority, as in the immediately preceding example. On the other hand, if the opposing party does not have legal training or legal representation, then you should express your arguments in terms that the party can understand. If you try to intimidate the opposing party with formal citations to authority, you might simply confuse or antagonize rather than persuade.

For example, the following excerpt of a demand letter to an insurance company's subrogation analyst assumes that the analyst has a sophisticated knowledge of business practices but has no formal legal training. The excerpt refers to three legal concepts: waiver, offer, and the "mailbox rule" governing the timing of acceptance. The author of the letter has tried to use these concepts in a persuasive manner without diverting the reader's attention to distracting citations:

> Even if Mr. Upton's premium had arrived after expiration of the grace period, his rights were preserved in the conversation between him and Diane Campbell, assistant to Dee Boston, on March 12. In that conversation, Ms. Campbell notified Mr. Upton that his claim would be covered but that she would delay processing his claim until he paid his late premium. Mr. Upton stated over the phone that he would mail his premium. In effect, Ms. Campbell waived any condition to coverage that would require Mr. Upton to deliver the premium to her within the grace period. She thus made the date of her receipt of the premium relevant only to the matter of processing his claim. Alternatively, Ms. Campbell may have communicated a new offer of coverage that invited Mr. Upton's return promise to pay the premium. If so, Mr. Upton accepted the offer either over the phone or, under the "mailbox rule," when he placed his premium in the mailbox.

C. Avoiding Concessions, Admissions, and Waiver

A demand letter is not the proper place to make concessions or admissions that may come back to haunt you later. Therefore, if you choose to adopt a conciliatory tone, do so in a way that does not preclude you from taking a stronger position in the future. For example, suppose that your client demands compensation based on a strong contract claim and a weak tort claim. To maintain credibility and to avoid antagonizing the opposing party, you might invoke only the contract claim to justify your client's demands in a demand letter. If so, you should remain silent about the weaker tort claim or refer to it only vaguely. If you affirmatively concede the weakness of that claim in writing, you could hinder your ability to pursue it later if newly discovered facts enhance its potential merit.

You should also avoid ambiguous conciliatory language that might grant unintended rights to the opposing party. For example, in a letter demanding payment of a liquidated sum owed, you should exercise caution before explicitly stating that the amount is negotiable. Such a statement is unnecessary because the opposing party is aware of the possibility of negotiating a settlement that compromises the amount owed. Moreover, your statement of willingness to negotiate might be construed as an offer or promise to negotiate in good faith, to which the opposing party can bind you by accepting the offer or relying on the promise. To keep all your options open, state your demands in an uncompromising manner, even though you may be willing to compromise if the opposing party offers a reasonable settlement.

VI. Demands and Threats

You should not send a demand letter unless your client has a well-defined goal that you can formulate into a straightforward demand to the opposing party. Moreover, to maximize the chances of achieving that goal, you must provide the opposing party with an incentive to satisfy your client's demand. If the opposing party is fair-minded and your demand is just, your persuasive presentation of the legal and factual bases for the demand should help induce him to satisfy the demand. In most cases, however, you can provide the greatest incentive to the opposing party by threatening to take actions that would be less attractive to the opposing party than satisfying the demand.

Thus, you must clearly state both your client's demand and the actions your client will take if the opposing party rejects the demand. To ensure prompt action, you should set a specific date by which the opposing party must satisfy your client's demand or suffer the adverse consequences of the threatened action.

If the relief to which your client is entitled is uncertain, your unstated objective may simply be to initiate settlement negotiations. More specifically, you may desire to induce your opponent to advance the first realistic settlement offer, which might reveal something about her evaluation of the case or her client's interests. If so, your demand letter might state the maximum possible liability and threaten formal action unless the opposing party acts to reach a settlement.

In other cases, your client may seek payment of a certain sum of money. For example, if your client is demanding the payment of amounts past due on an installment contract or liquidated damages clause, you should

- state the precise payment that your client demands;
- set a date by which the opposing party must deliver the payment to a specific address;
- depending on the circumstances, threaten to sue on the contract or take other appropriate legal action if the demand is not satisfied; and
- take care to satisfy any statutory or common law duties that apply to your transaction. For example, some attorneys or law firms may qualify as debt collectors subject to the provisions of the federal Fair Debt Collection Practices Act,[5] which will require some kinds of demand letters to disclose certain information and to refrain from making certain kinds of threats,[6] as illustrated in the final paragraph of the illustration immediately below.

The following excerpt from a loan collection letter illustrates the clarity, specificity, and directness for which you should strive. Notice that it identifies the risk of increased liability if legal proceedings are commenced: interest, costs, and attorneys' fees.

> If you desire to avoid legal proceedings, you must submit $22,000 on or before August 4, 2018, in cash, cashier's check, or certified funds made payable to Dawn Development, Inc. You must mail or deliver the payment directly to:
>
> Dawn Development, Inc.
> Suite 11000, Financial Plaza
> 1901 South Alma School Road
> Fairbanks, New Maine 10701
> Attention: Kathy Growl
>
> Take notice that time is of the essence. If Dawn Development has not received the above amount on or before August 4, 2018, it will immediately commence legal proceedings to collect the liquidated damages with interest, costs, and attorneys' fees.
>
> . . . .
>
> Notice: Unless you notify this office within 30 days after receiving this notice that you dispute the validity of any portion of this debt, this office will assume that this debt is valid. If you dispute the debt in a written notification sent to this office within 30 days from receiving this notice, this office will obtain verification of the debt or obtain a copy of a judgment and mail you a copy of the judgment or verification. If you submit a request to this office in writing within 30 days after receiving this notice, this office will provide you with the name and address of the original creditor, if different from the current creditor.[7]

To avoid any dispute about the opposing party's receipt of your demand letter, you should normally send the demand letter by registered mail or through a reputable delivery service that offers easy tracing of the letter. If same-day delivery is necessary for some reason, then you can consider hand delivery, faxing, or even attaching the letter to an email. A fax or email, however, is not likely to convey the sense of gravity and formality of an original letter delivered in hard copy.[8]

Finally, to preserve your credibility in future correspondence, you must confirm that your client is willing and able to back up its threats with action if your demand is not satisfied. As stated by one author, "Don't poke the bear unless you are ready for a fight."[9]

Exercise 21-1 and Sample Demand Letters

1. Collection Letter

Study the following collection letter and explain the purpose or purposes of each paragraph.

Scott L. Short
Stanley, Leeds & Cardon
100 W. Central Ave., Suite 2100
Fairbanks, New Maine 10701
July 21, 2018

CERTIFIED MAIL
RETURN RECEIPT REQUESTED
Arnold G. Hooper Hooper
Construction Co.
4094 Industrial Way
Fairbanks, New Maine 10713

RE: Damages for Delay in Completion of the Office Bldg. on Center St.

Dear Mr. Hooper,

Our client, Dawn Development, Inc., has directed us to prepare legal proceedings against you if you delay further in paying the liquidated damages owed under the Center St. construction contract.

As you have conceded in correspondence with our client, your firm completed construction on the Center St. office building 22 days beyond the deadline in the Construction Contract dated September 8, 2017 (attached). This delay has caused Dawn Development to suffer damages, which you and Dawn Development reasonably estimated at the time of contracting would be $1,000 for each day of delay in completion. Accordingly, pursuant to the liquidated damages clause in section 15 of the contract, you are liable to Dawn Development for liquidated damages of $22,000. Our client has informally requested payment of these damages on several occasions, but has not received a satisfactory response from you.

If you desire to avoid legal proceedings, you must submit $22,000 on or before August 4, 2018, in cash, cashier's check, or certified funds made payable to Dawn Development, Inc. You must mail or deliver the payment directly to:

Dawn Development, Inc.
Suite 11000, Financial Plaza
1901 South Alma School Road
Fairbanks, New Maine 10701
Attention: Kathy Growl

Take notice that time is of the essence. If Dawn Development has not received the above amount on or before August 4, 2018, it will immediately commence legal proceedings to collect the liquidated damages with interest, costs, and attorneys' fees.

Sincerely,

____

Scott L. Short
Stanley, Leeds & Cardon

Notice: Unless you notify this office within 30 days after receiving this notice that you dispute the validity of any portion of this debt, this office will assume that this debt is valid. If you dispute the debt in a written notification sent to this office within 30 days from receiving this notice, this office will obtain verification of the debt or obtain a copy of a judgment and mail you a copy of the judgment or verification. If you submit a request to this office in writing within 30 days after receiving this notice, this office will provide you with the name and address of the original creditor, if different from the current creditor.

2. The Bad Example

Study the following collection letter and explain why it is less effective than the letter in Problem 1 above. Identify and describe each defect.

Green and Gain
120 West Washington
Phoenix, AZ 85003
April 1, 2022

Mr. and Mrs. Joe Smith
5555 North 55th Street
Phoenix, AZ 85055

RE: Delinquent Loan #9-1403726-841

Dear Borrower:

We are counsel of record for the Bank of Phoenix (hereinafter referred to as "the Bank"). Our client has informed us that you are behind in your home loan payments, and has asked that we write you on its behalf to request that you take some action to bring your loans current. We understand that you presently are approximately $2,500.00 behind in your payments.

Over the past several months, the few loan payments you have actually made have been consistently late. While the Bank was happy to take whatever it could get from you, it would prefer that you try to make payments on time. If you are having difficulty making your payments, the Bank would be happy to consider and, if reasonable, would agree to an extension of your loan, a modification of its terms, or a second loan to see you through whatever difficulties you may be experiencing. If you desire to pursue this offer, please call your loan officer or some other authorized representative of the Bank.

Please be advised, however, that the Bank has no intention of waiting forever for you to make good on your commitments. Frankly, in our experience the Bank has very little patience with deadbeat borrowers such as you appear to be. The Bank has ruined the credit of thousands of borrowers who, like you, did not take their obligations seriously. Hundreds more have been forced into bankruptcy. Moreover, the Bank is a large, powerful institution which can afford to hire big law firms such as this one, against which the average debtor has little chance of prevailing.

We spoke to your attorney about this matter over the phone this morning but found him to be uncooperative. We sincerely hope that you adopt a more constructive attitude and pay up.

The Bank therefore suggests that you arrange to bring the aforementioned loan current by paying the amount hereinbefore stated or making such other arrangements as you and said Bank may subsequently agree upon.

Sincerely,

____

Bob Jenkins Green
& Gain

3. Settlement Letter

a. The settlement letter below is addressed to the opposing party's attorney in response to preliminary settlement discussions. It was written several months after suit was filed and shortly before a scheduled arbitration hearing. Explain the purpose or purposes of each paragraph. Precisely what does the letter demand? What action does the author of the letter threaten to take if the demand is not met?

b. Rewrite the letter so that it is appropriate for an unrepresented opposing party who has no legal training or knowledge. Summarize your analysis without citing to specific authority.

Charles Rehnquist, Esq.
333 S. Central Ave.
Phoenix, Arizona 85001
(602) 849-0101
June 2, 2022

Robert M. Phillips, Esq.
Kim, Phillips, Burley & Stewart
3301 E. Bethany Home Road, Suite B-111 Phoenix, Arizona 85012

RE: *Araiza v. Udave*

Mr. Phillips,

I met last Wednesday night with my clients, the plaintiffs in the suit against Max and Josephine Udave. All the plaintiffs are anxious to press their claims. Nonetheless, they have agreed to make the following settlement offer: They will withdraw their suit if Max and Josephine Udave pay them a total of $10,000, conditioned upon payment by noon on June 30, 2022. In light of my following evaluation of the case, I think you will find this offer to be quite reasonable.

I have no doubts about our ability to prove the claim for breach of contract. Indeed, your early correspondence and the defendants' answers to the complaint and interrogatories admit that Josephine failed to perform as promised. Even if she had acted in good faith and with best efforts, that would be no excuse for breach of the contract. Therefore, the defendants have essentially admitted to liability. The direct loss in value is easily computed: the difference between the value of each gown as promised ($900 each by your own correspondence) minus the value of the dress as delivered (we can prove that some are total losses).

In addition, the plaintiffs will be entitled to foreseeable consequential damages stemming from the breach. *See S. Ariz. Sch. for Boys, Inc. v. Chery*, 119 Ariz. 277, 280, 580 P.2d 738, 741 (1978). Those will include the plaintiffs' expenditures on specialized accessories that were suitable only for the wedding and that some plaintiffs were unable to use. *See A.R.A. Mfg. Co. v. Pierce*, 86 Ariz. 136, 142, 341 P.2d 928, 932 (1959) (victim of breach entitled to award of damages for wasted promotional expenditures). Those members of the wedding party who could not fully participate in the wedding, the sole event for which the specialized gowns were ordered, can also recover damages for that lost opportunity. *See, e.g., Mieske v. Bartell Drug Co.*, 593 P.2d 1308 (Wash. 1979) (in UCC case, upholding award of $7,500 for emotional value associated with contracting parties' loss of home movies of significant events). Indeed, the opportunity to participate in the wedding formed the basis for the contracts for the gowns.

All these losses are itemized in Count I of the complaint. They total approximately $20,000. Because the plaintiffs will certainly prove a breach of contract and will establish at least some of their alleged damages, they will also be entitled to an award of attorneys' fees, which could add thousands more to the total recovery.

Josephine's own theory of the case is that she breached the contract because she lost the ruffles. Coupled with her failure to warn the plaintiffs to obtain gowns from an alternative source, those facts should easily support the negligence claim in Count II. That claim provides even stronger support than Count I for an award of general compensatory damages, including damages for emotional distress.

Also solid are the claims for promissory fraud and consumer fraud in Counts III and IV. The consumer fraud statute prohibits use of deception, fraud, false promises, or suppression of material fact with intent that others rely, in connection with the sale of any merchandise. A.R.S. § 44-1522. "Merchandise" includes services. A.R.S. § 44-1521(5). Like the common law tort of promissory fraud, a claim under the consumer fraud statute will support an award of punitive damages. *See Schmidt v. Am. Leasco*, 139 Ariz. 509, 512, 679 P.2d 532, 535 (Ct. App. 1983). We should have little trouble proving a claim under either theory: The plaintiffs will offer abundant and vivid testimony describing the way in which Max and Josephine deliberately misrepresented that many of the gowns would be ready on time, thus inducing many of the plaintiffs to wait until the last minute and beyond, when in fact Max and Josephine knew that the gowns could not possibly be completed on time. In light of the recklessness or malicious intent associated with such actions, these claims potentially could add thousands of dollars in punitive damages to the compensatory damages detailed in Count I.

In sum, the plaintiffs are angry and confident. They are anxious to go to an arbitration hearing, and they are ready to enforce their judgment by attaching the Udaves' property. Indeed, I experienced some difficulty getting them to agree to propose this settlement offer. I can assure you that it is not a bargaining posture; it represents their current bottom line, before they have incurred significant legal fees. Despite their passionate views on this matter, however, they have compromised their full claims substantially. The $10,000 figure represents 50% of the compensatory damages for Count I, without costs or attorney's fees, and without any punitive damages.

This offer remains open until noon, June 15. Please call or write to me before then if your clients wish to settle.

Sincerely,

____

Charles Rehnquist, Esq.

4. Response to Demand Letter: Demand for Withdrawal of Claim

The following letter responds to a demand letter from an attorney for Framer Insurance Co. addressed to Michael Upton. Mr. Upton caused an automobile accident, resulting in injuries to Eileen Bradley, who was insured by Framer. Framer paid Ms. Bradley's claim for $10,000 in losses and medical expenses arising out of the accident. Framer then demanded that Mr. Upton reimburse Framer for Framer's payment to Ms. Bradley. Mr. Upton, however, claimed that he had liability insurance from Framer and that Framer thus was obligated to assume the cost of his liability to Ms. Bradley. The primary matter of dispute between Framer and Mr. Upton was whether Mr. Upton had validly renewed his insurance contract with Framer despite Framer's assertion that it received his late premium payment only after expiration of the policy's grace period.

a. Although it responds to a demand letter, the letter below is itself a demand letter, albeit a subtle one. What does it demand? What action does it implicitly threaten if the demand is not met? Should the author have stated the demand and threat more strongly?

b. Who is the audience for this letter? Assuming that Marilyn Branscomb is not a lawyer, would she likely consult with Framer's attorney, Jon Drake, before deciding whether to drop Framer's claim against Mr. Upton? If so, should the author have advanced a more formal legal analysis with citation to authority?

Charles Rehnquist, Esq.
333 S. Central Ave.
Phoenix, Arizona 85001
(602) 849-0101
January 28, 2022

Marilyn Branscomb
Subrogation Analyst for Framer Insurance
P. O. Box 3108
Mesa, Calzona 89211
Policy No. 881347 94

Dear Ms. Branscomb,

I represent Michael Upton in his claim for coverage under the above policy. I write in response to Jon C. Drake's letter dated January 7 to Michael Upton, in which Mr. Drake requests Mr. Upton to indemnify Framer for Framer's payment of claims to Eileen Bradley. I address this letter to you because Mr. Drake directed Mr. Upton to contact you. I'm sure that everyone hopes to resolve this matter before either party must incur the enormous legal expenses associated with litigation.

Mr. Upton is unwilling to pay the claim because he claims liability coverage under his policy and thus expects Framer to satisfy Ms. Bradley's claims. Mr. Upton recognizes that his insurance policy requires actual receipt of a late premium before expiration of the grace period. Even so, Mr. Upton is certain that the post office in fact delivered his premium within the three days remaining in the grace period, and he doubts Framer's claim that it received the premium a full week after it was posted five miles away. A jury would have the same doubts. Once Mr. Upton proves to a jury with his testimony and that of a witness that he posted the letter three days before expiration of the grace period, the jury will not likely believe that the letter took longer than the standard two to three days for delivery.

Mr. Upton is confident of his ability to prove his version of events before a jury, particularly in light of his previously communicated willingness to submit to a lie detector test. Of course, if litigation or other inquiry reveals that anyone within the Framer organization sought in bad faith to deny Mr. Upton coverage by covering up the facts, the resulting issues would transcend the relatively small dispute now before us. Thus, you should consider the possibility of a counterclaim to any claim that Framer might consider pursuing against Mr. Upton.

In sum, Mr. Upton is prepared to prove that he owes Framer nothing because Framer had a contractual duty to provide him insurance coverage for his liability to Ms. Bradley stemming from the March 12 accident. If Framer drops its claim, Mr. Upton will be happy to cease any further inquiry into possible claims he might have against Framer based on bad faith or other misconduct that Framer may have engaged in.

Sincerely,

____

Charles Rehnquist, Esq.

Checklist for Chapter 21

In a demand letter, you should

- ✓ use plain English whenever possible;
- ✓ adapt your format and depth of legal analysis to your audience and your purpose;
- ✓ use an introductory sentence or paragraph to identify your representative capacity, provide an overview of the purpose of your letter, or orient the reader in some other fashion;
- ✓ state the legal and factual bases for your demand;
- ✓ state your demands, including the time and place for satisfaction of the demands, and threaten to take legal action if the demands are not met; and
- ✓ stay abreast of common law and statutory regulation of demands in your transaction, and comply with the law in your communications.

Endnotes

1. *See* U.C.C. § 2-201(1) (2011).
2. *See* U.C.C. § 2-201(2) (2011).
3. *See* U.C.C. § 2-201(1), (2) (2011).
4. Carrie Sperling, *Priming Legal Negotiations Through Written Demands*, 60 CATH. U. L. REV. 107 (2010).
5. 15 U.S.C. §§ 1692-1692(o) (2012).
6. For a helpful discussion of the Act's requirements, see Scott J. Burnham, *What Attorneys Should Know About the Fair Debt Collection Practices Act, or, the 2 Do's and the 200 Don'ts of Debt Collection*, 59 MONT. L. REV. 179 (2000).
7. With minor changes, this paragraph quotes from one recommended by author Scott Burnham as offering language that would satisfy some disclosure requirements of the Fair Debt Collection Practices Act. *Id.* at 190. It might be included, in an excess of caution, as boilerplate language in all demand letters that seek payment of money, even if its terms do not always apply.
8. *See* Bret Rappaport, *A Shot Across the Bow: How to Write an Effective Demand Letter*, 5 J. ALWD 32, 48 (2008).
9. *Id.* at 36.

Appendices

In a legal method and writing course, you can best master a challenging writing assignment by preparing for and accomplishing your task in at least three separate steps. First, you should acquire information about the topic of your assignment by reading assigned portions of a descriptive text, such as the main text of this book, and by attending classes in which your professor lectures and leads class discussion. Second, you must become an active participant in the educational process by analyzing assigned problems and preparing legal documents, such as case briefs, office memoranda, and briefs. Third, you should welcome constructive criticism from instructors or peers, and you should thoughtfully react to their editorial comments by deciding which have merit and by revising your draft accordingly.

Along with the exercises in the main text, these Appendices provide you with the problems and other materials you need for the second step of the educational process: your active participation in research, analysis, and writing. The exercises in the main text are suitable for class discussion or for in-class writing exercises. They include policy questions, invitations to critique sample documents, an essay examination, and composition problems.

The Appendices include "problems" similar to the "exercises" in the main text: They provide further opportunities to think about and discuss fundamental questions of legal method and writing. Although an instructor could make these problems the subjects of formal writing assignments, they are primarily designed for individual review or for class discussion.

The "assignments" in the Appendices, on the other hand, are take-home assignments requiring formal written documents. They ask you to analyze a problem and draft a document such as an office memorandum or a pretrial brief. Many of the assignments requiring formal documents provide all necessary materials and require no supplementary research. Others, particularly the more complex ones, provide you with little or no authority and require you to perform all necessary research in the library.

The assignments that require research will inspire different analyses depending on when you perform them and what authorities have been issued at that time. For example, statutes or judicial decisions issued after the publication of this book might radically alter the nature of the issues originally intended to be raised. Similarly, one of the office memorandum assignments is set in the state in which your law school is located. Because your analysis of the problem in that assignment will depend on the law of your state, the assignment may be more interesting in some law schools than in others. For all these reasons, your professor may perform some "fine tuning" of some of the assignments by modifying the facts or otherwise adjusting the problems to avoid unintended difficulties raised by intervening laws or the laws of a specific jurisdiction.

Appendix I

Introduction to the Case Method of Study: Additional Text and Problems for Chapter 2

Your professors in all your classes likely will provide you with guidance in preparing case briefs for class discussion, even if only by example through the questions they ask about cases. If you do not receive sufficient guidance and instruction, you can turn to this Appendix for additional direction.

When you research cases for an office memorandum, you will employ many of the skills of close reading, interpretation, and synthesis that you develop over the first semester in briefing cases for class. However, in an office memorandum, you will present your case analysis in a different way than in preparing a case for class discussion. Accordingly, refer to Part IV of the main text for instruction on case analysis in an office memorandum.

I. Study of Cases in Your First-Year Courses

When preparing for law school classes, like Torts, Contracts, Property, and Criminal Law, you must analyze cases: judicial decisions, mostly appellate, published as "opinions," that resolve specific disputes. In those and similar courses, casebooks simplify your task. Rather than requiring you to search for unedited judicial opinions in the library, your assigned casebooks will group judicial opinions in logical fashion and will present them in edited form to isolate selected issues.

When preparing for class discussion, you should anticipate the possibility that your professor will call on you to recite the facts of the case, identify the issue and holding, explain the court's reasoning, opine whether the court would reach the same decision under slightly different, hypothetical facts, critique the court's decision or analysis, or synthesize (compare) the decision with other decisions on the same or a similar issue. Such preparation for a class of one to two hours should take you several hours of intense reading, thinking, and note-taking. This process of preparation is commonly referred to as "briefing" the case for class.

The resulting "case brief" is not an end in itself; seldom will a professor ask you to turn it in for review. It is simply a vehicle for class preparation. Accordingly, view the following recommendations as simply one way of preparing for a typical class. If you find that another method of preparing for a particular professor's class is more effective, by all means adapt your study techniques accordingly.

II. Preparing a Case Brief

A. General Approach and Format

Whether researching a memorandum problem or preparing for class, you should prepare "case briefs": written analytic summaries of appellate opinions. Although you will eventually develop shorthand techniques for taking notes on cases, during your first semester you should prepare formal, thorough case briefs to ensure that you develop skills of case analysis.

You should not be troubled if your instructors and textbooks recommend a variety of formats for case briefs. All the formats include essentially the same information; they vary chiefly in emphasis and organization. Below are outlines of two sample formats. If necessary, you can modify them to suit the requirements of a classroom instructor who asks students to recite parts of a case in a different order.

A	B
1. Identification	1. Identification
2. Issue(s) and Holding(s)	2. Facts
3. Facts	3. Procedural History
4. Procedural History	4. Issue(s) and Holding(s)
5. Reasoning	5. Reasoning
6. Evaluation	6. Evaluation
7. Synthesis	7. Synthesis

Although format B may be more popular, format A has the advantage of forcing you to frame the legal issue before stating the facts, thus ensuring that you state the facts with an appreciation for their legal significance. The issue and holding also provide an effective overview of the case brief.

Whichever format you select, you should start by placing the case in context in your study, as described in Section B below. Then, read the case completely before beginning to write. To state some elements of a case brief, you must first understand other elements; moreover, the organization of an appellate opinion may differ from that of either case brief format outlined above. Indeed, some elements of the case brief may not appear explicitly anywhere in the opinion. For example, the precise issue and holding of a decision may be only implicit in the court's statement of the facts, legal reasoning, and disposition. Consequently, before briefing a case, you should read and reread the entire opinion until you understand all its elements.

You might try this technique for reading and briefing: (1) Read the opinion once, at a moderate pace, to get a general idea of its content. (2) Then, study it carefully, at a deliberate pace, looking up any unfamiliar terms, and filling in the elements of your case brief. (3) Finally, read it again, aiming for deep understanding, and adjusting your case brief to reflect your additional study. Sometimes notes after the case will help clarify some passages that are difficult to understand.

During step 1, consider whether you identify with one side of the dispute, or with the judge writing the opinion, or a dissenting opinion. As you proceed to step 2, you can engage more actively with the case by adopting the role of a party's attorney, who must understand the case to explain it to a new client, or by adopting the role of the authoring judge who must persuade other judges to sign on to the opinion.

As you study the case, try to anticipate the questions that your professor will ask in class. It might help to review the class syllabus, the section headings in the casebook, and any notes in the casebook before and after the case. Pay special attention to any comments your professor made about the next case for study at the end of the previous class. All these things can provide clues to the points that your professor is likely to explore and emphasize when discussing the case.

B. Elements of a Case Brief

Before addressing the more formal elements of the case brief, take a moment to place the case in context in your studies. Glance at the class syllabus or the section heading in the casebook in which the case appears. Remind yourself of the topic that the class is exploring and make a quick note of that context immediately above the case name in your brief, such as: "Remedies/Damages/liquidated damages v. penalty clauses." This quick preliminary step can provide some helpful orientation before you study the case and summarize the following elements.

1. Identification of the Case

In preparing a case for class, you should begin your case brief with

1. the name of the case, which is usually taken from the names of two adversary parties;
2. the jurisdiction, in the sense of the geographical and political body, within which the court sits;
3. the level of the deciding court;
4. the date of decision; and
5. the page on which the case appears in the casebook ("CB"), which facilitates quick cross-reference between notes and casebook.

For example, the following notes identify a 1904 decision of the Supreme Court of Rhode Island, which appears in the student casebook at page 387:

Davis v. Smith, Rhode Island Supreme Court (1904), CB 387

To develop familiarity with citation form, you might want to record the full citation to the reporters in the library in which the opinion appears, if that citation is presented in your casebook. The following example includes such a full citation, along with an additional reference to the page on which the edited opinion begins in the student casebook:

Davis v. Smith, 26 R.I. 129, 58 A. 630 (1904), CB 387

By citing to the official Rhode Island Reporter, "R.I.," you have referred to the Rhode Island Supreme Court under commonly accepted citation form. Consequently, both examples above identify the authoring court in *Davis v. Smith* as the court of last resort in Rhode Island. That information is significant: It shows that the court is not bound by lower court decisions within Rhode Island or by decisions in other states, although such decisions might provide persuasive authority.

The early date of the *Davis v. Smith* decision, 1904, helps identify the decision's place in Rhode Island law. This decision adhered to nineteenth-century legal principles that minimized a landlord's duties and liability to a tenant's infant son for unsafe conditions, partly because the infant son was not, and could not be, a party to the lease. As discussed in Chapter 5, any aging decision can lose force or relevance over the years because of growth in the economy, technological advances, and changes in social attitudes and legal context. Such changes prompted the Rhode Island Supreme Court to overrule *Davis v. Smith* in 1967, stating that "[we] can perceive no reason to abide by a rule of law promulgated over a half century ago and leave unchanged a principle which in our opinion no longer serves a useful purpose in today's times." *Rampone v. Wanskuck Bldgs., Inc.*, 227 A.2d 586, 588 (R.I. 1967) (allowing employee of tenant to sue landlord in tort after she stepped in a hole in the floor, when the landlord had undertaken a contractual obligation to the tenant to make repairs).

The name of a case does not always clearly identify the original parties to the underlying dispute. A named party may be a representative of one of the original disputants or an assignee of its rights and obligations. For example, the dispute in *Hamer v. Sidway,* 27 N.E. 256 (N.Y. 1891), concerned the contract rights and obligations of William E. Story, Sr., and his nephew, William E. Story, II. The case name is taken from the parties to the lawsuit: (1) the executor of the senior Story's estate and (2) a person who acquired the nephew's contract rights through assignment.

Identifying the court may be problematic as well. Most court systems use "Court of Appeals" to refer to the intermediate appellate court and "Supreme Court" to refer to the court of last resort. In the New York state court system, however, the trial courts of general jurisdiction are the Supreme Court and the County Court; the intermediate appellate courts are the appellate divisions of the Supreme Court and the appellate terms of the Supreme Court; and the court of last resort is the Court of Appeals.

2. *Issue and Holding*

a. *Issue*

An "issue" is a material question of fact or law that arises from the claims, defenses, and arguments of the parties. An issue may be a question of law, such as whether Congress intended the term "sex" to encompass sexual orientation as well as gender in section 703(a) of Title VII of the Civil Rights Act of 1964. Except at the trial level, an issue rarely presents only a question of fact, such as whether the evidence shows that an employer exclaimed "Women can't perform this job!" when he rejected a woman's application for employment.

Most commonly, the issue before a trial or appellate court requires a combination of legal and factual analysis in the determination of whether the facts of a dispute satisfy a general legal rule. An example of such a question is whether certain conduct by an employer in fact created a discriminatory work environment, thus satisfying Title VII's rule regarding discrimination in "conditions ... of employment." By applying the rule to the facts and reaching a conclusion, the court not only resolves the immediate dispute before it, but it also refines the rule by adding more concrete substance to its abstract terms.

If you look for a concise statement of the issues in an appellate opinion, you may find only frustration. Courts do not always state the issues in simple terms before resolving them. When a court does formally state the issues, it may not state them with the narrowness and specificity to which you should aspire if you seek to maximize the development of your analytic skills. You may find clues to the precise question addressed by the court in the court's description of the trial court decision that it is reviewing, in its summary of the parties' arguments on appeal, in the emphasis it places on specific facts, and in its discussion of the law.

At a minimum, your statement of an issue should identify a substantive legal question that distinguishes the case from the bulk of case law in the casebook. In addition, you should specifically incorporate the facts of the case that are critical to the court's analysis and that therefore help to define the precedential effect of its decision.

For example, the following statement of the issue in *Wagenseller* obviously is too general:

> Did the trial court correctly dismiss the tort claim against the defendant?

This issue statement does not distinguish the case from countless others in a first-year casebook on tort law. The issue statement should identify the narrower topic of tort law presented in the case:

> Is an employer liable in tort for discharging an at-will employee for a reason that violates public policy?

This statement of the issue identifies (1) a legally significant relationship between the parties (employer/employee), (2) the nature of the claim (tort), (2) the basis for the claim (public policy), and (4) the obstacle to relief on a contract claim (by its terms, the employment contract is terminable at the will of either party).

Though the second statement of the issue is much more informative, it still leaves room for improvement. Your issue statement will better define the effect of the decision as precedent if you more specifically refer to the critical facts of the case:

> Is the employer liable in tort for violation of public policy when he discharged an at-will employee because of her truthful testimony in a hearing of the State Dept. of Health and Safety?

This statement of the issue identifies the source of public policy, and it gives sufficient factual details to permit an assessment of the importance of that policy.

The point at which the disadvantages of increased complexity begin to outweigh the benefits of enhanced specificity in the issue statement is a matter of judgment and personal style. As discussed in the next subsection, you can reduce the complexity of the issue statement by transferring some of the critical information to the statement of the holding.

b. Holding

The "holding" is simply the court's answer to the question presented in the issue. If you state the issue so that it is sufficiently narrow and specific to provide a basis for evaluating the effect of the decision as precedent, you may state the holding with a simple "yes" or "no." Of course, if a professor asks you during class discussion for the holding of a case without first asking for the issue, she expects you to offer more than "yes" or "no." In those circumstances, you should transform the issue into a detailed holding in the form of a statement:

> The employer committed the tort of wrongful discharge by firing an employee for a reason that violated public policy: because the employee had testified at a hearing of a state agency.

Even when pairing the holding with a detailed statement of the issue, you may wish the holding to convey further information than "yes" or "no." For example, if a fully descriptive statement of the issue would be unwieldy, you can move some of the critical information to the holding:

> *Issue*: Did the employer discharge the employee for a reason that violates public policy, thus rendering the employer liable in tort for wrongful discharge?
>
> *Holding*: Yes. By discharging the employee because she testified at a hearing of the State Dept. of Health and Safety, the employer violated public policy reflected in a statute authorizing the Department to gather information about workplace safety and to develop regulations based on that information.

Because narrowly drafted statements of the issue and holding represent an attempt to identify the effect of the decision under stare decisis, from a practical standpoint the precise contours of the issue and holding may not become clear until subsequent decisions interpret and apply them as precedent. Through that process of determining whether the prior decision is controlling, analogous, or distinguishable, subsequent decisions help explain—or may even redefine—the relative importance that various facts and policies played in the prior decision. In turn, this process helps the court explain the relative importance of various facts and policies to the resolution of subsequent disputes.

Consequently, the issue and holding of the decision cannot be identified with perfect certainty when analyzing that decision in isolation. Rather, each decision presents a range of possible statements of the issue and a holding. When preparing for class, you should try to state an issue and a holding that fall somewhere within a plausible range. Try also to appreciate how other statements nearer to either end of the plausible range would aid in the advocacy of either side of a subsequent dispute.

In a future case dealing with an employee's testimony to the State Dept. of Transportation, for example, an employer might argue that precedent on the tort of wrongful discharge should be limited to testimony before the State Dept. of Health and Safety, because the public interest in maintaining safe workplaces is especially great. The other party might argue that the precedent should be read more broadly to state a principle about the public interest in encouraging truthful testimony in hearings of any state agency.

3. Facts

a. Significance of Facts

Pressed for time, you may be tempted to skim over the facts of a case and rush to the middle of the opinion, searching for succinct statements of law that you can preserve in your notes. In the final analysis, however, legal rules are nothing more than statements of the legal consequences of specific facts.

Whether case law is based on statutory interpretation or common law, it generally develops gradually, with each new opinion adding refinements in the law through its application of legal standards to the facts of a new dispute. A court's statements about the law are fully meaningful only when read in the context of the facts of the dispute that the court resolves. Consequently, you should master the facts of a case with the same intensity that you devote to appreciating the court's discussion of legal principles.

b. Selecting Facts for Your Fact Statement

Your statement of facts should include all "material" facts, which are facts that have legal significance and therefore directly influence the court's holding and reasoning. Identification of material facts is not an exact science; rather, it is a matter of judgment that requires an appreciation of the factors that the court considered in reaching its decision. In your statement of facts, you may also refer in general terms to any additional background facts that are helpful to a full understanding of the dispute. At the least, your statement of facts should identify

1. the principal parties to the underlying dispute that gave rise to the legal proceedings,
2. the relationships between those parties, and
3. the events that led to the dispute.

You may refer to such facts as "historical facts" to distinguish them from "procedural facts," which are discussed in Subsection 4 below.

For purposes of general discussion, this book often uses the procedural term "plaintiff" to refer to the party who initiates a lawsuit and the term "defendant" to refer to the one against whom suit is brought. You can create a more concrete image of the underlying dispute, however, if you identify the parties with their more specific, formal names.

In addition, you should consider supplementing the formal names with labels that have substantive, rather than merely procedural, significance. Because statutes generally address broad categories of activities rather than individual cases, they often create rights and obligations in broad but carefully defined classifications of persons, such as "employers" and "employees" or "buyers" and "sellers." Similarly, although courts interpret statutes and develop common law in the context of individual disputes, a series of judicial decisions on closely related points may create case law that allocates rights and obligations according to membership within general classes of persons, such as "landowners" and "trespassers." Therefore, you can more clearly reveal the legal significance of material facts in your case brief if you identify the named parties or other important actors with labels that reflect undisputed and legally significant classifications, such as employer, buyer, seller, merchant, landlord, tenant, landowner, or invitee.

When you assign a label to a party or otherwise characterize a factual matter, do not prematurely state a conclusion on an issue that is disputed by the parties and that is later analyzed in the opinion. For example, your statement of facts should not refer to a seller as a "merchant" if the parties dispute whether the seller is a merchant for purposes of determining the seller's warranty obligations under the Uniform Commercial Code. Similarly, your statement of facts should not state that the defendant in a criminal burglary prosecution "broke into" a "dwelling" if "breaking" and "dwelling" are elements of the charged offense and if the parties dispute those elements.

Rather than stating disputed legal conclusions in your statement of facts, summarize the subsidiary facts that the court analyzes in reaching its conclusion. For example, in the first case in the preceding paragraph, you might state that the seller of a computer system did not normally buy or sell goods, and that his sale of the computer system was an isolated transaction, but that the seller's occupation as a computer repair person led the buyer to believe that the seller had special knowledge of the performance capabilities of different computer systems. In other parts of your case brief, you can discuss whether those subsidiary facts satisfy the legal definition of "merchant," a matter that the parties dispute.

c. *Mastering the Facts*

To truly master the facts, you must go beyond simply summarizing or reorganizing the opinion's fact statement. Otherwise, you may find yourself simply transferring words and phrases from the casebook to your case brief without truly comprehending their meaning. Instead, seek a conceptual understanding of the facts, one that creates concrete images of the parties and transactions. If necessary, prepare charts, timelines, or other graphics that vividly represent the relationships between multiple parties and events.

To fully appreciate this point, return briefly to the discussion of *Hadley v. Baxendale* at the beginning of Chapter 2. Notice how the charts summarize the transactions and legal proceedings in a rough timeline. Did those charts help you form a vivid image of the events? If so, imagine how your own charts or other graphics can help you visualize complex transactions or relationships among parties.

As a practical matter, moreover, preparing graphics will enhance your class performance in at least three ways. First, you will force yourself to thoroughly study and comprehend the facts, because you will not be able to represent the facts in a graphic form unless you truly understand what happened in the case. Second, by glancing at your graphic representation in class, you can quickly recall the facts. Third, by relying primarily on such a representation in your class recital of the facts, you will tend to describe the facts more naturally and spontaneously than if you mechanically read your summary of the facts verbatim from your notes.

4. *Procedural History*

a. *Elements of Procedural History*

In your statement of the procedural history of a case on appeal, you should identify

1. which party or parties originally brought legal action against which others,
2. the legal claims and defenses and the relief sought in that action,
3. the trial court's disposition along with the stage of the proceedings at which the trial court rendered its decision,
4. the dispositions of any intermediate appellate courts below the authoring court, and
5. the authoring court's disposition.

In some cases, it may also be helpful to summarize the arguments that the parties made to the trial or appellate courts.

The case name on appeal does not always reveal which party initiated the legal action in the trial court. In the trial court, the case name begins with the plaintiff's name. In some appellate courts, however, the case name begins with the name of the party who is dissatisfied with the trial court's decision and has thus appealed (the "appellant") or petitioned for review (the "petitioner").

b. *Significance of Procedural History*

The nature of the plaintiff's legal claim and request for relief in the trial court may provide a key to the appellate court's analysis. For example, classification of a plaintiff's legal claim as one in tort rather than in contract may determine whether the claim is barred by a statute of limitations or whether the plaintiff is entitled to punitive damages. Similarly, whether a contract is sufficiently definite to enforce may depend on whether the plaintiff seeks enforcement through an award of damages or through injunctive relief granting specific enforcement.

Moreover, by stating the dispositions of all the courts that rendered decisions in the case, you can identify precisely the ruling that the authoring court has reviewed. The "disposition" is the practical, procedural effect of the court's holding on the litigation. In an opinion of a trial court, it might be "action dismissed," "summary judgment for the plaintiff," or "judgment on the jury verdict for the defendant." In an opinion of an appellate court, it might be "affirmed," "reversed," or "reversed and remanded for further proceedings."

In stating the trial court's disposition, try to identify the stage of the proceedings at which the trial court rendered judgment. An appellate court gives varying degrees of deference to different kinds of trial court decisions. Therefore, the likelihood of reversal by an appellate court depends partly on the stage of the proceedings at which judgment is rendered and, in some cases, on the classification of critical issues as ones of fact or law.

For example, although appellate courts review without restriction the legal rules formulated by trial courts, they restrict their review of the factual findings made by a trial judge or jury after a full trial, overturning such findings only in unusual circumstances. On the other hand, a trial judge does not resolve disputes of fact when he uses summary judgment to dispose of claims before trial, and an appellate court will reverse summary judgment if it determines, without deference to the analysis of the trial court, that the parties genuinely dispute material facts. Further, on a motion to dismiss an action for failure of the complaint to state a claim for relief, both the trial and appellate courts simply assume the truth of the allegations of fact in the complaint and analyze the legal significance of those allegations.

5. *Reasoning*

a. *Rule and Rationale*

By carefully studying the reasoning of opinions, you will gradually develop a feel for the way in which judges decide cases. With that acquired knowledge, you can develop the ability not only to analyze a legal dispute and offer a reasonable prediction of its outcome in court, but also to persuade a court to reach a conclusion favorable to your client.

Unfortunately, published opinions provide only an imperfect guide to the decision-making process. For example, the published opinion may exclude some of the more pragmatic reasons privately expressed by panel members to one another and may focus instead on more conventional legal analysis. Because an opinion thus communicates a court's actual reasoning imperfectly, do not hesitate to read between the lines and to offer facts or policy considerations that you believe may have contributed to the court's decision, even though the court did not expressly identify them as critical factors.

On the most fundamental level, when stating a court's reasoning, note whether the court is interpreting and applying a constitution or statute or is developing common law. Many judicial opinions rely on two or more sources of law, sometimes in combination and sometimes applied to different issues. Beyond that, you should summarize the court's reliance on precedent, its analysis of policy considerations, its explanation of the significance of critical facts, and its adoption or recognition of a legal rule of general application.

Some opinions do not formulate or restate a general legal rule that controls the analysis. Instead, they simply define a dispute on specific facts, reach a decision, and provide a justification that is narrowly tailored to the dispute before the court. Such an opinion leaves you only with a "holding" in the narrowest sense. Using techniques described near the end of this appendix, however, you can synthesize several such cases addressing similar issues and derive your own rule of general application.

When you analyze cases for class discussion, you should reflect on how the court's opinion might apply to facts other than those presented in the dispute that the court resolved. Your professors will provide many opportunities for application of legal rules to new facts in classroom hypotheticals and in essay examinations. If you can anticipate some of their questions, all the better.

b. Holding and Dictum

One of your most challenging tasks is to distinguish the holding of a decision from dictum. Narrowly defined, a "holding" is the court's resolution of an issue before it, limited to the material facts of that dispute. It does not include statements in the opinion about the probable outcome of disputes not before the court.

"Dictum," on the other hand, is a statement in the opinion that helps explain the court's reasoning by addressing questions not squarely presented in the dispute before the court. With dicta, a court may compare its rule of decision with other rules that it does not apply to the dispute, or it may discuss how its rule of decision would apply to facts other than those presented in the dispute before it.

The issue, facts, and holding of a previous decision limit the decision's effect as precedent under stare decisis. Even a lower court that is absolutely bound by the holdings of the previous decision may choose not to follow the dicta of the decision.

Dictum in an opinion is not meaningless; it may have considerable persuasive value. Nonetheless, because dictum does not carry the full weight of a holding, you should take care to read all of the court's reasoning in light of its narrow, fact-specific holding. Do not confuse what a court says, or even what it says it is doing, with what it actually does in a case.

6. Evaluation

You should resist any tendency to defer to the reasoning of a judicial decision as the expression of the single "correct" analysis of a dispute. Many disputes present close questions that are reasonably susceptible to alternative, inconsistent resolutions. You should read a decision critically to determine whether you agree with the result and the reasoning. Constant practice in critically examining judicial opinions will help you develop the ability later to persuade a court to adopt or reject the rule or reasoning of nonbinding authority.

On one level, you should examine an opinion for doctrinal integrity by asking questions such as these:

1. Does the court analogize or distinguish precedent in a convincing manner?
2. Does it apply the appropriate standard of review?
3. Does it analyze a statute under accepted principles of statutory interpretation and construction?
4. Does the court place excessive emphasis on certainty in a general rule at the expense of equitable considerations in the context of peculiar facts?

On another, closely related level, you should examine the policy and practical implications of an opinion. For example, you might ask:

1. Does a decision that promotes economic security for employees unwisely reduce economic efficiency at the expense of producers and consumers?
2. Does a court-developed tort standard allocate risks among parties in a way that encourages them to conduct themselves in a manner that avoids harm to others yet encourages socially productive ventures?

7. Synthesis

a. A Bridge between Case Briefs and Course Outlines

Perhaps the most important and the most challenging element of a case brief is the "synthesis," in which you explore the relationships between two or more cases that address the same issue or closely related ones. After comparing the critical elements of each in a series of cases, you can refine your view of the holding of each case in the series. With synthesis, you can either (1) formulate a general principle that explains all the decisions or (2) compare and evaluate the inconsistent approaches of different courts or of the same court over time. By synthesizing cases, you take a critical step in legal analysis that will have special significance when you look ahead to final examinations: Synthesis forms a bridge between daily briefing of isolated cases and periodic preparation of course outlines.

When studying law, you cannot fully appreciate the legal significance of a single judicial decision without examining its role within a larger body of case law; yet you cannot master the larger body of case law without first gaining at least an imperfect grasp of its parts, first one case in isolation and then a growing group of cases. As you brief a series of cases, you gain new insights by examining the cases' relationships to one another. Those insights may cause you to modify your early, less sophisticated understanding of a case standing alone or standing with fewer cases in the series. Additionally, they may enable you to identify a general legal principle, or at least a set of accepted criteria, that helps to explain the decisions.

b. Reconciling Disparate Results

The first step in synthesizing cases is to compare the cases' substantive results as conveyed by their holdings, regardless of the procedural dispositions of the appellate courts. For example, assume that two appellate decisions from different jurisdictions, States *X* and *Y*, have addressed the question of whether a specific newspaper advertisement amounts to an "offer," defined at common law as an expression of willingness to enter into a contract that empowers the offeree to create a contract by accepting the offer. In Case *A*, an appellate court of State *X* affirmed a trial court judgment that a specific newspaper advertisement amounted to an offer to sell the advertised goods. In Case *B*, an appellate court of State *Y* affirmed a trial court judgment that another newspaper advertisement communicated only an invitation to negotiate rather than an offer to sell. If you are not yet prepared to abandon hope of finding at least limited uniformity among the states in their formulation and application of common law, you should be curious about the reasons for the difference in results.

Synthesis of Cases

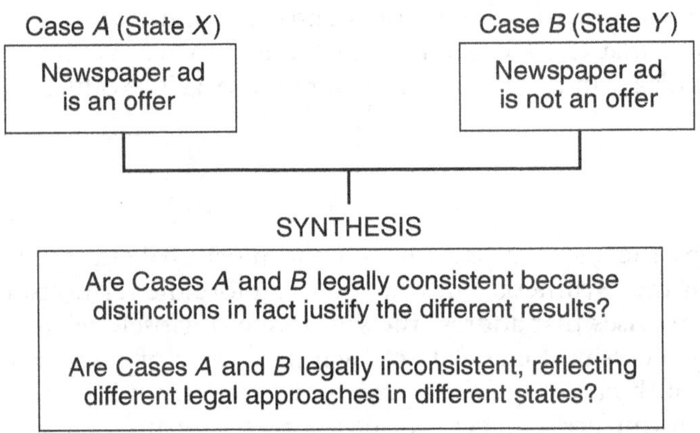

In the next step of the synthesis, you should determine whether Cases *A* and *B* are materially distinguishable and therefore warrant different results on application of the same legal principles, or whether they are legally inconsistent and simply represent different views of the law adopted by courts in different states. As a general approach, you should first attempt to reconcile the cases by searching for distinctions in facts, procedure, or both that support a conclusion that the cases are legally consistent. For example, unusually specific and detailed language of commitment in the advertisement in Case *A* might clearly communicate a willingness to conclude a contract for sale on a customer's assent. In contrast, more general language in the advertisement in Case *B* might leave important terms of sale unaddressed, suggesting a need for further bargaining before the advertiser is willing to commit to a contract for sale.

In these circumstances, you could compose a single legal rule that is consistent with the reasoning of both cases and that appropriately produces different results on application to the contrasting facts of the cases:

> A newspaper advertisement is an offer only if it expresses definite commitment, leaving no important detail for future negotiation.

With such a synthesis, you will better understand the holdings of Cases *A* and *B*, more firmly grasp otherwise abstract legal principles, and improve your ability to predict the outcome of a new case that presents the same issue on new facts.

If you fail to find material distinctions in facts or procedure between Cases *A* and *B*, you can safely conclude that the appellate decisions are legally inconsistent. In that event, you should analyze the reasons for the different views of the law. Perhaps States *X* and *Y* apply different legal approaches because they emphasize different policies. Such a synthesis helps you to put conflicting case law into perspective and to develop the ability to persuade a court in a future case to adopt one line of conflicting authority over another.

Different results in cases decided by the same court present particularly interesting questions of synthesis, because the court cannot depart from its prior decision under stare decisis without overruling the prior decision. If the cases are not obviously distinguishable but the court does not explicitly overrule the prior decision, you should search with special care for possible distinguishing features before concluding that the court has implicitly overruled the prior decision. Of course, the proper synthesis may lie in middle ground: A decision may limit the range of possible interpretations of a prior holding without completely overruling it.

c. Comparing Reasons for and Limits on Consistent Results

If two cases reach the same result, a synthesis should compare the facts and reasoning of the two cases to determine whether the courts were influenced by similar factors. For example, suppose that in Case *A* a court in State *X* held that a particular newspaper advertisement constituted an offer to sell the advertised goods. Suppose further that in Case *C* a court in State *Z* found a different newspaper advertisement to constitute an offer. Although both decisions find offers, a comparison of the facts may suggest that Case *C* represents a significant extension of the holding of Case *A*. Similarly, the reasoning of Case *A* might suggest that the court in State *X* would not have reached the same result if presented with the facts on which the court in State *Z* found an offer in Case *C*.

d. Limited Utility of a Case Viewed in Isolation

When you synthesize, you compare two or more cases. Therefore, when you prepare a single case brief in isolation, you will not include a synthesis, except perhaps in the form of a prediction of the questions that may arise later from uncertainty in the breadth of the holding of the case.

In a perfect world, you would read all opinions in a series of cases relating to a problem area before briefing any of them. You would then brief each case with an eye to the problems raised in the others, and finally prepare a single synthesis of the entire series of cases.

Unfortunately, class assignments and library research techniques seldom permit that luxury. As a more practical procedure, you should prepare a synthesis for each case brief in a series beginning with the second case. Each succeeding synthesis will reflect the addition of a case to the group of cases among which you can make comparisons, thus adding new insights to previous syntheses. If your casebook does not provide more than one main case on a topic, try to synthesize the main case with notes cases or hypothetical cases following the main case, or with hypothetical cases presented in class by your professor.

Checklist for Briefing a Case

In preparing a case brief, follow these steps:

- Place the case in context, noting its place in your current topic of study.
- Thoroughly read the entire case at least once.
- Identify the case. Include details that help identify the case's place in the overall case law of the jurisdiction and the case's value as precedent.
- State the issue and the holding as narrowly as possible without making your question cumbersome and unwieldy; tailor your statement of the issue to the facts.
- Summarize the material facts and the helpful background facts.
- Summarize the procedural history, including the dispositions in the trial court and on appeal.
- Summarize the reasoning of the court. Distinguish holding from dictum. Identify general rules recognized by the court and pay particular attention to the authority, policy analysis, and logic on which the court relies.
- Critically evaluate the court's holding and reasoning.
- Synthesize the case with others that present the same or a similar issue. Attempt to explain apparently conflicting results among the cases.

Exercises for Practice and Sample Case Briefs

1. Case Brief

Using the format set forth at the end of Chapter 2, read the following excerpt of the appellate opinion in *White v. Benkowski* and prepare a case brief. Do not be satisfied with the court's statement of the issue; try to improve it. Critically evaluate the court's holding and dicta regarding the availability of punitive damages; ask yourself whether you can defend the court's views on the grounds of economic efficiency, certainty in legal rules, equity in individual cases, the proper roles of compensation and deterrence, or any other policy considerations. You should not yet attempt to synthesize this case with any others, although you may comment on possible extensions or limitations to its holding that subsequent cases could introduce.

After completing your case brief, compare it with the sample in section 2 below.

WHITE v. BENKOWSKI
Supreme Court of Wisconsin
37 Wis. 2d 285, 155 N.W.2d 74 (1967)
[footnotes in the original omitted]

This case involves a neighborhood squabble between two adjacent property owners.

Prior to November 28, 1962, Virgil and Gwynneth White, the plaintiffs, were desirous of purchasing a home in Oak Creek. Unfortunately, the particular home that the Whites were interested in was without a water supply. Despite this fact, the Whites purchased the home.

The adjacent home was owned and occupied by Paul and Ruth Benkowski, the defendants. The Benkowskis had a well in their yard which had piping that connected with the Whites' home.

On November 28, 1962, the Whites and Benkowskis entered into a written agreement wherein the Benkowskis promised to supply water to the Whites' home for 10 years or until an earlier date when either water was supplied by the municipality, the well became inadequate, or the Whites drilled their own well. The Whites promised to pay $3 a month for the water and one-half the cost of any future repairs or maintenance that the Benkowski well might require. As part of the transaction, but not included in the written agreement, the Whites gave the Benkowskis $400 which was used to purchase and install a new pump and an additional tank that would increase the capacity of the well.

Initially, the relationship between the new neighbors was friendly. With the passing of time, however, their friendship deteriorated and the neighbors actually became hostile. In 1964, the water supply, which was controlled by the Benkowskis, was intermittently shut off. Mrs. White kept a record of the dates and durations that her water supply was not operative. Her record showed that the water was shut off on the following occasions:

(1) March 5, 1964, from 7:10 P.M. to 7:25 P.M.

(2) March 9, 1964, from 3:40 P.M. to 4:00 P.M.

(3) March 11, 1964, from 6:00 P.M. to 6:15 P.M.

(4) June 10, 1964, from 6:20 P.M. to 7:03 P.M.

The record also discloses that the water was shut off completely or partially for varying lengths of time on July 1, 6, 7, and 17, 1964, and on November 25, 1964.

Mr. Benkowski claimed that the water was shut off either to allow accumulated sand in the pipes to settle or to remind the Whites that their use of the water was excessive. Mr. White claimed that the Benkowskis breached their contract by shutting off the water.

Following the date when the water was last shut off (November 25, 1964), the Whites commenced an action to recover compensatory and punitive damages for an alleged violation of the agreement to supply water. . . .

The jury returned a verdict which found that the Benkowskis maliciously shut off the Whites' water supply for harassment purposes. Compensatory damages were set at $10 and punitive damages at $2,000. On motions after verdict, the court reduced the compensatory award to $1 and granted defendants' motion to strike the punitive-damage question and answer.

Judgment for plaintiffs of $1 was entered and they appeal.

Wilkie, Justice.

Two issues are raised on this appeal. . . .

1. Are punitive damages available in actions for breach of contract?

. . . .

Punitive Damages

. . . .

Over one hundred years ago this court held that, under proper circumstances, a plaintiff was entitled to recover... punitive damages.

Kink v. Combs is the most recent case in this state which deals with the practice of permitting punitive damages. In *Kink* the court relied on *Fuchs v. Kupper* and reaffirmed its adherence to the rule of punitive damages.

In Wisconsin compensatory damages are given to make whole the damage or injury suffered by the injured party. On the other hand, punitive damages are given

> . . . on the basis of punishment to the injured party not because he has been injured, which injury has been compensated with compensatory damages, but to punish the wrongdoer for his malice and to deter others from like conduct.

Thus we reach the question of whether the plaintiffs are entitled to punitive damages for a breach of the water agreement. The overwhelming weight of authority supports the proposition that punitive damages are not recoverable in actions for breach of contract. In *Chitty on Contracts*, the author states that the right to receive punitive damages for breach of contract is now confined to the single case of damages for breach of a promise to marry.

Simpson states:

> Although damages in excess of compensation for loss are in some instances permitted in tort actions by way of punishment ... in contract actions the damages recoverable are limited to compensation for pecuniary loss sustained by the breach.

Corbin states that as a general rule, punitive damages are not recoverable for breach of contract.

In Wisconsin, the early case of *Gordon v. Brewster* involved the breach of an employment contract. The trial court instructed the jury that if the nonperformance of the contract was attributable to the defendant's wrongful act of discharging the plaintiff, then that would go to increase the damages sustained. On appeal, this court said that the instruction was unfortunate and might have led the jurors to suppose that they could give something more than actual compensation in a breach of contract case. We find no Wisconsin case in which breach of contract (other than breach of promise to marry) has led to the award of punitive damages.

Persuasive authority from other jurisdictions supports the proposition (without exception) that punitive damages are not available in breach of contract actions. This is true even if the breach, as in the instant case, is willful.

Although it is well recognized that breach of a contractual duty may be a tort, in such situations the contract creates the relation out of which grows the duty to use care in the performance of a responsibility prescribed by the contract. Not so here. No tort was pleaded or proved.

Reversed in part by reinstating the jury verdict relating to compensatory damages and otherwise affirmed.

2. Sample Case Brief for *White v. Benkowski*

Compare the case brief that you prepared in Problem 1 with the following sample. Remember that the sample is only an example of a reasonable reaction to the opinion; it is not necessarily the best interpretation and evaluation of the opinion, and it certainly is not the only reasonable one. In particular, the "evaluation" is a matter of individual opinion.

Context: Remedies for Breach of Contract/Limits on Damages

White v. Benkowski, 37 Wis. 2d 285, 155 N.W.2d 74 (1967), CB 12.

Issue and Holding: Is Buyer entitled to an award of punitive damages for Supplier's malicious breach of a contract to supply water, even though Buyer established no independent tort? No.

Facts: The Whites (Buyer) and Benkowskis (Supplier) are neighbors. By written agreement, Supplier promised to supply Buyer's house with water from Supplier's well for 10 years, unless the well became inadequate or unnecessary. The relationship deteriorated, and Supplier maliciously shut off Buyer's water supply partially or completely on nine occasions for the purpose of harassing Buyer.

Procedural History: Buyer sued Supplier for compensatory and punitive damages, alleging only breach of contract. On a finding of malicious breach of contract, the jury awarded Buyer $10 in compensatory damages and $2,000 in punitive damages. On motions after verdict, the trial court disallowed punitive damages and reduced the compensatory damage award from $10 to $1. Buyer appealed. The appellate court reversed the trial court's reduction of the award for compensatory damages, but it affirmed the trial court's elimination of the award for punitive damages.

Reasoning: Prior Wisconsin case law, persuasive authority from other jurisdictions, and the views of commentators support the following common law principle: Even an intentional and malicious breach of contract will not support an award of punitive damages. In dictum, the court suggests that punitive damages could be awarded if the breach of contract also constituted an independent tort; however, Buyer failed to plead and prove an independent tort. The court did not explicitly overrule a nineteenth-century decision in which it had approved punitive damages for breach of a marriage contract, thus leaving open the question of whether the court will retain that exception and distinguish it from breaches of more ordinary contracts.

3. Case Briefs with Synthesis

Contracts are formed through a process of offer and acceptance. An offer is an expression of a willingness to enter into a contract. It gives to the party to whom it is addressed, the "offeree," the power to create the contract by assenting to the offer in a manner authorized by the offer. To constitute an offer, an expression must lead a reasonable person in the position of the offeree to understand that she has such power.

With that background, prepare a case brief for each of the following two cases. End the second case brief with a synthesis of the two cases. Do not assume that all the citations in these opinions are consistent with the current uniform citation style that you should use in your office memoranda. Compare your case briefs and synthesis with the sample that follows this exercise. For additional practice in synthesizing cases, perform Assignment 1 in Appendix III.

CRAFT v. ELDER & JOHNSTON CO.
Ohio Court of Appeals
38 N.E.2d 416 (Ohio Ct. App. 1941)

Barnes, Judge.

... On or about January 31, 1940, the defendant, the Elder & Johnston Company, carried an advertisement in the Dayton Shopping News, an offer for sale of a certain all electric sewing machine for the sum of $26 as a "Thursday Only Special." Plaintiff ... alleges that the above publication is an advertising paper distributed in Montgomery County and throughout the city of Dayton; that on Thursday, February 1, 1940, she tendered to the defendant company $26 in payment for one of the machines offered in the advertisement, but that defendant refused to fulfill the offer and has continued to so refuse. The petition further alleges that the value of the machine offered was $175 and she asks damages in the sum of $149 plus interest from February 1, 1940....

The trial court dismissed plaintiff's petition as evidenced by a journal entry, the pertinent portion of which reads as follows: "Upon consideration the court finds that said advertisement was not an offer which could be accepted by plaintiff to form a contract, and this case is therefore dismissed with prejudice to a new action, at costs of plaintiff." ...

We will now briefly make reference to some of the authorities. "It is clear that in the absence of special circumstances an ordinary newspaper advertisement is not an offer, but is an offer to negotiate—an offer to receive offers—or, as it is sometimes called, an offer to chaffer." Restatement of the Law of Contracts, Par. 25, Page 31.

Under the above paragraph the following illustration is given, "'A,' a clothing merchant, advertises overcoats of a certain kind for sale at $50. This is not an offer but an invitation to the public to come and purchase."

"Thus, if goods are advertised for sale at a certain price, it is not an offer and no contract is formed by the statement of an intending purchaser that he will take a specified quantity of the goods at that price. The construction is rather favored that such an advertisement is a mere invitation to enter into a bargain rather than an offer. So a published price list is not an offer to sell the goods listed at the published price." Williston on Contracts, Revised Edition, Vol. 1, Par. 27, Page 54.

"The commonest example of offers meant to open negotiations and to call forth offers in the technical sense are advertisements, circulars and trade letters sent out by business houses. While it is possible that the offers made by such means may be in such form as to become contracts, they are often merely expressions of a willingness to negotiate." Page on the Law of Contracts, 2d Ed., Vol. 1, Page 112, Par. 84....

"But generally a newspaper advertisement or circular couched in general language and proper to be sent to all persons interested in a particular trade or business, or a prospectus of a general and descriptive nature, will be construed as an invitation to make an offer." 17 Corpus Juris Secundum, Contracts, Page 389, § 46, Column 2. . . .

We are constrained to the view that the trial court committed no prejudicial error in dismissing plaintiff's petition.

The judgment of the trial court will be affirmed and costs adjudged against the plaintiff-appellant.

Entry may be prepared in accordance with this opinion. Geiger, P.J., and Hornbeck, J., concur.

LEFKOWITZ v. GREAT MINNEAPOLIS SURPLUS STORE

Minnesota Supreme Court
251 Minn. 188, 86 N.W.2d 689 (1957)

Murphy, Justice

This is an appeal from an order of the Municipal Court of Minneapolis. . . . The order for judgment awarded the plaintiff the sum of $138.50 as damages for breach of contract.

This case grows out of the alleged refusal of the defendant to sell to the plaintiff a certain fur piece which it had offered for sale in a newspaper advertisement. It appears from the record that . . . the defendant published the following advertisement in a Minneapolis newspaper:

> . . . .
>
> Saturday 9 A.M.
>
> . . . .
>
> 1 Black Lapin Stole Beautiful,
> worth $139.50 . . . $1.00 First Come
> First Served

The record supports the findings of the court that on . . . the Saturday[] following the publication of the above-described ad[] the plaintiff was the first to present himself at the appropriate counter in the defendant's store and . . . demanded the . . . stole so advertised and indicated his readiness to pay the sale price of $1. . . . [T]he defendant refused to sell the merchandise to the plaintiff. . . .

The defendant relies principally on *Craft v. Elder & Johnston Co.* . . . On the facts before us we are concerned with whether the advertisement constituted an offer, and, if so, whether the plaintiff's conduct constituted an acceptance.

There are numerous authorities which hold that a particular advertisement in a newspaper or circular letter relating to a sale of articles may be construed by the court as constituting an offer, acceptance of which would complete a contract. [citations omitted]. . . .

The authorities above cited emphasize that, where the offer is clear, definite, and explicit, and leaves nothing open for negotiation, it constitutes an offer, acceptance of which will complete the contract. The most recent case on the subject is *Johnson v. Capital City Ford Co., La. App.*, 85 So. 2d 75, in which the court pointed out that a newspaper advertisement relating to the purchase and sale of automobiles may constitute an offer, acceptance of which will consummate a contract and create an obligation in the offeror to perform according to the terms of the published offer.

Whether in any individual instance a newspaper advertisement is an offer rather than an invitation to make an offer depends on the legal intention of the parties and the surrounding circumstances. Annotation, 157 A.L.R. 744, 751; 77 C.J.S., Sales, § 25b; 17 C.J.S., Contracts, § 389. We are of the view on the facts before us that the offer by the defendant of the sale of the Lapin fur was clear, definite, and explicit, and left nothing open for negotiation. The plaintiff having successfully managed to be the first one to appear at the seller's place of business to be served, as requested by the advertisement, and having offered the stated purchase price of the article, he was entitled to performance on the part of the defendant....

Affirmed.

4. Sample Case Briefs with Synthesis

Both Evaluations in the sample briefs below note the importance of the quantity term. The cases don't specifically discuss the presence or absence of a quantity term; instead, that analysis reflects the kind of extra information that you might secure from class discussion.

Context: Contract Formation under Common Law/Offer

Craft v. Elder & Johnston Co., 38 N.E.2d 416 (Ohio Ct. App. 1941)

Issue: Did a newspaper advertisement for the sale of a certain electric sewing machine for $26 as a Thursday only special constitute an offer?

Holding: No. In the absence of special circumstances, the ad was only an invitation to negotiate.

Facts: Buyer alleged that Seller advertised a type of sewing machine worth $175 for sale for $26 in a shopping newspaper with citywide distribution. The sale price was good for Thursday only. On Thursday, Buyer attempted to purchase one of the advertised machines but was refused.

Procedural History: Buyer sued Seller for the difference between the value of the machine and the advertised sale price, plus interest. The trial court dismissed on the ground that the ad was not an offer to sell. The court of appeals affirms.

Reasoning: Relying mainly on secondary sources of the common law, the court applies a general rule of construction that newspaper advertisements are invitations to submit offers, rather than offers themselves, if they do no more than inform the general public of the price for described goods. The court suggests that an ad might constitute an offer in "special circumstances."

Evaluation: This decision makes sense. Seller did not specify any quantity limitations in the ad, nor did it limit who might respond to it. If the ad were an offer, Seller might be subjected to unlimited liability as innumerable buyers accepted the offer for more sewing machines than were in stock. A reasonable buyer would not interpret the ad to permit those consequences.

Lefkowitz v. Great Minneapolis Surplus Store, 86 N.W.2d 689 (Minn. 1957).

Issue and Holding: Did newspaper ad for the sale of specified quantities of described goods to the first arriving customers constitute offers to sell? Yes.

Facts: In a newspaper ad, Seller advertised "1 Black Lapin Stole," for sale at a specified date and time for $1, "First Come First Served." On the appropriate date, Buyer attempted to purchase advertised item for $1 and was refused.

Procedural History: The Buyer sued the Seller for breach of contract and was awarded $138.50 in the trial court. The Supreme Court affirms.

Reasoning: The court rejects Seller's argument that *Craft* is controlling; instead, it relies on authorities that recognize a newspaper ad as an offer if it is "clear, definite, and leaves nothing open for negotiation." This offer met that standard.

Evaluation and Synthesis: This decision also makes sense, because the ad identified not only the goods, but also the quantity available and the means of identifying which buyers could bind Seller to contracts. Thus, unlike the ad in *Craft*, these ads would not create the risk of unlimited liability for Seller if construed as offers. Accordingly, a reader could reasonably interpret them as statements of intention to contract, with nothing left for further negotiation. The cases are distinguishable on their facts and thus are legally reconcilable.

Appendix II

Introduction to the Legal System: Problems for Part II of the Main Text

Problem 1. Sources and Limits of Lawmaking Powers

Examine each government action described in the sections below. Which represents a legitimate exercise of legislative, judicial, or executive authority?

a. The Flag-Bashing Bill

The First Amendment to the United States Constitution provides in part that "Congress shall make no law ... abridging the freedom of speech, or of the press." Shortly before July 4, however, Congress sought to override the First Amendment by restricting speech critical of the American flag. Offended by a wave of public criticism of the American flag and the values for which it stands, Congress enacted the "Flag-Bashing Bill," which the president signed into law. Section 1 of that statute makes it an "unlawful publication practice for any person to publish any oral or written statement critical of the flag of the United States of America." Section 2 provides for fines of up to $5,000 for each violation of the statute.

Section 3 of the statute created the Flag Protection Commission (FPC), a federal agency, and granted it powers to investigate violations of the statute, to hold hearings on alleged violations, to impose fines for violations, and to issue rules and regulations to aid in its investigative and enforcement activities. Section 4 of the statute grants jurisdiction to the United States Courts of Appeals to review the FPC's actions, subject to further appeal to the United States Supreme Court.

b. The FPC Flexes Its Muscle

As the chief officer of the executive branch of the United States government, the president appointed several staunch flag enthusiasts to the FPC. Without delay, the FPC issued rules and regulations that, among other things, (1) describe procedures for FPC hearings, (2) authorize FPC hearing officers to impose fines of $1,000 to $10,000 for various kinds of violations of the Flag-Bashing Bill, and (3) define the statutory phrase "unlawful publication practice" to include any public criticism of the flag or the president's wardrobe.

c. Judicial Review

In the FPC's first major hearing, an FPC hearing officer found that a Washington, D.C., newspaper publisher had violated the Flag-Bashing Bill by publishing a critical commentary entitled "The Stars and Stripes—Do the Colors Clash?" The hearing officer fined the publisher $2,000. The publisher appealed to the United States Court of Appeals for the District of Columbia Circuit.

On appeal, the court of appeals overturned the hearing officer's decision. Contrary to the plain language, legislative history, and clear purpose of the Flag-Bashing Bill, the court found that the bill prohibited only oral criticism of the president's foreign trade policies.

The FPC appealed to the United States Supreme Court. The Supreme Court upheld the court of appeals' overturning of the hearing officer's decision, but on different grounds. The Supreme Court concluded that (1) the FPC had validly issued the rules and regulations on which the hearing officer had relied in this case, and (2) the hearing officer's findings and imposition of a fine were consistent with a proper interpretation of the Flag-Bashing Bill. However, the Supreme Court held that the statute was unenforceable because it violated the First Amendment to the United States Constitution.

Problem 2. Developing the Common Law and Interpreting Statutes That Modify the Common Law

In each of the sections below, fully explain the reasons for your conclusions. Express each step of your analysis.

a. Survival of the Fittest and the Common Law

If you have not already done so, perform Exercise 1-1 at the end of Chapter 1 in the main text. If you have already performed that exercise, review that exercise and your response to it.

b. The Justification of Self-Preservation

Assume that your court responded to *State v. Blight* by adopting the following common law rule and by remanding to the trial court for a new trial with jury instructions consistent with the new rule:

> A defendant is justified in killing another human being if the defendant is reasonably certain at the time of the killing that the killing is necessary to preserve his own life and that failure to kill the other will result in the death of both.

Do you support the rule? Apply this rule to the facts of *State v. Blight*. Should the jury acquit if instructed to apply this rule? Explain your answer in detail.

c. Mercy Killing and the Criminal Code

One hundred years after *State v. Blight*, your state has largely replaced the common law crimes with a comprehensive criminal code: a collection of statutes that defines criminal conduct and penalties, incorporating some common law principles and modifying or rejecting others. Section 101 of the criminal code defines the crime of murder as "the killing of another human being without justification." Section 101.A provides that "premeditated murder" constitutes first-degree murder, which carries a maximum penalty of life in prison. Section 101.G, enacted just last year, provides that "a desire to ease the suffering of a terminally ill person is not justification for ending the person's life prematurely." A state legislative committee report explained the purpose of the bill that later was codified as section 101.G:

> This bill makes it clear that euthanasia, popularly known as "mercy-killing," is not "justified" under § 101 of our criminal code and therefore is not excluded from our definition of murder. With this bill, the state declares its policies to promote the use of life-sustaining measures and to preserve the life of even a terminally ill patient for as long as possible, in the hope that a cure for the illness may be found before the patient dies. The physical and emotional suffering of terminally ill patients should be relieved through counseling and the prescription of pain-relieving drugs rather than the termination of life-sustaining medical equipment or treatment. Thus, even well-meaning friends or relatives who "pull the plug" on a terminally ill patient may be charged under our murder statute.

(1) Blight *Revisited*

Review Subsections a and b above. If facts identical to those of *State v. Blight* were presented to a jury today, should the jury convict the defendant of first-degree murder under the criminal code? How should the trial judge instruct the jury? If the state appellate courts have not yet interpreted section 101's reference to "justification," should the trial judge attempt to define that term for the jury? On what would it base its definition? Suppose that Blight has argued that the trial judge should not instruct the jury according to section 101.G, on the ground that section 101.G does not apply to his case. How should the trial court rule and why?

(2) The Pact

Emma Padilla was losing her battle against cancer. Although she continued to receive chemotherapy, it made her quite ill and offered her almost no hope of remission. Preferring to live her final days in familiar surroundings, she arranged for full-time nursing care in her home. She often spoke to her nurses about her desire to die and about her wish that no one prolong her life with heroic lifesaving measures.

One evening, Padilla suffered a seizure; her heart stopped beating, and she ceased breathing. Her night nurse, Jim Murrow, rushed to Padilla's side to administer cardiopulmonary resuscitation and to hook up a portable respirator and other lifesaving equipment. He stopped short, however, remembering Padilla's wish to die naturally. Murrow allowed Padilla to die, notified the hospital that had been treating Padilla with chemotherapy, and admitted to several colleagues that he had honored Padilla's wishes that he refrain from prolonging her life.

Is Murrow guilty of murder under sections 101 and 101.G of the criminal code? Fully analyze the law and the facts, taking care to advance arguments for both the defense and the prosecution.

Appendix III

Legal Method and Analysis: Problems for Part III of the Main Text

Problem 1. Analogy, Distinction, and Precedent

Read the materials for the Office Memorandum Assignment in Appendix IV. The only two Arizona cases provided in the materials, *Henderson* and *Fogleman*, deny any award of damages for emotional distress. The only case in your materials that approves of such an award for breach of contract is *Browning*, an early decision from another jurisdiction. Fully explain how you could distinguish the facts of *Henderson* and *Fogleman* from Araiza's case, and explain how you could analogize the facts of her case to those of *Browning*. Further explain how dicta in *Henderson* and *Fogleman* support an analogy to *Browning*.

Problem 2. Legal Policy and Application to Facts

Cheryl Watkins, an expert pilot, retained Flight Ready, a private aircraft service, to maintain her single-engine private plane based at Palm City Airport in Calzona. While flying from Palm City to a nearby town on a business trip, Watkins noticed that the passenger door of the cabin had sprung partially open. She knew that the partially open door would reduce the stability of the aircraft under certain conditions and that flying for more than a few minutes with the door open would be distracting, if not hazardous. She rejected the idea of making an emergency landing on the busy highway below or on the desert dotted with massive saguaro cacti. Instead, Watkins leaned across the passenger's seat to close the passenger door, even though her instructor had twice warned her never to do so. As Cheryl reached for the passenger door, the plane abruptly rolled to the right and spiraled into a sharp dive. Watkins was not in position to take control of the aircraft, and it crashed into the desert seconds later, killing Watkins instantly. A tape recorder found in the wreckage had recorded Watkins's comments during the emergency, allowing investigators to reconstruct the events.

In a wrongful death action brought by Watkins's survivors in Calzona, the jury answered several specific questions called "special interrogatories," submitted to it by the court. Specifically, the jury found that personnel for Flight Ready had negligently repaired a latch on the passenger door of Watkins's aircraft, which door had previously stuck in the closed position. The negligent repair caused the door to spring open during the flight. The jury also found that the partially open door had reduced the stability of the aircraft, causing it to roll and dive when Watkins shifted her position in the aircraft. Finally, the jury found that had Watkins remained in the pilot's seat, she likely could have maintained control of the plane and either reached her destination without mishap or survived an emergency landing on the desert. Following an instruction based on the doctrine of "contributory negligence," the jury denied Watkins's survivors any recovery.

Under the traditional common law doctrine of contributory negligence, a victim of a tort is precluded from recovering damages from the tortfeasor if the victim negligently contributed to her own injuries. At the time of trial, Calzona courts still applied the doctrine of contributory negligence as a defense in a tort action brought either by the victim or by her survivors. Accordingly, the trial court had rejected a jury instruction proposed by counsel for the plaintiffs that would have permitted the jury to apply the doctrine of "pure comparative negligence." Under the proposed instruction, Watkins's own negligence would not preclude the plaintiffs from all recovery; instead, their recovery would simply be diminished in proportion to which Watkins's own negligence contributed to her death.

In class discussion or a written essay, respond to the following questions:

a. In the process of developing its common law, should the Calzona Supreme Court abandon its contributory negligence doctrine by adopting a pure comparative negligence scheme? Discuss the policy arguments supporting both sides of this issue.

b. As a legislator, would you support proposed legislation that would create a modified comparative fault system in which a plaintiff would receive the benefits of comparative negligence if she is no more than 50 percent at fault but would recover nothing if she is more than 50 percent at fault? State your reasons for your support or opposition.

c. How would either a pure or a modified comparative negligence standard likely apply to the facts on remand?

Appendix IV

Office Memoranda: Assignments for Part IV

The assignment below presents a single issue for analysis. It is a "closed universe" problem: All the necessary authority is provided at the end of the assignment. The dispute in the assignment is set in Arizona, so the Arizona case law provided to you is mandatory authority. Of course, your professor can modify the problem by asking you to conduct research to supplement the materials provided to you in the Assignment, perhaps after setting it in a different jurisdiction.

The page numbers within the opinions in the original reporters appear in brackets in the reproductions of the opinions at the end of the assignment. Some of the opinions cite to other authorities in a form other than standard citation form. When you cite to any authority, adopt the citation form recommended by your professor, rather than other forms reflected in some of the opinions.

Office Memorandum Assignment
Single Issue
Jurisdiction: Arizona
Closed Universe

You are an associate in a firm that represents 15 young women and their mothers. They complain that a seamstress intentionally breached a con- tract to provide gowns for their use in a Quinceañera ceremony in Phoenix, Arizona.

A Quinceañera ceremony is a traditional "coming out" party for a woman on her fifteenth birthday. It is celebrated in many Hispanic communities throughout the world. The celebration consists of a Catholic mass, followed by a formal reception that includes a dinner and dance. The celebrant, known as the "Quinceañera," traditionally wears a gown that is nearly as formal and ornate as a wedding gown. She is attended by relatives, by godmothers and godfathers, and by 14 maids of honor. The maids of honor are typically peers and close friends of the Quinceañera. The maids traditionally wear fancy gowns that match each other either in color or pattern. Along with their male attendants, they participate in both the mass and the reception.

Your primary client, Trina Araiza, turned 15 last July 10. She and her 14 chosen maids of honor hired Ramona Udave to sew gowns of a particular pattern for the Quinceañera celebration. Trina's mother, Cristina, negotiated the contract with Udave. Because the Quinceañera and her maids of honor were minors, their parents cosigned the contract to ensure enforceability. On March 15, the Quinceañera participants provided Udave with material for the gowns and met with Udave so that she could take measurements. On May 5, Udave met with each participant for final fittings. At that meeting, each gown was only partially sewn, was partially held together with pins, and was not wearable.

Throughout May and June, Udave repeatedly assured all the participants that she was making normal progress on the gowns and that the gowns would be ready on time. In early July, Udave represented that she was putting the finishing touches on the gowns and that they would all be ready by the morning of the Quinceañera. Although some of the participants were anxious to see the gowns, Udave said that she never let her clients see her work until the last stitch was in place.

On the morning of the Quinceañera celebration, the participants arrived at Udave's shop to pick up their gowns. Udave repeatedly assured each of them that her gown was minutes away from completion and that each one should wait for the gown in the front room of Udave's shop. Udave kept the participants waiting for varying periods of time, some beyond 1:00 P.M., the time for commencement of the mass. Araiza herself received her gown at 12:30 P.M. At that time, she was nearly ill with anxiety. She dressed quickly and arrived at the site of the mass by 1:10 P.M. Her maids of honor, how- ever, were still waiting for their gowns and therefore could not yet participate in the formal procession that begins the mass. By 1:30 P.M. five of the maids of honor had arrived with their gowns. Although the gowns were unfinished and looked terrible, Araiza and her five maids of honor walked in the procession and began the mass. Araiza was emotionally distraught during the mass, partly because of the absence of two maids of honor who were designated to recite prayers with her; those maids of honor were still waiting at Udave's tailoring shop on Udave's representations that their gowns were nearly complete.

In fact, the remaining gowns were in the same condition as they had been during the March fitting, and Udave never completed them. Although Udave continued to represent that the gowns were nearly completed, the remaining Quinceañera participants left her shop shortly after the mass and attended the reception in casual or semi-formal clothes. Although they participated in the traditional reception procession and waltz, they felt humiliated because of their inappropriate attire.

Araiza and the maids of honor suffered embarrassment and other forms of emotional distress as a result of Udave's actions. Based on information they acquired after the Quinceañera ceremony, they are convinced that Udave intentionally ruined the Quinceañera because of her friendship with a bitter rival of the Araiza family.

Your supervising attorney, Daniel Adams, intends to explore various potential claims, including breach of contract, fraud, and negligence. He wants you to assume that he can establish only the contract claim, and he wants you to analyze the question whether the Quinceañera and her maids of honor can recover damages for emotional distress on their claims for breach of their collective contract with Udave. He knows that they can recover damages for other kinds of losses stemming from the breach, but he thinks that the damages for emotional distress may be problematic.

Using only the following research materials, prepare an office memorandum, five to seven pages in length, discussing this question. In reciting the facts of this dispute, summarize only the facts material to your analysis. You may assume that the Quinceañera and her maids of honor are parties to an enforceable contract and that any dispute regarding the contract will be governed by Arizona law. Because Mr. Adams intends to use your memorandum to help him prepare a brief that he will submit to an Arizona tribunal, he wants you to use parallel citations when citing to either of the two Arizona decisions. To help you find your way through those decisions, internal page numbers for the official Arizona Reports are noted in bold in brackets, and internal page numbers for the Pacific Reporter are noted in italics in brackets. When citing to the Alabama decision, you may cite only to the regional reporter.

Research Materials

CONTRACTS
E. Allan Farnsworth
(4th ed. 2004)

§ 12.17 Other Limitations, Including Emotional Disturbance. . . .

[**pg. 810**] A limitation more firmly rooted in tradition generally denies recovery for emotional disturbance (or "mental distress") resulting from breach of contract, even if the limitations of unforeseeability and uncertainty can be overcome. . . . Whatever the basis of the limitation, courts have not applied it inflexibly. Some courts have looked to the nature of the contract and made exceptions, as under the Restatement Second rule, when serious emotional disturbance was a particularly likely result of the breach.

FARMERS INSURANCE EXCHANGE v. HENDERSON
82 Ariz. 335, 313 P.2d 404 (1957) (Arizona Supreme Court)

[**pg. 337,** ***pg. 405***] WINDES, Justice.

The appellant, Farmers Insurance Exchange, issued to appellee, George Henderson, a public liability insurance policy insuring him against claims for death or bodily injury and property damage resulting from the operation of Henderson's car. The limit of the policy for death or bodily injury was $5,000 for one person and $10,000 for one accident and $5,000 for property damage. There was a collision between the Henderson car when operated by his employee, one Whitehead, and an automobile operated by Charles Breesman. Three actions were filed for damages resulting from the accident. One action was by . . . Breesman against Henderson and White- head. This . . . action was tried in the superior court. The present case is a suit by Henderson against the company for damages claimed to have resulted from the failure to settle the Breesman claim for an amount within its policy limits when opportunity was presented for such settlement. This failure caused Henderson and his wife to lose their business, because they were forced to sell the business to pay for liability in excess of their liability insurance limits. A jury trial resulted in a verdict and judgment against the company in the sum of $45,000. The company appeals. The appellant will be referred to as the company and individuals by name.

The principal questions presented for solution are the extent of the obligations of the insurer to the insured to settle within the policy limits a claim against the insured and, if liability is established, the correct measure of the insured's damages.

. . . .

[**pg. 342**, *pg. 408*] On the question of damages Henderson submitted and the court gave instructions that if the jury found the company breached its contract, it could assess damages for the following items: loss of the property as a going business and interest from time of loss, humiliation, pain and suffering, attorney fees incurred by Henderson, loss of earnings, expenses of seeking employment [*pg. 409*] including traveling expenses to that end, and his loss of business reputation and credit. Over the company's objection evidence on these items was admitted. Except as to the value of the business as a going concern and interest thereon from the time of its sale, the court erred in the admission of evidence and giving instructions on the foregoing items of damages.

The wrong involved is causing the destruction or conversion of insured's business property in satisfaction of the [**pg. 343**] company's obligation. The court correctly instructed that as a general rule the damages for the loss or destruction or conversion of a going business is its value at the time and place of destruction with interest. This is in accord with the pronouncements of this court. *Jones v. Stanley*, 27 Ariz. 381, 233 P. 598. The humiliation, mental pain, suffering and anguish incurred by the Hendersons was the direct result of the pecuniary loss suffered. If it is to be considered a breach of contract, to recover for these items the contract must be of such a nature that its breach would cause mental suffering for reasons other than the pecuniary loss. Restatement of Law, Contracts, section 341 . . . .

[**pg. 344**, *pg. 409*] The judgment is reversed with instructions for a new trial on the entire case as to all issues.

FOGLEMAN v. PERUVIAN ASSOCIATES
127 Ariz. 504, 622 P.2d 63 (Ct. App. 1980)

[**pg. 505**, *pg. 64*] HATHAWAY, Chief Judge.

In August of 1973, appellants were residents of Tucson, Arizona, and Mr. Fogleman was employed as a welder at a copper mine near Tucson. Appellees offered him employment at a mine operated by appellees at Quajone, Peru, and he accepted. The contract of employment was dated September 24, 1973, and was for a two-year period, employing Mr. Fogleman as welding supervisor at $1,700 per month plus housing allowance and other benefits.

Appellees terminated Fogleman's employment on March 8, 1974. Appellants brought this action alleging wrongful termination of the employment contract and seeking damages. After trial to the court, without a jury, judgment was entered in favor of appellants in the amount of $14,989.33, plus costs, together with interest commencing on the date of judgment. The trial court entered findings of fact and conclusions of law.

On appeal, appellants contend that they were entitled to an award of consequential general damages. . . .

[**pg. 506**, *pg. 65*] Appellants first contend that the trial court erred in not awarding consequential general damages because the evidence and findings support such an award. Specifically, the court found that appellees could terminate appellants' employment contract only for cause and that they did not have cause. This breach caused appellants economic loss of $14,989.33. In finding of fact number 10, the court found:

> *10. The wrongful conduct of the Defendants S.P.C.C., Fluor Utah and Peruvian Associates also caused Plaintiffs to suffer general damages, including emotional distress, anxiety, embarrassment, humiliation and other items listed on page 14 of Plaintiffs' Post-Trial Memorandum.*

The court refused to award consequential damages, perceiving the rule to be that such damages are not allowed in a breach of contract action, and so stated in conclusion of law number 15.

Appellants argue that consequential damages are allowable in a breach of contract action and that appellees' wrongful conduct was both a breach of contract and a tort, therefore such damages were allowable. The trial court's first finding of fact stated that the action was for breach of contract. . . . We do not have before us an appeal from a tort action, and appellants' citations for the proposition that damages for mental anguish are allowable in actions which sound both in contract and in tort, are not applicable. The appropriate measure of damages for an employee who has been wrongfully discharged is the unpaid balance of the salary less the sums earned during the remainder of the contract period. . . .

In *Browning v. Fies*, 4 Ala. App. 580, 58 So. 931 (1912), cited by appellants, a special situation was presented where the plaintiff had hired a carriage to transport him to church for his wedding. The defendant was aware of the reasons and the time frame for performance and that the failure of performance would, under the circumstances, expose plaintiff to particular consequences, alluded to by the court and for which the plaintiff was allowed damages. This case is inapplicable to the facts herein. . . .

[**pg. 507**, *pg. 66*] Affirmed as modified.

BROWNING v. FIES

58 So. 931 (Ala. Ct. App. 1912)

[**pg. 932**] Appeal from City Court of Birmingham; Chas. A. Senn, Judge.

Pelham, J. This is a suit for damages for the breach of a contract entered into between the appellant, who was the plaintiff below, and the appellees. Under the terms of the contract, the defendants, for the consideration of $5 paid to them by the plaintiff, agreed to furnish a carriage and team for the special purpose of carrying the plaintiff, his friends, and relatives from the home of the plaintiff near Rising Station to a church in Birmingham, Ala., a distance of about three miles, at which church the plaintiff on this particular occasion was to be married. The damages claimed and sought to be recovered were for the actual financial loss arising out of a breach of the contract, and damages for mental suffering, physical pain, humiliation, mortification, etc.

[The defendants] filed two motions to strike from each count of the complaint as amended the averments as to the plaintiff's having suffered great mental anguish, humiliation, distress, etc., on the ground that such allegations did not set up matters constituting proper elements for the recovery of damages. The defendants also separately moved to strike from each count of the complaint any claims for damages based on delay in reaching the place appointed for the marriage ceremony, for being compelled to ride to the church in a public street car, and for physical and mental pain and suffering, for humiliation, etc., etc., in consequence thereof, on the grounds that such damages were speculative, too remote, and not recoverable in an action of this nature. The court granted the defendants' motion to strike from the complaint these elements as claims of damage as to each count, and the plaintiff reserved exceptions to the court's ruling. On the pleadings as thus framed, the issues were tried before a jury....

The evidence without conflict showed that the plaintiff, on the day of the evening upon which he was to be married, went to the defendants' place of business in Birmingham, Ala., and entered into a contract with the defendants, who were engaged in conducting a public livery business, to furnish the plaintiff, for the use of himself, friends, and family, a carriage and team which was to be sent to the plaintiff's residence at or near Rising Station at 7:30 o'clock P.M. on that day to carry plaintiff and his wedding party to the church in Birmingham, three miles distant, where the plaintiff was to be married at 8 o'clock on that evening. The defendants made a charge of $5 for this specified use of the carriage and team, which amount was paid to the defendants by the plaintiff, who at the time of making the contract informed the defendants of the purpose **[pg. 933]** for which the same was to be used and the hour appointed for the ceremony, and the defendants agreed and contracted to furnish the carriage and team to be used by the plaintiff for this specific purpose. It was also shown without conflict in the evidence that the defendants made default and breached the contract and failed to send the carriage at the time and place as they contracted to do, and no excuse whatever was offered upon the part of the defendants for having failed to perform the contract. The plaintiff, on account of the defendants' breach of the contract, was compelled, in order to reach the church where his prospective bride and friends were awaiting his coming, to resort to a public street car in which plaintiff and his family and friends, at the expenditure of 30 cents for street car fare, attended the wedding appareled in "dress" or "evening" clothes. The plaintiff and the lady members of his family, unsuitably attired for riding in a street car and for walking along the public streets, had to walk for several squares from the place necessary to leave the car line in going to the church, and the wedding ceremony was delayed for 45 or 50 minutes on account of the failure of the plaintiff to reach the church on time. During this period of delay, the bride, family, minister, and friends in attendance at the church were kept waiting upon the delayed arrival of the prospective groom.

On the trial the plaintiff offered in varying forms questions to elicit evidence going to show that he suffered mental and physical pain, mortification, and humiliation, but on objection of the defendants he was not allowed to make such proof or to show any elements of damage of this nature. At the instance of the defendants, the court gave the following charge in writing to the jury: "If the jury believe the evidence, they can only find a verdict for the plaintiff for $5.30 with interest thereon from the 26th day of April, 1906." The plaintiff requested charges in writing, which were refused by the court, to the effect that the plaintiff was entitled to recover for any mental suffering and physical pain caused as a proximate consequence of the defendants' breach of the contract. The jury returned a verdict for plaintiff for $6.55, and, from the judgment entered on this verdict, the plaintiff prosecutes this appeal.

The main contention of appellant is that the court was in error in its ruling on the pleading and on the evidence, and its rulings on the charges in refusing to allow mental suffering and physical pain as an element of recoverable damages for breach of the contract.

The plaintiff's special or ulterior purpose in making the contract was disclosed at the time it was entered into and thereby became incorporated into it and thus afforded a substantial basis for the assessment of special damages. The special circumstances having been known and assented to by each of the contracting parties, each is deemed to have contracted with reference to them, and the party who breaches the contract may be justly held to make good to the other whatever damages, general or special, he has sustained which are the reasonable and natural consequences of the breach under the known circumstances with reference to which the parties acted in making the contract.

When a contract is entered into under special circumstances within the knowledge of both parties, the natural and proximate consequences of a breach of which will entail special damages upon the party not in default, the larger amount of damages may be recovered as having been in the contemplation of both parties. [Citation omitted.] This was also the English rule and the rule at common law. Damages recoverable for the breach of a contract are measured, not only by the actual loss sustained that naturally results as the ordinary consequence of the breach, but extend to consequences which may, under the circumstances of entering into the contract, be presumed to have been in the contemplation of both parties as the probable result of a breach. [Citation omitted.] And, if the special circumstances are communicated, they become an element of the contract. [Citation omitted.]

But are damages for mental suffering an element of the special damages recoverable? "Injury to the feelings—mental harassment—is an element of actual damages. 'Wounding a man's feelings is as much an element of actual damages as breaking his limb.' *Head v. Georgia Pac.*, 79 Ga. 358 [7 S.E. 217, 11 Am. St. Rep. 434]." *Birmingham Water Wks. Co. v. Martini*, 2 Ala. App. 652, 56 So. 833.

The right to recover special damages for mental anguish growing out of a breach of contract to send and deliver a telegram, as said in the recent case of *W. U. Tel. Co. v. Cleveland*, 169 Ala. 131, 135, 53 So. 80, 82, "has been settled in this court," citing the cases sustaining this proposition.

If damages for mental suffering are actual damages and recoverable as compensatory damages when proximately resulting from a breach of the contract, because of the nature of a telegram and the relationship disclosed bringing this consequence of the breach within the contemplation of the parties, as was held in *W. U. Tel. Co. v. Haley*, 143 Ala. 586, 39 So. 386, we cannot perceive under what rule or by what sound reason such *actual* dam- ages can be excluded as a proper measure of recovery in connection with the pecuniary loss sustained in any case where they flow naturally and as a direct consequence from the infraction **[pg. 934]** of a contract entered into under special circumstances known to both parties, and with reference to which they contracted....

This court has also held [citation omitted] that, for a breach of contract for transportation, a woman may recover for mental distress and worry due to having been prevented and delayed in securing stateroom accommodations while on her bridal trip.

In this particular case, considering the subject matter of the contract, the special purpose and exceptional use to which plaintiff intended to put the carriage, which was communicated and well known to the defendants, and with reference to which they contracted, it would seem that it was in the reasonable contemplation of the parties when the contract was entered into under the special known circumstances, that the immediate effect and proximate result ensuing from a breach of the contract by the defendants would cause the plaintiff inconvenience, annoyance, mental harassment, or distress, and make him to suffer physical delay with the attendant discomfort, as well as mental pain in consequence thereof. Certainly it is but common knowledge that some distress of mind must be the natural and proximate consequence of being delayed and not having proper conveyance to meet an appointment of such delicate nature.

The plaintiff by proper averments claimed damages in different counts of the complaint for physical discomfort in consequence of being delayed and not having proper conveyance to meet the special and particular appointment (undoubtedly of great moment to him), and for mental distress attendant upon and suffered in consequence of these physical inconveniences, delay, etc. The court was in error in not submitting these questions to the jury as a proper element of recoverable damages, and in limiting the recovery to the actual financial loss sustained.

A detailed discussion of the various assignments of error is unnecessary. The main proposition involved in each of all of them goes to the question we have considered and determined in what has been said.

Reversed and remanded.

Appendix V

Legal Writing Style: Problems for Chapter 9 of the Main Text

Problem 1. Conventions of Punctuation: Policy and Style

Described below are several conventions for use of commas, semicolons, and colons.[1] For each convention of usage,

1. describe the policies of composition that support the rule; alternatively, critique the rule or comment on it;
2. explain what practical problems may arise if the rule is ignored;
3. determine whether the rule should be viewed as sufficiently flexible to permit exceptions when adherence to the rule is not necessary to satisfy important policies or to avoid significant problems; and
4. consider alternatives to the approach described in the rule.

If helpful, illustrate your points with examples.

a. Independent Clauses

An independent clause is a clause with a subject and verb, structured so that it could stand alone as a complete sentence. You should separate independent clauses either with a period, thus creating two sentences, or with the following punctuation:

(1) In the absence of a conjunction, use a semicolon, not a comma:

> The roughest American team sport is football; basketball and baseball are comparatively gentle.

(2) Use a comma if the second independent clause begins with a coordinating conjunction, such as *and, but, yet, for, so, or, nor:*

> For two weeks after the earthquake, the tap water in Sarah's house was contaminated, but potable water was available in plastic containers at a nearby Red Cross outpost.

(3) Use a semicolon if the second independent clause begins with a conjunctive adverb, sometimes called an adverbial connective, such as *therefore, however, moreover, consequently, accordingly, nevertheless, thus.* Follow the connective with a comma:

> Basketball is not intended to be a contact sport; nonetheless, basketball players often deliver crushing blows to one another without incurring penalties.
>
> For two weeks after the earthquake, the tap water in Sarah's house was contaminated; however, potable water was available in plastic containers at a nearby Red Cross outpost.

(4) Multiple verbs of the same subject do not create independent clauses and therefore should not be separated with a comma:

> Joanie dribbled the ball past a defender and drove to the basket.

b. Lists or Illuminations

After an independent clause, use a colon to introduce a list, as when listing the elements of a rule:

> A claim under the due process clause requires proof of three elements: a protectable interest, deprivation of the interest by a state official, and the state's failure to afford procedural protections appropriate in the circumstances.

You can also use a colon to introduce a clause that illuminates the statement preceding the colon:

> Judge Crowder looked forward to oral argument: he learned much from well-prepared advocates, and he took a perverse pleasure in grilling those who were ill-prepared.

c. Parenthetic Words, Phrases, or Clauses

Use a comma or commas to set off parenthetic words or phrases and nonrestrictive clauses:

> One disgruntled patron in the back row, however, complained bitterly about the acoustics of the concert hall.
>
> Carlos Nakai, the flutist and leader of the band, had composed the finale while visiting the Yucatan peninsula.
>
> The audience stood and cheered for Carlos Nakai, who had composed the finale while visiting the Yucatan peninsula.
>
> The court held that, in light of the predominance of service activities, Article 2 of the UCC did not apply to the transaction.

Problem 2. Prehistoric Prohibitions

The following questionable clichés of composition are outdated; indeed, some never rose to the level of an accepted rule. Nonetheless, they still have currency among some editors. If you accept any of these "rules," justify it according to the directions in Problem 1 above. If you reject a rule or would limit it significantly, explain the reasons for your more flexible approach.

1. Never start a sentence with "because," "however," "and," or "but."
2. Never split an infinitive, as in "to severely limit his use of water."
3. Do not insert a comma between the last two elements of a series of three or more elements joined by a conjunction, as in "red, white, and blue."

Endnote

1. For further examples, *see* William Strunk, Jr., & E. B. White, The Elements of Style 1-9 (5th ed. 2009).

Appendix VI

Pleadings and Pretrial Motions: Assignments for Part VI

Assignment 1. Revision of Sample Complaint

Critically evaluate the following complaint for substance and style. In this actual complaint, the names of the parties and attorneys have been changed, and the text is single-spaced to conserve space in this book.

a. Specificity of Allegations

Identify the fact allegations that are especially detailed and redraft them to achieve greater generality. What are the advantages and disadvantages of each version?

b. Simplicity

Discard clichés or jargon in the sample complaint and replace them with simple, plain English.

c. Request for Relief

Each count in the sample complaint includes a request for punitive damages, as well as compensatory damages. Would a court be likely to instruct a jury that it could award punitive damages on the first count, for breach of contract? What tort, if any, does the second count allege?

IN THE SUPERIOR COURT OF
THE STATE OF ARIZONA
IN AND FOR THE COUNTY OF MARICOPA

Georgia Anne TUCKER, Plaintiff, v. James CLYDE, Defendant.	No. CIV-9X-79 COMPLAINT (Breach of Promise; Tort)

Plaintiff alleges:

I

This is an action for money damages exceeding $1,000.

II

Plaintiff is a resident of Cushing, Oklahoma. Defendant is a resident of Morris, Oklahoma. Defendant has caused an act to occur in Maricopa County, Arizona, out of which this cause of action arises.

COUNT ONE

(Breach of Promise)

III

At all relevant times, both Plaintiff and Defendant were over the age of 18 years, and in all respects capable of entering into a marriage contract.

IV

Plaintiff and Defendant were introduced and became acquainted with each other in September 1983. On or about December 8, 1983, Defendant proposed marriage to Plaintiff, and Plaintiff accepted. On January 17, 1984, the proposal and acceptance of marriage were reaffirmed when Defendant purchased a diamond engagement ring for Plaintiff.

V

Plaintiff and Defendant discussed their marriage agreement from time to time and on a great many occasions too numerous to mention herein. In the course of these discussions, Plaintiff and Defendant confirmed plans to be married in Hawaii on March 10, 1984.

VI

In January and February of 1984, Plaintiff and Defendant came to Phoenix, Arizona, for the purpose of locating and purchasing a home for their future marital residence. Defendant purchased a house located at 6052 East Cortez Drive, Scottsdale, Arizona. In addition, in preparation for the marriage, Defendant opened bank accounts, charge accounts, and utility service accounts in the names of James Clyde and Georgia Anne Clyde.

VII

At the insistence of Defendant and in reliance on the agreement to marry, Plaintiff gave up a profitable business as a hair stylist in Cushing, Oklahoma; borrowed and spent the sum of $12,000.00 to refurbish her residence in order to facilitate its sale; listed her residence for sale with a real estate agency; leased her residence to Defendant's son; withdrew her children from school; and moved her household possessions and her children from Cushing, Oklahoma, to Scottsdale, Arizona, at great expense and inconvenience.

VIII

On March 1, 1984, after having moved to Scottsdale, Arizona, Defendant presented to Plaintiff a prenuptial agreement that, among other things, listed the State of Arizona as the domicile of the parties and that provided for execution of the agreement in Maricopa County, Arizona. Plaintiff refused to sign the prenuptial agreement as written; however, despite Plaintiff's refusal to sign the prenuptial agreement, Defendant again renewed his promise to marry Plaintiff.

IX

On March 8, 1984, Defendant, Plaintiff, and three of Plaintiff's four children flew to Hawaii for the purpose of consummating the marriage, which was scheduled for March 10, 1984.

X

At approximately 8:00 a.m. on the morning of March 9, 1984, Defendant informed Plaintiff that he would not go through with the wedding. Since that date, Defendant has refused to carry out his promise to marry Plaintiff.

XI

On March 9, 1984, Defendant, Plaintiff, and Plaintiff's three children returned to Scottsdale, Arizona, where Defendant left Plaintiff and her three children in the house that was to have been the marital residence. On March 22, 1984, Defendant demanded that Plaintiff and her three children vacate the Scottsdale residence; for lack of other accommodations, Plaintiff was forced to return to Cushing, Oklahoma.

XII

By reason of Defendant's breach of promise to marry, Plaintiff has been deprived of Defendant's support and care for herself and her children, and of the commensurate standard of living that she would have enjoyed had the marriage been consummated. In addition to the foregoing, Plaintiff has suffered, and will continue to suffer, the following damages: a loss of past and future income as the result of Defendant's insistence that she give up her business; economic loss as the result of monies expended for refurbishing her residence in preparation for sale; economic loss resulting from the move from Cushing, Oklahoma, to Scottsdale, Arizona, and from Scottsdale, Arizona, back to Cushing, Oklahoma; and mental pain and anguish, wounded pride, mortification, humiliation, shame, and disgrace, which has directly impaired Plaintiff's health.

XIII

Defendant's actions in breaching his promise to marry were intentional or taken with reckless disregard for the rights of Plaintiff.

Plaintiff therefore requests judgment as follows:

1. past and future lost income in an amount to be determined at trial;
2. out-of-pocket expenses in an amount to be determined at trial, but not less than $12,000;
3. mental pain and anguish in an amount to be determined at trial, but not less than $10,000;
3. other compensatory damages in an amount to be determined at trial;
4. reasonable attorney's fees;
5. punitive damages in an amount to be determined at trial; and
6. such other and further relief as the Court deems just and proper.

COUNT TWO

(Tort)

XIV

Plaintiff realleges and incorporates into this count paragraphs I through XIII.

XV

Defendant stated to friends, relatives, and acquaintances of Plaintiff that Plaintiff and Defendant were engaged, that Plaintiff and Defendant were moving to Scottsdale, Arizona, and that Plaintiff and Defendant would be married on March 10, 1984.

XVI

After Defendant informed Plaintiff that he would not go through with the marriage, Defendant promised Plaintiff that he would provide her with the financial means to relocate wherever she desired so that she would not have to return to Cushing, Oklahoma, where she would experience the humiliation, shame, disgrace, pain, and anguish of explaining Defendant's failure to fulfill his marriage promise.

XVII

Defendant, after making the above-described promise to Plaintiff, forced Plaintiff to move out of the residence located in Scottsdale, Arizona, and refused to provide any financial assistance except transportation expenses to Cushing, Oklahoma.

XVIII

Defendant's actions in providing only transportation expenses for Plaintiff's return to Cushing, Oklahoma, were extreme and outrageous, were intentional, and were done with full knowledge of the emotional consequences to Plaintiff.

XIX

Plaintiff has suffered grievous mental pain, anguish, mortification, humiliation, shame, and disgrace; Plaintiff's mental and physical health has been impaired.

Plaintiff therefore prays for judgment as follows:

1. compensatory damages in an amount to be determined at trial, but not less than $12,000;
2. punitive damages in an amount to be determined at trial; and
3. such other and further relief as the Court deems just and proper in the premises.

Dated May 21, 1984

TICKER, STRANGER & NEAR

By ______________________
James R. Near
900 East Camelback Road
Scottsdale, AZ 85281
Attorney for Plaintiff

Assignment 2. Drafting an Answer

Review the sample complaint in Assignment 1 above or the revised version prepared by you or by a classmate. The defendant, James Clyde, is prepared to prove that Georgia Anne Tucker repudiated the marriage agreement when she refused to sign a written prenuptial agreement, that he never renewed his promise after Tucker's repudiation, that Tucker called off the wedding, and that he suffered severe disappointment as a result. Draft an answer on behalf of Clyde.

Assignment 3. Drafting a Complaint

Introduction to the Dispute: Office Memorandum
Multiple Issues
Jurisdiction: State in which your law school is located, or as dictated by your professor
Open Library

You are an associate with the law firm of Roberts and Cray. Partner Susan Cray asks you to prepare an office memorandum analyzing the claims of Charlotte Rembar, a potential client. The following is a transcript of your interview with Rembar. Fill in "20ZZ" with the current year, "20YY" with the year before the current year, and "20XX" with the year before "20YY." Alternatively, you can use the dates provided in the sample motion for summary judgment at the end of Chapter 15.

Associate: I understand that you have a problem with your employer.

Rembar: My ex-employer—he fired me November 20YY; that's my problem.

Associate: Did he tell you why he fired you?

Rembar: It was pretty obvious—he cut me off because I wouldn't go to bed with him.

Associate: Start from the beginning. Tell me about your job and your employer.

Rembar: I worked for Alexander Hart. He owns Comcon, a local computer consulting firm; they help businesses determine the best computer system for their needs, and they create custom computer programs for them. Alex is a real genius, and he hires the best consultants to work for them, so his business is booming. I started working there January 1, 20YY.

Associate: What was your position with the firm?

Rembar: I was one of his consultants; I designed computer systems and developed programs. I graduated from Stanford with honors in May 20XX with a degree in computer programming; this was my first decent job in the computer industry.

Associate: How many of you work at the firm?

Rembar: Alex works in the field himself as a consultant, and he had six of us working also as consultants. Other than that, he's got a secretary and a part-time accountant.

Associate: Is that his full work force? Has it ever been bigger?

Rembar: As far as I know, that work force represented substantial expansion for him from previous years; his firm has never been bigger.

Associate: Tell me about your termination.

Rembar: Well, Alex had an eye for me since the day he hired me. He was always flirting and asking me out on dates. I always thought of some polite excuse not to go out with him; I didn't want to offend him, but I don't like him that much, and I didn't think it would be good for our working relationship to get involved in dating. It started getting worse last fall, and near the end of October, 20YY, he called me into his office at the end of the day and flatly propositioned me. I refused, and he fired me.

Associate: Precisely what did he say, and how did you respond?

Rembar: First he asked me how I liked my job and my pay; I said I liked it fine. Then he said that he was in love with me and that he wanted me to go home with him that night and sleep with him and that I wouldn't regret it if I did. I didn't know what to say—I was so shocked. I think I just stood there with a stupid expression on my face for a few seconds; then I told him I had to go to a Halloween party, and I ran out of his office.

Associate: Did he fire you then?

Rembar: Not at that meeting. I was so distressed, I could hardly eat or sleep the whole weekend. I was worried about how we were going to maintain a decent working relationship if he was infatuated with me. I decided to talk to him about it the next morning, but I never got a chance. When I arrived at work, Alex called me into his office and told me that he didn't need my services any longer and that I had one week to clean out my office. I was literally speechless. I just walked out to my car and cried and cursed him. I got my last paycheck a week later.

Associate: Were you upset for a long time?

Rembar: Oh yes. I had trouble sleeping for a month. I was so nervous and depressed that I couldn't attend normal social functions. And I felt guilty—and stupid. I thought that I could have avoided all this if I had been more assertive in the beginning and told Alex more clearly that I wasn't interested. I started seeing a doctor and a counselor so that I could cope with it. I guess you've probably handled bigger problems than this, but I felt like my world was coming apart. This was my dream job—I was making $5,000 a month doing work that I love. When Alex fired me, I didn't know how I would ever explain it to other employers in job interviews. Luckily, I told the truth to the personnel manager at IBM, and she believed me. I started working there at the same salary in early January, 20ZZ.

Associate: How was your performance at Comcon?

Rembar: Great. I was the newest consultant, but I was better than two or three of the more experienced ones.

Associate: Did Alex ever praise your work, either orally or in writing?

Rembar: Sure. In my first month, he said I was learning fast. And in August, he complimented me on a particularly good job I did with one account. But he never put anything like that in writing.

Associate: Did he ever complain about your work, either orally or in writing?

Rembar: Never.

Associate: Do you want your job back at Comcon?

Rembar: No. I'm happy at IBM, and I don't want to ever work for that worm again. But I went through a lot of pain, and I think he owes me something for it.

Associate: Did you have a written contract of employment with Comcon?

Rembar: No, we just orally agreed that I would provide the consulting services for a starting salary of $60,000 a year. But he gave me a little policy manual to look at when I interviewed for the job. I've got a copy of it right here.

Associate: Did he say anything when he gave it to you?

Rembar: Yeah, he said that he believed in treating his consultants like professionals and that he could offer me better benefits and working conditions than I would get at the bigger firms. He encouraged me to read the policy manual to confirm that. He obviously wanted to give the appearance of a class operation so that he could attract the best consultants; he made a lot of money off of us.

Associate: I think that's all I need. I don't have authority to take your case; I'll have to report to the partners and get a decision from them. I'll get back to you by the end of the month. If we don't take the case, I'll help steer you toward some other attorneys who may be interested. In the meantime, read this explanation of our fee system and call me if you have any questions.

POLICY MANUAL
for Employees of Comcon

I. Introduction

The success of Comcon lies in its ability to recruit and retain the best employees available nationally. To promote a stable and productive workforce, Comcon provides attractive terms and conditions of employment, including those set forth in the following policies.

II. Salary

A. *Initial Salary ....*

B. *Change in Salary ....*

III. Holidays, Vacations, Sick Leave

A. *Holidays ....*

B. *Personal Leave ....*

IV. Termination

A. *Probationary Employment*

Each employee will work on probationary status during his or her first 60 days of employment. During this probationary period, Comcon reserves the right to terminate the employee for any reason or for no reason at all.

B. *Nonprobationary Employment*

Comcon reserves the right to terminate the employment of any employee who is not performing satisfactorily.

Based on the analysis in your office memorandum, determine what claims you could allege in good faith, and draft a complaint for an action in state court on behalf of Charlotte Rembar. You may assume that both parties agree

Ms. Rembar has received notice of right to sue by the appropriate state agency under Ariz. Rev. Stat. Ann. § 1481.D, or a similar statute in the jurisdiction in which your professor sets your assignment. You may also assume that your complaint meets all applicable limitations periods for any claim that you allege.

Assignment 4. Motion for Summary Judgment

Review (1) your Office Memorandum and Complaint in Assignment 3 above, and (2) the sample motion for summary judgment at the end of Chapter 15 of the main text. Do you agree with the decision of Hart's attorney to concede for purposes of summary judgment that the employee manual stated terms of Rembar's employment contract with Comcon?

Now imagine that the second sentence in Section I of the Comcon Policy Manual (Exhibit A of the materials supporting the motion) instead stated the following: "To promote a stable and productive workforce, Comcon endeavors to provide attractive terms and conditions of employment, as reflected in the following policies." On these terms, would you still concede for purposes of summary judgment that the employee manual stated terms of Rembar's employment contract? Add a section to the argument of Hart's memorandum in support of his motion for summary judgment, arguing that the employee manual did not state contract terms under the statutory standard but instead set forth Comcon's current polices, to which it was not contractually bound.

Assignment 5. Opposition to Motion for Summary Judgment

Review (1) Assignment 3 above, and (2) the sample motion for summary judgment at the end of Chapter 15 of the main text.

Prepare materials opposing Hart's motion for summary judgment, or opposing a similar motion on Hart's behalf supplied by your professor.

In preparing your opposition, you may assume the following premises or developments:

a. Your firm filed a complaint alleging four claims for relief: (1) breach of a promise of job security, (2) violation of the Arizona Civil Rights Act, (3) wrongful discharge in violation of public policy, and (4) infliction of emotional distress. In his answer, Hart denied that Rembar's contract contained any provisions for job security and denied the allegations of sexual harassment. He alleged that he discharged Rembar for poor performance.

b. Rembar stands by the information she provided in the initial interview, set forth in Appendix XX, and she is willing to swear to it in an affidavit. Your independent fact investigation has revealed some corroborating evidence from Leslie West, Alex Hart's secretary during Charlotte Rembar's tenure at Comcon. In a recent interview, West revealed that she and Rembar developed a close friendship and that she was distressed to learn of Rembar's discharge. After Rembar filed suit, Hart became irritable and unpleasant to work for; West voluntarily quit her job at the end of the year after Rembar's discharge. She has offered to support Rembar with trial testimony and statements in an affidavit. The following is an excerpt from your interview of West:

> *West:* That was on Halloween last fall, 2017. I saw Charlotte leave the office in tears at quitting time. The following workday, in the afternoon, Mr. Hart told me to process the paperwork to terminate Charlotte's payroll at the end of the week. When I said that I had thought Charlotte was one of his best consultants, he said, "Her consulting isn't my problem—it's her stuckup attitude." I asked him what I should put down on the paperwork as the reason for her termination, and he said something like, "I don't care what you put—just say that she has a negative attitude."

c. Through discovery requests, you have obtained copies of the contents of Rembar's employment file at Comcon. The file includes only a few insignificant notes and the two payroll action forms attached to Hart's motion for summary judgment.

d. In responding to the Motion for Summary Judgment, you may assume that both parties agree that Ms. Rembar has received notice of right to sue by the appropriate state agency under Ariz. Rev. Stat. Ann. § 1481.D, or a similar statute in the jurisdiction in which your professor sets your assignment, and you need not address that issue. You may also assume that your complaint met all applicable limitations periods for any claim that you alleged.

Assignment 6. Motion to Exclude Evidence

Review Assignments 3 and 5 above. Assume that you have successfully opposed Hart's motion for summary judgment and that the trial judge has scheduled a pretrial conference.

You are concerned about some embarrassing evidence that Hart has obtained through the discovery process. While a freshman at Stanford University, Rembar posed nude for a two-page spread in *Hustle and Bustle*, an adult magazine; some of the poses would strike the average juror as lewd and tasteless. Rembar explained that she posed for the pictures on a dare and that she didn't realize until later how lewd and revealing they would be. She regrets her decision to pose, and she insists that the pictures do not reflect her current personality or style of relating to friends or colleagues.

Hart probably learned of the magazine spread through one of Rembar's freshman college classmates or professors. In a discovery request, Hart requested confirmation of the event, along with a copy of the outof-print magazine. Pursuant to your state's counterpart to Federal Rule of Civil Procedure 26(c), you objected to the request on the ground that the information requested would be inadmissible at trial and that its production would result in annoyance, embarrassment, and oppression. The trial judge, however, compelled discovery on the ground that the information sought, whether or not admissible itself, might lead to the discovery of evidence relating to a claim or defense. *See* FED. R. CIV. P. 26(b)(1); *Kidwiler v. Progressive Paloverde Ins. Co.*, 192 F.R.D. 193, 199 (N.D. W. Va. 2000).

You now seek an advance ruling barring any reference to the magazine spread at trial. Draft a motion to exclude the evidence before trial.

INDEX